Negation, Subjectivity,
and
The History of Rhetoric

Negation, Subjectivity, and The History of Rhetoric

Victor J. Vitanza

State University of New York Press

Published by
State University of New York Press, Albany

For information, address State University of New York
Press, State University Plaza, Albany, N.Y., 12246

Production by Diane Ganeles
Marketing by Dana Yanulavich

Library of Congress Cataloging-in-Publication Data

Vitanza, Victor J.
    Negation, subjectivity, and the history of rhetoric / Victor J.
Vitanza.
        p.   cm.
    Includes bibliographical references and index.
    ISBN 0-7914-3123-1 (alk. paper). — ISBN 0-7914-3124-X (pbk. :
alk. paper)
    1. Rhetoric—History.   2. Rhetoric—Philosophy.   3. Negation
(Logic)   4. Subjectivity.   5. Sophists (Greek philosophy)
I. Title.
PN183.V58   1997
808'.009—dc20   96-3775
                                                          CIP

10 9 8 7 6 5 4 3 2 1

...for Vickie, Paul, David, Marty, and Roman—*All My Children*...

Contents

Acknowledgments

I would like to thank the following for their contributions to my thinking about historiography and discourse:

Graduate students (colleagues) with whom in the past ten years I have read rhetorical and critical theory: Lynn Worsham, Cynthia Haynes, Lorie Goodman, Michelle Ballif, Diane Davis (Mowery), Lisa Hill, Beverly Johansen, Joshua Kretchmar, Matt Levy, Dave Reeder, Tom Rickert, Collin Brooke, Doug Brown, Rebecca Sabounchi, Robert Cook, Chris Dacus, Jo Suzuki, Alan Taylor, and Corri Wells—especially, Cynthia for our discussions about Heidegger; Diane for reading sections of the manuscript; Lorie for always being a careful and understanding reader; and Lynn for getting me to see the necessity for articulating my views on the relationship between aesthetics and politics.

Other colleagues to thank: James Berlin, Robert Connors, William Covino, Sharon Crowley, Lester Faigley, Michael Feehan, Luanne Frank, Lynda Hass, Hans Kellner, Charles Kneupper, Steven Mailloux, Margaret Morrison, Barbara Biesecker, Janet Atwill, John Omlor, John Poulakos, Takis Poulakos, Susan Jarratt, Robert Reddick, Edward Schiappa, John Schilb, James Sosnoski, Jane Sutton, Gary Tate, and John Trimbur—especially Hans for his support of this project and his various contributions to it.

I would like to thank Nancy Wood, who made it possible for me to have a semester off to write most of this manuscript.

I would like to thank my wife, Toni, for her support in my writing this book, which, in many ways, would not have been completed without her. When I was brooding far too much over what I had written and mostly not written, she took me to Poland to work with faculty and students who for the first times in their lives—in the history of Poland—were working and learning in a 'democracy.' (I delivered four formal lectures and had many arguments with the students who believed that Capitalism would deliver them from their Socialist shackles.) While in that strange country, I read Heidegger's four volumes on Nietzsche and visited Auschwitz. When we returned from Poland, I finished the manuscript. And then along came Roman!

I would also like to thank Carola Sautter (my acquisitions editor), the staff at SUNY Press, and the readers of the manuscript.

And finally I would like to thank the following publishers for granting me permission to reprint articles (complete or in part) that were previously published:

" 'Some More' Notes, Toward a 'Third' Sophistic." *Argumentation* 5 (1991): 117–39. Copyright 1991 Kluwer Academic Publishers. Reprinted by permission of Kluwer Academic Publishers.

"A Feminist Sophist?" *JAC* 15.2 (1995): 321–49. Permission granted by *JAC: A Journal of Composition Theory.*

"Taking A-Count of a (Future-Anterior) History of Rhetoric as 'Libidinalized Marxism' (A PM Pastiche)." In *Writing Histories of Rhetoric,* ed. Victor J. Vitanza. Carbondale: Southern Illinois University Press, 1994: 180–216. Copyright by the Board of Trustees, Southern Illinois University. Reprinted by permission of the publisher, Southern Illinois Unverisity Press.

Introduction:
What Do I Want, Wanting to Write This ("our") Book?
What Do I Want, Wanting You to Read This ("our") Book?

. . . What we see in the return of the repressed is the effaced signal of something which only takes on its value in the future, through its symbolic realization, its integration into the history of the subject. Literally, it will only ever be a thing which, at the given moment of its occurrence, *will have been.*

—Jacques Lacan

I shall give birth to a centaur someday.

—Fredrich Nietzsche

I began writing this book so many times. I would sit and type what I thought I was going to type, and yet out came something else. More often than not, *something else!* I'm not sure who wrote this book. As a case in point, this very introduction is something else. For a period of several months—as I was finishing up the book manuscript—I made notes for this introduction. When it came time to write from the notes for this supposed-to-be-introduction, I tried and tried to write from them. And yet, something else kept appearing, haunting—humming on—the screen. The only part of this introduction that is actually from the notes is the opening paragraphs with their question ("What is it that you want?"); the rest is a departure. A wandering and wondering from the notes. What someone wants and what he or she gets, as is commonly experienced by and among many of us, are on occasion quite different. And yet, perhaps we always get what we want. Difference.[1] Yes, contrary to The Stones, I would now say: We always get what we want and seldom, what we need.[2]

1

While readers (audiences) have needs, writers have desires. While the living have their needs, the dead (rhetoric[s]?) *still* have their desires.[3]

> But who's talking about living?
> In other words on living?
> [...]
> Under the pretext of commenting upon a terribly indeterminate, shifting statement, a statement difficult to pin down, it gives a reading or version of it that is all the less satisfactory, controllable, unequivocal, for being more "powerful" than what it comments upon or translates. The supposed "commentary" of the "i.e." or "in other words" has burnished only a textual supplement that calls in turn for an overdetermining "in other words," and so on and so forth. In other words on living?
>
> —Jacques Derrida

I. Not a (traditional) Introduction
but a Letter to James A. Berlin

> ... instead of trying to define the other ("What is he?"), I turn to myself: "What do I want, wanting to know you?" What would happen if I decided to define you as a force and not as a person? And if I were to situate myself as another force confronting yours?
>
> —Roland Barthes

Dear Jim,

Books have a thousand-and-one beginnings. This book is no exception. My book is about beginnings, but not what we think of as traditional, common-sense beginnings, but intrusions or interruptions. One such beginning can be traced back to a challenging political question directed to me by you, who asked: "Victor, What is it that you want?" (You/It asked: *"Che Vuoi?"*)[4] You asked the question in the light of a discussion concerning Marxism, rhetorical theory, and history writing, which took place one night very, very late in Pittsburgh, after you and I had made our presentations at a session of the Marxist Literary Group at Carnegie Mellon University. The informal audience was composed of colleagues in rhetoric and critical theory. It was in the house of one of our guests.[5]

I answered in one, but a radical multiplicity, that I wanted "desire." Histories of unfettered desire. Desire in language (Kristeva 1980) and everything else (J. Butler 1987). Desire in *logos*, but also in *ethos* and *pathos*. And I wanted this desire reflected in writing histories of rhetorics. (Michel Pierssens in *The Power of Babel* had written: "to reinvent history as the history of desire" [1980, 34].) I did not want a desire by way of determinate negation, a Hegelian desire of "restrictive economy" (see Bataille 1988a, 25). Instead, I wanted and still want a desire by way of a "general economy" (25), which would be both affirmative and disruptive. The desire that I wanted was to be expressed in pararhetorics, paragrammaticisms. Prior to your question, I had already written in such a manner (a mannerist way of assemblages and series) so as to let this desire express itself.[6]

Such a desire/force is to be found in the Nietzschean corpus without organs. (Organs = ways of territorializing, or of deterritorializing and reterritorializing—denegating and renegating—the flow of desire. Without Organs = perpetual deterritorializing.) Nietzsche expresses this desire/force best:

> This world: a monster of energy, without beginning, without end; . . . a play of forces and waves of forces, at the same time one and many, increasing here and at the same time decreasing there; a sea of forces flowing and rushing together, eternally changing, eternally flooding back, with tremendous years of recurrence, with an ebb and a flood of its forms; . . . a becoming that knows no satiety, no disgust, no weariness: this, my *Dionysian* world of the eternally self-creating, the eternally self-destroying, this mystery world of the twofold voluptuous delight, my "beyond good and evil," without goal, unless the joy of the circle is itself a goal. . . . *This world is the will to power—and nothing more!* And you yourselves are also this will to power—and nothing more! (1968c, 550; Nietzsche's emphasis)

Yes, JB, I would unleash this desire/force that is all around us on writing, reading, and thinking about the grand narrative of *The* History of Rhetoric,[7] and I would do so not only for paraethical un/reasons but also for parapolitical ones that would become radical multiplicities. (The History is the history of an Error [Nietzsche, *The Twilight of the Idols*, 1968b].) I would unleash desire on the grand narrative; I would especially unleash it on the structures that enable the narrative, namely, discipline and punishment and metadisciplines and fascism.

We have read what Nietzsche says about this desire/force; now, let's read what the Nietzscheans Deleuze and Guattari say:

> If desire [force, will to power] is repressed, it is because every position
> of desire, no matter how small, is capable of calling into question the
> established order of a society: not that desire is asocial, on the contrary. . . .
> Despite what some revolutionaries think about this, desire is revolution-
> ary in its essence. . . . [N]o society can tolerate a position of real desire
> without its structures of exploitation, servitude, and hierarchy being com-
> promised. (1983, 116)

Therefore, Jim, here are two but-an-un/common *answer* to your question, "What is it that you want?" Two on the way to a Third (or some
more).

And so now you perhaps have an idea of what I'm talking about. With
a preliminary understanding of what I have in—and yet mostly out of—mind,
however, comes problems. And Why? Because finally, antinomian. Because
such a free-flowing desire/force would be against the very principle of *identity* itself. Yes, yes, yes, I would reintroduce the excluded middle (muddle).

Let me explain further: After almost completing this book, I read Kathy
Acker's *In Memorium to Identity* (1990). A Novel. Acker writes: "She learned
she must be several, if not numberless, parts" (260). Even closer to completion, I read Clarice Lispector's *The Passion According to G. H.*, in which,
G. H.—in attending to the ugly, the most despicable creature—disposes of
her identity, and takes on undifferentiated "vastness" (1988). She becomes-
animal. When I speak of adding force/desire to The History of Rhetoric, I
am saying, therefore, the same that Acker and Lispector say about their
characters.[8]

Yes, I would reclaim for The History—that which is under suppression,
repression, political oppression—its severalness, but its numberlessness, its
sublime vastness, and especially its parts that do not allow for systemization, for completeness, without exclusion, without purging. Why? Because
systemization *is* the result of exclusion. Wherever there is system (totality,
unity), there is the trace of the excluded. As Kenneth Burke keeps telling
us, congregation is established by way of segregation. As Catherine Clément
says: "The same goes for women as for madmen: in a *manifest* position of
exclusion, they keep the system together, *latently*, by virtue of their very
exclusion" (1981, 134; Clément's emphasis; cf. N. O. Brown 1966, 160–61).
Again as Clément says: "Somewhere every culture has an imaginary zone
for what it excludes, and it is that zone we must try to remember today. This
is history that is not over" (Cixous and Clément 1986, 6).

Therefore, yet again, I do not wish to write, read, and think in this major
disciplined language of "doing" history that produces The History "that is
not over"; rather, I would write, read, and think by way of and within—as
Deleuze and Guattari do—"a minor language." Which can be the site of an

"imaginary zone." I wanted, or at least it would start this way, "a minor literature," in the midst of *The History* of Rhetoric. (I would unleash this history that is not over, which is *in* an "imaginary zone," right in the midst of The History. Or vice versa! I would *fold* the two into each other, destroying the difference that allows for exclusion.) In wanting what I wanted, I thought that I wanted to write Kafka-like and yet V.V.-like. (I wanted to fold the two personae into each other.) I now realize that as I wrote this book "I" sat and wondered, and re/wrote and wondered, *How would Kafka write against* (contra to but along side) *The History of Rhetoric*? How would Kafka deOedipalize (denegate) The History? Perhaps I wanted to write like the other Victor/ian. I wanted, as Deleuze and Guattari say, in their discussion of a minor literature, "to become a nomad and an immigrant and a gypsy in relation to [our] own [dominant, academic] language" (1986, 19). I wanted to be a Rye-zomatic![9] I wanted on occasion to deterritorialize my writing without having to reterritorialize through the dominant discourse. And yet, I wanted more: I wanted, like Kafka, to make a language and be a stranger in it. How? I wanted to find language (*logos*) uncanny. Unhomely.

And why? Again, ever again, because this novelistic but nonetheless forceful and desirous "I" obviously does not want to formulate its identity by way of the dominate identity that is part and parcel of the dominant discourse. Does not want the imaginary (as Lacan sees it) to be structured by the bureaucracy (as Kafka sees it) of writing The History. Let's recall, as Deleuze and Guattari say, "there is no fixed subject unless there is repression" (1983, 26). I would be a subject-therefore-that-is-not-academic. Not repressed. Why? and How?

Because this "I" would become a series of flows, energies, movements, capacities, a series of parts and segments capable of becoming linked together in ways other than those which congeal them by standard academic operating procedures. (. . . un/just as these "Becauses" link but do not necessarily, legitimately link, or couple. Yes, I am for illegitimate couplings! As I will tout later, by way of Jean-François Lyotard and Ovid and Hélène Cixous, it is necessary to link [be social] but not how to link. Here, throughout, therefore, I link one traditional or revisionary machine to a desiring machine. George Kennedy's or Edward Schiappa's philological machine to Acker's desiring machine. Or Gorgias's revisionary-perspectival machine to Judith Butler's desiring machine. Or Marx's proletarian-classless machine to François Fourier's phalansteric machine [see Barthes 1976]. Or Martin Heidegger's Being machine to Nietzsche's becoming machine. Or in general our culture's binary machine to a desiring machine. Just link. Just link. Just link. These (hypertextual) linkages, to be sure, will be seen, more often than not, as irresponsible! By what criterion? By that of the dominant discourse, whether naively real or strategic? Yes, in the face of such so-called responsibility, I would be irresponsible. Therein lies minoritarian justice. For what has been repressed, suppressed, oppressed.)

And yet, I would want more: Yes, Jim, it may very well be that this "I" (that-is-a-"we," yet not a corporate "WE")[10] would even deny what an "I" would be in a minor language living within a major, dominant language! At times, I think that this "I" attempts, as I confided earlier, to denegate and disperse even all minor languages into wild, savage babylonianisms. Wild, savage particularities. As Michel Foucault says: "The purpose of history . . . is not to discover the roots of our identity but to commit itself to its dissipation" (1977, 162). I would be anti-oedipus. Anti-discipline. Anti(both)-victor *and* vanquished. There are many tactics without strategies—I repeat: without strategies—unleashed here, there, and everywhere in this book. As Deleuze and Guattari say: Writing has "nothing to do with signifying. It has to do with surveying, mapping, even realms that are yet to come" (1987, 4–5).

I think that this "I" that-is-not-an-expressive-I is concerned with the *future anterior*. After all, I would be far left of what it is to be humanistically possible. Hence, my social linkage of libidinalized Marxism. I would be wildly, savagely proleptic.

II. From Disorientation to Orientation?

The depressed narcissist mourns not an Object but the Thing.
. . .
Of this Nerval provides a dazzling metaphor that suggests an insistence without presence, a light without representation: the Thing is an imagined sun, bright and black at the same time. . . .

—Julia Kristeva

Solar energy is the source of life's exuberant development. The origin and essence of our wealth are given in the radiation of the sun, which dispenses energy—wealth—without any return. The sun gives without ever receiving.

—Georges Bataille

I have looked the sun in its face.

—Hélène Cixous

Let us pause, drop anchor, and ask, How are the other over-readers (as in *over-hearers, eaves-droppers*) responding to what has been said thus far? In another word, in this *letter*. Not that I would insist on their hearing the letter of the word. In part, I can hear them exclaiming, "Oh, so this is not really about history? But about writing novels? Hence, this is about 'rational reconstructions' (anachronisms, fictions) and not about 'historical reconstructions' (the way things 'really' were or intended)."

My response: No! And of course such a response on my part requires a lengthier answer, or redescription, which I give in chapter 1. (This No is a No to kNOw.)[11] As readers—for to be a reader is to be disciplined, Oedipalized—we bring our identities and, thus, our trained incapacities to what we read. We often find it the case that we do not like what we have read because *what*—or is it *how?*—we have read challenges our ever-so-fixed disciplinary identities. I ask, Why else read? For un/reasons other than being challenged or being dispersed? Writers who disperse me are writers (sky-writing flyers) who I would reread in dis/order to be perpetually dispersed. Yes, I would be "desiring and capable of other."[12]

This book takes a look and another look at those reading—writing, thinking—identities and capacities—and possible ears, both right and left—but does not settle for a Burkean, formalist ac*count*. It attempts to go beyond such ac*count*s (ears, both right or left) to radical multiplicities and for parapolitical un/reasons (third ears). Throughout, I make much of counting and accounting, of taking account of. I make much of the counting anti/system of 0, 1, and plenty; or of 1, 2, and some more.[13]

Why? Again: Because this "I" does not wish to reformulate but to "deformulate"; does not want to reterritorialize but perpetually deterritorialize. And why? (As a child, I ask perpetually the question Why? Why? Why? Does it unnerve my reader? If so, then good.) Again, because of and for—yes, yes, yes—parapolitical un/reasons. But *What* does this "parapolitical un/reasons" *mean*?

Allegorically, I am the character in the novel who goes around picking up what was refined out of The Novel, out of The History, and insists on putting it back into The Novel so that it can no longer be The Novel/The History. *Topologically*, I would put so much back in that it would explode and find itself as all outside. I would make of The History of Rhetoric a Klein jar, which is all outside and no inside, or which is neither. I would fold, and fold, and refold, perpetually. *Scavengerly*, I am the collector of ashes, of scraps, of waste, of that which has been excluded so as to purchase stability (*stases*, standpoints, etc.).[14] *Anti-psychoanalytically*, this "I" is the imaginary that comes back, eternally returns, to haunt, to ask haunting questions about, the symbolic (the negative, absence, the Black Sun). This "I" is here to denegate the principles of identity, contradiction, and excluded middle.

Hysterically-schizophrenically, I would denegate *physis*, so as to let it flowwwwwwwwwwwwvv&vv&vv.

Again, *What* does this "parapolitical un/reason" *mean*? The Nietzscheans Deleuze and Guattari answer:

> We will never ask what a book [or a paraconcept] means, as signified or signifier. . . . We will ask what it functions with, in connection with what other things it does or does not transmit intensities, in which other multiplicities its own are inserted and metamorphosed, and with what body without organs it makes its own converge. A book only exists through the outside and on the outside. A book in itself is a little machine; what is the relation . . . of this literary machine to a war machine, love machine, revolutionary machine, etc.—and an *abstract machine* that sweeps them along? We have been criticized for overquoting literary authors. But when one writes, the only question is which other machine the literary machine . . . must be plugged into in order to work. Kleist and a mad war machine, Kafka and a most extraordinary bureaucratic machine. . . . Literature is an assemblage. It has nothing to do with ideology. There is no ideology and never has been. (1987, 4; Deleuze and Guattari's emphasis)

There is, however, force/desire and how it variously but samely gets "fixed."

So can we amend Althusser *and* Deleuze/Guattari and say, first, there is force/desire, second, ideology (negation), then, writing (reading, thinking) history? After all is said and undone, this is what "thinking" is, thinking that is so reactionary because it is filtered through being-fixed, being-*physis*[neg.]. Or being-*nomos* (class, race, gender, national origin).[15] We know—write, read, think—semiotically across these *signs* of lack, absence. (No wonder thinking is reactionary!)[16] As will become more unclearly clear, I would denegate the fixedness of things, whether fixed absolutely or strategically. If I am told, "But you can't!" I will say, "Just watch." All this reminds me of Kristeva's child, who rejects the symbolic, who says:

> . . . *nausea* makes me balk at that milk cream, separates me from the mother and father who proffer it. I want none of that element, [that negative] sign of their desire; I do not want to listen, I do not assimilate it, I expel it. But since the food is not an "other" for "me," who am only in their [negative] desire, I expel *myself*, I spit *myself* out, I abject *myself* within the same motion through which I claim to establish *myself*. (1982, 3: Kristeva's emphasis; cf. Lispector 1988)

Do I sound like a holy brat? or better yet, a would-be orphan? What would be my purpose for hailing the audience to think of me as such? Like Antonin Artaud, when reading The History of Rhetoric, "I don't believe in father, in mother, got no papamummy" (1965, 247). "I" am not a subject; not an object. "I" am an abject.

Therefore, dear readers, do not ask *what* this book means but *how* it variously means. (It is, then, not so much What I want? but How to give?) This is—in the words of Bataille in *The Accursed Share*—an attempt at an "erotic" book without reserve (see 1993, vol. 2). In other words, a book of How(l)s. To give a gift. But, in asking about the *hows*, do not count the *ways* of the how(l)s. I purposefully and un/consciously parody (and yet, pastiche) both *what* and *how*. Mostly the *hows*. At times, I write (perform, give) in the most traditional manner and then in revisionary manners. You will see that I can imitate (i.e., make a copy of a copy, simulate, give) boring traditional academic prose, and make boring subversive nonacademic prose. (Yes, I can perform discourse under negation!) And I hope on occasion some not-so-boring nonacademic writing. On occasions, but mostly toward the end (re/beginning?), I perform in sub/versive, baroque mannerisms. In folds and folds after folds. Or such bad manners perform "me" or "us." But again, do not ask and then count the ways this book means! Unless by way of 1, 2, and "some more." And be always aware, the force/desire—yes, yes, yes—most importantly becomes farced. As Marx gasps—but few will accept his gasps—history is Bonapartisms (see Marx 1984). First, Tragedy; then, Comedy; and finally (re/beginningly?) FARCE (see Mehlman 1977).

In recalling to memory here the question—let's call it "The Pittsburgh Question"—I may have led some of my readers to think that I was attempting to give (to gift?) a representative anecdote for this my book. To be honest, I think that I am—and I know that I am—not. Hence, an un/kind of *nes/ yo* answer.

I am well aware that this all—and so soon in my deliberations—may be very difficult to follow, not because of any profundity, but because like the narrator of Lawrence Durrell's *Justine*, "What I most need to do is to record experiences, not in the order in which they took place—for that is history—but in the order in which they first became [in/]significant for me" (1969, 100). After all, I'm a novelist that would be a historiographer (hysteriographer, schizographer)! I'm a process writer! "I" am a desiring machine. Who would destroy, explode *the* sign.[17] Who would refuse to reterritorialize and commodify this process cum product so that it might be easily consumed. This is not social-epistemic production, but desiring production. I would deny commodification and search out for the extreme limits of Kapitalism. "I" am a desiring machine writing. As Deleuze and Guattari say,

> If this constitutes a system of writing, it is a writing inscribed on the very surface of the Real: a strangely polyvocal kind of writing, never a

biunivocalized, linearized one; a transcursive system of writing, never a discursive one; a writing that constitutes the entire domain of the "real inorganization" of the passive syntheses, where we would search in vain for something that might be labeled the Signifier—writing that ceaselessly composes and decomposes the chains into signs that have nothing that impels them to become signifying. The one vocation of the sign is to produce desire, engineering it in every direction. (1983, 39)

III. No Longer a Letter,
but a Dilemma-that-would-Become a Trilemma

But who's talking about living?
In other words on living?

—Derrida

And who's thinking about becoming-human?

—Anonymous

Tyrell: "Is this to be an empathy test? . . . Involuntary dilation of the iris?"
Deckard: "We call it 'voigt-kampff' for short."
Rachel: "Mr. Deckard, Dr. Edwin Tyrell."
Tyrell: "Demonstrate it. I want to see it work."
Deckard: "Where's the subject?"
Tyrell: "I want to see it work on a person. I want to see a negative before I provide you with a positive."
Deckard: "What's that going to prove?"
Tyrell: "Indulge me."
Deckard: "On you?"
Tyrell: "Try her."
Deckard: "It's too bright in here."

—*Blade Runner*

Honored members of the Academy! You have done me the honor of inviting me to give your Academy an account of the life I formerly led as an ape.

—Franz Kafka

For the sake of orientation (let's set aside disorientation for a while), I have been saying, among many things, that . . .

Victor, let me force—as you say, "farce"—my way into this, your discussion. If you're going to get this thing published and get it to the point of being an introduction so that the audience can at least be suckered into reading the first chapter and so on, you're going to have to make some negative—let's say, affirmative—sense here. Therefore, what's the bottom line here?

Okay, Jim. [Laughter.] This book that you, Dear Reader, perhaps are about to read is *not* a history of rhetoric, but a set of essays concerning and excursions into historiographies. It is not a grammar of historiographies; I have never written such a grammar, contrary to what some of my readers claim.[18] Instead and more specifically, it is ruminations on the question *What is it* to write histories of rhetoric? Or better put, ruminations on What is it that a writer gives when writing histories of rhetoric? I say rumination, for I am not interested in answering, but in interrogating the question perpetually, in guarding this question from being answered, not because there is no answer, or answers (there are, though there are not), but because there is a negative desire (a will to truth, to knowledge) that would have us insist on *an*—that would become *the*—answer to the question. The question *What is it* to write histories of rhetoric? is a pernicious one; it is a question predicated on the principles of negative dialectic (species-genus analytics, dividing practices, *diaeresis*, negative essentializing).

What is X? (such as What is subjectivity?, or What is a Sophist?) is a question that excludes and purges. Perhaps appropriate elsewhere, it is not appropriate here. I ruminate on this question in relation to the question of the Sophists. In my ruminations, I raise again, and very initially in my discussion, in the two opening excurses, the question of the relationship between aesthetics and politics. It is in this very rumination, that I speak most suspiciously about subjectivity and negation. And all in relation to writing The History of Rhetoric. It is here that I, so to speak, resurrect, or recreate the conditions of the possibilities for, the Sophists as sublime, sovereign subjects that-are-not-subjects. (I have to resurrect them because Edward [not scizzor-hands, but Edipus] Schiappa has killed them off.[19]) It is here that I speak of—by way of pastiche—Favorinous and Marx, as two hermaphrodite Sophists. Whose texts become the very desires that rush on to the end (rebeginning?) of this, my discussion. In the midst, all heaven (a Blakean exuberance) breaks—or should break—loose.[20]

In the midst (*in medias res* and *mise en abyme* and in parentheses), I concentrate on Isocrates and Gorgias, and I do so metaleptically. More specifically, I concentrate on *physis* (nature, Being) and *logos* (discourse, law) in relation to these Sophists. And specifically on How Isocrates engages in negative essentializing, and How Gorgias can be read as dis/engaging in such essentializing. Moreover, in these terms, I examine Heidegger's views and something called a Feminist Sophistic. Always, I am interested in parapolitics and paraethics. Event-ually, I rush on and hum on to what I have been calling variously a Third Sophistic and a Libidinalized Marxism (or libidinalized materialism). And again, all in relation to writing (as in a hysteriography and schizography of) histories of rhetorics.

Good, Victor. Now, what else?

Just as important, however, this book-that-is-not-a-book is ruminations—yes, excessive ruminations—on the contrary question *What do I want, wanting to know history?* What is it to know (to no)? This contrary question allows me to interrogate the *What is X?* question. Again, *What is it that I want wanting to write history?* As will become unclearly clear, I approach this question very indirectly. And yet, directly. (It is a question that comes from the hermeneutics of suspicion.) I examine *how* other historians have answered the question, What is it that I want?, variously in respect to the Sophists. The trio of historians that I work with here are, as I said, Edward Schiappa, but also John Poulakos and Susan Jarratt. I have learned much from them. I consider them and what they have to say of the greatest and most challenging importance. I hope that my thinking about their thinking will be received as an honoring of their—our different—thinking. (And yes, I play jokes on [FARCE] them!)

I am specifically concerned about their reliance on the negative, on negative essentializing, "to do history," though to be sure they employ the negative to varying degrees in respect to *physis* and *logos*.

What's wrong with the negative?

While the negative enables, it disenables. As I've said, it's mostly a disenabler because it excludes. Something *is* by virtue of Nothing, or what it *is not*. The formula: Species + genus + differentiae.[21] All determination is negation (*omnis determinatio est negatio*).[22] This dialectical procedure and scholastic saying are variously called today negative dialectic, species-genus analytics, or *diaeresis* ("dividing practices"). It is beautifully illustrated by Plato in *The Sophist*. Michel Foucault and Andrea Nye, among others, have written at great length about (against) it.[23]

The negative—or negative dialectic—is a kind of *pharmakon*, and in overdoses, it is extremely dangerous. (E.g., a little girl is a little man without a penis! Or an Aryan is not a Jew! And hence, they do not or should not—because in error—exist.[24]) The warning on the label—beware of overdoses—is not enough; for we, as KB says, are rotten with perfection. We would No. That is, say No to females, Jews, gypsies, queers, hermaphrodites, all others. By saying No, we would purchase our identity. Know ourselves. By purifying the world, we would exclude that which, in our different opinions, threatens our identity. (We have, Burke says, "the motives of combat in [our] very essence" [1969a, 305].[25]) Hence, we build gulags and ovens, so as to have a great, good place. My point in relation to my subject is that The History of Rhetoric *is* by ill-virtue of gulags and ovens! It is a monument built by ways of exclusion. I am against monuments, *edifying pretensions* (cf. Hollier 1989).

Let me in/cite in historiography one general example: Schiappa asks the question: The Sophists, oasis or mirage? He employs a dividing practice, either oasis or mirage. No matter how anyone, including Schiappa, needs or wants to say otherwise, with *this* formulation of the question, Schiappa destroys the conditions for the possibilities of the Sophists. (I go into greater detail in chapter 1.)

What to do in the beatific face of negative dialectic? (Why beatific? Such a dialectic carries us up to heaven, through the chimnies?; it's the engine of salvation history?! [Please excuse my sarcasms!]) Simply put, I would denegate the negative: The principles of identity, contradiction, and excluded middle. I would denegate identity politics and ethics. Why? I want everything that has been excluded, now reincluded, put back into The History of Rhetoric. You see, if we get meaning by way of excluding, by way of saying what something *is* by way of *what it is not*, then we have purchased a stable grand narrative and meaning by way of exclusion. The History of Rhetoric is purchasable as long as we purge it of *mirages*! Yes, I would radically destabilize! The final (beginning?) excursus speaks of How everything is to be reincluded. And again, How? By *denegating the negative*, by denegating both *physis*[neg.] (as well as *nomos*) and *logos*[neg.]. By denegating that which gives us the conditions of exclusion.

Earlier in my discussion here, I said, that "this book . . . is *not* a history of rhetoric, but a set of essays concerning and excursions into historiographies. It is not a grammar of historiographies." These are beginning examples of denegations. By denying business as usual, I denegate. To write *The*, or even *a*, history, as commonly done, is to engage in narrative by way of negation, which I would denegate. Narratives are usually written temporally as tick-tock, tick-tock, tick-tock, measuring out by negation. Grand Narratives especially are measured out in this fashion. I would, however, revalue measuring and would concern us all with tock . . . tick, tock . . . tick, tock . . . tick, that which is on the outside, the Other side, of tick-tock, tick-tock, tick-tock. Hence, I am thinking in terms of the *untimely* (Nietzsche 1968b, 67–104) and *haecceity* (Deleuze and Guattari 1987, 261–65, 296–97).

History is the gift that keeps on giving to us, and yet it is a very subtle, expensive giving. It is a gift that I and others have misgivings about. The History—as historians of rhetoric write it—gives a so-called gift of

remembrance and yet creates the conditions for forgetting. Some would give
The History so that some of us could forget it, be free of it!, all together
(Shorey[26]). Others are more seemingly beneficent in their giving so that we
might remember. Yes, How to give, *to gift?*, is the question that needs—
desires—to be reopened here and elsewhere. The issue of remembering as
forgetting is the issue here.

As I stated and will elaborate on now, I think histories, hysteries,
schiztories desire to be written the way Kafka writes his stories and letters.
In Kafka's case, while he deterritorializes Papa (and Mama, and the other
bureaucrats), he gets reterritorialized by archetypal, grand narrative readers who would re-write him. Papa's Oedipalized children, with downcast
heads, are ever faithful to Papa (and Mama). (We do not need to be about
our father's [or mother's] work! We no longer need "familial investments"
[Deleuze and Guattari 1983, 278].) On occasion, Papa's children have reread
me in this fashion (see Leff 1988, Kennedy 1988, Scott 1988).

Just as we have not known How to read Kafka, we have not known How
to read our history except archetypically *as*, say, a struggle for democracy.
That is, as a class and racial and gender struggle for a radical democracy,
which, I am sorry to say, is a deterritorialization for emancipation that only
ends up being reterritorialized. I am sorry to say such a thing! But not sorry
in any Oedipal, guilty sense of being sorry. I am also sorry that this explanation might be difficult to understand. But I do not feel guilty about what
I say not being easy to drift with. Grand narratives of emancipation do not
emancipate. (I am with Lyotard and Deleuze and Guattari and many others
on this point.) Clear and concise explanations do not emancipate. (I am with
the aforementioned and Lanham [1976] on this point.) Korax and others did
not give us the means of liberating ourselves, anymore than we teachers
empower our students when we make things—really muddled things of our
whirl—so clear for them! Once when we were liberated from the tyrants on
the isle of Sicily, Korax only reterritorialized us all, just as we reterritorialize
each other when we write The History, the ever so coherent History to be
consumed and assimilated. The issue finally (beginningly?) is not emancipation but *escape* altogether. How to escape? Vomit![27] By way of *intensities*
(see Deleuze and Guattari 1986; Lyotard 1993). If I cannot always and forever denegate the negative and let nature (*physis*) flowwwwwwwwwvv&vv&vv
decontextualized here, I do, nonetheless, disengage by way of intensities. On
occasion, kaierotic occasions, I have dis/engaged from The History by way
of intensities throughout this book and especially in the final (beginning?)
excursus. I hum.

Curiously enough, I am often described, by way of a dividing practice,
as being un(in)authentic or some how of less value because *I actually do*

not write histories but write *about* (i.e., paratheorize) histories (see Connors 1991, 66–71).[28]

But to get back to my earlier point about Schiappa and the Sophists, it is not a matter of reincluding the Sophists and others in The History, for there is the additional problem that we are not at home in the *logos*. Whether negated or denegated. (As I pointed out in an interview, we—just like Isocrates—place far too much faith in the *logos*. We think that all we have to do is reterritorialize from time to time our language game and, then, just engage in dialogue freely [!] and everything will eventually be okay.)[29] And therefore, while I ruminate over what has been said about the Sophists, I also ruminate over *logos*—whether under the sign of negation or denegation, but mostly under negation, when it is most dangerous. For Isocrates, the *logos* was a Greek *logos*[neg.] and not a barbarian one. The *logos* gave the *gift* of Greek culture, Hellenism. (I focus on how such a concept as *logos* is worked and played over by Isocrates and Gorgias, Heidegger and Nietzsche.) It is not just a matter of doing away with *physis*, some universal notion of it, and accepting *nomos*, our differences, but of perpetually denegating both *physis*[neg.] and *nomos*. And doing the same to *logos*. To be sure, differences are important and crucial, but I would denegate differences to become *différance*. (*Différance* = desire, force, will. Intensities.)

You're not suggesting that you include everything here that has been excluded, are you?

Of course not, anymore than I would suggest that someone else has excluded everything. If what has been excluded is deflected, it eternally returns. Therefore, it is present in its absence. What I am suggesting here and throughout is that for parapolitical reasons, I desire radically to include the excluded. I am talking about *radical* radicals of presentation. The specific *struggle* is against the dominant discourse that goes by the name The History of Rhetoric. Given that I'm a historiographer, I have to be concerned with the social, and especially in relation to the question, At whose expense is the social constructed? It is terribly expensive. I am a critic of not only traditional history writing but also revisionary (social-constructionist) writing. Hence, I would switch social-epistemic production with desiring production.[30]

As much as we don't want to, we are playing silly games with logic here. That's why we need to get on to a trialogue, which is what the book is all about. We need to get on to what Barthes, Christa Wolf, William S. Burroughs, Deleuze and Guattari, Butler, Cixous, and others call *the third way*.[31]

By overly including the excluded, do you not threaten meaning, that is, exclude (as you yourself have said) the conditions of its possibility?

Meanings are. Simply put, I would further problematize them. Create a lot of what, in the singular or plural, meaning would call *noise*. (I am not a pluralist, but a nosiest!) And I would do more than that. For the *that*, the readers have to read through the chapters and especially the excurses.

Moving now from the questions on the negative to questions on subjectivity: What is the relationship in your title between negation and subjectivity?

I repeat: "There is no fixed subject unless there is repression" (Deleuze and Guattari 1983, 26). And add, "between the act of producing and the product, something becomes detached, thus giving the vagabond, nomad subject a residuum" (26). It is the detached, the residuum that I'm after. It is "a third party" (56). Hence, by denegating the subject-under-negation, I would make it polytropic. In other words, allow the subject to be not only 1 or 2, but some more. Would have the subject undergo metamorphosis. I end (rebegin?) with excurses on this possibility. The tactic is massive de-oedipalizations, massive de-negations. Massive deconcentration, campy writing. For the most part, while traditional historians write, they Oedipalize; while revisionary historians write, they deOedipalize and then reOedipalize; while a sub/versive writes, s/he (it) perpetually deOedipalizes. Therefore, I'm attempting to denegate the negative and subjectivity while I'm attempting to denegate—perpetually deterritorialize—The History.

Where do you stand in relation to the Feminist Sophistic?

As with all "isms," I stand *against* it (both contra to it and along side it). I am not a "male feminist." I would not pretend to know *what it is* to be one.[32] I feel uncomfortable when I read Stephen Heath's and Paul Smith's uncomfortablenesses (Jardine and Smith 1987). And I think, by the way, that it is good to feel this uncomfortableness! I understand, however, that given the conditions of life for women on this planet, particular feminists must engage in negative essentializing, by arguing that females can do such and such while males cannot. Such is a negative deconstruction, while I, how-ever, would move on to affirmative deconstructions.[33] I understand that many women cannot afford to (acknowledge that they) use deconstruction. I understand that they have to fight fascism with fascism. I see women in our field engaging in a social struggle at the level of the performative![34] The situation requires extremes. I consider your question in an excursus enquestioned "Feminist Sophistic?"

Why do you have excurses?

For me excurses are more important than the traditional chapter. I agree with Roland Barthes:

> . . . I am increasingly convinced, both in writing and in teaching, that the fundamental operation of . . . loosening method is, if one writes, fragmen-

tation, and, if one teaches, digression, or, to put it in a preciously ambiguous word, *excursion*. I should therefore like the speaking and the listening that will be interwoven here to resemble the comings and going of a child playing beside his mother, leaving her, returning to bring her a pebble, a piece of string, and thereby tracing around a calm center a whole locus of play within which the pebble, the string come to matter less than the enthusiastic giving of them. (1983, 476-77)

Why do you employ so many parenthetical comments? Why so many parentheses?

I have been criticized for apparently overusing parentheses and brackets. I use *parentheses* (a rhetorical figure!) for many reasons. Parentheses are invaginations. Sometimes, I find that I must un/make particular comments of mine. (I must put my "I"/eye—so to s/peak—in parentheses.) When reading *en parentheses*, just laugh.

Why do you invest so much in Nietzsche? Why be a Nietzschean?

This is a good question after the questions on feminism and excurses. Let's think of it in terms of my favoring Nietzsche over Heidegger (or over Freud). There is that point in the book when I have to state my preference (chapter 6), however, without excluding he-who-I-hold-in-disfavor. Nietzsche deals with the body, with the surface of things, more than Heidegger does for me. Nietzsche is by far more of a materialist than Heidegger. For Nietzsche, the force or desire or will to power is here with us, in our bodies; for Heidegger, the Nothing (Being, force) is beyond; is as he says *in withdrawal*. Both speak of "originary" forces, but locate them in different places. On the one hand, Deleuze and Guattari and Butler and a significant number of feminists (see Patton 1993; Burgard 1994) go with Nietzsche; on the other, Derrida and very few feminists go with Heidegger.[35] As I said, I favor the conditions of possibilities put forth by Nietzsche, not Heidegger, though I would not dispel the latter (including Freud); for as I say, he is *one of us*. I would agree with Derrida and Spivak that we have to say Yes to the text twice (to the good and bad, to structures of violence), and I would agree with myself that we have to say Yes, three times.

In many ways this book (as you say) -that-is-not-a-book is difficult to follow. Does it have an organizing principle?

In one sense, No. It is a "book" that would be without organs. Or I wish it to be read as such. The table of contents, however, looks fairly conventional, except perhaps for the excurses. An organizing principle? Ludwig Wittgenstein writes: "the strength of the thread does not reside in the fact that some one fibre runs through its whole length, but in the overlapping of many fibres" (1968, §67). Will that do? Some of the fibres?

-the problem of the negative
-out of the impossible comes the possible
-possibilisms and compossible
-definitions (species-genus analytics, *diaeresis*)
-identity, contradiction, excluded middle
-counting, accounting, giving an account of (*logos*)
-the excluded third
-"trace," "différance," "writing," "woman" (Derrida)
-*to apeiron* (the indeterminate)
-remembering is forgetting (Lyotard, Kundera)
-naive essentialism, strategic essentialism, denegated essentialism
-the Sophists (first, second, and what I call Third Sophistic)
-redescriptons (Rorty), not arguments
-forces, wills, desires as folds (Nietzsche, Foucault, Deleuze)
-desire in language (Kristeva)
-subjectivity (sublime, sovereign subject)
-restrictive and general (libidinal) economies (Hegel, Bataille, Cixous)
-canny and uncanny (*Unheimlich*)
-scarcity and excess, potluck and potlatch, the gift, the sun
-history and novel
-hermaphrodites (the last sex?)
-politics and aesthetics, politics and ethics (Kant, Lyotard)
-the negative, positive, nonpositive affirmative (Foucault)
-problem of being reactionary
-active and passive nihilisms, and the middle voice
-"eroticism" of human beings and the "sexuality" of animals (Bataille)
-gender; sexuality; not one, not two, but radical multiplicities (Butler
    and Fausto-Sterling)
-the *polis* (locus of dialogue, dialectic) and the *pagus* (metamorphoses)
-will to truth and will to power (Nietzsche)
-Panhellenism and rape narratives
-traditional, revisionary, and sub/versive (history) writing
-historiography, hysteriography, schizography
-Isocrates and Gorgias
. . . the fibres (i.e., desires, forces, or wills to power) go on . . .

What do these fibres have to do, as indices, with The History of Rhetoric?
Of course, that will have been the question. Perhaps the list is disorienting
(deterritorializing). If so, then good.

Is this the postmodernist book that you wanted to write?

For me, while this book rages against traditionalism and modernism
(romanticism) and attempts to do so by way of postmodernisms, it is none-

theless still deeply invested in modernism. For much time, this bothered me, until I remembered that modernism is a byproduct of postmodernism, given Lyotard's understanding, and, therefore, they are inextricably intertwined fibres (see 1984b, 81). In parallel fashion, while this book rages against liberalism, it is nonetheless still deeply invested in its thinking, as so many of my colleagues' thinking is as well. For me, the *topos* out of the impossible (negative) comes the possible may be avoidable. At least, I would say so (incite so?) and thus attempt to a-void it with performative bravado.

I sense that's potentially a very ambiguous—and ambivalent—statement . . . "may be avoidable. At least, I would say so. . . ."

Yes, yes, yes, ambiguities *are*. And we are told to work hard to a-*void* them! YES = ambiguities.[36] For Freud, negation represented ambiguities, wherein No means Yes.[37] As I point out in the book, this is a bit of a problem! Derrida has an article entitled "A Number of Yes," which he ends (rebegins?), "Already but always a faithful countersignature, a yes can never be counted. Promise, mission, emission, it always sends itself off in numbers" (1988, 132). E-mission, E-mission, E-mission. Sometimes, if not all times, we have to dis/engage by way of *tropes* (mixing the alphabet and numbers), especially against *topoi*. Tropes allow us to open up places, spaces, if not completely turn them inside out. Yes, it is not a matter of going to the outside, but being an outsider while inside. And it is open (poetic) spaces, parastructures, that I'm ever searching for: homosocial spaces (Sedgwick), baroque territories/folds (Deleuze), bodies without organs (Deleuze and Guattari), a *pagus* (Lyotard), *"les domaines inférieurs"* (Genet), *dépays* (Cixous), exterior field (Deleuze), or temporary autonomous zones (Bey).[38] As I've said and will continue to say, it is savagely open numbers that I'm ever searching for: I spend a lot of time trying to revalue counting (accounting, giving an account of) in this book. I want to give (to gift, to give the gift of) a different account of how to relocate and revalue The History of Rhetoric.

You wear masks when you write. Why? And why so many?

We all wear masks. Remember, Nietzsche says, whoever wears a mask is profound. (Of course, I fool myself, and yet we are all fools.) We all wear either proper or *inpropria persona* when we write. (But this wearing of a mask does not mean that underneath or on the other side, there is a real, fixed, authentic person! I am not an essentialist of that sort.) And if we are confronted with different audiences (multiple desires, forces) and if we have different things (forces) to express, doesn't it follow that we need many different masks (folds[39])? Nietzsche remarks: "It is impossible for Dionysian man not to understand any suggestion of any kind, he ignores no signal from the emotions. . . . He enters into every skin [fold], into every emotion; he is continually transforming himself" (1968b, 73). He is *"polytropoi"* (1974,

282), is perpetually being-refolded. Richard Lanham understands this when he writes of *homo rhetoricus* (1976, ch. 1). So yes, I wear different masks, refold myself, engage in autoaffection in front of an audience that has its own deeply entangled k/not of disciplined forces. My "colligs" have variously called me an "Aristotelian gunslinger" (James Porter), "Clarebel the clown" (Hans Kellner), the "Paganini of the printed page" (Donald Stewart), "Mr. Natural" (anti-guru of R. Crumb's *Zap* comics) (Kellner again), "Evel Knievel" (still more Kellner), "the deconstructive demon" (you, Jimmie), "the great epistemological anarchist in the field" and "Gayatri Spivak, but on acid" (Robert Connors), "the V.V. Project" (Kenneth Burke), "Vitanzan Vitalism, . . . a kind of linguistic herpes that comes and goes" (George Kennedy)—the list of forces or folds continues. It is difficult maintaining this much intensity when writing and speaking, which each of us must, if we are not to fall into being appropriated or reterritorialized. On occasion, however, it is inevitable, and so we need a strategic academism. Or strategic dullness. In other words, on occasion, we need to write the fold of the dunciad. I engage, from time to time, in such a strategy in this book. [Laughter.]

You seem to focus on the persona, or as you put it, the fold, of a child a lot. Why?

If of a child, I would hope the persona is read as a postromantic or retrosymbolic child, for I would strip *physis* (nature, Being) of its negation and let it flow wherever it desires. (Perhaps the only powerful line of resistance/flight against the dominant discourse is the technology of perpetual foldings or deterritorializations. This would be a new notion of *ethos* or poly*ethoi*.) By postromantic or retrosymbolic, I mean that I would write as a child who was in the act of dispelling mother and father, the Lacanian symbolic. Other personae of the child? Milan Kundera's (see *Life Is Elsewhere* 1986; *Immortality* 1993). And then, Kathy Acker's child, who has such "great expectations" (1982). And most importantly, let's not forget Heraclitus's child, the player of games (fragment 52). A newborn "child" always tests the capabilities of the symbolic; and the symbolic, the capabilities of a "child." I would hope—in a Victor Vitanzan hope—that every new history of rhetoric would—I think it should—test the symbolic; and vice versa.[40]

And so like denegated physis, you flow on occasion, when you write, which makes it exceptionally difficult for your audience to follow your flow. Or as you say, your drift! Do you not have respect for, or feel a responsibility towards, the common needs of the audience?

I respect the audience so much that I would try to meet, more so, the suppressed, repressed, politically oppressed *desires* of the audience. (The word "responsibility" is one of those Panopticon words. I agree with Nietzsche that we have to be strategically irresponsible so as to be responsible.)

I not only like to quote Deleuze and Guattari and Barthes excessively but also Michel Montaigne who writes: "It is the inattentive reader who loses my subject, not I. Some word about it will always be found off in a corner, which will not fail to be sufficient, although it may be concise. I seek out [I desire?] change indiscriminately and tumultuously. My style and my mind alike go wandering" (1965, 186).

But I have to insist that this book-that-is-not-a-book is really *not* that difficult to read. I spend a lot of time parodying, but mostly pastiching, academic discourse. There are lengthy sections that read like a (German) dissertation! On occasions, I slip into an obsessive discourse, with all kinds of metacommentary (first, I'm going to do this; blah, blah, blah; then finally, I'm going to do this). Other times, I am hysteric (I'm confused, or so would an obsessive reader claim!). And then schizophrenic (switching codes, deterritorializing, refolding, and *VV*ery rapidly). Those would be my paraperformatives. How various readers receive them will have been determined by their interests (again, forces) and how I serve or do not serve them. (After all, as readers we turn the lever[41] in an un/certain way, so as to promote what we think our own interests are. This "our" is quite problematic.) I try to turn the lever so as to disclose what has been, heretofore, hidden in the text (*logos*). And that requires, on occasion, to rapidly shift styles and genres. Folds. Baroque mannerisms. Derrida speaks of "a new writing"; he says, "one must speak several languages and produce several texts at once"; and finally disclosing his source, he says, "what we need, perhaps, as Nietzsche said, is a change of 'style'; and if there is style, Nietzsche reminded us, it must be *plural*" (1982, 135; Derrida's emphasis. Cf. Cixous, with Clément, 1986; Cixous 1991, 1993a).

Which then raises the question of identity. You say that you want to denegate identity but you are into identifying with such people as Deleuze and Guattari, Barthes, Montaigne, Lyotard, Cixous, etc. How do you explain such an apparent contradiction?

Yes, I identify—if you wish to call it such—with the "postidentitarians."[42] If my readers think that this is a contradiction on my part, fine. However, there are a number of ways of thinking about identification. The one that I'm against is by way of the negative. You see, I, instead, identify with the third man/woman, or the excluded middles. What Derrida calls the trace. Allow me to quote another French man, Michel Serres:

> To hold a dialogue is to suppose a third man and to seek to exclude him; a successful communication is the exclusion of the third man. The most profound dialectical problem is not the problem of the Other, who is only a variety . . . of the Same, it is the problem of the third man. We might call

> the third man the *demon*, the prosopopeia of noise. . . . Dialectic makes the
> two interlocutors play on the same side; they do battle together to produce
> a truth on which they can agree, that is, to produce a successful commu-
> nication. In a certain sense, they struggle together against interference,
> against the demon, against the third man. Obviously, this battle is not always
> successful. In the aporetic dialogues, victory rests with the powers of noise.
> (1982, 67)

Or allow me to quote an American woman, Donna Haraway:

> . . . cyborg politics insist[s] on noise and advocate[s] pollution, rejoicing
> in the illegitimate fusions of animal and machine. These are the couplings
> which make Man and Woman so problematic, subverting the structure of
> desire, the force imagined to generate language and gender, and so sub-
> verting the structure and modes of reproduction of Western identity, of
> nature and culture, of mirror and eye, slave and master, body and mind.
> (1990, 218)

So I'm very interested in excluded thirds (or middles, muddles). I would
be Franco-American-Sicilian. I search for third subject positions-that-would-
not-be positions. I attempt to denegate the principles of identity, contradiction, and excluded middle. I search for the *last sex* of The History (see Kroker
and Kroker 1993).[43] There're others who make similar searches. Acker is at
it constantly. I try to uncover the last sex in everything. In the Sophists, it
is Favorinus, whom I speak of in chapter 1.

It may very well appear, however, that I want to purge all binary
machines and replace them with desiring machines. I'm not a puritan against
binaries. There are lots of binaries in this book. The point is more simply
that I would denegate all attempts to reduce everything to binaries (e.g., male
or female) and to exclude such last sexes as trinaries (hermaphrodites,
merms, and ferms).[44] As hard as I might try, I could never exclude all binaries, for they keep creeping back in. Parataxis becomes hypotaxis; hypotaxis,
parataxis. Just as anything that has been repressed, purged, excluded eternally returns such as thirds. And, yes, yes, yes, I would do what I am capable of doing when doing hystery and schizography to enable these thirds
to creep and ooze in and in and in, back into the The History of Rhetoric.
I want to denegate The History. "I imagine a child," as Kristeva says, "who
has swallowed up his parents too soon, who frightens himself [herself, it-
self] on that account . . . and, to save himself, rejects and throws up everything that is given to him—all gifts, all objects" (1982, 5–6).[45] As I ask in
the final (rebeginning?) excursis, "WHAT WILL HAVE BEEN ANTI-OEDIPAL
(De-Negated) HYSTERIES OF RHETORICS? WHAT WILL HAVE THEY
LOOKED, SOUNDED, READ LIKE?"

*What other tactics do you employ in confronting the problem of ex-
clusion and especially in relation to what you call parapolitics, or what
Lyotard calls "pagan politics"?*

Let's turn to Nietzsche's "Homer's Contest." Simply put, again, I would
include all (ALL). The tactic works this way: If the game predicated on the
negative excludes, then, the game depredicated on the negative such as
Nietzsche's, in "Homer's Contest" (1968a), and Lyotard's, in *Just Gaming*
(1985), *includes all* in the inside except that which would dominate ethically or politically by way of exclusion. Sam Weber explains Nietzsche's two
conceptions of struggle:

> On the one hand, struggle is seen as a means, it is subordinated to a finality
> determined outside the game (whose goal is thus identified with victory);
> on the other hand, the game (or struggle) is regarded as the end-in-itself.
> The first conception finds its most extreme . . . expression in what Nietzsche
> calls the *Vernichtungskampf*, the extermination struggle; the second, in
> contrast, identified with Greek society during the Homeric epoch, is des-
> ignated as *agôn* properly speaking, as *Wettkampf* (joust). . . . "The core of
> the Hellenic notion of the joust," writes Nietzsche, is that it "abominates
> the rule of one (*die Alleinherrschaft*) and fears its dangers: it desires, as
> a protection against the genius [the negative], another genius [a
> denegation]." (1985, 106)

As we know, he-who-would-win must be *ostracized*, excluded. Hence, the
principle of exclusion (negation) is excluded (denegated). Hence, a terminal
paradox. As Weber says, "Otherness . . . is . . . sought . . . *within* the game"
itself (106). In just gaming, we play the game in such a manner to protect
the incommensurability of language games (see Lyotard 1984, xxiii-xxv).
Why? Because "we" desire a pagan politics (parapolitics).[46] You see, unlike
Bartleby, I would prefer (not to) not. . . .

*A question ever remains here with us. Does this book represent
Kristeva's "black sun" of LACK (Freud) or does it represent Bataille's sun
of EXCESS (Nietzsche)? In other words, does this book represent either the
negative cum positive (the impossible cum possible) or the nonpositive
affirmative (possibilisms)?*

A Positive answer: The latter. I believe that we can emulate the sun when
writing histories of rhetoric. Or we can perpetually attempt such an emu-
lation. I try to here and elsewhere. Yes, yes, yes, it requires great risk. To
borrow an insight from Geoff Sirc, I, too, would turn that image of the sun
on each cover of *College Composition and Communication* into a Bataillean
sun, a Bataillean Pineal Eye. The sun as excess. The eye as eroticism without reserve. (I explain this further in the first two excurses.)

A less than positive answer: Both. There is, after all has been said and undone, *joyful pessimism*. Even Bataille writes: "the sickness of being vomits a black sun of spittle" (qtd. in Land 1992, 29). We are modernists and therefore we are paradoxically not much different in our sick nostalgia for the sun. However, whereas Plato/Socrates viewed this endless source of desire (will, drive, force) as ideal, we must see it as libidinal materialism. Whereas Plato would keep the sun outside of the cave, with our seeing only a reflection—after all, he would keep us there, and make us dependent on his giving ("gifting"), and hence make us suffer resentment and become reactionary—Bataille and others would have us see the sun (libidinal energy) in all things material, especially our bodies. We are bodies that desire and waste, and perpetually. Bataille puts it well, when he talks about "meeting" Nietzsche; Nietzsche, him. About friendship. About hope. About human limitations. Bataille says:

> Writing's always only a game played with ungraspable reality. And given the impossibility of enclosing the world with propositions, I wouldn't even want to try. I wanted rapturousness [exuberance] for the *living*—for non-believers who find happiness in the pleasures of the world—a rapturousness that seemed distant from them (and which, so far, ugly asceticism has jealously kept away from them). If people never had the urge to look for pleasure (or joy) and if the only thing that mattered was repose (satisfaction) and equilibrium, then, the gift I'm contributing would be without meaning. This gift is ecstasy, it's a fitful play of lightning. (1988b, 47; Bataille's emphasis)

Yes, yes, yes, I—"WE"—believe that it is possible and more favorable to desire to write histories of *rherotics* (rherotics = rhetoric + *eros*; rherotics of free-flowing desire, until they reach their limit. . . . [and then, once again . . .]).

Yes, we are modernists (loss, anguish), but first postmodernists (joy, exuberance). How could it be otherwise? Look at this very dialogue: Out of the impossible comes the possible! Desire inevitably reaches the moment of exhaustion, anguish, loss (death). What I am saying here can be read that way, and will be read that way. *As* a loss. When it is, rather, a rebeginning (this is good!). People invest when they read, whatever they need (and want) to invest. However, they, too, when reading, reach the moment of exhaustion. Readers, just like writers, have desires that get dissipated. Forces acting on themselves and other forces. And yet there is always a return of too muchness. (It is, so I would claim as I do throughout, not in our *nature* to be exhausted; it is, to be exuberant.)

And so, yes, Jim, we find ourselves perched on the summit of the volcano Aetna[47] . . .

. . . tHere, I sit listening and speaking to you. [Laughter.]

The chapter[s] . . . have been written not as by one speaker, but as a dialogue in which several speakers conflictingly participated. The representative of "the aesthetic" [is] a lean and scurvy fellow who blurt[s] out things in a somewhat violent fashion. "The practical" [is] a represented by a portly, not wholly articulate gentleman, of obviously high repute, who look[s] upon his adversary as a scandal. And there should [be] at least one other figure, somewhat drooping, who suffered the wrangling of the two, while feeling that both had their particular kinds of justification.

—Kenneth Burke

Flectere sinequeo superos, Archeronta movebo.
(If Heaven [or respectable culture] remain unyielding, I shall move Hell.)

—Virgil

I am writing machine. The last screw has been added. The thing flows. Between me and the machine there is no estrangement. I am the machine. . . .

—Henry Miller

When I write, I become a thing, a wild beast. A wild beast doesn't look back when it leaps; doesn't check that people are watching and admiring. Those who do not become wild beasts when they write, who write to please, write nothing that has not already been written, teach us nothing, and forge extra bars for our cage.

—Hélène Cixous

Chapter 1

⋗⋖

The Sophists?

Every question selects a field of battle.

—Kenneth Burke

As I read The History of Rhetoric—as it has been processually unfolded in this century—one of the foremost problems (or questions) has been that of the Sophists. But then, Have not the Sophists always posed a problem, from Plato to the present? Has not the problem always been What to do with the Sophists? (I will anticipate: Has not the problem always been What to do with the Jews/"jews," with the Gypsies, the Queers, the rootless; always been What to do with that-which-cannot-be-represented? The Others? The Waste? [see Lyotard 1990; Barthes 1978, 134-35, 209]). It is now time—for time is running out—that we come to understand that what we, or I, do with the Sophists, when writing histor(ies) of rhetoric(s), will have established the conditions of the possibilities for any (future-past) history of rhetoric. Again, the Sophists are *The* problematic that must be addressed here. To ignore them is to turn them into the Forgotten, which will *not* have remained forgotten. But to address them (How does one speak of, or even to, the Sophists?), to readdress[1] them, we, or I, must re/address them not directly or in any referential-representational mode. And certainly, we, or I, must not re/address them, most of all, in any definitional mode. (But I greatly anticipate myself.)

*How to Speak of the Sophists?, For They have been ex*Terminated: This, then, is the problem that I will examine, the question that I will interrogate, and address in this chapter and throughout this book. As a case in point, I will examine what I consider to be a typical way that the Sophists have been addressed, and most recently by Edward Schiappa (1991). Eventually, I will examine Schiappa's argument closely, but for now some of his conclusions are that

27

- "sophistic rhetoric" should be considered a mirage (8);
- the label sophistic-*anything* may be more misleading than useful (10; Schiappa's emphasis);
- "sophistic rhetoric" is largely a fiction (14);
- the principle of Ockham's Razor suggests that "sophistic rhetoric" is expendable (15);
- I believe that "sophistic rhetoric" is a construct that we can do without; a fiction, originally invented by Plato for his own ends. We no longer need to maintain the fiction for ours. (16)

There is much that we can learn from the particular ways that we have and still do *think* of the Sophist. (We must discover ways of thinking about the Sophists that are not reactionary-revengeful ways.) For Plato, the possibilities for *representing* the Sophists, is to be realized by way of *diaeresis* (division, naming) and purification (*Sophist* 226c). Plato—or the Eleatic Stranger—concludes, after throwing his net repeatedly, that the Sophist practices "the art of contradiction making, descended from an insincere kind of conceited mimicry, of the semblance-making breed, derived from image making" (268c–d). As we know, Plato continually speaks against *mimesis*, or representations three times removed (see *Republic*, bk. III; cf. Pefanis 1991, ch. 4). It is the three times removed, however, that I would desire and eventually in the name of a *nonpositive affirmative sublime.*[2] (I would re-claim for and re-add to The History of Rhetoric not only the Sophists but also all those contemporary dissemblers such as Nietzsche, Bataille, Foucault, Cixous, Deleuze and Guattari, J. Butler, Derrida, Lyotard, Dora, the Wolf Man, Judge Schreber . . . the list goes on.)

For Schiappa, the possibilities of representation are to be found in *diaeresis* as well, but without the intention of using them to capture the Platonic "real," or "ideal," though Schiappa, nonetheless, displays a modernist nostalgia for the "real," or so-called "actual." After all, Schiappa, like Plato, rejects the "mirage" (the three times removed) in favor of *the real thing.* And to boot, the classical, philological real thing. (Whether ideal or actual makes little difference here. My sense is that Schiappa is, at times, a Platonist, while, at other times, an Aristotelian, at least, in relation to "knowing," i.e., "theoretical sciences.") For Schiappa, no matter how much he claims that he is not a Platonist, the possibilities of representation are still determined by ontological conditions, whether some thing *is* or *is not* (cf. *Sophist* 236c–237b). Aristotle is a similar ontologist. It is no wonder, then, that when Schiappa asks the ontological question (Did the Sophists exist?) that he asks it in terms of whether the Sophists are an "oasis" or a "mirage." It is also no wonder that his answer—perpetrated and perpetuated by *diaeresis*, or species-genus analytics—is that the Sophists were/are, in fact, a "mirage," or a mere imitation without an original. They are three times removed. He concludes, therefore, that there is no reason whatsoever to refer to the Sophists or to sophistic rhetoric, except for whatever uses we might have for a construct that is "largely a fiction" (14). (Yes, we are being asked to choose disjunctively between either a "fact" or a "fiction."[3]) Schiappa's conclusion, concerning the Question of the Sophists, is arrived at because it is, he insists, "historically grounded" (16). (The issue here is not Schiappa, but the methods he, and we, associate ourselves with; and yet, the issue *is* Schiappa, for he is the method that he consumes and ask us, in turn, to consume so as *to forget* the Sophists, so as to make the Sophists the Forgotten.)

Foucault has warned us repeatedly of how subjects, or agents, become subjects by way of what he calls "dividing practices"; the subject is "objectified," so as to be excluded (1982, 208; see Rabinow 1984, 7–11). The subject is negatively essentialized. Schiappa and his use of dividing practices, of *diaeresis*, of species-genus analytics, represent the hermeneutics of forgetting, and hence the politics of forgetting. I will not drink from this cup! Schiappa's is a *knowing* that I would expel.

As Stanley Rosen reminds us, however, the more that philosophical (rhetorical) discourse has attempted to *term*inate the Sophists, the more that they, the Other, live on in the *body* of philosophical (rhetorical) discourse (1983, 321–22). The more that the Sophists are repressed, the more that they return, and not only within but also, as Gilles Deleuze and Félix Guattari would say, all along the surfa(r)ces of the body, the "miraculated" body (1983, 17). Hence, Schiappa and his method are not only a manifestation of congregation by segregation but also the eternal return of the repressed, suppressed, politically oppressed.

I will report in greater detail precisely what Schiappa's (Platonic, yet Aristotelian) argument is, but it will take me a while to get to the point of reproblematizing Schiappa's views concerning the Sophists. For first, I want to lay the un/groundwork (*abgrund*)—may I still use this word?—for re(ap)proaching this problematic of seeing (theorizing, spectacalizing) the Sophists. Where we begin, or rebegin, will have determined where we will have ended; will have pre/*determ*ined what we see as our possible choices/ alternatives. (The Sophists? Either Oasis or Mirage?) Have we not learned, at least, this much about beginnings and pre*determ*inations already from rhetoric?[4] There is an important lesson here for historiographers and would-be historians of rhetoric. Let us begin this reorientation—at least, in passing—by rebeginning on familiar grounds, for eventually I will switch us—very abruptly, perhaps rudely, and at length—to thinking on more unfamiliar grounds. We will have moved from the canny to the uncanny.

Therefore, let us first look at what Kenneth Burke through Paolo Valesio says about *representation* so that I later can introduce us to the more perhaps uncanny, unfamiliar ways of what Jean-François Lyotard and others have to say potentially about representing, seeing (paratheorizing) the Sophists.

Mechanisms of Exclusion, Negative Essentializing: Valesio, discussing his concept of "regional ontology" (not to be confused with any philosophical, total view of ontology), writes: *"[E]very discourse in its functional aspect is based on a relatively limited set of mechanisms—whose structure remains essentially the same from text to text, from language to language, from historical period to historical period—that reduce every referential choice to a formal choice"* (1980, 21; Valesio's emphasis). Valesio continues:

> The choice is only between what mechanisms to employ, and these mechanisms [persona, genre, mode of emplotment, dramatistic ratio, whatever] already condition every discourse since they are simplified representations of reality, inevitably and intrinsically slanted in a partisan direction. These mechanisms always appear (so much more convincingly if the discourse is more polished and well organized) to be *gnoseological*, but in reality they are *eristic*: they give a positive or a negative connotation to the image [oasis or mirage?] of the entity they describe in the very moment in which they start describing it. (22; Valesio's emphasis; cf. H. White 1978)

Now, in pointing out this formalist view of rhetorics and their possible different historiographies, I am not evidently telling Schiappa and company something that they do not already seem to know. (Again, ever again, a historian's choice of historiography, his/her choice of "mechanisms," will have de*term*ined, the conditions of any choice of history with its conclusions.) As I say, Schiappa suggests that he does sympathize with this understanding. I have in mind Schiappa's earlier article on rhetoric (1990b), in which he appropriates Richard Rorty's "The historiography of philosophy: four genres" (1984). Specifically, Schiappa focuses on the differences between *two* of Rorty's genres, namely, "rational reconstructions" (anachronisms, fictions) and "historical reconstructions" (the way things "really" were).

Rorty, in his exposition of these two historiographies, *bases* his distinction on Quintin Skinner's maxim, and most importantly whether we decide to "obey" or to "ignore" it (54). (Skinner's maxim: "No agent can eventually be said to have meant or done something which he could never be brought to accept as a correct description of what he had meant or done" [qtd. in Rorty 1984, 50; Skinner 1969, 28]). In qualifying his use of Skinner and *what he meant*, Rorty wisely implies: " 'what [Skinner] meant' is different depending upon who is asking such questions" (54)! The implications are that the

distinctions that Rorty makes between rational reconstructions and historical reconstructions are fluid, not fixed. Rorty's view of this maxim is a
provisional, pragmatic one: At one moment, epistemic (philosophical); at
another, forensic (rhetorical); at yet another, sophistic (playful). I myself find
the maxim problematic in the light of psychoanalytic and postpsychoanalytic
hermeneutics or ideology critique. As Marx says: "they do this [speak it, hear
it, mean it] without being aware of it" (1977, 166–67). The mechanisms of
denial and disavowal, basic defense mechanisms, cause me to pause and not
give assent to Skinner's (pre-critical) maxim, which is so nostalgic for
foundations.[5]

Now, when Schiappa appropriates Rorty's distinction between "rational"
and "historical reconstructions," he retraces in places precisely what Rorty
says: "Those alternatives [rational or historical] do not constitute a dilemma.
We should do both of these things, but do them separately. We should treat
the history of philosophy as we treat the history of science" (1984, 49).
Schiappa states the same: "I am not suggesting that historical reconstruction should be done to the exclusion of rational reconstruction. With Rorty,
I believe that both ought to be done, but done 'separately' " (1990b, 196).
So far, so good; or so one might think. But my sense of what Schiappa is
doing, which Rorty is *not doing*, is sorting sheep from goats (satyrs) as the
early Puritans did. (And so, Can Schiappa make Rorty say what he had not
intended? Of course. The more interesting questions for me, however, are
How is it that Schiappa reinvests Rorty? and For *what* purposes and out-
comes?, intended or not.) Schiappa's plea in reading Rorty the way he does
is more invested, I believe, in sorting out and privileging "historically
grounded" (would-be responsible) historiography over and against
fictionalized, therefore, ungrounded (irresponsible) historiography. There is
a moral and a logic here, in this not-so-hidden allegory, that I, as well as
others, personally do not wish to identify with. The logic, as I have suggested,
is that of a privileged position over supplementary position(s).

Let us read Rorty's article on historiography and Schiappa's appropriation of it within the context of Rorty's larger discussion. (Let us take a *scenic*
view.) And let us note first of all that Rorty is describing for us "The historiography of philosophy," not *the*, or *a*, historiography of *rhetoric*. What
Schiappa finds attractive in a decontextualized version of Rorty's thinking—
and of course this is ironic, given Rorty's ever-shifting standpoints elsewhere
(see 1979; 1989)—is a residual philosophical bias. In his article under consideration, Rorty turns from analytical philosophy to hermeneutical philosophy. This is fine and I assume that many of us in rhetoric applaud such a
shift. However, Rorty later in a book-length study, *Contingency, Irony, and
Solidarity* (1989), turns, and continues to turn, from hermeneutical

philosophy to sophistic (liberal) rhetoric. In writing about the differences between a "metaphysician" and an "ironist," Rorty says that, in part, for ironists "anything can be made to look good or bad by being *redescribed*" (73; my emphasis. Cf. Burke 1984b, 39–44; and 1969a, xv–xxiii, 3–517). How many of us in rhetoric would be willing to give assent to Rorty's shift from philosophical (hermeneutical) metaphysician to a sophistic (posthermeneutical) ironist? Would Schiappa? I ask about Schiappa because he does not in his article incorporate Rorty's earlier statement concerning historiography into this processual unfolding of Rorty's thinking about writing history.

Whereas Rorty is fluid, provisional in his use of Skinner and in his historiographical distinctions, Schiappa is fixed; whereas Rorty is an "ironic" formalist (cf. K. Burke), Schiappa is a traditional-philological-"metaphysical" formalist.[6] The difference here, then, lies between the new philology (as practiced, say, by Nietzsche and Rorty) and the old philology (as practiced by Ulrich Wilamowitz-Moellendorff and Schiappa). The two have radically different notions of "describing" the world: Again, for Rorty, the ironist believes in no "final vocabulary" (1989, 73) and, thus, in redescriptions (anything *can be made to look* either good or bad, like an oasis or mirage, a fact or fiction) while the metaphysician, in descriptions (anything *is* either good or bad, etc.). I would redescribe redescriptions—which is my interest as I work through this playbook—in terms of forces (desires, wills) being brought to bear on an already existing re/description, or force (cf. Deleuze 1988, 94–123).

In any case, if Schiappa has a penchant for laying the ground work for a historiography of philosophical rhetoric, Why in the world—I cannot not ever ask—should the various "we's" or "I's" agree that *the*, or *a*, history of rhetoric be determined by the conditions or rules and regulations established by the interests and investments that de*term*ine *the historiography of philosophy*? Why should we or I use the same "mechanisms" (Valesio)? If Rorty in his discussion of the historiography of philosophy wishes—if Schiappa wishes for a decontextualized reading—that the history of philosophy be based on the same conditions as the history of science (1984, 49), there is no necessary, compelling reason why historiographers of rhetoric should follow his (momentary) predisposition toward philosophy. (Unless, of course, it's for a laugh!) And there is no reason that we should follow Schiappa's subtle plea for a so-called responsible historiography when it is based on this predisposition toward philosophy. (Unless, of course, it's for a farce!)

I am well aware that I have not by any means sufficiently argued my position that Schiappa "really has" a bias in favor of "historical reconstructions" at the expense of so-called "rational reconstructions." After all, I am an "ironist" not a "metaphysician." I agree with Rorty "that a talent for speaking [writing, thinking] differently, rather than for arguing well, is the chief instrument of cultural change" (1989, 7; cf. 8–9).[7] To argue is not my purpose here, that is, to make Schiappa agree to something that he never intended! My purpose is to redescribe perpetually by way of new idioms. (More so, I would mix idioms while I redescribe *and* redescribe so as to create the conditions for the possibility of new configurations.) However, it could be countered, by what Rorty calls a "metaphysician," that I am reading into Schiappa's argument ("redescribing") my own bias and that, therefore, I should be dismissed out of court. I agree that I have a bias. How could I humanly not! Is that not what court is all about, a place for people to speak their various biases and have them heard and not heard? (I will take up this issue of not being heard [the issue of silence] later in reference to Lyotard's concept of the *differend*. And I will situate it, as Lyotard does, in court, in the forensic.) I also maintain that it would be extremely difficult to locate in Schiappa's argument the precise place, or places, where his feigned balanced-view is slightly, subtly tilted. I could cite all the other historians and historiographers that agree generally with my position, some quite reputable. But what would that prove, as far as Aristotelian inartificial proof goes?

Finally, however, I cannot emphasize enough that I am not interested (invested) in "proving" this subtle tilt in Schiappa's article; rather, I would hope to compel the reader to see that the *Question of the Sophists* must be guarded, held ever open; for if not, then, as I will aver throughout this book, we will have continued to engage in pernicious, reactionary thinking. We will have continued to engage in negative essentializing. Such thinking is vengeful thinking. I take seriously, as well as playfully, Nietzsche's view, as Heidegger interprets it, that "revenge is the fundamental characteristic of all thought so far"; in other words, Nietzsche "thinks of revenge metaphysically . . . not only psychologically, not only morally" (1968, 97, 98). As Heidegger continues to describe it, this thinking that is vengeful is strictly modernist thinking. What goes for thinking = nostalgia. The "It Was" real has become "It Is Not." Oh, how traditional philologists suffer from this loss, inflict their revenge on the past ("It Was"); oh, how they negatively desire to know/no what was really/actually said or done! Traditional (Modernist) philologists, therefore, invest in historical reconstructions (the way things *real*ly were [intended]) instead of rational reconstructions (anachronisms, fictions)! Oasis or Mirage?

Therefore, my interests and investments are in demonstrating and performing that instead of favoring rational over historical reconstructions or vice versa, we should affirmatively deconstruct the favoring, the privileging. And I will rely less on logic, or inference, as Schiappa does (after all, he wants to be a traditional-modernist-philologist); but will lie, in an extra-moral sense, by *throwing a metaphor* in(to) the Question concerning the Sophists (after all is said and perpetually undone, I desire to be an ironist-cum-humorist).[8] Dear reader, do you find this a shocker? This is the abrupt shift that I spoke of earlier. The shifts will have become even more rapid and expansive as we continue here and mostly elsewhere. I will throw a meta-phor—by the way of Favorinus—into this discussion toward the end, so as to reopen, perpetually reopen, the Question of the Sophists.

What I propose to do, therefore, is to demonstrate and to perform just why Schiappa's argument to diminish and then to exclude "the Sophists" and "sophistic rhetoric" is dangerous and pernicious, and why it must be resisted and disrupted. In dis/order to accomplish this end for perpetual rebeginnings, I am going to establish the conditions for the possibilities of both revisionary but especially sub/versive readings of Schiappa's award-winning and influential article.[9] Specifically, I am going to use a constella-tion of language games (really paragenres, both hybrids and "sports") that requires that I reinvent myself as a "critic," more so a "paracritic," which means, in turn, that I will have to establish an *improper, proper persona* from which to criticize Schiappa's position.[10] (Therefore, my discourse[s] will not be classically well-organized or even polished [Valesio].) After suggesting a new ethos, I will then turn to a discussion of Lyotard's *The Differend*, so as to further establish the conditions for rethinking the Sophists and sophistic rhetorics. So you see it will take a while to get to Schiappa's article, but the getting-there (becoming-there) is as important as arriving-there (being-there), and in fact there may be no difference.

> . . . excess reveal[s] itself as truth.
>
> —F. Nietzsche

Therefore, unlike virtually all of my colleagues, but definitely like Barthes in *The Pleasure of the Text*, my parathinking about the question of writing histories of rhetorics is driven by the desire to have a *Society of the Friends of the Text (or Hysteries and schizzies of Rhetorics)*:

> . . . its members would have nothing in common (for there is no necessary agreement on the texts of pleasure) but their enemies: fools of all kinds, who decree foreclosure of the text and of its pleasure, either by cultural conformism or by intransigent rationalism . . . or by political moralism or by criticism of the signifier or by stupid pragmatism or by snide vacuity or by destruction of the discourse, loss of verbal desire. Such a society [of

rhetoric] would have no site, could function only in total atopia; yet it would be a kind of phalanstery, for in it contradictions would be acknowledged, . . . difference would be observed, and conflict rendered insignificant (being unproductive of pleasure). (1975, 14–15)

Yet, desiring *some more*, just as Barthes himself ever desires *still more*, I would accept the "fools" and the jokers as I accept myself. (And hope that my [good] readers, in turn, will have accepted me.) For how else, as Barthes says, could I be "the writer [who] is always on the blind spot of systems, adrift; . . . be the joker in the pack . . . [or] the dummy in the bridge game; necessary to the meaning (the battle), but deprived of fixed meaning; [my] place, [my] (exchange) *value* . . . varies [as floating signifier] according to the movements of history, the tactical blows of the struggle" (35; Barthes's emphasis).

> A wild practice . . . , one that does not provide the theoretical credentials for its operations and which raises screams from the philosophy of "interpretation" of the world. . . .
>
> —Louis Althusser

If possible, however, I would desire to be even a wilder card than a joker. (A wilder jester at court than ever previously tolerated. My "I" would be a floating, drifting signifier.) And to that end (or beginning) I would have us move on, perpetually, to a *third place* outside this dispute (*paradoxa, dissoi logoi*), to that of a sub/versive paralogy (*dissoi paralogoi*). We will have eventually been there. (We will have perpetually returned to, ventured there to that wild place, that-which-has-been-repressed place, because of discipline, metadiscipline.) Let's cut and paste, blast and uproot. Let's, hereafter, dis/engage in anacoluthons and asyndetons. Our motto: *Tmesis*.

> It is equally deadly for a mind to have a system or to have none.
>
> Therefore, it will have to decide to combine both.
>
> —Frederich Schlegel

In addition, I will be, not only like Barthes but also again like and yet un/like Lyotard, less interested in *sentences* (after all, I desire to unhinge them), and less interested in *speech acts* (after all, I would dispel author/ity), and will be, even more than Lyotard, more interested in what I will have called *theos-tricks* or *theatricks*. This latter quasi-subject position is based on my casuistic stretching of Lyotard's notion of "paganism" (1985, 16–18) and is related to my notion of a Third Sophistic (or *Society of the Friends of the Text or Hysteries and schizzies of Rhetorics*).[11] Whereas Lyotard links his notion of paganism to Aristotle (27–29), I would, as excessively suggested, move beyond, way beyond, Aristotle to a view linked up with Diogenes of Sinope and even more so with Ovid. (The choice for me, as Peter Sloterdijk best states it, is not between Plato *and* Aristotle—or a so-called bad cop and a good cop/y—but between Plato *and* Diogenes of Sinope [1987, 103].)

What is both needed and more so wanted, therefore, are ways of pro-visionally-temporarily negotiating with exclusionary structures of violence (politics, litigation, the *polis*, binaries) and then ways of re/including greater, greater, excessively greater—but I cannot say "numbers of"—the suppressed, repressed, politically oppressed (or *differends*, re/situated in the *pagus* or *les domaines inférieurs* or temporary autonomous zones or homosocial space or Baroque deterritorializations). And yet this is a conservative suggestion of what I'm about. (As we trek though this book-that-is-not-a-book, there will have been more radical re/considerations. For finally, I will not have wanted to even negotiate with narratives of violence!) What I will have suggested is that what is wanted is a movement, but not necessarily a *political* movement, from "1" to "2" (*polis*) to "some more" (third) subject positions (*pagus*, TAZs, perpetual deterritorializations). As Rorty says: "freedom [is] the recognition of contingencies" (1989, 26). At least, on occasion! For I would also trek with the unaccountable (chance, hazard).

> It is necessary to link, but the mode of linkage
> is never necessary.
>
> —J.-F. Lyotard

I. The *Differend*,
Incommensurable Phrases in Dispute
(or, Preparing the Way to Toss a Metaphor)

If you, dear reader, have made it to this point, you are a more gracious (sado-masochistic) reader than most. Bravo! Much of what I will say about the radical form of dissensus (or expulsion of the principle of expulsion) comes out of Lyotard's discussion in *The Differend* (1988a). From this point on, it would be helpful, beneficial, to forget (like Nietzsche's cows) the opening section of this chapter, especially if *you*, dear reader, are wondering about "connections" or what mode of linkage it might have with what is to follow. (You see, it is the so-called . . . illegitimate lineage that I am after. The "uncivilized." The negated so that there might be—so we have been told—a civilized. It is the excluded middle [muddle] that I am after. And therefore my rude interventions, disruptions, and perhaps annoying waywardness.) For my more immediate aims, however, the discussion that follows has two purposes: (1) To introduce any new reader, or rereader, to *The Differend*, that is, to *my way* of reading, stretching, this remarkable sophistic book; (2) and to suggest how the discussion in the book, at key points, might be even more radicalized for Sophistic rhetorics of radical dissensus. In more traditional sense, I am laying the un/ground work, or the conditions, for rethinking the Sophists after Schiappa has systematically excluded them or redescribed them as mere "fictions." (In other words, if you catch my drift, I would denegate Aristotle's *Sophistic Refutations* so as to get to Lyotard's *Sophistics*. After all has been said and undone, I would reclaim the Sophists but without redomesticating them. And that will require Other in[ter]ventions, con-fabulations.)

The Fate of the Three Classical Speech Acts (forensic, epideictic, deliberative discourses): Let's rebegin by examining the central term of the title of the book: For Lyotard, a *differend*, as opposed to a *litigation*, "would be a case of conflict, between (at least) two parties, that cannot be equitably resolved for lack of a rule of judgment applicable to both arguments. One side's legitimacy does not imply the other's lack of legitimacy. However, applying a single rule of judgment to both in order to settle their differend as though it were merely a litigation would wrong (at least) one of them" (1988a, xi). The distinction, then, is that though we have rules to settle *litigation*, we have no rules for settling a *differend*. Hence, we have epistemic violence: While litigation enables one side, it disenables the other. It is difficult to remedy this problem because no final set of rules can be developed to accommodate the *differend* into the discourse of *litigation*, for the simple reason that the introduction of rules—statements based on *how*—only introduce new *differends* (see 181). Though there is no final set of rules, this does not mean, however, that there are not perpetual attempts to universalize rules by a (synecdochic) genre of genres, which *is* the act of real epistemic violence (see 128–150). The cure (the *pharmakon*), however, becomes, for Lyotard, "some more" *differends*.[12]

What Lyotard has in mind with this definition of the *differend* and the primary example that he opens with is what in The History of Philosophical Rhetoric is called *forensic* discourse. (This discourse centers around questions of fact, value, and quality: Is it? What is it? What quality is it?) Lyotard's primary example is the War-Crime Trials and how examinations of the transcripts disclose on occasion that the Jews and others were further

victimized, that is, silenced, by the very rules of evidence that were specifically designed to allow them to speak in their defense. But the violence and
silence does not stop with the trials. For now, Lyotard tells us, there is a
group of historians who are saying that, as they look through the court
transcripts, *they can find no evidence of the holocaust*: One historian writes,
"I have tried in vain to find a single former deportee capable of proving to
me that he had really seen, with his own eyes, a gas chamber" (3–4). Lyotard
gives an account of the rule (or the question, Is it?) and how it informs reasoning: "To have 'really seen with his own eyes' a gas chamber would be the
condition which gives one the authority to say that it exists and to persuade
the unbeliever. Yet it is still necessary to prove that the gas chamber was
used to kill at the time it was seen. The only acceptable proof that it was
used to kill is that one died from it. But if one is dead, one cannot testify
that it is on account of the gas chamber" (3–4).

(Oh, sophisticated reader, do you see where I might be event-ually taking
all this? Well, if so, do not project too much, do not fill in the enthymeme
too quickly!)

Lyotard with Adorno on "What happened to the beautiful death?": But
Lyotard does not stop with the problem of forensic discourse. As I read the
book, Lyotard is equally concerned with the apparent impossibility of *epideictic*
and *deliberative* discourses as well. This impossibility is in great part linked
with *the sign of Auschwitz*. It's a "sign," as Lyotard sees it, at the end of the road
of history, a "sign" that Adorno himself had already summoned in his *Negative
Dialectic* (1987). It is a "sign" that is a counter-product of a perfect metaphysical identification (noncontradiction, excluded middle), or a way of achieving
perfect understanding, or congregation/integration, by way of exclusion/
segregation, which is touted to be the end of all Hegelian onto-theological
History. And how? Adorno answers: "Genocide is the absolute integration"
(362; cf. Plato, *Sophist* 226d, 227d). For Adorno, *metaphysics*—which attempted to link life with death in obligatory terms—*is "absolute integration."*
Genocide (Genus-cide) is the segregating and silencing of the *differend*. As
Deleuze says, if the "lineage" (1983b) is not proper, the species *is* illegitimate
and, therefore, it must be systematically exiled, ex-*term*inated. As Catherine
Clément says: "Somewhere every culture has an imaginary zone for what it
excludes, and it is that zone we must try to remember today. This is history that
is not over" (Cixious and Clément 1986, 6).

For Lyotard, it is a question of violence done both to human beings and
our resources of language. He asks, How can one engage in epideictic discourse after Auschwitz? How can we, say, as Gorgias and Isocrates had said
about the Athenians, that the Jews, the Gypsies, the Poles, the Queers, and

Others died the true, the good, the beautiful death? As Adorno wrote: "Auschwitz confirmed the philosopheme of pure identity as death" (1987, 362). Auschwitz, as the locus of the *differend*, the excluded, is the very embodiment of epistemic violence. As Lyotard says in his "Hegel" Notice: "We wanted the progress of the mind, we got its shit" (91). Philosophically, rhetorically, historically, Athens has enabled (made a necessity) Auschwitz: If for Nicole Loraux (1986), epideictic discourse *invented* Athens, for Adorno and Lyotard, Auschwitz put an end to epideictic discourse, in fact, silenced all discourse, past or future—that is, judicial (that which would have righted the wrongs) and deliberative (that which would have attempted to prevent the wrongs from ever happening again). But let's not despair too deeply, for, in Lyotard's view, Auschwitz did not lead to the end of history; as is expressed in the final chapter of *The Differend*, Auschwitz is paradoxically (but negatively) both the end, the impossibility of history, but also the beginning, its eternally returning possibility: *Auschwitz is*—as the last chapter of the book "entitles" it—one of "The Sign[s] of History." (As we will eventually see, in a *litigation*, which is determined by cognitive rules and regimens, often a *differend* is created, and *silence* is created; but the creation of this *differend* and its state, silence, "does not impose the silence of forgetting"; on the contrary, the *differend* "indicate[s] that something [variously referred to as a 'feeling' and a 'sign'] which should be able to be put into phrases cannot be phrased in the accepted idioms" (1988a, 56). And, therefore, it is necessary to bear witness to this silence and consequent sign/feeling, and to discover idioms for them (13).

Wittgenstein and Lyotard, on Silences; or Let's Rethink Linkages: In order for Lyotard to establish his concept of linkage—to link is necessary, but how to link is *not* necessary[13]—Lyotard must retell the whole history of philosophy and rhetoric. (He has, in a sense, to reestablish "the sign of the history of philosophy [and rhetoric].") The book *The Differend*, therefore, vacillates between what Lyotard calls "presentations" (or "phrases," which are antithetical to numbered "propositions" as we find in Wittgenstein's *Tractatus* [1961]) and what Lyotard calls "Notices," or "Reading Notes," which are his "readings" of the "signs" of the history of philosophy. He has "Notices" on Protagoras, Gorgias, on Plato, Aristotle, Kant, Hegel, and others. This is a whole continuum of critical coordinates, or "signs," or perhaps rude in(ter)ventions that Lyotard has to establish in dis/order to rethink linkages.

If someone were going to read *The Differend* for the first time, I would suggest that what has to be understood about Lyotard in this work, is that he is not an advocate for traditional philosophy and Enlightenment-emancipatory thinking such as is perpetrated by an early or mid-Wittgenstein or a Habermas. (Lyotard sees the impulse to philosophize systematically, in the name of the language game of knowledge or of *litigation* or of universal pragmatics, *as* ethically and politically dangerous.) If not an advocate for traditional philosophy or its rhetoric, he is then an advocate for the language games of avant-garde art. (Lyotard, like the latter Adorno, is very much a child like and of Nietzsche.)

In dis/respect to the language game of knowledge, therefore, we might come to see that the book *The Differend* is a loose continuation of Wittgenstein's thinking, but a continuation that attempts to move beyond the impossibilities of *litigation* (traditionally situated in the *polis*) to the possibilities of the *differend* (situated in the *pagus*). In other words, whereas Wittgenstein starts out with the *Tractatus*, an exploration of the grounds for formal logic and its connections with nature, he then continues by way of amends with *The Philosophical Investigations* (1968), a development of his concept of "language games"—which is a concept further developed by Austin, Searle, et al. Many people in our field—widely defined as criticism, rhetoric, communications—are happy with this movement from the *ideal* to the *actual*, from Plato (bad cop) to Aristotle (good cop/y). But others of us are not so happy, though we are *cheerfully pessimistic*: For Wittgenstein reaches the end of the rules and falls into silence (as later Heidegger does!), not just in the *Tractatus* but even in his *Investigations*; but though he reaches the end of his road, he stops short of the *pagus*. In the simplest words, Wittgenstein stops short of "magic," or what he calls "bewitchment" in language (1968, 47e). Wittgenstein leaves some of us, at this point, consequently, with a "feeling" and a "sign" of what has been silenced/re-pressed, what has been systematically excluded/negated.[14]

Therefore, my linkage: I see the movement from the *Tractatus* (formal logic, the true) to *Philosophical Investigations* (informal logic, the good) to *The Differend* ("paralogic," the negative sublime). This movement—like Kant's movement in his three critiques—creates, however, a greater level of *contingencies* among the three discussions of the true (pure reason), the good (practical reason), and the beautiful (the aesthetic). Lyotard and Kant's latter thirds, the *paralogic* and the *aesthetic* (negative sublime), foster this loose-ness, but also a danger.[15]

The concept of *differends* becomes for Lyotard—as he would envision it as an extension of Wittgensteinian (and Heideggerian) silence—"the unstable state and instant of language wherein something which must be able to be put into phrases cannot yet be." He writes: "This state includes silence." But not the silence of forgetting! As we know, Wittgenstein, after kicking his ladder away, had concluded his *Tractatus* with proposition no. 7: "What we cannot speak about we must pass over in silence." However,

Lyotard continues—by virtue of a *paralogic* linkage—where proposition no. 7 leaves off: "This state [of silence] is signaled by what one ordinarily calls a feeling: 'One cannot find the words,' etc. A lot of searching must be done to find new rules for forming and linking phrases that are able to express the differend disclosed by the feeling, unless one wants this differend to be smothered right away in a litigation. . . ." And then, he writes: "What is at stake in a literature, in a philosophy, in a politics perhaps, is to bear witness to differends by finding idioms for them" (1988a, 13; cf. 80). The key words here are "to bear witness" and to find "idioms." The concepts of bearing witness and searching for new idioms are reminiscent of the Sophistic antitradition of making the weaker argument the stronger (159), or I would add now *making the feeling hold precedent over the argument*. (Feyerabend, a modern-day Sophist, has called this activity "counter-induction" [see 1978, 1988]. This is the same Feyerabend who has influenced Lyotard in his writing *The Postmodern Condition* [1984b].)[16]

In "presentation" no. 137, Lyotard extends this concept of the *differend*. (Let us now return to and relink up with the war-crime Trials.) Lyotard says:

> By forming the State of Israel, the survivors [of the holocaust] transformed the wrong into damages and the differend into a litigation. By beginning to speak in the common idiom of public international law and of authorized politics, they put an end to the silence to which they had been condemned. *But* [let's not miss Lyotard's more important point] the reality of the wrong suffered at Auschwitz before the foundation of this state remained and remains to be established because it is in the nature of a wrong not to be established by consensus. . . . What could be established by historical inquiry would be the quantity of the crime. But documents necessary for the validation were themselves destroyed in quantity. . . . The result is that one cannot adduce the numerical proof of the massacre and that a historian pleading for the trial's revision will be able to object at great length that the crime has not been established in its quantity. But [Lyotard continues] the silence imposed on knowledge does not impose *the silence of forgetting*, it imposes *a feeling*. . . . the *silence* that the crime of Auschwitz imposes upon the historian is a *sign* for the common person. *Signs* . . . are not referents to which are attached significations validatable under the cognitive regimen, they indicate that something which should be able to be put into phrases cannot be phrased in the accepted idioms. (1988a, 56–57; emphasis mine)

Then referring to those historians who wish to claim that there was *no* holocaust, Lyotard writes: "They will say that history is not made of *feelings* and that it is necessary to establish the *facts*. But, with Auschwitz, something new has happened in history (which can only be a *sign* and not a *fact*) . . ." (57; emphasis mine).

By Way of Finally Beginning. Some Further Ruminations on Non-Humanism, the Pagus, Differend, *and the Sign of History*: In "presentation" no. 63, Lyotard recalls, from language theory, the distinction among *designation, nomination,* and *signification.* (Notice here the drift toward a third term.) Or, in other words, the distinction among an *ostensive* phrase, a *nominative* phrase, and a *subjunctive* phrase. Or still again, a distinction among *showing* the facts, *naming* them properly, and *signifying* not facts but "feelings." It is this third concept of *signification*—a concept that is excluded due to the epistemic violence of the rules of litigation—that we need to readdress, finally in relation to Lyotard's non-Humanist position, and in relation to the possibilities of my perpetual search for third subject/object positions.[17]

The question, for Lyotard, *is,* How to link *feeling/sign* to designation and nomination? The answer is "to just-link." (Yes, there is a pun on this word "just," as in "justice.") Lyotard says that the conjunction *and* "signals a simple addition, the apposition of one word with another, nothing more." Lyotard favors *parataxis* over *syntaxis* (or *hypotaxis*). He says:

> Conjoined by "*and,*" phrases or events follow each other, but their succession does not obey a categorical order ([i.e., the order of] *because; if, then; in order to; although* . . .). Joined to the preceding one by "*and,*" a phrase arises out of nothingness—here is the problem of the negative again—to link up with it. Parataxis thus connotes the abyss of Not-Being [cf. Heraclitus, Gorgias, Heidegger] which opens between phrases, it stresses the surprise [remember, Wittgenstein said there are no surprises in nature!] that something begins when what is said is said. '*And*' is the conjunction that most allows the constitutive discontinuity (or oblivion) of time to threaten, while defying it through its equally constitutive continuity (or retention). (1988a, 66)

It is in this statement that we have the oxymoronic yoking of a loss of control and an appearance of control, of non-Humanism and Humanism, of *kairos* and *chronos,* of "tock-tick" (*and* as nothingness, threatening discontinuity) with "tick-tock" (a momentary reestablishment of continuity, or retention). Linking "tock-tick" and "tick-tock," Lyotard tells us: "For there to be no phrase is impossible, for there to be *And a phrase* is necessary. It is necessary to make linkage. This is not an obligation . . , but a necessity, . . . To link is necessary but how to link is not" (66). This is what *paralogy* is all about—"just-linking." For Lyotard, *paralogy,* not rules, precedes consensus. This is Lyotard's game of the future-anterior, or of *prolepsis,* with the rules developing out of the processual realization of them—with questions, out of the answering of them; and with "WEs," out of the elaborating of the question. Once realized, however, the rules are to be discarded for another future-anterior, or avant-garde, language game. This is the *just-game* of "paganism," as in playing the game without criteria. It is a game of sophistic anti-foundationalism. The just-game of "paganism" is played out in the "*pagus*, on the border zone where genres of discourse enter into conflict over the mode of linking" (151; cf. 1885, 73–83). (But this game, as admitted by Lyotard himself, is not only sophistic but also Aristotelian!)

Lyotard points out that Marxists and Capitalists, however, do not want to play the (just) game this way, the pagan way. (Nor, I would add, do Aristotelians.) Both systems of thought are informed by what Lyotard calls "the economic genre," which demands *litigation* at the expense of the *differend*—demands *litigation*, which in turn demands centralism and monopoly and the suppression of heterogeneity. (This economic genre, as I will make clear in the forthcoming excurses, is a restrictive economy, not a general economy.) Marx, Lyotard says (171–72), heard the cry of the proletariat, which, indeed, was voicing the "feeling" of "communism, the free linking of phrases, the destruction of genres." This "feeling" was *signal*ing a finality of history. But we must ask, What went wrong? It was simply the economic genre, which favors/demands *litigation* over the *differend*; which favors hypotaxis over parataxis; which pretends to be the genre of genres.[18] Marxism demands *litigation* as centralism and monopoly, *not* unlike its alleged antithesis, capitalism. Moreover, it was (is) Humanism (anthropologism), which goes wrong, namely, the belief that human beings actually choose, or make, their own history; and the belief that sometimes human beings, as when making a grammatical error, choose incorrectly their own history, and it is just a matter then of learning to choose correctly.[19]

Lyotard says: "It is not the people that is fickle, but 'language.' . . . [Still more importantly, he says:] Maybe prose is impossible. It is tempted on one side by despotism [syntaxis, hypotaxis] and on the other by anarchy [parataxis]. It succumbs to the seduction of the former by turning itself into the genre of all genres. . . . But the unity of genres is impossible. . . . Prose can only be [the people's] multitude and the multitude of their differends" (158). Lyotard continues: "The wisdom of nations is not only their scepticism, but also the 'free life' of phrases and genres. That is what the (clerical, political, military, economic, or informational) oppressor comes up against. . . . Prose is the people of [radically heterological] anecdotes" (158–59). Deleuze and Guattari speak similarly in terms of "a minor literature" (see 1986). Lyotard is primarily non-Humanist, which means for him that human being is, more so, the function of language than vice versa. He makes it clear in his closing two "presentations" that human being is the function of the *differend*, though human being attempts to take charge in the grand narrative and in the proper name of *litigation*. What is left to human being is to come to understand that we are best, at home, when re/located at the site of the unhomely, the *"pagus,* a border zone where genres of discourse enter into conflict over the mode of linking." And therefore as an avant-gardist, Lyotard hails "Joyce, Schöenberg, Cézanne: *pagani* waging war among the genres of discourse" (1988a, 151). To insist on the traditional philosopher's ideal of the *polis*, however, will only return us to deep trouble. After all, as Lyotard says, for 2,500 years "We wanted the progress of the mind, we got its shit" (91).

II. The Included Third:
The Death of Rhetoric and History and the Sophists, and their Rebirth in the the Sign of a "Third Sophistic"

To hold a dialogue is to suppose a third man and to seek to exclude him; a successful communication is the exclusion of the third man. The most profound dialectical problem is not the problem of the Other, who is only a variety . . . of the Same, it is the problem of the third man. We might call the third man the *demon*, the prosopopeia of noise. . . . Dialectic makes the two interlocutors play on the same side; they do battle together to produce a truth on which they can agree, that is, to produce a successful communication. In a certain sense, they struggle together against interference, against the demon, against the third man. Obviously, this battle is not always successful. In the aporetic dialogues, victory rests with the powers of noise.

—Michel Serres

. . . we do not need the fiction of "sophistic rhetoric" as a way into pressing contemporary issues.

—Edward Schiappa

Let us return to the beginning of this chapter. Or return to the improper name of the repressed—the Sophists. What needed to be said by way of preparation, or rude in(ter)vention, has been said. What remains is what *desires* to be said. What remains is to include what has been excluded. Let us, therefore, return to the Question of the Sophists.

I agree with, though paradoxically/ironically, Schiappa's major point, namely, "that we cannot identify a defining characteristic of 'the sophists' that allows us to narrow the group to a degree sufficient to adduce a common perspective or set of practices" (1991, 8). We not only cannot identify a defining characteristic, but also, I would insist and incite, we *do not have to*. Schiappa, however, writes: "Scholars defending 'sophistic rhetoric' typically *must engage in some act of defining* what the terms mean to them, or else rely on readers' intuitions as to what the terms denote" (15; my emphasis).[20] I do not think so!

When Schiappa insists on "defining" (limiting, as a single rule of judgment) and, more generally, when he insists on engaging in traditional philosophical/philological rules of judgment, he is no longer engaging in a *litigation* but in what Lyotard has called a *differend*. I would add that Schiappa is engaging in a very violent and potentially dangerous and pernicious *differend*. Schiappa's thinking is much like the contemporary revisionary historians' thinking who would deny—given the rules of evidence in the courtroom—the less-than-factual testimony of the holocaust survivors (Lyotard 1988a, 3–6). As I summarized Lyotard's position earlier, in respect to the war-crime trials, what is said in the courtroom, and more recently in the scholarly journals, and in U. S. Senate hearings (Hill vs. Thomas) gets ruled out of court as not "facts" but feelings, emotions, intuitions, etc. (Again, the rules and regimens that are exclusive to one side's argument are used not only to shape, but to find, the other's argument lacking.) Hence, history gets rewritten: No holocaust. In our case here, The History of Rhetoric gets rewritten: No "sophistic rhetoric." (It is both this *method* and this kind of history that the method creates, therefore, that I would denegate. There is, I would incite, *justice* in such denegations.)

To recapitulate and to move on: When we move out of *litigation* and create the (ontological) conditions for the possibilities of a *differend* (which is the using of rules and regimens proper to one party and not the other, and using them as the means of excluding *the other*), we inevitably purify, silence, and exclude. And we do so traditionally by asking, Is it? What is it? And What quality is it? As Derrida says, "One cannot name [sophistic-*anything*] within the logocentric system—within the name—which in turn can only vomit it and vomit itself in it. One cannot ever say: what is it? That would be to begin to eat it, or—what is no longer absolutely different—to vomit it" (1981b, 25).

Yet, Schiappa asks, What is it? As I made clear, Adorno in his *Negative Dialectic* warns us of the inherent destination of ontological thinking, which is the thinking of, and the thinking warranted by, the question "Who were the sophists?" (Schiappa 1991, 5) and "What is sophistic rhetoric?" (8). Though Schiappa seems to be aware of the dangers behind thinking of "a 'correct' definition of a word in any absolutist, metaphysical sense" (15), he, nonetheless, engages in this kind of correct-thinking, when he employs species-genus analytics, *and* when he, more importantly, does so *with the sole purpose of excluding* those historians who are incorrect. Adorno writes: "Genocide [Genus-cide] is the absolute integration" (1987, 362). Burke similarly writes against employing segregation to justify integration/congregation (see Desilet 1989, 76; Burke 1970, 4–5). Schiappa, however, writes: "Sophistic rhetoric" (apparent species) is not distinguishable by any genus and differentiae. He concludes: ". . . *we do not need the fiction of 'sophistic rhetoric'* " (14; Schiappa's emphasis). Throughout his article, the species "Sophist" and "sophistic rhetoric" are dismissed, except at the end, when he comes back around, though not really, to saying that both might have some value as a "reservoir"—but this last stance seems greatly disingenuous, especially since, in the remaining paragraph Schiappa returns, once again to excluding both concepts (16).

Allow me to continue with *why* I think that the kind of thinking Schiappa engages in, as an historiography of exclusion and a hermeneutic of forgetting, is not only in practice dangerous but also puzzlingly ironic (or perhaps confused, which in some ways I take to be, in dis/respect to Schiappa's mode of historiography, unintentionally virtuous, for an act of con-fusion—such as an act of metalepsis—is akin to and a beginning sign of virtuosity). Though Schiappa says that the Sophists and their rhetoric are both "a fiction, originally invented by Plato for his own ends" (16), Schiappa, nonetheless, goes on to use the very in/terror/gating method (*diaeresis*) that Plato and later Aristotle, though differently, used in the first place, according to Schiappa, to create the very concept of "sophistic rhetoric." My sense, then, is that what Schiappa does—and without any conscious irony (or confusion)—is to recapitulate Plato himself. What Plato creates, Schiappa ex-creates. What a versatile methodology! It destroys no matter what! My provisional conclusion, however, is that the concept of "sophistic rhetoric" or "Sophist" itself is not the culprit as Schiappa would have it. Nor is the culprit necessarily Plato, unless we make our judgments based on Humanists predispositions. I would say, again, that the culprit is the very *method (or process) itself* that produced the so-called Platonic concept—or as Schiappa might have it, "effect"—sophistic-*anything*; and produced this person/thing called "Plato." From a non-Humanist perspective, the concept here and the personage are functions of the methodology (strategy). But all this can be seen in even darker ways, for my sense is that in language (*logos*) itself there is this (potentially fascistic-Hierarchical) force that predisposes us to do as we do. (Again, we are a function of our methodology, which more often than not is a negative essentializing methodology such as species-genus analytics, *diaeresis*. It is our methodology that enables us to create and ex-create.)[21]

If so, then, there is another point to be made in this connection: Schiappa says that we should not read "history backwards" (7).[22] Schiappa, however, reads history backwards when he employs species-genus analytics, as I said, on those historical figures that have been called Sophists. But more importantly, he reads history backwards when he centralizes PLATO as *the measure* of The history of philosophy and philosophical rhetoric so that he might negatively reessentialize and purge the Sophists from the Republic of The History of Rhetoric.

This needs some further explaining: Sarah Kofman has brilliantly demonstrated how the so-called presocratics—some of whom have been labeled "Sophists"—were systematically misrepresented, misappropriated, and then characterized as *children*-thinking-philosophy. She demonstrates, in this case, when history is read backwards, how much epistemic violence can be done. She says that Plato, Aristotle, and Hegel (the Platonic lineage) each characterizes these early thinkers as infants-yet-doing-their-best. As Kofman says, it is assumed—given the rules and regimens of judgment, which have been initially informed and privileged by Platonic thinking—that "the later [grownup] philosophers [Plato et al.] can help [these early thinkers] grow from childhood to adulthood, from metaphorical obscurity to conceptual clarity" (1987, 43). The primary example, which Kofman calls on, is found in the various characterizations of Heraclitus. (I am not suggesting that Heraclitus *is* a Sophist, though I prefer to think, perhaps childishly, of him *as* a Sophist.) Heraclitus, with his so-called obscurity and lack of clarity, is variously interpreted as a poet not a philosopher and as dealing in *alogia*, the absurd (Plato); or as a bad writer, with a poor knowledge of grammar and punctuation (Aristotle); or as in need of being translated into speculative reason (Hegel) (41–44).

My point, then, is that Schiappa's whole article is arranged along this Platonic, Aristotelian, Hegelian line (lineage) of thinking. Quite ironically, like Plato, Schiappa in our own century intellectually acts (thinks backward) so as to rekill off not just potentially a Heraclitus but anything Sophist(ic). If not rhetorical infanticide, Schiappa, again, like his predecessors, engages in Sophist-cide by way of Genus-cide. But ironically again, the very act of killing off "sophistic rhetoric" only reassures that it will live on stubbornly (cf. Rosen 1983, 321–22). And why? Because quite simply we are left (far left) with a void and a (Wittgensteinian, Heideggerian) silence. Lyotard writes:

"This state [of silence] is signaled by what one ordinarily calls a feeling: 'One cannot find the words,' etc. A lot of searching must be done to find new rules for forming and linking phrases that are able to express the differend disclosed by the feeling, unless one wants this differend to be smothered right away in a litigation. . . ." And then, he writes: "What is at stake in a literature, in a philosophy, in a politics, [in writing histories of rhetorics] perhaps, is to bear witness to differends by finding idioms for them" (1988a, 13; cf. 80). Again, Lyotard might say: "[Schiappa would argue] that history is not made of *feelings* and that it is necessary to establish the *facts*. But, with [the death of sophistic rhetoric], something new has happened in history (which can only be a *sign* and not a *fact*). . ." (57; emphasis mine).[23] Continuing along this same subjunctive-argumentative line, Lyotard would point out that philosophical philologists and rhetoricians (of the Ulrich Wilamowitz-Moellendorff[24] and Schiappa type), however, would not want to play the (just) game this way, the pagan way. Both systems of thought are informed by what Lyotard calls "the economic genre," which demands *litigation* at the expense of the *differend*—demands *litigation*, which in turn demands centralism and monopoly of (The) history (of Rhetorik) and the suppression of heterogeneity. Schiappa, Lyotard would say, cannot hear the cry of the other revisionary and sub/versive historians and hysterians, who, indeed, are voicing the "feeling" of "sophistic rhetoric," that is, "the free linking of phrases, the destruction of genres" (171).

So much for, at best, subjunctive argumentation. I have another way of dealing with Schiappa's injunctive argument, with more obvious redescriptions (desires, forces, wills). Let us retrope quickly and search for a way of avoiding the problem of the *differend* altogether, which gets us to the next section. . . .

What would be different has not begun as yet.

—T. Adorno

With the death of sophistic rhetoric, we are left with a feeling.

—[indirectly, J.-F. Lyotard]

After "sophistic rhetoric": In this section, I will continue the discussion of a-voiding (de/negating) the problem of the method of species-genus analytics, which has given us, in my extended example, the *differend*. Thus far altogether, I introduced myself as an "ironist" (Rorty) cum humorist (Deleuze and Guattari); I discussed Lyotard's concept of the *differend*; and I discussed the death of history but, then, its rebirth in a "feeling" and in "a sign of history." (I've had to perform all these things so as to get myself to a position that would allow me to think and speak.) Then, bringing us up to date, I just-linked the discussion of Lyotard's *differend* analogically with Schiappa's discussion of "sophistic rhetoric," pointing out that Schiappa, in his act of Genus-cide, creates a *differend* and hence kills off, once again, sophist-*anything*, but that, nonetheless, sophistic rhetoric lives on as a "feeling" and a "sign" in revisionary and sub/versive historians and hysterians' views; lives on as "the sign of sophistic rhetoric."

I will continue this discussion in the following way: In dis/order to escape the situation of the *differend*, in reference to the questions of What is sophistic rhetoric? or What is rhetoric?, I simply would *not* ask these ontological questions, as I attested earlier, with the purpose of answering them. (I do not even like them when framed as a plural, What are. . . ?) Why do I suggest this as a post-Heideggerian tactic? For the simple reason that any attempt to answer *the Question of Being* definitively only leads to a political nightmare, to exclusion, and to rites of purification. (Heidegger himself stands as an example of someone who failed finally to realize and practice his own post-hermeneutic and showed only a contempt for Being [cf. Lyotard 1988a, no. 197; 1990, 51–94].)[25]

The *last man* asks, "What is it?" (see Nietzsche 1968a, 129).

Instead of going to Heidegger himself, I would at this provisional point turn to Derrida (1978, 140–53) and to Gayatri Spivak, who have recently made much of *the Question of Being*.[26] Borrowing from Derrida, Spivak writes: "Heidegger suggests that *Dasein* is ontically programmed to ask the ontological question, and not to be able to answer it" (1989a, 209)[27] Being—its Question—is, indeed, highly problematic: As I have attempted to point out, we do insist, nonetheless, on answering its Question, whether it be the Question of rhetoric, or sophistic rhetoric, or of woman. Spivak sees the ontological question (What is it?) as an inevitable one, but not necessarily one that we must inevitably capitulate to. She says, therefore, following Derrida, that we must "negotiate [with this/these] structures of violence" (212). The structure of the ontological question is violent, as I have suggested, because it is preconditioned to have us believe that it must be answered (that it is irrepressible) and that it has a "correct" (Platonic absolute or Aristotelian actual) answer. (Again, I am well aware that Schiappa says that he is against "correct" ontological answers, but I am also keenly aware that he has practiced traditional philological analysis "correctly" so as to exclude. As Stephanie Jed argues, "the practice of philology has important political implications" [1989, 11].) The structure of the ontological question is so violent because it *pre*-excludes. And it does so with a professional, disciplinary *alibi*! While it harbors resentment, it does not know of this *ressentiment* (see Nietzsche 1969, 73–82; Deleuze 1983a, 111–47). Another way of character- izing the ontological question is that it contains the conditions for the possibility of a *differend*. (E.g., What is a woman? Historically the answers have been, Woman does not exist. Or A woman is a man who has no penis.)[28]

And therefore How are we to negotiate with this in/terror/gating struc- ture of violence? Spivak points to two steps that Derrida (a post-Heideggerian) has taken: The first, *negative* deconstruction; the second, *affirmative* deconstruction (1989a, 112; cf. Derrida 1992, 134–36). The first "guards the question," "keeps the question alive," by switching and shuffling the bina- ries, so that *an* answer does not become The answer; so that histories/ hysteries do not become The history. The first, in other words, shifts the synecdochic relationships from macro- to micro- and, then, vice versa (see Burke 1969a, 326). The second, however, attempts to move outside of the binary (machine) of possible answers. The second busts out of the synec- dochic relationships, out of context (the *polis*) and gambols out satyrically toward the *pagus* (homosocial space or temporary autonomous zones or baroque deterritorializations). The second is composed of "calling to the absolute other" (Spivak 1989a, 212). Calling to "woman." (Now I interpo- late, so as to include yet others.) Calling to "sophistic rhetoric." Calling to *becoming*-all-these-things. Calling to the Uncanny (*Das Unheimlich*). *Becom- ing*-animal. Becoming-dog (Diogenes of Sinope). *Becoming-minoritarian*. Becoming-Deleuzian and Guattarian (see 1987).[29]

As I have come to understand it for myself, the second (which is a third) is once ever again a Trotskian permanent revolution of calling, calling, calling to the Other or a vocation that would be a perpetual vacation from answer- ing the Question of Being or the Question of the Sophists. This, then, is what I might mean by becoming-*sophistikytes*.[30]

And therefore, just-how are we to call by vacating? My sense is that we would dis/engage in (see Adorno's logic[s] of disintegration [1987, 144– 46]) . . . we would dis/engage in what I have been variously calling (a) *dissoi paralogoi*, (b) *mis*representative antidotes, (c) and *theos*-tricks, theatricks (see Vitanza 1994a, 249–51). All are the How(l)s of "redescriptions." That is, the forces, desires, wills. I have variously dis/engaged in them here, but will make them somewhat more specific intermittently and especially in the closing excursus. First, tacitly presented; then, more explicitly presented. These three dis/count for my (eventual, unfolding) notion of a Third Sophistic (or *So- ciety of the Friends of the Text (or Hysteries and schizzies of Rhetorics*).

. . . I would now go on to the concluding (rebeginning?) section and to a discussion of the *pagus*, so as to characterize further my idea of a Sophist.

. . . Hydra-headed Sophist. . . .

—Plato

Man [*Mensch*] is an animal organism with (like others) an unmistakably bisexual disposition. The individual corresponds to a fusion of two symmetrical halves, of which, according to some investigators, one is purely male and the other female. It is equally possible that each half was originally hermaphrodite.

—Freud

Biological theories of sexuality, juridical conceptions of the individual, forms of administrative control in modern nations, led little by little to rejecting the idea of a mixture of the two sexes in a single body, and consequently to limiting the free choice of indeterminate individuals. Henceforth, everybody was to have one and only one sex.

—Michel Foucault

I shall give birth to a centaur someday.

—Nietzsche

Single vision produces worse illusions than double vision or many-headed monsters.

—Donna Haraway

III. Favorinus: The Most Typical Sophist

My idea of the *pagus* (TAZs and baroque deterritorializations and *les domaines inférieurs*) is simple. As we think we know, being exiled from the *polis*, for the Greek or the Roman, was a fate worse than death. (We try so hard to have the canny, homely, instead of the uncanny, unhomely!) Only beasts, barbarians, and the gods lived outside the civic (synecdochic) space of the *polis*. They were excluded by and because of Genus-cide, which constantly created the space (scene-agents) of disciplinary, canny societies. Beasts and others were excluded to and, therefore, lived in the *pagus*, literally the *country*. The country that I am referring to, however, is not a sentimentalized, romanticized, Rousseauistic country. It, instead, is a wild, savage (de

Sadean, de Ridean, de Manian, de Salesian, etc.) country. If any country at all. It is an *atopos* of Third subject/object, Sophistic positions-that-are-not-positions. It is, as Hélène Cixous calls it, *dépays*, uncountry (see 1993a, 131). There, nothing is fixed by a genus, everything is fluid. Nothing is fixed by way of negation. It is perhaps an uncivilized (ironic-cum-catechrestic) space, where creatures are voicing the "feeling" of "sophistic rhetoric," "the free linking of phrases, the destruction of genres" (Lyotard, 1988a, 171). This is an Ovidian (nondisciplinary) space. This is the site of metamorphoses. Of Fourier's phalanstery (see Barthes 1976).

I have in, but mostly out of, mind, in respect to Ovidian (nondisciplinary) space, the story of Salmacis (who is a wood nymph and is protean but is in the form of a pool) *and* the boy named Hermaphroditus (who is the son of Hermes and Aphrodite and who steps into the pool). There is so much that can be spun, spun, and punned out of this little narrative, but let us hallucinate, which is a way of becoming a *pagani*, on one particular pun. Towards the conclusion of the story, Hermaphroditus—when overwhelmed by and undifferentiated from the nymph whom he steps into—inven(s)tories hope in the possibility of petitioning the gods. He prays: "O father and mother, grant me this/May every [O]ne hereafter, who comes diving/Into this pool, emerge half man [and woman]" but neither One or the Other (Ovid 1967, 93). His/Her, Her/His petition is fulfilled. Hermaphroditus's loss cum gain, his loss of differentiation (i.e., his denegation) becomes others' gain (their denegation).[31] In the translation of the *Metamorphoses*, the pool is referred to as a "contamination"—which perhaps, in respect to "the excluded third" might be a possible locus cum radical paraloci for an Empedo/clean abyss, out of which crawl monsters as satyrs, satyrs as monsters (in that, of course, they would not be Platonic or Aristotelian proper creatures, proper species, proper names). This, indeed, would be a new creation, but not *ex nihilio*! For this is not a negative abyss as it is for Lyotard (*The Differend* [1988a]) or for Bataille (*Guilty* [1988b]), but an affirmative (or nonpositive affirmative) abyss as it is for Nietzsche (*Beyond Good and Evil* [1966]).

I am making two points here so as to get on to a third: First, I am talking about the abyss as an erotic parabase. Recall what N. O. Brown says in *Life Against Death*: "language is an operational superstructure on an erotic base" (1959, 69). When I say "language" (*logos*), I do not mean, however, Platonic (*Phaedrus*) or Aristotelian (*Rhetoric*) "language/*logos*," and I specifically do not mean Saussurean *la langue* (as system/synecdoche), or *le parole* (as individual speech act/metonymy), but just Lacanian *lalangue* (as Babel, wild/savage baby-lonianisms, interruptions/asyndetons.) This kind of language, *lalangue* (baby-lonianisms), will have de*term*ined our new (grotesque) parasubjectivities. Second, I am talking about reconceiving and revalorizing a discarded locus of what is generally/generically called *con-fusion*, variously called gender confusion (Butler 1990a, 1990b), sexual/biological confusion (Foucault 1980a; Irigaray 1985a), or logical confusion (Serres 1982). I castrate this male Hermaphroditus so as to destroy "him" and everything that he represents, so as to make him a third. It is necessary, as Deleuze and Guattari and Cixous say, that there be death of the masculine. (And of the feminine.) Later, of course, I must castrate (i.e., denegate) castration (negation) altogether (see Deleuze and Guattari 1983, 295). And in "his"/"her" place?[32]

Andrea Nye, in *Words of Power* (a feminist history of logic), discusses Parmenides's poem, and in reference to its "teachings" says: "If a female mixes with a male [i.e., as a hermaphrodite, mixed genders in one], the result is both female and not female, impossible by the rule of noncontradiction" (1990, 14). (For centuries, we have forced these biological contradictions to be subject to and of forensic discourse and we have placed these so-called "freaks" into carnival side shows.) After Parmenides's "freaks" and women, it is—as Plato, or the Eleatic Stranger, explains—the Sophist who dis/engages in these confusions: "Making contradictions with words, opinionated mimicry of a dissembling kind, illusion-making generated from image-making, a kind of production, human not divine, of a magic show of words" (*Sophist*, 268c–d). In dis/respect to writing The History of Rhetoric or even histories of rhetorics, then, I would con-fuse, con-fuse, con-fuse it all. And in "his"/"her" place?

I would, therefore, claim that, in fact, if one needs "facts," *the most typical Sophist is Favorinus.*[33] Philostratus, in his *Lives of the Sophists*, tells us that Favorinus, both a philosopher and a Sophist,

> was born double-sexed, a hermaphrodite, and this was plainly shown in his appearance; for even when he grew old he had no beard; it was evident too from his voice which sounded thin, shrill, and high-pitched, with the modulations that nature bestows on eunuchs also. Yet he was so ardent in love that he was actually charged with adultery by a man of consular rank. Though he quarreled with the Emperor Hadrian, he suffered no ill consequences. Hence he used to say in the ambiguous style of an oracle, that here were in the story of his life these three paradoxes: Though he was a Gaul he led the life of a Hellene; a eunuch, he had been tried for adultery; he had quarreled with an Emperor and was still alive. (1968, 23)

Now, first of all, what is meant by the (paradoxical?) statement that Favorinus is *the most typical Sophist*? This attempt of mine at *theatricks*, or at a performative *mis*representative anti*dote*, which Habermas would see as a performative contradiction, is a replaying of—after all is said and undone,

I am playing with—Victor Shklovsky's statement that "The assertion that *Tristram Shandy* is not a novel is common; for persons who make that statement, opera alone is music—a symphony is chaos." Then Shklovsky wonderfully, theatrically adds: "*Tristram Shandy* is the most typical novel" (1965, 57).

Yes, the statements about Favorinus and *Tristram Shandy*, and the homological relationship between the two, are paradoxical. A novel such as *Tristram Shandy* is so novel that it escapes defining—being limited, being typical—in any classical, philosophical sense. After all is said and undone, it is, however, a "novel," that is, a "novelty." And though we cannot satisfactorily define what a novel is, though its *name* will always consequently be improper, and its form will always be at best a bastardized form of philosophical literature (cf. Aristotle, *Poetics*), we nonetheless have such "things" (species that are not "species") that are protean—Socrates hated the Proteus myth—and we do live quite well with "them." They are, indeed, I would insist and incite, quite liberating. We might call such an understanding of novelty a "feeling," or a "sign," whereas Schiappa would insist on calling it an "intuition," but he would see "intuition" as less than what he would need. For me, by counterviolating the *genus*, by just-vomiting it up (as Sterne just-counterviolates the very [would-be philosophical] form of the novel itself when writing *Tristram Shandy*), I would force/farce us—we historians cum hysterians—to attend to the form of and the narrative of violence known as species-genus analytics; and for me, this our coming into awareness of what I have been calling *Genus-cide*, through its counterviolation, would thereby constitute the very existence of "sophistic rhetoric" in paradoxical structures, say, as embodied in (the sign of) Favorinus, or as expressed simultaneously in being dead but alive (as sophistic rhetoric is [see Rosen 1983, 321–22]), or as reembodied and reexpressed in becoming a satyr.[34]

Therefore, I would contend that when we—historians cum hysterians and schizographers of rhetorics—set out "to write" histories, what is at stake in writing history, or histories, of rhetorics *should be put perpetually into question* (cf. Lyotard 1988a, 139). We would, therefore, "write" hysteries. If Hermaphroditus (in Ovid's *Metamorphoses*) had his prayer to the gods, I would borrow one from Euripides's *Bacchae*, so that "we" might have "ours," and call it "A Dionysian's Prayer." Each of these Third Sophistic prayers (Hermaphroditus's and Euripides's chorus's prayer) is beyond the *One* and *Two* or the *Many* (which are complementary) in Kenneth Burke's "A Dialectician's Prayer," in which Burke ends by petitioning: "And may we have neither the mania of the One/Nor the delirium of the Many" (1966, 65), etc. "A Dionysian's Prayer," in contrast to Burke's petition, would go and go, and amble and amble, gambol and gambol—when writing hysteries of rhetorics—

would trotsky and trotsky, would put itself perpetually into question, and nomadically, as

> O Dionysus, reveal thee!—appear as a bull to behold,
> Or be thou seen as a dragon, a monster of heads manifold,
> Or as a lion with splendours of flame round the limbs of him rolled,
> Or. . . . (1017ff)

Excursus: The Negative, Aesthetics, and the Sublime (terror)

As for a politics of the sublime, there is none. If there were,
it could only be the Terror. But in politics, there is an
aesthetics of the sublime.

—J.-F. Lyotard

Most simply put, I am now turning to what is normally called the theory
chapters, but which I would abnormally redescribe (Rorty) as *the spectacle
excurses*. It is difficult to describe exactly what is going to happen in this
and the following excursions, though I will attempt to do so, and excessively.
Obsessively, yet hysterically! What will happen here is that chapter-time will
stop, while excursion-time will start up. Eventually, I will return to chapter-
time, as is often typical in eighteenth-century novels. What will happen here
in excursion-time will be a moving away from Lyotard (as developed in
chapter 1 and initially here) to Georges Bataille (as developed fully in the
second excursion), and yet a remembering of Lyotard (toward the close of
the second excursus). For many readers, these excurses may appear to be
a stumbling block, or just more irritating theory talk; they are, however,
unnecessarily necessary. In the two excurses, I have taken great freedoms
in redescribing what I have read so as to say what I would think wants to
be said about the Sophists, The History of Rhetoric, nature (*physis*), language
(*logos*), aesthetics, the sublime, and many other conceptual starting places.
Again, simply put, I would have the reader drift with what wants to be
thought and rethought and rethought, and rechewed and rechewed.

In chapter 1, I said that I would have to return to the problem of the
negative,[1] primarily because Lyotard, in his discourse tactics such as *paralogy*,
works from the *negative*. As a way of dealing with this problem, I stated that
I would have to "casuistically stretch" Lyotard's paralogical discourse, founded
on the negative, to what I would call *dissoi paralogoi* (or *polylogoi*),
unfounded on radical excess, or affirmation. Such a stretching is achieved,

57

in respect to the ethico-political horizon, by way of a poetic/aesthetic view of discourse. I am not going to aesthetics for a new foundation, for such an aesthetics would, nonetheless, be subject to a Kantian negation. Much like Lyotard, perhaps, I would go to the space *between* politics and aesthetics for an ungrounding.

While the negative has its problems, the affirmative, or any attempt to denegate or desublimate the negative, also appears to be problematic. As Lyotard says: "A politics of the sublime . . . could only be the Terror" (qtd. in Carroll 1987, 180). Could only end in the return of a Third Dionysus? Though I generally agree with this assessment, I do not think that it holds, or should hold, for writing (rethinking) histories of rhetorics. What Lyotard's statement amounts to—quite ironically here—is the establishment of a *differend*: He judges a politics of the sublime by way of the negative, not the affirmative (denegation), or what I will later call, with the help of Foucault, *the nonpositive affirmative* (1977). Lyotard, in other words, privileges the negative over the affirmative as Kenneth Burke does when he rejects "Nietzsche's cult of Yea-saying" (1966, 433). I am suggesting, therefore, that The History of Rhetoric must be denegated, must be written, if it can be called *writing*, across what Kant calls not the "beautiful" but the "sublime," more specifically, "the mathematical sublime" and beyond to the "Dynamic" (1991, 94–117; Part I, Bk II, §25–29); or what Herbert Marcuse sees as "a non-repressive mode of sublimation which results from an extension rather than from a constraining deflection of the libido" (1962, 154). This beyond to the "Dynamic" will have had an uncertain linkage with what I will later refer to in chapter 2, as Gorgias's penchant for *dynamis* and not hegemony (*hegemon*). Yes, yes, yes, I would libidinalize The History of Rhetoric.[2] Herein, then, is the beginning of the spectacalizing of the libidinal and the libidinalizing of the spectacle.

Before attempting this goal—for I must build up to it—I am going to attempt a pedestrian excursion into the relationship between *lack*, that is, the negative (as scarcity or dialectic) and *excess*, that is, the affirmative (as denegation of the negative). I will further problematize this binary (machine) by reforming it into a trinary (i.e., a desiring machine): Now, respectively as *topos, e/utopos, atopos*. Lest the reader get too comfortable with this trinary, I will still further problematize it, at the very end of this excursion, with another trinary. Throughout, I will attempt to turn binary machines into desiring machines, to turn one's and two's into three's, and primarily in relation to *a sublime-ethical subject*. (Though I will not spend time giving an exposition of Deleuze and Guattari's tactics of schizography such as assemblages and series, I will make free use of them [see 1986, chs. 6–9].) It's that way on the way to being engulfed by the mathematical sublime. As I proceed, therefore, I will incrementally, but provisionally, announce what my various intentions are becoming. You, Dear Reader, will know as I know. And yet, these words may be those of a trickster. Who can tell?

Following this pedestrian discussion of the binary and then the trinary reconceptual starting places, I will investigate Lyotard-Kant (in relation to the beautiful-sublime), Bataille-Hegel (in relation to the profane/sacred, custom/nature, taboo/desire), and finally will return to the Bacchanalian conclusion of chapter 1: The chorus's invocation of the terror, or its calling for the return of the Third Dionysus, the god of perpetual transformations. In this Baccalanalian conclusion I will attempt to rebegin by returning to Lyotard's earlier discussion of a libidinalized economy; though it appears that Lyotard would re/Kant and, therefore, repress his earlier statement concerning such an economy,[3] I will have us listen to its eternal return. (Whereas I end chapter 1 with the vertiginous image of Favorinus as a hermaphrodite, I will end the second excursus with the image of the text of Marx as a hermaphrodite. Both images represent a sublime-ethical, humorous subject; both are un/founded on third [Sophistic] subject positions.) Let us not forget that what's repressed (suppressed, politically oppressed) returns. (Again, it is the *mad* text of Marx that returns as a hermaphrodite. And Kafka's mad text that returns as an ape addressing the academy on the nature of the sublime.) It is these returns that I would incite and exploit as newer sublime *rebeginnings*.

> It is only as an *aesthetic phenomenon* that existence
> and the world are eternally *justified*.
>
> —F. Nietzsche

Aesthetics and Politics: Before I begin to rebegin, I must additionally, but briefly, if not ever obsessively, acknowledge the problem of aesthetics and politics.[4] Or the problem of the aesthetization of politics. (After all, the problem of the negative and the problem of the aesthetic, or specifically the sublime, were made for each other.)[5] Geoffrey Bennington, in his *Lyotard Writing the Event* (1988), returns us to the *question* of the problem of aesthetics in his discussion of Lyotard's *Differend* (1988a). Bennington says that in the absence of any criteria for making a judgment, Lyotard "links the aesthetic and the political in a way which is bound to worry all those who immediately sense Fascism in the association of those two terms" (164). More to the point, Bennington writes: "It naturally remains to be seen whether Lyotard is aestheticizing politics or politicizing aesthetics" (164). Bennington's concern is rooted in Walter Benjamin's "The Work of Art in the Age of Mechanical Reproduction," in which Benjamin claims: "the logical result of Fascism is the introduction of aesthetics into political life" (1969, 242); and further claims:

"all efforts to render politics aesthetic culminate in one thing: war" (242). For support, Benjamin cites Emilio Marinetti, the founder of Futurism, and his "war is beautiful" and *"l'art pour l'art."*[6] That the Fascists and Communists have used art/aesthetics to twist the political lives of its members cannot be argued against; that all persons or groups who link art/aesthetics with the political would by necessity twist political lives, however, does not logically or experientially follow. To be sure, the issue for me here is not merely a question of logic, which *is*, as I pointed out in the introduction and again in chapter 1, the very seat of negation itself, but more so a searching for ways of dealing with the problem of an absence (i.e., a negation) of criteria for making political judgments and secondly a searching for ways of reincluding all that, heretofore, has been excluded, or purged. My claim is that whereas Kant's "beautiful" (subject to reason, rationality) necessarily excludes, his "sublime" (the mathematical and dynamic sublime, which he fears) is the paralocus of reinclusion. What I say of Kant's views and choices, I will eventually say of Hegel's in relation to "determinate" and "abstract" negation. (Dear reader, if you recall in my introduction that I spoke of *desire, force, will*, you will have a chance of understanding these terms and concepts again, but in the name of the "sublime" [and "abstract" negation].)

Others who have taken up the problem of linking politics and aesthetics have been less inclined to make Benjamin's strong claim but are, nonetheless, against such a link. I have in mind Jürgen Habermas, who would scare us away from the aesthetic to what he calls uncoerced consensus building, or a communicative model of rationality as warranted assertability (1987, 294–326). I will in passing take up Habermas's view and what I see to be its shortcomings. For the most part, I will as suggested take up the discussions of others. Though primarily concerned with moving beyond Lyotard's discussion, I will build on Martin Jay's statement that "whatever their inadequacies . . . Lyotard's . . . thoughts on the potentially benign links between aesthetic judgment and politics serve as useful reminders that not every variant of the aesthetization of politics must lead to the same dismal end" (1992, 56).[7] To be sure, my position will be more radical than Jay's or even Lyotard's, though I would not claim, as Nietzsche does, that existence and the world can "only" be justified as an aesthetic phenomenon (1967, 52). My claim, as it develops processually here, is that *the negative*—or the Kantian *beautiful* or Hegelian *determinate*—and its influence on politics and the aesthetic is the culprit, not politics or the aesthetic itself. In other words, to return to Habermas, I do not believe that it is possible to have an uncoerced consensus based on a communicative model of rationality as warranted assertability; such a model is, though ever so subtle, the very epitome of the negative itself, that is, of exclusion as effected by logic and of purgation as effected by politics.

As early as Plato, dialectics meant to achieve something positive by means of negation.

—Th. Adorno

Excess revealed itself as truth.

—F. Nietzsche

A Dreary, Ugly Series of Paragraphs, But Necessary to Irritate: Lyotard's symptomatic *topos*—like that of Freud and Jacques Lacan and like Kenneth Burke, and so many other critics—is *Out of the impossible* (i.e., lack) *comes the possible* (excess).[8] This *topos* is a residue of classical and modernist ontologies/metaphysics. It is to be found in Heidegger's thinking his "fundamental ontology" (see 1962, 28–35, 62–63; 1977, 95–112). It is an extremely dangerous conceptual starting point, for it enables us to espouse that out of *no* comes *yes*, or that *no* really means *yes*. This latter interpretive maneuver is, to be sure, the downside of the modernist "hermeneutics of suspicion" as practiced by Freud and Marx (see Ricoeur 1978, 32–36). As a case in point, the more adamantly that Dora says "no," the more that Freud takes this "no" for a "yes" (see Freud, 1962, *SE* 7: 57; cf. 19: 234–39).

As I announced, my own symptomatic *atopos*—like that of Nietzsche, N. O. Brown, Marcuse, Deleuze and Guattari, and Judith Butler—is *excess*, or affirmation.[9] The primary reason that I gave for having to return to the problem of the negative was the perhaps equally incipient problem of the (nonpositive) affirmative, or excess, which I will eventually explore, as promised, in respect to the mathematical sublime and beyond. The point that I am making, in yet other terms, is that while the *topos* (*polis*?) of negation is problematic, the *atopos* (*apolis*, statelessness) of excess itself is perhaps equally problematic. It can be ascertained that if we exclusively favor "yes" and altogether ignore "no" (or if we altogether denegate the negative), then, we theoretically return to a state of nature (*physis*), or statelessness, prior to the taboos, or prohibitions, that contain us (see Aristotle *Politics*, 1253a.19–39; Freud 1961, 46–54; cf. Eagleton 1991, 275–77). This, to be sure, would be a view of nature without any negative whatsoever (see K. Burke 1966, 9; N. Jay 1981, 48). Such a return prior to the taboos, of course, would be a setting aside of Virgil's *Aeneid* and an accepting of Ovid's *Metamorphoses*; would be a return of and to Dionysus or, better put, the Third Dionysus. However, as Habermas says: "[W]hen the containers of an autonomously developed cultural sphere are shattered, the contents get dispersed. Nothing remains for a desublimated meaning or a destructured form; an emancipatory effect does not follow" (1987, 11; cf. 91–105).

And therefore, it would seem—Does not common sense insist?—that I would have to admit that it is finally not enough—Ambiguous statement?— to lower the curtain of the previous chapter with the mad chorus calling for the return of Dionysus. What occurs in Euripides's *Bacchae*—what so violently occurs—cannot not be readdressed. To this Terror, as I have suggested, I will ever return. And to this madness (Dionysian excess), I will ever return. For it is a return of the eternally repressed that I am primarily interested, and especially in relation to writing histories cum hysteries cum schiztories of rhetorics cum rherotics.[10] First, however, allow me to make other pedestrian distinctions, and thereby rebegin by moving from *two* (the binary of lack-excess) to *three*. (Yes, Dear Reader, I am ignoring the logic of Habermas's argument, and especially his concept of Enlightenment "emancipation," for each creates only another *differend*! And, consequently, leaves me with a sign and a feeling.)

I. A Threefold of Conceptual Starting Places

> I no longer fear a lack of aesthetics. . . . I still don't foresee what else I may have gained. Maybe I'll learn of it little by little. For now, the first timid pleasure that I feel is being able to say that I have lost my fear of the ugly. And that loss is a very great good. It is a delight.
>
> —Clarice Lispector

A Garden of Delights: Borrowing now from Roland Barthes (1977, 49), I would insist on three notions of the possible, namely, *topos*, *e/utopos*, and *atopos*. (I borrow, but again I stretch.) The first, *topos*, is determined by the negative (i.e., species, genus, differentiae). It is associated with commonplaces, *doxa*, mystifications. It is an exclusionary-purification strategy. It is, as I have suggested, Genus-cide. The second term, *E/utopos* is not finally different from *topos*; for as a conceptual starting place, it, too, is determined by the negative, but it takes this negative and attempts to create political success. It is political in that while it acknowledges the political failure of *topos* (or *polis*?), it fantasizes, like an unrequited lover, for the great, good place. *Atopos*, however, is another matter altogether (see Barthes 1978).

Atopos is boundless, is undetermined or at times, either underdetermined or overdetermined. It either finds itself—in dis/respect to *topos* or *e/utopos*—denegating the negative for a starting place of total excess; or better, it finds itself as without any lack whatsoever, as therefore affirmation or excess. (This is what Kant would refer to as the mathematical sublime and beyond, or Hegel, the abstract negative, or Bataille, a general economy.) Whereas *topos* or *e/utopos* engage in strategies with tactics, the latter dis/engages in tactics alone. Whereas the first two engage in finitude, the third dis/engages by way of infinitude. Whereas the first two engage in territorializing and reterritorializing (both editorializing), the third dis/engages in perpetual deterritorializings (decodings, denegations). It is often argued, in disrespect to *atopos*, that it is apolitical. If apolitical, *atopos* is so only by virtue of resisting and disrupting a politics-by-negation (i.e., integrating by excluding and purging, or establishing the beautiful by excluding the ugly). *Atopos* dis/engages in an aestheticized parapolitics. It is almost already like Fourier's "Domestics": Barthes explains, "The area of Need is *Politics*, the area of Desire is what Fourier calls *Domestics*. . . . [P]olitics is what forecloses desire, save to achieve it in the form of neurosis: political neurosis or, more exactly: the neurosis of politicizing" (1976, 84–85; Barthes's emphasis).

In relation to such traditional concepts as *ethos, pathos,* and *logos,* the third conceptual starting place, *atopos,* sees them all as radically multiple: *Ethos* is a Nietzschean-Hélène Cixous's hysteric and a Nietzschean-Deleuze and Guattari's schizo (Nietzsche writes that he is all the names of history); *pathos* is Kant's aestheticized *sensus communis,* that has re/become Nietzsche's Dionysian-tragic chorus, or deSade's polymorphous perversity from the dark side of reason; and finally *logos* is a Heraclitean, Nietzschean, Heideggerian "storm." Put in darker Kantian terms, *ethos, pathos,* and *logos* are in a perpetual sublime infinitude. The terms are "dark" because in Kantian and, then, Freudian perspectives this infinitude suggests the death instinct at work (see Weiskel 1976; Hertz 1985). Which I would turn pharmakonically into a remedy, so as to kill off both the common-sense and Humanist (Mascu-Lenin-ist) thinking-speaking-acting subject for a sublime (mad) subject. No, not a Mad Max. Nor a mad Maxine. But an Over-Maximum. (These references, terms, and apparent metaphors may be obscure and this tactic absurd, but they have been and will continually be rediscussed, as I toss other metaphors into the discussion.)

Let us turn now to negation (lack) and affirmation (excess), and further elaborate their possibilities. What I have made fairly clear by now, I hope, is that whereas *negation*—which is the principle of definition or rhetorical invention—is a strategy that de*term*ines what something is by way of *excluding* (the Sophists do not exist! Woman does not exist! The mathematical sublime or aesthetized politics exist, but each is dangerous!, considering what they lead us to), *excess,* or nonpositive affirmation, on the other hand, is a tactic that denegates negations by way of *reincluding*. (The Sophists are hydra-headed, or they are hermaphrodites, or ugly. Women are a radical multiplicity of sexes. Or, more radically sublime, there are more than one or two genders and sexes. With the return of the excluded middle or third, there are more than one or two or countable *ethoi*; in fact, there is a sublime *ethos*).

Topos, E/utopos, Atopos: What needs to be made still more clear, however, is that this distinction between negation and excess is more complicated than I have thus far suggested, if we keep in mind the threefold of *topos, e/utopos, atopos*, and especially the latter two. *E/utopos*, unlike *topos*, attempts to include more than it excludes; for it looks outside the traditional boundaries set by species-genus analytics. *E/utopos* can be politically used, say, in the pedestrian form of "affirmative action"; in other words, it can be used to look beyond racist and sexist boundaries to include those who, heretofore, have been excluded. And yet, excluded from what? Capital! It is, therefore, either a liberal strategy or possibly a strategic liberalism. And why? Because *it is a strategy*—it has a destination—and, therefore, a discourse, or signifying, practice that is still determined by way of negation, so that it can reach for its destiny, or great, good place.[11] Which is, yes, Capital! Moreover, the issue for me is not to get more people *in* Capital, but to get us all *out* of Capital, that is, *out* of the destiny of negation itself! Capital, like various Freudianisms and Marxisms, is a negating principle, though it masquerades as excess.

Lyotard is certainly well aware of this problem of both Capitalism and Marxisms (see 1988a, 171–73; 177–79), though in *Libidinal Economy*, he suggests that the tensors of Capital are the very cites to locate ourselves (1993, ch. 2). What is so insidious about Capital, mostly Capital, is that it has maintained so successfully—even in spite of the various critiques of post-Marxisms—the grand illusion that each of us, as subjects, is, or can, be "free"—as if there *is* an "each" and as if there *is* "freedom" instead of "necessity" under Capital [see Zizek 1989, 21–22].) Capital also represents itself as denegating the negative while it most insidiously negates us all. Therefore, I do not believe in this kind of "affirmative action," nor do I believe, as Lyotard suggests, that Capital is the extreme limit. I have more faith in Deleuze and Guattari's tactic of searching for the limits of Capital and moving beyond. And yet, this moving beyond is not outside of, not an *escape* from Capital, but a space inside/outside Capital (see Deleuze and Guattari 1983, 240–62; Deleuze 1988, 70–93). To realize a space outside of a necessity into flight would be a new condition for excess. And yet, How? By becoming-animal. Deleuze and Guattari write: "To become animal is to participate in movement, to stake out the path of escape in all its positivity, to cross a threshold, to reach a continuum of intensities that are valuable only in themselves, to find a world of pure intensities where all forms come undone, as do all the significations, signifiers, and signifieds, to the benefit of an unformed matter of deterritorialized flux, of nonsignifying signs" (13). Their example is "Gregor [Samsa, of 'Metamorphosis,' who] becomes a cockroach not to flee his father but rather to find an escape where his father didn't know to find one, in order to flee the director the business [*sic*.], and the bureaucrats [yes, all of the Capitalists], to reach that region where the voice no longer does anything but hum: ' "did you hear him? It was an animal's voice," said the chief clerk' " (1986, 13).[12] But understand: "escape doesn't consist in fleeing—quite the contrary. Flight is challenged when it is useless movement in space, a movement of false liberty; but in contrast, flight is affirmed when it is a stationary flight, a flight of intensity" (13; cf. 35). Flight is a "schizo [sublime] voyage . . . a line of escape . . . [a] flight [that] takes place in place, in a pure intensity" (71).[13]

> I closed my yes, waiting . . . my panting to become something more than the panting in that groan that I had heard as though it were coming from the depths of a dry, deep cistern. I kept feeling the groan, incalculably far within me, but it was no longer reaching my throat.
>
> This is madness, I thought. . . . [W]hat I knew very well was not madness but was, my God, a worse truth, the horrible truth. But why horrible? Because it wordlessly contradicted everything I had been accustomed, also wordlessly, to think.
>
> —C. Lispector

Intensity? Is this difficult to follow? Of course, it is: For it is, in positive terms, the hum of the sublime, which designifies the loss of the subject of enunciation that would say what "s/he" means and mean what "s/he" says. (It is a denegation of subjectivity.) Oh well, I find it difficult to explain myself, just as Kafka's Ape finds it difficult in his "Report to an Academy": "I fear that perhaps you do not quite understand what I mean by 'way out.' I use the expression in its fullest and most popular sense. I deliberately do not use the word 'freedom.' I do not mean the spacious feeling of freedom on all sides." (Kafka 1971, 253). A way out be-comes with a *hum* and departs with a human being. Lispector's H. G., in *The Passion According to H. G.* (1988), experiences such a way out by way of a deep groan that becomes more and more intense until it becomes the hum of the intensity of becoming-non-human (becoming-denegated). If you still do not yet understand, Dear

Reader, then, continue to listen for an intermittent hum, in the body of this writing, but especially toward the end (new beginning?). Listen for a hum in your body of writing. In others' bodies of writings. A hum. A body in metamorphosis. Like: hummmmmmmmmm. Hummmmmmmmmmmmmm^n.

> The unconscious does not coo sweet lyrics or unroll immaculate and measured prose, it howls and raves like the shackled and tortured beast that our civilization has made of it, and when the fetters are momentarily loosened the unconscious does not thank the ego for this meagre relief, but hisses, spits, and bites, as a wild thing would.
>
> —Nick Land (about Henry Miller's writing)

> A cockroach is an ugly, shiny being. The cockroach is inside out. No, no, I don't mean that it has an inside and an outside; I mean that is what it is. What it had on the outside is what I hid inside myself: I have made my outside into a hidden inside.
>
> —C. Lispector

My main complaint against *e/utopos* is that it does exclude; in another politically charged word, it does *purge*. (Now, as previously suggested, I don't have anything against *vomiting*, but I do against *purging*, if you catch my drift!) As we recall from my opening discussions, Barthes explains, "seen from today (i.e., after Marx), politics is a necessary purge" (1976, 88). Lest we forget, I am forever looking for an infinite play of differences without any exclusion (Barthes 1977, 85–86). And in relation to writing-à-la-Fourier histories-cum-hysteries of rhetorics. And yet, I would go beyond Barthes; I would go with Foucault and with Deleuze and Guattari to more Deleuzian extreme-sublime limits, if limits at all, within, yet beyond Capital. (I agree with all those who say that the unconscious is the unplace, i.e., the place without negation.)

There is another form of *e/utopos* (this time, a movement from negation/lack to *apparent* affirmation/excess); it has many advocates, though fewer than it initially had, that claim that as a conceptual starting place, it can help realize a great, good place, outside of Capital. Though it has been extremely effective in changing, in part, the status quo, and effective as a means of constructing arguments for change, it still, nonetheless, works from, begins with, the negative, in other words, takes "the risk of [negative] essence" (Spivak 1989b) and, therefore, has within its strategy the logical necessity and the practical potential to exclude others. This strategy unfortunately invites everyone to be reactionary.

This particular *e/utopian*ism, like *topian*ism, first of all works from a view of the negative, as I have suggested, that is Hegelian, a view of the negative that discards while it sublates, or preserves. (Though I claim this starting point to be Hegelian, I would also contradictorily claim it to be Heideggerian.) Hence, this double movement of discarding and preserving is what is meant when Gayatri Spivak speaks in terms of taking the risk of strategic (negative) essence. Essence gets dismissed in positivistic-scientistic terms but gets preserved, or reclaimed, in strategic (rhetorical?) terms. And yes, as Spivak says, this is risky, but as she also claims, it is well worth the risk. The locus for politics here—I should say, for *e/utopian* politics-by-negation—is the essential differences between female and male. This *e/utopian*ism has as its basic strategy *negative deconstruction*, a privileging of female over male. I am thinking of the kind of *e/utopianism* suggested and practiced variously by Marguerite Duras (women over men), Julia Kristeva (herethics over ethics), or Gayatri Spivak (strategic essentialism). All are engaging in negative essentializing (forms of negative deconstructions), which exclude and, yes, potentially purge. Whether practiced by males or females, the strategy is for me unacceptable. I would, therefore, denegate such negative strategies. I argued in chapter 1 that negative essentializing allows Schiappa to say *there are no Sophists*. (Other men have similarly argued that *there is no female*.) I will point out in chapter 5 similarly that Heidegger equally practices, though differently, a negative essentializing. Thereafter, I will discuss, in the excursus that follows chapter 5, Susan Jarratt's similar, though still different, negative essentializing in the name of a *feminist sophistic*. All inevitably exclude, negatively purge. Such exclusion, I see, as the real terror of politics. (And yet, as will become unclearly clear in the excursus "Feminist Sophistic?", I would preserve! Am I contradicting myself? Yes, if a reader insists on staying with the principles of identity, contradiction, and excluded middle; No, if a reader can give up readership and take up with schizoshipless.)

If not *e/utopos*, therefore, *atopos*. The tactic that I favor, as I have suggested elsewhere (1990, 1993d), is searching for *third, non-synthesized subject positions-that-are-not-subject-positions*. When I speak of a denegation of the negative, I am not speaking of a traditional synthesis-consensus, but of a radical constellation-dissensus. (And certainly a more radical dissensus than John Trimbur espouses partially in my name [see 1989].) I would like to see, in rewriting histories of rhetoric, how to include what, heretofore, has been excluded or purged. This attempt would, then, take *some form* of sublating (i.e., throwing away but preserving). And yet, this tactic, no doubt, will have to deal with the problems of sublimation (sublation is sublimation and vice versa). I am really talking about a more radical form of sublation than Hegel suggests or than Spivak sees in Derrida's readings (see Spivak 1983). For now, however, the parapolitics that I would, in part, dis/engage in is that which denegates a traditional or a modernist *ethos* (or speaking, thinking subject) and "identity politics" (see Butler 1990, 1–6, 142–49), and does so by avoiding the *topos* that there is only one sex (Freud, Lacan) or two sexes (common sense) and, instead, by working with the *atopos* of "there are as many sexes as bodies" (see Deleuze and Guattari 1983, 294–96; Barthes 1977, 69; Irigaray 1985; Butler 118–19; Fausto-Sterling 1993). Hence, a sublime *ethos*. I would/will do the same to *pathos* (consensus) and *logos* (discourse, reason). Why? So as to avoid such bureaucratic, Oedipal triangulations and substitute in their place a proliferation of series (see Deleuze and Guattari 1986, 54–55; Barthes 1976, 101).

But remember, as I forewarned, this ex-position is all processual and, as such, it is possibly a sublation—sub/version—itself. (Dear reader, if you are already lost, once again, simply learn to drift!) Though the negative (*topos*, *e/utopos*) is dangerous, I may not be able to throw it away without having to preserve it. And the same especially goes for the affirmative-excess (*atopos*). Mine is an Montaignian essay.

A recapitulation: Instead, I am talking about, pointing us to, an excess that is itself *either* excluded by and that escapes dialectic, division, *diaeresis*, definition *or* I am talking about preferably an excess that is for some of us more of a "feeling" and a "sign" (Lyotard), but a feeling and a sign that is not de*term*ined by, again, negation, as with Lyotard, but a feeling and a sign of *exuberance*, as with the poet Blake. (Let me further simplify these two: I refer to an excess, on the one hand, that is the by-product of *diaeresis*, and I simultaneously talk of an excess, on the other, that is *exuberance*. Or, borrowing from Thomas Sebeok, I might call the latter "esperable uberty" [1988, 1], by which he means an "expected or hoped for rich growth, fruitfulness, fertility, copiousness, abundance.")

Excess, Excess, Excess: Yes, yes, yes. Drawing from Blake and from others, Georges Bataille in *The Accursed Share* writes: ". . . energy is always in excess; the question is always posed in terms of extravagance. The choice is limited to how the wealth is to be squandered" (1988a, 23). Instead, Capital works with, and thus creates the conditions for, a model of scarcity, or supply and demand (lack), to benefit the few. (Bataille here in response says that we must no longer work with a "*restrictive* economy," but with a "*general* economy." This he calls a Copernican, economic revolution for both thinking and ethics [25].)

Along these same lines, Norman O. Brown—the revisionist of Marx and Freud—who speaks of Bataille, writes:

> That Copernican revolution which Freud thought he was inaugurating, by showing that the human ego is not even master in its own house, is not complete until the human ego is forced to admit another master, *the Dionysian principle of excess*: Nietzsche called it drunkenness. It takes a madman like Nietzsche, and a libertine like Bataille, to challenge the homeostatic pleasure-principle in terms of another definition [*sic*.] of pleasure and another definition of life. (1991, 183; my emphasis)

Brown continues: "In Bataille's Heraclitean vision we are suffering not from some repressed longing for death but from excess of life—the Dionysian principle of excess, Blake's principle of exuberance. There is a contradiction built into the pleasure-principle: there is no such thing as satis-faction; there is no such thing as 'enough.' There is a built-in need for toomuchness, for flamboyance (flaming), for exaggeration. . ." (183). And finally: "That is why, in the last resort, there is [no traditional philosophy or rhetoric] only po-etry. We cannot live without imagination; adoring and exaggerating life; lavishing of itself in change [which The History of Rhetoric has suppressed!]. This property of the imagination is not a human aberration, but a manifes-tation of the fundamental nature of life" (183; cf. 1959). This, then, would be a view of nature (*physis*) without any negatives.

Counter-Repression, Repression, Repression. No, no, no. If Lyotard were to attempt this statement (and he has), he would put it, however, in *negative*, Kantian terms: He might add, with the help of Slavoj Zizek or Jacques Lacan, that there is another contradiction, this time, in the political economy: There is no such thing as satis-faction in a(ny) political relationship; there is no real/ity to it, no rational consensus behind it; finally no great, good place (*e/utopos*, only *dystopos*) to be realized, objectified. Therefore, there is only the "taste" (à la Kant) for it, which manifests itself in the desire for a sublime object of political reality (as fantasy or ideology). *And therein lies the most dangerous condition for humanity!* Wanting, desiring what cannot be grasped (see Lyotard 1984b, 81–82).

A "taste," a "desire" for the Thing (Das Ding): The term "The Thing," appropriately chosen as the title for a horror film (traditional and revised), is a term that needs explaining. Put simply, it is Kant's Thing-in-itself (*da Ding-an-sich*), which resists being realized, but which we pursue, nonetheless, and at great expense to ourselves and others. It is philosophy's super-entity upon which everything, every idea, can rest. It is God, or foundationalism, center, presence, *arche*, itself. Having explained the Thing in this manner, however, I must now recall that this (monotheistic) God, this presence, is "radical negativity," is absence itself. Refining this point in Lacanian terms, Slavoj Zizek writes that the Thing, which Lacan calls the Real,

> cannot be inscribed, but we can inscribe this impossibility [radical negativity] itself, we can locate its place: a traumatic place which causes a series of failures. And Lacan's whole point is that the Real is *nothing but* the impossibility of its inscription: the Real is not a transcendent positive entity, persisting somewhere beyond the symbolic order like a hard kernel inaccessible to it, some kind of Kantian 'Thing-in-itself'—in itself it is nothing at all, just a void, an emptiness in a symbolic structure marking some central impossibility. (1989, 172–73; Zizek's emphasis; cf. Burke 1969a, 23, 24–25; Derrida 1972; Zizek 1993).

(*"The Thirst for Annihilation"*: Parenthetically, I should say, as is commonly said in theological circles, God has always been a *topos* founded on Nothing [Burke 1969a, 21–37; 1970]. Historically, we have addressed Him [paradoxically] as NOthing that is SOMEthing. And yet, what happened when God was killed, declared dead? What happens to the phrase *via negativa*? What was dis-played—when Baubô was unveiled—was death. And, therefore, how and to whom do we now—but is there a difference?—address our petitions? Our inner experiences? Our humming?

Of all the commentators on this *topos* of out of *the impossible cums the possible*, Nick Land [1992] is the most brilliant and yet troubling.[14] He is brilliant by ill-virtue of his intrepid resistance to academic style [he, too, could be the ape reporting to the academy; the creature, within, humming to its audience]; he is troubling because he writes by way of the word "annihilation" and the word "negative" [nothing, absence]. Land writes: "Modernity is virtual thanocracy guided insidiously by zero; the epoch of the death of God. There is no God but (only) zero—indifferentiation without unity—and *nihil* is true religion" [91]. Land writes about Georges Bataille, whom I will take up with soon as we progress [?], regress [?], become-intense, yet serene [?], in my discussion. What Land does is to write incessantly of the negation of negation, but continues to display this immense "thirst for" death, this boundless necessity to speak of ALL THIS in terms of NEGATION. And never lets up. There is no sense of a celebration of hope or of life. And I think that I understand why: He begins with the historical narrative of the Death of God, and instead of revaluing value so as to get out of Nihilism, he follows Bataille into the abyss of zero, out of which *there is* possibilities. Out of death there is life! He does not get out of the binary;

for him, now everything begins with zero. Hence, life is always determined by way of death, zero, negation. It is death against life.[15]

And yet, Land's ends and my rebeginnings are the same though different in our common principle of negating negation [i.e., absolute, sovereign negation], in our common principle of a general economy [without reserve]. However, while Land insists on counting from zero to 1 [122], I incite [on] counting from 1 and 2 to *exuberance* [nonpositive affirmation, excesses]. And yet, we both start from Nietzschean material conditions as libidinal [desire, will to power, force, energy, drive (*Trieb*), negentropy] [see Land, ch. 2]. Hence, Land's reading of Bataille's "Thirst" is another expression of a desire for free-flowing desire, for excess. It's just [unjust?] that individual identity must perish. This happens to G. H. It will have happened to all of us. It's that way when the excluded middle [muddled matter] is not so much reincluded but acknowledged as negentropy or H-value. As libidinal matter [see 37–47].)

The Return of Excess, Excess, Excess: Yes, yes, yes. There is yet another contrary view to Lyotard and Zizek and Lacan (and K. Burke and others), specifically, in dis/respect to their embracing the negative. And that is the perverse view of Gilles Deleuze and Félix Guattari, who are more optimistic than Nick Land's Bataille. Deleuze and Guattari identify capital and Oedipalization as the negating principles of a subject's desire, as principles of lack (*manque*) that are a "countereffect of desire" (1983, 27). They write: "the traditional logic of desire is all wrong from the very outset: from the very first step that the Platonic [and Aristotelian] logic of desire forces us to take, making us choose between *production* and *acquisition*. From the moment that we place desire on the side of acquisition, we make desire an idealistic (dialectical, nihilistic) conception, which causes us to look upon it as primarily a lack: a lack of an object, a lack of the real object" (25). And of course knowing is Oedipalized and Capitalized. Our desiring production (machines) get mercantilized (cf. Lyotard 1984, 5; 1993, chs. 4–5). What we as subjects, therefore, desire is knowing/Noing (see Aristotle *Metaphysics*, 980a). But Lacan says that we cannot know, except in the form of "going through the fantasy" (see Zizek 1989, 195) so that we might learn that there is only the sublime object of our desire, which is *NOthing*. However, Deleuze and Guattari, writing of a non-Platonic and non-Aristotelian desire, say: "Desire does not lack anything" (1983, 26). And say: "The real is not impossible; on the contrary, within the real everything is possible, everything becomes possible" (27). And they say still a great deal more about a materialist, libidinalized Marxism, which I will leave for much later.

II. Kant-Lyotard

A popular joke tells of the meeting between a sadist and a
masochist; the masochist says: "hurt me." The sadist replies:
"No."

—G. Deleuze

The sublime is not a pleasure, it is a pleasure of pain.

—J.F. Lyotard

Having undergone this zig-zag movement, I want to return us more
fully now to how Lyotard examines the problem of excess, but by way of his
discussions of Kant and the aesthetic (specifically, the mathematical sublime
and beyond).[16] And of course the political. I want to examine Kant's view of
the ethic (ethos, subject) *of sublimity*.[17] Which means that I want to distinguish between Kant's notion of the unbounded (mathematical and dynamic)
sublime and the bounded *beautiful*.

Kant speaks to this problem as "the mathematical sublime" and, therefore, in terms of numbers, counting, and finally being confronted with the
uncountable (1991, 98–109; Bk II, §26–27). When confronted with *hypsos*
(height, the metaphor of the sublime-as-power, as "monstrous" or "colossal" [94–95, 100]), the mind of the subject suffers from not being able to
stop counting, on *ad infinitum*; in this state, Kant says,

> the mind . . . hearkens now to the voice of reason, which for all given
> magnitudes . . . requires totality, and consequently comprehension in *one*
> intuition, and which calls for a *presentation* answering to all the above
> members of a progressively increasing numerical series, and does not
> exempt even the infinite . . . from this requirement, but rather renders it
> inevitable for us to regard this infinite as *completely given* (i.e., given in
> its totality). (1991, 102; Bk II, §26; Kant's emphasis)

While the mind of the subject is on the verge of experiencing (apprehending) the sublime, the infinite, or excess, it pulls back from the abyss of the
sublime with the help of the understanding and reason and opts (in the eyes
of later theoreticians) for the beautiful (99, 104, 107, 115–18; or Bk II, §26–
29). The mathematical-infinite sublime subject is thereby, through the
intervention of *comprehensio aesthetica*, replaced by the beautiful-but-lim-
ited subject. (Possibilisms [excesses] are replaced by the impossible [lack]
to realize the possible.) For Kant the retreat is necessary, for without it there

is supposedly/theoretically only destruction and death. Culture is a compromise formation, settling for a part that would be total, instead of the whole that would be annihilation.

This is an important casuistic stretching of Kant, which I perform by way of Thomas Weiskel, who writes, "insofar as there is an insistence upon realizing man's infinitude either imaginatively... or materially, ..., the sublime moment... must disappear" (1976, 44). E/utopian Marxist, like Lucien Goldmann, Weiskel argues, "think... in terms of beauty" so as to think it possible to achieve a correspondence between individual human beings and a social totality; so as to achieve the totality promised by the new social harmony. In contrast, "in Goldmann's aesthetic... the sublime must simply drop out. For the judgment of the sublime comes into play precisely insofar as man cannot attain the totality" (45).

While Lyotard does acknowledge this movement of the Kantian subject from sublime to beautiful, and while he discusses the sublime as prior to any political concerns, he concentrates on other unacknowledged consequences of Kant's thinking: Instead of agreeing that the Kantian beautiful is the viable source of the political subject, he argues that Kant *inadvertently goes so far into the heterogeneous that he brings about an excess of phrases and genres*. It is this heterogeneity (i.e., excess as nothingness), therefore, that Lyotard sees as the *locus* of a political-sublime subject. But it is a locus that does not make for "a political 'program' "; it is a locus that the subject only "can bear witness to" (1988a, 181). The tactic is un/founded on the principle that it is necessary to link, but not how to link (29).

I stress that it is this locus of heterogeneous phrases and genres—as a new mathematical sublime and beyond—that determines the subject. Lyotard is not a Humanist in his discussion of Kant. I stress that while the beautiful subject might be able to engage in a e/utopian politics of redemption by way of *litigation*, the sublime subject can dis/engage in such a politics but is simultaneously and productively aware of the problem of the *differend*.[18] And finally I stress that it is difficult at this point to characterize Lyotard's view of phrases and genres and, then, subjects as solely founded on the negative or freed from the negative, passing over into the nonpositive affirmative. However, my sense is that the negative of phrases and genres is, for Lyotard, the locus of inventing the political subject. Lyotard insists on stating and restating the *topos* of *impossible* (nothingness) *cum possible* (75, 138, 144).

Let us take a closer look at Lyotard's discussion of Kant's view of aesthetics on the sublime as negative presentation.[19] In his "Kant 4.4–5" notices, Lyotard writes:

> Enthusiasm is a modality of the feeling of the sublime. The [subject of the] imagination tries to supply a direct, sensible presentation [the object, the Thing] for an Idea of reason. . . . It does not succeed and it thereby feels its impotence, but at the same time, it discovers its destination, which is to bring itself into harmony with the idea of reason through an appropriate presentation. (1988a, 165)

In other words, though enthusiasm, as a modality of the sublime, expresses a desire (a taste) for it knows-not-what, the imagination must necessarily *fail* because reason (the cognitive) cannot supply such an objectless object (or Thing); therefore, such enthusiasm is left only with a "feeling," which is left in the speaking-thinking-acting subject. (This is a "feeling," as I said in chapter 1, that Schiappa leaves us with when he says that we cannot supply the Sophists, which are only an objectless object!)

This is all potentially dangerous; for the would-be sublime subject, unrequited and in pain—repeatedly so—begins to embrace this pain and to turn it into pleasure and joy.[20] Lyotard says: "It is the joy of discovering an affinity within this discordance" between the cognitive and aesthetic faculties. But this affinity—attraction and repulsion—is not equal, for "nature (including human nature and including the natural history of man, such as in *a great revolution*) is still and always will be 'small in comparison with Ideas of reason' " (1988a, 165–66; emphasis mine. See Kant 1991, 106–09, or Bk II, § 27).

Lyotard continues: "What is discovered is . . . *the destination of the* [would-be sublime] *subject*, 'our' destination, which is to supply a presentation for the unpresentable, and therefore, in regard to Ideas, *to exceed* everything that can be presented" (166; emphasis mine). Not getting what it desires from the cognitive faculty, " 'our' destination," nonetheless, gets "a supremely paradoxical presentation [from the aesthetic faculty], which Kant calls 'a mere *negative presentation*' . . . 'a presentation of the infinite' " (166; emphasis mine).[21]

Kant explains that when reason, or the cognitive faculty, comes up short, the aesthetic has a tendency to rule without any rules or boundaries. (In other words, a rational subject has the tendency in relation to the mathematical and dynamic sublime to become a sublime, transgressive thinking-speaking-acting subject. [See Lyotard 1994, 89–146.]) Kant speaks of the subject in this state as experiencing "a feeling of being unbounded." As Lyotard explains, "enthusiasm is . . . on the edge of dementia, it is a pathological outburst, and as such it has in itself no ethical validity, since ethics requires one's freedom from any motivating pathos" (1988a, 166). Kant warns that it is, therefore, imperative to temper "the ardour of an unbounded imagination [of a subject] to prevent it rising to enthusiasm" (Kant 1991, 127–28). Unlike thoughts well-regulated by the judgment of cognition, "the feeling of the sublime," Lyotard explains, "judges without a rule" (1988a, 169; cf. 1985, 3–43).

What Kant sees as a "pathological outburst," however, is not just out there, but is locatable in what Kant calls "*sensus communis*" (see Kant 1991, 82–85, 150–54, or § 20–22, 40). Let us keep in mind now that this common sense—a totality that is not a totality—is not predicated on the beautiful but the sublime. In this common sense, Kant says, "the assertion is not that every one *will* fall in with our judgement, but rather that every one *ought* to agree with it" (84; Kant's emphasis). Again, no determinate rules of cognition stand, as a motivation for the sublime subject, behind this common sense. There is "consensus which is nothing more than a *sensus* [a feeling, a sign] which is undetermined, but *de jure*." This feeling of the sublime, then, is in political situations, *but* at its Kantian best it is there only in the form of "a sentimental anticipation of the republic" (168). Or another way of putting it: "The community [that exists in anticipation of freedom] is already there *as taste*, but it is not yet there *as rational consensus*" (169; my emphasis). Hence, the terror, the terror, the terror!

For those of us who, in various ways, identify with rhetoric and not philosophy, there is most likely a question now about why no attention is paid to the second critique, that of practical reason. (The parallel, of course, would be with Aristotle's *Nicomachean Ethics*.[22]) Throughout the Plato-Aristotle-Kant tradition, philosophers have located themeselves across the trinary of the true, the good, and the beautiful, or knowledge, politics, and desire, or the cognitive, the ethico-political, and the libidinal-aesthetic. Philosophers and even many rhetoricians have felt extremely uncomfortable with the third term and concept, desire-aesthetics. As should be obvious, Kant manifests this uncomfortableness when he insists on thinking of the third critique in terms of the first and not the second.

Lyotard is aware of this problem. In the "Kant 4.5" notice, he raises the question of the unexplored, possible relationship between the second and the third critiques, for this possible relationship might neutralize the potentially sado-masochistic relationship between the first and third critiques. If this could be done, we could then applaud ethics, politics, and rhetoric. But, as Lyotard says in relating Kant, *this cannot be done*: "The *sensus communis* is . . . in aesthetics what the whole of practical, reasonable being is in ethics. It is an appeal to community carried out *a priori* and judged without a rule of direct presentation. However, in the case of moral obligation [second critique] the community is required by the mediation of a concept of reason, the Idea of freedom, *while* in the phrase of the beautiful [third critique], the community of [*pathos*] is called forth immediately, without the mediation of any concept, by *feeling* alone" (1988a, 169; emphasis mine).

It is important to understand, therefore, that the third critique is an attempt to describe the indescribable and not any idea or concept of political freedom, though the *sublime* and *freedom* might be seen as analogical. Lyotard writes: "Great changes, like the French Revolution, are not, in principle, sublime by themselves. Qua object, they are similar to those spectacles of (physical) nature on whose occasion the viewer experiences the sublime. . . . The sublime is best determined by the indeterminate. . . : 'the sublime in nature [. . .] may be regarded as quite formless or devoid of figure'. . . . The same ought to apply for a revolution" (167). But it does not, at least, in Kantian thinking.

In "Kant 4.6" notice, Lyotard briefly addresses Kant's attempt to argue, or to find a way out of this problem of the mathematical sublime as a calling from the indeterminate (infinitude), by claiming that while thinking-speaking-acting subjects are susceptible to the sublime, "culture is [nonetheless] requisite for judgement upon the sublime in nature," and that culture has its "foundations" not outside of but "in human nature" (Kant 1991, 116, or § 29). Kant perpetually attempts to locate subjectivity, or to find in human beings, some resource, such as culture (*nomos*, duty, the symbolic) that will save them. Kant speaks of a culture of skill and of will (95–97, or § 83), as Aristotle spoke of *phronesis* (the virtue of practical wisdom).[23]

Lyotard himself does not place much credence, however, in Kant's appeal to culture as a means of neutralizing or, at least, resisting the mathematical sublime and its impact on subjectivity. In tentatively closing his final Kant notice, Lyotard says, "[w]ith the sublime, Kant advances far into heterogeneity" (169; cf. Lyotard 1991b, 222–23; 1994, 140–58). Picking up on and finding fault with Kant's solutions to the problems posed by the sublime and their connection with ethico-political problems (see Kant 95–96, or § 83), and then immediately with Marx's solutions and Capital's solutions (171–81) to these problems, Lyotard ends (rebegins?) his book by placing hope not in culture but in "the heterogeneity of phrase regimens" (181): What Kant could not resolve as radical heterogeneity, Lyotard turns into a postmodern virtue that is virtuosity. Yet, to the very end of his book, Lyotard continues to think of heterogeneity in terms of the negative. His thinking of heterogeneity is almost identical with John Dewey's "infinitation of the negative" (1938, 192). Lyotard would have us bear "witness to the nothingness which opens up with each occurring phrase and on the occasion of which the differend between genres of discourse is born" (141). This nothingness (or can I say, this act of potlatch?), then, is what establishes the conditions for the possibilities of a sublime subject. Lyotard is indebted to Heidegger, who I will interrogate in chapter 4.

Is legitimacy to be found in consensus obtained through
discussion, as Jürgen Habermas thinks? Such consensus does
violence to the heterogeneity of language games.

—J.-F. Lyotard

Can one engage in politics without finality?

—J.-F. Lyotard

As is fairly well known by now, Lyotard in *The Postmodern Condition*
(1984) has taken issue with the Enlightenment, with the attempts by
Habermas to rehabilitate the idea of the Enlightenment and consensus
(*homologia*), and with what Lyotard calls metanarratives of emancipation,
which he sees as doing violence to the heterogeneity of language games (xxv).
Lyotard continues this critique in *The Differend* on any form of discourse—
generally Kantian-Enlightenment discourse—that would homogenize heterogeneous discourses, that would have one genre of discourse or language
game be privileged over another. In *The Postmodern Condition*, he called
this privileging "terrorism" (1984, xxiv, 46, 63).

In dis/order to resist and disrupt the hegemony of any one dominant
genre, Lyotard extends Wittgenstein's notion of language games. Lyotard writes:
"You don't play around with language.... And in this sense, there are no
language games. There are [however] *stakes* tied to genres of discourse. When
these stakes are attained, we talk about success. There is *conflict*, therefore"
(1988a, no. 188; emphasis mine). When Lyotard says, "you don't play around
with language," he is separating himself from others who are seen as engaging in an apolitical game of "free play," which is a phrase and notion from
Kant's third critique. When Lyotard says the object of the game is not to win,
he is equally separating himself from those "terrorists" who would bring the
game to an end (see 1984, 10; 1985, 73–100; cf. 105–108). Instead, Lyotard
directly speaks of language games as the *loci* for politics.

But in being political, Lyotard does not think of politics in any classical or modernist way; he thinks less in terms of a Humanist subject (one
that makes history) and more in terms of a poststructuralist or postmodernist
sublime subject (one that is greatly deterritorialized by heterogeneous
phrases and genres). Lyotard explains, "the conflict ... is not between
humans or between any other entities; rather, these result from phrases. At
bottom, one in general presupposes *a* language, language naturally at peace
with itself, 'communicational,' and perturbed for instance only by the wills,
passions, and intentions of humans. Anthropocentrism. . . ." (1988a,
137–38). Though invested in the political, Lyotard challenges Habermas's

investment in a pragmatics that would have genres as a function of addressors as beautiful subjects. For Lyotard, the *logos* is not—and cannot be—at peace with itself and neither can subjects.

I am spending time commenting on these passages because in them we can find specifically how Lyotard situates the sublime subject well within poststructuralism and postmodernism while still, nonetheless, situating the subject *in the political*. More to this point, he writes:

> Were politics a genre and were that genre to pretend to that supreme status, its vanity would be quickly revealed. Politics, however, is the threat of the differend. It is not a genre, it is the multiplicity of genres, the diversity of ends, and par excellence the question of linkage. It plunges into the emptiness where "it happens that . . ." It is, if you will, the state of language, but it is not *a* language. Politics consists in the fact that language is not a language, but phrases, or that Being is not Being, but *There is's*. It is tantamount to Being . . . which is not. It is one of its names. (1988a, 138; Lyotard's emphasis)

Lyotard's thinking against any one Enlightenment language game and his thinking about a heterogeneity of language games, for radical dissensus, should be more obvious here. That these genres are heterogeneous should lead to the additional conclusion that the sublime subject is equally heterogeneous. If there is no container (genus, genre, synecdoche), there is no contained. If politics is not a genre, there can be no true or good or beautiful political subject!

A Return to Aesthetics: Lyotard's idea of the heterogeneity of language games and what's at stake in and between or among these games comes from the failure of the Kantian aesthetic, which we have seen "advances far into heterogeneity" (1988a, "Kant 4.5" notice). Hence, in the face of such excess and radical multiplicities, Lyotard opts for avant-garde language games as a means of "plunging into the emptiness." Of the Question of Politics! But this is only half the story; for modernism longs, broods nostalgically in the midst of "the emptiness" for a return to a so-called peaceful moderation and unity (see 1984, 81–82). And why? Because the political has a tendency to become the genre of genres (to become The Answer of answers), which has happened with Marxism or Capitalism favoring the economic genre (Answer) over all other genres (see 1988a, 141, 173–79). Hence, again, the necessity for the aesthetic intervention of the postmodern.

As Lyotard says, it is not just the political (the *polis*), but also the avant-garde artists, or *pagani* (the *pagus*) that can perpetually put what is at stake in the ethico-political life into question:

When Cézanne picks up his paint-brush, what is at stake in painting is put into question; when Schönberg sits down at his piano, what is at stake in music, when Joyce grasps hold of his pen, what is at stake in literature. Not only are new strategies for "gaining" tried out, but the nature of the "success" is questioned. . . . Everything is political *if* politics is the possibility of the differend on the occasion of the slightest linkage. Politics is *not* everything, though, *if* by that one believes it to be the genre that contains all the genres. It is *not* a genre. (139; my emphasis)

Lyotard speaks even more directly to the relationship among the *polis*, genres, and differends: "In organizing itself around the empty center where deliberation takes place—namely, the conflict of phrases and their judgment—the Greek *polis* did not invent politics[;] it placed the dialectical and rhetorical genre or genres in the governorship of phrases, thereby allowing their differend to flow, in the form of litigations right out into the (empty) milieu of political institutions" (1988a, 141). The *polis*, therefore, could not invent politics, because the *polis* itself is the (changing) function of politics, just as politics itself, if not allowed to become the genre of genres, is the (changing) function of how to accommodate a differend without excluding it in a litigation. However, lest we forget, the history of the *polis*, which is the history of *phrases at civil war*, is the history of *excluding the other* (1985, 67–68; cf. 107–08). The *polis* creates itself by creating the Ovidian *pagus* (the paralocus of excluded thirds). What the genre of politics, the genre of genres does, then, as Lyotard states, is to "leave a 'residue' of differends that are not regulated and cannot be regulated within an idiom, a residue from whence the civil war of 'language' can always return, and indeed does return" (1988a, 142).

Forget Bataille?: Lyotard, in his next numbered presentation, distances himself from Georges Bataille and his rereading of Marcel Mauss's *The Gift* (1967). Lyotard claims that "to call this residue the 'accursed part' [*part maudite*] is useless pathos. As for a politics centered on the emotions associated with sacrifice . . . that would be human, all too human." Lyotard continues: "In coddling the event [i.e., the sacrifice], one puts on a Horrorshow *à la Grand Guignol*. One's responsibility before thought consists, on the contrary, in detecting differends and in finding the (impossible) idiom for phrasing them. This is what a philosopher does. An intellectual is someone who helps forget differends, by advocating a given genre, whichever one it may be (including the ecstasy of sacrifice), for the sake of political hegemony" (142).

What Lyotard implies here about Bataille's views of writing (which is the same he states about Habermas, namely, that he wants one genre at the expense of all others) appears, in this case, to me to be very wrong-headed. To be sure, both Lyotard and Bataille have different solutions to the problem of language, of the subject, specifically, of the lordship and bondage relationship, and the kind of politics that this relationship fosters. It is this very difference that I will discuss in the next section of this excursus, which is a difference that will allow me to further develop the point that I earlier discussed in terms of negation (lack) and affirmation (excess). An understanding of these terms and their heuristic possibilities, especially that of *atopos*, will eventually give some insight into my own double (hydra-headed, Third Sophistic) view of historiography and hysteriography, and their possible sublime-mad subjects.

III. Hegel-Bataille

The abyss is the foundation of the possible.

—G. Bataille

In response to Lyotard, I would have to say that Georges Bataille does not advocate any genre of discourse, except for his non- or paragenre of "sovereignty." This non-genre of sovereign writing destroys the subject/ agent (the dialectic) and all forms of subordination. If Lyotard is uncomfortable with Gorgias's radical negativity and with Gertrude Stein's radical parataxis (see 1988a, 14–16; 67–68), it is understandable that Lyotard would be equally, if not more so, uncomfortable with Bataille, whom he would see as a terrorist, not because Bataille searches for the genre of genres, as Lyotard insists he does, but because Bataille would not think in terms of genres at all and, therefore, would lean, as I would stretch him, in the extreme opposite direction: Bataille is not just interested in incorporating *differends* into litigations, as he does when he speaks of de Sade, but is also—and perhaps more so—interested in divesting himself and us of litigations altogether. Bataille, in a word, is an *outlaw*. But having said as much, I must admit that while Lyotard is working out of the negative in search of the affirmative or, in other words, is a postmodernist who is a modernist (see 1984), Bataille himself on occasion works out of the negative while searching for the nonpositive affirmative. At best, I can say that they differ in degree, with Bataille, yes, more antinomian. It is not difficult to understand, then, why Foucault pays hommage to Bataille (and Blanchot) as the thinker of the nonpositive affirmative (see Foucault 1977, 36).[24]

Non-knowledge communicates ecstasy—but only if the
possibility (the movement) of ecstasy already belonged, to
some degree, to one who disrobes himself of knowledge.

—G. Bataille

In this section, I will focus on, first, George Bataille's examination of
two Hegelian negatives (determinate and absolute) and their possible
subjectivities, and Bataille's privileging the absolute, which Hegel dismissed
as terroristic and madness itself. In discussing these two negatives, I will
summarize Bataille's readings of de Sade and his reading of anthropology's
view of nature/custom, *physis/nomos*. (Bataille affirmatively deconstructs not
only Hegel but the anthropologists as well.) Second, I will concentrate on
Bataille's examination of two kinds of political economies (restricted and
general, or scarcity and excess), and Bataille's selecting the one that Capital
or Marx did not select (i.e., general). This deconstruction of a general political economy enables Bataille to explore his concept of excess. It is this
very concept that I want, finally, to link up with the sublime (terror); I will,
contrary to the norm, tactically incite us to begin thinking about the possibility of a sublime subject and its politics, specifically, in relation to rewriting—to dispersing into a proliferation of series—The History of Rhetoric.

Two Kinds of Negatives: Bataille's every remark is in response to Hegel,
specifically his *Phenomenology of Spirit*. Bataille was one of the participants
in the now famous Alexandre Kojève seminar on Hegel. As Jacques Derrida
says: "all of Bataille's concepts are Hegelian" (1978, 253). What Bataille is
attempting to do, however, is to find a way to write himself out of the
Hegelian lordship/bondage (master/slave, domination/subordination) dialectical relationship; he is, as he says, attempting to disrobe himself of
knowledge. And why? Because, he explains, "Non-knowledge communicates
ecstasy" (1988c, 123). In order to get to this non-knowledge and ecstasy,
Bataille takes on Hegel (and the Enlightenment tradition) by searching for
a third term, which for him is "sovereignty." (As before, I am speaking of yet
another sublime subject.) The word, "sovereign/ty" is not to be confused with
lordship-*Herrschaft*. In Hegel's dialectic, there is lordship (master) and
bondage (bondsman, servant, slave) (see Hegel 1977, 111–19; Kojève 1986,
ch. 1); in Bataille's addition of a third term, there is "sovereignty" (see 1985,
145–49; 1988b, 41; 1988c, 55). In dis/order to get to this term and what it
represents (which is nothing, but a "nothing" that is exuberance), Bataille
has to perversely rethink (or unthink) Hegel's two kinds of negation, which
are "determinate" and "abstract" negatives. (He achieves this rethinking by

reading Hegel across Nietzsche and Blake, two outsiders in dis/respect to both philosophy and poetry.)

Lordship/Servant: Allow me to summarize briefly, the lordship-servant relationship, and summarize only with the purpose of getting to the third term. For Hegel, the self—that is, our sense of self—is intimately linked with another self, or other. He writes: "Self-consciousness exists in and for itself when, and by the fact that, it so exists for another; that is, it exists only in being acknowledged" (1977, 111). Each consciousness, to achieve self-consciousness has, therefore, *to recognize* the other. Hegel continues: "They *recognize* themselves as *mutually* recognizing one another" (112; Hegel's emphasis). But this mutual recognition is less mutual and almost immediately more unequal, for there is a "splitting-up . . . into the extremes which, as extremes, are [dialectically, agonistically] opposed to one another, one being only recognized, the other only recognizing" (112–13; cf 116).[25]

What happens now, Hegel writes, is that "the relation of the two self-conscious individuals is such that they prove themselves and each other through a life-and-death struggle. They must engage in this struggle, for they must raise [the uplifting of the dialectical process] their certainty of being *for themselves* to truth. . . . And it is only through staking one's life that freedom is won." (Recall Lyotard's constant use of the phrase "what is at stake.") Hegel continues: "The individual who has not risked his life, may well be recognized as a *person*, but he has not attained *to the truth* of this recognition as an independent self-consciousness. Similarly, just as each stakes his own life, so each must seek the other's death" (1977, 113–14; emphasis mine). What is at stake here, however, is doubly difficult: For not only must one self-conscious individual struggle with the other—risk death—but this same individual must also not kill the other, for both are dependent on the other for recognition. To kill the other would be to fall into "abstract negativity," or abstract skepticism (the "empty abyss" [51]).

Bataille's Deconstruction of Hegel, a Return to the Two Negatives: Now comes the distinction that we have been working towards, the distinction that Bataille deconstructs. Hegel writes that the two individual self-consciousnesses must come to understand—and they do in Hegel's *Bildungsroman*—that "[t]heir act [of one killing the other] is an abstract negation, not the negation coming from consciousness [determinate negation], which supersedes in such a way as to preserve and maintain what is superseded [what is called "*Aufhebung*" and translated as "sublation"], and consequently survives its own supersession [sublation]" (114–15). This Hegelian language is thick. Hegel explains: With this understanding—that there can be no annihilation without annihilating one's self—there comes about "a pure self-consciousness" and a "merely immediate consciousness, or consciousness in the form of *thinghood*. . . . [O]ne is the *independent* consciousness whose essential nature is to be for itself, the other is the *dependent* consciousness, whose essential nature is simply to live or to be for another. The former is lord, the other is bondsman" (115; emphasis mine). In other terms, instead of one subject killing the other and, therefore, killing itself, the subject sublates/sublimates the other.

It is this diremption and reconciliation that make for Hegel's view of The History of Spirit, as well as The History of meaning, of philosophy and of discourse. Hegel writes:

> . . . the life of the Spirit is not the life that shrinks from death and keeps itself untouched by devastation, but rather the life that endures it and maintains itself in it. It wins its truth only when, in utter dismemberment, it finds itself. It is this power, not as something positive, which closes its eyes to the negative, as when we say of something that it is nothing or is false, and then, having done with its turn away and pass on to something else; on the contrary, Spirit is this power only by looking the negative in the face, and tarrying with it. This tarrying with the negative is the magical power that converts it into being. (19; cf. Zizek 1993)

To have a better sense of this History—and later what Bataille is going to do with it—we need to take a closer look at Hegel's distinction, implied in the above quote, between *determinate* and *abstract negation*. (This distinction is important in relation to a sublime subject.) Hegel favors determinate negation, favors "tarrying with the negative." For Hegel, the latter term (abstract) refers to a binary that is static and not dynamic, not dialectical in his transcendental sense. The former (determinate) is transcendental. In a parallel fashion, Hegel makes a distinction between untrue and true Science. "Natural consciousness," he writes, "will show itself to be only the Notion of knowledge. . . . The road can therefore be regarded as the pathway of doubt, . . . as the way of despair [or scepticism]" (49). He continues:

> This is just the scepticism which only ever sees pure nothingness in its result and abstracts from the fact that this nothingness is specifically the nothingness of that *from which it results*. For it is only when it is taken as the result of that form which it emerges, that it is, in fact, the true result; in that case it is itself a *determinate* nothingness, one which has a *content*. The scepticism that ends up with the bare abstraction of nothingness or emptiness [i.e., "abstract negation" (see 114)] cannot get any further from there, but must wait to see whether something new comes along and what it is, in order to throw it too into the same empty abyss. But when, on the other hand, the result is conceived as it is in truth, namely, as a

determinate negation, a new form has thereby immediately arisen, and in
the negation the transition is made through which the progress through
[sic] the complete series of forms comes about of itself. (51; Hegel's
emphasis)

With this scenario of struggle and reconciliation in mind, and of *determinate negation* and *abstract (radical) negation (cum affirmation)*, we can now
listen to how Bataille revises (affirmatively deconstructs) it, specifically in
relation to his notion of *sovereignty* and *excess*, or as I have been suggesting, a notion of a sublime subject.

> Hegel, by elaborating a philosophy of work . . . cancelled out
> chance—and laughter.
>
> —G. Bataille

> There is . . . an aspect of the transition from animal to human
> so radically negative that no one talks about it.
>
> —G. Bataille

> Even laughter may yet have a future. . . . Perhaps laughter will
> then have formed an alliance with wisdom, perhaps only "gay
> science" will then be left.
>
> —F. Nietzsche

Bataille's Sovereignty: If we listen carefully, we hear Bataille bursting
out *in laughter*, over and over again (see Derrida 1978, 255). But how are we
to understand (Hegelianize!) this laughter? Bataille explains that Hegel so
desired *serious*, absolute knowledge that he blinded himself (cf. Nietzsche
1969, 116; 1974, 74–75). Hegel's perverse economy is that of *determinate
negation*, which restricted Hegel from seeing that "there is in understanding
[itself] *a blind spot*: which is reminiscent of the structure of the eye" (emphasis
mine). Another Oedipal problem? Bataille, in *Inner Experience*, explains at
greater length:

> In understanding, as in the eye, one can only reveal [this blind spot] with
> difficulty. But whereas the blind spot of the eye is inconsequential, the
> nature of understanding demands that the blind spot within it be *more
> meaningful* than understanding itself. . . . To the extent that one views in
> understanding man himself, by that I mean an exploration of what is

possible in being, the spot absorbs one's attention: *it is no longer the spot which loses itself in knowledge, but knowledge which loses itself in it.*

. . . [D]esire, poetry, laughter, unceasingly cause life to slip in the opposite direction, moving from the known to the unknown. Existence in the end discloses the blind spot of understanding and right away becomes *completely absorbed in it. . . .*

. . . Even within the closed completed circle (unceasing) *non-knowledge is the end* and knowledge the means. To the extent that it takes itself to be an end, it sinks into the blind spot. *But poetry, laughter, ecstasy are not the means for other things.* In the "system," poetry, laughter, ecstasy are nothing. Hegel gets rid of them in a hurry: he knew of no other end than knowledge. His immense fatigue is linked in my eyes to horror of the blind spot. (1988c, 110–11; emphasis mine)

Bataille opts for "the blind spot of existence," for the "horror," for *abstract negation,* which gives him his third (eye/"I") term, "sovereignty." And gives us another notion of a sublime subject. What this all means is that Bataille takes the greatest *risk* of all, the risk beyond that of lordship, the risk of saying No to No (to know, knowledge) or takes the risk as, Derrida says, of "the absolute loss of meaning" (1978, 255). Possibly, the horror! the terror of the sublime! Bataille writes: "There is no longer subject-object [master/slave], but a 'yawning gap' [because self-consciousness is no longer] between the one and the other and, in the gap the subject, the object are dissolved" (1988c, 59). Recall that "self-consciousness" is a product of negation and as such self-consciousness unites the subject and object. Let us recall that Nietzsche had written that "slave morality" is founded on a No, while a "noble mode of valuation" is without guilt, resentment, or negation (1969, 36–39). Following Nietzsche, Bataille revalues the (Hegelian) subject by similarly establishing "sovereignty." (Later, the Nietzscheans Deleuze and Guattari revalue the [Hegelian-Freudian] subject, which is Oedipal by establishing schizo-[sublime]-subjects [1983].)

But this is no mere irrationalism, for Bataille's is, as I would now label it, *the risk of a strategic (nonpositive affirmative) essence.* (This risk stands in stark contrast to *the risk of strategic [negative] essence,* which Gayatri Spivak and others engage in.) As stated, this is no mere irrationalism. Bataille is not saying that "anything goes." What he is saying is that so much has gone, has been excluded, negatively purged, that we must reclaim and revalue it.

Bataille's *general economy* of life is not homogeneity, nor *typical* heterogeneity (a systemization of differences), but *radical* heterogeneities. Bataille desires to include all that has been excluded by Hegel's dialectical procedure. As Habermas explains: "From the start, Bataille applied the concept of the heterogeneous to social groups, to the outcasts and the marginalized, to the counterworld . . . of those elements that are placed outside the boundaries of social normality—be they pariahs and the untouchables, the prostitutes or the *lumpenproletariat*, the crazies, the rioters, and revolutionaries, the poets or the bohemians" (1987b, 212; see Bataille 1985; cf. Marx 1984, 75–76). Because these elements are excluded (negated, prohibited), there is what Bataille is going to refer to as "normal"—or as I would say, "customized"—human beings. (He will affirmatively deconstruct this process: Because there are norms, purchased at the expense of the other, there is going to be the return of the repressed.)[26] It is inevitable. And therefore, we find him turning to criminals, outsiders, who occupy *les domaines inférieurs*. Who live in the sun. Since Bataille *goes there*, we will have gone there. (But having said these things, I must ever repeat that Bataille acknowledges the negative in ways that I—yes, with bravado, on occasion—am not willing. Instead, I would will. . . .)

In *going there*—say, to Bataille's de Sade—my interests lie specifically in How desire (*physis*) gets distributed to and exchanged within this underside of civilization (local *nomoi*). Yes, we will take up with Bataille's de Sade before taking up with the accursed share. With negentropy. With "the curse of the sun" and libidinalized matter (Land 1992, ch. 2). With the sublime, the ever so "ugly."

Excursus (contd.): The Negative, Aesthetics, and the Sublime (terror)

III. Hegel-Bataille (contd)

> There is thus, in each man, an animal shut up in prison like
> a convict, and there is a door, and if one cracks the door the
> animal tears out like a convict finding an exit.
>
> —Bataille

I have been concerned with What happens When—instead of selecting, as if any of us selects!, absolute negation—we select *determinant negation*. What happens When we do this? What happens When we deny
our denial of animality, or deny our humanity-in-animality? I want now
to see What happens when Bataille selects de Sade (denegated desire) as
a prime example of a sovereign man, or *absolute negation*. What happens when the negative is stripped away and total undifferentiation is
lived, *yet* lived by a post-philosopher through the *mask* (fold) of a
monster, so that he might interrogate the other side of reason. (The other
side of the sun. Of the Pineal eye.) Yes, what is being interrogated is the
other side of reason, the monsters that sleep while reason/rationality
holds on to such linkages as identity, noncontradiction, and excluded
middle. The other side known as the accursed share, for which we will
eventually get an expository explanation. But first action, sufferance, and
then an explanation.

> De Sade said over and over again in different ways that we are
> born alone[;] there are no [fixed] links between one man and
> another.
>
> —Maurice Blanchot

87

Bataille-(Sade)-Hegel, The Return of the Repressed: Bataille in *Death and Sensuality* (1962) has two chapters on de Sade: The first, "De Sade's Sovereign Man"; the second, "De Sade and the Normal Man." I cannot give near as lengthy an exposition and appraisal of this discussion as it deserves. But I do want to point to a few of Bataille's concepts that will further explain, but complicate, Bataille's concept of *sovereignty*, of the radical heterogeneous, sublime "man" and "woman." I will parenthetically insert de Sade between Bataille and Hegel, with the purpose of further discussing radical, denegated forms of sovereignty. (I'm always concerned with the return of the repressed.) Have I, however, left Kant behind? No; for, as Nick Land says, "the age of Kant is tangled with that of Sade" (1992, 60; cf. Klossowski 1991). And Hegel (60–61)? Who was equally concerned with the other side of reason as monstrosities (see Desmond 1992, ch. 4)? Left and right here share a middle, muddle.

But two caveats are in order. Such a notion of subjectivity as radically heterogeneous—sovereignty as unfounded on absolute negation—is difficult to discuss, for the standards of normalcy, based on determinant negation, would demand immediate purging of such monstrosities, which would be realized by way of "demonstration" (de-monstering). And herein paradoxically lies "our" (human beings's) problem. For, that *God* (de-termination, de-monstering) *is dead* (absolute negation) leaves us with a "desire" that is "amoral savagery" (see Land 1992, 136). The reader must work hard at not allowing this revulsion (?) to cause him or her to think in a reactionary manner. If not, then, nought.

A further complication arises with Bataille's employing the term "sovereign" (or "sovereignty") equivocally, paradoxically. Contra-logically. *Sovereignty* is usually contrasted with *servitude* and it is easily associated with the Hegelian lordship and bondage (master/slave) dialectic. Hence, there is a possible contradiction here; however, as I said earlier, *sovereign* or *sovereignty* is a third term outside of the dialectic. Sovereignty—outside of dialectic, and specifically in relation to Bataille's discussion of de Sade—is a "persona" in novelistic-dialogic form that refuses servitude and silence; that refuses to make separate exclusionary distinctions such as civilized and barbarous, implying that one is superior, the other inferior; that one is speech, or language itself, while the other is *bar-bar*, silence itself. These two contra-voices could very well be considered the *logos* speaking itself.

The best way once again to explain this problem of equivocation, paradox, is to summarize Bataille's reading of de Sade. My purpose, then, is to pick up where I left off in the previous excursus on the sublime subject and to continue here at length the Bataille-Sade connection in relation to sovereignty.

Bataille in his two chapters on de Sade initially spends an inordinate amount of time explaining to his readers—whom he indirectly calls "normal man"—that, yes, de Sade is repugnant. Bataille writes: "Sexual instincts to which de Sade gave his name [are] pathological." He continues: "I have already said that I have no quarrel with this point of view. Short of a paradoxical capacity to defend the indefensible, no one would suggest that the cruelty of the heroes of *Justine* and *Juliette* should not be whole heartedly abominated. It is a denial of the principles on which humanity is founded" (1962, 183). However, Bataille then says: "But there remains this question. Would it be possible wholly to avoid the denial of humanity implicit in these [perverse] instincts? . . . Is our being ineluctably the negation as well as the affirmation of its own principle [which is for Bataille the essence of unlimited eroticism]?" (183–84). Later when we look at the nature/culture pair, Bataille will focus on nature (*physis*) as essentially erotic and sacred as opposed to culture (*nomos*) as prohibitive and profane, as taboo. Contrary to what Blanchot says (in the headnote preceding this section), there is something that *links* all human beings: The essence of eroticism (212), which we "normal" human beings know better than to risk! Bataille writes: "Vice is the deep truth at the heart of man" (184). And then he speaks of "The two poles of human life" (185). (Allow me parenthetically to say that it is at this point that Bataille, given Nick Land's reading, gets into his exploration of libidinal materialism [force, desire, will, drive, etc.]. Bataille, instead of taking on the method of displacement practiced by Plato and Aristotle, reincludes and attempts, then, to give an a*count [logos]* of monstrosities, which are not One but Zero. Yes, counting to zero. Monstrosities are undifferentiated Zero. [Hence, we have the movement from Homogeneity to radical Heterogeneity. Or as I, in spite of Land, would say the movement from *animal sexuality*, then to human being's denial of such sexuality (along with somatic dejecta) and the acceptance of *limited eroticism*, and finally to the inevitable outburst of *limitless eroticism* (the third, or de Sade, the Kantian sublime-ugly, the energy that cannot not be spent) Hence, whereas Land counts Zero, One, return to Zero, I count One, Two, "some more." Whereas Land wants to focus so much on death, I would speak to the movement beyond death. To be sure, we must die before moving on.[1]] My saying of this beckons the saying of the most ancient fragment that we have, namely, that of Anaximander. In this fragment, it is generally understood that "*to be as determinate* was the primal ontological sin by which limited things tear themselves free from the unlimited, *to apeiron*" [Desmond 1992, 200; Desmond's emphasis]. Hence, human being is both animalistic/bestial *and* human.)[2] Human being must, cannot not, return to the unlimited.

In one of the most important passages on language (*logos*) in *Death and Sensuality*, Bataille says:

> There are two extremes . . . civilisation and barbarism—or savagery. But the use of these words is misleading, for they imply that there are barbarians on the one hand and civilised men on the other. The distinction is that civilised men speak and barbarians are silent, and the man who speaks is always the civilised man. To put it more precisely, since language is by definition the expression of civilised man, violence is silent. Many consequences result from that bias of language. Not only does "civilised" usually mean "us," and barbarous "them," but also civilisation and language grew as though violence was something outside, foreign not only to civilisation but also to man, *man being the same thing as language*. Yet observation shows that the same peoples are alternately barbarous and civilised in their attitudes. . . . If language is to be extricated from this impasse, *we must declare that violence belongs to humanity as a whole and is speechless, and that thus humanity as a whole lies by omission and language itself is founded upon this lie.* (186; emphasis mine)

This distinction between "civilisation and barbarism" suggests the collapse of the other distinction between *physis/nomos*, nature/culture. (As we will see in chapters 3–5, Isocrates and Heidegger both play a major role in accepting this view of *logos* as separating Greeks from Barbars.) If we believe that nature is checked by culture, we fool ourselves; if we ("normal men" and "women") think that we differ from the lower animals and abnormal human beings, we delude ourselves. *Physis*-nature, though repressed and negated, always returns and without our being aware, for it returns under the auspices of the negative (see Freud *SE* 7: 57; 19: 235–36).

Let's examine this issue of "civilisation and barbarism" more closely and in relation to *logos* (language). We are speaking in terms of *ethos* (a sovereign, sublime subject), but we are also examining *ethos* in relation to *logos*. Now, as I approach a more complicated discussion of Bataille's notion of sovereignty (radical heterogeneity), some interesting things are developing in respect to my earlier discussions of Lyotard and the *differend* in chapter 1. Bataille writes again: "Common language will not express violence. It treats it as a guilty and importunate thing and disallows it by denying it any function or any excuse." (186). "Common language" of "normal man" here is comparable to the language and speaking-writing-acting subject of Lyotard's *litigation*, or of the dominant, hegemonic discourse, which creates *differends*. It is litigation (the genre of judiciary-forensic discourse) that enables civilized human beings to speak, but it is the same genre that silences others and makes them into barbarians, ab-normals, or "jews" (see Lyotard

1990, 3). While litigation creates what Lyotard would call the "Forgotten," it also creates what Foucault calls the "counter-memory" (1977). The question that I hope will eventually become clear and acceptable is Who will speak for those who are silenced? Or Can someone else speak for them? If not, then, Will they ever be able to speak for themselves? Derrida and Gayatri Spivak have wrestled with these questions and have concluded that the "mad" and the "subalterns" cannot speak for themselves, nor can anyone else speak for them.[3] To be sure, this conclusion is de*term*inistic.[4] Bataille, however, has quite another view of this problem. His is that there is a strategic place from which to speak for the silenced, the place of *sovereignty*.

To get to this view, I will explain the two sovereigns. The *first sovereign*—attached to a dialectical lordship/bondage relationship—is responsible for creating silence and, therefore, admits *no link* whatsoever with audience nor with a victim; he hides himself, just as so-called "normal man" does, within the veil of "the language of authority" (1962, 187) or of "common language" (177–79, 186). But the *second sovereign* transgresses the veil, or barrier of silence and common language, and lets be spoken (hears and listens to) what desires to be spoken (heard); lets be remembered what has been forgotten. Bataille argues that de Sade *provides the linkage*, which "normal" language does not allow, between the torturer and the victim, between violence (silence) and speech (cries for justice) (see 186–190).

In this way, Bataille argues, de Sade justifies himself before us, justifies specifically the manner in which he wrote. The language that forms this linkage, de Sade's "expression of violence," however, "changes violence into something else. . . : into a reflecting and rationalised will to violence" (1962, 191). Therefore, the question remains, Is de Sade speaking for both the master and the slave? When de Sade speaks for anyone, if this can be called speaking, he speaks nonhumanistically for that part of language that has been silenced, that part, once again, that Foucault calls the "counter-memory." De Sade's language is that of "transgression" (1977, 33–36). When de Sade speaks, it is less for individual sufferers (both monster and tortured, both objects) and more so for generalized violence (to human beings and to language). When the author de Sade engages in the "philosophical dissertations" that interrupt the dialogue, Bataille says, "we face de Sade's books as a terrified traveller might once have faced giddy piles of rocks. We flinch away, and yet. . . . Mountains are something that can only appeal to man in a roundabout way, and the same with de Sade's books." He continues: "But humanity has nothing to do with the existence of those lofty peaks. . . . Mankind . . . call[s] for second thoughts. . . . De Sade's philosophy, anyway, is not to be classed as madness. It is simply an excess, an excess to make our heads reel, but the excess of our own extravagance. We cannot ignore this peak without ignoring our own nature" (192). We so-called "normal" people—or a part of us that we would deny—are sublime.

Excess revealed itself as truth.

—F. Nietzsche

Transgression contains nothing negative.

—M. Foucault

Bataille does not romanticize de Sade as a Promethean, porno-, comic-book rebel; he does not play him exclusively off of, nor separate him completely from, the way he is normally portrayed, namely, as a monster. What Bataille is attempting is to reestablish a way of reconsidering the possible *link* that exists, though denied, between nature and culture, in his matching terms, respectively between death (excess, the erotic) and taboos (the negative). This *link* with its images of mountains and human giddiness, also suggests the sublime, but before it is attached to any (stabilizing, if this is possible) object.

In this section, I am going to continue a discussion of this link in respect to the incest taboo and Bataille's thinking about it, specifically his reading of the anthropologists Marcel Mauss and Lévi-Strauss. These considerations are important because they will give us finally an insight into Bataille's *economy of life*, an economy that is not based on the negative, but primarily on the denegation of the negative or on nonpositive affirmation, excess itself—that is, an economy not based on master/slave dialectic, on Hegel's "determinate negation," or homogeneity, but on Hegel's dreaded "absolute negation," or radical heterogeneity, which gives us Bataille's ethical, but mad and sublime subject, that is, his "sovereign/ty." An understanding of this economy will, in turn, allow us to understand Bataille's Nietzschean aesthetic (the denial of the principle of individuation) and particularly his potential view of the sublime.

Two Kinds of Political Economies, Nature and Culture: Bataille in any number of works, but again especially in *Death and Sensuality*, discusses the *link* between taboos and death and transgressions against taboos (cf. 1993, vol. 2).[5] He writes: "There is in nature and there subsists in man a movement which always *exceeds the bounds* [recall Lyotard's reading of Kant's sublime as "the boundless"]. Indeed it is by definition that which can never be grasped, but we are conscious of being in its power: the universe that bears us along answers no purpose that reason [the Kantian cognitive] defines, and if we try to make it answer to God [foundationalism, determination], all we are doing is associating irrationally the infinite excess in the presence of which *our reason exists without reason itself*" (1962, 40; emphasis mine).

Prohibitions, then, have an economic purpose: Bataille says, "[T]hey are there to make work possible [and] productive; during the *profane* period allotted to work consumption is reduced to the minimum consistent with continued production. *Sacred* days though are feast days. Then things which usually are forbidden are permitted or even required. . ." (68; emphasis mine). Bataille writes, therefore, that "Man is a fundamental contradiction" (140–42). Borrowing from and building upon Lévi-Strauss (*Elementary Structures of Kinship*), Bataille contrasts nature (*physis*) with culture (*nomos*), or animals with human beings. He focuses on the prohibition of incest, or the *rules of linkage*, by which *homo sapiens* made (and make) their transition from nature to culture. In this taboo, Bataille says, there is a "paradox" (196), for out of this particular anthropological representation of prohibition comes affirmation (207). We have the *topos* again: Out of the impossible comes the possible.

Bataille examines Lévi-Strauss's (with Marcel Mauss's) discussion of the rules of coupling, or the factors which prohibit, yet permit marriage. The incest taboo is a sign of the potential for "effusion" (excess, violence) which must be controlled in some social manner. Women are coded contradictorily as sacred subject, or a "luxury" item, and as a profane, or "bartered," subject (see 1962, 205). Bataille writes that from the point of view of anthropologists, "Women rank [in primitive societies] on a level with celebrations. A woman given in marriage has after all the same sort of significance as champagne has in our customs" (206).[6] Continuing in his exposition of the anthropologists, Bataille writes:

> [W]omen seem primarily important as *a means of communication* in the strongest sense, the sense of *effusion*. Consequently, they have to be *objects of generosity* on the part of their parents in whose gift they are. The parents must give them away, but this happens in a world where each act of generosity contributes to the cycle of generosity [reciprocity] in general. I give away my daughter. I shall receive another woman for my son or my nephew. Thus throughout a limited group based on generosity there is an organic and pre-arranged communication. (206; emphasis mine)

(Here, then, is the very epitome of rhetoric and its history!)[7]

Having summarized Lévi-Strauss's view of the incest taboo, Bataille now turns to what he sees as a scandal—namely, the unacknowledged "ambiguity of Lévi-Strauss's doctrine," which centers on the gift of a woman, with the expectation of reciprocity. Bataille writes: "This fits the duality of the gift-exchange, the institution [of] 'potlatch' [which] is calculation in the highest degree and at the same time calculated interest are loftily ignored" (1962, 210). Gift-giving (or potlatch) can create a lordship/bondage relationship, or the conditions for the possibility of subordination and rivalry (in debt), not reciprocity and good feelings (cf. 1985, 121–23; 1988a, 63–77). Returning to the unacknowledged ambiguity of Lévi-Strauss's doctrine, Bataille says: "But it is rather a pity that Lévi-Strauss has paid so little attention to the bearing of *eroticism* on the potlatch of women" (1962, 211; emphasis mine).

It is at this point that Bataille adds to Lévi-Strauss's doctrine by deconstructing it. *Potlatch* is like *eroticism* in that both come "from an alternation of fascination and horror, or affirmation and denial" (211). (It's as if we are again speaking of the sublime here! Attraction and repulsion. Homeorrhesis.[8]) Bataille points out, in addition to these dyads, that there is another in the difference between *marriage* (profane, work) and *eroticism* (sacred, play), with marriage socially structured and eroticism rejected. The point that Bataille is getting to, the manner in which he is going to deconstruct Lévi-Strauss's, as well as Hegel's, doctrine, is that he doubts that the exchange of a gift for a future reciprocal gift is founded primarily and independently on the incest taboo (negation) but more so on eroticism, "sexual taboos taken as a whole," in which there is a still greater negation (212). Therefore, he writes: "I believe indeed that this pattern of reciprocity is of the *essence* of eroticism" (212; emphasis mine).

However, "man" has not and evidently cannot live with such a conclusion, for he would have to favor exclusively a *negative essence* (taboos, marriage, profane) over an *affirmative essence* (eroticism, sacred). Bataille writes: "The rise of *work*, taboos which can be grasped historically in a subjective way, long lasting *repugnances* and an insurmountable *nausea* mark the contrast between man and the animals[9] so well that for all the remoteness of the event in time the facts are obvious" (214; emphasis mine). He continues:

> I think the following statement will hardly be contested: that man is the animal that does not just accept the facts of nature, he contradicts them. Thus *he alters the exterior world of nature.* Out of it he makes tools and manufactured *objects* which make up a new world, the human world. Similarly *he contradicts his own nature,* he educates himself, he refuses to give free rein to the satisfaction of his animal needs, needs that *a true animal* will satisfy without reservations. (214; emphasis mine)

Then Bataille concludes: "*It is not for us to give pride of place to one or the other,* to enquire whether education, in the form of religious taboos, is the consequence of work, or whether work is the result of *a mutation in the field of ethics.* But in so far as man exists there exist also work on the one hand and denial of the animal element in man's nature on the other" (214; emphasis mine). However, later in an even greater Nietzschean vein, he writes:

> But where others may see a trap, I see the *sovereignty of chance*. Chance, inescapably the final sentence, without which we are never sovereign beings. At some moment or another *I must either abandon myself to chance* or keep myself under control, like the religious vowed to continence. The intervention of will, the decision to keep clear of death, sin, and spiritual anguish, makes nonsense of the free play of indifference and renunciation. Without such free play, the present instant is subordinated to preoccupation with the time to come. (250–51; emphasis mine)

This theme of chance (hazard) and risk will become major throughout the work of Bataille as it was previously major in Nietzsche's thinking. *Amor fati*. Abandoning one's self. Sounds a little risky(que)? I will stress this theme intermittently, even, and especially, through the closing sections and lines of this book-that-is-not-(would-not-be)-a-book. NOT be work. But novas of intensities.

Here we have, then, the essential parallels with master/slave dialectic and sovereignty, and with homogeneity and heterogeneity: A to and fro between negation and affirmation, work and play, profane and sacred, marriage and eroticism, civilized man and animal man, One and Zero (see Bataille 1993, 227). Master/slave dialectic and homogeneity, then, are the products of human being's attempt to say *No* to nature (*physis*, i.e., violence, death, excess, play, the sacred), which has its parallel in Hegel's *No* of a "determinate negation"; and the products of human being's attempt to say Yes to culture (*nomos*, i.e., reason, life, scarcity, work, the profane). Sovereignty and heterogeneity, however, are the by-products of homogeneity; they represent what has been excluded (purged). Therefore, Bataille's is an attempt *to acknowledge* that, in fact, we human beings do say *Yes* to nature (violence, death, excess, play, eroticism); and that thereby, we do engage in transgressions (61–62).[10] Again, Bataille establishes this acknowledgement by saying No to Hegel's "determinate negation" and Yes to "absolute negation," the abyss, zero. (This, however, is not the abyss of nothingness, but the abyss of a sublime eroticism [see Bataille 1988b, 109; N. O. Brown 1959, 69]). This is not a patent acceptance of "anything goes" or of violence or of especially incest, but is an acknowledgement of violence, or of "a [necessary] transgression of the limit" (1962, 144); this is not an unconditional *Yes*, but an acknowledgement of the equally dangerous *No* of disavowal; this is an acknowledgement of the inextricable "link" (40) that exists—recall Blanchot and Lyotard—between social continuity (taboos) and discontinuity (death of

God/foundationalism). This is an acknowledgement of what philosophy, specifically Hegel, could and cannot *admit*, for this im/possible linkage of the homogeneous and wildly heterogeneous is "the horror of philosophy" (213; cf. Desmond 1992).

Therefore, Bataille has to reject Hegel (philosophy) so that he might have radical heterogeneity. (Recall what Lyotard says of Kant's investigation of the sublime and its effect of going so far into heterogeneity that it effects genres. [Cf. Land, ch. 1.]) Bataille defines philosophy as *"the sum of the possibles* in the sense of a synthesis, or nothing" (1962, 254; emphasis mine). In this light, Bataille says, "it is difficult to live and to philosophize simultaneously. . . . [H]umanity is made up of separate experiences and *philosophy is only one experience* among others. Philosophy finds it harder and harder to be the sum of experiences, in [its] specialist's peculiar narrow-mindedness" (254; emphasis mine). In numbers, experience is Zero (indeterminate), while philosophy is One (determinate). Therefore, Bataille opts for transgression and an economy of excess. And a sublime (sovereign) subject that would be the by-product of such an economy.

The Accursed Share: I want now finally to turn to a discussion of Bataille's "general economy." (We are steadily making our way to Lyotard's *Libidinal Economy*.) If we recall, Bataille's is an economy that contrasts with a Hegelian "restrictive economy" and that is un/founded on the following doctrine: Namely, that "On the surface of the globe, *for living matter in general*, energy is always in excess; the question is always posed in terms of extravagance. The choice is limited to how the wealth is to be squandered" (1988a, 23; Bataille's emphasis).[11] Let's look at the sun. And listen to the sun. So as to hear what Bataille is saying, and saying paradoxically in respect to "excess"; otherwise, we will continue to get stuck in an even more restrictive economy, which *is* Late Capital, or multi-nationalism. Habermas, a critic who is extremely critical of things Bataillean, has, nonetheless, an accurate understanding of what Bataille means by excess. Habermas writes: ". . . Bataille understands 'excess' quite literally as the transgression of those boundaries drawn by [capitalistic] individuation" (1987b, 230). Yes, Dionysus must transgress Apollo.

The Sun: "light, desire, and politics"[12] : The sun—say, from Plato (the allegory of the cave) to the modernists (the gory of the Enlightenment)—is ever politicized (see Irigaray 1985a, 243–364). He who can gather and control this energy (force, desire, will) for his own interests will have the power of the state (stasis). *Dynamis* (power) would, then, be hegemony. Here's Bataille's (topological) twist on all of this:

> I will begin with a basic fact: The living organism, in a situation deter-
> mined by the play of energy on the surface of the globe, ordinarily re-
> ceives more energy than is necessary for maintaining life; the excess
> energy (wealth) can be used for the growth of a system (e.g., an organ-
> ism); if the system can no longer grow, or if the excess cannot be com-
> pletely absorbed in its growth, it must necessarily be lost without profit;
> *it must be spent, willingly or not, gloriously or catastrophically.* (1988a,
> 21; emphasis mine)

Continuing:

> Solar energy is the source of life's exuberant development. The origin and
> essence of our wealth are given in the radiation of the sun, which dispenses
> energy—wealth—without any return. The sun gives without ever receiv-
> ing. Men were conscious of this long before astrophysics measured that
> ceaseless prodigality; they saw it ripen the harvests and they associated its
> splendor with the act of someone who gives without receiving. It is nec-
> essary at this point to note a dual origin of moral judgments. In former
> times value was given to unproductive glory, whereas in our day it is
> measured in terms of production: Precedence is given to energy acquisi-
> tion over energy expenditure. (28–29)

There are numerous other passages and an extended argument and "data"
in *The Accursed Share* to support this argument. But quantity of information is not the problem here. Understanding and acceptance of contradictory statements are the problem. Yes, Bataille's readers must stand themselves
on their heads. (They—we—need a camera obscura.) If this were not enough,
Bataille is perverse in his use of scatology and what some "normal" readers
might call degeneracy. (How, then, to discover the Gestalt switch? so as to
enter into Bataille's blinding vision?) I will give mere shadows first; the
blazing sun later. The shadows as *notes:*

I.

- *The sun is the locus of excess.* (Corollary: It gives without reckoning.)
- There is the desire of excess not shortage.
- The excess must be spent, but when spent there is only still some more
  excess, which, in turn, must be spent either gloriously or catastrophically.
- Human beings have attempted to emulate the sun, which leads to acts
  of sacrifice and wars (Aztecs), and to potlatch (resentment, rivalry).
- Men do *not* know how to give without reckoning, expecting a return.
  (Men, in attempting to emulate the sun, take their fellowmen and all
  women, and turn them into use value [objects] and exchange value

[cementing bonds, b(u)y excluding women]; turn them into the means of communication.)

- Capital attempts to emulate the sun, but inverts it. (In a *particular* economic situation, more often than not, there is, or may appear to be, scarcity; in a *general* situation, however, there is always excess. [See 1988a, 22–23.] We are given [via Plato-Kant-Hegel lineage] to the particular [the Apollonian, the principle of individuation], not the general [Dionysian]. Moreover, Capital inverts excess to scarcity. With scarcity comes the need-turn-desire to acquire. We are not natural consumers but unnatural acquirers. Hence, Capital's need for each of us to think we are individuals-who-lack, so that Capital can extend each of us the sun's dream of excess.[13] Yes, Capital has appropriated the sun. Capital, unlike the sun, however, gives credit [access to excess] but demands a greater debt. "Individuals" are taught to compete [engage in potlatch and rivalry].)
- Capital (or Socialism, which does not take excess into account) must again spend, *after* equal distribution, its ever remaining excesses without return; for, ever and again, there will have been excesses. And imminent catastrophes.

II.

Man will escape his head as a convict will escape his prison.

—Bataille

However, let us return to . . .

- *The sun is the locus of excess*. (Counter-corollary: It gives without reckoning. *And yet*, the sun destroys us. Bataille writes: "The sun is black." "The sun is nothing but death." "The sickness of being vomits a black sun of spittle" [qtd. in Land 1992, 29].) The sun is the possible, *and yet* the impossible. In glory, we fall to exhaustion. We are spent, Zero.
- If "I" had only forgotten the question!
- The sun (contradictorily) is excess without lack, and yet lack. The sun is *Possibilisms*, and yet the *possible cum impossible*. (For Bataille, human being's predicament is having to live with both, and especially catastrophe.)

    How did this doubleness come about? Bataille's answer (like Nietzsche's answer) is by way of the history of an error.
- Hollier's *nyanza* (no answer) from Bataille's *L'Impossible*: "On the road to Thebes, Oedipus meets a sphinx who asks him a riddle: what animal walks on four feet in the morning, on two [. . .]? He is the first to figure

out the answer ('man'), and he causes the death of the sphinx [half animal, half female]. (But, asks Bataille, 'Would not the answer be: "I forget the question"?' " (Hollier 1989, 85). What is X? What is a Sophist? However, hubristic Oedipus says, *Anthropos*; says, One.[14]

It is out of this basic doubleness (contradiction) that Bataille recommends a new ethical-political economy, one that would have to engage in unproductive expenditure without reserve. A Heterology.

> Men committed to political struggle will never be able to yield to the truth of eroticism. Erotic activity always takes place at the expense of the forces committed to their combat. But what is one to think of men so blinded as to be ignorant of the motives for the cruelty they unleash?

> —Bataille

Ethics Reversed; Hence, Politics Reversed: Bataille calls for a recognition of and partial abandonment to irrationality and waste. Un/namely, to unlimited eroticism. To libidinal parapolitics. Bataille says: "the extension of economic growth itself requires the overturning of economic principles—the overturning of the ethics that grounds them. Changing from the perspectives of restricted economy to those of general economy actually accomplishes a Copernican transformation: a reversal of thinking—and of ethics" (25; Cf. 1985, 118). His comment about ethics here is twofold: He suggests that we must be ethical in our distribution but we must also be counter-ethical in a way that might appear unethical (even irrational). We must come to understand that it is in our nature, or essence, to engage in waste of energy, to be *sovereign*. On the one hand, our essence that-is-under-negation demands that we spend our energy productively, profanely; while, on the other, our essence that-would-be-denegated, demands that we spend non-productively, sacredly.

I cannot, as Bataille cannot, reemphasize enough that *this excess* (of solar energy, of libidinal energy, found in libidinal matter... this is not idealism but a materialism) not only *must be* but also, no matter what, *will be* spent either *gloriously* or *catastrophically*.

If spent gloriously, it must be spent in two possible ways: First, it must be given, say, by "a transfer of American wealth to India without reciprocation" (40). This, then, is a giving without an expected return. Bataille, therefore, argues: "If a part of wealth . . . is doomed to destruction or at least to unproductive use without any possible profit [if it is to be spent in a sacred manner], it is logical, even inescapable, *to surrender commodities without return"* (emphasis mine; cf. Spivak 1990, 96–98). Bataille would thus avoid altogether, or at least discover a way to live with, the problem of potlatch. "Henceforth," Bataille continues to argue, "The industrial development of the entire world demands of Americans that they lucidly grasp the necessity, for an economy such as theirs, of having a margin of profitless operations" (25–26). Once this redistribution has been made, however, there *must still be* an excess.[15]

Second, this remaining excess, therefore, must be spent without placing it back into production, as Late Capital or multi-nationalism demands, so that more items can be exchanged or purchased; this excess, which is to be spent gloriously, *must be sacrificed*. No profit must be made from its sacrifice! Whereas Capital wastes to manipulate supply and demand, heterologists waste to avoid catastrophe. (As Nick Land says, "Capitalism . . . is (the projection of) the most extreme possible refusal of expenditure" [1992, 56].) Heterologists waste only after all *animal* demands and desires, except one, have been satisfied.[16] That one? Glorious expenditure.[17]

If spent catastrophically, this excess energy will be spent in war, in a holocaust, as history has demonstrated. In war or in serial killings.[18] That is, it will be spent in a kind of "sacrifice" that we cannot any longer engage in. Bataille warns: "After a century of populating and of industrial peace, the temporary limit of development being encountered, the two world wars organized the greatest orgies of wealth—and of human beings—that history has recorded." To make things even worse, these wars appear to be profitable. Bataille says: "[T]hese orgies coincide with an appreciable rise in the general standard of living: The majority of the population benefits from more and more unproductive services; work is reduced and wages are increased overall" (37). Hence, to avoid future wars and the apparent benefit from them, we must expend this excess energy in other ways than catastrophically, which gets me to a more specific discussion of an alternative view of sacrifice.

For his understanding of the sacred, Bataille turns to a study of the Aztecs and their sacrificial rites. His conclusion is that the sacred has been profaned, heterogeneity has been turned into homogeneity, excess into lack, and subject (sublime-sovereignty) into object. Bataille writes: "sacrifice [e.g., as performed by the Aztecs, can restore] to the sacred world that which servile use has degraded, rendered profane" (55). Lest there be some common-sensical misunderstanding, Bataille is not calling for human sacrifice to the gods or even animal or vegetable sacrifice! What he is calling for, however, is for us to realize the danger of potlatch, which creates a rivalry and negative essentializing; and for us to see that this shift from sacred to profane, from subject to object, has reified all of us, has turned us all, especially females, into object-relationships, or commodities.[19]

Therefore, the question remains: What is to be sacrificed? In dis/order
to answer this question it is necessary to examine Bataille's notion of objectification, individuation; his notion of Hegel's lordship/bondsman.
(But a caveat: I am from this point on focusing on only one, though primary,
aspect of the sacred/sacrifice, and that is the counter-ethical side, in other
words, on the negation of, say, ab-jection, or ob-jection, so that we might
return, as Bataille suggests, to an ab-original *ethos*, or to sublime-sovereignty.
[Cf. Spivak 1990, 10.] The counter-ethical requires that, first, the labor/play
distinction be negatively and affirmatively deconstructed; that prohibitions
be denegated; and that, third, morality be rigorously critiqued [cf. Habermas
1987, 230–33]. In dis/order to dis/engage eventually in an aesthetic of the
sublime, i.e., to dis/engage in excess energy—for we cannot not—it will be
necessary, therefore, in every case, to dis/engage by way of a general
libidinalization.)

Let us return to Bataille's notion of objectification, individuation; his
notion of Hegel's lordship/bondsman. As Bataille says: "Servile use has made
a thing (an object) of that which . . . is of the same nature as the subject. . . .
It is not necessary that *the sacrifice* actually destroy the animal or plant of
which man had to make a thing for his use. They must at least be destroyed
as things, that is, insofar as they have become things [objects]. Destruction
is the best means of *negating a utilitarian relation* between man and the
animal or plant" (1988a, 55; emphasis mine). The practice of such a sacrifice or "destruction" (or denegation, affirmative deconstruction, or general
libidinalization) is to be realized by stepping out of the Hegelian lordship/
bondage relationship.

What must be realized is that religion is not historically what religion
does today. Religion has always practiced sacrificial rites. With the advent
of rationality, of objectification, of commodification, however, these rites have
fallen into master/slave relationships, and so have human beings. Bataille
says: "Religion is . . . always a matter of detaching from the real order, from
the poverty of things [objects], and of restoring the divine order. The animal or plant that man uses . . . is restored to the truth of the intimate world;
he receives a sacred communication from it, which restores him in turn to
interior freedom" (57–58). Bataille continues: "The meaning of this profound
freedom is given in destruction, whose essence is to consume profitlessly
whatever might remain in the progression of useful works. Sacrifice . . . does
not have to destroy as fire does; only the tie that connected [or linked] the
offering to the world of profitable activity is severed" (58).

With this idea of sacrifice better described, Bataille now can lay the
additional groundwork for his new ethics: "The world of intimacy is as
antithetical to the real world as immoderation is to moderation, madness

to reason, drunkenness to lucidity. There is moderation only in the object, reason only in the identity of the object with itself, lucidity only in the distinct knowledge of objects. The world of *the subject* [the new sovereign, not unlike Nietzsche's *Übermensch*] is the night: that changeable, infinitely suspect night which, in the sleep of reason [in the blind spot], produces monsters." And then, Bataille finally announces his new (but old, for previously lost to the world) creature:

> I submit that madness itself gives a rarefied idea of the free "subject," unsubordinated to the "real" order and occupied only with the present. The subject leaves its own domain and subordinates itself to the objects of the real order as soon as it becomes concerned for the future. For the subject is consumption insofar as it is not tied down to work. If I am no longer concerned about "what will be" but about "what is," what reason do I have to keep anything in reserve? I can at once, in disorder, make an instantaneous consumption of all that I possess. This useless consumption is what suits me, once my concern for the morrow is removed. And if I thus consume immoderately, I reveal to my fellow beings that which I am intimately: Consumption is the way in which separate beings communicate. (58)

IV. "Dionysus," the Transgressive Historian

... this victor over God and nothingness—he must come some
day.—

—F. Nietzsche

My intention in the foregoing discussions of Lyotard and Bataille has been less to contrast, in some traditional manner, the two paraphilosophers than to use them as a starting point for an excursion into still other ways of rethinking (unthinking) subjectivity, specifically, a sublime ethos, in relation to writing histories of rhetorics. In passing, I have suggested a few ways that Lyotard and Bataille are similar and different. Since this is not my extensive purpose, I am not here going to bring the two back together now in order to summarize their differences in some grand finale to this excursion. What I will say, however, is that whereas I found Lyotard extremely helpful in chapter 1 for my discussion of Schiappa's treatment of the Sophists in general, I will find Bataille equally helpful, and intermittently so, in the remaining chapters, especially in the last extended excursis. (However, lest I appear to favor Bataille over Lyotard, let it be understood that I am not finished with Lyotard, for I will return to him, as I have suggested, eventually, in relation to his earlier work *Libidinal Economy*, which will be a return that will force me to go back further to Deleuze and Guattari's libidinal-economic discussions in *Anti-Oedipus*.) What I do want to do in this final (rebeginning?) section to this excursus, and what I am resetting into motion for the entire book, is to return now to Dionysus as I left the god, being invoked, in the closing section of the previous chapter. After all, it is Dionysus that has been placed under negation and it is Dionysus (the most sublime of thinking-speaking-acting [performative] subjects) that I would denegate in dis/order to open up writing histories (hysteries) of rhetorics to new possibilities.

Drawing loosely on what I have said about my reconceptual starting places (*topos, e/utopos, atopos*), what I have said about Kant-Lyotard and then about Hegel-Bataille, I will now discuss more pointedly what the role of aesthetics would be in any future (anterior, metaleptic, hys-teric) histories of rhetorics. I will discuss how the ethical subject—and consequently how the *polis* and politics—must be aestheticized so as to get to what has been systematically forgotten. To achieve this end, or new beginning, I will now set aside my previous trinary and select momentarily and provisionally another trinary.

Thirds: In my discussion of Bataille, I referred to his apparent use of the *physis/nomos* distinction. I say "apparent" because I believe that Bataille does not work exclusively with binaries; instead, he takes the ready-at-hand language of philosophical and rhetorical discourse, which does work with binaries (thereby excluding thirds), and he reformulates this language by way of reestablishing subtle trinaries (thereby reincluding thirds). Lyotard does the same in the case of litigation/*différend*. If we recall that nature (*physis*), as well as essence, has been placed under negation, has been repressed, or excluded, in favor of custom (*nomos*), what we have, then (I'm constructing this as a tautological statement), is what I would call *physis*[neg.] and *nomos*[neg.], both of which are conceptual starting places that are under negation. Bataille, however, thinks in terms of denegating nature (*physis*[deneg.]) so as to remind us of our prior, denegated *physis*, our animality, our excesses uncurbed. Hence, the trinary: *physis*[neg.]-*nomos*[neg.]-cum-*physis*[deneg.].[20]

But there is a forever possible misunderstanding here, for this is, once again, not a binary (machine) of positive-negative. Therefore, it will be necessary to think of this ab-orginal *physis* as not simply a positive but, as Foucault explains, a "nonpositive affirmation" (1977, 36). Whereas Foucault tells us Blanchot calls this reconceptual starting place "contestation" (36), Foucault also calls it "transgression" (29–52). But there is still another

possible misunderstanding—because of our penchant for appropriating virtually everything in terms of binaries—which is owing to the word "ab-
original," which strongly suggests the myth of origin. This misunderstanding
should not be; for the concept of origin, or a nostalgia for one, comes into
being only with an act of negation (see Foucault 1977, 37). To this attempt
to rethink the possibility of thirds, we will return throughout. (For me, and
I think for Bataille and Cixous, aboriginal means not subjective/objective but
abjective.)

Isn't all this misunderstanding stuff a riot?

Physis: To further explain what this denegated, or "nonpositive affirmative"—and for some, dreadful—*physis* might mean, I want to turn to a
statement that Hayden White (1978) made concerning the absurdist critics
(and historians). I am going to quote White at length. He says:

> For the Absurdist [historian], criticism's role [in dis/respect to The history
> of rhetoric] is to take the side of nature against culture. Whence the cel-
> ebration . . . of such antisocial phenomena as barbarism, criminality, insan-
> ity, childishness—anything that is violent and irrational in general. The dark
> side of civilized existence—that which, as Nietzsche said, had to be given
> up or repressed or confined or simply ignored, if civilization was to have
> been founded in the first place—has simply been avoided by the Normal
> critics [recall Bataille] who define their principal task as the defense of
> civilization against all of these things. (269)

White continues:

> Absurdist criticism achieves its critical distance on modern culture, art, and
> literature by reversing [deconstructing?] the hitherto unquestioned assump-
> tion that "civilization" is worth the price paid in human suffering, anxiety,
> and pain by the "uncivilized" of the world (primitive peoples, traditional
> cultures, women, children, the outcasts or pariahs of world history [the
> abject]) and asserting the rights of the "uncivilized" against the "civilizers."
> Absurdist criticism is informed by the intuition that art and literature [and
> writing The History of Rhetoric] are not innocent activities which, even in
> their best representatives, are totally without complicity in the exploitation
> of the many by the few. On the contrary, by their very nature as social
> products, art and literature are not only complicit in the violence which
> sustains a given form of society, they even have their own dark underside
> and origin in criminality, barbarism, and will-to-destruction. (269)

Lest there be still yet another misunderstanding, White does not identify at all with the absurdists; in fact, as a liberal and a formalist (a prac-

titioner of negation), he criticizes their over-dependence on irony, or catechresis (see 270–82). White reads these absurdist critics as simply "reversing" (negatively deconstructing) the *physis/nomos* binary (machine) and does not see them as dis/engaging in displacement (affirmatively deconstructing) the binary and as moving to third subject (or sublime) positions, which I am attempting throughout.

And to achieve these third subject (or sublime) positions, it is necessary to aestheticize the ethical subject, and consequently the *polis*, and politics, so as to get to what has been systematically (synecdochically) excluded and forgotten. The abject. We must attend to the abject, the other in ourselves and in other selves. In other Bataillean words, what I am saying (again) is that what must be *sacrificed*, therefore, are master-slave relationships, and sacrificed for sublime "sovereignty." We have master/slave relationships in the narrative of The History of Rhetoric because we have a sublimation that is a desexualization (a determinate, negative, restrictive economy); instead, what we desire is a sublimation that is polymorphously perverse, that is libidinalized. Like Bataille we must set aside Hegel's choice of a "determinate negation" and accept, in an absurdist moment, an "abstract negation"; must set aside a "restrictive economy" and accept a "general economy." Therefore again, what I am suggesting is that some more of us must take the risk of nonpositive-affirmative essence (*physis*). This setting aside, without sublation, of restrictive sublimation, would be sovereignty.

In what follows, I want to examine this question of aesthetics and the sublime still more closely. I desire to turn more directly to Nietzsche, Herbert Marcuse, and Foucault; for each speaks for aestheticized (sublime) subject position(s).

> Morality is preceded by compulsion; indeed, it itself remains compulsion for some time, to which one submits to avoid disagreeable consequences. Later it becomes custom, later still free obedience, and finally almost becomes instinct: then, like everything long customary and natural, it is linked with gratification—and now is called virtue.
>
> —F. Nietzsche

> . . . man would rather will *nothingness* than *not* will.
>
> —F. Nietzsche

Nietzsche: Perhaps Nietzsche is the most critical of a negated-substantial subject. Virtually everything he wrote is an attack on Humanist, bourgeois subjectivity or individuation. If there is a subject, he argues, it is an effect of language, culture. He best says in *Genealogy of Morals*: ". . . there is no such substratum; there is no 'being' behind doing, effecting, becoming; 'the doer' [performer] is merely a fiction added to the deed—the deed is everything" (1969, 45; cf. 1966, 23–29; 1968c, 267–71). This passage has been often cited to argue that there is ab-originally no fixed essence other than what has been fixed by "theoretical" or "decadent man" (see 1967, 80; 1968b, 29–34).

For Nietzsche, then, the political-ethical subject is the *aesthetic subject*. Human beings can be represented only by masks. As Nietzsche tells us in *The Birth of Tragedy*, Dionysus, at first, never appeared on stage; later, however, the god appeared but wore a mask (see 1967, 66). As Nietzsche says: "whatever is profound loves masks" (1966, 50–51), and is undergoing metamorphosis. If, however, the god Dionysus should become a singly and stably represented god (or if he should perish), there is then hope for a "third Dionysus" to return, to be reborn again, from Demeter (74).

Before examining this subject that is not One, nor a systematized Many, but a Radical Multiplicity (and perpetually so in transformation), I want to summarize how Nietzsche develops his concept of the aesthetic (sublime) subject. It is in *The Birth of Tragedy* that he contrasts both Apollonian and Dionysian, the "aesthetic Socrates" (1967, 83) and "artistic Socrates" (92; cf. 98). There is a possible misunderstanding here because of the use of the word "aesthetic." Nietzsche is differentiating respectively between (and deconstructing) scientific optimism and cheerful pessimism, consciousness and unconsciousness, individuation (Hegelian "recognition") and loss of individuation, lyric and tragedy, the Platonic Socrates with the Dionysian Socrates.

Nietzsche writes: For "*aesthetic Socratism* . . . 'To be beautiful everything must be intelligible' " (84); similarly, "to be beautiful everything must be conscious" (86). The "aesthetic Socrates," to know himself, would favor a genre of genres (Lyotard); would favor a lordship/bondman dialectic (Bataille). This is a knowing of self that is based on a will to truth and a will to knowledge (death). Instead of "aesthetic Socratism," Nietzsche favors "artistic Socrates," or the nonrational, radically multiple mad-sublime subject. On the one hand, the "aesthetic Socrates" hails every citizen and concept in the agora to be rationally *linked* together (recall Kant-Lyotard and Blanchot); on the other hand, the "artistic Socrates," who turns from a "hunger for insatiable and optimistic knowledge" to a "tragic resignation and destitute need for art," *practices music* (98; cf. 1974, 272).

Rationalism—an "optimism" that contributes to "decadence"—is not to be seen and used as a means of understanding the world or ourselves. (Be gone all dividing practices: the laws of identity, contradiction, and excluded middle.) Nietzsche warns: ". . . the existence of the world is justified only as an aesthetic phenomenon" (1967, 22; cf. 52, 59). For Nietzsche, Heraclitus sees existence as a child playing a game, which perhaps only "aesthetic man" can grasp. Heraclitus "could only say, 'It is a game. Don't take it so pathetically and—above all—don't make morality of it' " (1987, 62–64). Like Heraclitus, other pre-Platonic Greeks were cheerfully pessimistic; then, with the advent of a Parmenidian Plato, Greeks became theoretical-scientistic men, which means that they consequently became pessimistic without the resources of cheerfulness or laughter (see Nietzsche 1987; 1967; 1974). Greek rationality could never deliver what it had promised and, therefore, Nietzsche concludes: "Truth is ugly. We [necessarily then] possess art lest we perish of the truth" (1968c, 435).

Nietzsche attempts, therefore, to return us to the "gay science" (see 1974), in disrespect to both negative science and negating morality. He sees European thought as pathological (1974, 35). "Mortality," he writes, is "a will to negate life" (1967, 23; cf. 1969). Nietzsche prescribes an aesthetic-sublime-pagan view of existence for a return to health, an aesthetic based on polytheistic, gods "just gaming" with and against each other, and not a view based on a monotheistic, omnipotent-omniscient God (cf. Lyotard 1985, 42–43).

> The concept of the whole does not lie in things, but in us. These unities that we name organisms are but again multiplicities. There are in reality no individuals, moreover individuals and organisms are nothing but abstractions.
>
> —F. Nietzsche

I want now to return to the radically multiple (sublime) subject position that Nietzsche develops in response to the Humanist, bourgeois subject, or individuation. (This, again, would be a sublime subject that would be unac*count*able.) Nietzsche writes: "*My hypothesis*: The subject as [radical] multiplicity" (1968c, 270; my emphasis. See Thiele 1990, ch. 3.) The best passage by Nietzsche to cite to explain this multiplicity, I think, is in one of his very last letters, one to Jacob Burckhardt, the Renaissance historian. In it, Nietzsche writes, "I am every name in history." He signs the letter "Dionysus" (1968a, 686–87).[21] Many readers may see the letter as the product of a diseased mind. For these readers, however, it is easy to point to Nietzsche's earlier writings in which he is dealing with the same aesthetic-sublime subject that is radically multiple, that is Dionyian. Besides the discussion of subjectivity in *The Birth of Tragedy*, there are other discussions in, say, *Twilight of the Idols*: "In the Dionysian state . . . the entire emotional system is alerted and intensified: so that it discharges all its powers of representation, imitation, transfiguration, transmutation, every kind of mimicry and play-acting, conjointly." Nietzsche sees this Dionysian state as comparable to that of the "hysteric, who also assume[s] any role at the slightest instigation. . . . Dionysian man . . . is continually transforming himself" (1968b, 73; cf. 1974, 282). It is this "transforming," like the masks, that has been repressed, negated. Dionysus is under repression, especially in The History of Rhetoric. Nietzsche had warned very early:

> Apollo could not live without Dionysus! . . . The . . . "barbaric" [is] as necessary as the Apollonian. . . . The individual, with all his restraint and proportion, succumbed to the self-oblivion of the Dionysian states, forgetting the precepts of Apollo. *Excess* revealed itself as truth. [However] it is equally certain that, wherever the first Dionysian onslaught was successfully withstood, the authority and majesty of the Delphic god exhibited itself as more rigid and menacing than ever. For to me the Doric state [Sparta] and Doric art are explicable only as a permanent military encampment of the Apollonian. Only incessant resistance to the titanic-barbaric nature [a denegated *physis*] of the Dionysian could account for the long survival of an art so defiantly prim and so encompassed with bulwarks, a training so warlike and rigorous, and a political structure so cruel and relentless. (1967, 46–47; Nietzsche's emphasis)

I find, like so many others before me have, this series of discussions on the aesthetic-sublime subject in Nietzsche to be a seed plot of ideas. I will return to discuss them repeatedly.

> In the symptom, the abject permeates me, I become abject. Through sublimation, I keep it under control. The abject is edged with the sublime.
>
> —J. Kristeva

> His [Orpheus'] language is song, and his work is play.
>
> —H. Marcuse

Marcuse: I want now to turn to the issue of how this "transforming" can take place, and when focusing on capability, I want to take up more directly the issue of aesthetics and the sublime. I will employ Herbert Marcuse, specifically his *Eros and Civilization* (1962; cf. Brown 1959). And then I will turn to Foucault, his *Language, Counter-Memory, Practice* (1977). To be sure, we are now faced with the problem of removing (or denegating) the sublime, or sublimation, and thereby dispersing abjection (Kristeva) and thereby possibly (?) confronting the politics of terror/horror (Lyotard). Or Should we be so sure that a denegation, or desublimation, of the libido, both in the *body* and in *language*, will necessarily give us this terror/horror? (It is this Question of the horror, the terror, that I would interrogate, *not* just here, but throughout.)

Marcuse, in his reading of Freud, argues that culture exist by ill-virtue of sublimation. Therefore, it has been reasoned repeatedly that *if* we remove sublimation, we end culture. However, it has to be equally pointed out, as Freud and Marcuse and others have that "sublimation [as in culture (*nomos*)[22]] involves desexualization" (75; cf. Brown 1959, 158–59). For Marcuse, sublimation is what "alters the balance in the instinctual structure. Life is the fusion of Eros and death instinct." But

> culture demands continuous sublimation; it thereby weakens Eros, the builder of culture. And desexualization, by weakening Eros, unbinds the destructive impulses. Civilization is thus threatened by an instinctual defusion, in which the death instinct strives to gain ascendancy over the life instincts. Originating in renunciation [negation] and developing under progressive renunciation, civilization tends toward self-destruction. (76)

For a solution to this problem of desexualization, Marcuse turns to an Orphic Eros—a surrogate Dionysus—which announces the "Great Refusal," that is, the great refusal to desexualize or negate libido. He sees Orphic Eros as a "non-repressive mode of sublimation which results from an extension rather than from a constraining deflection of the libido" (154).

Marcuse, then, discusses the aesthetic dimension, arguing that from Kant to the present, the third critique is a document concerning ethical-political liberation; and suggests that while the cognitive (knowledge) has been privileged, the sensuous (the body) has been only a mere supplement (cf. Eagleton 1991). Not only has the body been desexualized but also has the corpus of The History of Philosophy (and I would add, of The History of Rhetoric). Marcuse writes: "In this history, the foundation of aesthetics as an independent discipline counteracts the repressive rule of reason" (1962, 165).[23]

Following his discussion of aesthetics, Marcuse discusses the possible transformation of sexuality into eros and argues for "the possibility of non-repressive sublimation," "without desexualization" (190). But this sublimation, he warns, must not be achieved on the individual (neurotic) level, but on the social level.[24] Marcuse says: "Reactivation of polymorphous and narcissistic sexuality ceases [then] to be a threat to culture and can itself lead to culture-building if the organism exists not as an instrument of alienated labor but as a subject of self-realization" (191–92).

And how is this subject going to achieve self-realization? I am going to casuistically stretch this statement by Marcuse to read that the reactivation of polymorphous and Dionysian sexuality is a threat to Capitalistic culture and history (philosophical and rhetorical) because it denegates, desublimates and destabilizes, and perpetually resexualizes the subject to be not one but a radical multiplicity, to be polymorphously perverse both in work *as* play and mind *as* body. What I am variously reaching for here is an aesthetic-sublime subject that is millions, an aesthetic-sublime subject, or *ethos* cum *ethoi*, that would embody (across its bodies) deterritorialized, rhizomatic writings of the histories of rhetorics (see Deleuze and Guattari 1987, 23–24). What Marcuse is discussing is a desublimated culture (*nomos*); what I am talking about, *au contraire*, is a desublimated nature (*physis*). What I am placing at stake is the very praxis of writing histories of rhetorics. (What I would re/include is Nietzsche's mad-sublime philosopher, Zarathustra-Dionysus, and re/include Bataille's-Foucault's mad-sublime subject. And eventually, Lyotard's mad-sublime text [sex] of Marx.)

> The space of language today is not defined by Rhetoric, but by the Library: by the ranging to infinity of fragmentary languages, substituting for the double chain of Rhetoric the simple, continuous, and monotonous line of language left to its own devices, a language fated to be infinite because it can no longer support itself upon the speech of infinity.
>
> —M. Foucault

Foucault: At this point it might seem most obvious that I would turn to Foucault's *History of Sexuality* and *Madness and Civilization*. Instead, I want to move from the body (its desublimation, its liberation) to language, or *logos* (now, its desublimation). Now, I want to discuss briefly and finally what Foucault calls "counter-memory" (1977), namely, that which heretofore has been repressed, sublated, sublimated (negated while preserved). Derrida calls counter-memory "the trace," that which is excluded to a third position (see 1976). This discussion will take us back to Nietzsche and Bataille, who both wrote of madness (or excess, transgression) in language, and forward to Lyotard, who writes of the mad, hermaphrodite Marx. Yes, yes, yes, we move hermaphroditically in two opposite directions.

What is at issue, in a previous term, is "sovereignty" in language, or now "transgression," which is not again contra to anything. As Foucault says: "Transgression contains nothing negative" (1977, 35; cf. Land 1992, ch. 3). Transgression is a "nonpositive affirmative" (36), which means it is a third element: The negative, the affirmative, and the nonpositive affirmative. It is a transgression that is not subject to the law (negation), but can be seen as abject to it. What the law of non-contradiction (dialectic, dialogic) has been in our culture, transgression (*dissoi-logoi, dissoi* para*logoi*?), Foucault says, may be in our future cultures (33). Transgression is not something lost and we suffer nostalgically for; it is yet to be (37). Transgression has been, however, always already in language (*logos*); it becomes, for Foucault, intermittently present in the thinking of both Kant and de Sade, when the aesthetic and pleasure perversely appear in the face of reason. It is noticeable, as in de Sade's works, "where a rational order is linked to an order of pleasure" (39, 40). It is a philosophy of eroticism, of excess; it is the *aesthetics of excess* (see Weiss 1989). As Lyotard says, Kant (and de Sade) "advances far into heterogeneity" (1988a, 169). Yes, yes, yes, nes/yo . . . s/he does.

I want now to quote at length a passage on transgression as a wild, savage heterogeneous element in language that has been negated by the ontotheological tradition, and by philosophical rhetoric itself. If Socrates/Plato and others developed dialectics, Nietzsche-Bataille-Foucault search for a nondialectic, transgressive language (40). Foucault writes:

> In a language stripped of dialectics, at the heart of what it says but also at the root of its possibilities, the philosopher is aware that "we are not everything"; he learns as well that even the philosopher does not inhabit the whole of his language like a secret and perfectly fluent god. Next to himself, he discovers the existence of another language that also speaks and that he is unable to dominate, one that strives, fails, and falls silent and that he cannot manipulate, the language he spoke at one time and that has now separated itself from him, now gravitating in a space increasingly silent. Most of all, he discovers that he is not always lodged in his language in the same fashion and that in the location from which a subject had traditionally spoken in philosophy—one whose obvious and garrulous identity has remained unexamined from Plato to Nietzsche—a void has been hollowed out *in which a multiplicity of speaking subjects are joined and severed, combined and excluded.* (41–42; emphasis mine)

As Foucault continues in this discussion, he begins to speak of the unspeakable: "[T]he possibility of the mad [Dionysian] philosopher." He explains: "In short, the experience of the philosopher who finds, not outside his language. . . , but at the inner core of its possibilities, the transgression of his philosophical being; and thus, the nondialectical language of the limit which only arises in transgressing the one who speaks" (44). Again, this transgression "is not that of breaking prohibitions, but of seeking the limits of the possible"

(61). We move from work to play to "madness [?]." If there be possibly "mad philosophers," there must be *mad-sublime rhetoricians*! Who would listen to silence. (If so, then we will have had to investigate How to listen? How to interrogate *the exuberance* within the silence of questioning.)[25]

I am far from finished with the problematic of politics and aesthetics. And the sublime-mad subject. I now make a metaleptic turn (Dear Reader, are you getting dizzy?), so as to keep a promise to return to Lyotard's *Libidinal Economy* (originally published, 1974; translated, 1993); for it is in this work that I would bring together some of the scattered themes thus far discussed, but would keep them compossible,[26] and yet nonpositive-affirmative possibilities.

Lyotard's earlier study *seriously questions* what Bataille and others have said about a libidinal, desublimated [general] economy that would inform a subject, namely, whether or not these denegated possibilities are even possible! And, therefore, we cannot not continue without a look back to the other, or "evil," Lyotard. The fundamental difference between Nietzsche-Bataille-Foucault-Deleuze, on the one hand, and the Lyotard of *Libidinal Economy*, on the other, is that Lyotard sets the limits of libidinal interests well within Capital itself. Hence, there would be no escape from Capital or even a means of resisting or disrupting it. The sublime subject would be an effect of Capital and not any parapositions beyond Capital. Deleuze, however, sets the limits of libidinal interests and the way these interests dis/inform schizo-subjectivity (the sun) way beyond Capital altogether. It is necessary to redescribe Marx the hermaphrodite (1993, 96) in paradoxical terms beyond Capital, and not as the very product of Capital itself. *Libidinal Economy* and *Anti-Oedipus* are at—hermaphroditic?—odds with each other. Perhaps the hermaphrodite's heuristic value must be set aside for the schizo's aleatory value. In any case, let's get intense, yet remain serene.

V. Lyotard and the (subjectively invested) Desire Named Marx

We must come to take Marx as if he were a writer, an author full of affects, take his text as a madness and not as a theory. . . .

—Lyotard

And, therefore, I would now re/turn to Marx *as* a hermaphrodite, or mad (potentially schizo-) economist. A solar economist. A solar psychologist. A solar sociologist.[27] In the section "The Desire Named Marx," Lyotard exclaims:

"We [Libidinal Economists] no longer want to correct Marx, to reread him or to read him in the sense that the little Althusserians would like to 'read *Capital*': to interpret it according to 'its truth'. We have no plan to be true, to give the truth of Marx, we wonder what there is of the libido in Marx, and 'in Marx' means in his text or in his interpretations, mainly in practices. We will rather treat him as a 'work of art' " (1993, 96). And therein and thereby Lyotard begins his scandalous reading, which I would extend scandously-neurotically beyond its limits.

The *text of Marx*—I must emphasize, the *text* of, not Marx himself; and to reemphasize, the *mad text* of—in Lyotard's performance of it, reads: "The old Man [Marx] is also a young woman to us, a strange bisexual assemblage" (1993, 96). What Lyotard notices in the text, and invites us to notice, is that "The old Man" of the text is dis/engaged in perpetual invention; is dis/engaged in "the perpetual postponement of finishing work on *Capital*, a chapter becoming a book, a section a chapter, a paragraph a section, by a process of cancerization of theoretical discourse, by a totally pulsional proliferation of a network of concepts hitherto destined on the contrary to 'finalize,' to 'define' and to justify a proletarian politics" (96–97). Marx's work becomes an aestheticism (a fetishism). While the young woman of the text needs the finished work *Capital*, the old man desires pursuing every aspect and detail of his art. While the young woman of the text would have what Lyotard calls the *dispostifs* (or investments) take on "compromise-formations," that is, take on political forms that would at last stabilize the libidinal flow (specifically, Marx's libidinal flow) in terms of, say, the German Party or the Bolshevik Party, the old Man of the text dis/engages by way of postponement (97). Lyotard writes: "We say that this postponement, which results in the 'Economy' never being completed, and in the calculations of *Capital*, Book 3 being false, already demonstrates a whole *dispositif* [investment], a libidinal monster with the huge fat head of a man full of warrior's thoughts and petty quarrels, and with the soft body of young amorous Rhénane—a monster which never achieves the realization of its unity" (97). In classical Freudian terms, of course, this inability to postpone this aesthetic flow (or this constant revisionary process) is the same inability to postpone *thanatos* (or the negative, the death wish).[28] Or, in any case, this is how Lyotard would have us read this aesthetic flow (17, 22–23; see Pefanis 1991, 92–92). Lyotard suggests that the old man Marx is working from the negative and Capital, while the little girl Marx is working from *eros* and Socialism (the life principle). At this point, we should be able to conclude that this potentially sublime subject is a Kantian (sublime) negative presentation.

Lyotard tells us that this "monster" is "not exactly the centaur [a traditional icon of the libido]; rather, it would be the hermaphrodite, another monster in which femininity and masculinity are undiscernibly exchanged, thereby thwarting the reassurance of sexual difference" (1993, 97). At this point, the revaluing of sexuality that I have been propounding thus far— in the improper name of not One or Two sexes, but a sublime million—might be seen as being perpetuated by Lyotard. And yet he writes: "But it is exactly this [thwarting the reassurance of *sexual difference*] that is in question in the 'Economy,' and we maintain, dear comrades, the following thesis: the little girl Marx, offended by the perversity of the polymorphous body of capital, requires a great love; the great prosecutor Karl Marx, assigned the task of the prosecution of the perverts and the 'invention' of a suitable lover (the proletariat), sets himself to study the file of the accused capitalist" (97). What happens, given Lyotard's libidinal scenario is that Marx gets caught in a libidinal flow without end. The mad text of Marx becomes not only a hermaphrodite but a schizo-man-who-is-not-a-man caught in sublime-libidinal flows upon flows, but all nonetheless determined by the negative.

Thus far, Lyotard has described the mad text of Marx as manifesting two contrary voices: One of perpetual process (perpetual addition and revision of and by the text); the other of product (a call for resolution/unity of the text and for a political party to redeem the past). As Lyotard continues, he introduces the parallel theme of dysfunctional love (we love whom we hate; hate, love), and "we" (you, Dear Reader, and I) are inadvertently returned to what I discussed in terms of a sublime (Sadean-Kantian) love, subject to and of the negative. Lyotard identifies in the text of Marx the question, "What happens when the person assigned to the prosecution is as fascinated by the accused as he is scandalized by him?" His response:

> It comes about that the prosecutor [Marx] sets himself to finding a hundred thousand good reasons to prolong the study of the file, that ... the lawyer submerged in the British Museum in the microscopic analysis of the aberrations of capital is no longer able to detach himself from it, that the organic unity, that this swarming of perverse fluxes that is supposed to have to produce (dialectically), never stops moving away, escaping him, being put off, and that the submission of petitions is kept waiting interminably. What was happening then throughout the thousands of manuscript pages? The unification of Marx's body, which requires that the polymorphous perversity of capital be put to death for the benefit of the fulfillment of the desire for genital love, is not possible. The prosecutor is unable to *deduce* the birth of a new and beautiful *(in)organic body* (similar to that of precapitalist forms) which would be child-socialism, from the pornography of capitalism. (97–98; Lyotard's emphasis)

Let me continue to emphasize that Lyotard in his extended description is developing and adding to a set of Freudian themes: The more prominent themes are *perpetual process vs. product* (resolution for social action), which is associated with obsessive-compulsion; and *dysfunctional love* between the two aspects of the bisexual text (dysfunctional politics between "child-social-ism" and "the pornography of capitalism"), which is associated with Freud's general theory of perversion, the libido, and Oedipus complex. What we see being added now in this most recent description of the mad text of Marx is the theme of *Capital as a schizophrenic process* (the "polymorphous per-verse body of capital" itself). This latter theme becomes more and more explicit as Lyotard continues, especially when Lyotard says that Marx comes to understand, even if only implicitly, his "work cannot form a body, just as capital cannot *form a body*." (Lyotard is completely invested in a Freud-ian, negative hermeneutic.) He continues:

> This absence of organic, "artistic" unity gives rise to two divergent move-ments always associated in a single vertigo: a movement of flight, of plung-ing into the bodiless, and thus of continual invention, of expansive additions or affirmations of new pieces (statements, but elsewhere musics, techniques, ethics) to the insane patchwork—a movement of *tension*. And a movement of institution of an organism, of an organization and of organs of totalization and unification—a movement of reason. Both kinds of movement are there, effects as force in the *non-finito* of the work just as in that of capitalism. (102; Lyotard's emphasis)

It is *as if* Lyotard has Marx peering into a sublime abyss. What is considered dysfunctional is that Marx invests in sexual attraction (and repulsion) not affection, in the sublime and not Kantian beauty. (The pre-Socratic fragments are sublime; Plato's and Aristotle's completed texts are beautiful.) *Thinking* itself has become a perpetual process without reaching a *praxis*; has become dysfunctional. (Recall the joke concerning the sadist and the masochist's perfect "love" relationship.) Thinking, reading, writing, speaking, acting—all have become here in the mad text of Marx so much symbolic Capital manifesting itself latently or patently as a schizophrenic process. These endless, aphoristic processes are all sublime. Hereafter, we should refer to the mad *and* sublime text of Marx. (Recall all—the various libidinal install-ments—that I reported earlier that Lyotard has said about Kant and the "mathematical sublime" and the problem of the *non-finito*.)

We are now at a point where we can state—perhaps as investments!—how Lyotard differs fundamentally from Deleuze and Guattari, how the mad text of *Libidinal Economy* differs from that of *Anti-Oedipus*. And, therefore, why I must reject but preserve Lyotard's text.

- First of all, though Lyotard gives much credence to *nonpositive affirma-tion*, or an ab-original *physis* (as "figural difference" or "the libidinal band/

skin"), he, nonetheless, gives even greater credence to the negative (as "the great zero"). The former manifests itself when there is no particular investment (*dispostif*) but only a polymorphous perverse movement or flow, such as that performed by the old man Marx; the latter comes into being when there *is* a particular investment, such as that demanded by the little girl Marx. I emphasize: Lyotard sees no escape from the negative whatsoever; and, in fact, both will remain dysfunctional, contributing to a sublime-libidinal, but negative subject/object. Lyotard is thoroughly a Freudian as well as a Kantian hermeneut and, therefore, is given to the negative.

• A corollary to this first investment is that for Lyotard *all* economies are libidinal. Therefore, it would only be redundant to speak of a libidinalized Marx. (This corollary is owing to the Freudian theory of perversion, of libido, and of the Oedipal complex.)

• Second, though there is this polymorphous perversity, this schizoidness (sublimeness), as manifested in the mad text of Marx (and in Lyotard's examples of Judge Schreber and Chinese erotics), is the epitome of Capital. In this view, Lyotard would be in general agreement with such critics as Jürgen Habermas and Fredrich Jameson, who, contrary to Deleuze and Guattari, see Capital as schizophrenic. (There is most likely an equivocation here in relation to the term "schizophrenic.")

With these two investments and corollary, therefore, it is easy to see how Lyotard attempts to respond to Deleuze and Guattari. If all of this is the case, and I think that it is a fairly accurate, though quite general, representation of what Lyotard is saying, then, a *sublime* subject, or agent (such as a Judge Schreber or a Deleuzian Schizo), would not be of benefit; a sublime subject of a free-flowing libidinal economy would not work, or rather play, very well in escaping Capital. Though I think this is generally accurate in relation to what Lyotard is saying, I do not think that his conclusion serves the other interests of his image of the hermaphrodite (which I would see as a third sublime-subject position). To be sure, the hermaphrodite strongly suggests a dysfunctional love relationship. However (now I begin a pharmakonic turn on Lyotard), when I read *Libidinal Economy*, I hear, of course, more than I have represented as Lyotard's two major investments: I hear another Lyotardian implicit investment behind the scandal of this image of a bisexual Marx; I hear Lyotard the "bisexual," hermaphroditic Kantian-Freudian philosopher/sophistic rhetorician himself or the mad text of Lyotard itself. Hence, the question can now become, Is there a way to rescue Lyotard's own mad text of Marx-as-hermaphrodite so that he (Lyotard's writing) might be a locus (that-demands-not-to-be-a-locus) beyond Capital? Is there a way to divest Lyotard's mad text?, not to heal it, but to make it enjoy a wilder, more savage Nietzschean madness! I think there is *if* we would only reinvest, or more so perpetually divest, Lyotard's *demand* that there is "no affirmative region" as a *desire* to be told there is a nonpositive affirmative pararegion. Initially, it is necessary to read the mad text of Lyotard as *hysterical*, so that we can get on to reading it as *schizoid*.[29] Therefore, to the hysteric Lyotard, I would say that there is a nonpositive affirmative pararegion and there are investments outside of Capital, though paradoxically originating within economies such as Capital itself. (There is more than One economy, more than Two; there are sublime millions! Recall Bataille's libidinal materialism, his negentropy.)

Allow me to explain further: I was careful not to call Lyotard's response to Deleuze and Guattari *arguments against*, but a set of *investments* (*dispostifs*). Arguments and investments are means of linking. And therefore I would reinvest. Following the Lyotard of the *Differend*, I would now remind us that though it is necessary to link (to invest), it is not necessary how we link (reinvest). Deleuze and Guattari, first of all, have more subjectively invested in not linking (investing) their view of schizophrenia with the negative. They are well aware of how purposeless such an activity would be, namely, that there could be no sublime, anti-oedipus subject/molecular group. For Deleuze and Guattari,

> Desire does not lack anything; it does not lack its object. It is, rather the *subject* that is missing in desire, or desire that lacks a fixed subject; there is no fixed subject unless there is repression [the negative]. Desire and its object are one and the same thing: the machine, as a machine of a machine. Desire is a machine, and the object of desire is another machine connected [linked] to it. Hence the product is something removed or deducted [or excluded, as in the excluded middle or "thirds"] from the process of producing: between the act of producing and the product [the act that Lyotard's mad text of Marx exemplifies], *something becomes detached, thus giving the vagabond, nomad subject a residuum* [emphasis mine]. The objective being of desire is the Real in and of itself. [This Real is in reference to Lacan's theory of desire, which is predicated on the negative.] As Marx notes, what exists in fact is not lack, but passion, as a "natural and sensuous object." Desire is not bolstered by needs, but rather the contrary; needs are derived from desire: they are counterproducts within the real that desire produces. (1983, 26–27)

Deleuze and Guattari, in divesting their thought from the negative, continue: "The real is not impossible; on the contrary, within the real everything is possible, everything becomes possible [sublime]. Desire does not express a molar lack within the subject; rather, the molar organization deprives desire of its objective being" (27).

If the first point is that the schizophrenic processes are not linked with the negative, the second is that the schizo (its paraprocesses) are resistant and disruptive of Capital. Where Deleuze and Guattari might agree with Lyotard is that Capital produces schizos, but again where they would not share a common investment is that they maintain that Capital cannot control (reOedipalize, or renegate) schizos. In fact, what Capital produces in the form of the schizo becomes not only useless waste (a "residuum" [a trace] that cannot be reappropriated to serve the interests of Capital), but what it produces also resists and disrupts any attempts by Capital to recodify/ reterritorialize this so-called waste back into Capital. With this difference Deleuze and Guattari link up with, invest in, the view that *not* all econo- mies are similarly libidinal. Capital may be libidinal, but it does not at all express its libidinal flows as paratactically and hyperbolically as a schizo can and does. Let's take a closer look at how Deleuze and Guattari's *schizo- sublime artist* (or subject group) can go beyond Capital and return perpetu- ally to resist and disrupt Capital. I will only suggest what this *beyond* is, so as to leave a fuller suggestion for much later and intermittently until we reach the conclusion (rebeginning) of this book. It might help to think of this beyond, however, as the *pagus* ("the border zone where genres of dis- course enter into conflict over the mode of linking") and to think of schizos as *pagani*.[30]

Scrambling the Codes/Desiring-Production: Felix Guattari, a psychia- trist, had noticed, prior to collaborating with Deleuze on *Anti-Oedipus*, that patients suffering from schizophrenia (not unlike Judge Schreber or Lyotard's Marx) were divulging cognitive-somatic processes that resisted and disrupted totality (see Guattari 1980). This very process becomes the means, in *Anti- Oedipus*, of not only resisting totality but also, as both Guattari and Deleuze say, of resisting the *negative*, as it re/manifests itself through Oedipalization or capitalization. The paratheorists argue, as Lyotard later does, that Capital/ ism itself creates the conditions of the possibilities for schizophrenics. ("Our society produces schizos the same way it produces Prell shampoo or Ford cars, the only difference being that the schizos are not salable" [1983, 245].) As Bataille would say, they are sovereign and *useless* (see 1993, 197–211). Capital *de*codes and *de*territorializes so that it might *re*code and *re*territorialize by way of Capitalist axioms, which allow Capital to drain off surplus value created by schizo processes. Deleuze and Guattari point out, however, that there is a pharmakonic value in these processes by ill/virtue of the fact that the schizo "deliberately seeks out the very limit of capitalism: [the schizo] is its inherent tendency brought to fulfillment, its surplus product, its proletariat, and its exterminating angel. [The schizo] scrambles all the codes and is the transmitter of the decoded flows of desire" (35). Hence, it has to be understood that for Deleuze and Guattari the schizo process, often characterized as *the* problem (of poststructuralism and postmodernism), is only initially a product of (Late) Capital but finally the very pharmakonic means of eventually resisting Capital (cf. Lyotard 1988a, 178–79).

Deleuze and Guattari have studied the *paraprocesses* of schizophrenia (the rapid switching of codes that perpetually deterritorialize the axioms of Capital) so as to arrive at the means of a political "breakthrough" (1983, 278; see esp. 134. Cf. Brown, *Love's Body* 161). They study the "schizo-revolutionary type" and its "interest/investment" in following "the *lines of escape* of desire," that is, the lines, or flights, that take us beyond the negative/synecdochic structure of capital (277, 278; their emphasis),[31] and help create the conditions for the possibilities of a sublime-mad subject.[32]

Early in *Anti-Oedipus*, the authors quote Henri Michaux, who "describes a schizophrenic table ["carpentered" by a patient] in terms of a process of production which is that of desire." (There is a wonderful parallel here with Lyotard's Marx producing a mad text called *Capital I, II, III, ad infinitum*. Yes, an ac*count*ing to infinity. Marx, the sublime accountant.) Let me quote this lengthy passage first and then briefly comment on it:

> Once noticed, it continued to occupy one's mind. It even persisted, as it were, in going about *its own business*.... The striking thing was that it was neither simple nor really complex, initially or intentionally complex, or constructed according to a complicated plan. Instead, it had been desimplified in the course of its carpentering.... As it stood, it was *a table of additions*, much like certain schizophrenics' drawings, described as "overstuffed," and *if finished it was only in so far as there was no way of adding anything more to it, the table having become more and more an accumulation, less and less a table*.... It was not intended for any specific purpose, for anything one expects of a table. Heavy, cumbersome, it was virtually immovable. One didn't know how to handle it (mentally or physically). Its top surface, the useful part of the table ... was disappearing [so] that the thing did not strike one as a table, but as some freak piece of furniture, an unfamiliar instrument ... *for which there was no purpose*. A dehumanized table, nothing cozy about it, nothing "middle-class," nothing rustic, nothing countrified, not a kitchen table or a work table. A table which lent itself to no function, self-protective, denying itself to service and communication alike. There was something stunned about it, something petrified. Perhaps it suggested a stalled engine. (6–7; emphasis mine)

Deleuze-Guattari-Michaux's table is "mapped" transsemiotically across parataxis (additions) and paralogy (not necessarily tied together). Simply put, the "carpenter" of the schizophrenic table is shifting from one semiotic system to another to produce the effect of excess tables ("more an accumulation"), while the table verges on no longer being a *sign* ("less and less a table"). In Deleuze and Guattari's language, the "carpenter" is engaging in "a positive absolute deterritorialization on the plane of consistency or the body without organs" (1987, 134; 135–36). They say: "the schizophrenic table is a body without organs" (1983, 8), which means it is a table that is a performance of the "carpenter's" free-flowing desire, or that it is *de*territorialized (not identifiable as one kind of table [middle-class, rustic, countrified, or a kitchen table]). Moreover, it is not functionable. This schiz table is outside the genus of Capital; outside the practical acquisition process but in the desiring-production process. Needless to say, this "carpenter" would not be allowed in Plato's Republic—this "carpenter" who produces an "identity that constitutes a *third term* in the linear series: an enormous undifferentiated object" (7; emphasis mine). If Capital re/codes us for the sake of the market—to desire particular "things" (fetishes [rustic-idyllic tables for those of us who live in urban squalor])—this schizo table, or the *process* of this table's becoming, *de*codes us. Perpetually! For Deleuze and Guattari, this is affirmation; for Foucault, this is nonpositive affirmation. For Lyotard, this could have been Marx's affirmation if he (Lyotard/Marx) had not begun with the negative investment.

It has been a long trek, with various libidinal installments along the ways, from Kant to Deleuze and Guattari's schizo-sublime subject; consistently, however, what has established a continuity in a nonclassical sense is power that would not be traditional power but a will to power as Nietzsche described, a sublime power (the will to power = the sublime) without any negation, that is, suppression, repression, political oppression.[33] Yes, yes, yes libidinal interests. Now, perhaps, it is time to slow down the pace, the intensities.

I ended the previous chapter with a hanging quote from Euripides *Bacchae*. I now end so that I might rebegin later with another problematic passage, one that is contrary to Foucault's position. Silence, silence is the issue. *Silence* as a form of the *sublime*. Later, we will return, via this quote, to a failed Heidegger, who sat and listened to the silence. Sat and listened for revelation. From Camus's *The Myth of Sisyphus*:

> . . . A revolution is always accomplished against the gods, beginning with the revolution of Prometheus, the first of modern conquerors. It is man's demands made against his fate; the demands of the poor are but a pretext. . . .
>
> Yes, man is his own end. And he is his only end. If he aims to be something, it is in this life. . . . Conquerors sometimes talk of vanquishing and overcoming. But it is always "overcoming oneself" that they mean. . . . Every

man has felt himself to be the equal of a god at certain moments. At least, this is the way it is expressed. But this comes from the fact that in a flash he felt the amazing grandeur of the human mind. The conquerors are merely those among men who are conscious enough of their strength to be sure of living constantly on those heights and fully aware of that grandeur. . . .

There they find the creature mutilated, but they also encounter there the only values they like and admire, *man and his silence*. . . . (Camus 1955, 65; Camus's emphasis)

Chapter 2

꧁꧂

Helen(ism)?

"casuistic stretching" is indigenous to historicism.

—Kenneth Burke

There is no event, no phenomenon, word or thought which does not have a multiple sense. A thing is sometimes this, sometimes that, sometimes something more complicated— depending on the forces (the gods) which take possession of it.

—Gilles Deleuze

Meta-Commentary: In chapter 1, I was mostly concerned with the philological-historiographical methodology of species-genus analytics (*diaeresis*, dividing practices), which is an inventional procedure that comes to know-ing/no-ing by way of exclusion. (Nothing is something by ill/virtue of not being some other thing.) The principle of identification by way of division is perhaps best summed up as congregation by segregation. The steps of the methodology should be familiar to us as being both Platonic (*Sophist*) and Aristotelian (*Poetics*). I have perversely selected Aristotle's *Poetics* as an example and have not gone to his other works so as to conjure up his attempt to regulate poetic (desire in) language (see Kristeva 1980, 23–35).

Aristotle applies the steps of the methodology rigidly to *logos* so as to have an acceptable aesthetic (see 1447a). Aristotle applies the same steps just as rigidly to "desire" in his opening statements to *Metaphysics* ("All men by nature desire to know" [980a]). The steps, or divisions, establish the conditions (or controls) for thinking about the desire to know. Again, the steps of the methodology, when applied to poetic (desire in) language, are *species* (poetry), *genus* (imitation), *differentiae*, which include *means* (imitation in language alone), *object* (persons engaged in action), *manner* (mode of presentation). Like Plato, Aristotle would, by these steps, control the flow of the

123

mimetic arts.[1] To be sure, Aristotle, unlike Plato, saw value in imitation, but value determined, nonetheless, by way of *diaeresis*. Like Plato's Stranger (*Sophist*), Aristotle weaves and casts a net. (Aristotle's attitude toward division, however, is ambivalently expressed in his works. [See Nye 1990, 53, n26.]) Like Plato and Aristotle, Schiappa would, by the same divisive steps, by weaving and throwing the same net, decide what would be acceptable ("oasis") or not acceptable ("mirage") for inclusion in The Republic of The History of Rhetoric. Since the Sophists form no species, they are not. Plato and Schiappa, however, leave us with a feeling and a sign, in which Sophists and sophistic-*everything* live on.

Whereas the Platonic-Aristotelian-Kantian lineage searches for commonalities, I search for particularities so as to recall what has been excluded. Like mathematicians, this tradition of purgers, as Tarski would say, dream a nightmare of "the 'we' of an ideal republic which is the city of communication maximally purged of noise" (qtd. in Serres 1982, 68). Maximally purged of counter-memory of the trace. Identity by way of division; identity, noncontradiction, and the excluded middle; or suppression, repression, and oppression are their major weapons. Noise, noise, noise. Here comes the Noise, my antidote.

Therefore, in searching for and defending radical particularities, "I" would practice a tactic of cacography and epigraphy; would be the demon, the prosopopeia of noise (see Serres 67). Such an "I" would be a sublime/sovereign subject, one-cum-radical multiplicities. As Deleuze and Guattari say: "There is no fixed subject unless there is repression" (1983, 26). Hence the necessity against necessity (identity, suppression): A change in the conditions of the possible, a change from negative conditions to nonpositive affirmative "conditions." To the compossible. Those conditions I discussed throughout the two excurses on aesthetics and the sublime, but again a sublime that would not be Kantian (a negative presence), but a sublime that would be a hysterical cum Dionysian schizo. A sovereign sublime. I would have such a schizo—heretofore, systematically excluded from The History of Rhetoric—reincluded in a hystery and schiztories. That would, then, be the perpetual rebeginning(s).

And what would be, so to speak, unleashed? Once again, Nick Land writes: "The unconscious does not coo sweet lyrics or unroll immaculate and measured prose, it howls and raves like the shackled and tortured beast that our civilization has made of it, and when the fetters are momentarily loosened the unconscious does not thank the ego for this meagre relief, but hisses, spits, and bites, as any wild thing would" (1992, 124–25).

Dear Reader, am I asking too much of you. Are you now simply incredulous? If so, and I think so, let's rebegin and with dividing practices so as to ease you into what has been locked up in the attic, in the basement, in the walls. I am now going to turn more directly to The History of Rhetoric.

This present chapter is transitional, establishing a *metaleptic* linkage—it's important to link but not how to link—between Isocrates and Gorgias. Moreover, it is an attempt to establish a linkage between Isocrates and negative essentializing, as a caveat, while at the same (opportune) moment it is an attempt to disestablish and then reestablish a linkage between Gorgias and nonpositive affirmative essentializing, as a hope for a better life. (It will take a long while to pick up, theoretically, where I far left off in the excurses on aesthetics and politics; it will take a long while to get to a sovereign, Dionysian Gorgias, but we will get there.)

However, there is more, especially in relation to Isocrates; for I describe what I see as a *negative essentializing* that goes politically wrong, from Isocrates to Heidegger. The sublime subject, when determined by negation, or by the *topos* "out of the impossible comes the possible," leads more often than not to imperialism/fascism, as my immediate interests illustrate, in history writing. (Let us not forget that my primary interests here lie with The Historiography of Rhetoric.) What I will focus on most specifically/obsessively—before I place it in dispersion, before I throw it to the gods, to Nietzsche's infinite play of differences, to Fourier's phalanstery—is the key concept of "Helen(ism)." Actually, it is "Panhellenism." In any case, either is a code word for "Imperialism." And in relation to "*logos*." (And in relation to "*mythos*," narrativizing The History of Rhetoric in terms of rape narratives. Yes, Helen[ism], as a master metaphor, does double duty here, signifying imperialism over *logos* and *mythos*. Helen[ism] becomes *the trope of rape*, which is used both to inform and legitimate The narrative of The History of Rhetoric.)[2] But I get way ahead of myself. Therefore, simply at this point I will say that both Gorgias and then Isocrates speak in favor of "Panhellenism." Allegedly, Gorgias influenced Isocrates. (While Gorgias played, Isocrates took the game of discourse seriously.) "Panhellenism" = "imperialism." Not only in historiography but also—lest I mislead my readers—in political education and everyday political life. Isocrates becomes our model of the great educator.

My discussion is a radical intervention into the *representations* of "Isocrates" and "Gorgias," for I wish to reclaim them as different allegorical personages, representing a negative-positive subject and a denegated (sovereign, sublime, nonpositive affirmative) subjectivity. (I'm after a certain, as Deleuze and Guattari say, comic effect [1986, ch. 2]: If Freud constructed a certain Oedipalization of the universe of education, and Jaeger, a certain Isocratezation of the universe, I would exaggerate to the point of absurdity and paralogy, way beyond Werner Jaeger's absurdity of St. Isocrates.) Isocrates and Gorgias are complementary given their different views of and on *logos*. Together they are almost Heideggerian.

Though complementary with Gorgias, Isocrates is problematic because of his penchant for unity (gathering [*Lese*]).[3] I say this about Isocrates, knowing very well that other historians see Gorgias as problematic because of his penchant for dispersion (laying [*legen*]). As Heidegger says of Heraclitus's Fragment B 50: "The Laying that gathers has, as [*Logos*], laid down everything present in unconcealment" (1984, 70). I have no interest, however, in simply blaming one rhetor (Isocrates) and praising the other (Gorgias). At least, not in any naive, serious way. Instead, I wish to say "Yes" twice to the possibilities of the text of The History of Rhetoric. Saying Yes twice means dis/engaging in a negative deconstruction, saying Yes to not only the privileged but also the supplementary representation. (Which I have begun above by switching Isocrates and Gorgias not only metaleptically there and through the next five chapters but also by now slightly privileging the one over the other.)

Specifically, then, as for "Isocrates": Whereas he is generally and globally discussed in favorite, privileged terms in The History, I would now take up and inquire into the opposite terms. I will eventually have to respond to Jaeger's sanctification of Isocrates as the patron saint of Humanism. I would, therefore, in opposite terms, dis/engage by way of *dissoi logoi* (ancient negative deconstruction), saying Yes to what has not been admitted about the heritage of Isocrates and hegemony. As for "Gorgias": Whereas generally he has not been lavished with as much praise as Isocrates, he nonetheless has been recently celebrated, if not also sanctified, by a small cadre of new historians, whom Schiappa would dismiss.[4] If Gorgias has been recently praised, I will continue this Yea-saying to a third degree in the most radical Nietzschean-Dionysian terms; for I am drawn by incessant, insatiable desires of a sign and a feeling.

Therefore (I am speaking in parallel fashion now with the above discussion), while the so-called *actual* personages ("Rational Reconstructions") are important to many historians, for me the *conditions* ("Historical Reconstructions") for interpreting/representing them are more important. The actual is a subset to the conditions for the possibilities of interpretation. (To paraphrase Deleuze, the "actual" is only one force [or god] that can take a hold of a thing. The imperialistic "actual" always leaves us with a sign and a feeling of something left—far left—unspoken of or unseen or forgotten.) In saying Yes a second and eventually a third time, I would try to reclaim what has been far left of what is thought possible, which will have been done in "Gorgian" terms.

For comic effect, I have now recognized, paid homage to, the corps of engineers, with their meta-commentaries of flow charts, which subordinate hydraulic force to conduits, pipes, embankments. Eventually, for joyful-pessimistic effect, however, I will have invited an earthquake, a chaosquake, to root them all up, down, sideways, inside/out—all scattered, dispersed. Diaspora. . . .

. . . *Victor, Victor, VV project, hey!, Whoa! What are you doing? Victor, let me force—as you say, "farce"—my way, once again, back into this, your discussion. I thought that we decided in the middle of your introduction that you were not going to do this wild, savage stuff! Recall, you need to at least establish the illusion of a proper, academic ethos.*

I'm sorry. I have been reading too much Kathy Acker and Kafka lately. I am getting ready to do just what you have been suggesting now and for as long as I am capable.

Good. Give us an apparent binary. You can always trash it later.

It is impossible to understand how they have gotten through, all the way to the capital, which is so far from the border. However, they are here, and each morning their number seems to grow. . . . To talk with them, impossible. They don't know our language. . . . Even their horses are carnivorous.

—Kafka

Hegemon (hegemony)/*Dynamis* (dynasty): Before we get to this discussion of "Helen(ism)"—yes, lest we forget, we are talking about Helen(ism) here—and to what has been left unsaid or forgotten, I want in this transitional discussion to review a set of common differences (*differentiae*) between Isocrates and Gorgias, which are best discussed by John Poulakos, specifically, in his article "Early Changes in Rhetorical Practice and Understanding: From the Sophists to Isocrates" (1989). Though Poulakos examines the two rhetors across a set of common points of comparison, he does not take up the point or charge of *imperialism* (whether openly political, or in a wider sense ethical, moral, philosophical, or hermeneutical). It is Poulakos's discussion, therefore, that I must extend—or casuistically stretch—so that what now desires to be said, in the light of what I have already said, will have been said.[5] I will interrogate Poulakos's reading of Isocrates's view of *logos* as "hegemonic capacity" and Gorgias's view as "dynastic power" (311). (Whereas formerly I was working with the contrast between unity and dispersion, the contrast, now then, is between *Hegemon* and *dynamis*, with the former in my mind associated with the negative/positive [the Zero and One binary (machine), or the One and the Two] and the latter being associated with, and therefore reclaimed, in terms of a nonpositive affirmative sublime ["some more"].) Put most simply, I hesitate repeatedly to have *Hegemon* and *dynamis* as complementary, for the pull toward *unity* (as expressed in imperialism [Panhellenism], again whether political or ethical or hermeneutical) more often than not places *dispersion* in unconcealment. Hence, here and through out I will err (and casuistically stretch) by overcompensating in favor of radical dispersion. (The justification will become more unclearly clear as we make our way to Heidegger's penchant for unity over dispersion, his lapse from guarding the question of and partial contempt for Being.)

Several conceptual starting points will be established: First, that Isocrates should be distinguished from the other Sophists, for his view of rhetoric (and *logos*) is different; second, that the differences, in general, between the other Sophists and Isocrates are owing to "cultural circumstances of the 5th and 4th centuries B. C.," which include "the emergence of the city-state," the founding of Isocrates's school, and the development of writing over orality (1989, 310–11). (I am going to concentrate here on all but the orality/literacy issue.)[6]

*Rhetoric and Language (*logos*)*: Poulakos says that while Gorgias emphasizes the "dynastic power of language [*logos*] to impose, to undermine, to violate, to deceive, and to distort," Isocrates emphasizes its "hegemonic capacity to collect, to unify, to lead, to shape, and to facilitate" (311). Moreover, "while Gorgias stresses [language's] power to rule arbitrarily over people, Isocrates emphasizes its ability to lead them to worthwhile ends" (311). And again, "while Gorgias dwells on logos' psychological impact on the individual, Isocrates underscores its civilizing influence on society" (311).

The Emergence of the City-State: The Sophists, in general, challenged the old ruling order. In particular, "Gorgias was one of those responsible for overthrowing the old intellectual regime and replacing it with the dynasty of logos, a dynasty invested with unlimited powers," which could "deconstruct prevailing views" (312). (An interruption and a word of caution are necessary before we proceed: Poulakos, in describing Isocrates as well as Gorgias, puts forth a view that would be, given the prevailing conditions of interpretation, Isocrates's view of himself. Poulakos is not making a distinction here so that he can critique. As he says: "Which of the two notions [dynastic or hegemonic notions of *logos*] is superior is not at issue here" [315]. Therefore, when I say that I am going "to stretch" Poulakos's discussion, I am saying that I intend to paracritique the conditions of this Isocrates.) In contrast, Poulakos continues, "Isocrates seems to have accepted the new logocratic regime but to have been more interested in its potential for beneficial results and less in its awesome powers" (312). Therefore, Isocrates's "rhetoric sought to construct arguments for a pan-Hellenic awareness, arguments to replace war with peace, social chaos with order, and political weakness with strength" (312). Poulakos says that Isocrates's "better known works . . . are appeals to end the political turmoil and intellectual disorientation of the times, to harmonize individual and collective purposes, and to restore Hellas' sense of greatness" (312). (I interrupted previously because Poulakos knows as well as each of my learned readers—and this will eventually be one of my primary points—that Isocrates would have Greeks purchase harmony at home at the expense of waging war against the barbarians. Isocrates is a proto-imperialist.)

At this point, as I continue to stretch Poulakos's discussion, I am going to begin to focus on two aspects: Isocrates's school (hence, the themes of education and *paideia*) and Isocrates's view of *logos*. Both these themes and their analogical relationship, more so than other themes, are as I stated central to my next two chapters on Isocrates.

(a) *The Opening of Isocrates's School*: What Poulakos is interested in contrasting now are "the differences between the sophistical and Isocratean educational practices" (316). He writes that with the new school "rhetoric stopped being a nomadic show on the road and was given for the first time an institutional home" (316).

The analogy that Poulakos is working with here and that I especially want to stretch, is that while Gorgias, in particular, has a view of *logos* that places old power into dispersion, Isocrates has a view that gathers people together; therefore, in analogical fashion, while Gorgias and other Sophists have a view of education that is geographically decentered, Isocrates's is centered. Whereas one is closer, in respect to *logos* and education, to the Nietzschean Deleuze's concept of nomadic thinking (1977), the other is *polis*-based.[7]

Poulakos continues: "Whereas the sophistical [program of education] had construed rhetoric as the key to social survival and political prominence, the Isocratean turned it into an expression of and a guide to pan-Hellenic welfare" (317). "Pan-Hellenic *welfare*"? I would feel better if the phrase had been written as Pan-Hellenic *warfare*.[8]

As I stretch Poulakos's article, I will begin to paracritique what has become known as "Isocrates's [educational] heritage," which develops into Germanic views of language and education (see Finley 1975, 193–214; Lyotard 1983, 31–37). My point concerns the tyranny of Greece over Germany and, consequently, of the rest of us; my point is that it is not that far from Isocrates's school in Athens, as Isocrates advertises it in *Against the Sophists*; it is not that far as we move through Fichte, Schleiermacher, von Humboldt in Berlin at the University; it is not that far until we come finally to Heidegger's school in Freiburg-in-Breisgau, as he advertises it in his "Rector's Address."[9]

The Opening of the French and Prussian-German Schools: Since I will later discuss M. I. Finley's critique of Isocrates, I want now only to suggest, indirectly through Lyotard, just how Isocrates's view of education can be seen as raising its ugly head through the Prussian ministry of education. (What I am saying here about Isocrates's view of education can be said about Plato's and Aristotle's views as well.) Lyotard, in the *Postmodern Condition: A Report on Knowledge* (1984b), which was written for the Conseil des Universités, Québec, discusses two views of education that were developed during the Enlightenment for the purposes of legitimizing knowledge. The first is French; the second, Prussian-German. Whereas the first favors the "social subject" (the citizen) as the basis for legitimization, the second favors a "speculative subject" (the Spirit, reason, *logos*) as the basis. The first, however, only appears to favor the social subject; for, as Lyotard explains, "the State resorts to the narrative of freedom every time it assumes *direct control* over the training of the 'people,' under the name of the 'nation,' in order to point them down the path of progress" (32; emphasis mine). Hence, the State leads; the people follow. There is no sovereign subject! The second view of education, the Prussian-German, and subject of knowledge, as Lyotard further explains, "is not the people, but the speculative spirit. It is not embodied, as in France after the Revolution, in a State, but in a System. The language game of legitimation is not state-political, but philosophical" (33). There is no sovereign subject! (For there to be a sovereign, sublime subject, as I will point out later in discussing Heidegger's view of education, and will point out especially in the excursus "Feminist Sophistic?", there would have to be, in the terms of Hélène Cixous, a libidinalized education.)

What Lyotard makes clear is that in both cases subjectivity or agency, as a locus of *freedom of choice*, is not possible. In the first there is only the illusion of agency, with the State, or nation, in control; in the second there is not even an illusion. Lest there be a misunderstanding, agency, as traditionally constructed by the State or philosophy, as I have announced throughout, is to be resisted and disrupted. (I have sketched out the old and the new conditions for a sovereign, sublime subject, and will continue to do so in the two chapters on Gorgias and beyond.) Likewise, It should be clear by now that I and myselphs find no home in the politics of identity as described in these two pedagogical-political visions, nor as advocated either by Humanism in general or by rhetorical and composition studies.[10] I would insist that the latter two—Humanism and rhetorical and composition studies—like the French model of education can only work at creating the illusion that "human beings make history." For me, subjectivity is idiomatic. (It should not fall prey to faith in logic [as in "sentences"], or to faith in grammar/utterances [as in "speech act performatives"].) What I have advocated, however, is a search for third-subject positions (sovereignty) as a means of resistance and disruption and the establishment of newer places. (Subjectivity should rise to a new paganism ["theatricks, theos-tricks"].) Such a "subjectivity," which I will discuss at greater length in the chapters on Gorgias (there, in terms of self-overcoming and the middle voice) and in the final (beginning?) excursis (there, in terms of "wild, savage" practice), is without any form of negation. Hence, *physis*[neg.] (or negative essentializing) would become denegated as *physis*[nonpositive affirmation].

But I need to emphasize a point even further here, namely, that the second model, the (Greek-)Prussian-German, is especially dangerous, for it rests nervously on a view of the *logos* as beneficent. This model of education is Greek and is not only Platonic but also (with differences) Isocratean. (Let us simply remember Isocrates's hymn to the *logos*, in the *Nicocles* [ll. 5–9] and the *Antidosis* [ll. 253–57] as *one old beginning* for this model.) The speculative spirit, reason, the *logos*—so these philosopher-educators posited—will help us become enlightened. To be sure, Heidegger has his doubts about that Platonic-Christian view of *logos* and had his remedy, which was a guarding of the question of Being—though sadly, when he became the *Führer* of education, he dropped his guard. Heidegger, unlike Isocrates, was aware that the *logos* "gathered" but also took away. (Jürgen Habermas, consequently, continues the Prussian-German tradition, though allegedly with a difference. He would have a *logos* realized in an intersubjective communication that would be noncoercive.) But I have anticipated myself too much here. Education, pedagogy, *paideia* are the point here; *logos* is the next. (They are inextricably intertwined.)

(b) Logos *that Gathers, Yet Excludes*: One of the aspects of language that Poulakos is not concerned with, given his stated purpose, is the nature (*physis*) of discourse (*logos*), specifically, whether or not it is under, or founded on, negation (hence, *physis*[neg.] and *logos*[neg.]). In considering this issue of negation, or denegation, I will stretch Poulakos's discussion perhaps now beyond recognition altogether. (I am a topologist: I would stretch forms, deform forms, not already discovered in our nature that is under negation.) As Deleuze says, in his Nietzschean way, "A thing [in Poulakos's discussion, *logos*] has as many senses as there are forces [gods, farces] capable of taking possession of it" (1983, 4).[11]

As I will discuss in chapters six and seven Gorgias's (Untersteiner's) view of *logos*, which presumes a Gorgian view of knowledge as tragic, Gorgias's *logos* would, then, be understood as partially-apparently under negation (hence, *logos*[neg./pos.]) However, this *logos*—its binary of negative/positive—is exploded by way of a *kairos* that is un/founded on *nonpositive affirmation*.

(I go on to reinterpret Gorgian *logoi* in other ways as expressed in yet other extant works; I achieve this end, or new beginnings, with other protocols of reading.) Now in respect to Isocrates's view of *logos*, however, I would generally characterize it as negative (hence, *logos*^neg.). The primary characteristic of the Isocratean *logos*^neg. is that it exhibits solidarity but by way of exclusion. This characterization, however, needs further explaining. Simply put, for now, Isocratean *logos*^neg. is perhaps best understood if contrasted not just with Gorgias's view, but also with Heraclitus's view of the *logos*.

Isocrates, Almost an Innocent: . . . places great trust in the *logos*; he does not seem to think at all that it might misguide him and others.[12] In his hymn to *logos*, Isocrates says: "there is no insitituion devised by man which the power of speech has not helped us to establish. For this it is which laid down laws concerning things just and unjust, and things base and honourable" (*Nicocles*, ll. 6–7). The *logos* has given him and his kind Hellenism. The linkage that I am going to eventually investigate, then, is among Isocrates's view of *logos* and Hellenism and Panhellenism. Let us recall that Isocrates's goal is to unite the various city-states, or in other words, his goal is Panhellenism, which would be achieved by waging war against the barbarians. In contrast, Heraclitus sees the *logos* and human beings' relationship to it in more problematic terms. Heraclitus (fragment 53) sees *logos* as *polemos* (battle, strife). As Heidegger says, "*Polemos* and *logos* are the same" (1959, 62). If logos is *polemos*, there is reason to pause and think twice and, then, "some more." There is every reason to question *logos* as being beneficent.

Therefore, while Isocrates gives us no evidence of understanding that the *logos* as *Hegemon* (guide, prince) is split, Heraclitus gives us ample evidence: On the one hand, the *logos* may give the splendor of Hellenism and may put an end to agonistics among the city-states; on the other hand, *logos* purchases this apparent stability and liberation at the price of waging war, perhaps perpetually, against the barbarians. Again, there is no evidence that Isocrates understands this split in the *logos* and its cost. Heidegger interprets: "Men are forever with the *logos*, yet forever removed from it, absent though present; thus they are the *axynetoi*, those who do not comprehend" (1959, 130; cf. 1984, 59–78).

While hegemony-as-imperialism might be a way of seeing, it is also a way of not seeing, or of rationalizing, the consequences. I might say now, as Marx would say (see 1977, 166–67), "Isocrates does it while not knowing he does it"; in other words, Isocrates is in a state of mystification. Heraclitus, however, knows that he is doing it and, therefore, is more likely to be careful, though, given his tragic view, this knowledge will not prevent him and others from tragic acts.[13] The further differences between Isocrates and Heraclitus, however, are going to require a lengthy rumination not only with respect to Isocrates and Heraclitus but also with respect to Heidegger, who found himself on numerous occasions having to explain his discussions of Heraclitus's view of *polemos* and his own views with dis/respect to his support of National Socialism (see Neske and Kettering 1990, 21). Heidegger himself is a tragic character.

Gorgias and Heraclitus: I would signify *logos* for Heraclitus in the same manner as I have for Gorgias, namely, as *logos*[neg./pos.]. Heraclitus does express the *playfulness* of Being, or Nature, in the form of *parody*, if one were to employ the reading protocol that determines parody; but Heraclitus expresses even more so—given my penchant for the protocol that determines pastiche—the playfulness of Being in the form of *pastiche*, as I will redescribe Gorgias in a different protocol of reading in chapter 6. (For Gorgias, as for Nietzsche, truth is a fable and, therefore, lying in an extra-moral sense [as *apate*, deception] is the *only* means of communicating. Again, the truth of *logos* may be, but human beings are *axynetoi*, those who do not comprehend. If the world, from a post-modern perspective, from a Bataillean perspective, is de/composed of libidinalized matter, is in an un/state of negentropy, How could we, human-beings, understand? We, consequently, act, suffer, learn, only to act again, never really learning in any progressive sense. Only in a joyful pessimistic sense.[14])

Specifically what I have in mind here in reference to the playfulness of Being—however problematic it might be—is Heraclitus's fragment 52: "The course of the world is a playing child moving figures on a board—the child as absolute ruler of the universe."[15] About Heraclitus and this fragment, Nietzsche writes: "In this world only play, play as artists and children engage in it, exhibits coming-to-be and passing away, structuring and destroying, *without any moral additive, in forever equal innocence*. And as children and artists play, so plays the ever-living fire. It constructs and destroys, all in innocence" (1962, 62; emphasis mine). These, indeed, for many, if not all of us, are disconcerting words!

Two points need to be made here and investigated more fully later: First, not only is Isocrates innocent (and does not know it) but also Heraclitus, Nietzsche, and Heidegger are innocent (but do know it); second, a politics in and for itself, given this view of *logos*[neg./pos.], is less likely, while an aesthetic that would perpetually interrogate a politics is more likely, if not necessary (cf. de Man 1983). However, it is unacceptable to me, as I think it is to these personages, to take this Heraclitean fragment and use it as a means of establishing a view of aesthetics for its own sake. (As I stated in the two excurses on aesthetics, art for art's sake is unacceptable.) What is left at stake, then, is to work from this fragment in ways that would not simply be political (for often such ways are politically reactionary), but would be complexly *parapolitical*. Such play would be without criteria such as the play of Wittgenstein's "language games" (1988, §66–§84) and the play of Lyotard's "just gaming" (1985). Let us recall that Nietzsche—subjunctively concluding what Heraclitus might say about *logos*, Being, the game, and a possible politics—writes: "Don't take it [not knowing why there is flux and indeterminateness] so pathetically and—above all—don't make morality of it!" (64). Why not make a morality of it? All that any of us has to do, in seeking an answer, albeit ambiguous, is to return to re/reading *The Genealogy of Morals* and the literature that has developed out of this volume and others like it. Nietzsche writes: "The slave revolt in morality begins when *ressentiment* itself becomes creative and gives birth to values. . . . slave morality from the outset says No to what is 'outside,' what is 'different,' what is 'not itself'; and *this* No is its creative deed" (1969; Nietzsche's emphasis). In my usage, then, *politics* is to ressentiment/the negative as *parapolitics* ("pagan politics") is to the nonpositive affirmative. Nietzsche, in his appropriation of Heraclitus, wants to say Yes to everything in life (*amor fati*). In agreement with Heraclitus, Nietzsche writes in *Ecce Homo*: "a Yes-saying without reservation, even to suffering, even to guilt, even to everything that is questionable and strange in existence [the uncanny]" (1969). If not, then Nought, which means a cycle of revenge. Is such a stance-which-is-an-ever-shifting(protean)stance possible?[16]

This begs for further explanation: If the game predicated on the negative (resentment, morality, genius, genus, the definitive answer to a question, and what goes for political thought and action in terms of capitalism or vulgar socialism) excludes, then, the game depredicated (denegated) on the negative such as Lyotard's "just gaming" (as in "Homer's contest") includes all in the inside except that which would dominate ethically or politically by way of exclusion. Sam Weber in his discussion of Lyotard writes:

[A]s in *Just Gaming*, Nietzsche's argument [in "Homer's Contest"] takes as its point of departure the distinction between two conceptions of struggle: on the one hand, struggle is seen as a means, it is subordinated to a finality determined outside the game (whose goal is thus identified with victory); on the other hand, the game (or struggle) is regarded as the end-in-itself. The first conception finds its most extreme, but also most consequent, expression in what Nietzsche calls the *Vernichtungskampf*, the extermination struggle; the second, in contrast, identified with Greek society during the Homeric epoch, is designated as *agôn* properly speaking, as *Wettkampf* (joust). . . . "The core of the Hellenic notion of the joust," writes Nietzsche, is that it "abominates the rule of one (*die Alleinherrschaft*) and fears its

dangers: it desires, as a protection against the genius [the negative], another genius [a denegation]." (1985, 106)

He-who-would-win must be *ostracized*, excluded. Hence, the principle of
exclusion (negation) is excluded (denegated). Hence, a terminal paradox. As
Weber says, "Otherness . . . is . . . sought . . . *within* the game" itself (106).
In just gaming, we play the game in such a manner to protect the incommensurability of language games (see Lyotard 1984, xxiii–xxv). Why? Because
we desire a pagan politics (parapolitics).

My purpose in employing Heraclitus here has been (is) for other reasons than a mere contrast with Gorgias and Isocrates; for it is Heraclitus
that allows me to introduce Heidegger, who is deeply influenced by his own
readings of Heraclitean fragments (see 1984, 59–78, 102–24) and who similarly has a view of *logos* that I would characterize as *logos*$^{neg./pos.}$. This is not
to say, however, that Gorgias, Heraclitus, and Heidegger have the exact same
view of *logos*: My sense is that their views are identical in kind but differ
respectively and progressively in degree. In their acting (performing) them.
Or In my acting (performing) them, their sublime fragments. My purpose
in employing Heidegger here, likewise, is for other reasons than a mere
contrast; for it is Heidegger, as reintroduced by Samuel Ijsseling, that allows me *metaleptically* to reread Isocrates, who deeply influences German
thinking, a thinking that is reactionary, and who conversely is, yes, deeply
influenced by Greek thinking. (As I proceed, *metalepsis* as a heuristic, or
reading protocol, will become more unclearly clear and perhaps its revaluing more acceptable.)

Gorgias/Isocrates and Heidegger: While Gorgias carries the *logos* from
city-state to city-state, and while Isocrates, as Poulakos says, would bring *logos*
home (to the city-state), Heraclitus and more so Heidegger would say (and
Heidegger does say) that there simply is no at-homeness, or being-at-home.
Isocrates may establish a school at home, but he does not realize that he and
others cannot go home again. Canniness is no longer; uncanniness (*Unheimlich*)
or strangeness (*deinon*) with its violence *is* always already within *logos* (see
Heidegger 1959, 146–65; 1962, 233–33). Hence, to struggle against it or to try
to purify the uncanny with its violence from *logos* only brings about more of
the same, the eternal return of tragedy. A politics that would be rational
(optimistic) contributes to such violence. Hence, the Nietzschean suggestion
of joyful pessimism, the gay science; the Lyotardian suggestion of just gaming.

Yes, I am purposefully employing "our" revised understanding of
Heidegger to reread Isocrates, especially in relation to the *logos* as unhomely.
And I will continue this tactic, affirming it more so, as I proceed through

the next two chapters. If *logos* is our guide (*Hegemon*), let us be perpetually suspicious of it. Michael Allen Gillespie explains, and I will quote him at length, that the

> experience of Being [*physis, logos*] . . . is in Heidegger's view fundamentally tragic. The experience of the abyss of Being . . . gives birth to politics and ethics but at the same time also opens up the fundamental mysteriousness of existence and casts man out of the everyday realm in which the prevailing order is accepted as a given. Those who are struck by Being in this way become preeminent as creators and founders but "become at the same time *apolis*, without city and place, alone, alien, without a way out in the midst of being as a whole, at the same time without statute and limit, without structure and order because as creators they must first ground all this." (1984, 139; qt. from Heidegger 1959, 152–53)

Gillespie continues:

> Like Antigone and Oedipus, or for that matter Heracleitus, they are beyond good and evil, pariahs cast out not by their fellows but by their experience of the abyss of Being, which calls everything into question and directs them in a new and as yet uncharted direction. The experience of Being for the early Greeks is thus in Heidegger's view the experience of homelessness and nothingness that drives them to the attempt to establish a new home, a new *ethos*, and hence a new ethics and politics through the articulation of new gods, heros, virtues, and laws, according to the clue given them by the particular character of the revelation of Being itself in and as the question "What is being?"

Again in reference to politics, Gillespie writes:

> Like Heracleitus such men seem apolitical, but this is only because they are not concerned with some immediate public use like those within the polis. They are concerned with what is far more important, the ground of the polis itself in Being. Thus, whatever public opinion may think of such men and however resolutely they may seem to abandon political life, their attendance upon the question of Being and the gods is the source of all ethics and politics and thus the authentic political act. In this heroic-tragic sense, battered, blinded, and cast out, they thus represent for the Greeks the highest human possibility. (139–40)

This lengthy passage, concerning Heidegger's views of the pre-Socratics, especially Heraclitus, can be read in many different ways.[17] (Heidegger's stretching will be my concern, especially in chapter 5, though, to be sure, my stretching will inevitably overlap with Heidegger's dis/similar stretching.

But in my stretching, in my calling on the gods for different senses, there will be those of my readers who will hear devils. There lies the difference between gods and God.) My stretching of it, however, is that the *polis* is not only the *political locus* but also, if not more so, the necessary *aesthetic locus-cum-radical loci* of *apolis*, of *pagus*, of bedlam, of *chora*, of T.A.Z., of *les domaines inférieurs*, of the uncanny, of gulag, of *oikos* (private-yet-social lives!). Recall that, following "Homer's Contest," I would re/include all (ALL) back into the polis; I would light out for the *pagus*, the TAZ, in dis/order to return all (ALL) the excluded back into the *polis*. Hence, my aesthetics would save writers of rhetorics from the truth, or any variant thereof. It should be evident by now that I agree with Lyotard when he says

> The word aesthetic has an insulting connotation in Marxist-French, which shows the links in this language with that of the bourgeoisie. . . . "Aesthetics" has been for the politicist I was (and still am?), not at all an alibi, a comfortable retreat, but the fault and fracture giving access to the subsoil of the political scene, the great vault of a cave on which the overturned or reversed recesses of this scene could be explored, a pathway allowing me to skirt or divert it. For the operations concealed in the production of ideologies can be induced from those of desire exhibited in the production of "works" of art. Hence the equation: aesthetics = workshop for the forging of the most discriminative critical concepts. (1984, 15–16)

But first pedagogical imperialism, a.k.a. the *Paideia*, or play *(paizo, paisdo)* with children (see Krell 1972, 77), is the issue.

Chapter 3

꧁꧂

Isocrates, the Paideia, and Imperialism

For Nietzsche, revenge is the fundamental characteristic of all thought so far.

—Martin Heidegger

Jewgreek is greekjew. Extremes meet.

—James Joyce

With the irruption of the sexual instinct, educability is for all practical purposes at an end. For society must take as one of its important educative tasks to tame and restrict the sexual instinct when it breaks out as an urge to reproduction, to subject it to an individual will which is identical with the bidding of society.

—Sigmund Freud

State? What is that? Well then, open your ears to me, for now I [Zarathustra] shall speak to you about the death of peoples.

State is the name of the coldest of all cold monsters. Coldly it tells lies too; and this lie crawls out of its mouth: "I, the State, am the people." That is a lie! . . .

"On earth there is nothing greater than I: the ordering finger of God am I"—thus roars the monster. And it is only the long-eared and shortsighted who sink to their knees!

—Friedrich Nietzsche

In many ways this particular chapter does not "fit" directly into the discussion of this book. (In this sense, it is yet another interruption, and intrusion of the uncanny.) I am not suggesting that politics and pedagogy do not belong together; they do, most assuredly. What I am suggesting, however, is that in this book I have avoided for the most part any direct discussion of education and the State; and I have avoided such a discussion because it is my intent to discuss at much greater length such matters in the sequel to this book on historiographies of rhetoric.[1] And yet, this chapter does "fit." I am after the conditions of a libidinalized educational paratheory. One way of thinking about this chapter, then, is that it looks forward to a sequel, while it, nonetheless, looks back and examines the interrelationships among The History of Rhetoric, the State, and education (including libidinalized versions). Therefore, the chapter might be read as a glance at what will be discussed as I continue this discussion later (in terms of Isocrates's, Jaeger's, Heidegger's, Cixous's views of education) and a look at how it does, after all is said and undone, fit here in an uncanny, canny way.[2]

Contrary-Critical (Revisionary) Coordinates: As I tried to suggest and illustrate, thus far, different hermeneutical predispositions, or coordinates, or will to forces (gods) at play, can give us quite contrary readings. It is semiotically across revisionary coordinates—contrary to traditional—that we can see differences. The differences of the issues, more often than not, are deeply political. (At best, these revisionary readings are negative deconstructions.) And what about sub/versive coordinates and their differences, contrary to traditional and revisionary? The differences of these issues and interests are dramatically aesthetic, ethical, and political. (At best, these sub/versive readings are affirmative deconstructions.)

Given my predispositions, I find Isocrates's notion of *Panhellenism* to be highly problematic. It becomes a forerunner of "manifest destiny" and of the Third Reich; it has within it the conditions of a philosophy/rhetoric of history and politics that is imperialistic. Panhellenism is a dangerous *master trope*.[3] To be sure, there will be many readers who will argue that my comparison between Panhellenism and the Third Reich is too metaleptic, or too anachronistic. In a way they are correct; yet in other ways, deeply "mistaken" (Burke 1984, 41). To insist on a reading protocol according to numbers on a particular calendar, from one to thirty or to thirty-one, or from one to twelve, or from decade to a century, in terms of periods and, then, in one direction, is only one possible protocol, or language game, among others, albeit a canonized protocol of reading among historians of rhetoric (cf. Nietzsche 1974, 335).

My being anachronistic here is not my unique act; for one of Martin Heidegger's own contemporaries drew an identical relationship between Isocrates's views of Hellenic history (destiny) and Nazi Germany (the Third Reich). Hence, the eventual and, I would insist, inevitable historiographical-Oedipal triangle among Isocrates, Heidegger, and National Socialism. I am referring to Georges Mathieu, in *Les Idée Politiques d'Isocrate* (1925),[4] who points to an "analogy" between Isocrates's *"panhellénisme du ive siécle"* and *"pangermanisme"* of the twentieth century; Mathieu specifically says that many German historians begin to employ easily Isocrates's views to justify the Third Reich's ambition (destiny?, fascisms) *to unite* (by way of expulsion, purging) all of the Germanies and the rest of the continent and beyond (218–22).[5] The grand narrative goes: Today, Germany; tomorrow, the world! Greeks and Germans. Germans and Greeks! Such an ungrand narrative must be, cannot not be—I will incite right here and now and everywhere—responded to. Reb Derissa (Derrida) helps:

> Are we Jews? Are we Greeks? We live in the difference between the Jew and the Greek. . . . We live in and of difference, that is, in *hypocrisy*. . . .
>
> Are we Greeks? Are we Jews? But who, we? Are we (not a chronological, but a pre-logical question) *first* Jews or *first* Greeks? And does the strange dialogue between the Jew and the Greek, peace itself, have the form of the absolute, speculative logic of Hegel, the living logic which *reconciles* formal tautology and empirical heterology. . . ? Or, on the contrary, does this peace have the form of infinite separation and of the unthinkable, unsayable transcendence of the other? To what horizon of peace does the language which asks this question belong? From whence does it draw the energy of its questions? Can it account for the historical *coupling* of Judaism and Hellenism? And what is the legitimacy, what is the meaning of the *copula* in this proposition from perhaps the most Hegelian of modern novelists: "Jewgreek is greekjew. Extremes meet"? (1978, 153; Derrida's emphasis)

Since *desire* is under negation, *libido* must have reached for the absolute other (see Derrida 1978, 321).

Above: Is this stylistic—perhaps cryptic—intervention of mine understood? While the grand narrative of unity is the product of Greek (Platonic) and Christian (Pauline and Platonic) tradition, the ungrand view of the grand narrative is the by-product (?) of the Jewish counter-tradition, in which "Derissa" often writes.[6] I am alluding to Talmudic commentary—as Christopher Norris reminds us—with its "multiple insets and other such graphic devices which refuse any clear demarcation between 'primary' and 'secondary' texts" (1987, 229). Yes, we are talking about an attack on a so-called established academic research protocol by a forgotten one. We are not talking about mere, empty playfulness here. In terms of the gesture toward the Talmudic: "Authority" reverses to counter-authority; then counter-authority displaces to no author/ity. Or "primary" and "secondary" texts are blurred so as to reach, as I have been saying, for "tertiary" texts.

The question of Derissa's text: While Hegel would unite the differences by possibly excluding the other, and hence the trace; while Joyce would unite and yet attempt to include the trace, which makes his texts so difficult; What, then, are "we" (who long to attend to the Other more fully) do? Whereas the Graeco-Christian (and German) tradition tends to long for unity by way of logocentricism, the Jewish-Talmudic counter-tradition does not. And does not in its style of writing, which is a Derissaian and a Victa Nyanzian, though different, style of writing. My unclear clarification and no answer: Hence expect such perpetual, though intermittent, interventions especially in the forthcoming chapters on Isocrates and Heidegger, who are subject to logocentricism, because of "a figural logic and wayward 'economy' " (see Norris 228), though differently. Therefore, expect my in(ter)ventions, interruptions, and irruptions. How else should "we" write in the face (and trace) of such history? Today, in(ter)ventions; tomorrow, the whirl!

To this view I will eventually return. For now, however, let us get to the business of what our contemporary historiographers have to say about writing histories of Isocrates and, then, quite specifically, about the *paideia* (often associated with Isocrates) and about "its heritage." Here, therefore, I move from Poulakos's contrastive reading of Isocratean *hegemony* and Gorgian *dynamis* to other historians' critiques (negative deconstructions) of Isocrates. The analogy, or ratio, that I will explore is as follows: Arnaldo Momigliano and M. I. Finley are *to* Werner Jaeger's *paideia as* Georges Mathieu is *to* 1920s and 1930s German historians' call for Pangermanism. The crucial linkage here is with both Isocrates's *paideia* and Panhellenism. Hence, illustrated, I will read (metaleptically) in this direction: Mathieu/ Finley/Momiliagno —> Jaeger —> Isocrates. (In the next chapter, I will read similarly: Heidegger —> Isocrates.) However, this protocol is not just metaleptic; for as I reread history and perform these readings, it will be necessary to shuttle not only backwards but also forwards simultaneously (dialectically), so as eventually to reach for a nonsynthesized third, or "some more." In the final excursis of this book, I will call this protocol the *future-anterior.*[7]

The historiographical strategy being employed by these historians, such as Momigliano and Finley and initially by myself here, is revisionary, negative deconstructive. It's a reopening of the question of Isocrates and his apologist-historians so as to consider the question's opposite—with what has been privileged being considered supplement; and supplement, privileged.

As I proceed beyond this chapter on pedagogy, however, I will be dis/engag-
ing, once ever some more, in affirmative deconstructions in relation not only
to pedagogy but also historiography (hysteriography and eventual
schizography) itself (themselphs). I will expend more time and resources on
calling to the other, that which is beyond the binary engine of history, so
that I might reinclude into The History of Rhetoric what has been systematically negated, purged, and forgotten. As we proceed, through this chapter and the next, the reading will (or may) become difficult. I will zig-zag,
for reasons I have given. The reader similarly will have to zig-zag. (We will
have to dis/engage in Grammar "Z."[8])

I. About Werner Jaeger's *Paideia*
and the "Crisis" Of German Hellenism;
or, Let us Gossip

When not writing history themselves, historians *talk about* other historians; that *is*, after all, what in part prompts this, my book, an open discussion about such "talk."[9] As stated, I will here be concerned with talk about
Werner Jaeger's *Paideia: The Ideals of Greek Culture* (first published in 1939
[vol. 1], 1943 [vol. II], 1944 [vol. III]).[10]

For M. I. Finley, Jaeger remains a "central, and ambiguous, figure" in
Greek Studies (1975, 78). For Arnaldo Momigliano, Jaeger's *Paideia* is "a
symbol of one aspect of the 'crisis' through which Greek studies are passing, namely, the divorce of the study of Greek political ideas from the study
of politics"[11] (Finley, 79; see Momigliano 1955, 230). Moreover, for
Momigliano, Jaeger's *Paideia* has as its aim an "aristocratic [elitist] educational idea" (Finley 79; see Momigliano 1969, 51–52). For Momigliano, a Jew,
Jaeger carries with him to the United States something of the German
"*Geist,*" which Momigliano sees as problematic in relation to history writing (Finley, 78). Simply put, such abstractions as "spiritual bond," which
inform historical thinking, remove the historian away from the material
conditions, which shape history itself and all historical writing.

Institutionalized Silence: Finley makes much of these complaints in his
review of Momigliano's collected reviews, *Contributo alla storia degli studi
classici e del mondo antico*.[12] It is here that Finley and Momigliano speak
their mutual complaints against Jaeger. However, before critiquing Jaeger
on each of these complaints, Finley by way of Momigliano has to point out
that in Greek, or Classical, Studies there is a commonly accepted attitude
of silence towards one's colleagues, especially along political lines. Obviously,

this silence can only perpetuate the crisis in Classical Studies. Finley explains: "there is nothing uncommon about the study of great historians of the past *against their intellectual or political background*. Publications pour out on Herodotus and Pericles, Thucydides and the sophists, Tacitus and the senatorial opposition to autocracy, on Gibbon, Macaulay and Burckhardt" (1975, 76; my emphasis). Finley points out, however, that historians are curiously silent about their contemporaries. If there is an exception to this institutional silence, it is to be found in Momigliano's writings. Finley says:

> What gives Momigliano's work its unmistakable stamp . . . is the consistent and complex counterpoint he weaves—between . . . the ancient world and the modern, *including our own*. . . . [N]o other classical scholar is so conscious of the importance, and so willing to accept the responsibility, of analysing the writings of *his colleagues and contemporaries* [such as a Jaeger] *with the same methods, and according to the same canons*, which we all regularly employ in examining the Greek and Roman writers of history. (76; emphasis mine)

Finley continues:

> Whereas the impact of nationalism on the historiography of the First World War, or of Nazism on German historiography in general, has become a fairly respectable subject of historical investigation, there appears to be *a taboo* against similar inquiries outside a restricted range of men and events, a taboo not shared in other disciplines, such as philosophy, economics and sociology. At the very least, a man must be dead for a generation. (77; my emphasis)

This silence, however, is not practiced by both Finley and Momigliano, who do not "forgive and forget" (Finley 77). As Finley points out, Momigliano critiques his own native historians for turning their collective backs on the social conditions, institutions, hegemony that produce history. Momigliano sees Italian classicists as blind to "the influence of Nazism on ancient history" (qtd. in Finley 77; Momigliano 1966, 699--08). Why the taboo and the silence? Momigliano writes: "One is the tradition of the *academic encomium* which wishes to keep silence about anything unpleasant, even if essential. The other is the habit of treating the history of historiography as *a Sunday pastime*, when one is weary from genuine historical labours and has not enough energy to read books, only to leaf through them" (1966, 708; my emphasis).[13]

Momigliano's Complaints: Having identified that there is general silence and why there is such silence, Momigliano, then, begins to critique Jaeger, whom again Momigliano sees as representing the epitome of the crisis in Classical Studies. Here is a sampling of what Momigliano says:

> The antijuristic current, to which I would attribute long-term effects, is that which is represented in Greek history by W. Jaeger's *Paideia*. . . . In [this work] concrete situations, economic and juristic relationships, institutions, are left on one side. Jaeger speaks of Paideia [which is an "abstraction"], but the history of education in antiquity has been written by a very different historian, the Frenchman H. I. Marrou. (1966, 300–1; cf. 1969, 51)

Momigliano continues:

> It would be erroneous to say that this historiography is a child of Nazism: this would not only go against chronology [Jaeger left Germany in 1936 for the United States], but also against the fact that distinguished scholars like W. Jaeger were themselves victims of Nazism. Nor should we forget the conspicuous contribution of Jaeger, [R.] Heinze and certain of their disciples to the understanding of Greek and Roman ethics. (1966, 300–301)

Having made these concessions, however, Momigliano argues: "This historiography [of Jaeger], *with its scant grip on reality*, bears the mark of an epoch of *political dissolution*. . . . That this historiography could degenerate into Nazism [one of the worst forms of negative essentializing] was a danger, which was confirmed by some of Jaeger's pupils who had remained in Germany" (1966, 300–1; my emphasis).

Further Complaints: Momigliano, in "Perspective 1967 of Greek History," in general criticizes German historians or, better put, German Greek Studies, but in particular criticizes the *Paideia* trilogy as a program exclusively for an aristocratic idea of education (1969, 43–58). He characterizes what he sees as eight problems. The third problem focuses on the *paideia* as elitist (47). Just as important is the fifth problem, which says that "to understand Greek it is necessary to think in Greek or, alternatively, in German" (47; cf. Heidegger 1959, 57). The initial part of the proposition may be ideally acceptable (classicists do need to know Greek); the second, concerning thinking "in German," however, is problematic (there can be no necessary, exclusive isomorphic relationship between Greek and German; and if someone insists, his or her view must be resisted). In discussing the fifth problem—the alleged linguistic link between Greek and German—Momigliano specifically attacks the use of a modern language to translate, and in some cases to hide, Greek "abstractions" such as "Paideia, Eunomia, Areté, Hairesis" and attacks the use of what he calls "Heideggerian language" to translate Heraclitus and Plato (47). The eighth problem, which grows out of the fifth, is that there is an intellectual-political continuum among and running through Greece, Rome, and then *Germany* (48; cf. E. M. Butler 1958). This continuum excludes all others and contributes to the first problem, which is a separation of Greece from the orient.

What Momigliano is pointing to in Greek Studies is the colonization of German by Greek, and Greek by German, and specifically the influence of this colonization on Italian historians. In this *"Perspettiva"* and elsewhere Momigliano warns his fellow Italian classicists against what he sees as the German invention of classical philology, as practiced in our century by Werner Jaeger (cf. 1966, 267–84; 699–708). Momigliano (1969, 52) favors, instead, the work of M. I. Finley and Jean-Paul Vernant. (

What Jaeger Himself Says: Momigliano's charges are serious. Let us, therefore, look closer at what Jaeger himself has to say: In the introduction to *Paideia* (see 1965, xv–xvii), Jaeger makes much of what he sees as the connection between Greece *and* Rome, saying that, indeed, they are part of a continuum. As Jaeger develops his discussion, Germany especially follows in the historical footsteps of Greece and Rome. (Jaeger excludes Asia, specifically the Chinese, Indian, Babylonian, Jewish or Egyptian culture, for "none of these nations has a word or an ideal which corresponds to real culture" [xvii; cf. Bernal 1987, 1991].)

In making the connections that he needs, Jaeger writes: "Greek history had become part of the life of the world-wide empire of Rome. . . . [Greek and Rome] were the first to develop the classicist theology of the mind. . . . Both [were based on] an *abstract timeless* conception of the mind as a realm of eternal truth and beauty high above the troubled destinies of any one nation" (xvii). He writes: "Augustus envisaged the task of the Roman empire in terms of Greek culture" (xvii). And then Jaeger, making a final connection, says: "Similarly, the German humanists of Goethe's time regarded the Greeks as the perfect manifestation of true human nature in one definite and unique historical epoch" (xxv). Jaeger mentions no other country's poet, humanist, or historian who has regarded the Greeks as the Germans had.

The Jaeger-Nazi Connection: Assessing Jaeger's statement, Momigliano writes: "If one looks at Greece as a political organization, Rome is the next step: Hellenism is just a transition between Greece and Rome" (1965, 338). *And then*, Hellenism is just a transition between Rome *and* Germany *and* possibly the Third Reich? To be sure, Momigliano does not explicitly identify this further connection with Jaeger; nor does he explicitly reject the incipient connection. Let us recall that Momigliano has already warned us against thinking that Jaeger is a proto-Nazi.[14] And yet, if we look closer, Momigliano apparently *is* saying that Jaeger practices a kind of history writing that is—for the lack of a better way of putting it—predisposed to Nazi historiography. Momigliano's strategy is to construct a synecdochic (or part-whole) argument; in this way, he is able to critique Jaeger professionally on apparently less serious issues (i.e., *paideia* as an abstraction and as an elitist view of education) while he is able to attack German Studies on a more serious issue (quasi-Nazi). However, if Jaeger epitomizes Greeks Studies, then, Momigliano indirectly attacks Jaeger himself for being quasi-nazi. Calling on his fellow Italian historians, Momigliano says Greek Studies, with Jaeger as its head, *must be* "decolonized" (1969, 43, 55, 58).

The Jaeger-Isocrates Connection: Along with the Greece-Rome-Germany continuum and parallel, Jaeger constructs another, this time between Isocrates and himself. (The hero of the *Paideia* story is not Plato, though he is commonly considered to be of greater intellectual weight; instead, the hero is Isocrates—either the pragmatic or xenophobic political strategist— in his constant attempts to argue for Panhellenism and war against the barbarians. [Cf. Marrou 1964, 79–80.]) Though Finley and Momigliano do not point out this particular connection, I do so as to strengthen their argument and so as eventually to link all this discussion of German thinking about historiography with Heidegger's philosophizing about *logos*. Eventually, the critique with its various connections will stretch from Nazi-historiography, through German Studies and Jaeger, to Heidegger and, finally, back to Isocrates. (It is simply a matter of splicing together Momigliano's critique of Jaeger [and Isocrates] with Ijsseling's reading of Heidegger and Isocrates.) The conceptual glue that holds together the connections is hegemony, hegemonic discourse, *Hegemon*, and *paideia*, culture, *Geschlecht*.[15]

Jaeger rather explicitly begins his introduction with the argument present in Isocrates's eulogy to (the hegemony of) *logos* (*Nicocles* 5–9; *Antidosis* 253–57):

> The natural process of transmission from one generation to another ensures the perpetuation of the physical characteristics of animals and men; but men can transmit their social and intellectual nature only by exercising the qualities through which they created it—reason and conscious will. Through the exercise of these qualities man commands a freedom of development which is impossible to other living creatures. (1965, xiii)

And then, Jaeger glues the Greco-Roman continuum together, similarly as Isocrates ties all Greeks and others together, not by blood, but by the abstraction *culture* (1965, xv; see Isocrates, *Panegyricus*, 1980, 149). Jaeger writes:

> Our kinship with Greece is not merely racial, however important the racial factor may be in understanding the nature of a people. When we say that our history begins with the Greeks, we must be sure of the meaning which we attach to the word history. History, for example, may connote the exploration of strange half-understood new worlds. . . . We study even the remotest peoples with closer attention, and try to enter into their minds. *But* history in this quasi-anthropological sense must be distinguished from the history which is based on a true and active *spiritual kinship*. . . . *Only* in this type of history is it possible to achieve true understanding of *the inner nature of a race*. . . . (1965, xvi; emphasis mine)

Looking from the past to the future, Jaeger muses: "It is impossible to say whether at some time in the future the whole human race will be *united by a spiritual bond* of the kind described here; and the question has *no bearing* on our present study" (xvi; emphasis mine). It may very well be that Jaeger is not thinking of the German Spirit (*Geist*) as the spiritual bond,[16] nor especially of Nazism itself with its cult founded on blood and spirit, but what is clear here is that he is thinking in terms of a unification that is akin to *imperialism*, whether historiographically, militarily, or whatever.

Jaeger is working in the German tradition of the word *Geschlecht*, just as Fichte had (in *Addresses to the German Nation*, 1968) and Heidegger had (in various lectures). Fichte had written in the seventh discourse: "Whoever believes in spirituality and in the freedom of this spirituality, and who wills the eternal development of this spirituality by freedom, wherever he may have been born and whatever language he speaks, is of our blood [*Geschlecht*]; he is one of us, and will come over to our side" (qtd. in Derrida 1987, 194, n. 2; Fichte 1968, 108; cf. Isocrates 1980, 149). Blood here is apparently not biological, but spiritual. However, as Derrida discloses, *Geschlecht* is virtually impossible to translate, with its various other meanings of "sex, race, species, genus, gender, stock, family, generation or genealogy, community" (162). Derrida, in his reading of Heidegger, associates the word with "monster" and "to show" or "demonstrate" (i.e., de-monster) (166). The word has a meaning realized in species-genus analytics, in sorting out human beings from monsters (or the other), in distinguishing male from female (186–87), in naming and surnaming (187), in distinguishing between one and two (189). The word is linked with "gathering" and "sorting" (182, 192).[17]

According to Jaeger, there was, for Isocrates, such a hegemonic gathering in the development of Athens and Greece. Going back to mythic-primitive times, Isocrates speaks of the time when "man first put behind him the wild, bestial life of nomad and savage [and] begins his history of culture with the appearance of agriculture" (1986b, 76). Jaeger's reference is to Isocrates's use of "the legend of the wanderings of Demeter" and her "settled peaceful life," which enabled the development of "a higher moral code" (76–77; see Isocrates 1980, 135, or *Panegyricus*, ll. 28–29). Hence, Isocrates devalues a nomadic life, as Poulakos suggests (1989, 311–12, 316), and favors a settled, canny life. Here, then, we can most easily see *Geschlecht* at work (the separation of monster, or beast/savage, from human being; and the separation of nomadic from agricultural, static life). Here, again then, we can see the development of a nationalistic ideology and the myth of the state (see Cassirer 1966).

Be that as it may, the connections among Isocrates, Fichte, Heidegger, and Jaeger—their thinking concerning the dividing practice of "them and us" as realized across *Geschlecht*—will become perhaps clear as we progress into the next chapter. The partial connections are stressed by Momigliano, who goes so far as to associate parts of these connections with Nazi thinking. Though as far as I can determine Momigliano does not reflect directly, as Derrida does, on the tradition of the word *Geschlecht*, he certainly works in several of his *Contributi* with the sense of the word and how it is typical of German thinking and its philological-historiographical approach and how it is specifically typical of Jaeger's thinking about the legacy of Greece (and Germany) to the rest of the world. Momigliano, therefore, searching for a way to dispel this German influence, calls for a "decolonization" of Greek Studies (1969, 53).

Decolonization?: But what does Momigliano's call for decolonization mean? and have we given too much away? Let us recall once again that Momigliano says, "this [Jaeger's] historiography could degenerate into Nazism" (1966, 300–301). Why else put out a general call for Greek Studies and Jaeger's historiography to be *decolonized*? The only answer can be to avoid *re*creating the conditions of the possibilities for the political problems of the thirties. And, therefore, we are back to the continnum Greece-Rome-"Nazi" Germany. Or in its most extreme form, "Germany today; tomorrow the world," which *is* a banal parody[18] of what *was* Greece. In making this judgment, however, I think that all of us finally have to ask, *once again*, Does this kind of historiography not encourage and foster—most probably—such banal parodies? However, can I stop with this question, without tracing it back even further and ask, Does not Isocrates himself, whom Jaeger especially admires and imitates, have a view of Panhellenism that more often than not leads to banal parodies? These are extremely difficult questions to answer, as I have tried to indicate by weighing what Momigliano himself has to say concerning them.

In any case, we must never forget—as Gayatri Spivak tells us, by way of an interpretation of Althusser—that "we think ideology before we can think history" (1990, 54). The history of ideas approach—Jaeger's approach—can and, more often than not, does lead to the ideologies of the Enlightenment master metaphor or grand narrative that would save the world by destroying it. The view of going back to origins can and does lead to, even unintended, banal parodies. (While Habermas would go back to Enlightenment principles in an attempt to rework them, Lyotard would resist and disrupt "the mutterings of the desire for a return of terror" [1984, 82].) Decolonization can be a form of resistance and disruption.

The issues that Momigliano has raised here must be returned to; they are in great part reunderstandable in terms of the differences between modernism and postmodernism. For now, however, I would move on from Momigliano's reading of Jaeger's reading of Isocrates to Finley's reading of Isocrates, which gets us much closer to the idea that Isocrates (as well as Jaeger and later Heidegger) has a view of education as elitist.

II. About Finley's "Heritage of Isocrates"

Finley's essay is about Isocrates and education and its role in maintaining the *polis*; it is an essay that is very critical of Isocrates. He begins, however, by not referring to Isocrates at all but substantially to Ernest Robert Curtius, in his *European Literature and the Latin Middle Ages* (originally published, 1948; translated, 1953), and to F. R. Leavis, in his *Education and the University* (1943).

Curtius and Leavis: Finley's purpose, as I read it, is to reestablish the argument for the perennial claim—this time, by the modernists Curtius and Leavis—that "we" are in a state of *crisis* and decline in the West, but that there are ways of extricating ourselves. Finley's ultimate purpose is not so much to question the standing claim but more so to critique the various (*paideia*) proposals for resisting the crisis and decline. The crisis, more often than not, is an opportunity for historians or philosophers or educators to call for a return *to the splendo(u)r that was*, so that "we" (they?) might be saved.[19]

Finley points out that for Curtius and Leavis the cause of the crisis and decline was not the clash between the Allies and the Axis (i.e., WW II), which they lived through, but the Industrial Revolution. (Heidegger has a similar view [1977, 283–318].) As we might by now expect, the claim is that the Industrial Revolution brought about a crisis and decline in the West *because* it was really a *revolt against tradition*.[20]

Curtius and Leavis respectively offer two solutions to the crisis: A return to the humanism of the Middle Ages *and* a return to seventeenth-century England as a model for schools. Curtius sees the Middle Ages as a time of intellectual freedom to pursue knowledge and to foster great minds, as defined by tradition. He writes:

> The middle of the eighteenth century witnessed not only the beginnings of that great economic change which is termed the Industrial Revolution. It saw also the first powerful revolt against cultural tradition, which is marked by Rousseau. This tradition was restated by the universal genius of Goethe. But it was restated for the last time. Goethe has not been succeeded by another universal genius. He had a very clear consciousness of belonging to this tradition. He pointed to Homer, to Plato, to Aristotle, and to the Bible as its foundations. *He was stepping in the shoes of the Elders* [a sort of *Areopagus* of Literary thinkers], many of whom he thought greater than himself. History was to him a sequence of great minds which commanded respect and loyalty. . . . He is the last link of that golden chain. Yet he is not too remote from us. We can still grasp that link. (1953, 587; emphasis mine)

Leavis, in chapter two of *Education and the University*, sees the Seventeenth-century as important: It was "a key phrase, or passage, in the history of civilization . . . at one end in direct and substantial continuity with the world of Dante, . . . at the other a world that has broken irretrievably with the medieval order and committed itself completely to the process leading directly and rapidly to what we live in now."[21] Which is? Leavis's answer: "Capitalism 'arrives,' finally overcoming the traditional resistances, so that its ethos becomes accepted as law" (1943, 48–49). His intention is to use the seed-plot of ideas in his century of choice to resist:

> The study of the Seventeenth Century is a study of the modern world. . . . [But] the Seventeenth Century is *not* the modern world, and the study of it . . . would have the necessary comprehensiveness, complexity and unity: it would be a study in concrete terms of the relations between the economic, the political, the moral, the spiritual, religion, art and literature, and would involve a critical pondering of standards and key-concepts—order, community, culture, civilization and so on. (49)

Thirty years later in *Nor Shall My Sword* (1972), Leavis picks up where he left off, but this time he critiques C. P. Snow's two cultures. Against what he calls Snow's "technologico-Benthamite spirit," Leavis advocates William Blake's view of "the individual [as] the agent of life." (Now we have Blake, and also Charles Dickens [185], substituted for Dante, in an argument that is reminiscent of T. S. Eliot's view on tradition and the individual talent.) Against Snow's statement that "the condition of the individual . . . is tragic," but "there is social hope [in science and technology]," Leavis advocates that the individual is our hope and he is "inescapably social"; the individual, such as Blake, is "a focal conduit of the life that is one, though it manifests itself only in the myriad individual beings, and his unique identity is not the less a unique identity because the discovery of what it is and means entails a profoundly inward participation in a cultural continuity—a continuous creative collaboration, something that must surely be called 'social' " (171-71).[22]

Along these same lines, Leavis attempts to dismiss the negative meanings often associated with the word "elite." He writes:

> The word "élitism" is a product of ignorance, prejudice and unintelligence. It is a stupid word, but not for that the less effective in its progressivist-political use, appealing as it does to jealousy and kindred impulses and motives. It is stupid, and perniciously so, because there must always be 'élites,' and, mobilizing and directing the ignorance, prejudice and unintelligence, it aims at destroying the only adequate control for 'élites' there could be. (1943, 169)

He continues:

> I think it would be essentially misleading to apply the term at all to *the real educated class* we need, though the word 'élitism' is being used, and will in the name of 'democracy' go on being used, to destroy any possibility of its being developed. We who are determined not only to resist, but to defeat and reverse the destructive drive should face that truth in all its formidableness [e.g., to defeat Snow who, by the way, Leavis at a point later associates with "post-Marxist enlightenment." (213)] (169-70; my emphasis)

And then finally in the chapter entitled "Élites, Oligarchies and the Educated Public," Leavis returns specifically to the idea of *the university*, claiming that though Blake and Dickens are dead and perhaps their likes are no longer possible, we nonetheless have their works (185), around which *we* must "collaborate" in "the form of creative quarrelling." (Curtius had made a similar point: Goethe "is not too remote from us. We can still grasp that link.") Leavis specifically says:

It is not unanimity that characterizes a real educated public. . . . In the creative community of collaboration that would form in the university the members would generate between them . . . a language that made *creative quarrelling possible*; that is, made possible the implicitly collaborative interplay of different bents and convictions. (205; emphasis mine; cf. Graff 1987)

The university and students that Leavis has in mind, however, are "represented by Oxford and Cambridge, [which had, he says] a distinct and strongly positive organic life, rooted in history" (206). Here, we will have *the real élite* ("the real educated class"), according to Leavis, to protect us against *the false élite* (169).

Finley's Critique: In my attempt to examine closely what Leavis has to say, I have left Finley far behind. Finley continues by briefly discussing Aristotle and then by concentrating at greater length on both Plato and Isocrates—contrasting their views of education and its role for the *polis* and the State. Hence, Finley's approach thus far has been to present the problem of the crisis and its solutions *a*chronologically, with, first, the moderns (such as Leavis) and, then, the ancients, with Aristotle first (generally acceptable as the great compromiser), then Plato (unacceptable as "the great propagandist" [Popper]), and finally Isocrates (most palatable). What better way to highlight the generally accepted contrast between Plato/Isocrates, so that this contrast, which privileges Isocrates, could eventually be demonstrated to be only an insidious form of *false consciousness*.[23]

Finley reminds us that Plato had a view of education that "would produce an élite of perfect and perfectly rational rulers" (197). His was a perfectly rational theory blending metaphysics, ethics, and psychology (*psyche*). For Plato, the *psyche*/soul was tripartite, with each part unequally distributed to human beings and, therefore, unequally in society. With this view of psychology in mind, Plato proposed for each part of society—which has now been divided into three *classes*—"an appropriate kind of education, the highest form," Finley explains, "being reserved for the naturally qualified few, whose *psyche* would be trained in a lengthy, difficult process, until they were capable of apprehending the Absolutes, and then of ruling with absolute justice" (197).

The view of "an *élite* of perfect and perfectly rational rulers" dispensing "absolute justice" is a far cry from the Aristotelian view of the prudential judge, who understands, contrary to Plato, that there is *no science of the political*. Which is, of course, a general view that Isocrates had first advocated, in his redefinition of "philosophy" (see *Antidosis* 270–71), so that he might in turn redefine the role of education for the *polis* and State. But lest there be a misunderstanding, Aristotle is not like Isocrates, nor vice versa, in relation to the concept of "Philosophy."[24]

Finley's View of Isocrates: If, as Isocrates concludes, there can be no science of speaking well or of the political, as Plato would have it and Aristotle knew we could not, then, there must be some other way of realizing noble (just and honest) political rule. For Isocrates, Finley reminds us, "[political] virtue [*areté*] cannot be taught, though virtue is the aim of life." And then Finley reminds us: "anyone with a predisposition to virtue *and a proper station in life* can become 'better and worthier' if he is eager to speak well and to persuade" (198; Finley's emphasis). What is in italics here is crucial to Finley's argument. Isocrates specifically says:

> I consider that the kind of art which can *implant honesty and justice in depraved natures* has never existed and does not now exist. . . . But I do hold that people can become better and worthier if they conceive an ambition to speak well [through the faculty of rhetoric], if they become possessed of the desire to be able to persuade their hearers, and, finally, if they set their hearts on seizing their "advantage." (*Antidosis* 274–75; cf. 192; emphasis mine)

We might ask, where here or elsewhere in Isocrates, as Finley concludes, is there a reference to *a proper station in life*? or a "citizen élite"?

Isocrates says: " . . . ambition . . . desire . . . set their hearts." We must ask, what *determines* and *controls* this ambition, desire, and what sets their hearts *to speak well*? What keeps it from being false instead of true? It is, for Isocrates, clearly not racial or in the blood, but cultural (see *Panegyricus* 50). Which means theoretically that anyone steeped in Greek culture, in Hellenism, or *paideia*, is someone who is *not* depraved but is honest and just. Barbarians obviously would be excluded. But does this mean, therefore, that all Greeks have such virtues? Not necessarily. They must be inhabitants in the Greek world *and* have (had) a proper station in life. In other words, it was necessary for them to have acquired at a very early age a certain predisposition toward virtuous character. Or, put in other terms, Isocrates is suggesting, in great part here, that "debating and writing" *can be learned, but not taught*. Why? Because virtue or excellence (*areté*) had to have already been implanted into the individual speaker *in order to learn to speak well*. In this way, Isocrates is like Plato before him (see *Meno* 95ff) and Aristotle after him (see *Metaphysics* Bk. 2, Ch. 3; *Nicomachean Ethics* Bk. I, Ch. 3). But whereas Plato had a theory of learning as recollection, Isocrates and Aristotle had a theory of learning as having the right "predispositions," which means (again) coming from "the right families," or the elite.

In our continuing attempt to answer the question What controls ambition and desire?, let us turn to *Areopagiticus*, Isocrates's later discussion of how "to live as a citizen" and not just "to live."[25] For Isocrates, there was a danger in too much democracy, or freedom, or too much loose speech, which he felt there was after the "Social War" (355 B.C.). The problem that he was confronted with, as Plato was before him, is how to distinguish between true and false words. Isocrates differs from Plato on this issue. For Isocrates, what is true is what reflects the culture, *paideia*, which was steadily being threatened by radical democracy. He addresses this danger (of false speech) in his speech on "the public safety": What he calls for in *Areopagiticus* is a rejection of a broad, radical democracy and a return to aristocratic rule, a return to the days of Solon and Cleisthenes. Specifically, what he calls for is a return of the *Areopagus*, which was a council of the *elite* [or "Elders" as Curtius would have it, or "great minds" as Leavis would have it] who would have complete, unimpeachable authority over daily life in the *polis*, especially education, which it was believed would establish the right predispositions "to live as a citizen," in both the children and especially in the adults (see 1982, 20, 37–, 44–47). (Isocrates believed in "continuing" education.)

Let us return to Finley, who unequivocally says that this "ancient heritage" of Isocrates is problematic. He schematizes it into three elements and a corollary, which are clearly Isocratean:

First, "there is a belief in the possibility and virtue of training the mind."

Second, there "is the belief in the supreme value, for public life or the life of the citizen . . . of a fundamentally literary education, under which [is] include[d] history and philosophy as well as languages and literature. A corollary is that such education should concentrate on the best literature . . . past literature."

And third, there "is the identification of most non-vocational education with high culture, believed to be accessible only to a very small minority, an élite" (1975, 202). Finley says: "this [ancient] heritage is still a living one" (203).

It is a heritage that has given us distinctions between high and popular culture; and between liberal education and specialized, technological education.

Concluding his article, Finley borrows a distinction from Durkheim, a distinction "between 'pedagogy' and 'education,' between formal schooling and the no less important education taking place all the time outside school" (208). (This is a distinction that is similar to the "teach-learn" distinction that I have used earlier.) This distinction is especially enlightening in that it allows Finley to give us a better, concluding understanding of Isocrates's educational-political program for the *polis* and the State. Finley writes:

"Isocrates' programme was pedagogical [teach], and it was designed for members of the ruling élite, a socially and culturally homogeneous group, whose common values were formed and repeatedly reinforced by their continuous association and shared experience [learn], at first within the family and then outside, in the army, in the dining clubs, in their political activity" (208). He adds:

> Higher education continued to be so based until the end of the nineteenth century; the structure and needs of society may have changed radically from one era to another, but not the fact that it was a homogeneous élite who received the pedagogy as one part of a larger common education. The link between school and *scholé* [ease, idleness, leisure] remained unbroken. A minority of outsiders were admitted, to be sure, but they were recruits into the élite, either as full members or as men to be admitted to the councils of the élite or, at the least, as their future retainers. (208)

All this begins to change radically in the twentieth century, as the student population becomes "heterogeneous." More so than ever, Finley says, "We have a large and growing student population who share the same system of *pedagogy* [taught] while not sharing the same *education* [learned]. . . . Those who come to it from outside the élite normally come with an impoverished cultural capital, a different and inadequate 'set of master patterns,' and their pedagogy is not reinforced by their continuing non-school associations" (209; emphasis mine).[26]

With Finley, then, Isocrates does not fare well. Finley concludes his article with a few suggestions that are terribly anti-climatic and that are not worth repeating here. (The real purpose of his article is to call attention to a problem, which is "the heritage," and not to offer solutions.)

Decolonization, the Uncanny, and the Will to Power: I would now take my first step towards Isocrates and historiography (and education) by way of a negative (revisionary) deconstruction (reversal) of both Jaeger and Isocrates, a decolonization backwards and forwards. What is (far) left now is the next stumbling-stammering step, un/namely, an affirmative deconstruction, which would be also a form of affirmative (sub/versive) decolonization (dispersion). What is (far) left here, however, I will only suggest, for it is the continual purpose of these various excurses and chapters to work and play their way on to the final (beginning?) excurses where nonpositive affirmations will have taken place repeatedly.

I would, therefore, point to *decolonization* as an acknowledgement of the *uncanny*, the *unhomely*, not only in historiography but also in education. Instead of centering historiography and education around Dante or

Goethe or Leavis's Blake, or possibly the so-called common human being,
I would decenter them around such an uncanny character as a deoedipalized
Oedipus, the so-called "criminal" and excluded element. (We don't need
obsessive canonized views of historiography [and education]; rather, we desire
hysterical decanonizations.)

I would stretch these perverse judgments even further. The issue is not
just historiography and education but it is our very fundamental(ist) view
of language (*logos*) and how it predisposes us to dwell in language. I am
referring now to philology as our favored means of thinking about language.
Jaeger and his commentators are philologists. In discussing Jaeger, I with-
held any reference to his possible counterpart, namely, Erich Auerbach, who
in "Philology and *Weltliteratur*," would appear to take a very opposite view
of history writing. Auerbach writes:

> Our philological *home* is the earth: it can no longer be the nation. The most
> priceless and indispensable part of a philologist's heritage is still his own
> nation's culture and language. Only when he is first separated from this
> heritage, however, and then transcends it does it become truly effective.
> We must return, in admittedly altered circumstances, to the knowledge that
> prenational medieval culture already possessed: the knowledge that the
> spirit [*Geist*] is not national. (1969, p. 17)

While many of us might welcome Auerbach's call to philologists to shift from
their nationalistic tendencies to prenationalistic ones, a few of us might still
find Auerbach's view of philology as highly problematic. The fundamental
assumption that language (*logos*) and, then, philology as the science of
language and, therefore, as the means of purchasing a home for us in language, is specifically what I see as being highly problematic. Philology, as
espoused here, is still an abstraction that would be a will to mastery over
language; that would have us forget uncanniness and its effect on our
material conditions, or that would relegate uncanniness and its effects to
some so-called science of the uncanny, such as psychoanalysis. (Such a so-
called science would have as its aim not the remembering but the systematic forgetting of the "counter-memory.") Auerbach's philology is not
Nietzsche's or Heidegger's. Auerbach's is more in the tradition of Ulrich
Wilamowitz-Moellendorff.

My position is, especially in the next chapter, that we are not at home
in our world/whirl of language. Any and every attempt to assume that we
are has or will have created for human beings dangerous situations. There
is no "philological home." However, there is negative essentializing. Therefore, we must find some way to live productively with uncanniness. Nietzsche
has his way; Heidegger has his. I would favor Nietzsche's (and his commen-

tators') over Heidegger's, which would mean that I would employ the un-canny as a means of radical decolonization.

On the Way to Decolonization: If there is no philological home, there is, more so, no philosophical (ontological) home. (With this statement, I am addressing philosophical rhetoricians. With this mis-statement, I am speaking as sophistic rhetoricians.) Therefore, I would insist on—would more so incite us—to remember what Nietzsche said of the *dogmaticism* versus the *will to power*. He said in *Beyond Good and Evil* that not only do (all too human) human beings philosophize, but the "gods, too, philosophize" (1966, 232). In other words, the gods, too, have no metalinguistic position from which to determine, or measure, the nature of things (cf. Lyotard 1985, 16, 42–43). Nietzsche writes that "life *is* will to power" (203; Nietzsche's emphasis) and that will to power is "the essence of the world" (99). It is the affirmative play of the differences of things and ideas that he advocates. To deny this affirmative play, this will to power, and to insist on the will to truth, is to insist on death. Is to insist on hegemony! To deny this affirmative play is the "most dangerous of all errors so far" (3). To deny this nonpositive affirmation and, instead, to stand truth on her head and to deny perspective (3), as Plato would and did realize it, that is the most dangerous of "a dogmatist's errors," the most dangerous of a historiographer's (and educator's) errors. The will to power "is the *primordial fact* of all history" (204; Nietzsche's emphasis). "A world that is supposed to have its equivalent and its measure in human thought and human evaluations—a 'world of truth' that can be mastered completely and forever with the aid of our square little reason" (1974, 335)—that is a dangerous world. It is an impoverished world that allows for "an interpretation that permits counting, calculating, weighing . . . and nothing more" (335).

Therefore, how would I decolonize? How would I denegate hegemony? By reintroducing the *uncanny* (the unhomely) and the *will to power* (the affirmative play of differences) into historiography and education and philology. As Nietzsche says in *Beyond Good and Evil*: "*Measure* is alien to us; let us own it; our thrill is the thrill of the infinite, the unmeasured. Like a ride on a steed that flies forward, we drop the reins before the infinite, we modern men [*sic*], like semi-barbarians—and reach *our* bliss only where we are most—*in danger*" (1966, 153).

Chapter 4

❦

Isocrates, the Logos, and Heidegger

When I write, I become a thing, a wild beast. A wild beast doesn't look back when it leaps; doesn't check that people are watching and admiring. Those who do not become wild beasts when they write, who write to please, write nothing that has not already been written, teach us nothing, and forge extra bars for our cage.

—Hélène Cixous

"You [the tight rope walker] have made danger your vocation; there is nothing contemptible in that. Now you perish of your vocation: for that I will bury you with my own hands."

—Zarathustra, Nietzsche

. . . *den Führer führen* [to lead the leader]. . . .[1]

—Karl Jaspers

Where have I been; where am I going?: "*Measure* is alien to us; let us own it; our thrill is the thrill of the infinite, the unmeasured." Is it? Or should it be? Ought it be? Let's take a closer look, lest I be accused of inviting us all to leap into the infinite (play of differences) without first having a look. And yet, to look into this abyss, for too long, for more than a glance, Would it not blind us?

The statement from Nietzsche, with which I concluded the previous discussion, is problematic, if considered in relation to certain parallels between Isocrates and Martin Heidegger, which are the major considerations of this chapter. It is problematic, let us recall, because as Nietzsche says, "like a rider on a steed that flies forward, we drop the reins before the infinite [sun] and reach our bliss only where we are most—*in danger*" (1966, 153;

159

Nietzsche's emphasis). Or it is dangerous because we have been taught to both fear and mistrust the infinite. (We are taught to count in terms of one or a binary [machine], and never a vertiginous infinity [machine].) Since Nietzsche, however, the problem of a being-who-would-be-without-measure (or who would be by way of a perpetual-revaluing, or -deterritorializing, of value) has become for society and philosophical rhetoricians even more problematic; for such a way of being (or *becoming-sublime*) has, indeed, *become paradoxical* and, therefore, not easily resolved. As Nietzsche says: "the value of life cannot be estimated [reckoned, counted, given an account of]" (1968b, 30). To estimate life here would be to exclude the ugly by way of the principle of the excluded middle; would be to de-monster life, or that which is a vital part of life itself. And traditional philosophical types would give an account of how to resolve the paradox and to set out to resolve such a decadent state of mind (by only falling, paradoxically, as Nietzsche would say, into "decadence," into rationality and morality).[2]

The Paradox: Nietzsche's statement concerning measure is problematic because as Isocrates demonstrates (actually, "monstrates") unwittingly for us, an unmeasured view of *logos* is dangerous; *and* because as Heidegger demonstrates ("monstrates") for us, a fall back into a measured (negated) view of *logos* (or being$^{neg.}$, essence$^{neg.}$ [*Wesen*]) is equally dangerous. Another way of putting this paradoxical statement is that both an unmeasured and measured view of *logos*, both a will to power (a naive radical, rhizomatic multiplicity) and a will to truth (one perspective over all others) can be equally dangerous; or an unmeasured, unhomely (uncanny), view of *logos* that does not stay perpetually unmeasured, that is, in dispersion, or that is the product of the extreme will to truth, can be dangerous. Isocrates, as I will redescribe him, is an innocent thinking that *logos* is good, while Heidegger is well aware that *logos* can be extremely dangerous, but unfortunately opts, politically, to control *logos* and helps, directly or indirectly, to bring about a catastrophe. He appears to continue this thinking post-1945. But let us not miss the point here: Isocrates, like Heidegger, finally called on *logos* as a means of congregation by way of segregation. Theirs was a tightly measured *logos*. (Let us not miss the point here: In talking about *logos*, I am talking about the sun; and vice versa. Recall Bataille who says that the energy of Being, or of desire—that is, of the Sun—must be spent both for construction and destruction. Deconstruction [or waste, expenditure, *dépense*] can manifest itself for good [giving, wasting, without expected return[3]] or for terrible catastrophe [war]. This is the cycle of *potlatch*, violence.) Hence, my favoring perpetual deterritorializations; my favoring *logos*$^{nonpositive\ affirmation}$ and *physis*$^{nonpositive\ affirmation}$.

To be sure, I have not resolved this paradox, or the danger that it exhibits. Dear Reader, Did you really expect me to? Instead, I have accepted the risk (the hazard). He-who-would-be-all-the-names-of-history cannot afford to be a rationalist, that is, a coward. My favoring the radical, rhizomatic many is a subjunctive pretension of mine to take on the new figure of the tight rope walker,[4] for if I or another does not, then, there is no chance— and always in the face of hazard—of becoming the *Ubermensch* (the sub-lime, sovereign subject-that-is-not-a-subject/object). While most reject the risk, I cannot not take it.

The Paradox ReStated in other Words: Nietzsche's statement concern-ing measure is problematic because as Bataille has pointed out, an unmea-sured view of *the sun* (or desire, will to power, Being, essence [*Wesen*], or excessive-pre-ontological energy, thermospasm, negentropy, libidinalized un/ states of energy/intensities) is dangerous; *and* because as Bataille-Lyotard-Nick Land point out, a fall back into a measured, controlled view of *the sun* (its excesses) is equally dangerous, for excess will be expended catastrophi-cally. Icarus sought out the sun, on his wings, not unlike Nietzsche's "rider on [his] steed." And the tight rope walker. And then, there is Prometheus. Once ever Again: The calling (vocation cum vacation) of the sun cannot not be voided. We must chance (hazard) it; there is no such thing as choice here. (Bataille makes this point repeatedly. No choice.) And yet, we must come to understand, in accepting the gift of the sun, we must accept also its immense danger.

From the Earth to the Sun: Our home is not the earth. Our home is the sun. The philological sun. The *potlatch* of the sun. Our home, rather unhome, cannot be nationalism (race, gender, class), cannot be *Geist*, can-not be the earth only. These are all based on a restrictive economy. Our un/ home is the sun. Our general-libidinal economy. The earth (as the locus of philology-as-"necessity") is Capital, the worst decadence; the sun (as the radical *loci* of *logos*-as-"luxury") is our future-anterior beyond Capital. About language Nick Land writes:

> Poetry, Bataille asserts, is a "holocaust of words." A culture [of philology] can never express or represent (serve) capital production, it can compro-mise itself in relation to capital only by abasing itself before the philistinism of the bourgeoisie, where "culture" has no characteristics beyond those of abject restraint, and self-denigration. Capital is precisely and exhaustively the definitive anti-culture.
>
> Capitalism, then, is (the projection of) the most extreme possible refusal of expenditure. [. . .] It is not that capital production "invents" the crisis

which comes to be named "market saturation," it is rather that capital production is the systematic repudiation of overproduction ["luxury"] as a problem. (1992, 56, 57)

These, to be sure, are difficult words to take, for they seem—so we have been taught to think—to say the opposite. When Nietzsche speaks of Socrates and Plato being decadent, it seems the opposite, with Nietzsche as decadent and Socrates anti-decadent. We need to begin to think in reversals. Nietzsche, Freud, and Marx taught us that everything is inverted as in a camera obscura; hence, we must turn it all on its head (see Marx and Engels 1978, 154).

Poetry, a "holocaust of words": This especially is troublesome, and will be even more so as we progress into a discussion of Heidegger, the *logos*, and the Holocaust of this century. Classical philology would fix words, or give an account (*metalogos*) of words (*logos*); would utilize a dividing practice (species-genus analytics) on words. Rhetoric would expect a sense of decorum in the use of words. Poetry, however, would make words burn, not simply destroying them, but destroying/constructing them, turning over the various, heretofore, fixed or decorous meanings. Whereas philology would create the conditions for purging "noise" (excluding what it, by rule, denotes as noise), poetry—wild, savage[5] poetry—would reinclude desire in language, the heterogeneousness, the semiotic (see Kristeva 1980, esp. 23-35; 133-47). This is all better put by Julia Kristeva, who writes:

> [P]oetic language, in its most disruptive form (unreadable for meaning, dangerous for the subject), shows the constraints of a civilization dominated by transcendental rationality. Consequently, it is a means of overriding this constraint. And if in so doing it sometimes falls in with deeds brought about by the same rationality as is, for example, the instinctual determination of fascism . . . Poetic language is also there to forestall such translations into action. (139-40)

"To forestall"? Is this a Kristevan hope? Was it Heidegger's hope? To be sure. And yet, it is my hope, or the *loci*, as I have suggested, of my hope. I agree with Hélène Cixous that there is hope (*Espérance*) in the unconscious (1989); for if not, then, there simply is no hope. Nope! Poetic language cannot— nor does Kristeva or even Cixous claim that it can—guarantee freedom from fascism. Or death. Or hell. Cixous ("jewoman") writes of Etty Hillesum, older sister of Anne Frank, who also wrote a journal at Auschwitz, where she died in 1943; and "read Rilke while sitting on a trash can in a tiny corner of the Jewish Consul, which had as a mission the expedition of the Jews to the oven. It was really a circle of the *Inferno*. She read Rilke in this world where the people hastened to not die, not die, to kill, she wrote this. It is what one can best hope for poetry: that it will serve in the face of death. Etty read Rilke right up to death. Rilke saved her, but she saved Rilke" (1989, 6).

There is something in *logos* that both binds and sets us free, or so we hope.[6] And I do hope. Without being the philologist, we can sense, as others have, that poetic language (wild, savage language) can "forestall" (Am I beginning to sound like Freud toward the end of *Beyond the Pleasure Principle?*) *thanatos.* Yes, yes, yes, I think that poetic language, as viewed here, is the principle of *eros.* Hence, the necessity to link but not how to link; hence, the necessity (cum escape) in writing hysteries of rh*erotics*. Kristeva writes: ". . . we have (a) Platonistic acknowledgement on the eve of Stalinism and fascism: a (any) society may be stabilized only if it excludes poetic [and adolescent, baby-lonian, pre-ontological] language. . . . The question is unavoidable: if we are not on the side of those whom society wastes in order to reproduce itself, where are we?" (1980, 31). Poetry is not dead after the Holocaust; it must be more and more alive so as to forestall other Holocausts. Or to help us through our holocaust.

Logos *Matters*: Land tells us that "Bataille's matter [libidinal matter] is that which must be repressed [politically oppressed] as the condition of articulation, whereby immanent continuity is vivisected in transcendence" (1992, 122). In other words, as Michel Serres says, the third must be excluded, purged (1982). Hence, the trace (Derrida). The sign and the feeling (Lyotard). Hence, we must bear witness, must search for new idioms. For what has been repressed desires and will have returned. Language does matter. Classical philology, our home? Pragmatics, our home? Auerbach's earth, our home? NOPE. Land writes:

> The ahistorical [obsessive], descriptive, and normalizing study of language usage is pragmatics, which can be contrasted with the historical [hysterical], epidemic, and aberrational experiments in flow summarized as "libidinal-" or "base materialism." Base materialism is the plague of unilaterial difference, which is a difference that only operates from out of the [Dionysian] undifferentiated. Thinking of this kind is flagrantly inconsistent with the principle of identity. . . . The human animal rebels unilaterally against its animality, just as life differentiates itself against and within the undifferentiable desert of death. . . . For any ardent materialism truth is madness. (1992, 123-24)[7]

Yes, *logos* matters. Henry Miller, in *Tropic of Cancer*, writes:

> Yes, I said to myself, I too love everything that flows: rivers, sewers, lava, semen, blood, bile, words, sentences. I love the amiotic fluid when it spills

out of the bag. I love the kidney with its painful gall-stones, its gravel and what-not; I love the urine that pours out scalding and the clap that runs endlessly; I love the words of hysterics and the sentences that flow on like dysentery and mirror all the sick images of the soul; I love the great rivers like the Amazon and the Orinoco, where crazy men like Moravagine float on through dream and legend in an open boat and drown in the blind mouths of the river. I love everything that flows, even the menstrual flow that carries away the seed unfecund. I love scripts that flow, be they hieratic, esoteric, perverse, polymorph, or unilaterial. I love everything that flows, everything that has time in it and becoming, which brings us back to the beginning where there is never end: the violence of the prophets, the obscenity that is ecstasy, the wisdom of the fanatic, the priest with his rubber litany, the foul words of the whore, the spittle that floats away in the gutter, the milk of the breast and the bitter honey that pours from the womb, all that is fluid, melting, dissolute and dissolvent, all the pus and dirt that in flowing is purified, that loses its sense of origin, that makes the great circuit towards death and dissolution. (qtd. in Land 1992, 130; H. Miller 1961, 257-58)

Kenneth Burke—our Papa who art in scatology—best understands the relationship between fascism and language and the people of representative anecdotes (*logos*). (Recall Lyotard who says: "The wisdom of nations is not only their scepticism, but also the 'free life' of phrases and genres. That is what the (clerical, political, military, economic, or informational) oppressor comes up against in the long run. Prose is the people of anecdotes" [1988a, 159].) In Burke's reading of Hitler's *Mein Kampf*, in which Burke points out how Hitler refers to the Habsburg Empire as Babel/Babylon, he writes: "So, you had this Babel of voices; and, by the method of associative mergers, using ideas as imagery, it became tied up, in the Hitler rhetoric, with 'Babylon,' Vienna as the city of poverty, prostitution, immorality, coalitions, half-measures, incest, democracy (i.e., majority rule leading to 'lack of personal responsibility'), death, internationalism, seduction, and anything else of thumbs down sort" (1957, 172). It is obvious where Hitler's vision is going, which is to keep the system together, blatantly, by virtue of exclusion. That is, by way of *negative essentializing*. As we know, Hitler did exclude (purge), *by silencing* all the mixed voices—with their misrepresentative antidotes—as manifested in both language (*logos*) and people and *by essentializing* the "Jews." Burke writes: "The wrangle of the parliamentary is to be stilled by the giving of *one voice* to the whole people, this to be the 'inner voice' of Hitler, made uniform throughout the German boundaries, as leader and people were completely identified with each other" (177; my emphasis). This was the holocaust of voices that led to the One, Unified Voice that led to the other Holocaust. Henry Miller wrote in *Sunday After the War*: "Man [sic] will be forced to realize that power must be kept open, fluid and free. His aim will be not to possess power but to radiate it" (qtd in N. O. Brown 1959, 305).

Both Isocrates and Heidegger Trust Logos *(the Sun), But Differently:* Isocrates trusts naively, for he never suggests that *logos* might speak through human beings in any dangerous, imperialistic manner, unless it be democratically (*demos* = mob) spoken. Heidegger trusts guardedly, for he states that for modern human beings, as for the ancient Greeks, *logos* speaks in an uncanny manner. It is their respective attitudes toward *logos* that got them and us into trouble. My assessment of Isocrates is that he, too, along with Plato, established the conditions of the possibilities for imperialism and colonization. My assessment of Heidegger is that he did not finally keep his guard, did not perpetually deterritorialize the various voices of the *logos*; he did not, as Jean-François Lyotard says, remember the Forgotten, and, therefore, Heidegger compromised with National Socialism (1990), with, heretofore, the worst form of imperialism and colonization.

I anticipate myself here with these thoughts, to which I will return at length; but I would say now that the possible, exploratory analogy between Isocrates and Heidegger is, for me, compelling. While Isocrates put naive trust in the *logos*, he also put naive faith in Philip of Macedon. While Heidegger did not put complete naive trust in the *logos*, but in essence (*physis, Wesen*), he also put naive faith, even if only momentarily, in Hitler. Like a modern-day philosopher king, Heidegger would lead the leader![8]

Therefore, I return to Isocrates and this time to Heidegger *questioningly*, and return to take a closer look at Isocrates's hymn to and innocent faith in the *logos* (the sun) and a closer look at Heidegger's interrogation of Being and *logos* and innocent faith in the will to truth, specifically, in a fascistic politics.

The Ear of the Other; or, How does One-cum-a-Radical-Multiplicity *Listen to the Sun?:* In reference to the *logos*, I spoke of its paradoxical nature. I might have spoken of its duplicity or, best put, its triplicity. And always its complicity. No one has dealt with the problem of *logos* (and Being and time) and the problem of speaking and reading and thinking—both, or all these, problems are the same—more than Jacques Derrida. (Not even Heidegger!) If it was the fortune of various thinkers—Hegel, Nietzsche, Freud, Marx, Heidegger—to discover the duplicity of language and to discover their and our need to be suspicious of *logos*, it is the fortune of Derrida to be presently discovering that there is a left *and* a right political interpretation and *praxis* (in terms of history and education and philology) of each of these thinkers, whether that interpretation be rudely forced or not, or even crudely farced. (The question about language and these thinkers is *How is this possible?* and *Can we identify the source of this duplicity?*, or even *triplicity?*, and *complicity?*)[9]

Derrida's *Ear of the Other* (1985, 3–38, esp. 32–33) is an examination of Nietzsche's *Ecce Homo* (1969) and especially *On the Future of Our Educational Institutions* (1964). Nietzsche, best of all, in his quasi-autobiography, knew that he and his language were political "dynamite" (see 1969, 326–27); he compares his "glad tidings" with those of Christ (327). We have simply to recall Nietzsche's *Anti-Christ*, in which he sees (St.) Paul interpretating, or misappropriating, Christ's teachings, by turning Christianity into a religion of guilt (see Nietzsche 1968b; cf. Kazantzakis 1960). Which is turning it into a religion of being-reactionary (see Deleuze 1983, 111-46). Derrida wrestles with this problem of discourse—both intentionality and aberrant readings—and says that we must not excuse Nietzsche because the Nazis appropriated his writings for their own perverted, reactionary ends. Derrida says:

> It would still be necessary *to account for* the possibility of this mimetic inversion and perversion. . . . [T]he law that makes the perverting simplification possible must lie in the structure of the text "remaining". . . . It cannot be entirely fortuitous that the discourse bearing [Nietzsche's] name in society, in accordance with civil laws and editorial norms, has served as a legitimating reference for ideologies. There is nothing absolutely contingent about the fact that the only political regimen to have effectively brandished [Nietzsche's] name as a major and official banner was Nazi.
>
> I do not say this in order to suggest that this kind of "Nietzschean" politics is the only one conceivable for all eternity. . . . No. The future of the Nietzsche text is not closed. But if, within the still-open contours of an era, the only politics calling itself—proclaiming itself—Nietzschean will have been a Nazi one, then this is necessarily significant and must be questioned in all of its consequences. . . . I do not believe that we as yet know how to think what Nazism is. The task remains before us, and the political reading of the Nietzschean body or corpus is part of it. I would say the same is true for Heideggerian, Marxist, or Freudian corpus, and for so many others as well. (30; emphasis mine)

At no time does Derrida argue or imply that the Nietzschean (or the Marxist!) text should or ought to be discarded. (As for Derrida, so for me; as for me, so for Derrida: At no time is anything to be forgotten, unless it is an affirmative forgetting.) Instead, a "Nietzschean" text must be attended to. But *how* such a text is to be attended to is crucial; for in remembering the past and the Forgotten, we must not, in remembering, in calling to the past, be driven by the spirit of revenge. We write history and we educate—or so we say—so that we will not repeat the mistakes of the past; the problem, however, is again that when we remember, we more often than not, do so by way of the spirit of revenge.[10] How *banal*! What, then, to do?

This acknowledgment of the duplicity of the "Nietzschean" text and a willingness not to blame or shame it away are to be realized by way of what Derrida calls "guarding the question" of the duplicity-rhetoricity of Hegel's or Nietzsche's or Heidegger's or Marx's, or still others' texts. (Even Derrida's and mine.) It is a guarding of a question that is a refusal not to forget the Forgotten, but in remembering the Forgotten is a complementary refusal to become reactionary. Reading Derrida, Gayatri Spivak takes this problem of the *logos*, of language, specifically of the Nietzschean or Heideggerian texts in her own terms of *"taking the risk of saying 'yes' to Heidegger, Nietzsche, and Derrida"* (see 1989a, 212; Spivak's emphasis). Both Derrida but especially Spivak would call this "saying 'yes' " a necessary "negotiation with structures of violence" (211), which are inevitable in language (*logos, physis,* the sun).

Again, Derrida asks: "Is there anything 'in' the Nietzschean corpus that could help us comprehend the double interpretation and the so-called perversion of the text?" If he could locate this perversion "in" the text, he and we might extricate or exorcise it. Derrida's answer to this question, rather his guarding of it, is in (Nietzschean) terms of *ears.* Derrida re/discovers, "The ear is uncanny. Uncanny is what it is; double is what it can become. . . " (1985, 32–33). Derrida takes Nietzsche's image of the ear—Nietzsche's own answer to the problem of his own text—as his clue. Derrida homeopathically suggests that the duplicity, the double bind, that we can find ourselves in when reading "Nietzschean" texts, exists not only "in" the text, but in the (our) "ears." After all, we have a left *and* a right ear.

Sara Kofman (1987) directs her attention to the duplicity of *logos,* but in Heraclitus, and how various commentators—Plato, Aristotle, Hegel, Nietzsche, Heidegger—have read what is called Heraclitus's "obscurity" in a variety of ways. For Kofman, Nietzsche sees Heraclitus's so-called obscurity as owing

> to the distortion between two types of forces [wills to power], two points of view, . . . or between two ears which cannot get along (hear each other) without misunderstanding, without entering in a dialogue of deaf ears. The correct (harmonious) understanding of a text is not determined by the size of the ear . . . but rather by its sharpness. It is to Ariadne's small ears that Dionysus speaks. To the intuitive ears of women who know how to "understand" without demanding logic or demonstration, without attempting to "unveil" truth. . . . Women's small ear is this *third ear* mentioned by

> Nietzsche, the artistic ear which, positioning itself beyond metaphysical
> oppositions such as truth and falsehood, good and evil, depth and surface,
> clarity and obscurity, is capable of hearing (understanding) an incredible
> (unheard) language incommensurable with vulgar language and its logic
> or metaphysical presuppositions. (48; emphasis mine)

Therefore, What are we to do when confronted with this duplicity in
the text, with these two ears of the text and the audience? (Or the triplicity
of the sun, with its perpetual challenge and demand to desire and to give,
to produce, to consume, and to waste?) Derrida's (and Spivak's) answer is
that we need a new politics of reading. Kofman's answer, however, is another
question: "Do we have to choose between . . . two ears?" (1987, 54).[11]

Beyond these two views, yet close to Kofman's, Deleuze speaks of
Nietzsche's nomad thought that develops "the notion of style as politics"
(1977, 143). Writing in aphorisms, not sentences (propositions) or speech
acts (pragmatics), Nietzsche "hang[s] thought on the outside" of philosophical thinking (147). To use a traditional protocol of reading, as Derrida and
Spivak do, as Aristotle did, is to approach Nietzsche's writing as a reader in
the "despot's bureaucratic machine," not a nomad in "a nomadic war machine" (148). Deleuze writes:

> An aphorism means nothing, signifies nothing, and is no more a signifier than
> a signified: were it not so, the interiority of the text would remain undisturbed.
> An aphorism is a play of forces, the most recent of which—the latest, the newest,
> and provisionally the final force—is always the most exterior. Nietzsche puts
> this very clearly: if you want to know what I mean, then find the force that
> gives a new sense to what I say, and hang the text upon it. . . .
>
> At this point, we encounter the problems posed by those texts of Nietzsche
> that have a fascist or anti-Semitic resonance. We should first recognize here
> that Nietzsche nourished and still nourishes a great many young fascists.
> There was a time when it was important to show that Nietzsche had been
> misappropriated and completely deformed by the fascists. Jean Wahl,
> Bataille, and Klossowski did this in the review *Acéphale*. But today, this is
> no longer necessary. We need not argue Nietzsche at the level of textual
> analysis—not because we cannot dispute at that level, but because the
> dispute in no longer worthwhile. Instead, the problem takes the shape of
> finding, assessing, and assembling the exterior forces that give a sense of
> liberation, a sense of exteriority to each various phrase. (145–46)

And then most importantly Deleuze says:

> The revolutionary character of Nietzsche's thought becomes apparent at the
> level of method: it is his method that makes Nietzsche's text into some-

thing not to be characterized in itself as "fascist," "bourgeois," or "revolutionary," but to be regarded as an *exterior field* where fascist, bourgeois, and revolutionary forces meet head on. If we pose the problem this way, the response conforming to Nietzsche's method would be: find the revolutionary force. (146; emphasis mine; cf. Nietzsche 1969, 265)

Hence, the aphorism = the sun. In its face and light, we are challenged to produce, consume, and waste. How we respond to this challenge, this gift (this "there is . . ." [*Es gibt*]) will determine or not determine our reading(s). Do we have the instinct for aphorism/sun or have we placed ourselves in eclipse? The aphorism = sun = Dionysus, which, as Nietzsche says, is "a means to understanding the older Hellenic instinct, an instinct still exuberant and even overflowing: it is explicable only as an *excess* of energy" (1968b, 108; Nietzsche's emphasis).

To Kofman's question "Do we have to choose between . . . two ears?" (Or, How do we listen to the sun?), my answer, which is not an answer (after all, I am "Nyanza"[12]), is to turn duplicity into a triplicity; I will not choose exclusively between Derrida's political reading (his protocols) and Kofman's more blatantly Nietzschean reading of Heraclitus, but guard the question of both Derrida and Kofman—with a tilt toward the latter—by continuing to call out to the Other for a third position. I drift nomadically toward and within the *exterior field* (Deleuze) of no definitive, even strategic definitive, answer. Often, this is read despotically as only a ludic response and not political (see Ebert 1991). I am not interested in despotic signifiers and politics, in the naive/cynical legal (contractual), institutional, or bureaucratic organizational machinic drives (wills to truth), but in an infinite place of differences (will to power). I am interested in an "advent of a new politics [parapolitics, pagan politics]" (Deleuze 1977, 149). One cum a more radical mutiplicities than, heretofore, thought.

IIIA. About Ijsseling's Isocrates, the Power of, and the Hymn to, the *Logos* (the Sun?), and Heidegger

We are going to shift—and carry these thoughts about reading with us—now to a view of Isocrates that is very unlike that espoused by Finley, or by any other historian or critic. Samuel Ijsseling, in *Rhetoric and Philosophy in Conflict* (1976), is less concerned, at least directly, with the influence of rhetoric on the *polis* and education and more concerned with how The History of Rhetoric has been told and can be retold. I do not wish, however, to overstress his view of The History at the expense of his view of the *polis* and education; for The History of Rhetoric *is* The History of the *polis* and education. But I would also point out that, as I read Ijsseling, The Histories of Rhetoric, language, *polis*, and education are tied very intimately to Heidegger's "History of Being," which specifically is concerned with two questions: What is Being? and Who is Man (i.e., *anthropos*), human being? Which leads to a third question: Where is human being's home? If such a being can have a home. (And, to be sure, there is another question: The question of "there is . . ." [*Es gibt* . . .], which is the question of What gives? Being gives. Then, the question of How are we to give in the face/light of Being's/the sun's giving?)

In his opening chapter, Ijsseling tells his audience about "the rehabilitation of rhetoric." It is a rehabilitation (or *de*criminalization), as the reader proceeds through the book, that is influenced not by rereadings or rediscoveries of Aristotle (Chaim Perelman), but by rereadings of such nineteenth-century thinkers as Nietzsche, Freud, and Marx (the three hermeneuts of suspicion), and by Heidegger. (It might be thought from a traditional point of view that such a rewriting/revision of The History of Rhetoric is not a *de*criminalization but a *re*criminalization of The History. And a *re*criminalization of The Histories of Rhetoric, language, the *polis*, and education.) The influences are hermeneutical, and begin with Heraclitus, then, Nietzsche *and* Heidegger's reading of Heraclitus and their subsequent critique of metaphysics. Inevitably, this influence leads to considerations of the uncanny. (Hence, my quip about *re*criminalization.)

What we have in Ijsseling's history is a subtle rereading/revision of The History of Rhetoric semiotically across The History of Being. Such a "Heideggerian" rereading of The History raises the ancillary question of What is human being's place in history (What is being given/revealed to human being? and What is expected from this being and How expected?). In Heideggerian terms, once that we discover that human beings are "thrown" into time/historicity, into our homelessness, the question becomes What is it to be at home? This question, rewritten for more specific purposes, becomes What is it to be at home in rhetoric? (Some variations of the question: Are we a function of rhetoric, or Is rhetoric a function of us? Is rhetoric a function of *logos*, or Is *logos* a function of rhetoric?) The three hermeneuts of suspicion all argued and demonstrated that we are, more so, a function of rhetoric, and that rhetoric is a function of *logos*. Hence, in part, their suspicion. (But I am getting ahead of Ijsseling and of myself here.)

After a discussion of the so-called rehabilitation of rhetoric, Ijsseling goes on to emphasize what I will call the *Isocrates-Heidegger connection* (which Ijsseling discusses in chapter three), and goes on much later to emphasize what, in passing, I will call the *Nietzsche-Freud-Marx connec-*

tion (which he discusses in chapters thirteen and fourteen).[13] Hence, Ijsseling retells the story achronologically, metaleptically (by way of reversal on its way to displacement); for Ijsseling again wishes to retell the story according to the question raised by Heidegger, which is a question that Nietzsche himself initially had raised but did not pursue—namely, *the Question of Being,* which is also, as I referred to it earlier, the ancillary question that entitles Ijsseling's last chapter, "Who is Actually Speaking Whenever Something is Said?" Again, Is the speaker a function of *logos,* or *logos* a function of the speaker?

It will take me a while before I get to the Question of Being, but every comparison between Isocrates and Heidegger, every examination of the troublesome words *logos, doxa, physis* will be a working toward what I have referred to as *"the connection"* and *the question.*

General Summary: Ijsseling's history of rhetoric—which is ostensibly a history of the rehabilitation of rhetoric as told via the narrative of the conflict between philosophy and rhetoric—is quite *a*typical. The chapters do not, in any traditional sense, logically follow. What a reader might expect— as is very typically expressed in chapter two, "Plato and the Sophists"—is a continuation of what has come to be known as *"The* History of Rhetoric," as in *the grand narrative of The Enlightenment History of Rhetoric.* The logic of the narrative is less that of traditional, chronological history and more that of a (Kafkan) novel. (As Ijsseling writes, so do I.) It is in chapter three, "Isocrates and the Power of *Logos,*" that *the story* veers from what we expect of traditional narrative. Into intensities, series, flows.

In the second chapter, Ijsseling is as about lackluster as any writer using a current-traditional perspective can get; but then in chapter three, instead of sticking to the traditional party line on Isocrates—via Jaeger and Marrou— Ijsseling abruptly gives the reader a set of intensities (not intentions) from which to think about The History of Rhetoric. This different slant is brought about by Ijsseling's abrupt, strange yoking of Isocrates *with* Heidegger. Ijsseling's inclusion of Heidegger is rather daring, eccentric and a "threat" to the stability and integrity (coherence) of The History; and secondly, Ijsseling's inclusion of Heidegger turns traditional historiography *on its head,* allowing most radically Ijsseling to "read" history *a*chronologically—that is, metaleptically—with Heidegger *influencing* a reading of Isocrates.[14]

Therefore, with Ijsseling's hermeneutical principle in mind—which is a (Nietzschean)-Heideggerian "linguistic/rhetorical turn"—let us take a look at what he has to say about Isocrates's view of *logos* and Heidegger's view of *logos, doxa,* and *physis.* These words and concepts are inextricably connected with the problem of The History of Being. And as I have said, How these words/concepts are defined de*term*ines our view of not only history, rhetoric, language, but also of the *polis* and education and philology, and finally of each human being's *place* in dis/respect to these Western institutions. (Be they ever so homely or unhomely.) After all, if it is the *logos* that defines us as human beings (as *Zoion Logon echon*) and as political animals (as *Zoon politikon*) and, therefore, as distinct and separate from beasts and barbarians, as Isocrates insists in his hymn to the *logos*, then much, rather obviously, is at stake in this word *logos*—one of the most difficult, if not most mysterious, of unearthly words.

What Heidegger attempts *to account for* is what *logos* meant for the pre-Socratics and Plato and others. It is the Platonic view of *logos* that, according to Heidegger, inaugurates "The History of Being." (Which is really a series of histories of Being; for each new age redefines *logos* for its own ends and thereby reconstructs Being.) My point is that when we study The History of Rhetoric, we simultaneously are studying The History of Being. What we have, however, in this joint study is the postmodern conditions of the possibilities for rhetorics unconstrained by Platonic or Aristotelian Being(s). After all, there are others' Beings, of which we have no histories/ hysteries. To historicize is to place these Others' Beings under negation. Hence, my earlier calls for hystericizing and histories of Desire.[15]

But, for a Heidegger, matters are more difficult; for let us not forget, Heidegger's Being(s) is (are) withdrawing. From us. If Being(s) is (are) withdrawing into exile, human being begins to see, will have begun to see, its uncanniness. While Being withdraws, Nihilism sets in. Being sees its uncanniness. Indeed, The History of metaphysics sets in; for this History *is* The History of Being's withdrawal, its uncanniness (see Heidegger 1991, 4: 215). If in a manner of speaking, Being's (Beings's) withdrawal *causes* The History of Metaphysics, or Philosophy, or Nihilism, What effect, then, might The History's (metaphysical and physical time's) or Nihilism's effect have on The History of Rhetoric? Heidegger's problem—the question of the withdrawal of Being—would become my paraquestion, un/namely, that of the question of the return of what has been repressed, suppressed, politically oppressed. Which is a paraquestion that I take up with and more fully interrogate in the final excursis.

To round out this discussion: Ijsseling's histories have led me to see the problem of The History of Rhetoric, specifically in Heideggerian terms, and yet also in Nietzschean, Freudian, and Marxist terms. While Ijsseling presents the conflict between rhetoric and philosophy in incipient terms of the will to power (*kairos*, or many competing forces at play) and the will to truth (death, Nihilism), I would still represent the conflict in yet more radical terms. It is not a Platonic or Aristotelian *kairos*, nor a Heideggerian *kairos* that I would reach for, but a Nietzschean *kairos*, that is, a reaching for the *un*measured.[16] Is this dangerous? *Yes*. Is this dangerous? *No*, when I consider the alternative of The History, whose so-called authors "would rather will *nothingness* than *not* will" (Nietzsche 1969, 163; Nietzsche's emphasis).

A *Roadmap For what Follows*[17]: What I will say about Ijsseling's view of Isocrates will be at greater length and depth than what I have said about Jaeger's and Finley's views, though what I have to say is an extension of that earlier discussion. It is actually more than an extension; for I see it as a culmination of thinking about Isocrates and about writing histories/hysteries-cum-schizographies of rhetorics.

What I intend to do, then, by way of introduction, is to survey Ijsseling's discussion of *logos*—specifically, what *logos* means for Isocrates and how his view of *logos* is similar to Heidegger's. Then, I will examine Heidegger's intricate counterphilological interrogation of the concept of *logos* (along with *doxa* and *physis*). With this distinction between Isocrates and Heidegger in mind, I will elaborate on what I call the *Isocrates-Heidegger connection*, which will be a brief transitional comparison that will allow me to continue a discussion of Heidegger and how he precisely extends but differs from his predecessor Isocrates. But this "connection," I wish to stress, is *no mere* comparison, for the "connection" tells us something about The History of Rhetoric—The History of an Error—that we, heretofore, have not known or been willing to admit. The "connection" enables us to think what has been systematically unthought—un/namely and un/timely, that "rhetoric" is intimately connected with The History of Being and, consequently, is a "Philosophical Rhetoric" (i.e., a rhetoric of the *one* and/or *many*), not a Third Sophistic Rhetoric (i.e., radically open rhetorics of heterogeneous *multiplicities*). After this section, I will center on a further, more in-depth explanation and analysis of the pre-Socratics's meanings of *logos/doxa* and what Heidegger calls "unconcealing-concealing," and the Platonic meaning of *logos* and *doxa* and what Heidegger calls a "permanent decision."

For Heidegger, it is Plato and others who desire to put an end to the *pre-Socratics's (or rather Heraclitus's) perpetual questioning of Being*, in order to put an end to "unconcealing-concealing," or to heterogeneous multiplicities—to put an end in the form of a permanent unconcealing, or revealing of truth and I would add, to put an end to hysteries of rhetorics. In another word, to put an end to the sun.[18] This end, for Heidegger, is the inauguration of The History of Being; for me, it is simultaneously the inauguration of The History of (Philosophical) Rhetoric.

The consequences of all this re/thinking done by Isocrates and Heidegger—especially its political ramifications for rhetoric, language, the *polis*, education—will inform my final discussion of Ijsseling's book, a final discussion that I will call "the Isocrates-Heidegger *dis*/connection." (Dis/connection = decolonization.) It is a final discussion that speculates on the concept/word *logos* in relation to imperialism, hegemony, and ideology. It is a final discussion that will take up Isocrates's attitude toward the barbarians and specifically the Persians; and will take up Heidegger's role with the Nazis and his/their attitude toward "the jews."[19] It is a discussion that articulates and speculates on the pros and cons of Isocratean and Heideggerian thinking, which is a reactionary thinking.

The Hymn to Logos, *as* Hegemon (Dynamis?): Ijsseling begins his discussion with a close look at what has come to be known as Isocrates's "hymn, or eulogy, to *logos*" (*Nicocles* 5–10; *Antidosis* 253–57). For Ijsseling, the hymn is concerned with Who is actually speaking whenever something is said?, and, therefore, is concerned with the question What is Being? Isocrates's answer to this one-and-the-same question is *logos*, but let us see how he arrives at this answer and what it means for him and us. Isocrates says:

> Because there has been implanted in us the power to persuade each other and to make clear to each other whatever we desire, not only have we escaped the life of wild beasts, but we have come together and founded cities and made laws and invented arts; and, generally speaking, there is no institution devised by man which the power of speech [*logos*] has not helped us to establish. (*Nicocles* 6–7)

Logos (the power to speak, to persuade and be persuaded) is creator of all culture (*paideia*): It directs our public and private affairs and gives us our concept of justice and self-control. It divides us from the beasts and the barbarians. (Recall, as I discussed in chapter 3, the term *Geschlecht*, as signifying a de-monstering.) Because of *logos* (the sun), we have a home.

Isocrates continues: ". . . the power to speak well is taken as the surest *index* of a sound understanding, and discourse which is true and lawful and just is the outward image of a good and faithful soul. With this faculty we both contend against others on matters which are open to dispute and seek light for ourselves on things which are unknown." And then he writes: "Speech is our guide" (7–9). Here, we have Isocrates's answers to Who is speaking? and What is Being? The word "guide" in Greek, Ijsseling points out, is *hegemon*, which means not only "guide," but also "prince" or "leader." (It obviously also gives us our word "hegemony.")

As I have said earlier in my discussions of Jaeger and Finley, if *logos* (speech, discourse) creates culture (*paideia*), culture then, in turn, may influence the state by *educating* (in the sense of "learning," instead of "teaching") *its leaders* in *areté* (in political virtue, or excellence). This issue of political virtue is important for both the *leaders* and the *followers*, which is evident in Ijsseling's selection of Isocrates's own conclusion to the hymn: "Therefore, those who dare to speak with disrespect of educators and teachers of philosophy deserve our opprobrium no less than those who profane the sanctuaries of the gods" (9). Ijsseling is the only one—in comparison to Jaeger, Marrou, and Finley—who cites this rather startling passage. Why startling? Because to disagree, here, means *to commit a sacrilegious act.* (This statement is most emphatic: It ends the hymn to *logos*.)

We will return to the concept of *hegemon* and to the association of educators and philosophers with the gods, and to the questions of Being and Man: For the concept and the association and the questions will help us think about the larger implications of associating Heidegger with Isocrates—not only in relation to thinking, writing, reading histories of rhetoric but also in relation to structuring educational institutions and the *polis*. The issue is that of *hegemon* and *hegemony*. Of Influence. Of political interest. After all, the embedded questions are What is Being?, Who is "Man" (*anthropos*)?, and "Who is Actually Speaking. . . ?" Or What is the source of *hegemony*?

How these questions, as well as the rephrased question, are answered— if answered at all—is crucial: In the first *and* last chapters, Ijsseling poses the question "Who is Actually Speaking Whenever Something is Said?" It is this question—heretofore, not articulated since common sense already offered an answer and deflected such a question from being reasked—that gives us *a history of the answers* (or errors), gives us The History of Being—The History of Man (*anthropos*) as having spoken *and* having been spoken. (Much is de*term*ined by one or the other answer; even more is de*term*ined if the question is definitively answered.)

Ijsseling's history and in particular his third chapter, on Isocrates-Heidegger, is a *tour de force*: In it he tells us that insofar as both he and we know The History of Rhetoric *authentically*, namely, *as* a problem, we know it only *questioningly*. (Cf. Heidegger 1959, 206.) What is put into question here, therefore, is the Enlightenment grand, or master, narrative of The History of Rhetoric. And it is put into question perpetually. What we get in Ijsseling's history is not *The* History but a *pastiche* of radical, multiple histories; it is as if he used the "cut up method" (Brion Guyson and William S. Burroughs) on extant and possible histories, on traditional philosophy and counterculture philosophy, and arranged the "cuttings" in a collage/montage. Ijsseling's history is The History (or Nova) that Exploded insofar as it is History as Perpetual Questioning. This is the Heraclitean, Isocratean, Nietzschean, Heideggerian legacy that Ijsseling identifies history with. It is the legacy of questioning, not answering. It is the legacy of the Possible, of Possibilism*s*. However, it is Possibilisms not based on the negative (i.e., out of the impossible comes the possible); for such a *topos* is the very nature of traditional Being; but it is Possibilisms of the nonpositive affirmative. Whereas Plato, Aristotle, Kant, and company work out of the negative, and whereas Freud, Marx, and Heidegger attempt to work out of the positive but only reposition Being/being in the reactionary negative, Nietzsche plays within the nonpositive affirmative. (As we progress into this my discussion, it will become more evident just how Heidegger thinks and practices from the negative.)

Logos/Doxa: Let us return to Ijsseling's (and Heidegger's) questioning of the history of the words/concepts *logos* and *doxa*, and examine them, first, very generally and, then, more specifically. Ijsseling tells us that *logos*, during the 6th and 5th centuries B. C. undergoes a shift in meaning: Initially, it was *logos* as speech/writing (the orator's monologue or poet's myth); then later, it is *logos* as reason (dialogue, dialectic). It is the "philosopher"/sophist Isocrates, who maintains the view of *logos* as speech/writing. Other philosophers—beginning with Parmenides-Plato and moving through Locke, Kant, and Hegel—begin to think of the *logos* as the guide of (pure) reason (*ratio, Vernunft*) (See Heidegger 1959, 188). Plato characterizes a distinction between, on the one hand, ordinary *logos* (monological speech) as *doxa* and, on the other, *logos* (dialogical speech) as *episteme*. He favors the latter view of *logos*. Unlike Isocrates's hymn to *logos*, Plato's, like Parmenides's before him, *is* a Hymn to Pure *Logos*/Reason.[20] (Plato, after all, wanted/wants to answer the question of Being definitively! He desires to master our desire.)[21]

Ijsseling tells us, however, that in Greek culture, in particular in sophistic culture, the word *logos* had many other meanings such as *number, account, connection, arrangement*; and that the word *doxa* meant not *mere opinion*, as it is *revised* by Plato and is most often translated still today to mean, but also meant "brilliant, esteem, glory, fame, honor"—all of which were *transitory*. Which finally might mean, according to Ijsseling *and* Heidegger, that prior to Plato's revision, "the essence of being [in *logos*] lay partly in appearing" (*doxa*) (Ijsseling 1976, 24; Heidegger 1959, 102–03). This aspect of the word—appearing, appearance—will play an important part in Heidegger's view of *logos* as unconcealing/concealing. In addition to this interpretation of *logos*, there is yet a different one expressed in the Greek idiom *logon didonai* which means "to give an account of" (Ijsseling 1976, 20). The telling of a story is the giving of an account, which the Sophists both embraced and enacted.[22]

Up to this point I have let Ijsseling speak for the connection between Isocrates and Heidegger. Let us now have Heidegger tell The Story (or stories); for, indeed, it is Heidegger who partially tells Ijsseling's history-cum-histories; I say "partially" because as I read Ijsseling's histories, the primary story teller is Nietzsche and, then, Heidegger, with Freud and Marx thrown in as additional interlocutors. Hence, heteroglossia. Specifically then, let us take a closer look at Heidegger's view of *logos* in relation to the concepts expressed in the phrases *on the way to*, or *by way of*, language. Heidegger is very direct. He explains: "We do not merely speak *the* language—we speak *by way of* it." (Again, "Who is Speaking Whenever Something is Said?") We speak *by way of* language "solely because we always have already listened to the language. What do we hear there? We hear language speaking. But— does language itself speak? How is it supposed to perform such a feat when obviously it is not equipped with organs of speech? Yet *language* speaks. . . . Language speaks by saying, *this is* [there is, *Es gibt*], by showing" (1982, 124; cf. Cixous 1989, 7). Heidegger continues:

> What it says wells up from the formerly spoken and so far still unspoken Saying which pervades the design of language. Language speaks in that it, as showing, reaching into all regions of presences, summons from them whatever is present to appear and to fade. We, accordingly, listen to language in this way, that we let it say its Saying to us. No matter in what way we may listen besides, whenever we are listening to something we are *letting something be said to us*. (124; Heidegger's emphasis)

Now it is crucial to understand that, for Heidegger, all that "we speak" *by way of logos*/language is not *episteme/physis* (certain knowledge). Heidegger's view of *logos*/language, or "speaking/saying," is *perpetually an act of concealing/unconcealing*. (As Bataille's sun enables and disenables.) For Heidegger, this Being/essence cannot be realized, completely revealed, or unconcealed. Any and every attempt to unconceal or answer definitively is to perpetrate an act of violence on Being and on human being. Moreover, Being is withdrawing.

Let us return and recall that, if not Parmenidean-Platonic *episteme* (as certain knowledge), then, what "we speak" *by way of logos*, in Heidegger's view, is *doxa*. But it is not *doxa* as "mere opinion," but a *doxa* that is, nonetheless, "partly" *episteme/essence*; for, as Heidegger tells us, "the essence of being [in *logos*] lay *partly* in appearing" (*doxa*) (1959, 102-03; Heidegger's emphasis). *Logos*, he tells us, was "the interwovenness of being [*physis*], unconcealment, and appearance" (109). Moreover, *doxa* meant glory: "I show myself, appear, enter into the light. . . . Glory [which is the highest state of Being/*physis* for the pre-Socratics Greeks] is the fame . . . in which one stands" (103)—which was/is also *transitory*, or subject to falling back into concealment.

By this way, then, *doxa* in *logos* and *logos* in *doxa* are concealed and unconcealed to us. In other words, *logos* speaks *doxa* which is an unconcealment and simultaneously a concealment of *some aspect* of *episteme*/truth, which can never be completely gathered, or unconcealed. Unless rudely forced! Let us further consider the implications of unconcealing-concealing and their rudely forced, sometimes farced destiny under Platonic/Aristotelian thinking.

Logos, Doxa, Unconcealing-Concealing: Ijsseling tells us: "The word logos is fundamental to Heidegger's thought, where it points to an original event of unconcealing and concealing . . . which takes place primarily in speaking" (1976, 23). The *logos* is an auditory experience/event. In Heidegger's own poetic words—in his translation of Heraclitus, fragment B 50—*logos* is "the Laying that gathers, lies before us as gathered" (1984, 75). If "the Laying" is thought of as *grounds, foundings*, it may be easier to think of it as *logos*, as that which gives us *grounds*, or guides us, so that we might *gather*; or gives us grounds, or the *way*, so that we might *unconceal* what has been *concealed* (cf. 1982, 125). But—Heidegger is very emphatic—these *grounds cannot be known*, nor *can the unconcealment be permanent*, as the Greeks, especially Plato (as Ideal) and Aristotle (as actuality) *desired*.

Instead of lamenting not being able to know ultimate grounds/foundations, Heidegger laments the loss of a sense of *wonder* and *possibility* that the pre-Socratics originally experienced—a sense of wonder and possibility that contributed to the golden age (the *Ur-sprung*, as Heidegger would have it) of their thought. Heidegger sees the Sophistic and Platonic and Aristotelian will-to-grounds/foundations as, in his word, an unfortunate favoring of "unconcealment" over "concealment" (1959, 106); he favors, instead, as expressed in Greek tragic poetry, that "abyss of Being," that irresolvable struggle between "unconcealment and concealment," that "confused, intricate struggle between the powers of being and appearance" (1959, 106). He favors pondering the Question of Being; the productive state of confusion expressed in the pre-Platonic and pre-Aristotelian view of *physis*, which did not denote/connote the *separation* of *physis/logos* from *doxa*, but its inclusion. Again, as Heidegger says: "The essence of being [*logos/physis*] lay partly in appearing [*doxa*]" (103).[23]

Thus far, we have examined the importance of the concept and word *logos* for Isocrates, and have similarly examined not only its importance for Heidegger but his counterphilological reading of *logos* and how it meant both *physis/doxa* and then came to mean exclusively *physis* (*episteme*), altogether separating *doxa* and lowering its value. Isocrates and Plato as contemporaries, therefore, had diametrically opposed views of *logos*. In discussing *logos*, we have also become aware of how, for Isocrates, *logos* is our *hegemon* (guide, prince, leader), and finally how Isocrates's concept of *logos* fostered a view of Panhellenism that was, as Jaeger phrased it, a "nationalist ideology" (1986b, 77). What we have not done thus far, however, is to examine more closely what I call *the Isocrates-Heidegger connection.* It is their near common view of language that will be our central concern for now.

The Isocrates-Heidegger Connection: It is easy for Ijsseling to draw a parallel between the Isocrates of "the hymn to *logos*" (in *Nicocles* and *Antidosis*) and the Heidegger of *An Introduction to Metaphysics.* A central and similar notion held in common by Isocrates and Heidegger is that *logos* (discourse) *is our guide.* Implied in this statement is that *logos* (culture, discourse, language) is the ground and constitution of communication and community; and therefore that *logos speaks us always already before we,* individually or collectively (can), *speak.* For Isocrates, *logos* was *the way to* culture/*paideia.* Without *logos* as a guide, there would be only darkness and barbarity, which is represented by Isocrates as a Asian-Persian threat to Hellenism. (Hence, Isocrates's call for Panhellenism and his call later for a united war against the Persians, in *Evagoras* and *Panegyricus* and the letters *To Philip.*)

Similarly, for Heidegger, "It is in words and language that things first come into being and are" (1959, 13). It is important, however, for me to point out what I mentioned earlier: That in Heidegger's view Being, with its constant dance of concealment-unconcealment, withdrew on its own rather mysterious accord. It was not human being, whether a Parmenides or a Plato, who caused Being to fall into evidently permanent concealment. (For Nietzsche, however, it is *anthropos.*) It is such thinkers as Plato and Heidegger's contemporaries who desired/desire to recapture and control unconcealment, to construct a ground/foundation for establishing the difference between true and false words, reality and appearance. They, Heidegger would say, refuse to "station [themselves] in the storm of Being." They "betray the fact that we bestir ourselves only to drive storms away. We organize all available means for cloud-seeding and storm dispersal in order to have calm in the face of the storm. But the storm is no tranquility. It is only anesthesia; more precisely, the narcotization of anxiety in the face of thinking" (1984, 78).

But though withdrawn, the now *Abyss of* Being is still, according to Heidegger, to be sought after, still to be our guide—but as the pre-Socratics (or Socrates) sought after and pondered it, by "station[ing] ourselves in the storm of Being." If not, then we make tentative answers to questions into dogmatic answers and we fall into *in*authenticity. We repeat the original fall away from "Being," only again to suffer a "forgetfulness of being."

Heidegger's whole point in everything he writes is that we are engaged today in an *in*authentic use of language. We try to control language (*logos/ physis*)[24]; for when language gathers us to questions such as What is Being? and Who is "Man" (*anthropos*)?, we attempt to answer them definitively, that is, we practice a strategy of limitation. It is these answers that cause us to suffer a "forgetfulness of being," that prevent us from pondering the mystery of Being. Again, for Heidegger, it is some of the Sophists[25], Plato, and Aristotle, and the moderns who steer us away from the Question of Being; but it is Socrates who constantly ponders it, in fact, who lives *questioningly*. As Heidegger says: "The true problem is what we do not know and what, insofar as we know it *authentically*, namely as a problem, we know only *questioningly*. To know how to question means to know how to wait, even a whole lifetime" (1959, 206; emphasis mine). To wait for *kairos* to speak; to wait for *Moira* (destiny, fate) to speak; to wait for the revelation of Being.[26]

But if we do not wait, but are quick to answer or finally to answer definitively, then again, as Heidegger would see it, we know language *in*authentically, and, therefore, "we no longer know what is at stake in language" (1959, 51). Heidegger's is an account of what has come to be(ing)—man's *"barbarization" of language* (51) and *"forgetfulness of be- ing"* (of *Dasein*, being-there [19]) and, consequently, his *falling away from his proper place in history*. Which is, again, to ponder the question "What is Being?" Or "What is perpetually possible?" (This *proper place*, according to Heidegger, is one assigned exclusively to Germany, which is caught in the "pincers" of Russia and America [37–38]. Recall Hegel's statement in *Phi- losophy of Right*: "The world-spirit, in its onward march, hands over to each people the task of working out its own peculiar vocation. Thus in universal history each nation in turn is for that epoch . . . dominant. Against this absolute right . . . the spirits of the other nations are absolutely without right" [qtd. in Cassirer 1966, 273–74.]) Heidegger asks: "What if it were possible that man, that nations in their greatest movements and traditions, are linked to being and yet had long fallen out of being, without knowing it, and that this was the most powerful and most central cause of their decline?" (1959, 37). Like Isocrates before him, Heidegger sets out not only to diagnose the decline from a golden age, from greatness (as manifested in "the forgetful- ness of being") but also to offer a prognosis in the form of "the disclosure [unlocking] of being" (19). There are definite *political* implications here, to which I will return.[27]

Metaphysics, Humanism, and Heraclitus: As a corollary to their view of *logos,* neither Isocrates nor Heidegger has any use for metaphysics. Though Heidegger wrote *An Introduction to Metaphysics,* the book is, as M. A. Gillespie says, an attempt, like so many other efforts of Heidegger's, to liberate us from metaphysics, which Heidegger sees as "nihilistic" (1984, 134–49; cf. "Introduction" to *Being and Time,* 1962). To our knowledge, Isocrates never wrote a piece entitled *Against the Metaphysicians,* but it is clear that when he addresses the concerns of metaphysics, he sees them as futile and as a waste of time. In this capacity as "a practical thinker" who wishes to redefine a "Philosopher," Isocrates is a forerunner to Heidegger (see *Antidosis,* 270–71, for Isocrates's "Philosopher"; also see Schiappa, 1995b).

I am not by any stretch of the imagination suggesting, however, that Isocrates and Heidegger are intellectual equals, anymore than I suggested earlier that Isocrates is equal to Plato (cf. Marrou 79). (Such a comparison, like all such comparisons across great periods of time, are senseless; I will, however, keep up the pretense.) But what is the conspicuous and remarkable achievement realized by Isocrates is his maintaining the *speaker-spoken paradigm* (with the speaker being-spoken), and the maintaining of it *without* relying on some Platonic transcendental signifier. After all, for Isocrates, without *logos* there would be no *paideia;* without *paideia,* there would be no Hellenism, or Helene, only barbarians and barbarisms.

Isocrates's primary influence in this case is most likely Heraclitus, while Plato's is Parmenides.[28] I say Heraclitus because it was he, as best as we know, who abstractly initiated the paradigm. Similarly, it is Nietzsche much later who rereads Heraclitus and brings about the reversal again, in the form of a metalepsis; then it is, to a degree, Freud (with his view of the unconscious) and Marx (with his view of the base and superstructure, or ideology), and finally back to the future it is Heidegger (the historian of Being).

Heidegger, however, has his own slant on Heraclitus, which I will sketch out here; for it is crucial to a reading of his rector's address, which I am working my way towards. In discussing Heraclitean fragments 73, 34, and 50, in *An Introduction to Metaphysics,* Heidegger discloses that for Heraclitus it is *logos,* not human being, that "brings together." (Again, recall the German word *Geschlecht* as it is associated with the words "laying" and "gathering," which, as Derrida writes, "resists the forces of dissemination or dislocation" [see Derrida 1987, 182, 192; cf. Heidegger 1984, 59–78].) It is the *logos* that *guides* (lays and gathers and hearkens), speaks through human beings that they are beings, so that they might ask the question, What/Who is *anthropos?* (see Heidegger 1959, 128–29). (Later in "The Rector's Address," it is not only *logos* but essence [Being, essence, *Wesen*] that does and should guide.) Heidegger writes: "Heraclitus means to say: Men have hearing, they hear words, but in this hearing, they cannot 'heed,' i.e. follow what is not audible like words, what is not a *discourse*, a *speaking*, but indeed the *logos*" (1959, 129; Heidegger's emphasis). Then, carrying out the rest of his redescription, Heidegger concludes:

> Thus, properly understood, Fragment 50 proves the exact opposite of what is [by some] read into it. It says: do not attach importance to words but heed the *logos*. Because *logos* and *legein* already signified discourse and to speak, but since these are not the essence of the *logos*, *logos* here is opposed to *epea*, discourse. Correspondingly, the hearing that is a follow-ing . . . is contrasted with mere hearing. Mere hearing scatters and dif-fuses itself in what is commonly believed and said, in hearsay, in *doxa*, appearance. True hearing has nothing to do with ear and mouth, but means: to follow the *logos* and what it is, namely the collectedness of the *essent* itself. (129)

After this statement, Heidegger emphasizes: "We can hear truly *only if we are followers*. But this has nothing to do with *the lobes of our ears*" (129; emphasis mine). If we do not follow the *logos*, we are "*axynetoi*, those who do not comprehend" (130).

In concluding his discussion of Heraclitus, Heidegger makes two ad-ditional points. The first is that "only those who [stand in the being of the *essent*] can master the word; these are the poets and thinkers. The others stagger about in their obstinacy and ignorance." The second is that "because being as *logos* is basic gathering, not mass and turmoil in which everything has as much or as little value as everything else, *rank and domination are implicit in being*. If being is to disclose itself, it must itself have and main-tain a rank. That is why Heraclitus spoke of the many as dogs and donkeys" (1959, 133; emphasis mine). What is developing in this redescription of Heraclitus is progressively disconcerting, namely, only a select, or elite, few can hear and all is hierarchical or hypotactic. However, it may very well be that Heidegger is merely attempting in a disinterested way, the philological way, to accurately represent what Heraclitus says. I think not. For a line or so later, Heidegger is injecting his own counterattitude concerning a popu-lar reading of the *polis* as the cite of a developing democracy. He writes: "Nowadays a little too much fuss is sometimes made over the Greek polis. If one is going to concern oneself with the polis, this aspect [of *logos*] should not be forgotten, or else the whole idea becomes insignificant and sentimen-tal. *What has the higher rank is the stronger*" (133; emphasis mine).

The connection between Isocrates and Heidegger is closer and closer. However, the connection begins to become a little unsavory, given recent history; for the other connection—namely, that with National Socialism—

becomes also close and closer, credible and more credible. To be sure, there are differences between Isocrates and Heidegger, but I am not, as I have repeatedly stated, working out a simple comparison and contrast; instead, I am working toward understanding the conditions of the possibilities for hierarchical education, politics, philology, and history writing. Whereas for Nietzsche, human, all too human beings had ears, which were uncanny and which might be Heraclitean donkey's ears, for Heidegger, ears are not the point at all. Rank and domination are the point. Species and Genus are the determinants. Rank and domination become steadily more and more visible in some of his works.

The Isocrates-Heidegger Dis/connection, or Some Troubling Specula-tions: Ijsseling, towards the end of his discussion of Isocrates-Heidegger, raises the *question*, which is presented as a Platonic question in the form of an objection—namely, if *logos*/language (what it has to say, how it guides us) is not controlled or stabilized in some way, if the ambiguities are not removed or at least not *accounted* for, if questions are not finally answered with a degree of certainty and confidence, How, then, will we ever know what is the true, good, and beautiful, that is, what is the good, virtuous-ethical life in the *polis*? (1976, 23). It is important to stress that this Socratic-Platonic question assumes an *a priori* answer as all Platonic questions long for, whereas the Heideggerian question is *proleptic*, with the question(s) arising out of their Being/being experienced, or in some cases answered. Therefore, if from a Platonic point of view some pre-Socratics and Heidegger appear not only dangerous but also logically absurd, Plato appears just as danger-ous and absurd from a pre-Socratics-Heideggerian view. (I am well aware that there is a question of Aristotle here as well and intend to approach it intermittently and especially towards the end of this chapter.) How do we *account* for this apparent contra/*logos*? Quite simply, Plato, as I have pointed out, has a radically different notion of *logos* than Heidegger and the pre-Socratics have. It is Plato who separates *doxa* (opinion, appearance) from *episteme* or *physis* (knowledge as certainty or of reality), thus destroying the pre-Socratics meaning of *logos*, by insisting on the concealment of *doxa* or by insisting on its being projected onto the Sophists. That is, on to a scape-goat. That is, by *negative essentializing*. But it is Heidegger, however, who attempts a return to *logos* as both *doxa* and *episteme*, as concealment/unconcealment. Or so it appears on numerous occasions.

Another way of saying all this, while making an additional point, is that, for Heidegger, there is no way to control or to stabilize or for that matter to ameliorate *logos*. In Heidegger's view, which is influenced by his read-ings of Heraclitean fragments, *logos* is both irresistible and violent (*polemos*, *kampf*), while it establishes the grounds for what *will have become* the true, good, and beautiful. (Recall Bataille's view of the sun.) *Logos*, as it *guides* human being/*polis*, therefore, is pre-political, pre-ethical; for it is what de*term*ines, in the first place, such concepts and their appropriate praxies.[29] There is Being, then, language, and finally "man." In his "Letter on Human-ism," Heidegger writes: "Man is not the lord of beings. Man is the shepherd of Being" (1977, 221; cf. 193).

The Heideggerian response, therefore, is that this problem that Plato and others raised is a false problem itself, in that there is *no way* to sta-bilize or to give ourselves or others *a guarantee* about the meaning of words, or of questions-answers, and consequently about the true, good, and beautiful. For Heidegger, "Error is the space in which history un-folds. In error what happens in history bypasses what is like Being" (1984, 26). To desire to play the game with security is to relinquish our originary relation with Being. We are by birth wanderers, nomads, drifters; we are by birth subject of and to Being, its absence and its presence. Though particular human beings may, from time to time, bring about the *polis*, it is Being itself, in its withdrawal, that determines human beings' ac-tions and the kind of *polis* they establish. This view of human being is, according to Heidegger, human being's fate, which is more so the fate of the *polis* than of any individual (see Gillespie 1984, 152; cf. Bernstein 1992, 79–141).

And why is there not *a* Platonic/dialectic/accoun*t*able *way* to stabilize or to assure or to give ourselves or others *a guarantee* about the meaning of words? (Let us not forget that this *is* the question, for if Being is to be our guide, what it has to say to us must be, or so we would hope, reliable.) Why is there not a guarantee? Quite simply because human beings cannot *understand* Being (*physis/logos*)—though the pre-Socratics *experienced* Being, in a fundamentally tragic way when they *stood in the storm of Being*, a storm created by Being's withdrawal, its concealing/unconcealing itself (1984, 78). Put in another way and contrary to what traditional philosophers and rhetoricians have come to maintain, Being has no point of stasis that is not unequivocal. Stasis is paradoxical. Tragic.[30] Let us see what Heidegger *specifically* says about this relationship between Being/being, and about standing in the Storm. (Bear in mind as we proceed that we are moving towards a discussion of "The Rector's Address" and its kinship with Isocrates's hymn to *logos*.)

What is it to Experience Being? (the Sun): To be a (human) being— as Heidegger perceives that state of being—is to be, like Oedipus, cast out of the *polis*, to be a wanderer. It is to be *apolis*. How does this come about? Simply put, this state of uncanniness, or unhomeliness, comes about when human beings confront Being. And when confronting Being, human beings come to understand that they do not make history; Being makes history in so far as it reveals and conceals itself through being's actions. (Let us not forget, history is Being revealing itself through *logos* that, in turn, speaks through human being. What human beings understand is that they cannot understand; hence, being's knowledge is "negative knowledge" [cf. de Man 1983a, 75].) Again, Being is a storm, in which human being can stand, though not Platonically—that is, assuredly—only uncannily. Being is struggle (*polemos*). In its midst, *there* is the originary abode, which being must dwell in (1977, 232–34). Heidegger says:

> Only in *polemos,* in the conflict/war which sets (being) [i.e., both mortal and immortal] apart. It is only such conflict that *edeixe,* that *shows,* that brings forth gods and men in their being. We do not learn who man is by learned definitions; we learn it only when man . . . projects something new (not yet present), *when he creates original poetry, when he builds poetically* [i.e., brings into unconcealment]. (1959, 144; emphasis mine)

This statement concerning *polemos*/war, no doubt, is greatly unstable and politically haunts Heidegger. And, hence, he also stands in the storm of controversy.

But then how does human being create, build poetically, bring into unconcealment?: We are told, first, that "Man is *to deinotaton,* the strangest of the strangest [the most uncanny]"; and once again, that "man is violent" in his making. Heidegger explains further:

> We are taking the strange, the uncanny . . . as that which casts us out of the "homely," i.e. the customary, familiar, secure. The unhomely . . . prevents us from making ourselves at home and therein it is overpowering. But man is the strangest of all, not only because he passes his life amid the strange understood in this sense but because he departs from his customary, familiar limits, because he is the violent one, who, tending toward the strange in the sense of the overpowering, surpasses the limit of the familiar. (150-51)

Aristotle, in his rationalist approach, might call this strangeness, uncanniness, perversity in human being "incontinence" (see *Nichmachean Ethics,* Bk. 7). And Aristotle, in his view of knowing, doing, and making, characterizes the maker-poet as acting *by virtue of the polis.* However, with Heidegger's going back to the future, going back to the pre-Socratics, the *maker* acts *after* (prior to) *virtue.*[31] The Heideggerian difference here is a metaleptic one.

Where does poetic human being create?: In the *polis*. But as Heidegger says,

> *Polis* is usually translated as city or city-state. This does not capture the full meaning. . . . The *polis* is the historical place, the there *in* which, *out of* which, and *for which* history happens. To this place and scene of history belong the gods, the temples, the priests, the festivals, the games, the poets, the thinkers, the ruler, the council of elders, the assembly of the people, the army and the fleet. (1959, 152; Heidegger's emphasis)

But then Heidegger adds an important qualification:

> All this does not first belong to the *polis*, does not become political by entering into a relation with a statesman and a general and the business of the state. No, it is political, i.e. at the site of history, provided there be (for example) poets *alone*, but then really poets, priests *alone*, but then really priests, rulers *alone*, but then really rulers. (152; Heidegger's emphasis)

Hence, though in the *polis*, the poet/maker is, at first, *apolis, avirtuous, apolitical*. What statement concerning ethics and the *polis* could be further from both Plato and Aristotle's views?

The *polis* is *not*, Heidegger tells us, the result of rational-political deliberation, but the result of an Oedipus confronting the Abyss of Being, of Tragedy, of Nihilism, of *polemos* (struggle, conflict, war), which, contrary to what we normally think, is *not*, for Heidegger, the ground for despair, but possibilisms. (Albeit possibilisms based on negation.[32]) Oedipus cannot deliberate—by way of rational discourse alone—with Being, for human being cannot understand Being. Again, the point of stasis gives only negative knowledge. The *logos* is uncanny; Being is uncanny. Oedipus is engaged in thinking, which cannot be realized by way of *techné* (See 1977, 196–97). Instead, as Heidegger sees it, human being can more productively-poetically stand in *the storm of Being*, which is what Oedipus does. Heidegger says: Those beings who stand in the storm found the *polis* while they "become at the same time *apolis*, without city and place, lonely, strange, and alien, without issue amid the essent ["existents," "things that are"] as a whole, at the same time without statute and limit, without structure and order, because they themselves as creators must first create all this" (1959, 152–53).

Again—and I emphasize—the originary experience of Being for the early Greeks, as Heidegger posits, was that of being strange, alien, homeless, being a wanderer or nomad (see Gillespie 1984, 139).[33]

These mythic, human beings—Oedipus, Heraclitus, and others—may appear to be apolitical, but such a conclusion would be only a misunderstanding, Heidegger would argue, for these mythic beings or human beings are not concerned with *the business of the polis* because they are pondering *its various possibilities of changing grounds*. They stare, Heidegger says, "in the ever darker depths of a riddle, depths [of the Abyss of Being] which as they grow darker offer *promise* of a greater brightness" (1984, 78; emphasis mine; cf. Nietzsche 1966, 228–29). (Is this what Heidegger perhaps thought he was doing—staring into the abyss—when silent about the Nazis, during and still after the Holocaust?) For Heidegger, this "promise" that he speaks of was a promise that may result in a new order, a new *polis* with its hegemony.[34] (Out of *dynamis* would come hegemony?) Whereas, from Plato on, human beings had taken a turn away from a closeness to Being, Heidegger would have us reclaim this originary closeness.

The problem that Heidegger is dealing with here, then, is what he calls "the original ethics" (1977, 235). Mythic beings or human beings are in search of "man's essential abode" (236), which, for Heidegger, is a search for *ethos*. Though Plato and Aristotle investigated ethics—and, of course, quite differently—theirs are originary, but inauthentic; for "in the course of a [say, Platonic] philosophy so understood," as Heidegger writes,

> science [*episteme*] waxed and thinking waned. Thinkers prior to this [Platonic or Aristotelian] period knew neither a "logic" nor an "ethics" nor "physics." Yet their thinking was neither illogical nor immoral. But they did think *physis* in a depth and breadth that no subsequent "physics" was ever again able to attain. The tragedies of Sophocles . . . preserve the *ethos* in their sagas more primordially than Aristotle's lectures on "ethics." (232-33)

Heidegger would have us, some of us, "find the way to [our] abode in the truth of [Heraclitean] Being" (239), not unlike that found by the tragic heroes of Sophocles. According to Heidegger, however, we human beings abandon (the abyss of) Being. Therefore, Heidegger speaks of "the homelessness of contemporary man from the essence of Being's history" (217).

Before continuing, let us appraise these statements. First of all, it is clear here that Heidegger's is an aesthetic prior to a political view of *ethos*, though not a Nietzschean aesthetic view. (I have spoken earlier of this view in contrast to other aesthetic views, and I will speak of this topic more as I develop the final excursis.) Secondly, there is a possible nonproductive confusion with or equivocation in Heidegger's talk about homelessness; for while pondering (the abyss of) Being, Heidegger's select mythic beings are homeless (nomads, wanderers), *and* while not pondering Being, the rest of us are also homeless. Evidently, there is a difference in terms of authentic and inauthentic homelessness; and yet, authentic here can only form with homelessness an oxymoron. Man's being is authentic only when it "guards," or is the "shepherd" of, the Question of Being; when not guarding the Question, human being is inauthentic. If Being were ever to reveal itself to human being, our homelessness would cease. Or so it would seem.

Heidegger's philosophy is one thing, but his actions, as we will see, are another—hence, further nonproductive confusions. And yet, I would make something of them; for Heidegger, as Lyotard (1990) and so many others have stated, fails finally and then repeatedly to guard the Question of Being. He engages in negative essentializing (*physis*[neg.]), in the worst inauthetic "being"-cum-possible.

The Return of the Eternally Repressed: We began the discussion of this section with what I called the Platonic question (problem) of determining whether or not words/*logos* (as our *hegemon*/guide, prince, leader) were true or false. I raised the question of either the or a *way* of knowing that would tell us what we need to know about *logos* and Being. We would like to know (*episteme*) because we do not want to make any more errors than we already (human, all so humanly) do. (Perhaps we recall Heidegger's saying, "He who thinks greatly, errs greatly." Or we even recall Oedipus's fate. [Qtd. in Gillespie 1984, 174–75.]) We are, therefore, back to—eternally back to—the question of determining whether the *logos* guides truly or falsely, which as we said is *in itself* a false (i.e., spoken at cross-purposes) question. Therefore: "What are we to do?" This has become more and more from Plato through Heidegger to the McIntyre and Stout exchange (1984; 1988) a *pedagogical* question. At midpoint, still hung up *in utero*, I must continue to ruminate. Allow me, while summarizing, to advance. Allow me, while historicizing, to hysterize. After all, it is the tactic of the uncanny that I am dis/engaging in here.[35]

At best, Heidegger, given his pre-Socratics view of *logos*, makes the question for himself an *authentic* one by telling us that we—or at least some of us—must await the return/revelation of the Abyss of Being, and while awaiting, we must do three things: We must *destroy metaphysics* (as he himself attempts in his History of Being [see Rapaport 1989]); then when the opportunity comes, we must *situate ourselves in the Abyss/Storm of Being*; and finally, we must *respond to the revelation* (let the Being/*logos* be our guide/*hegemon*).[36] Unlike Nietzsche, Heidegger is very goal driven. Though he might appear to be nomadic, he is not!

As I have said, to Plato and perhaps most of us, such a response—given Heidegger's own criteria—is *not* authentic, but inauthentic and downright dangerous. Moreover, the Heideggerian response, as a prescription or prognosis, perhaps sounds to our ears simply ludicrous. If it does, it is primarily because Heidegger's *philosophy of history* is very contrary to the commonly accepted view. (I might add, however, that it sounds different only to certain intellectuals or academics, for I suspect that it does not sound so strange or ludicrous to certain evangelist preachers or ministers.) Heidegger did not see history as The History of the Enlightenment (as a Grand-historicist Narrative of Emancipation, from the slavery of ignorance to the freedom of rationality), but saw history as destiny, *Moira*.[37] Whereas the Enlightenment view of history depicts events as chronological and as Platonic and as Aristotelian rational-understandable causal links, Heidegger's view depicts events not based on *chronos* but on *kairos*, and, therefore, sees events as *not* being rational-understandable. It is *kairos* that creates, through a revelation, a radically new future. The consequences of Heidegger's view of history as *kairoetic* are sweeping. Gillespie explains:

> In establishing *a new future* the revelation of Being also establishes *a new past*, a new tradition that is appropriate to or commensurate with this future. Being thus unfolds itself *not merely forward but also backward* out of the kairos. Each revelation of Being gives rise to a new history or tradition and every history is thus a selection or re-collection of what has been, according to the new goals and standards that Being establishes. (158; emphasis mine)

Time, from a *kairoetic* perspective, is greatly different from that of *chronos/* traditional Historicism. And also different is the kind of politics that each allows for and subscribes to.

Heidegger tells us that Historicism gives us inauthentic politics and, quite differently, his *kairoetic* view of history allows for the possibility of "authentic" politics—that is, a politics in line with The Question of Being. Gillespie tells us:

> There is in [Heidegger's] view no inevitable or irresistible necessity that impels man toward one particular goal. This does not mean that man has no goal. Rather, man dwells in the question of his goal, i.e., in the question of Being as the question of the character and relationship of the *has been*, i.e., the tradition, and the *to be*, i.e., the goal, as they appear in the *is*, i.e., the kairos. Man's place in the world arises out of his dwelling within this question and his attendant listening and corresponding to it. . . . How man is to be, the character of the ethical and political constellations of human being can be apprehended only within the kairos of this aporia. (164)

What is necessary to recall is that Heidegger's is not *initially* a philosophy of choice. He is not a Humanist. (See his "Letter on Humanism," 1977; cf.

Rapaport 1989, 104–74.) The *logos* is a powerful force that acts on us, when we are in an authentic relationship with it. (It is *logos* that establishes the grounds, or conditions, for subsequent political action.) After acted on by the *logos*, we then choose, if at this stage such an action can still be considered "choice."

In describing Heidegger's view of *logos*, the uncanny, and *kairos*, I have not in the least suggested how his view of these concepts differ from my discussion of them in previous or in later chapters. It is not enough, of course, to assume that the reader can infer how I differentiate my view from Heidegger's view. Moreover, simply because I identify with Nietzsche instead of Heidegger is not enough, for most readers would see little difference between the two. It is my eventual purpose, however, to distinguish myself and my reading of Nietzsche from Heidegger. As we proceed now into "The Rector's Address," I will more specifically be laying the groundwork for differences. It still is, as I have repeatedly stated, the conditions of the possibilities for a historiography that would lead to *unification* (variously imperialism, colonization) by way of exclusion that I am searching for. I see these conditions, which are a *nostalgia*—the conditions for being *homesick*, in the face of the *unhomely* (*nostos*/home + *algia*, *algos*/pain, sick)—as being modern. Hence, I would search for postmodern conditions. That are *without guilt*. Heidegger was deeply into philosophical guilt (yes, another word for the negative).

Chapter 5

❦

Heidegger, Wesen, and "The Rector's Address"

Then there is Heidegger the Nazi, that is: the dues-paying member of the NSDAP from 1933 to 1945 (card number 312589, Gau Baden).

—Thomas Sheehan

IIIB: Being/*Logos*, *Hegemon*, Imperialism, and The Rector's/Rhetor's Address

It is with "The Rector's Address" (1985a) that we see Heidegger's particular view of history and what role education is to have in that history. We also see where he goes astray. In examining this address, I will take into consideration Heidegger's 1945 retrospective essay "The Rectorate 1933/34: Facts and Thoughts" (1985b), which functions as an *apologia* for his speech under the National Socialist party.[1] I will not, however, discuss, except in passing, Heidegger's connection with the NSDAP and Nazism. I think he was connected.[2] However, I agree more so with what Ijsseling has recently said: "For me, the only appropriate motivation for a philosopher [or rhetorician] to judge Heidegger and National Socialism is the desire to become aware of National Socialist tendencies in our own thinking" (1992, 7). After all, whether we want to acknowledge it or not, *Heidegger is one of us*! We are all connected with fascism.[3] I would add also that I am suspicious of those critics who have made their careers, in part or whole, on bludgeoning Heidegger over and over again. There is something pathological about it all. I am reminded of what Peter Sloterdijk has to say about Marx's scathing attack on Max Stirner in *The German Ideology*; it is, in its excessiveness, psychopathological (see 1987, 92–97). I also am reminded of Freud's statement that criticisms of Others are more often than not self-criticisms.

191

Let us now turn to "The Rector's Address" and examine some pertinent passages. As I proceed, I will occasionally call upon such commentators as Richard Wolin, Charles Scott, and Phillipe Lacoue-Labarthe.

"The Leaders are Themselves Led": Heidegger was elected by his colleagues to the Rectorate. On May 27, 1933, Heidegger, at the University of Fariburg delivered his acceptance speech. His opening statement reads:

> The assumption of the rectorate is the commitment to the *spiritual* [Heidegger's emphasis] leadership [*Führung*] of this institution of higher learning. The following of teachers and students awakens and grows strong only from a true and joint rootedness in the *essence* [*Wesen*] of the German university. This essence, however, gains clarity, rank, and power *only when first of all and at all times the leaders are themselves led* [*die führer selbst Geführte sind*]—led by that unyielding spiritual mission that forces the fate of the German people to bear the stamp of its history. (1985a, 470; emphasis mine)

Like any philosopher or rhetor, Heidegger looks, in this deliberative, partly epideictic, speech, for a way to ground/found his argument.[4] It should come as no surprise that he decides on "spirit" (*Geist*) and "essence" (*Wesen*). Like many German thinkers, he invests much in Spirit. It is this transcendental essence—present-though-absent in the Question (or abyss) of Being—that leads, or should lead, "the fate of the German people." ("The Rector's Address" precedes, by thirteen/fourteen years, Heidegger's "Letter on Humanism," with its theme of being led.)

The immediate, primary parallel that I would draw between Isocrates and Heidegger is that between *logos* (as *hegemon*) and essence (as guide). Both are "implanted" (*eggenomenou*)[5] and "imprinted" (*Gepräge*) on the people. Both lead, or guide, or choose the people. Lacoue-Labarthe points to "spiritual leadership [*Führung*]" as "hegemony," as "conducting or . . . guiding" (1989, 276). Heidegger says that essence is to guide the university and its faculty and students ("the leaders themselves are led [*die führer selbst Geführte sind*])"; but also that essence, in guiding the rector, allows the rector, in turn, to guide the faculty and the students. Hence, we get the *Führer* principle. Or we get what Lacoue-Labarthe calls the "hegemony of hegemony" (276–77); that is, essence leads the leaders who lead the others. (As I suggested earlier, Jaspers claims that Heidegger believed that he was to "lead the leader," Hitler himself.) A corollary to this statement that essence is to lead is that the essence of the German people (*deutsches Volk*), likewise, is to lead, the rector, who, in turn, is to lead the institution, that is, the faculty and the students. As we continue, this essence becomes science, knowledge, as practiced by the pre-Socratics, or so Heidegger would think it. However, in the context of my discussion in chapter 2, Heidegger has a greater kinship with Isocrates (the principle of hegemony, compounded) than with Gorgias or Nietzsche (*dynamis*) or any pre-Socratic.

In every case, it is essence leading Heidegger (the poet, the surrogate prince, anointed guide, analogically the adviser to Nicocles) so that he might lead the leader, who (by proxy?) might lead the chosen people. (Recall the potential relationship between Isocrates and Archidamus and, then, ten years later between Isocrates and Philip of Macedon.)[6] The "guiding" connections are essence-Heidegger-the *Führer*. However, let us not forget that if all power is finally centralized in Hitler, to guide or to interpret essence for Hitler, as Heidegger would, then, is to be an all-powerful guide. I am exaggerating my point here to make it. But as Wolin discloses, Joseph Sauer (the vice rector) reports that Walter Eucken "complained" that Heidegger "saw himself as the greatest philosopher since Heraclitus" (1990, 188, n. 53). There is much narcissism here, finding one's place in the history of philosophy and the Third Reich. But this may all be sour grapes, with narcissism endemic to all parties.

"Self-Governance": After his opening statement Heidegger takes on the concept of "self-governance," which he later associates negatively with the concept of "academic freedom." To achieve "self-goverance," Heidegger says, it "must be grounded in self-examination. Self-Examination, however, presupposes that the German university possesses the strength to *self-assertion*. Will we enact it? And how?" (1985a, 471; Heidegger's emphasis). The educational system, Heidegger says, is "the *primordial*, shared will to its essence. [It is] *grounded in science*, [and] by means of science educates and *disciplines* the leaders and guardians of the fate of the German people. The will to the essence of the German university is the will to science as will to the historical mission of the German people. . ." (471; emphasis mine). As Charles Scott explains, "On the one hand, the faculty and students must mold their passion to essence. On the other hand, essence must be approachable by powerful, willful exertion" (1990, 150).[7]

Greeks and Germans, and Historical Being: Next, Heidegger makes the link between "science" *and* Greek philosophy, which is also a link between the Greeks *and* the Germans. (Which is an explicit link Hitler makes in *Mein Kampf*: "The struggle that rages today is for very substantial goals: a culture is fighting for its existence, a culture that involves thousands of years of development and that embraces Greece and Germany together" [qtd. in Farias 1989, 100]. Let us also not forget Jaeger's same link in 1939 [in German][8] and Heidegger's in 1959, 37–38; 57.) Heidegger writes: "Only if we again place ourselves under the power of the beginning of our spiritual-historical being (*Desein*). This beginning is the setting out of Greek philosophy. Here, for the first time, western man raises himself up from a popular base and, by virtue of his language, stands up to the *totality of what is*" (1987a, 471; Heidegger's emphasis). Scott reads this passage as Heidegger's establishing a parallel between Greece and Germany, in that just as "Greek philosophy rises above the Greek *Volkstum*, that is, above the Greek national, ontic, and ethnic character," German philosophy and the university should do the same (1990, 153). Scott writes: "one could expect at this point a severe critique of German political culture, and why such a critique is not forthcoming focuses our own questions [of political concern] about Heidegger's address" (157; cf. Heidegger 1977, 218-19).

The Poet ("the work") Leads the Polis ("the works"): As Wolin stresses at length, Heidegger's view of the Greeks and especially the Greek *polis* is highly problematic (1990, 114–17). Whereas we rightly or wrongly think of Greece as the cradle of democracy, Heidegger did not. Like Isocrates, but perhaps more so, he viewed democracy in extreme by negative terms. Heidegger viewed the Greek *polis* as a work of art, or as "the work for the works" (see Heidegger 1977, 149–87). (Here we have Heidegger's aesthetic, not Nietzsche's.) Wolin explains that the Heideggerian artist and his [*sic*] art, to be "authentic," must open up the relation between Being and (human) beings. That is, the relation between "the Work for the works." It must not be internal (lyrical, romantic, or modern) art, but epical, as Homer's was for the Greeks, since Homer's was "an 'authentic repetition' of the Greek beginning" (1990, 110). If Homer is one poet, Heraclitus is another. Analogies between Greece and Germany abound in Heidegger's mind: As Wolin points out, Hölderlin is analogous with Homer, and Heidegger himself, with Heraclitus. These "authentic" artists (Plato, Isocrates, Heidegger) are to guide by way of an originary ethics. The artist is to be "the 'voice of the Volk,' " while "world-creating, history-founding" (110).[9]

In further explaining Heidegger's view of the artist, Wolin cites a passage in *An Introduction to Metaphysics* that I quoted earlier in another context. The passage can now explain that the *polis* can be the site of Being, where real poets and leaders are given the opportunity authentically to create and build political space. Heidegger writes:

> *Polis* is usually translated as city or city-state. This does not capture the full meaning. *Polis* means, rather, the place, the there, wherein and as which historical being-there [*Dasein*] is. The *polis* is the historical place, the there *in* which *out of* which and *for* which history happens. To this place and scene of history belong the gods, the temples, the priests, the festivals [etc.].

All this does not first belong to the *polis*, does not become political by entering into a relation with a statesman and a general and the business of the state. No, it is political, i.e., at the site of history, provided there be . . . poets *alone*, but then really poets, priests *alone*, but then really priests, rulers *alone*, but then really rulers. (qtd. in Wolin 1990 115; Heidegger 1959, 152; Heidegger's emphasis)

Wolin says this passage is "latently totalitarian: when the state—and the 'destiny of a historical *Volk*' that is its *raison d'etre*—are accorded unchallenged ontological primacy as 'the work for the works,' the autonomy and integrity of the other spheres of life (social, cultural, religious) disappears" (115–16). He continues: "The Greeks could solve this potential danger via the institution of direct democracy." (Let us not also forget that there is Nietzsche's view and account of *Vernichtungskampf* [the extermination struggle], which Nietzsche argues against in "Homer's Contest," in favor of *agôn* as *Wettkampf* [joust], with no one dominating over others.) However, for Heidegger, Wolin says, "the opposite is true: since his twentieth century polis/state is integrally tied to the *Führerprinzip*, it becomes a *Führerstaat*, a new form of political tyranny, which political space shrivels up into the person of the *Führer* and his sycophantic entourage" (116). (Recall Kenneth Burke's review of Hitler's battle.) That the leader is to be "authentic" does not stop him [*sic*] from actually being "inauthentic."

The Closing of the Question of Being: As Heidegger continues, his references to "spirit" and "essence" begin to speak for extreme unity (totality) and to border on racism:

If we will the essence of science understood as the *questioning, unguarded holding of one's ground in the midst of the uncertainty of the totality of what-is, this* will to essence will create for our people its world, a world of the innermost and most extreme danger, i.e., its truly *spiritual* world. For "spirit" is neither empty cleverness, nor the noncommittal play of wit, nor the endless drift of rational distinctions, and especially not world reason; spirit is primordially attuned, knowing resoluteness toward the essence of Being. And the *spiritual world* of a people is not the superstructure of a culture, no more than it is an armory stuffed with useful facts and values; it is the power that most deeply preserves the people's strengths, *which are tied to earth and blood* [my emphasis]; and as such it is the power that most deeply moves and most profoundly shakes its being (*Dasein*) (474–75; Heidegger's emphasis).

In reference to unity (totality), Scott says, Heidegger's "thought is overwhelmed by the ideas and ideals of unity, which are firmly associated with the *Führer* principle and by the German ethos of which he is a part" (1990, 161). For a philosopher who speaks for guarding the question, he here only closes it. Little by little, more by more, Heidegger engages in *negative essentializing*, closing down the Question of Being. The limited, unity, the determinate (individuation) is favored over the unlimited, disunified, the indeterminate (or Anaximander's *to apeiron*). Or *Physis*[neg.] is favored over *Physis*[nonpositive affirmation]. Heidegger is in line with National Socialism; how could he *think* that he thinks otherwise? How could he think that his thinking, as Nietzsche understood thinking, is an exception to being-reactionary? (Or is this Heidegger's "error[,] the space in which history unfolds" [1984, 26]?)

In reference to blood, it is here, in speaking of culture (*paideia*)/spirit and blood, that Heidegger differs from Isocrates, who advocates an "intellectual nationalism" not a "racial nationalism" (1980, 149; see Jaeger 1986b, 79). And yet, Is Heidegger speaking in terms of biology? As I stated earlier in chapter 4, in my discussion of the word *Geschlecht* (one meaning of which is "blood") and its historical context in German thinking, Derrida quotes from an unpublished letter, in which Heidegger says that he meant "national" not "nationalism," not "a biologicist and racist ideology" (see Derrida 1987, 165).

Organizing the Body: Heidegger next makes a connection between the German Student Body and "the new Student Law," which was proclaimed on May 1, 1933, in order to organize students under the *Führerprinzip* so as, in turn, to consolidate all universities under the Nationalist Socialist State. Unity, unity, unity. Schiller's perfect aesthetic society, as totality, is being realized (see Schiller 1967, 300; de Man 1984, 263–90). It was this radical student body, totally committed to the *Führer* (the local leader such as Heidegger at Freiburg and *The* Leader Hitler at Berlin) and its essence (*logos* as guide, *hegemon*)—as negative essence—that was to reshape the faculty and to redefine the concept of "academic freedom":

> Out of the resoluteness of the German student body to be equal to the German fate [*Moira*] in its most extreme distress, comes a will to the essence of the university. This will is a true will in that the German student body, through the new Student Law, places itself under *the law of its own essence* and in this way for the first time determines that essence. To give the law to oneself is the highest freedom. The much celebrated "academic freedom" is being *banished* from the German university; for this freedom was not genuine, since it was only negative. It meant primarily freedom from concern, arbitrariness of intentions and inclinations, lack of restraint in what was done and left undone. (475–76; emphasis mine).

The concluding section focuses on the three bonds/services, the first two of which were part and parcel of the National Socialist Party, *Labor*

Service, Armed Service, and finally that which Heidegger added, *Knowledge Service* (476). Unity, unity, unity. Greek-German Unity! Heidegger says: "The three bonds . . . are *equally primordial* to the German [negative] essence. The three services that stem from it . . . are equally necessary and of equal rank" (477; Heidegger's emphasis). Heidegger ends his speech with a reference to the "battle [*polemos*] community of teachers and students," and with a reference to Germany's "historical mission," and to the quote, or misquotation, from Plato: "All that is great stands in the storm" (479–80; see *Republic* 497d, 9). This passage is typically translated as "everything great is at risk" or ". . . precarious" (see Wolin 1990, 90; cf. Derrida 1993, 196–203).

Heidegger, much unlike Nietzsche, practices a reactionary thinking and aesthetic. We can see that he seeks unity/totality (congregation) at the price of exclusion (segregation). That he was *given to such totalizing*—in spite of his statements to the contrary—Heidegger had suggested already in his 1929 inaugural address, "What is Metaphysics?" He said:

> The various sciences are far apart and their subjects are treated in fundamentally different ways. This uncoordinate diversity of disciplines today can be held together only through the technical organization of the universities and faculties and through the practical intent of their subject matters. The rooting of intellectual disciplines in the grounds of their being has died away. (qtd. Lacoue-Labarth 1989, 273; see Heidegger 1977, 96; cf. Heidegger 1990, 43)

Heidegger had thought (thinks) ideology first, Being next.

Many of these statements and images, which were common *topoi* among German intellectuals, came to haunt Heidegger. (Come to haunt us, for let us never forget Heidegger *is* one of us.) It is his *language* (culture), which indicates his sympathy with the Nazis. It is his actions, which indicate his sympathy with the Nazis. He was numbered (ac*count*ed for) among them: 312589, *Gau Baden*. That Germany was in a national, economic mess after World War I, and that the 1930's were a time during which there was a hope for a "revolution" to regain a sense of national honor under National Socialism (see 1985b, 483; and letter to Herbert Marcuse in Farias 1989, 284–85) are all easy to understand; and that finally a handful of *criminals* got hold of the party is equally easy to understand. (The time was ripe for bandits.) However, such understandings cannot warrant an excuse or much less our acceptance.

> We can never know what to want, because, living only one life, we can neither compare it with our previous lives nor perfect it in our lives to come. [. . .] But . . . whether they [the

communists] knew or didn't know is not the main issue; the main issue is whether a man is innocent because he didn't know. Is a fool on the throne [such as Oedipus] relieved of all responsibility merely because he is a fool?

—Milan Kundera

Again, I am not going to delve deeply into the politics of Being and Nazism, for there are studies aplenty. It is Heidegger's language and its concomitant (reactionary) thinking that I wish to continue to look at in passing; for it is language (*logos* as our guide/*hegemon*-cum-*Führer*) that is the issue for me here. And *our* relationship to it. It is not, therefore again, just a simple matter of "us" and "them"; we ourselves are potentially Heidegger.

As I stated previously, Heidegger's *logos* and his *physis* (essence, *Wesen*) are both positive and negative (hence, *logos*[pos./neg.]). However, it is a *logos* and a *physis* that, in this address and in his actions, emphasize a negation, an exclusion, of others; that favors Greeks-Germans over all others. (Recall Derrida's questions: Are we Jews? Are we Greeks? Or do we live in the difference between the two?) Moreover, Heidegger's is a negation that practices forgetfulness. His is a practice of being a *leader* not a *guardian* of the Question of Being. As Lyotard writes:

> How could this thought (Heidegger's), a thought so devoted to remembering that a forgetting (of Being) takes place in all thought, in all art, in all "representation" of the world, how could it possibly have ignored the thought of "the jews" [i.e., the Other], which, in a certain sense, thinks, tries to think, nothing but that very fact? How could this thought forget and ignore "the jews" to the point of suppressing and foreclosing to the very end of the horrifying (and inane) attempt at exterminating, at making us forget forever what, in Europe, reminds us, ever since the beginning, that "there is" [*Es gebt*] the Forgotten? (1990, 4)

What Heidegger finally does is to engage in *negative essentializing*. (I have spoken in previous chapters repeatedly about the danger of negation, which is usually brought about by way of a grandnarrative. E.g., today Germany, tomorrow the world.) Therefore, it must be stated now, given the motif that I have employed throughout this book, Heidegger finally engages in *logos*[neg.] and *physis*[neg.].

This view of the *logos*, however, is not just Heidegger's. It is Greek— the Greek of our western heritage; it is the general view of *logos*. Hence, lest it appear that I am critiquing only Heidegger, or only National Socialism, I critique our collective views of *logos*. As Ijsseling suggests and I repeat, "the only appropriate motivation for a philosopher [or rhetorician] to judge Heidegger and National Socialism is the desire to become aware of National Socialist tendencies in our own thinking" (1992, 7). This *logos* that I have been examining, therefore, is not just a German *logos* (cultural, *nomos*[neg.]) but a transethnic-transracial *logos* (*physis*[neg.]). None of us is safe, for we inevitably and innocently have *logos* as our guide.

My sense is that at some level of thinking, Heidegger is aware of this problem of negation, though he is not willing to admit it, or if to admit it, to resolve it. As I read Heidegger, it *appears* that he is engaged contradictorily, on the one hand, in the *will to power* (to an infinite play of differences) and, on the other, and much to his and others' deprecation, in the *will to truth* (to a finite play of sameness). As I said, he engages in *logos*[pos./neg.]. Now, I say "contradictorily" because Heidegger, for a crucial historical period of time, appears to feign the will to power itself, that is, the perpetual interrogation of the Question of Being; hence, though it might appear in the first case that he might encourage such perpetual interrogation, such a will never to forget, he, nonetheless, strives for the will to truth (unity, Hitler's National Socialism), which is the will to forgetfulness. After all, he sits and waits for the revelation of Being, in other words, for the "truth." In both cases, he inevitably practices negation.

This is all rather complicated, and certainly not as easily put as I have introduced it here. Therefore, a closer examination is necessary. First, under the rubric of *the will to power*, I will examine Heidegger's argument based on philology; then, his argument based on time. His first argument goes such and such: *I said/meant this, not this. The audience did not understand me.* His second argument: *I spoke not really to you my contemporaries but to a man a thousand years henceforth.* This latter argument is also tied up with Heidegger's distinction between "error" and "truth" (see 1984, 26).

As I proceed under this rubric of the *will to power*, I will be laying the groundwork for the second rubric, Heidegger's *will to truth*. My hypothesis is that Heidegger—because he would not acknowledge the reasonableness of his audience's other possible interpretation of what he had to say (that there are both right ears and left ears)—moved strategically from a will to power (many competing meanings) to a will to truth (one meaning, "my" meaning). This argument about what a Greek word means parallels his penchant for political unity (or National Socialism). Though Heidegger would have us guard the Question of Being, he would have it answered. (He opts for revelation.) Though Heidegger eventually denounces Hitler, he never denounces the possibilities of National Socialism. Again, the hypothesis is that though Heidegger speaks of the will to power and interrogation,

Heidegger finally favors a will to truth and the answer. His is a nostalgic (modernist) philological longing for the saying of Being. He would find a home for some (oasis), while he would directly or indirectly find a locus of exclusion (mirage) for Others.

Will to Power (to an infinite play of differences): Heidegger, in his "The Rectorate 1933/34: Facts and Thoughts," which is a commentary on, and defense of, "The Rector's Address" is aware of the trouble that he is in with his language (*logos*), a language that expresses his penchant for German abstractions with quasi-allegorical multiple interpretations, many of which are not at all flattering to him or to his work. There is the additional problem of Heidegger's moral-political silence. Here we are again with the Platonic problem of getting language to mean only what the author consciously intends and what the language "precisely means." Since Heidegger is a radical nonhumanist and since he believes that Being speaks—though not clearly, because withdrawing—he has placed himself in a difficult position of not being able to defend himself against common-sense charges of what he does nor does not mean. Normally, someone would not have to defend himself or herself to the degree that Heidegger finds that he does. Because of his party membership, however, what he says as a philosopher, as a thinker concerning education, will be read in especially narrow political terms. (Here *ethos* greatly informs *logos*.) As we know, Heidegger has problems defending himself. Yet he tries, and in trying, tries to redefine his problem not as a rhetorical failure on his part but, most explicitly, as the failure of the audience to hear his attempt at what Heidegger calls *originary* thinking. It could be said that his audience—specifically, his critics—need to hear his words mean one thing (that which will serve their interests), while Heidegger himself needs to hear his words mean one other thing (that which will serve his interests). Left ears; right ears. The infinite play of these words, what we call Heidegger's words, are being divided up, or determined, by the various wills to truth (narrowly defined interests). Both various members of Heidegger's audience and Heidegger himself employ different gods (forces) to read Heidegger's (or the *logos*'s) meaning.

Let us now turn to Heidegger's word. Specifically, it is Heidegger's use of the Greek, Heraclitean word *polemos*, which gets primarily interpreted by others as "war"—that is, as Heidegger's being in support of a war to be fought by Germany to regain/reclaim its destiny in the world, Pangermanism, a war that, I might add, is similar to Isocrates's call for a war against the Persians so that there might be a resurgence of Panhellenism. This point about Heidegger's wanting war may be debatable, but about Isocrates's it most certainly is not. (The reference, in Heidegger's case is to his statement concerning the "battle [*polemos*] community of teachers and students" [1985a, 479]. To be sure, this analogy is not uncommon. As I have pointed out, Leavis and Gerald Graff themselves have spoken of such a struggle, though the moment—i.e., the historical moments—of saying it are dramatically different for them. And then, there is Nietzsche's use of it [1969, 273]. *Kairos* can make for a truly opportune moment, in both happy and unhappy, productive and counterproductive ways for the rhetor.)

In his defense, Heidegger says: "We [should] not think [*polemos*] as war and, furthermore, appeal to the supposedly Heraclitean proposition 'War is the father of all things' to proclaim war and battle as the highest principle of all being and thus to offer a philosophical justification of the warlike" (1985b, 488–89). Many commentators see this statement, however, as only a false alibi. If it were not for Heidegger's repeated conduct (his *ethos*), his statement concerning *polemos* might be more acceptable (see Wolin 1990, 91–95; cf. Derrida 1993, 210–16). As Heidegger continues in his defense, he gets deeper and deeper into explaining *the* meaning of—as a way of defending himself from—Heraclitus's fragments. (All rests on fragments!) He attempts to defend himself by conducting a seminar on pre-Socratic Greek; however, such esoterica—given the circumstances—only exacerbates his problem.

As Heidegger continues his "The Rectorate 1933/34: Facts and Thoughts," he attacks his audience. It is as if, for Heidegger, the ear is not at all uncanny![10] What is pathetic, yet ironic, is that Heidegger shifts in his own defense from will to power (differences, *différance*) to will to truth (unity, sameness). He will not admit that his use of *polemos* could have meant what his audience—yesterday and today—took it, indeed, literally or suspiciously to mean. Heidegger did not or could not see that his use of *logos* would be semiotically read across his *ethos* and the spirit of the time (*Geist*).

But it is not just the word *polemos*, for Heidegger attacks his 1933 audience for not understanding the word "Self-Assertion" in the title. He writes, "The address was not understood by those whom it concerned; neither was its content understood, nor was it understood in this respect: that it states what during the time I was in office gave me the guiding thread [hegemonic thread?] for distinguishing what was essential from what was less essential and only external. To be sure, the address and with it my attitude were grasped even less by the party and the relevant agencies" (1985b, 489–90).

Heidegger will not admit of other possible interpretations of his text and interrogate them. (He, too, would be an advocate of Skinner's axiom that a thinker cannot be made to agree with an interpretation of his/her work that they did not intend!)[11] Heidegger ponders the abyss of Being, stands in the storm (Heidegger 1968, 17; 1984, 78) and greatly commits an error (1984, 26)—at least, from his audiences's point of view—but he cannot admit to the possibility of such an error. And yet, Oedipus does!

At best, Heidegger seems, on occasion and in retrospect, to argue that in 1933–34 he was *apolis* venturing toward a yet-to-be-born new *polis*. Not having made it to the other side of Hitler's (or Heidegger's own) philosophy of history—not having realized his hoped-for "repetition" of what-was-but-had-not-yet-been—would obviously not permit Heidegger finally to say that a new (or primordial, originary) order had been established.[12] Instead, Heidegger blames the audience. He blames Hitler. He even blames Nietzsche for misleading him (see Wolin 1990, 141). He simply sits in silence and waits.[13] (Is it happening? Is the revelation at hand?) Being silent, after all, is the task of thinking itself, the task "that would be authentic saying" (Heidegger 1982, 52–53, 11–136). As Lacoue-Labarthe reminds us, Heidegger in a televised comment in reference to his essay "The End of Philosophy and the Task of Thinking" says: "A thinker yet to come who will perhaps one day approach the task of effectively assuming that thinking for which I am attempting to lay the ground, will have to come to terms with something Heinrich von Kleist once wrote: 'I stand aside for one who is not yet here and I bow, over a distance of a thousand years, before his mind' " (qtd. in Lacoue-Labarthe 1990, 106; for Heidegger's essay, see 1977, 369–92). If there had been some tiny amount of conscious self-deprecation, self-mocking in this statement, it would have possibly undercut the pathology of it all. (Compare Nietzsche who in *The Gay Science* writes: "We must find the *hero* no less than the *fool* in our passion for knowledge. . . . [And vice versa, for] Nothing does us as much good as a *fool's cap*" [1974, 164]. Nietzsche also claimed that he was posthumous man, but he also knew that he would be greatly misunderstood—knew why he was a destiny—and that people hungry for negative power would misuse him, would close down the aphorism by electing one meaning instead of thinking the differences. He knew of right ears. [See 1969, 326–27].) It is, indeed, sad to see Heidegger not being able to admit to, or even entertain the idea with, Herbert Marcuse, in their exchange of letters, that the Holocaust was an evil act; instead, he simply compares it to another "evil" act—the placement of the East Germans into the hands of the Soviets (see Farias 1989, 283–87). Marcuse evidently was not the man for whom he and his thoughts must continue to await! And yet, let me emphasize, from Heidegger's point of view, though silent about the Holocaust, he nonetheless speaks, for he maintained that silence *is* a form of speaking. Which few can hear and understand. We, instead, would read silence as a tacit admission of guilt! We listen as reactionaries.

Yet, given Heidegger's quasi-allegorical language, *something* by ill-virtue of negation, indeed, *was in a sense heard and understood*. Heidegger is like the character, played by Peter Sellers, in the novel/film *Being There (Da-Sein)*: The character, a half-wit gardener speaks of gardening but he is taken, even by the President of the United States, as speaking about State Politics. *Logos* is dangerous! (As I have pointed out, Christ in Kazantzakis's *Last Temptation* suffers from the confusion of his Father's voice, the *logos*, which speaks in doubleness and places him in a double bind, makes him into a hysteric [see Kazantzakis 1960; Zizek 1989; Vitanza 1993].) It can be "that way" *on the way to language*! If for the Son of Being, so for being. If for Heidegger, so for humankind. If for the Greeks, so for their heritage.

We are not at home in *logos*; and yet, as Heidegger writes, "language is the house of Being. In its home man dwells. Those who think and those who create with words are the *guard*ians of this home. Their guardianship accomplishes the manifestation of Being insofar as they bring the manifestation to language and maintain it in language through their speech" (1977, 193; cf. Rapaport 1989, 104–74). Heidegger knew this uncanniness of *logos*: It is the hallmark of his philosophizing, and eventually of his life, which he unfortunately did not guard (against) and, then, attempted to deny.[14] He has written: "We must guard against the blind urge to snatch at a quick answer in the form of a formula" (1968, 48). Heidegger put far too much faith in the *logos*. He did not practice, as in a newer praxis, a hermeneutics of suspicion. (As Ernesto Laclau suggests, the *logos* itself is a "Stalinist phenomenon" [see Zizek 1989, 212].) He was not suspicious for "what does call for thinking?" (Heidegger 1968, 48). To be sure, we must stand in the storm of the *logos*, but we must not put our singular or collective faith in the ontological vocation (Being's [negative] possibilities of calling, or revealing, to us).[15]

Having said this about Heidegger, however, my more important point is that Being—finally and at bottom—for Heidegger is a negative essentialism. It is fundamentally absent. Hence, the greater possibilities of nostalgia (homesickness). This is not to suggest that if Being were present, for Heidegger and philosophical types, that it would not be in the form of the negative (1977, 110). This is a difficult point to make clear, which I will attempt to make clear in relation to Gorgias, chapters 6 and 7. Being (*physis*) is conceived of traditionally as a negative essentialism. Hence, lest we forget, whereas Heidegger would see Being in negative terms, I would—following Nietzsche, Bataille, Deleuze and Guattari, and Judith Butler—denegate those terms.[16] (Let us continue this discussion in the next section.)

Will to Truth (to a finite play of sameness): Thus far, in discussing the Heideggerian will to power, I have tried to suggest that Heidegger's will *is* to truth (unity, totality), not power (affirmative play of differences). Now, I want to point still more specifically to his incipient rage for will to unity.

I have already suggested Heidegger's numerous attempts to establish unity by way of negative essence, but let us round out this discussion by returning to his penchant for a special Greek-German narrative unity.

If Isocrates believed we are to follow the *logos*, to allow it to be our guide/*hegemon*, this *logos* tragically led the German people and Heidegger astray. While Heidegger was following the *logos* as it revealed itself through Being (*physis*[neg.]), Heidegger's countryman Nietzsche had already turned his back on the Metaphysics of Being (see 1969, 45) and, instead, embraced an attempt to revalue values, which Heidegger would have nothing to do with. And why? Heidegger read Nietzsche as the last metaphysician (see 1991, 3: 8; 1977, 217–18). Heidegger, however—to return to what I was saying earlier—is a *negative* extension of Nietzsche. Heidegger reestablishes a (negative) metaphysics, and, therefore, himself may very well be the last metaphysician. The last man. Whereas Nietzsche and his recent commentators desire perpetually to denegate Being and *logos*, Heidegger finally keeps Being in a state of negation (unified by way of exclusion). It can be argued, however, that there is no way to escape metaphysics, and I would agree. In this light, I would claim that Nietzsche is one of very few, among a countertradition, of nonpositive affirmative metaphysicians, while Heidegger is a negative metaphysician.

An aside: It may be that, as Lacan would argue, the Question of (negative) Being is a fantasy; if so, then, this "fantasy," as Zizek explains Lacan's view, "is a means for an ideology to take its own failure into account in advance" (1989, 126). Heidegger must have known at some level that, contrary to his understanding of Nietzsche, he was going astray with his thinking, namely, that he was Being-reactionary (see 1968, 88–110). I might, likewise, say—if we are to be perpetually suspicious—that the Question of (nonpositive affirmative) Becoming is a fantasy. My position is that fantasy is all there is. Likewise, failure. I am no liberator, emancipator. Mine is not such a proclamation. And yet, I move into the future anterior, like Nietzsche, with a cheerful pessimism (1967, 17–18). Dispersion is the name of the game.

Let me explain greater how, in fact, Heidegger is a negative metaphysician, how he keeps Being in a state of negation (*physis*[neg.]). Lacoue-Labarthe has argued cogently that while Heidegger ostensibly in "The Rector's Address" talks about his theory of education in terms of a "spiritual mission," he is actually putting forth a political "doctrine of hegemony" (1989, 295). Lacoue-Labarth traces this stance back to *Being and Time* itself, where Heidegger speaks of the possibility of human relationships, of history. In 1927, Heidegger published the following statement:

> If fateful Dasein, as Being-in-the-world, exists essentially in Being-with-
> others, its historizing is a co-historizing and is determinative for it as

destiny [Heidegger's italics]. This is how we designate the historizing of the community, of a people. Destiny is not something that puts itself together out of individual fates, any more than Being-with-another can be conceived as the occurring together of several Subjects. Our fates have already been *guided* [my emphasis] in advance, in our Being with one another in the same world and in our resoluteness for definite possibilities. Only in communicating and in struggling [*polemos, Kampf*] does the power of destiny become free. (qtd. Lacoue-Labarthe 1989, 285; see Heidegger 1962, 436. Cf. Derrida 1993, 210–16)

Lacoue-Labarth reads this passage along side passages in "The Rector's Address," such as those that speak of the affinity and chosenness of both Greek and German essence, and asks: "But why, in spite of everything, should this privilege [of being chosen to lead, of being the hegemony of hegemony] be accorded to the *German* people? Why this mission, confided to it, of completing science?" (285; Lacoue-Labarth's emphasis; cf. Derrida 1993, 198). Indeed, why not Others? As is clear, Heidegger speaks from his nationalism, just as Isocrates before him. What is possible for Heidegger is determined by the impossible (the negative). His educational and political views have to be nationalistic, exclusionary.[17]

If, as I have claimed, Heidegger is a negative extension of Nietzsche, so is Nazism. To be sure, Nietzsche also gets appropriated by the Nazis, along with many other of our important thinkers. Be that as it may, however, Nietzsche was not a nationalist; he was a cosmopolitanist. He constantly critiqued and warned against German nationalism. In *Ecce Homo*, he writes:

"German" has become an argument, *Deutschland, Deutschland über alles* a principle; the Teutons represent the "moral world order" in history—the carriers of freedom versus the *imperium Romanum*, and the restoration of morality and the "categorical imperative" versus the eighteenth century.—There is now a historiography that is *reichsdeutsch*; there is even, I fear, an anti-Semitic one—there is a *court* historiography, and Herr von Tritschke is not ashamed—(1969, 319; Nietzsche's emphasis. Cf. 1974, 338–40; 1968b, 60–66.)

Nationalism, supernationalism as the Nazis practiced, was—and still is—negation. The Nazis misappropriated everything of Nietzsche's and others by ill-virtue of negation, *diaeresis*, for example, as aryan/nonaryan. There is nothing that cannot be negatively essentialized.

Negative essentializing. . . .

Excursus. A Feminist Sophistic?

Deckard: "She's [Rachel's] a replicant, isn't she."
Tyrell: "I'm impressed. How many questions does it usually
take to spot one?"
Deckard: "I don't get it, Tyrell."
Tyrell: "How many questions?"
Deckard: "Twenty to thirty crossed referenced."
Tyrell: "Took more than a hundred for Rachel, didn't it?"
Deckard: "She doesn't know."
Tyrell: "She's beginning to suspect, I think."
Deckard: "Suspect? How can it not know what it is?"
Tyrell: "Commerce is our goal here at Tyrell. More human than
human is our motto."

—*Blade Runner*

I want to continue here with a discussion of negative essentializing. As the title of this excursus might imply, I am going to interrogate Susan Jarratt's notion of a "feminist sophistic" as she discusses it in *Rereading the Sophists: Classical Rhetoric Refigured* (1991). In many ways this excursus sustains the discussion of the problems of negative essentializing as explored in chapter 1 and as continued throughout the chapters on Helen(ism), Isocrates, and Heidegger. This excursus both sustains and looks forward to a refiguring of Gorgias, Helen, and The History of Rhetoric: As chapter 2, "Helen[ism]," was a transition into the discussions of Isocrates and Heidegger's views of the *logos*, this excursus is a transition into and a linkage with the forthcoming chapters on Gorgias and the final (rebeginning?) excursis. While it was first necessary to reclaim the Sophists from negation and reclaim them in the name of a Third Sophistic, it is here necessary to speak of possible differences between a *Feminist Sophistic* (Jarratt) and a *Third Sophistic* (Vitanza), which, while similar and complementary, nonetheless, differ in political strategies and tactics.

207

And so wherever the Dionysian prevailed, the Apollonian was
checked and destroyed. But . . . it is equally certain that,
wherever the first Dionysian onslaught was successfully
withstood, the authority and majesty of the Delphic god
exhibited itself as more rigid and menacing than ever. For to
me the *Doric* state and Doric art are explicable only as a
permanent military encampment of the Apollonian.

—Nietzsche

Differences: Before continuing, we need to spend a little more time with
the Apollonians, that is, with Schiappa and Jarratt,[1] who first of all, do differ
in their attitudes toward *mythos* and *logos*, though they are similar in their
optimistic acceptance of reason/Enlightenment as cure. Schiappa, who thinks
in terms of fiction versus fact, would most likely say that *mythos* and *logos*
are different, with the latter superior to the former. *Mythos*, after all has been
said and undone, is the other of reason! Hence, he would go on to say (and
does) that we do not need the *mythos* called the Sophists. Jarratt's strategy
is different: Instead of privileging *mythos* over *logos*—as one might expect—
Jarratt introduces *nomos* as a middle term. Why? So as to establish a social-
epistemic space (*locus* or ground) within or upon which differences (race,
class, gender, nationalisms) can be identified and argumentively negotiated.
Nomos, however, stands with reason! *Nomos* is always structured under the
sign of the negative and, hence, necessarily excludes.

Second, while Schiappa engages in history rewriting by way of negative essentializing (there is/are *no* Sophists), Jarratt engages in revisions by
way of a similar, but very different essentializing ("only women" can [. . .],
etc. [*Rereading* 71]). To gain political leverage, Jarratt engages in a form of
essentializing that says, "only women can do such and such. . . ." In this
second difference, Jarratt is engaging in a simple negative deconstruction,
or reversal, of what men have been saying (only men can) for centuries. Only
women can = Feminist Sophistic.

Schiappa finds *nothing* essential among the so-called Sophists when he
attempts to define them by way of *diaeresis* or species-genus analytics (synecdoche); therefore, he dismisses them simply as a "mirage." Ah, the Phallic
Father. Jarratt, however, by way of *nothing*, finds *something* different between males and females. (The analogy, or refiguration, here is between
Sophists and women, who in Jarratt's eyes are similar because both have been
excluded.) With this heuristic analogy (Sophists = women), Jarratt is able
to reclaim—differently from Hegel or Grote's reclamations—the
marginalized groups known as Sophists and women for *the* or *a* history of

rhetoric. (Lest we forget, the reclamation, however, is achieved by way of exclusion! The rationale? What goes around comes around? A temporary love of power/fascism to overthrow power? Ah, the Phallic Mother!)

The political goal is of the utmost importance. A reader can misread Jarratt's "only women" statement, however, as being a form of naive essentialism.[2] Instead, Jarratt says: Helene Cixous's "practice can be described as strategic rather than essentialist" (70). Jarratt signals to us with the auxiliary "can" that she is engaging in a strategic misreading, a redescription, or partial casuistic stretching; hence, Jarratt's is not a naive, but a sophisticated, strategic essentialism. (Albeit, based on the sign of the negative!) In many ways, Schiappa insists on our thinking in masculinist terms (dividing practices); Jarratt insists in feminist terms (argumentative negotiations), and yet with a residual emphasis on a dividing practice (*diaeresis*) of female privileged over male. Essentially, it can be said, Jarratt reverses Schiappa. In their strategies, both are Doric. Rationality, whether it be old philological rationality or critical-pedagogical rationality, reign supreme in the form of the three principles of reason: identity, non-contradiction, and excluded middle (see N. Jay).

I. A Feminist Sophistic

The Liberal Temper Extended: In an earlier characterization of Jarratt's historiographical principles, I interpreted her as a "liberal" (1994c, 207), by which I mean that her reading of the Sophists is somewhat comparable to Eric Havelock's reading of them; to wit, the Sophists express "a liberal temper," or a penchant for democracy (see 1982, ch. 7).[3] It can be productive to see Jarratt in this tradition of thinking, for she is an advocate of a radical democracy, that is, for the inclusion of the excluded, yet exclusively women. (Jarratt's is a casuistic stretching of the project of the liberal temper: If there is to be a democracy, then, it should be for everyone, especially women. And yet, this democracy should be a new form, perhaps one predicated on feminist values.) Jarratt's pedagogy is linked up with what is labeled today as "critical pedagogy," that of Paulo Freire, Henry Giroux, Stanley Aronowitz, and Ira Shor (1991,107–12), which appears to pay its due to women as well as men.[4]

If Jarratt's expressing a liberal temper, how specifically so? There are any number of ways, but I would concentrate on two: The first is by way of a *middle term*, *nomos*, to be placed between the present-day extremes of *mythos* and *logos*, or orality and literacy; the second is by way of *strategic misreadings*.

A Middle Term, Nomos *(*Mythos/Logos*):* The search for a middle term—
though, not the excluded middle— is crucial for an understanding of Jarratt's
goal of emancipation. Instead of attempting to choose sides in the *mythos/
logos* or orality/literacy debate, Jarratt situates herself historiographically by
way of a middle term, *nomos.* Starting with social-political history, Jarratt
argues, from Jean-Pierre Vernant, for an event that can be described as the
historical refiguring of "political space" during the Mycenaean period. Instead of being determined by way of king to council to warriors and land-
owners, another political locus came about. Jarratt/Vernant say, "villagers,
each holding under a feudal arrangement a section of land called a *damos,*
met in a common space" for the purposes of "negotiating" (Jarratt, 40;
Vernant, 1982 32–34). They continue: "It was clearly not the interior of the
palace but rather a 'middle space,' in which 'those who contended with words
. . . became [even] in this hierarchical society a class of equals' " (40; Vernant
46). This space, Jarratt suggests, "created contexts for rhetorical discourse"
(40). Eventually, statutes (*thesmoi,* from the gods) are replaced by democratic reform (*nomos*) (41), which can be followed linguistically. An older
form of the word, *nomós,* meant "pasture," then "habitation," and most
importantly "habitual practice, usage, or custom" (41). *Nomos* becomes the
locus of *homologia.* As *nomos* is refigured as middle space, so is the agent
refigured. Jarratt now has a budding ethical subject.

> *Strategus* (Greek): Office or command of a general,
> generalship.
>
> —*OED*

> It's always clearly a question of war, of battle. If there is no
> battle, it's replaced by the stake of battle: strategy. Man is
> strategy. . . .
>
> —Cixous

Strategic Misreadings: At this point, Jarratt moves us from ancient
Greece to our contemporary scene of *logo/phallocentrism,* which still favors
a binary (machine) and hierarchical way of structuring society and language.
Males are privileged over females; logic over emotions; history over fiction;
mind over body; philosophy over sophistics; substance over style. (And oasis
over mirage.) It is necessary still today not only to include women but also
to rethink *logos* as "discourses of the 'other' " (63). In an attempt to further
expose these exclusions, Jarratt turns to the work that "has gone on under

the names of rhetoric in Nietzsche, of post-structuralist theory, which also claims Nietzsche as a forerunner, and of feminism" (*Rereading*, 66).[5] Jarratt ignores Nietzschean texts and concentrates on Derrida's reading Nietzsche's reading (*Spurs*) on the feminine, and on Gayatri Spivak's ("Displacement") reading Derrida's reading Nietzsche. This is all done very exclusively, as we will hear.[6] What Jarratt is questioning through Spivak's reading is both deconstruction and post-structuralism—whether or not they can be helpful to feminists, or to a reclamation of women and a female-sophistic style of discourse that would be appropriate for writing histories of rhetoric and for political discourse (in the middle space, *nomos*). Jarratt's answer is that deconstruction and post-structuralism *cannot* be helpful (66–69). There is, in Jarratt's and many other feminists' understandings, the problem of undecidability in deconstruction.[7]

Jarratt calls on Spivak's critique of Derrida in "Displacement and the Discourse of Woman." About deconstruction, Spivak writes: "a deconstructive discourse, even as it criticizes phallocentrism or the sovereignty of consciousness (and thus seeks to displace or 'feminize' itself according to a certain logic), must displace the figure of the woman twice over" (1983, 173). About Derrida, she writes:

> I learn from Derrida's critique of phallocentrism—but *I must then go somewhere else with it*. A male philosopher can deconstruct the discourse of the power of the phallus as "his own mistake." For him, the desire for the "name of woman" comes with the questioning of the "metaphysical familiarity which so naturally relates the we of the philosopher to 'we-men,' to the we in the horizon of humanity." This is an unusual and courageous enterprise, not shared by Derrida's male followers. (173; emphasis mine)

What I take Spivak to be saying is that deconstruction in the hands of a man, even Derrida, can only work to uncover for a man " 'his own mistake' " (173). It is important to note—for Jarratt does not point this out—that Spivak is quoting Derrida's own *autocritique* in his own words.[8] For Spivak, however, to "go somewhere else with it" (note, she does not say, without it) does not necessarily mean that she must abandon deconstruction (post-structuralism), as Jarratt would have us hear Spivak. I take the phrase "go somewhere else with it" to mean that Spivak is saying that she must do something other than what Derrida does with deconstruction in relation to the feminine. While deconstruction will not remove a male from his own history but only make him aware, Spivak does not need to be made aware. (That is, until a few years later, when she writes a sequel to this article!) Therefore, if Jarratt calls on Spivak's proper name, we need to be aware that Spivak is not saying No to deconstruction. (It is understandable that many feminists do not want to be

Derridaughters[9]; hence, the political and ethical necessity not only to reverse such a familial linkage but to displace it altogether. But let us hear it as such a strategy, namely, putting words in someone's mouth so that we might hear by way of the dividing practice of either right or left ears.)

But there is more at stake here than Spivak's attitude toward deconstruction, and that is *how* what she says in this 1983 article on displacement is to be read (appropriated)—either as a ground upon which to read in a feminist (woman's) way or as one deconstruction before another or as both. Yes, I'm bringing up the issues of appropriation and undecidability. After all, as good Sophists, we should all insist on the virtues of *dissoi logoi*. Therefore, I want to focus on Derrida's notion of *relever*, or turning the lever, so as to promote a particular interpretation that serves a reader's interest (see Derrida 1982, 88–108; 123–36). It is a matter now of learning how *to hear* what else is becoming-said. And yet, in dis/order to hear by way of not just two ears but a 'third,' we have to realize that the interests to be attended to are greater than either female or male. Hence, my interests in going beyond simple *dissoi logoi* toward *dissoi paralogoi* (which is a neologism of *dissoi logoi* and paralogy [see my 1987a, 52, 55–56]). In relation to the question concerning undecideability, I want to turn a lever showing how Spivak in a later article turns a lever so as once again to resituate herself via Derridean deconstruction and its reading of the question of woman.

Q: How have you changed in the last twenty years?

A: I ask less of deconstruction and I value it more.

—Spivak[10]

Spivak Reconsidered: The essay that was a sequel is published six years after "Displacement and the Discourse of Woman" and is entitled "Feminism and deconstruction, again: negotiating with unacknowledged masculinism." This article is difficult to summarize because often Spivak's meaning comes from juxtaposition and quick reversals that are only reversed once ever again. We are fortunate because Spivak has written an abstract of her own article:

> *Argument*. It is not just that deconstruction cannot found a politics, while other ways of thinking can. It is that deconstruction can make founded political programs more useful by making their in-built problems more visible. To act is therefore not to ignore deconstruction, but actively to transgress it without giving it up. . . . Feminism has a special situation here because, among the many names that Derrida gives to the problem/solution of founded programs, one is "woman." I explain in the essay why feminism should keep to the critical ways of deconstruction but give up

its attachment to that specific name for the problem/solution of founded programs. . . .

This is a more charitable position on the usefulness of deconstruction for feminism than I have supported in the past. It is a negotiation and an acknowledgement of complicity. This is the result of my recent teaching stint in India, which persuaded me that the indigenous elite must come to terms with its unacknowledged complicity with the culture of imperialism. Patriarchy/feminist theory is standing in for imperialism/postcoloniality here. (1989a, 206)

What comes through in Spivak's summary—and in the article—is that deconstruction is a way of reading and examining (political) programs and not a program in itself. To discard deconstruction because it does not have a political program in itself, or because it cannot found such a program, would be pointless; for deconstruction, in its strategies of reversal and displacement, in its various conditions, makes a politics possible, and yes, a materialist politics against the dominant discourse (see Spivak 1990, 46–47; 104–05). Those of us in rhetoric im/proper need to understand that the argument to reject deconstruction would be comparable to the argument to reject rhetoric itself because it has no content, truth, and politics!

It is also important to understand, however, why Jarratt does not simply go to rhetoric per se to establish the conditions for the possibility of a feminist liberation, and why, instead, she, by way of an exploratory analogy, goes to the Sophists-as-alien (other) to rethink the conditions for a feminist refiguring of The History of Rhetoric. Both deconstruction (reversal and displacement) and especially sophistic rhetorics (*dissoi logoi*, parataxis)—as Jarratt admittedly or not practices both of them—determine, underdetermine, and overdetermine content. We may displace deconstruction and traditional rhetoric but will have to replace either or both with the return of the different-yet-same.

That some writers slavishly imitate deconstruction and sophistic rhetoric for the sheer performative play for play's sake, of course, is inexcusable. However, some of us examine, by way of performance, our colleagues' political-theoretical-performative activities. Let me claim in nested-boxes that some of us (both men and women) examine *the conditions of the conditions* for the possibilities of becoming political. Having said as much, however, I am persuaded that a man such as V.V. cannot be a male feminist, if for no other reason than on provisionary ethical grounds, by which I mean that women (without the "help" of men) should determine their own past and destiny.[11] It may very well be that the only way that we-men can "help" is to self-de(con)struct the very idea of masculinity in dis/respect to writing The History of Rhetoric. Spivak's strategic essentialism suggests that this is the case. I recall her advice to a male student[12]:

I will have in an undergraduate class, let's say, a young, white male student, politically-correct, who will say: "I am only a bourgeois white male,
I can't speak." In that situation . . . I say to them: "Why not develop a certain
degree of rage against the history that has written such an abject script
for you that you are silenced?" Then you begin to investigate what it is that
silences you, rather than take this very deterministic position—since my
skin colour is this, since my sex is this, I cannot speak. (1990, 62)

In suggesting the possibility of a male speaking, Spivak goes so far as to attack
topoi that would exclude as "pernicious position[s]" (62; cf. Fuss 1989).
Spivak does not mince words: "I don't have any problems with starting from
the position that 'Women are universally oppressed by men.' . . . but when
it becomes a door-closer, that's when I begin to have trouble" (1990, 117).
Spivak's sophistic brilliance lies in recognizing our means of saying No to
both M/F and F/M ways of excluding.

Spivak in her summary of her argument points out that deconstruction
is not a program in itself, but the *means* of perpetually investigating such
programs. (I would remind us that Spivak places faith in Derrida's search in *The
Ear of the Other* for the means of a "new politics of reading" that does "not excuse
a text for its historical aberrations," and expects us to "admit that there is
something in the text which can produce these readings" [1990, 107; Derrida
1985a, 3–38].) The other thing that Spivak's summary points out is the necessity *to negotiate with structures of violence* and, therefore, her own *complicity*.
Negotiation is a word that Jarratt herself identifies with (1991, 40–42), though
perhaps she does not wish to negotiate by way of, or to admit that she is *complicit
with*, Derridian deconstruction, but a Spivakian deconstruction, whatever that
difference might be. Male or Female? Oasis or Mirage?

Spivak Reconsidered, again: Precisely what is it that Spivak now understands—that she did not see before—about Derridian reading practices
of reversal and displacement? She says that it is the *concept-metaphor
woman*. This understanding is crucial, for Spivak is concerned in this article as usual with female sexuality—its pre-ontological, ontological/episte-
mological, and axiological conditions for its possibility. (Again, it is such
conditions of possibility that deconstruction uncovers and examines.) What
Spivak acknowledges is that *whoever* deals with female sexuality at the level
of the pre-ontological—again, *whoever*, which, I take, to include both males
and females, for Spivak is speaking of Jacqueline Rose and of herself, too—
whoever deals with female sexuality must *inevitably* use this pre-ontological notion of female sexuality, or concept-metaphor woman, and must use
it "inside male-dominated historical narratives of propriation" (1989a, 210).

Spivak offers no alternative to rethinking woman *outside* of this narrative.[13] This concept-metaphor woman in so-called male-dominated narra-

tives contributes, she claims, to "the emergence of woman as 'catachresis,' as a metaphor without a literal referent standing in for a concept that is the condition of conceptuality" (211). What appears to be suggested here is that narrative per se[14] is "masculine" and consequently creates the effect/supplement of woman as catachresis. However, what Jarratt and very few critics bother to point out—and yet Spivak does—is that in Derridean thinking the critique of phallocentrism, in search of The Truth (of the end of man), *began with a critique of anthropomorphism.* Spivak says, "Derrida . . . see[s] that *anthropos* is defined as 'man' as a sign that has no history. So Derrida then begins to worry about the history of 'woman' " (1990, 14; cf. 53. See Derrida 1982, 109–36).[15]

Spivak continues: "Any programme [feminist(s) or otherwise] which assumes continuity between the subject of epistemology/ontology and that of axiology (the assigning of values) must also assume that the latter is a referent for the former" (1989a, 211). In more Derridean-Nietzschean terms, now, Spivak says:

> According to Derrida, if one looks at propriation in the general sense in Nietzsche, one sees a question that is "more powerful than the question, 'what is?' " . . . because before one can even say that *there is being,* there must be a decision that being can be proper to itself to the extent of being part of that proposition. . . . Outside of all philosophical game-playing, the irreducible predicament pointed at here is that the ontological question cannot be asked in terms of a cleansed epistemology, for propriation organizes the totality of "language's process and symbolic exchange in general." (211; see Derrida 1979, 111, 113)

To ask the question What is X (Sophist, woman)? is to already have answered it, because the pre-ontological terms predetermine (what will *count* as) the answer to the question. Hence, the violence of negative dialectic! Similarly, as Althusser/Spivak say, we think ideology first, history second (Spivak 1990, 54). We must attend to the naming of Sophist and woman and others, but *how* we attend is always already predetermined, no matter who we are, and predetermined by way of structures/narratives of violence. (Is it clearer now that liberation requires more than a middle space! and that, according to Spivak, there is no getting away, at least in negative essentialism, from structures of violence!)

At this point in the article, therefore, Spivak deconstructs her previous position. Pulling another lever, she says:

> I believe that in "Displacement and the discourse of woman," I missed the fact that in Derrida's reading of Nietzsche in *Spurs,* there is an insistence that "woman" in that text was a concept-metaphor that was also a *name* marking the pre-ontological as propriation in sexual difference.

[. . .] I hope [that I] will make clear how crucial it is not to ignore the
powerful currents of European anti-humanist thought that influence us,
yet not to excuse them of their masculism while using them. This is what
I am calling "negotiation." (1989a, 211)

Therefore, again, the question: Can deconstruction be used in *naming
of woman*? Spivak says Yes, because it is best suited for negotiating with
structures/narratives of violence. The strategy is that of misreadings or
essentialism, but also *strategic* misreadings or essentialism. The steps are
reversal and displacement. Their source? Jarratt claims Spivak (1991, 70;
Spivak 1983, 186). Spivak claims Derrida,[16] who claims Nietzsche and
Heidegger.[17]

Having taken note of Spivak's *reversal* of her earlier reading, let us now
take a look at how Spivak returns to and refigures Derrida's reading in *Spurs*
of Nietzsche's proposition concerning "woman." (It is important to take a
look at this reading, for Jarratt in her view of feminist sophistic *rejects
Derrida's reading outright* [see 1991, 66–67].) Spivak says that we-men and
we-women can—by strategic misreadings—"read Nietzsche's text in a way
that suggests that the name of woman makes the question of propriation
indeterminate." (Here, to make it indeterminate is good, at least, initially.)
Spivak continues: "Let us look at the Nietzschean sentence: 'there is no truth
of woman, but because of that abyssal self-apartness of truth, this non-truth
is "truth" ' " (1989a, 211). This passage from Derrida's Nietzsche is Spivak's
translation. Barbara Harlow's translation is somewhat different: "There is no
such thing as the truth of woman, but it is because of that abyssal divergence of the truth, because that untruth is <<within.>> Woman is but one
name for that untruth of truth" (1979, 51). The last sentence, "Woman is
but one name for that untruth of truth," allows us to hear that "woman"
is a concept-metaphor, which Spivak had not recognized.

After reading this proposition on the question of propriation (proper
naming)—Spivak suggests, as Nietzsche does himself—that the word, or
concept-metaphor, "woman" can be displaced and replaced with another
concept-metaphor.[18] It can be replaced with "man," which had *always already*
itself been replaced with "woman," because of the discovery of the impossibility of *anthropos*/"man."[19] What was previously privileged becomes supplementary and vice versa. Other terms that "truth" can be replaced with, besides
"man" and "woman," are "power," "writing," and "différance." (We have
nothing but concept-metaphors.) Now that it is understood that "woman"
is another concept-metaphor itself, all is interchangeable. Such is simple
negative deconstruction.[20] And yet . . .

While such a deconstructive move might be good for we-men, Spivak
argues, it is not good for we-women, or many feminists, because such inde-

terminism (lack of substantial woman[21]) makes it impossible to be political. In this way, apparently, once the truth of "woman" becomes a concept-metaphor and no longer a fixed concept (hence, immanently lost), it must be reclaimed and restabilized for strategic, political purposes. While we-deconstructionist-men, then, would be indeterminate, we-feminist-women would be strategically determinate. Hence, the theatre of a Feminist Sophistic!

Or so it might seem, for as I have been pointing out, Spivak is not necessarily making this point about deconstruction and strategy in this later article. She writes: "My previous position on this essay of Derrida's [*Spurs*] was polemical. I suggested that it was not correct to see the figure of woman as a sign for indeterminacy. . . . But today, *negotiating*, I want to give the assent *for the moment* to Derrida's argument" (1989a, 212; emphasis mine). "For the moment" is a typical Spivakean qualification made even about strategic feminism: "I must say I am an essentialist *from time to time*" (1990, 11; emphasis mine. Cf. 32-34, 117-18; and "In a Word," 1989b). This qualification is typical of deconstructive processes. Spivak always has *to put into question the name of the name* (see Derrida 1982, 27), which is guarding the question, whatever the question of being or becoming might be.

Now comes Spivak's very, very different move. While she admits that deconstruction cannot be done without and is willing to negotiate with it, she announces that the concept-metaphor "woman" *must be done away with altogether*! (We are now really a long ways from where Jarratt begins and ends with Spivak! Are you, Dear Reader, hearing something different yet?) While Spivak will continue to use other metaphors such as "power" and "writing," she will no longer employ "woman." Why? Because couched in the midst of structures of violence, the term begins to take on masculine characteristics.[22] Spivak says: "We must remember that *this particular name*, the name of 'woman,' misfires for feminism. Yet, a feminism that takes the traditionalist line *against* deconstruction [comparable to Jarratt's line?] falls into a historical determinism where 'history' becomes a gender-fetish." She continues: "Guarding this particular name for the graphematic structure is perhaps the most essentialist move of all. . . . If we lose the 'name' of woman for writing, there is no cause for lament" (1989a, 217).

Ironically, therefore, it is the very un/name of "woman" that challenges not just men but women themselves. Losing the name of woman (in both senses) does not mean, however, losing deconstruction. Spivak writes: "Let us say . . . that we have to deconstruct our desire for the impasse, neutralize the name of 'woman' *for deconstruction* and be deconstructive feminists in that sense. If we want to make political claims that are more useful all round than the general bourgeois academic feminist toothsome euphoria this seems now to be the only way" (218; Spivak's emphasis). General bourgeois academic feminist toothsome euphoria! To recapitulate: What must be lost is both a naive, so-called notion of woman as real *and* a deconstructive notion of "woman" as concept-metaphor. Spivak is displacing anything known as "woman" or "feminine," and yet is not, for she engages in a replacing (a negotiating and a sublating) of *something*, so that she and others might continue the struggle against sexisms.

   Spivak/Derrida and Derrida/Spivak: Now, let us ask, What does it mean for Spivak to negotiate? Or as she also puts it, say Yes to the text twice? As I have tried to suggest subtly here—at times, in terms of Jarratt's language; at other times, in my own—to negotiate is to situate ourselves in *the middle space* of such concept-metaphors as *différance*, though not as "woman." This is important to understand: For to say that any of us does not negotiate in this way, but practices strategic misreadings in another way, and without "*différance*," such as Jarratt claims must be done, is to forget where the conditions of such possible misreadings come from, unnamely, *différance*. (*Nomos*, as a middle term, is not *différance*, which is the excluded middle!) Therefore, it may be possible to forget the concept-metaphor "woman" but not that of "*différance*" (or "writing," "power"). Again, Spivak does not forget, for I think that she is well aware that to forget is finally to fall into being determined by conditions in some prior but nameless sense.[23] Spivak writes: "*Différance* is, and it cannot be repeated often enough, only *one* name for the irreducible double bind that allows the very possibility of difference(s). . . . [D]*ifférance* as the ungraspable ground of propriation *is* (but the copula is a supplement) sexual difference" (1989a, 214; Spivak's emphasis). Sexual difference? How many? One, Two, or Countless?[24]

   What I do not understand in Spivak's discussion and revision of her former article, however, is Why it is not equally possible to throw away the concept-metaphor "man," which Derrida states is being replaced? I again have in mind Derrida's closing discussion in "The Ends of Man" (in *Margins* [1982]). It is here that he speaks of "The strategic bet" and "A radical trembling [that] can only come from the *outside*" (134). He points to two possible strategies that we-men might dis/engage in: One being "To attempt an exit and a deconstruction without changing terrain. . . . Here, one risks ceaselessly confirming, consolidating, *relifting* (*relever*), at an always more certain depth, that which one allegedly deconstructs"; and a second, "To decide to change terrain, in a discontinuous and eruptive fashion, by brutally placing oneself outside, and by affirming an absolute break and difference" (135). To realize these ends, Derrida calls for "A new writing [that] must weave and interlace these two motifs of deconstruction. Which amounts to saying that one must speak several languages and produce several texts at once" (135). Derrida speaks of "a change of 'style'; and if there is style,

Nietzsche reminded us, it must be plural" (135). Then, Derrida begins to speak in terms of *a passing beyond outside of sexual identity altogether*. The first of these strategies is *negative* deconstruction; the second, *affirmative* deconstruction. While the first stays in the binary, the second calls out to the other so as perhaps to pass out of the binary to countless genders and sexes (see Derrida and McDonald 1982; cf. Derrida 1980).

At this point, now, let us re/turn to the question of exactly Why Spivak, in still other terms, is willing to negotiate with structures of violence? As I said before, one reason is that for Spivak it is impossible not to, for in her estimation the pre-ontological reasons demand so. And yet, What might she additionally mean by this impossibility? To answer this secondary question, let us first take another look at what Spivak has in mind in negotiating, and then align it with Derrida's strategic bet. What I am most concerned about is Spivak's attitude toward the second, affirmative deconstruction. While she will engage in it, she will not disengage by way of it. (Which is where I cum we are going!)

Explaining Derrida's notion of saying Yes to the text twice,[25] Spivak describes the first step as "keeping the question alive" or "guarding the question" (or "*the question of the difference between the epistemological/ ontological, and the axiological*"); and the second as "calling to the absolutely other" (or "If sexual difference is indeed pre-comprehended by the ontological question then, miming Derrida's Nietzsche, *we* might think 'philosopher,' by way of the same historical narrative that gave Nietzsche 'woman,' as *our* wholly other. And thus we 'women' might indicate, or even figure forth and thus efface, that call to the wholly other as *taking the risk of saying 'yes' to Heidegger, Nietzsche, and Derrida*") (1989a, 212; Spivak's emphasis). Let us recall, however, that in the second instance, saying Yes to Heidegger and others is only saying Yes semiotically across a new protocol of reading politically. While Spivak will engage in negative deconstructions and in affirmative ones, she will not disengage in or by way of the latter. (Will not, in other words, dis/engage herself from narrative, the structure of violence, which she would negotiate with!) The reasons, obviously, are political. This will need some explaining here.

In her post-colonial interviews, Spivak explains that when Derrida moved from his negative to his affirmative phase, "I think what he began to realise is not that you have to say no to whatever positive stuff you're doing, that is to say 'keeping the question alive.' But that deconstruction *obliges you to say yes to everything*. You have to say yes to that which interrupts your project" (1990, 46–47; emphasis mine). Consequently, "you can't have a political program which doesn't say no to something. So, a political program cannot base itself upon affirmative deconstruction, because then it will very quickly come to resemble pluralism, and I think pluralism, as a political program, has already shown its dark side, especially in the United States" (47). She continues:

> On the other hand, when you are within the political program, choosing from among the yeses the possibility of saying yes to something which interrupts you does bring an end to the vanguardism of theory. . . . It's a responsibility to the trace of the other in the self. But then you haven't based yourself on affirmative deconstruction. Politics is asymmetrical, it is provisional, you have broken the theory, and that's the burden you carry when you become political. (47)

I agree with Spivak here, as far as the logic goes. From a more practical point of view, however, this kind of activity being described and, I would say, diluted here will not get the job done. The job? A radical reassessment and change in our attitudes toward what most interests Spivak, namely, sexism. And for me, *sexism in The History of Rhetoric*. My sense is that in Spivak's argument, the reference to "pluralism" is an attempt, intended or not, to displace the issue. It is one thing *to refigure* The History (one could build a *career* on it perpetually); and quite another thing *to destroy* its conditions and then *perpetually to deterritorialize* them. I think that Spivak knows this, for she as much admits it toward the end of her 1989a article, when she quotes at length Thomas Nagel's view that " 'It certainly is not enough that the injustice of a practice of the wrongness of policy should be made glaringly evident. People have to be ready to listen, and that is not determined by argument' " (Nagel 1979, xiii; Spivak 1989a, 219-20).[26] To listen? To hear? Not by argument, but by. . . ?

What am I (VVariously) saying? Neither argument nor polite, logical philosophical redescriptions will change the writing of The History of Rhetoric! There is *terrible power* in saying Yes to everything. Especially, to all that has been systematically excluded. (To the trace. To everything in the outside of the excluded middle!) Especially to the incomprehensible. Terrible powerful re-*Juvenal*zations in the perennial return of the ever-repressed. If someone follows logic, as Spivak insists on here, s/he wins (to be read, loses). If someone cum-a-radical-many wants change, it is necessary "to Yes" everything. Even and especially the incomprehensibles. The heretofore disposables. To Yes the excluders by saying No to their No. By saying No to all reactionary thinking and acting. In another word, by denegating the excluders' No. So as to let flow that nonpositive affirmative desire imminent in all of us. I say: Yes 'em to death!

Nothing is more powerful in bringing about change than a universal YES. I, too, would negotiate with structures of violence, but by way of parodic

YESs. YESs. YESs. Not Yes in any submissive way. But in the most disruptive, farcical way. YES is uncountable![27] YES is neither masculine nor feminine, both of which are (signs of) NOs. Yes to everything, therefore, must run along side Yes and No as Spivak believes she must employ negation *in the particular case*. Major revolutionary force (desire, will), however, must be brought to bear on sexism—and all the other conditions of exclusion—so that eventually the more normal force of argument—again, No in Spivak's particular case—might seek out its secondary ways. If such ways are even then necessary!

Change is not a matter of "evolution" as Jarratt suggests (1991, 19),[28] nor is it a matter of saying "let us none the less name (as) 'woman' that disenfranchised woman whom we strictly, historically, geo-politically *cannot imagine*, as literal referent" (1989a, 220; Spivak's emphasis). This is all too inconsequential in the short and long run. Change, call it revolution, is brought about because of massive campaigns of *tactical disruptions* against the dominant, strategic discourse. By way of massive, perverse redescriptions. Change is brought about by reintroducing "the excluded third." The trace. The excluded middle, which some NOers would call the (ludic) muddle. And yet, this is not to say enough, for it must also be said that change must be perpetual. Change can be not just in the form of No, which, given the structures of violence, can mean Yes, but also in the form of Yes, which can mean No. Nes/Yo.

There is a time for trickery—not just historical deception (*apate*)—so as to cut up and scatter The History. The Narrative. Tmesis. Tmesis. Tmesis. Not just parataxis, parataxis, parataxis. Which falls inevitably back into hypotaxes. But Tmesis today; tmesis tomorrow. Tmesis will have been.

Or another scenario: First, revolutionary discourse; then, renormalizing (reterritorializing) discourse. And yet, I-cum-a-radical-many would desire perpetual deterritorializing, while the reterritorializing is going on and on and on. The History of Rhetoric, just as Foucault says about knowledge (1977, 154), is for cutting up. Laughter?! As Nietzsche says, Yes, "Even laughter may yet have a future" (1974, 74). As Deleuze in Nietzsche's im/proper names says, Yes, "Laughter—and not meaning. schizophrenic laughter or revolutionary joy, this is what emerged from the great books" (1977, 147; cf. Deleuze and Guattari 1983, 316–18).

Lest I be (too) misunderstood, I have *not argued* throughout the foregoing (catch my drift?) that Jarratt has not done her homework carefully. Such an argument would be really neither here or there; for I am thoroughly persuaded, given my understanding of a feminist's necessity to determine (or over- and under-determine) her own terms, that Jarratt is warranted in her performances to stretch casuistically her terms whatever way and wherever she so desires. Let flow, flow, freely flow y/our ship of fools. (We all do it; some of us, however, simply are not aware of it or will not acknowledge it. Or cannot hear it. And perhaps for political un/reasons!) As Cixous says: "Thanks to a few [writers] who were fools about life" (Cixous and Clément 1986, 99). I would, therefore, say Yes to Jarratt's text. YES. And then, continue to give (gift) my own foolish redescriptions, my own stretchings. And How would I continue such redescriptions? By way of Georges Bataille's general economy, not a restricted one; that is, by way of a libidinal economy (see *The Accursed Share* [1988a, 1993]).

If there is going to be a Feminist Sophistic, or rhetorical feminisms, it/they will be and should be, again, determined by women, not "men" who now must remain under erasure. After all, I also say Yes to Derrida's refusal of humanism! I would complicate this all now with the following question. Shall we call a refusal to acknowledge men, such as Jarratt's refusal to acknowledge Spivak's acknowledgement of Derrida and Paul de Man, a Nietzschean affirmative forgetting? Indeed, in disorder to remember we must forget! Therefore, Jarratt turns away from Derrida to Spivak and, as a "case," to Hélène Cixous. Jarratt's turn is very brief (1991, 71–74) and then (again) highly selective.

> Whose degrading do you like better, the father's or the mother's? . . . We are pieced back to the string which leads back, if not to the Name-of-the-Father, then, for a new twist, to the place of the phallic-mother.
>
> —Cixous

> I inhabited Jean Genet.
>
> —Cixous

Strategic Misreadings, once again: I will not spend as much time with what Cixous variously says as I did with Spivak, but will only refer to a few passages in *The Newly Born Woman* and passages from later books[29] to qualify and problematize (re-open, for a new hearing) Jarratt's refiguring. But a caveat: From here/hear on the music, not from the sirens but from the excluded middle or excluded third, might drive you schizo. But do not have your Self/Subjectivity tied to repression (negation), for it will do you, Dear Reader, no good to attempt to listen from that mis/vantage point! For the temptation and passion, the seduction, is too sublime to ever avoid!

In introducing Cixous, Jarratt compares Cixous's writing style to that of the Sophists, then, qualifies this analogy by saying, "I would like to argue that the way she situates her practice rhetorically—within a cultural, political, historical context—tempers the charge. Cixous describes women's writing as bisexual, partaking in the heterogeneity of bisexuality. Right now, she says, it is *only women* who are capable of such a performance" (1991, 71; emphasis mine). This is the passage that Jarratt quotes from Cixous: "For historical reasons, at the present time it is woman who benefits from and opens up within this bisexuality beside itself, which does not annihilate differences but cheers them on, pursues them, adds more: in a certain way *woman is bisexual*—man having been trained to aim for glorious phallic monosexuality" (Cixous and Clément 1986, 85; Cixous's emphasis; cf. Cixous 1981, 254).

Again Jarratt reads this passage as saying "it is *only women* who are capable of such a performance." This is quite a stretch. *Only women!* Jarratt indirectly acknowledges that Cixous is not a naive essentialist and, therefore, speaks of her in terms of custom, convention (local *nomoi*).[30] Which is still heavily indebted to the negative! Cixous does say that "[men have] been trained to aim for glorious phallic monosexuality." I will not quibble with this statement's meaning as to whether it intends *some* or *all* men. Obviously, it is *some* men. How many? I suspect less than (some) more. I would argue with Jarratt, however, over Cixous's meaning as to whether she intends all women or some women. For Cixous speaks of women as also being under the sign of negation, castration.[31] The real point here, however, is not degree but kind (sexuality, gender). Cixous does not say here or anywhere else that I can locate only women and not men. Against the charge *only women*, Cixous would say:

> There are some exceptions. . . . Men or women: beings who are complex, mobile, open. Accepting the other sex as a component makes them much richer, more various, stronger, and—to the extent that they are mobile— very fragile. It is only in this condition that we invent. Thinkers, artists, those who create new values, "philosophers" in the mad Nietzschean manner, inventors and wreckers of concepts and forms, those who change life cannot help but be stirred by anomalies—complementary or contradictory. That doesn't mean that you have to be homosexual to create. But it does mean that there is no *invention* possible, whether to be philosophical or poetic, without there being in the inventing subject an abundance of the other, of variety: separate-people, thought-people, whole populations issuing from the unconscious, and in each suddenly animated desert, the springing up of selves one didn't know—our women, our monsters, our jackals, our Arabs, our aliases, our frights. (Cixous and Clément 1986, 83–84; cf. Deleuze and Guattari 1983, 295–96)

But let us not lose sight of the idea that Jarratt's interpretation is a casuistic stretching. Or perhaps we need a stronger word. If Jarratt would not have Spivak learning affirmatively from Derrida, she would not have Cixous learning affirmatively from "men." This, then, would be part of Jarratt's negative deconstructive (essentializing) strategy. Part of her forgetting!

Cixous Reconsidered: The issue here I will claim is that for Cixous— men and women, male and female—are not *fixed* biological or cultural categories. Moreover, for Cixous the words "men/male" and "women/feminine" are not exclusively biological; they are, instead, concept-metaphors.[32] I agree with Cixous when she exclaims: "There is phallocentrism. History has never produced or recorded anything else—which does not mean that this form is destinal or natural. Phallocentrism is the enemy. Of everyone. Men's loss in phallocentrism is different from but as serious as women's. And it is time to change. To invent the other history" (Cixous and Clément 1986, 83). The issue, as Cixous says, is not whether someone is biologically-essentially either male or female but whether someone is "dispersible, desiring and capable of other" (89).[33] Or whether someone is capable of One cum Radical Multiplicities. Of entering difference.[34] Cixous is playing around with a *libidinal economy*, which she refers and alludes to repeatedly. She, as I spoke of Bataille earlier, is interested in a *general economy* and not a *restricted* one (e.g., 78-83). She is, like Deleuze (anti-philosopher) and Guattari (anti-psychiatrist), interested in "becoming-woman" (85), interested also in women becoming-woman, "the other woman she will be" (89). Interested in woman becoming-animal. Many men and fewer woman, in one sense, are both fixed, that is, determined semiotically across the sign of negation/lack. Women, as well as men, must become sovereign, sublime subjects-that-would-not-be-subjects. Cixous—no doubt about it—is influenced by Bataille. Her novel *Portrait du soleil* is predicated on Bataille's notion of a general, libidinal economy as put forth in his first volume of *The Accursed Share* (1988a*).* (See Shiach 1991, 81–82.)

Again, these women are not biological women, but a concept metaphor for a general, not a restricted, economy excessively becoming. If women must disengage by becoming-woman, so are men, by becoming-woman.[35] For it is *in* Kleist or Shakespeare or others that we find some radical multiplicities or

> elsewheres opened by men who are capable of becoming woman. . . . who let something different from tradition get through at any price—men who are capable to love love; therefore, to love others, to want them; men able to think the woman who would resist destruction and constitute herself as a superb, equal, "impossible" subject, hence intolerable in the real social context. Only by breaking the codes denying her could the poet have desired that woman. Her appearance causing, if not a revolution, harrowing explosions. (Cixous and Clément 1986, 98)

The case of Kleist: Cixous recalls, "I said I owed my life to Kleist. For a long time I lived on the knowledge that he had existed. I owed him not only the will to live but the will to live several lives. To be more than one feminine one or masculine one, to catch fire and burn, to die of life because he caught fire, took on body, pain, and death for me" (1986,112). The references to catching on fire are to Cixous's earlier comment about and allusion to Bataille's image of the sun, as a denegated sign of excess (negation of negation), as a general, instead of a restricted, economy.[36] This is her image of being "a bit vulture, a bit eagle" (perhaps a phoenix), being consumed in flames and rising out of the ashes (99; cf. 88).

The case of Genêt: It is after this earlier description of men who are capable of becoming woman that Cixous writes, "I inhabited Jean Genêt" (99). Verena Andermatt Conley points out,

> the newly born one [from ashes?] is also a female version of the then much discussed writer Jean Genet. *"La jeune née"* or *"la Genet,"* especially evokes Derrida's *Glas* that erected contrastive readings of Hegel and Genet in 1974. . . . The title can also be read as *là je-une-nais*, there I am being born as one, *là*, always in movement, *une*, not as castrated. The title does not crown the work but, through poetic tone, remains undecidable. . . . The text welcomes others who dare to open themselves to sexual uncertainties, or who dare to identify with women. These men [Cixous] finds in artists like Genet, but also Kleist, even Shakespeare. (1992, 37)

What is valuable about this reading is that the title of Cixous's and Clément's book, *La jeune née*, roughly translated as *The Newly Born Woman*, while it is about woman/"woman" crossing borders, it is also about man crossing borders. The title gives entitlement to not only woman but also man! This possible reading is validated by Cixous herself, who in *Three Steps on the Ladder of Writing* says in characterizing Genet's "crossing borders between sexes, between species," being born: " 'I was born in Paris. . . .' That's the beginning, that's how autobiographies begin. But then *The Thief's Journal* begins with: 'Convicts' garb is striped pink and white.' *Je nais* later. There is phonetic play between *je nais* (I am born) and Genet. This is the theatrical setting up of everything connected with passing, with the frontier, birth, transition, descent, ancestry. He exists, he enters" (Cixous, 1993a, 124; cf. 130; also, see Cixous and Clément 1986, 166).

The case of *imund*: And now, as Cixous recalled, "I owed my life to Kleist," I in turn can say that I recall: I owe my life to Cixous.[37] And I-man again can produce discourse. It is one thing to rage against the masculine discourse that has silenced we-men (as Spivak argues we should do), and quite another thing to be " '*imund*,' [i.e.,] to be unclean with joy" (Cixous 1993a, 117), to write this *imund* as Cixous suggests.[38] To come un/clean when

writing? However, I cannot stress enough that what Cixous is saying comes
from Clarice Lispector, her novel *The Passion According to G. H.*, in which
the unclean, the consuming of the unclean, is the means of misidentifying
with, attending to, the other. But *this other* is not the beggar in the street,
who would exist in our minds, as the object of our charity, but this other
is *the nonhuman*: Lispector is calling for the setting aside and the losing
of *homo sapiens*, human species, of species-analytics, of differentiation altogether. (We will return so that we might hear all this somewhat better in
terms of a Third Sophistic, for Cixous has very little, if anything, to do with
a Feminist Sophistic, as limited by Jarratt, and more to do with a perpetual
moving toward a Third.)

In Cixous's references to Kleist and Shakespeare becoming-woman, she
says and I repeat, "Her appearance causing, if not a revolution, harrowing
explosions" (1986, 98). At the end of the Spivak section, I raised the question of Evolution? or Revolution? or Explosion? An answer? It is in Cixous,
in her writing, that we find radical multiplicities saying Yes to *everything
else*. To we-Sophists who would write histories of rhetorics, she says, "We
have no *woman's* reason to pay allegiance to the negative" (85; Cixous's
emphasis). Oh, to be sure!, Cixous says No to the negative (to "He-Bible"[39]),
which allows her, thereafter, to say Yes to everything else: By which I mean,
she says Yes to The Excluded, The Abominable, The Repressed. The un/clean.
The Unhuman. She writes:

> When *"The* Repressed" of their culture and their society come back, it is
> an explosive return, which is *absolutely* shattering, staggering, overturn-
> ing, with a force never let loose before, on the scale of the most tremen-
> dous repressions: for at the end of the Age of the Phallus, women will have
> been either wiped out or heated to the highest, most violent, white-hot fire.
> [Again, the Bataillean sun.] Throughout their deafening dumb history, they
> have lived in dreams, embodied but still deadly silent, in silences, in voice-
> less rebellions. (1986, 95; Cixous's emphasis)

This Repressed will have returned to The History of Rhetoric. The Third
Dionysian, general economy must, shall, will have returned.

What I have tried to indicate, thus far, about Cixous is that she has not
locked out males. She does not say "only women." Moreover, I have suggested
and will continue now to suggest what Cixous is up to as she explores the
body and the *imund*, the unclean, or that which is excluded, because forbidden. Cixous moves to a consideration of *third* (beyond subject/object)
positions.

Threes: Women more than men, Yes. Women and Men and the "feminine"/"becoming-woman," Yes. A Woman's body, a man's body, "the third
body," Yes. Cixous is moving in threes, moving toward what will have been.

Her movement is neither toward *One* nor *Two* but a *1001*. Her movement is toward desiring machines; toward the future-anterior; downward towards death, dreams, and roots (see *Three Steps* [1993a]). Toward the Third Dionysian.

In *The Third Body* (*Le troisième corps*, 1970), written five years before *La jeune née* (1975) and *"Le rire de la Méduse"* (1975), there was and will be (will have been) a reading as writing. As Verena Andermatt Conley explains: "A third body is synthesised from biography and quotation, self and other, writer and reader. Writing is not born as much from 'experience' or the description of a pre-existing reality." Instead, "it is invented from reading, from the investment of affect in living and textual 'scenes' " (1992, 17). The writing, drawn from many sources (Jensen, Kleist, Freud, Kafka, Poe, Joyce, Lispector, Genet, and others) is a pastiche effect of third bodies of literature.

Still in *Révolution pour plus d'un Faust* (1975), Cixous is playing with threes, a paralogic of nonsynthesized thirds, to shatter mirrors and theaters of representation: Cixous writes:

> The joker says to me: "Here, listen with your *third ear*, and if you have it, open your third eye, and think with the third thought, because here, the first wisdom and the second wisdom which adjust through joining like flower that the water binds and two eyes for sight and ears for opinion and belief, they will not suffice. The ear has to be invented for the third wisdom and the armoured eye for him who sees the invisible and who dresses his head in the full sun. . . . And I develop a third language here, inaudible and audible and neither audible nor inaudible." (qtd. in and trans. by Conley 1992, 27-28; emphasis mine).

The joker invites the "me" to become thousands. As Conley points out, the reader, then, is invited to become thousands.[40] That is, to become 'feminine,' that which is not subject to the law of being, that which moves toward perpetual becoming, crosses borders. From this Cixous begins a new language for a new politics. Hers is a libidinalized economy, exploding a fixed Marxist community, Conley argues, a libidinalized economy "made up of a polyphony of voices who write their stories and history, interminably" (30).[41] This new—or the most ancient—*ethos* has to have a new space in which to become.

Space (*locus*) for Cixous, as Conley argues, is a search "for passages, doors or exits to the female's imprisonment. . . . 'Sorties' is written *in medias res*. It locates moments of exclusion in various discourses of the past and projects openings toward the future. History is not a discourse of abstraction but is comprised of personal, singular stories" (Conley 1992, 38–39; cf. 41–42. Also see Shiach 1991, 78–79. See Cixous, *"Coming To Writing,"* 1991, 1–58).

Space as writing (unnatural, forbidden writing, as consuming and identifying with the ugly, despicable, the other) is what Cixous rethinks. (Actually, what Lispector thinks.) Why do Lispector/Cixous want to write in this way? They want to write the " '*imund*,' to be unclean with joy" (Cixous 1993a, 177; cf. Lispector 1988, 63–65). It is a space outside, yet paradoxically inside. As Lispector's G. H. says: "The cockroach is inside out. No, no, I don't mean that it has an inside and an outside; I mean that is what it is. What it had on the outside is what I hide inside myself: I have made my outside into a hidden inside" (69). G. H. takes within herself "the cockroach mass" (163). Yes, she eats the unspeakable creature (172). But when she consumes the ugly—the other, that which is now on the outside of the roach—she breaks "the law" (the negative) that says "I should live with person-matter and not cockroach-matter" (163). Not with libidinal matter. And when eating it, experiences a release into a sublime, ugly-but-not-ugly "vastness" (97), into "nonperson" (165), and experiences an "attentiveness to living" (43). G. H. undergoes absolute denegation and experiences life in a general economy, un/namely, that of becoming-animal. She leaves her species to be with an Other: "life is divided into qualities and species, and the law is that cockroaches will be loved and eaten only by other cockroaches; and that a woman, at the moment of her love for man, that woman is experiencing her own species" (163).

Dear Reader, How do you respond to such writing/thinking? Do you laugh Hollywood's laughter? Snicker the cynical laughter? Laugh (Bataille's) laughter. Kafka's "Metamorphosis" is also humorous. Poor Gregor Samsa, poor Gregor. And Mark Amerika's *The Kafka Chronicles*? Yes, we are supposed to laugh. A minoritarian literature is humorous (see Deleuze and Guattari, *Kafka*). But laugh a laughter as affirmation without reserve. There is no irony here (or should not be), but humor (see Irigaray 1985a, 349; Deleuze and Parnet 1987, 68–69). Kafka's prose is filled with human beings becoming-Other-beings. Cockroach, dog, ape. Are you repulsed at the thought? Good. For then you have experienced your negative relationship with the other. G. H. says that attending to the other is not even comparable to "kissing a leper" (Lispector 1988, 162). It is more despicable than such. It is a joining with the absolute other:

> In such a metamorphosis, I lose everything I have had, and what I have had has been myself—all that I have is what I am. And what am I now? I am: a standing in the presence of fear. I am: what I have seen. I don't understand and I am afraid to understand, the matter of the world frightens me, with its planets and its cockroaches. (59)

> Listen, in the presence of the living cockroach, the worst discovery was that the world is not human, and that we are not human. (61)

Dear Reader, does this mean that in losing our identity as human beings that we can no longer be political? No longer have talk about identity politics? No longer employ the alibi of being-political as a cover for being-reactionary? for dishing and shoveling out heavy loads of punishment so as to reform everyone? [THERE SHOULD BE REALMS OF LAUGHTER IN RESPONSE TO THESE QUESTIONS!!]

Let us return to Cixous, who wants to reclaim the unclean, and reclaim with joy. (Pessimistic joy; joyful pessimism.) She wants to know *how to give*. What is it that "woman" wants? Cixous wants to know *how to attend to the other*. Not woman. She does not make the stupid mistake that Freud or Lacan makes. She wants to know How to give. And without expected return. Her answer is Go to the nether (Hell) world (cf. Lispector 1988, 113, 119, 124). She takes us there and teaches us *(all of us)*, with the help of Kafka-Lispector, how to give, without expecting a return. This is the giving of Bataille's sun: "an economy without reserve" (Cixous and Clément 1986, 86). This is the giving of a general, libidinal economy:

> The purpose of Those Bible [the book of NOs] is to forbid the root [the unfixed world, the world of the excluded, the filthy, the abject, the leper, the AIDS sufferer, or more so any of these people who are made to feel like a cockroach]. This is what I wanted to bring to the surface, though we will not remain here; instead our ladder will grow down into the earth.
>
> Writing . . . comes from what Genet calls the "nether realms," the inferior realms. We'll try to go there for a time, since this is where the treasure of writing lies, where it is formed, where it has stayed since the beginning of creation: down below. (1993a, 118)

Being more specific, Cixous continues:

> It is deep in my body, further down, behind thought. Thought comes in front of it and closes like a door. . . . Somewhere in the depths of my heart. . . . Somewhere in my stomach, my womb, and if you have not got a womb—then it is somewhere "else." You must climb down in order to go in the direction of that place. . . . I know besides that what also prevents us in our society from going there is not our inability—because *all of us* are able—but our cowardice, our fear. Our fear, since we know perfectly well that we will reach the dangerous point where those who are excluded live—and we hate exclusion. (118; Cixous's emphasis)

Having said, quoted, and read all this, we must now keep two points in mind. Becoming-animal is a way of attending to the other, but it is also a way of escape while staying in place. It is a way of becoming-minoritarian, the most sublime—not beautiful but apparently ugly—parapolitics. Pagan politics. And the place of such a politics?

Space as nature (*physis*) is what Cixous primarily reclaims, but it is
a space (*locus*), if not already noticed, thoroughly denegated. In *Three Steps
on the Ladder of Writing*, Cixous speaks very directly about her view of nature
and culture (*nomos*):

> The natural word, the word *nature*, has a sad fate: it was taken up in the
> great disputes, aimed in particular at people like myself who work on the
> sexual scene and who have been accused by a certain group of unenlight-
> ened people of using this word to mean a feminine or masculine nature—
> something I have never been able to conceive of—as if "nature" existed in
> opposition to "culture" [*nomos*], or there were such a thing as pure nature.
> These disputes come from continents newly plunged in darkness. For a while,
> to flee the field of these sterile disputes, I no longer used the word *nature*,
> even through I adore it. Then I adopted it again. As soon as I use it in the
> domain of writing it begins to move, to twist a little, because in *writing* this
> is what it's all about. As soon as there is writing, it becomes a matter of
> passage, of all kinds of passages, of delimitation, of overflowing.
>
> We cannot forget Ovid's *Metamorphoses*. There are metamorphoses of all
> kinds and genders here. Writing runs them through the other world, which
> is the world of writing [Derrida's concept-metaphor "writing"]. The primi-
> tive civilizations that preceded us, our mothers, believed in trance, in
> transformation, in transition, in transfer: one species passed into another,
> one realm became another, from the human to the mineral to the vegetal,
> in a generalized, infinite, magnificent, and unbounded way. By the word
> *nature* I don't necessarily mean the concept. I don't want to return here
> to philosophic thinking. . . . I prefer to remain in the poetic space.
> (1993a,128-29; Cixous's emphasis)

This space is reclaimed not only by climbing the ladder down but also by
a rapid crossing of borders (switching of codes). Outside, while paradoxically
inside. Yet denegated. Cixous writes: "We [we-creatures] could go back ten
thousand years, before the time of 'country,' and imagine the birth of borders.
. . . Who invented the borders? Borders [species + genus, the negative] don't
exist. . . . They are as incredible as unicorns. Thus we might enter [crossing
borders, switching codes] History, which is always a History of borders. Today
. . . People are swollen with *home-neid* (home-envy)." Cixous continues: "It is
primarily a need for the proper, for a proper country, for proper name, a need
for separation and, at the same time, a rejection of the other. . . . I want the
word *dépays* (uncountry); I'm sorry that we do not have it since the uncountry
is not supposed to exist. . . . People like Genet or Clarice are inhabitants of the
uncountry, of the incountry, of the country hidden in the country [outside, yet
inside], or lost in the country, of the other country, the country below, the country
underneath" (1993a, 131).[42] (Recall the uncanny, unhomely.)

It is in this space (the zone of a denegated nature, or as I have signified it previously as *physis*[nonpositive affirmation]) and this *dépays*/"uncountry" (recall Lyotard's *pagus*) that Cixous writes and reclaims histories. Reclaims the excluded. In the uncanny. Both real and fictive stories, interwoven. About those who have suffered exclusion. First, however, she must negate the excluding force. She must undergo self-denegation. Far from Spivak, Cixous does not take the risk of strategic essentialism; instead, she risks:

> In the beginning, there can be only dying, the abyss, the first laugh.
>
> After that, you don't know. It's life that decides. Its terrible power of invention, which surpasses us. Our life anticipates us. Always ahead of you by a height, a desire, the good abyss, the one that suggests to you: "Leap and pass into infinity." Write! what? Take to the wind, take to writing, form one body with the letters. Live! Risk: those who risk nothing gain nothing, risk and you no longer risk anything.
>
> In the beginning, there is an end. Don't be afraid: it's your death that is dying. Then: all the beginnings. (1991, 41)

Her politics?[43] As Conley explains, a politics of the end of the necessity of politics, which would be "located beyond a space of exclusions" (1992, 47; cf. Shiach 1991, 6–37). Is this space beyond the *nomos*? Yes!, for such is ever a locus of exclusion: the modes of cooperation are the modes of being-co-opted and excluded. Consensus is cohersive. The *nomos* perpetuates the principle of excluded middle/muddle! Then, where is this non-Euclidean space? As stated previously, it is nature (*physis*), but Ovid's *dépays* (uncountry) and not the nature of the binary *physis/nomos* (see Cixous 1993a, 129–31), both of which are constructed under the sign of the negative. Ovid's nature-"uncountry" is the nonpositive-affirmative, a "third" (or radical infinity) beyond negative/positive. It is a becoming without borders, without the traditional philosophical principles of identity, non-contradiction, and the excluded middle. It is the practice (praxis) of the *imund*.

II. "Some More" *Différances*

What I have been attempting to say—by way of rereading both Spivak and Cixous, though they are very different[44]—is that there is always the danger in using words like "men" and "women," "male" and "female," in reactionary thinking, and in engaging in a dividing practice (*diaeresis*), in a negative essentializing, that would further drive a counterwedge between two sets of the human species. Yes, *strategic essentialism* is a form of *negative essentializing*! And yet, it is not always the case, for in great part *how* it is to be read is owing to what I would call the history of its use by a particular critic. I think that Spivak is careful and vigilant enough to interrogate herself perpetually; she is most sincere and performative in attempting to look around corners, asking herself constantly What is it that I have subjectively invested in making such a statement? Therefore, I think any expositor of what Spivak performs textually must make this as evident as possible to would-be Spivaks[45]; if not, then Spivak's name and constantly self-questioned intentions get ap/propriated as an alibi for negative essentializing.

But let us return to the problematic of doubleness. The words—"men" and "women," etc.—are used in a double sense throughout much of the writing done by feminists. I would add now that this doubleness is a tactic and perhaps necessary confusion. (Spivak is very careful, however, to point out how Derrida uses these and similar terms in quotes, as cues to help readers from being confused; Cixous does not use such diacritical marks but nonetheless makes implicit and explicit distinctions. Both Spivak and Cixous intermittently call on their readers to be careful when they think that they might go astray in fixing these words into literal "things.") It is one defense among others in the war that women have been forced to fight against sexism, against their very exclusion throughout what goes for (The) His-story (of Rhetoric), yesterday and today. If this tactic/strategy were denied them, by any arguer, there would be nought.[46]

I would now turn to a Third.

A Feminist Sophistic (negative essence) and a Third Sophistic (nonpositive-affirmative essence): I will attend only briefly to the implied difference in moving from One (unity) to two (binary, unity) to three (dispersion, infinity), for in numerous ways everything that I have written since 1987 and in the above discussion speaks to this difference. What is it that I want? What is it that I will have given? To say No to No! To the conditions of the negative, which master and enslave all of us. Saying Yes can mean No; saying No can mean Yes. I would destroy such conditions. Why? Because to say Yes to the text twice, to turn the lever twice is to reverse perpetually, to engage in *dissoi logoi* (or *to fix* the reversal, which is, more often than not, the case historically). To simply reverse endlessly is to bring about change while unfortunately maintaining the conditions of dominance over others. I would not desire, therefore, to say Yes to the text only twice, but thrice ('some more,' to infinity). But what does this mean? Simply, I would include everything that has been excluded because *imund*. Contrary to Schiappa and Jarratt, I see the Sophists as potentially saying Yes to every-thing! *except* reactionary thinking and acting, which they say No to! That's why for Schiappa, the Sophists do not exist (only things under the sign of the negative can be seen [theorized] when looking by way of the negative). And that's why, in part, Jarratt, in Order to be political, must be a strategic (negative) essentialist. Neither Schiappa nor Jarratt, to serve the interests of their own research protocols, can do Other/wise. Finally then, if there is to be exclusion, the very principle of exclusion itself must be excluded! And how? Again, by attending to the other, embracing the *imund*!

It is a Third Sophistic that I espouse. A denegated essentialism. It is *the risk of a strategic (nonpositive affirmative) essence* that I espouse. Having re/announced such an espousal, I make no pretense that other theorists, paratheorists, pragmatists, historians/historiographers, magicians, freaks should or ought to follow. There is no following. Only a drifting. A fractal drifting. A folding/refolding into fractals, which is the new asubjectivity. I am not the fool of the epistemic-court, not of social-production (a binary-machine); I am the fractalized fools of desiring-production.[47] Which will have been. *It is happening!*

Conjugate yourself in the future exterior. Go ahead.
Do not let the interior past weaken you.

—Cixous

As I proceed through the Vastness of the future-anterior, I would perform by way (VVolfean vvaves[48]) of a general, libidinal economy. It is not a matter of male/female or female/male; it is (the matter of) everything that has been excluded because of disjunctive logic, which gives us congregation (consensus) by way of segregation. I would trek with Anne Fausto-Sterling: Five sexes and counting. I am counter-infected with Cixous. *Je suis* in Sick-zoo. (Unto the death of Death): "When I write, I become a thing, a wild beast. A wild beast *doesn't look back* when it leaps; doesn't check that people are watching and admiring. Those who do not become wild beasts when they write, who write to please, write nothing that has not already been written, teach us nothing, and forge extra bars for our cage" (Cixous, "We Who Are Free," 218; Cixous's emphasis).

Now WE must turn to Gorgias/Helen so that we might reclaim her from being appropriated as negation (Helen/ism).

Chapter 6

❧

Gorgias, Accounting, and Helen

There is, according to Kant, a sense of the sublime—he calls it the mathematical sublime—arising out of sheer cognitive exhaustion, the mind blocked not by the threat of an overwhelming force, but by the fear of losing count or of being reduced to nothing but counting—this and this and this— with no hope of bringing a long series or a vast scattering under some sort of conceptual unity. Kant describes a painful pause—"a momentary checking of the vital powers"—followed by a compensatory positive movement, the mind's exultation in its own rational faculties, in its ability to think a totality that cannot be taken in through the senses.

—Neil Hertz

It's not that we or I need to start over again; it's just a matter of continuing to start over interminably. Moving forward I echo back to my earlier discussion of the Sophists and aesthetics. Not desiring to dismiss the Sophists and not wanting to have an aesthetics out of the Kantian sublime (predicated on the negative), I move on perpetually. To be sure, there are dangers. I have discussed in the preceding chapters on Isocrates and Heidegger what I see as some of those dangers. (Some we must set aside; others, embrace.) There is no going forward without turning back. (Let us ever remind ourselves of this situation.) Though we go forward, we do so by ill/virtue of repression (negation, disavowal). Yet we must go forward in some ways by a dis/engagement from negative essentializing. And so . . .

Most specifically, in chapter 1, I attempted to rediscover the possibilities of the Sophists in the very embodiment of Favorinus: A second (or Third?) Sophistic hermaphrodite, a biological contradiction and transgression, or, as I put it, "a sign" of the possibilities of the return of the eternally repressed.

Yet another way of saying all this is that I attempted to reestablish the conditions for the possibilities of what Foucault calls "nonpositive affirmation."

I want now to return to the question of predispositions towards history writing, which I have discussed elsewhere (1987b; 1993b; 1994a) and intermittently here, and return to the possibilities of the Sophists. To the Forgotten. I will attempt a return in the name of a "Third Sophistic." This return will be facilitated, this time, by way of an unusual counting system, or a new trinary/trilemma.[1] I will reinitiate a counting, or ac*count*ing, system of *one*, *two*, and *"some more."* What is being reinitiated here is a rethinking of the *logos*, or *the giving of an account*. (*One* and *two* are signs of negation; *"some more"* is a nonrepresentational sign of nonpositive affirmation.) *"Some more"* might be understood here as *Ta arreta* (irrational numbers or surds), but to interpret "some more" in this way would be to de/value it by way of the *logos*[neg.]. There simply is no way to have an intimation of *"some more"* in this way. Or again, perhaps *"some more"* might be understood here as *Arreton* (denegation of *rheton*, the unspoken, inexpressible, unutterable, not to be divulged). And yet, this, too, is no way to have an intimation of "some more." In both cases, such attempts would be to create what I referred to in chapter 1, in my discussion of Lyotard, as a *differend*, judging or valuing one phrase by the rules and regimens of an entirely different or incommensurable genre of thinking. What *"some more"* is all about, however, is to speak and write of The History in such *wild, savage* (dancing?) terms that the new histories would sound ab/surd. What *"some more"* would do, then, is to speak the unspoken, the Forgotten, the not yet divulged. How we narrate history, if narrate at all, is determined by how *we* give ac*counts*. *Logoi, alogoi, dissoi logoi, dissoi* para*logoi*.

Once I have ruminated on ac/counting, I will be concerned with *how* (far) such thinkers as Plato, Aristotle, and various Sophists could count. A determination of *how* (far) will suggest these thinkers' various attitudes towards *logos* as rational, irrational, nonrational, or whatever. The motive for revaluing counting is to discover a way of rereading Gorgias. Specifically, what I am interested in rereading—revaluing—is Gorgias's "On the Nonexistent" and his defense of "Helen." Commentators on Gorgias's work view Gorgias's thinking as from the negative. (It could be claimed that Gorgias invites us to read him that way; after all, he does—apparently—indulge in a negative nature, non-Being, *physis*[neg.].) I will attempt less a reversal of this way of thinking about Gorgias's texts (by way of negative deconstruction), which would only maintain the binary (machine), but will attempt more so a search for a desiring (machine) of a third position (by way of affirmative deconstruction), which would get us out of the binary readings of, say, Helen, to the possibilities of *"some more"* readings. Derrida says that we need a new politics of reading, a reading of politics: Here is mine. I am thoroughly persuaded that if we are to reclaim the Sophists, it must be done by searching for third ("*some more,*" sovereign, sublime) subject positions. Favorinus is but one-cum-a-radical-many embodiment(s) of such a sublime subject position; there are "some (more) others." I am thinking in terms of a radically different economy not *restricted* but *general.*

Discussing the possibilities of a Third Sophistic in rereadings of Gorgias's text will allow me to initiate a reinvestigation of a sublime-sovereign subjectivity. Extending Untersteiner's reading, I am going to suggest, somewhat differently and contrary to recent feminist readings (Suzuki 1989, 15; Jarratt 1991, 69; Biesecker 1991, 80 n.18), the possibilities of rethinking Helen as a non-Humanist subject. (I place very little value in the authorial fantasy, or the author effect, or a reactionary-being.) Avoiding such a subject position does not mean, however, that Helen as a subject must necessarily be returned to a position of victim. It is Helen's *sovereignty* that I am searching for, not her mere return to a master/slave dialectic, to a reactionary state of being, that is, active or passive nihilism because of *ressentiment.*

My discussion of Helen will only be preliminary and suggestive, for toward the end of this chapter, I will return to a more general discussion of gender that would not be determined by negation. What this will mean is a return to Nietzsche and his view of subjectivity and then a revaluation of various Nietzscheans (such as Deleuze and Guattari and Judith Butler) and their various views of gender. This latter section of the chapter is preliminary and suggestive; for I discuss agency and gender again but more fully in chapter 7, and primarily in relation to Helen. We will not easily be done with "Helen" and the problem of negation and gender; for Helen becomes not only, for many of us, one of the subjects/objects of a feminism but also she becomes Helen(ism). The ethical-political ramifications are already forever with us.[2]

One last note in respect to Helen: There is *the theme of rape*, which cannot not be dealt with, and which, if dealt with at all in Helen's case, is usually discussed in passing and then in terms of an "elopement" or "seduction" (see Jarratt 1992). In this chapter, I make only passing reference to this *rape*; I have discussed it in terms of Panhellenism in chapter 2, note 2.[3] My claim there is that the History of Rhetoric (of culture) is The History of Oppression, The History that is founded (that legitimizes itself) semiotically across canonized rape narratives. This theme of oppression is made much of in the final (rebeginning?) excursis. Let us now, however, return to the subject(s) of the possibilities of the Sophists. To re/begin with, I find it advisable, ever so, to restate my historiographical predispositions.

I. A Third Sophistic

In what follows, therefore, I am going to take the liberty of thinking unabashedly in print about what has not, heretofore, been so readily thought concerning the Sophists—namely, that besides the alleged "First" and "Second" Sophistics, there is a "Third Sophistic," which we are always already in the midst of and which radically differs from the previous two. For the sake of quickly locating the present, or Third Sophistic, we might historically identify with the following centuries and personages: Whereas the "First" Sophistic is dated as occurring in the 5th century B.C. and the "Second" in circa 2nd century A.D., a "Third" Sophistic belongs in the 19th-20th centuries. Whereas the representative Sophist of the first might be Protagoras and of the second Aeschines, representative Sophists of the most recent period might be Nietzsche, Jacques Derrida, Jean-François Lyotard, Michel Foucault, Judith Butler, Hélène Cixous, Gayatri Spivak, and others.

But a caveat is in order: This quick method of locating a "Third Sophistic" can lead to misunderstandings. Before proceeding I must disclose a predisposition that informs my thinking, which deals with what is implicit in the logic of *one, two,* and then *three.* Such a logic is bound relationally by ways of cause/effect and hypotaxis, which is typical of historical narrative. When Philostratus writes of the "second" Sophistic (1968, 481) and G. W. Bowersock writes of Philostratus's history (1969, 8–9), both traditional historians are predisposed to view a causal, periodic connection and development between the "First" and the "Second" Sophistics.

To understand my idea of history (writing), and my idea of a "Third Sophistic," it is necessary to think of a contrary, non-traditional status for historiography and for sequencing. The notion of a "Third Sophistic," as I espouse it here, can be more accurately understood according to the *topoi* of "antecedent and consequent" rather than "cause and effect"; according to radical "parataxis" rather than "hypotaxis." (Or according to flows of desire, assemblages, series, etc.) The particular view of history (writing) to which I am predisposed might be understood loosely as "annalist" or "serial" or as radically "paralogical" (see Lyotard 1984 and 1988a). Or as desiring-production. It is a view that is poststructuralist and postmodern in that it acknowledges an incredulity toward covering-law models or grand (causal) narratives of history (writing), such as an Hegelian or Marxist dialectical view of history as leading to ethical and political emancipation. It is a view of history (writing), instead, that dis/engages in just-drifting. Just-desiring.

With this predisposition I do not wish to suggest that traditional causal connections and developments are not at all to be constructed, but only that they should not be privileged as *a priori.* (I know, I'm not being revel(perluc)utionary enough. Give me time to build up to vast intensities. Give me time, and yourselves time, to rev up the desiring-machine!) I will sketch out one possible continuum and set of relationships between philosophical and sophistical rhetorics and another between the first two Sophistics and a Third. When we reach a Third, the "string" or continuum and the relationships among its parts will have changed radically. When we reach a Third, we will be at a point of having realized that the First and Second Sophistics do not (necessarily) precede a Third Sophistic; for this Third is not diachronic, but sub/versively already forever counterdiachronic. Whereas the First and Second Sophistics are told metonymically *as cause/ effect*, this Third will here be told metonymically *as contingency*. This Third is counter in that it is against any view of historical (revolutionary) eschatology. It is made possible by a view of history that is Nietzschean-Foucaultian, that is "effective history." It is "effective" in that it "differs from traditional history in being without constants"; it is " 'effective' history [in that] it will not permit itself to be transported by a voiceless obstinacy toward a millennial ending" (Foucault 1986, 153–54).

With this predisposition in mind, we might now begin to think in terms of a Third Sophistic. But before attempting a more detailed discussion, it is also necessary to understand that my discussion will be founded, so that it can be eventually un-founded, on yet another category/trio of thinkers. We have categories so that we might "destroy"/"disperse" them by allowing them to engage in a sophistic-rhetorical "diaspora"—that is, to dis/engage in a holiday from any pull toward the infinite or the transcendental—so that we, in turn, might also drift freely. We have categorical "knowledge," as Foucault says, "not . . . for understanding [but] for cutting" (1986, 154). Does perhaps, then, Foucault mean a . . . "cutting loose"? . . . does he perhaps mean a "drifting"? What is wanted here is to imagine so. The provisional category, or paracategory, that I have in mind—a most helpful and loose one-cum-a-radical-many for my project—comes from John Poulakos (1984), who works with Plato (as ideal), Aristotle (as actual), and the Sophists (as representing the view of the "possible").[4] Looking at the Sophists as interested in the "possible" will allow me to discuss—at least, in passing—the First and Second Sophistics and, then at greater length, a "Third" which, as I see it, allows for the kinds of aesthetic-pagan-political "dispersion" that I am after. And, indeed, I am "after" much and look "forward" to even *some more*. I must look forward to "some more" because the thirdness of the "possible," *as* Poulakos employs it, is Heideggerian (see Heidegger 1962, 63), and consequently incipiently founded again on negation. The possible that I will eventually be searching for, *count*ing on, will be un/founded on a nonpositive affirmation, on an excess, developed by Nietzsche, discarded by Heidegger early in his writing but then eventually returned to, and later reclaimed by Nietzscheans such as Deleuze and Guattari, Foucault, and Judith Butler.

IIA. On Our Ways to the "Possible";
or Learning How to Re/Count
"One, Two, and Some More"—Plato and the Sophists

Since I wish to drift toward some notions of a Third Sophistic, I will spend very little time on the First and especially the Second Sophistics. (A rudimentary scholarship is already available on these two Sophistics.[5]) But to get some sense of "continuity," so that this continuity might be undone, unraveled, *de*negated, or *counter*questioned, let us in passing begin with a working understanding of *the difference*[6] —that of the "subject/agent"— between "Platonic/Socratic thought" and "Sophistic thought," and focus on two commentators, respectively G. W. F. Hegel and Ernst Cassirer.

It is often said that Hegel is "the rehabilitator" of the Sophists. He draws such a characterization by having both Socrates and the Sophists engage in "thought about thought." But as expected, there is a difference, and one that unequivocally favors Socrates and philosophy. What is meant by the phrase "thought about thought" is what Hegel calls a "double character." It is both subject and object in a special (interpretive) relationship. At first, "the subject, when it reflected on the absolute, only produced thoughts." What followed as a revolutionary "Notion," however, is that the "thinking subject likewise really belongs to the totality of the objective." For Hegel, "it comes to pass in Philosophy [in Socratic and subsequent philosophy] that although the 'I' is the positing, yet the posited *content* [my emphasis] of that which is thought is the object existent in and for itself." The experience of thought about thought for the Sophists, however, is different. Hegel writes: "To the Sophists the content is mine, and subjective" (1974, 351). The inauguration of the "agent," then, is accomplished in these two ways: The Platonic/Socratic notion of the "speaking/thinking-subject" is linked to *physis* (nature); the Sophistic is linked generally, but by no means always, to *nomos* (law, convention, custom.)[7]

This distinction has a profound and inevitable influence on both the idea of how the "subject" is constituted and on the idea of will and on ethics (the individual) and politics (the social as universal). Hegel describes the struggle concerning "the absolute end, of the end of man"—that which will anchor individual human beings so as not to wander aimlessly, as if there is something wrong with "drifting"! He writes: "As regards content ["the posited content"], the standpoint of the Sophists differed from that of Socrates and

Plato, in that the mission of Socrates was to express the beautiful, good, true, and right as the end and aim of the individual, while with the Sophists the *content* was not present as an ultimate end, so that all this was left to the individual will" (1974, 366; emphasis mine). And to its "drifting."

Cassirer similarly says: "The very term 'man' was understood and interpreted by [the Sophists and Socrates] in two divergent and even opposite ways. To the sophists 'man' meant the individual man. The so-called 'universal' man—the man of the philosophers—was to them a mere fiction. They were fascinated by the ever-shifting [drifting?] scenes of human life, especially of public life. It was here that they had to play their roles and to display their talents." And then Cassirer writes: "What [Socrates] is asking for is the unity of the will" (1966, 57).

The point of this distinction between "socratic thought" and "sophistic thought" is the failure of both subjects or "the failure of the ethical subject." Let us chart out these additional distinctions so as to better understand this paradoxical, fortunate failure. If Plato/Socrates counted to *one*, it can be said that the Sophists counted to *two* and eventually, as I will urge, to a Third Sophistic *some more*. Plato/Socrates in the *Theaetetus* speaks of the party of *one*, or those who are for "a unity which stays still within itself" (180d), and the party of *two*, or those "who move like flowing streams" (160d, 180d). What I am still suggesting here and throughout is that there are more than two parties; there is, yes, *a third party*. It is, from a Platonic point of view, more anarchistic, or neoanarchistic, than Plato might have thought!

Let us look more closely so that we might come to see what happens when counting to *two*, we eventually get to "*some* (radical) *more*." In what follows, I am going to sketch out what I see are some basic permutations and combinations of the ethical subject in respect to the *physis/nomos* distinction, which I will, again, recharacterize as *physis*neg, *nomos*neg, and *physis* (as a nonpositive affirmation). (If there is a subject, whether fixed to an absolute or to local *nomoi*, that subject is necessarily under negation.)

Plato/Socrates identify their subject(s) with the Parmenidian ideal of nature as *one* (*physis*). Hence, as Hegel explains, "thought about thought"— and this means the thought of the ethical subject—is made objective (or made into negated *logos*). But then, Plato has absolutized his own interpretation, which Hegel himself, in turn, eventually achieves in the name of religion and *Geist*. Each is engaged in a crypto-subjectivity. In contrast, Protagoras—the protofather of Humanism—inverts "thought about thought" (*logos*) by making it subjective. He emphasizes *nomos* in his "man-measure" doctrine (*Theaetetus*, 160d). The full statement reads: "Man is the measure of all things, of things that are as to how they are, and of things that are not as to how they are not." Protagoras decenters himself from the Parmenidian Ideal to individual/subjective perceptions and thoughts. His emphasis is on the individuality of a "speaking/acting subject" as agent. But the implications of what he says are more radical than they appear because the logical consequences of his decentering is not just from the Ideal but also from the whole of the human race: Individual "measurement"—or perception such as taste—becomes individual and unique (152a 6–9). Where does this particular "thought about thought" take us? An answer is that such *dissoi-logoi* reasoning (or anti-reasoning) leads to negative (but eventually to nonpositive affirmative) consequences, which are an explosion, detonation of the ethical subject. The subject is left "drifting." In new but ancient *loci*.

Speaking of the logical consequences of Protagoras's thinking, Kerferd says: "If all [individual] perceptions are true [and they would be if there is no objective criterion for "thought about thought"], it follows that no perceptions are false" (88). If no perceptions are false, we have a linguistic statement with two incipient anti-foundational thoughts, or what I would rather paradoxically refer to as the two *topoi* of "the possibility of/within impossibility"—the first, the impossibility of contradiction; the second, the impossibility of saying what is false (*Euthydemus*, 283–286d; Kerferd 1981, 85ff.). These two *topoi* are devastating for the (traditional) possibilities of *logos* (law, reason, rationality). Moreover, with such thinking, or should I say Un-thinking, the ethical subject becomes detached (through self-consciousness) from all other ethical subjects (which for Hegel is the inauguration of the unhappy consciousness or alienation); but we have—at least, from my ethical-subjective perspective—come closer to the possibilities of a Third Sophistic. Let us continue on to Gorgias and his even more radical relationship to the *physis/nomos* controversy and especially his view of *logos* and the ethical subject.

Gorgias believed that the *logos* (of *physis*, which he emphasized over *nomos*) could not communicate the truth. Untersteiner writes: "If man, as happened for Helen, comes into immediate contact with *logos*—with the divine transformed into logical power—*logos* in its working *splits into two opposite directions* which with their antithetical existence destroy the ideal of a rationality to be recognized in all nature [*physis*]" (1954, 140–41; emphasis mine). One—as we have seen already in Protagoras's thinking—has become Two. Are there threatening consequences, and if so how? Untersteiner's view of Gorgias is that he is "not a skeptic but a man of tragedy" (143). In respect to ontology and epistemology, Gorgias is caught between two (or more) irreconcilable choices. He does not, however, fall into inaction (scepticism), for he acts (tragically): Untersteiner writes, "Epistemology, . . . [in] the realm of the practical, becomes *will*, decision, which was realised in a [*kairos*] endowed with the property of *breaking up the cycle of the antitheses* [the irreconcilable differences of Being (*physis*) and Not-Being] *and creating something new, irrational*" (166; emphasis mine; cf. E. C. White 1987, 20). *Logos* here functions as a super nova. Express! Let me emphasize that it is this dispersion/scattering of the antitheses that leads to "something new, irrational," something revolutionary here; and for me, this is a Third Sophistic Moment (Occasion), and one based on a particular Gorgian notion of *kairos*. And it is this "moment" that tells us something about the nature [*physis*] of the Gorgian "subject"—namely, that the "decision" is not the subject's, but is "willed by [*kairos*]" (181; cf. Miller 1987, 174–77). Here we have a view of the subject as a function of *logos/kairos*.[8] In respect to ethics, Gorgias, as before, sees a tragic split between divine law (which is irrational and corresponds with *kairos*), and human law (which is rational and corresponds to human logic). Ethical action, for Gorgias, is the result of the persuasive force of divine *logos*, which is dispersed by *kairos* and which aims at the "right thing at the right moment" (see Untersteiner 1954, ch. 7).

> For how could one outdo Gorgias who dared to say that of existing things none exists or Zeno who tried to prove the same things to be possible and again impossible? . . . [T]he theories of the early sophists, of whom one said the number of existing things is limitless . . . but Parmenides and Melissus said it is one and Gorgias none at all.
>
> —Isocrates

> But an age which regards as real only what goes fast and can be clutched with both hands looks on questioning as "remote from reality" and as something that does not pay, whose benefits cannot be numbered. But the essential is not number; the essential is the right time, i.e., the right moment [*kairos*], and the right perseverance.
>
> —Martin Heidegger

What I have attempted thus far is to get to the possibility of being able to talk about "counting." Kenneth Pike tells us: "In many languages of the world counting has never been developed. In some languages of New Guinea . . . people . . . count: *one thing, two things, many things*, and then must stop; one man translated his counting system into Pidgin English for me as *one fellow, two fellow, plenty fellow*" (1982, 23; Pike's emphasis). Jacques Lacan was very interested in how far his patients could count (see Schneiderman 1983, 1–8; Ragland-Sullivan 1987); to Lacan, we will eventually in passing return. For now let us ask: How far could Plato/Socrates count? The answer, I believe, is *one*. They wished to anchor their view of the *logos* and the subject in an indivisible/Parmenidian *one*. How far could Aristotle—with whom we will deal in a while—count? It is a complicated answer, but he does tell us quite explicitly in the *Physics* (Bk 1, ch. 5–6), that he counts *two* (as "contraries") and *three* (as "substratum"), but "neither One nor Innumerable" (189a). (This "three" is not the same as Pike's "many things," of which I will refer to as "some more"/"radical multiplicities"/"possibilisms"; it is also important to note that Aristotle explicitly says that there cannot be a *four* +, or an "innumerable" [189a 20].) Therefore, Aristotle counts: *Two, three*. But let us not be fooled: Aristotle is playing a shell game with only *one* primary pea, if any at all. His notion of counting to *three* (as "substratum") is a generic synthesis/unity of the prior *two* (the "contraries"): It is a *three*-cum-"One" that is "differentiate[d] . . . by . . . means of contraries, such as density and rarity and more and less" (189b 99–100). Hence, while agreeing to the possibility of *twos*, he still has his crypto-*one*, which he calls a *three*. Moreover, he says, "it is possible that there should be more than one primary contrariety" (189b 20–25), thus emphasizing unity/*one*ness again.

Now let us ask, how far could Protagoras and the other Sophists count? The answer, at the most general level, is to *two* (the *two* of *dissoi logoi*)— to a plurality limited to contested-contraries.[9] The Sophists of the First Sophistic were attempting to account for individual perceptions without the will-to-unifying them (as Plato and Aristotle were attempting for political ends). The Sophists' thinking—specifically, Protagoras's—led to the two notions of the impossibility to contradict and to state a falsity. With such a view, how can anyone unify? And yet, the early Sophists were locked into thinking across contraries and therefore, though "relativists," were bound, even if only incipiently, to homogenizing their heterogeneities. If not, then things would, indeed, fly apart; but then, with the early Sophists, things were always already on the verge of flying apart for these drifters and nomads.

And Gorgias, whom I see as a proto-Third Sophistic thinker, how would he count? The answer is *one, two*, and *some more*. Things do fly apart. The binaries are exploded when *kairos* intervenes and makes *something new, irrational* (Untersteiner 1954, 161). And when flying apart, what has happened to "Helen" as ethical subject? She has become fragmented not only because of the intervention of *kairos* in "her" decision, but also because she becomes a set *topos* down through the centuries, with various arguments being brought for and against her (see Suzuki 1989). There are, indeed, many "Helens," in infinite regress. And in many ways *kairos* has made Helen into the mother of feminist discourses. (It is this "Helen" that I must return to later; for when appropriated by a particular Feminist discourse, she becomes subject to *ressentiment* and consequently becomes potentially reactionary.)

IIB. On Our ways to the Possible; or Learning How to Re/count "One, Two, and Some More"—Aristotle and the Sophists

Let us now shift to a different vignette, but maintain a slight imbrication with the former, and change our focus, this time, to Aristotle and the Sophists, as *one*/certainty, *two*/probability, *some more*/possible. When Aristotle dealt with certainty, it was by way of formal/syllogistic logic, a logic founded on the principles of identity, contradiction, and excluded middle, which are supposed to keep things from flying apart. Our interest in rhetoric, however, focuses us on Aristotle's dealings with probability, which are philosophical. This leaves us with the possible, which John Poulakos associates with the Sophists. Aristotle does deal with the possible/impossible (*Rhetoric* 1392a) as one set of four common *topoi*; but his conception of them is based on a binary logic that is informed by the principles of logic in relation to probability. That is, it is founded on negation and, therefore, I will not trek with this notion of the possible. What I will be attempting to do here, however, is to reread Gorgias, for a Third Sophistic, in such a manner that this binary of possible/impossible is exploded by the introduction of a third element into numerous nonpositive affirmative possibilities (i.e., wills to power).

Poulakos points out that Aristotle (in Book 9 of the *Metaphysics*) favors *energeia* (the actual) over *dynamis* (the possible, the potential), with the "actual" being prior to the "possible" and therefore superior. The "actual," for Aristotle, is the world of facts. Poulakos says:

> Unlike his predecessors, who posit the world as it is not (Sophists) or a world that ought to be (Plato), Aristotle's starting point is the world as it is, in its positive structure and tendencies. Accordingly he grounds his Rhetoric in the actuality of facts or events and their proof, reminding us at the same time of the superfluousness of everything else, i.e., ethical and pathetic appeals, stylistic graces, and dramatic delivery. (1984, 217)[10]

Poulakos continues:

> By insisting on the primacy of facts, [Aristotle] endeavors to grant the world
> its own objective status and lift the linguistic spell cast on it by the Sophists.
> Aristotle assumes that the world can be known and reproduced accurately
> by linguistic means. . . . The Sophists, however, are not that confident in man's
> ability to know the world as it is; nor are they altogether sure of any cor-
> respondence between objective reality and language. For them, what mat-
> ters is not "pure" fact but fact as perceived, interpreted, and communicated.
> A fact is not something closed or finished; because it is subject to human
> speech, it remains open, unfinished, recurring each time it is *recount*ed
> [emphasis mine]. In short, a fact is essentially a linguistic fact. (218)

(I have already pointed out how both Protagoras and Gorgias viewed the world
of facts as unfinished, either caught in contradictions or irrationalities.)

Poulakos towards the end of his discussion calls on Martin Heidegger,
who in his deconstruction of Aristotle, says "higher than actuality stands *possibility*," and "possibility signifies what is not yet actual and what is *not at
any time* necessary" (Poulakos 1984, 222; Heidegger 1962, 63). Such a
favoring of what was the Aristotelian supplement (the possible), as we know
by now, issues in Heidegger's critique of western metaphysics. (What is issued,
to be sure, is a new currency for a new economy. Let us, however, be careful
of overly fantasizing about the new!) What Poulakos is attempting is a similar critique of western Aristotelian, philosophical rhetoric, by way of his own
favoring of the supplement Sophism-as-"possibilism" over the previously
favored philosophism-as-"actualism," with its concomitant impossibilism; and
it is a critique that I welcome, but which I wish *to extend* to my own
postmodern (Nietzschean) perspectives. To repeat: Whereas Poulakos issues
his new economy by way of Heidegger, I issue mine by way of Nietzsche. (This
issuing, however, may be no difference. Strong poets, however, may have to
make it appear, deceptively, so.) As I say, I wish to extend, stretch, casuistically
if necessary. I take my lessons in this act, then, from both Heidegger *and*
Nietzsche. But mostly from a third, stretched "Nietzsche." A reader can only
but stretch.

This my extension—as might be expected—is beyond *one* or *two* . . .
all the way to a radical, Third Sophistic *some more*, which can be seen—
if read from an Aristotelian bias—as working out of the *topos* of the *impossible* that makes for *possibilism*. (Cf. E. C. White's discussion of Aristotle,
1987, 22ff.; Ricoeur 1978, 11.) This is the way of philosopical-rhetorical
invention: What is invented, what is produced, is brought forth by way of
negation or No-thing. It is the way of species-genus analytics, *diaeresis*, as
I described it at length in chapter 1. However, *I would prefer not to not*. I

would prefer that the *possible* not be read singularly across either a Platonic or Aristotelian, philosophical conceptual starting place (*topos*); for, as I have already suggested, that *topos* is one founded on negation (know-ing by no-thing) itself, which ethically-politically "subjects" subjects. (As Deleuze and Guattari say—and I will say repeatedly—if there is a subject, there is repression [1983, 26; cf. Foucault 1982, 208–26].) If I am to finally suggest ways of reportraying Helen(s), it must be done, instead, by way of nonpositive affirmation. The theater of representation must be changed. Be change. If I am going to escape the history of Being, Nihilism, it must be done as I seek it. (Which may be in/determined by way of style, a writing style alone.) It is not enough to simply stop where Gorgias stopped with his four defenses of Helen, for we must have some more in dis/order to get the un/kind of linkage that I am after and as I will ruminate on in the next chapter.

Though I identify with Poulakos, as well as many others, in deconstructing Plato and Aristotle (Neel 1988; 1995), I think, however, that there is always a serious, potential problem with Poulakos's identifying with *the Heideggerian possible* and identifying this notion of the possible with the Sophists.[11] Moreover, contrary to what Derrida says, I find Heidegger's notion of Being and its relation to the possible (impossible) equally problematic. (To this point, I will return.) First, the easy part, namely, associating the Heideggerian possible with the Sophists. Heidegger in his deconstruction of Plato and Aristotle does not, in his own thinking, replace them with the Sophists. He could not because he associates the Sophists with the withdrawal of Being. If Heidegger identifies with anyone, it is a few so-called pre-Socratics but especially Socrates himself, who he says stood in the storm of the withdrawing of Being (see 1959, 106; Gillespie 1984, 141–42). Having denied this connection between the Heideggerian possible and the Sophists, however, I would not myself disagree with it if enacted in terms of casuistic stretching. (Therefore, I stand with but not with Poulakos on this point of mis/identification.)

Now to the more important and difficult issue concerning Heidegger's possible, specifically, whether or not it is founded on the negative or positive or a third notion of a possibility: There are readers of Heidegger who think that even in or around *Being in Time* that Heidegger does see his fundamental ontology as outside of the negative. Derrida—Heidegger's primary apologist—claims that Heidegger does see his notion of Being and the possible as outside, that is, as outside of any category of species or genus (1978, 141). If so, then, Being and its *incipit* possibilities are neither negative or positive but in a third position-that-is-not-a-position. Or if so, we might begin to think of reversing the *topos* to possible cum impossible (pure possibility would be a power [call it *dynamis*], which when entering predication becomes impossible). As we proceed, perhaps this will become more unclearly clear.

Let's take a closer look. Heidegger describes his relationship with this *topos* of the impossible cum possible (or again, the possible cum impossible) extensively in "What is Metaphysics?"; he writes, "For human existence the *nothing* [the impossible] makes *possible* the openedness of being as such. The nothing does not merely serve as the counterconcept of beings; rather it originally belongs to their essential unfolding as such" (1977, 106. Also, see 1977, 196, 238; 1962, 294; 1991, Vol. 2, 129–32; 173–75; 193–95). Hearing all this "nothing," we might think that we hear references to the negative (*physis*^neg.). Derrida, however, has an ingenious reading of this "nothing" (the impossible). In "How to Avoid Speaking: Denials," Derrida writes:

> One could read *What is Metaphysics?* as a treatise on negativity. It establishes the basis for negative discourse and negation in the experience of the Nothing which itself "nothings". . . . The experience of anguish puts us in relation to a negating . . . which is neither annihilation . . . nor a negation or a denial. . . . It reveals to us the strangeness . . . of what is . . . as the wholly other. . . . It thus opens up the possibility of the question of Being for *Dasein*, the structure of which is characterized precisely by what Heidegger calls transcendence. (1992, 122)

Derrida, in "Violence and Metaphysics," puts forth a similar argument. He says that Levinas argues that "the Heideggerian 'possibilities' remain powers. Although they are pretechnical and preobjective, they are nonetheless oppressive and possessive" (1978, 97). Derrida argues, however, that "Being itself commands nothing or no one. As Being is not the lord of the existent, its priority (ontic metaphor) is not an *archia*. The best liberation from violence is a certain putting into question, which makes the search for an *archia* tremble." He emphasizes: "Only the thought of Being can do so, and not traditional 'philosophy' or 'metaphysics' " (1978, 141). Levinas would have a nonviolent language. However, Derrida responds: ". . . nonviolent language would be a language which would do without the verb *to be*, that is, without predication. Predication is the first violence" (147; Derrida's emphasis). Therefore, having made his technical point that Being *is* pre-ontological, Derrida concludes: When we call on the possible, we call on "the economy of war," from which we cannot escape (148; cf. K. Burke 1969a, 305). (Nietzsche, of course, would not see this economy as war but as Heraclitean play.) Derrida concludes: "Are we Jews? Are we Greeks? We live in the difference between the Jew and the Greek, which is perhaps the unity of what is called history" (153). (Nietzsche, however, asks Whether we will nothingness or not will? [see 1969, 163].)

So what has been said? Namely, that Heidegger's notion of Being and possibilities are outside of any categories (species, genus) and therefore outside of the negative. In other words, this nothing is a nothing-that-is-not-nothing. However, when Being and its possibilities are realized, violence—actualized violence—presents itself. In other words, as Kenneth Burke and Jacques Lacan would have it, when we leave the imaginary for the symbolic, we take on the moral-political negative and become subjects "rotten with perfection" (Burke) or subjects given to "the fantasy to seize reality" (Lacan; Lyotard; Zizek). It appears, given Derrida's qualifications to his interpretation, that Being (and its originary possibilities) can be a source for resisting violence: "The best liberation from violence is a certain putting into question, which makes the search for an *archia* tremble." However, when it comes to writing history, we will forever be writing the history of nihilism—which means in error—unless we can find a way to make an *archia* tremble. (I have spoken of these possibilities earlier in Derridian terms of guarding the question and calling to the other.)

I do think that Derrida's argument is compelling, especially when he extends his reading of Heideggerian Being (*Dasein*) in terms of gender. On several occasions, Derrida speaks of Heidegger's (silent) attitude toward gender (and genre, species, genus). In "Choreographies" (an interview), Derrida speaks against "a 'reactive' feminism" (1982, 68) and " 'essentializing fetishes' (truth, femininity, the essentiality of woman or feminine sexuality as fetishes)" (70), and speaks for *Dasein* as "neither the human being . . . nor the subject, neither consciousness nor the self. . . . These are all determinations that are derived from and occur after the *Dasein*." He continues: "*Dasein* is neuter" (74; cf. Krell 1986, 27–46). Derrida quotes Heidegger: " 'The neutrality means also that the Dasein is neither of the two sexes. But this a-sexuality (*Geschlechtlosigkeit*) is not the indifference of empty invalidity, the annuling negativity of an indifferent ontic nothingness. In its neutrality, the *Dasein* is not the indifferent person-and-everyone (*Niemand und Jeder*), but it is originary positivity and the power of being or of the essence, *Mächtigkeit des Wesen*' " (74) From Heidegger, Derrida begins to speak in terms of "polysexual signatures" and of "a sexuality without number" (76). Such un/thinking, of course, interests me here and throughout my discussion. A year later, Derrida, in his lectures on *Geschlecht*, further discusses "sexual difference, ontological difference." Repeating much of what he had already said in the interview, Derrida restates Heidegger's view of the "originary positivity" and "power of essence" as "the positive and powerful source of every possible 'sexuality' " (1993, 72).

So far—so it might seem—so good; but these views (theories) of Derrida's reading of Heidegger have been appropriated so as to serve other interests, specifically Gayatri Spivak's reading of feminism and deconstruction. And, most assuredly, to strategic essentialism (of which I have spoken earlier). However, even if Derrida's reading of Heidegger had not been appropriated, I would still have problems with such a reading, for the simple reason that Derrida's is Heideggerian and, consequently, questionable, ever questionable. Is this a tautological statement? Of course. Why? Because Derrida, in his defense of Heideggerian thinking by way of Heideggerian thinking itself, has created a *differend*. And yet it is an ingenious reading. Which, nonetheless, must be resisted. And therefore we must find a way to make the Heideggerian *archia* itself tremble. I think that I have in chapters 4 and 5 demonstrated that I *can* say Yes to the Heideggerian text twice, at least in part. And, I hope, make that text tremble. Throughout, especially toward the end (rebeginnings?) of this book, however, I say Yes to the Nietzschean text three times (Yes, Yes, Yes). My existential choice away from Heideggerian to Nietzschean texts, however, has primarily to do with the commentators on these respective texts. Derrida but especially Spivak develop their readings in ways that, I think, extend a kind of essentialism that I am attempting to fully denegate. (I am most troubled by Derrida's reading of Nietzsche in *The Ear of the Other* [1985a]; and troubled by Spivak in any number of discussions [1989a, 1989b], as I have tried intermittently to suggest.[12]) Instead, Foucault, Deleuze and Guattari, Judith Butler, and others develop their reading of Nietzschean texts in ways that are most helpful (hopeful [yet pessimistically hopeful]) in the light of my reworking essentialism, specifically, in terms of nonpositive affirmation. (Nietzsche, as one of the hermeneuts of suspicion, was most suspicious of his texts; and his commentators are just as suspicious of his as well as their own texts.) Though I can give partial assent to Heideggerian texts, there is still the problem of Heidegger himself and his own questionable relationship to his texts as well as his actions. He appears to become more and more a romantic, sentimental, out-of-touch-poet, especially out of touch with the Other (cf. Rorty 1989, ch. 5). Most importantly, I favor Nietzsche because he deals with the body, with the surface of things, more than Heidegger does. In terms of the will to power and subjectivity, Nietzsche speaks of a *pathos* of embodiment, a "muscular sensation" (1966, 25), while Heidegger says, "We do not 'have' a body; rather, we 'are' bodily" (1991, vol. 1: 99).[13] Nietzsche is by far more of a (libidinal) materialist than Heidegger could ever be. (I think that Derrida is more of a libidinal materialist, in his redescriptions, than Heidegger could ever become.) For Nietzsche, the force or desire or will to power is here with us, in our bodies; for Heidegger, the Nothing (Being, force) is beyond; is, as he says, in withdrawal. Both speak of "originary" forces, but locate them in different places. Here and beyond. The "here" of Nietzsche is the beyond here within us (see Deleuze 1988, 94–123).

Heidegger, as Lyotard says, demonstrates a certain contempt for Being: "How could this thought (Heidegger's), a thought so devoted to remembering that a forgetting (of Being) takes place in all thought, in all art, in all 'representation' of the world, how could it possibly have ignored the thought of 'the jews' [the Other], which, in a certain sense, thinks, tries to think, nothing but that very fact?" (1990, 4). What Heidegger does, then, in Lyotard's estimation, is to engage in *negative essentializing*. (We, human beings, are given to such essentializing.) When we say, "There is. . . ," we reset the conditions for the possibilities of negative essentializing. And for potlatch! The sun shines. (Recall my earlier discussion of this phenomenon in relation to Mauss, Levi-Strauss, and Bataille in the excurses on aesthetics.) The "gift" issuing from "there is/it gives (*Es gibt*) Time and Being" can create, as Bataille says about the potlatch of the sun, the conditions for being-reactionary. Given Heidegger's reasoning, since Being has withdrawn, the "It" (the gift), as David Krell says, "resists all depiction" (see Heidegger 1991, vol. 4, 216, for Krell's comment in a footnote.) Whereas Bataille suggests a way around this problem, a way of emulating the sun, the "It," Heidegger does not. We must, as he does, simply sit and listen and wait for revelation. In the meantime, we are in the conditions of deep trouble. For sure, we are always in these conditions, but Heidegger's is especially deep trouble, for his conditions are in the negative. If Heidegger's Being cannot be depicted, represented, How then does it differ from Lacan's notion of the Real? Put simply, it does not. Both Being-withdrawn and the Real are the negative. Which only intensifies the conditions for the possibilities of being-reactionary. Hence, the counter-necessity of rapidly switching from one "There is. . ." to another "There is. . ." and switching without the so-called benefit of the principles of identity, contradiction, and excluded middle. (To be Derridian, once again: The *pharmakon* is ever necessary.) But had not Nietzsche issued this statement earlier? in terms of "joyful pessimism" and "neuroses of health" (1967, 21)? Other questions remain: Are we Hedeggerians? But finally: Are we Nietzscheans? Are we not the difference between the two. Becoming the third, "Nietzschean." We shuttle, while switching codes rapidly, between their differences. "Nietzschean."

The problem that I'm confronted with is that I want to throw away but maintain a Heideggerian view. I want my Heidegger and Nietzsche, too. But of course, I would, for reasons given above, set aside Heidegger's view of the possible (which, after all, is founded on the negative) and embrace Nietzsche's for yet other reasons. "Nietzsche." Heidegger's own view, or revision, of Nietzsche is reason enough. To avoid Heidegger. When Heidegger speaks and writes of Nietzsche, he philosophizes him, *systematizes* him (see 1991, Vol. 1, 18–24); and he grossly *misappropriates* him (see 1991, Vol. 4, 147–49, 188–

96, 199–250). He reads (resystematizes) Nietzsche in terms of his own *Being and Time*; and he misappropriates (makes improper) Nietzsche in terms of "value thinking" (204). Concerning the latter, revaluing value did not mean a returning it to, metaphorically here, a different counting system that was indebted to the negative, but a discounting system that would take it *out of*, and yet stay within, such indebtedness. This is what Nietzsche was aiming for and this is what he meant about living dangerously (1966, 224). (I take up this issue of value more fully in chapter 7.) My sense is that Heidegger's "debt" to Nietzsche—his need/desire to match Nietzsche's gift to him—is so great that he thinks that he stands in Nietzsche's shadow. I'm thinking, again, in terms of a Bloomian anxiety of influence and most emphatically in terms of Heidegger's confronting the indebtedness of having to match potlatch. (See Krell 1986, 138-51.) And what of potluck?

Having established a difference but nonetheless an identity with, but without, both Heidegger and Nietzsche, I want now to return to Helen(s). And the conditions for the possible (possibilities) of a Third Sophistic.

III. Still "some more" Helens

For me the number three is important, but simply from the numerical, not the esoteric point of view; one is unity, two is double, duality, and three is the rest. When you've come to three, you have three million—it's the same thing as three.

—Marcel Duchamp

In writing the previous and present sections, I am attempting to rethink (become ever-suspicious about) an earlier, published discussion of mine (see 1991, 127–29), in which, at this point, I characterized subjectivity in terms of the *topos* "out of the impossible comes the possible," or "out of negation comes affirmation." I achieved this reading by way of Lacan's discussion of the *real* (the impossible) and its trilemma (imaginary, symbolic, real), which I eventually paralleled with Gorgias's trilemma (in "On the Nonexistent or on Nature"). While it was a reading of Gorgias across these Lacanian *topoi* that allowed me to reach for a non-Humanist subjectivity (one in dispersion), it was also these *topoi*, however, that returned my thinking about Gorgias— and a Third Sophistic—back to the problem of the negative, specifically, to a model of subjectivity based on *lack*. It was Bernard Miller's reading (1987) of Untersteiner's incipient reading of Heidegger's notion of *kairos* that, likewise, kept me indebted to the negative.

I now desire to reestablish more suitably the conditions for the possibilities of "Third Sophistic" subjectivities, or radical-but-nonreactionary
Helens. I would be more blatantly and fully "Nietzschean," now, in my
readings of Untersteiner's reading of Gorgias's "On the Nonexistent or on
Nature" and "Encomium of Helen." As I continue serially to unfold this
notion of subjectivity that is a sovereign subjectivity, what I will attempt
here, therefore, is the difference between a view of strategic (negative) essentialism (which takes the risk of negative essence) and what I have been
calling a view of strategic (affirmative) essentialism (which will have taken
the risk of nonpositive affirmative essence). I spoke in chapters 4 and 5
of "danger"; here are two kinds, the latter of which I would trek with. With
such a view and risk, I will have been "Nietzschean" (in a sense, post-Hegel
and ante-Heidegger). I will have reinterpreted, re/engaged in *something
new, irrational*. And I will have attempted to do all this on a Sophist, whom
I claim to be a proto-Third Sophistic rhetor, but who is apparently deeply
indebted to negation. (It will take me a while [wild?] to do all this, so
patience is required.)

> A wild practice . . . one that does not provide the theoretical
> credentials for its operations and which raises screams from
> the philosophy of "interpretation" of the world. . . .
>
> —Louis Althusser

"On Nature" (*physis*^{neg}, essence^{neg}): There are numerous, rather ingenious readings of Gorgias's "On the Nonexistent or On Nature." It could be
argued that this plurality demonstrates that Gorgias and his text are already
in dispersal and, therefore, any form of subjectivity based on it would also
be in dispersal. Such a claim and argument, however, would miss my larger
point, namely, that though there are numerous, competing interpretations
of Gorgias's trilemma, these interpretations are simply a working out of the
available permutations and combinations of the *topos* of the impossible cum
possible, or the *topos* of from lack comes excess.

In this light, I want to suggest two different ways of rethinking Gorgias's
"On the Nonexistent or On Nature," two ways that might allow us to think
in yet unthought affirmative terms. First, I want to resuggest that there is
no difference between Parmenides's version of nature (*physis*) and Gorgias's
version. *Both are predicated on negation*. Hence, we have *physis*^{neg}. Second,
I want to examine the claim—and its undisclosed, unselfconscious significance for us—that Gorgias's trilemma is to be read across the genre of
parody, specifically a parody of Parmenides's poem (Guthrie 1971, 193–94;

E. C. White 1987, 32; Consigny 1991). In examining this claim, I want to establish a counter-statement that Gorgias's trilemma can be read in yet other ways, with quite different results, specifically, across the paragenre and conventions of *pastiche*. (Each way, or how this text can be read, brings into being different "texts.")

The first suggestion would say, then, that there is not a difference between Parmenides (Plato) and Gorgias, in that they both work from the negative; however, they do employ their workings (labor and play) from the negative in different ways. The second suggestion would say that Gorgias is not necessarily identified by way of a Parmenides, or a Plato, or by way of a Heidegger (or Poulakos) but heretically misidentified by way of a Nietzsche (or Victor Anza Vita[14]). With this second suggestion, I will be attempting to rescue Gorgias's texts (both "On the Nonexistent" and "Helen") from negative readings, so that we might think from the conditions of the possibilities of nonpositive affirmative readings.

> ... the one that IT IS ... is the way of credibility, for it follows Truth; the other, that IT IS NOT, and that IT is bound NOT TO BE: this I tell you is a path that cannot be explored; for you could neither recognise that which is not, nor express it.
>
> —Parmenides

> As early as Plato, dialectics meant to achieve something positive by means of negation.
>
> —Theo. Adorno

> The evidence of the body reveals a tremendous multiplicity.
>
> —Nietzsche

Whereas Parmenides (and Plato) argue that there is *some thing* instead of *nothing*, Gorgias argues there is *nothing* instead of *some thing*. (This *difference* is typical of the beginnings of The History of Philosophy, the origins of the incarceration of *logos* and of *ethos*, or subjectivity.) But as I have suggested—sophistically and fundamentally—there is *no difference*; for Parmenides's *some thing*, or "it is," is based on negation, specifically, on the principles of identity, non-contradiction, and excluded middle. As these principles get refined by Socrates and Plato, they inform the unfolding of dialectics. Let's take a closer look at Parmenides's didactic poem on existence (nature, Being, *physis*[neg.]), and then at Plato's, or the Stranger's, argument in the *Sophist*. I will eventually return to Gorgias's view of non-Being.

Parmenides is a subject (agent) of desire: He *desires* to know, but this desire will be limited (see Butler 1987; cf. Aristotle *Metaphysics* 980a). In his poem (I.11–14)[15] Parmenides desires *logos*; to this end, he is escorted by maidens (*Dike* and *Ananke*) to the forbidden doors of *the* goddess who would teach him knowledge of *logos*. *Dike* (justice) opens these doors, which allows Parmenides, then, to enter and behold the subject of desire. (The sexual imagery—door and penetration—are rather obvious here.) The goddess teaches that there is *some thing* (Baubô?) instead of *nothing* (2.3–4). The other maiden, *Ananke* (necessity) separates Being from non-Being. And why? The goddess says that Being constitutes choice, whereas non-Being makes choice impossible. Therefore, the goddess warns that the masses (*demos*) live in non-Being. She, therefore, tells Parmenides: "I debar you from that way along which *wander* mortals [the *demos*] knowing nothing, *two-headed* [of two minds], for . . . they are carried along as deaf as they are blind, amazed, uncritical hordes" (6; emphasis mine).

What is occurring in the poem is best described as *diaeresis* (or as Foucault would have it, and Schiappa would realize it, a "dividing practice" [see Foucault 1982, 208–26]) so as to establish and to maintain a certain order. (It is, of course, reasoned—given the conditions—that without this dividing practice there is no symbolic order, hence, only a mass of the indistinguishable, or what Nietzsche would refer to as will[s] to power.) Andrea Nye explains that both *Dike* (justice) and *Ananke* (necessity) are personifications of logical necessity, that is, the law (*logos*) of non-contradiction (1990, 12–13). But the handmaidens, after all, only assist the goddess, who, Parmenides tells us, "in the centre . . . guides [divides] everything; for throughout she rules over cruel Birth and Mating, sending the female to mate with the male, and conversely again the male with the female" (12.3–6). And yet, there is, nonetheless, the possible abomination of abominations:

> When a woman and man mix seeds of Love together, the power [of the seeds] which shape [the embryo] in the veins out of different blood can mould well-constituted bodies only if it preserves proportion. For if the powers war [with each other] when the seed is mixed, and do not make a unity in the body formed by the mixture, they will terribly harass the growing [embryo] through the twofold seed of the [two] sexes. (18)

In her reading of this passage, Nye argues that the goddess "describes for Parmenides the unfortunate biological effects of such mixings. In fertilization, if the male principle or the female principle prevails, then, there will be well-formed bodies, but if there is no unitary sexual identity, the sex of the offspring will be tormented by 'double seed,' that is it will have both male and female characteristics" (14). In a word, it will be a *hermaphrodite* (such a Favorinus? such as the desire named Marx?). Nye continues: "But to mix masculinity and femininity is unthinkable. The cryptic fragment 17 illustrates concretely the requisite division [*diaeresis*] between 'is' and 'is not': 'On the right boys, on the left girls [in the womb],' a segregation which popular theories of generation and cosmic origin *did not respect*" (14; emphasis mine; see Vernant 1990). Parmenides's predisposition regarding this issue of mixing, it must be emphasized, was not the dis/order of his day; though Parmenides along with Plato and Aristotle and company have apparently won the day, there are repressed voices (thoughts) returning to tell us all that this dividing practice is a lot less biological than we have been conventionally led to believe. Anne Fausto-Sterling and others are now demonstrating that there are at least five sexes, if not an infinite continuum of other sexes (1993).

If there is a mixture, a confusion, in the body, it will, Parmenides says in section 16.1–5, have an effect on the mind and its thoughts: ". . . according to the mixture of much-wandering limbs which each man has, so is the mind which is associated with mankind: for it is the same thing which thinks, namely the constitution of the limbs in men, all and individually; for it is *excess* which makes Thought" (emphasis mine). It is a mixture in and of the body, via wandering limbs (wandering wombs!), which cause a thinking that is characterized as mad, insane, or in excess. Stated another way, without negation (division) there is what I have been referring to as the conditions for the possibilities of nonpositive affirmation (which includes an aesthetic of excess, the body of the subject speaking, the subjectivity of hysteria and madness).

> The whole Socratic dialectic: nothing can be named as "beings" except those same things which all the same men see in the same way in a setup that does not allow them to see other things and which they will designate by the same names, on the basis of the conversation [dialogic] between them. Whichever way up you turn these premises, you always come back to *sameness*.
>
> —L. Irigaray

But division (*diaeresis*), negation, or exclusion, is ever insisted on. Up to this point, the thinking is fragmentary in more ways than one. However, what Parmenides has begun, Plato, or the Eleatic Stranger, in the *Sophist* continues in order to refine.[16] Let's now turn to this dialogue so as to pick up some of the themes (counting, *diaeresis*, negation, subjectivity) so as to see just how the Stranger changes Parmenides's poetry into dialogue, or dialectic.

The Stranger immediately gets in trouble. Early in this dialogue, in his attempt to follow the path of thinking that Parmenides has put forth, the Stranger finds himself, horror of horrors!, in a contradiction (238d). He says, "We shall find it necessary in self-defense [therefore] to put to the [dialectical] question that pronouncement of father Parmenides" (241d). And what is that pronouncement? That it is only possible to say *what is*. And the contradiction? That Parmenides's and now the Stranger speak of *"what is not."* (*What is* paradoxically/contradictorily leads to *What is not*.)

The Stranger, along with Theaetetus, imagines himself in a dialogue with "the Hydra-headed Sophist," who, he says, "has forced us against our will to admit that 'what is not' has some sort of being" (240c). What was suppressed/repressed, politically oppressed, has returned. The Stranger's discussion begins with numbers and counting: " 'Something' is always used of a thing that exists. . . . To speak of 'something' is to speak of 'some one thing' " (237d). He concludes: ". . . among things that exist we include number in general. . . . We must not, then, so much as attempt to attach either plurality or unity in number to the nonexistent" (238b). The Stranger continues, "I [however] who laid it down that the nonexistent could have neither unity nor plurality, have not only just now but at this very moment spoken of it as one thing, for I am saying '*the* nonexistent' " (238e).

Therefore, the question perversely presents itself, How can a lover of wisdom argue against a Sophist (such as Gorgias) who says there *is* nothing? To speak with a Sophist, even to admit that there is such a thing as a Sophist, is to surrender oneself to contradiction. (Remember Schiappa's refusal to admit the Sophists.) Therefore, how can one defend oneself from such an apparent inevitable trap? Further developing what Father Parmenides said, The Stranger sets out to find a way (*poria*) by counting, or determining, "how many *real* things there are" (242c; emphasis mine). The Stranger takes Thaetetus through a long disjunctive process of deciding (see Deleuze and Guattari 1983, 13, 25–30) on whether there is either One or Many, whether there is either "real being" or "becoming" (248a). Oasis or Mirage? The Stranger, then, introduces the possibility of a "third" way of thinking, which is a combination of both real being and becoming. This possibility of all three together, however, is ridiculed as only "magnificent entertainment" (251b–c). (The Sophists are known as being great entertainers! Or the P. T. Barnums of the philosophical world!) And yet, the Stranger allows that one of the three possibilities is acceptable, while the other two are not (252d). To determine what is and what is not possible—here we go again!—it is necessary, the Stranger says, to find some "guide" or "science" such as "dialectic" to sort out what conjoins and what does not, just as the guide of grammar tells us which letters of the alphabet conjoin and do not conjoin (253a–d). (Recall Isocrates's relying on a guide [*hegemon*].)

It is at this point, then, that the Stranger reintroduces the means of difference, or *diaeresis* (division). He begins this discussion by having Theaetetus ask, "What is the difference?" The Stranger proceeds to distinguish between the philosopher and the Sophist. (Notice that he is still speaking of the Sophist but, as will become clear, under different terms.) As we well know by now, the question "What is the difference?" is an archi deBunker question, which has a difference (ambiguity, a hydra-headed one) that either we or language itself or both cannot answer (see de Man 1979). So as to anchor difference, however, the Stranger introduces (the necessary fiction of) *ideal forms*, which includes five forms that can in certain ways be linked together. They include "existence" (*it is*), and "motion" and "rest," which cannot be linked together but can be linked with "existence"; for, after all, motion and rest *do* exist. The Stranger's discussion of these three leads him to conclude that there are two others, namely, "sameness" (linking together) and "difference" (not linking together) (254a–255e).

In chapter 1, I explained this logic of difference by negation, which is philosophical—philological-rhetorical logic. Though there appears to be both difference *and* sameness, what Plato and the Stranger reintroduce and emphasize *is difference*. As Nye points out, whereas Parmenides concentrates on the logic of "what is, is" (on the logic of tautologies), Plato and the Stranger now find it necessary to add to this logic (possibly through "parricide" [241d]) the means of differentiating how "anything is different from anything else, or that anything does not exist" (1990, 23). They ask, then, "What's [in the] difference?", which is the question of species-genus analytics. As I explained, the procedure for determining difference is quite simple and, by now, rather automatic: A *species* has meaning by virtue of its placement in a *genus*. This species is *in* this genus because it is not like, or is different from, those things that cannot be placed in this genus. Moreover, this species differs from all other species in this genus by virtue of a long list of *differentiae*. The logic of identification is the logic of negation: We can never say what some thing is, but can say what it is not (see K. Burke 1966, 913, 419–79): Or still, in more contemporary terms, the metaphysics of presence is the metaphysics of absence (Derrida 1972). We have *some thing*, then, because of *no thing*. Politically and ethically such thinking by division is so dangerous because it relies on congregation by segregation.

In speaking at length about Parmenides and Plato/the Stranger, we apparently have left Gorgias far behind. Or have we? Let us recall, Gorgias says, "Nothing exists." My contention at first and at the close of the discussion, thus far, has been that in order to say that *some thing is*, it must be said from the *topos* of nothing. In one sense, Non-being is nothing and cannot determine a choice; and yet, in another sense, as I have illustrated with species-genus analytics (*diaeresis*), it is what *does* constitute choice. Therefore, Parmenides's and Plato's (the Stranger's) redescriptions of Being, Nature (*physis*) is, at bottom, the same as Gorgias's redescriptions of Being. Both are of *physis*neg.

The first sense—that is, Parmenides and Plato's—I would call a fetish or fantasy that is not aware of itself *as* a fantasy structure. (This again is the metaphysics of presence that does not know that it is based on absence.) The second sense—Gorgias's—I would also call a fetish or fantasy that *is* aware of itself *as* such. (This, then, is the metaphysics of absence.) The first sense posits an everlasting "real"; the second, only a nostalgia for the loss of the real. For me, the two senses of Yes-as-no and No-as-"yes" are one and the same in that they are, as Zizek would say, both *sublime objects of ideology* (1989).

What I am saying here about Yes-as-no and No-as-"yes" should not simply be construed as a modernist, or Derridian/Lacanian, view appropriating a pre-modern, or classical, view. (Nor should this comparison of mine be seen as only an anachronistic one, but an assemblage.) The argument for Yes being no (or for that matter No meaning "yes"), which would be in a sense a modernist argument, does not come about because, as modernists might say, *God is dead*, does not come about because of antifoundationalism, or intellectual atheism; for as I pointed out earlier, "God" was "No" before God, so to speak, died: The onto-theological tradition itself had already defined "God" as "*pure* affirmation," that is, as radical negativity. This point is ancient; it is called *negative theology*. Certainly, for rhetoricians of all sorts, Kenneth Burke has reminded or taught us about this notion of a negative theology in terms of the paradox of Being, or substance (1969a, 21–58; 1970, 17–23). This can get humorous: Heidegger, in his appropriation of Nietzsche, has him down as practicing "a negative theology" (1991, Vol. 2, 95).[17] And yet, Nietzsche thought Dionysus, the anti-Christ! Let us laugh, schizophrenic laughter. Heidegger, where is your Nietzsche? Under negation?

Therefore, in simple terms, *there is*, but *there is not* any difference between Being and Non-Being. When Gorgias says that Nothing exists, he is and is not simultaneously Parmenides, Plato/the Stranger, and himself. The Stranger was well aware of finding himself, or Parmenides, in a contradiction ("that things that are, are not, and that things that are not, are"!): There being no difference between *it is* and *it is not*, which was a problem for him. Hence, the necessity for ideal forms. (See *Sophist* 240–41.)

Gorgias recapitulates, though metaleptically, the rise and fall of The History of Philosophy and Philosophical Rhetoric. He simply and directly states, therefore, what is at the very bottom-that-is-not-a-bottom. Nothing.

Which desires, however, to be Some (Kantian sublime object of desired) thing. It is this kind of desire (of nothing, lack), however, that must be negated itself or denegated. I would not go for Ideal forms to fix things, save them from contradiction and, as the Stranger says, silly games— to "conceive of reality as a third thing over and above [the] two" (250b–251c), but would denegate the forms and let things become not just fuzzy, but flow, wherever. *Physis*ⁿᵉᵍ must be denegated for a nonpositive affirmative *physis*. Must be denegated for a sublime, sovereign subject-that-would-not-be-a-subject. But beyond subjects to Nietzsche's various notions of will(s) to power. As Nietzsche says: "The Evidence of the body reveals a tremendous multiplicity" (1968c, 218, or no. 518). I have insisted on this throughout. What this will (to power) means is a redescription of Gorgias. It is a purposeful denegative turn away from What is? and a return to How are? (The mad text of Gorgias itself supports such a will to how/l.)

If the Stranger tries to resolve the problem of whether *it is, is,* or *it is not,* by appealing to a third kind that, as a mixture of the two statements, allows him logically to differentiate himself as a lover of wisdom from a Hydra-headed Sophist; and if I try, in passing, to resolve temporarily/provisionally the problem of the bifurcation by collapsing the two apparent kinds (Being and non-Being) into one; I would now return the discussion to another third unkind—or to Cixous's uncountry, *dépays*—that I have throughout been developing as not the *negative* and not the *affirmative* (which is insidiously and incipiently the negative), but is what Foucault has called the nonpositive affirmative. This entire discussion from Parmenides to Gorgias can, in The philosophical narrative that I have been denegating, only keep us indebted to the problem of the negative, or the *topos* of the *impossible/possible*; therefore, we must move on to this third unkind.

In both doxagraphic versions of "On the Nonexistent"—the so-called Aristotelian MXG and Sextus Empiricus versions—Gorgias allegedly says: Nothing exists; if it does exist, we cannot know it; if we could know it, we could not communicate it. (This is Gorgias's trilemma, which as I have argued [1991] is remarkably close to Lacan's trilemma of the imaginary, symbolic [the no], and real [the No].)

One interpretation of "On the Nonexistent" raises the question about whether Gorgias is "serious" about his argument, or whether he is parodying Parmenides (Guthrie 1971; cf. Consigny 1991). But is there a difference here? For parody, or satire, implies, or has as one of its generic conventions, playfulness with the purpose of seriousness. It also has the convention of original, or origin. To parody some "thing" or "thought," it is necessary to imitate in the appropriate stylistic, conventional manner, some original "thing" that the parodist wishes to poke fun at, with the primary purpose of improving on the "thing." With this understanding, we should be able to see that the ontology and epistemology of parody is that there is Being to work toward, to try to achieve, but also that there is Being, or original, that can be copied. "Original and copy" is the *topos* that informs the genre of parody and, at that, a highly Platonic *topos*. We simply have to recall Plato's attitude toward and theory of *mimesis* (see *Republic*, Bk. 3). (Remember, I would deal with those things, eventually all things, three times removed!) I do believe that Gorgias's argument can be read—given one's preferences of reading protocols—as a parody, or joke, on Parmenides, or for that matter can be read as a *dissoi-logoi* argument, or as possibly any other kinds of arguments. Such readings, however, do not provide precisely what I desire. Instead, I want to suggest that it is equally possible and productive—under different conditions of possibility—to read Gorgias's argument about Being, Nature (*physis*^{neg}), not as a parody but as a *pastiche*. (As a pastiche, Gorgias's trilemma can be seen, then, in Nietzschean terms.) One of the primary conventions of pastiche is that there is no origin, original, that is, no No. Pastiche is a paragenre that denegates a grand narrative founded on cause-effect, or on any other negative *topos* or *e/utopos*. Pastiche is informed by the post-ontology and post-epistemology that a copy is a copy of a copy of a copy, ad infinitum. (Here, then, infinite regression is embraced or, we might say, a Platonic third [mimetic] order is embraced. Here, then, I will reinclude whatever Plato and company have excluded.)

This shift in genres, or reading strategies and protocols, brought to bear on Gorgias's "On Nonexistence" will allow me to rethink both Gorgias's views and our various views of Helen. I partially agree with Untersteiner when he says that Gorgias's epistemology is founded on tragedy. Untersteiner devotes a chapter-length discussion to Gorgias and aesthetics (1954, ch. 8), and very importantly for my argument mentions and quotes Nietzsche in his opening discussion, in reference to the distinction between Socrates's view of reason/rationalism, which was, in Nietzsche's words, " 'strictly onesided, in contrast to the predominantly aesthetic culture of Greece which was current until then' " (185). The distinction that Nietzsche makes, of course, in *The Birth of Tragedy* is between an "Aesthetic Socrates" and an "Artistic Socrates" (1967, 83, 86, 92).

There is a possibility of an unproductive misunderstanding here, for we must insist on and emphasize Nietzsche's view of tragedy and not Aristotle's (or Arthur Miller's). I am going to dis/engage in a bit of a digression (mini-excursion) here. (As Barthes says, "fragmentation . . . digression . . . excursion" [1983, 476].) I want to talk about Nietzsche's views of *tragedy, justice, apate (deception)/aesthetics*. These views are inextricably tied up with pastiche (as a way of writing, dancing); and tied up with Being/being (nothing of fixed, negated essence exists). Nietzsche was diametrically opposed to will to truth (fixed, negative essentializing); he was for will to power (the affirmative play of differences).

Tragedy. Nietzsche, as a new philologist, speaks of Athenian tragedy in terms of a "pessimism of strength" (1967, 17). This pessimism is "a joyful pessimism." What brought about the death of this pessimism of strength was the rationalism that would give us optimism. A Knowing (Noing) that would give us not just hope, but the very answers that we have been led to expect from life. A rationalism practiced by Socrates and Euripides; a rationalism of theoretical man, of the principle of individuation and self-consciousness, of aesthetic socratism; a rationalism that demands that everything must be "conscious" to be beautiful and good, that we know ourselves, and that we think and do nothing in excess. All of these views of optimism and rationalism, for Nietzsche, are signs of "decline," not advancement (21).

This all begs for further explanation, which I will do briefly and in terms of threes again. The distinction is often made between the binary (machine) of pessimism and optimism. For Nietzsche, tragedy is not pessimism, for Nietzsche thinks *beyond.* As he says, he is interested in a "pessimism 'beyond good and evil' " (1967, 22). But there is an added twist. For Nietzsche, there is no difference between pessimism and optimism. (The parallel I want here is *with* my earlier statement that there is no difference between Not-Being and Being, absence and presence.)[18] The end(s) of man, given the conditions of Knowing (Noing), is (are) pessimism, or nihilism, both active and passive. Theoretical Man (or Onto-Theological Man, Optimistic Man) cannot deliver what he promises. Why? Because he expresses his desire by Knowing (Noing). Whereas there was a joyful pessimism, now there is only pessimism. (A reactionary optimism has replaced joy.) Again the result is nihilism. Whereas there was excess, now there is the negative. The scheme that we might keep in mind, then, so as to understand Nietzsche is *pessimism, optimism,* and *joyful pessimism* (the one, two, and some more). Or the scheme might perversely be read *joyful pessimism, optimism,* and *pessimism.* (Yes, it is necessary, here, to be contrary.)

Justice. Marxism is given to tragedy (see Eagleton 1981, 159–62). Nietzsche would agree with Marx that the "ground" of existence (life) is suffering (1967, 45), though Nietzsche would disagree about how to remember and "act" in relation to such suffering. Nietzsche refers to Silenus, the companion of Dionysus, who says that it would be better never to have been born (42–43). The Greeks had two ways of dealing with this suffering (terror): One, aesthetically (by way of joyful pessimism); the other, rationally (optimism). The first, at least in an Apollonian way, was accomplished by way of "the Olympian middle world of art" (44). Having the gods themselves live the life of man, the Greeks thereby "revers[ed] the wisdom of Silenus" and were in "harmony" with "nature" (44). However, this was the Apollonian (be it aesthetic) "fix" on the conditions of humanity. And, therefore, such a fix is right of us, for we must be far, far left of Apollo; far, far left of what is humanly (humanistically) possible. And how?, by "excess" (46).

Nietzsche speaks of "neuroses of *health*" (1967, 21; Nietzsche's emphasis). A Dionysian madness. He would now take those Apollonian gods and unite them with a billy goat, so as to have a satyr. Or to have gods-satyrs who would *dance*! He will have nothing to do with "the eternal No," or "a will to negate life" (23). He will have nothing to do with that "permanent military encampment of the Apollonian" (47). He finds that he has to say No to No. He has to denegate. He has to denegate the lyricist (48–50). That is, the principle of individuation, which is the sign of the repression, suppression, political oppression (cf. Deleuze and Guattari 1983, 26). He would not so much explode the subject rather than implode it. He would return to a Dionysian subject that-would-not-be-a-subject, but an *Ubermensch* (a sovereign, sublime subject). He says that he would set aside the Apollonian (Platonic) Dionysus, who, no matter how represented, is determined by way of the principle of individuation. Nietzsche writes: "In truth . . . the hero is the suffering Dionysus of the Mysteries, the god experiencing in himself the agonies of individuation, of whom wonderful myths tell that as a boy he was torn to pieces by the Titans" (73). Nietzsche continues:

> But the hope of the epopts [those initiated into the mysteries] looked toward a rebirth of Dionysus, which we must not dimly conceive as the end of individuation. It was for this coming *third Dionysus* [emphasis mine] that the epopts roaring hymns of joy resounded. And it is this hope alone that casts a gleam of joy upon the features of a world torn asunder and shattered into individuals; this is symbolized in the myth of Demeter, sunk in eternal sorrow, who *rejoices* again for the first time when told that she may *once more* give birth to Dionysus. (74; Nietzsche's emphasis)

As Josef Chytry points out, Nietzsche wants, first, to set aside the "purely political path of the *imperium romanum*" (world domination); and second, to set aside the "Schopenhauerian ideal of 'India,' the Buddhistic' desire for an ecstatic state," that transcends time and space in favor of a "political exhaustion in 'ecstatic brooding.' " In place of these two options, Nietzsche calls for a Third Dionysus (1989, 326; cf. Habermas 1987, 91-105).

Tragedy, Justice, Apate/*Aesthetics.* There is no *rational* way to "fix" the world that would not be reactionary; there are only aesthetic ways. Nietzsche takes to body and soul, Heraclitus's fragment stating that we should take the world aesthetically, not morally, religiously, or I might add, politically (Nietzsche 1962, 57–65; cf. Deleuze 1983, 17–25; Krell 1972). As Nietzsche translates Heraclitus: "It is a game. Don't take it so pathetically and—above all—don't make morality of it!" (1962, 64). As Nietzsche in/famously states, "the existence of the world is justified *only* as an aesthetic phenomenon" (1962, 22, 52; see Nietzsche 1968c, 451–53; Heidegger 1991, Vol. 1, 67–76). With an aesthetics of excess, then, there is the condition of the possibilities for *apate* (deception in an extra moral, Gorgian sense). With them both, there is the possibility of affirmative forgetting, the possibility of *amor fati* (which would be a No to being-reactionary.)

> He must cry and weep—but he is laughable even when he weeps. And with tears in his eyes he shall ask you for a dance, and I myself will sing a song for his dance: a dancing and mocking song on the spirit of gravity.
>
> —Nietzsche

Dionysus, a Dancing God! Rationality (the principles of what were refigured as *logos*) must be denegated. Identity—along with contradiction and excluded middle—must be denegated. (I cannot incite this enough. I want some more incitements!) As Nietzsche says, "the essence of nature is now to be expressed symbolically; we need a new world of symbols; and the entire symbolism of the body is called into play, not the mere symbolism of the lips, face, and speech but the whole pantomine of dancing" (40). We need a symbolism of affirmation. We must say No to the Platonic and Aristotelian logic; to the Freudian and Lacanian symbolic; to the Kantian and the Burkean symbolic. To the spirit of gravity. To the burden of guilt, of too much fixed (by way of repression, suppression) meaning, order, value. Which is purchased at the expense of the excluded, the purged, the Forgotten. As Nietzsche's Zarathustra (Dionysus, Christ) says, "I would believe only in a god who could dance" (1968a, 153; cf. 214). And as Zarathustra also says, "with tears in his eyes he [the god Cupid, a joyful pessimist] shall ask you for a dance, and I myself will sing a song for his dance: a dancing and mocking song on the spirit of gravity" (220).[19] As Emma Goldman said, "If I can't dance I don't want to be part of your revolution" (qtd. in Derrida and McDonald 1982, 66). The heaviness of thinking and writing revolutions (the negative essentializing of revolutions) are our "spirit of revenge" (Nietzsche

1968a, 251; see 249–54). We must dis/engage by self-overcoming. When we write, we must dance; we must write and think "the innumerable" (Derrida and McDonald 1982, 76).[20] Dis/engage by way of "choreographies." As Derrida elsewhere says, "a fictive beginning, a false entrance, a false exit, a kind of writing [dancing] of innumerable number—these will still have to be reread by you" (1981a, 305; cf. Ulmer 1994).[21] Innumerable sexes. Dionysus was (is) innumerable sexes.

> "I," you say, and are proud of the word. But greater is that in which you do not wish to have faith—your body and its great reason: that does not say "I," but *does* [i.e., performs] "I."
>
> —Nietzsche

From either One or Two Sexes to an "Excluded Third" of a Radical Multiplicity of Sexes/Genders, Helens/Hellenes: I want now to turn more fully to the Nietzschean Judith Butler, specifically to her *Gender Trouble* (1990a); my exposition of a brief section of her book should not by any means stand as a substitute for having read and studied it in great detail. With that understanding, let us proceed, and to do so we must here begin with Nietzsche, which is where Butler begins and traces Nietzsche through Deleuze and Guattari, and then through her own position of gender/sex as not essentialist but as "cultural performance." Butler's position (see 1990a, 26–29) stands in contrast to the positions of Lacan (a post-Hegelian who, as I have said, works out of the negative or lack), Irigaray (a post-Lacanian but nonetheless a reformulator of Lacan's concept of lack to excess), and M. Wittig (a quasi-Nietzschean who bifurcates a subject position as both humanist and non-humanist). Let me emphasize: Whereas Butler, in respect to gender and sex/uality, is working out of affirmation, Lacan, Irigaray, and Wittig are working in negation, that is, in the metaphysics of substance/presence. (This is Butler's assessment.) Whereas Butler (and Wittig) are working out of a "post-genital politics" (1990a, 27), Lacan and Irigaray have much invested in a negative form of genital politics. (This, too, is Butler's characterization.)

I'm not going to survey the latter group, but instead report in passing on Nietzsche and Deleuze and Guattari and then focus on Butler, who with the help of her precursors finds a way out of the master/slave dialectic or structural binary (machine) of male/female. After all, it's the way out of the *polis*—constituted by prohibition and determined by genus, scene, container (synecdoche)—that I (and others) desire; or it is, in non-positive affirmative terms, the perpetual ways of the *pagus* that we desire. What I am going to be concerned with now is how a subject (agent) can be situated outside of gender and sex/uality, or genus, scene, container (synecdoche)—all of which are, as Butler phrases them, "political categories" (1990a, 1). If situated inside genus, there is only One sex (Lacan), or Two sexes (capital). But if situated outside, if situated in the excluded third, Butler states, there are "as many sexes as individuals" (118; 6). Let's re/turn to Nietzsche.

And begin with Nietzsche's epistemology, for it is his contrary (anti-Enlightenment) epistemology that Butler runs with. Nietzsche writes of the "subject" (agent), or his rejection of the metaphysics of substance: ". . . there is no such substratum; there is no 'being' behind doing, effecting, becoming; 'the doer' is merely a fiction added to the deed—the deed is everything" (1969, 45). For Nietzsche, there is no essence/essentialism, which would have been determined by the negative, behind human beings and behind "male" or "female." Butler will pick up on the notion of "the deed is everything."

Deleuze and Guattari—being deeply influenced by Nietzsche—work out of the same post-epistemology. There is no fixed essence. (They believe in an essence as desire, but one cum radical many that is the opposite of the metaphysic/epistemology of substance, which is based on negation.) For them, in their "mysterious" way: "the phallus is not one sex, but sexuality in its entirety" (1983, 294; cf. Irigaray 1985b). Continuing they say: "Marx says something even more mysterious: that the true difference is not the difference between the two sexes, but the difference between the human sex and the 'nonhuman' sex" (294). For them, "desiring production" produces *molecular aggregates* (bodies without organs or schizo-flows), which supply an infinite number of sexes, which might be called, in this state of constant flux and nondifferentiation, " 'nonhuman' sex." This number (n+) is channeled and controlled by "social production" (by capital) so that there will be *molar representations* of sex, an "*anthropomorphic* [human] *representation of sex*": One sex (for Freud, the "female" [the locus of lack] has no sex) or Two sexes (for the sake of social-molar illusion) (294). Sexuality is constructed through social production.[22]

Let's return to Deleuze and Guattari, who are equally satirical: "If the woman is defined as the lack in relation to the man, the man in his turn lacks what is lacking in the woman, simply in another fashion: the idea of a single sex necessarily leads to the erection of a phallus as an object on high, which distributes lack as two nonsuperimposable sides and makes the two sexes communicate in a common absence—*castration*" (1983, 295; Deleuze and Guattari's emphasis). They continue: "We maintain therefore that *castration* [negation] *is the basis for the anthropomorphic and molar representation of sexuality.* Castration is the universal belief that brings together and disperses both men and women under the yoke of one and the same illusion of consciousness, and makes them adore this [j]oke" (295; Deleuze and Guattari's emphasis; my switching of "y" to "j"). Deleuze and Guattari continue:

> The molecular unconscious, on the contrary, knows nothing of castration, because partial objects lack nothing and form free multiplicities as such; because the multiple breaks never cease producing flows, instead of repressing [negating] them, cutting them at a single stroke . . . ; because the syntheses constitute local and nonspecific connections, inclusive disjunctions, nomadic conjunctions [parataxis, paralogy]: everywhere a microscopic transsexuality, resulting in the woman containing as many men as the man, and the man as many women, all capable of entering—men with women, women with men—into relations of production of desire that overturn the statistical order of the sexes. Making love is not just becoming as one, or even twos but becoming as a hundred thousand. Desiring-machines or the nonhuman sex: not one or even two sexes, but n sexes. . . . The schizoanalytic slogan of the desiring-revolution will be first of all: to each its own sexes. (1983, 295–96)

Butler, like Nietzsche and Deleuze and Guattari, moves beyond a molar/capitalistic male and female. Gender especially, but sex as well [she has the hermaphrodite Herculine Barbin in mind], are both simulation/simulacrum "without reference or circumference." (I borrow this latter phrase from Baudrillard [1988, 170; cf. Burke's "scope and reduction" in 1969a, 59–124].) That is, without reality or genus, but with a perpetually threatening nostalgia for the Modernist (Lacanian) *real*. This is how, working with a postmodernist epistemology, Butler defines "gender":

> Gender ought not to be construed as a stable identity or locus of agency from which various acts follow; rather, gender is an identity tenuously constituted in time, instituted in an exterior space through a *stylized repetition of acts*. The effect of gender is produced through the stylization of the body and, hence, must be understood as the mundane way in which bodily gestures, movements, and styles of various kinds constitute the illusion of an abiding gendered self. This formulation moves the conception of gender off the ground of a substantial model of identity to one that requires a conception of gender as a constituted social temporality. . . . Gender is also a norm that can never be fully internalized; "the internal" is a surface signification, and gender norms are finally phantasmatic, impossible to embody. (1990a, 140–41; Butler's emphasis)

This definition is quite revolutionary in its postmodernist epistemology. With it, Butler takes on Jameson's critique of Postmodernism, which he partially achieves across the distinction of "pastiche" and "parody" (1991, 16–19).

Jameson says: Pastiche "is a neutral practice of . . . mimicry, without any of parody's ulterior motives, amputated of the satiric impulse, devoid of laughter and of any conviction that alongside the abnormal tongue you have momentarily borrowed, some healthy linguistic normality still exists." He continues: "Pastiche is thus blank parody, a statue with blind eyeballs: it is to parody what that other interesting and historically original modern thing, the practice of a kind of blank irony, is to what Wayne Booth calls the 'stable ironies' of the late eighteenth century" (17). Pastiche is a mere copy of a copy, with no socially-productive purpose, while parody is a mimicry of an original with the primary purpose of satirizing to improve. Now whereas Jameson sees pastiche as a failing and parody as a virtue, Butler sees value in reversing this characterization. It is this very reversal of pastiche over parody that discloses the counter-epistemology of Postmodernism that Jameson does not recognize and that discloses a paratheory of affirmation.[23] Let me explain by beginning with Butler's discussion of "drag queens," which will exemplify her interpretation of gender.

Relying on the work of the anthropologist Esther Newton (in *Mother Camp*), Butler writes: ". . . the structure of impersonation reveals one of the key fabricating mechanisms through which the social construction of gender takes place. I would suggest as well that drag fully subverts the distinction between inner and outer psychic space [species-genus analytics] and effectively mocks both the expressive model of gender [the so-called stable "I"] and the notion of a true gender identity [negative essence]" (1990a, 136–37). Butler quotes Newton:

> At its most complex, [drag] is a double inversion that says, "appearance is an illusion." Drag says . . . "my 'outside' appearance is feminine, but my essence 'inside' [the body] is masculine." At the same time it symbolizes the opposite inversion; "my appearance 'outside' [my body, my gender] is masculine but my essence 'inside' [myself] is feminine." (137)

What we have in the "drag" is a performance of contradiction and/or paradox. (Recall the Klein jar, which some people see as having no inside or outside.) The two implicit epistemologies that are colliding and in collusion here are one that works from an original that can be copied (or parodied) and another that plays from a copy that can only be copied (or pastiched). What the "drag" can disclose is "the imitative structure of gender itself— *as well as its contingency*" (137; Butler's emphasis). Butler explains:

> Indeed, part of the pleasure, the giddiness of the performance is in the recognition of a radical contingency in the relation between sex and gender in the face of cultural configurations of causal unities that are regu-

larly assumed to be natural and necessary. In the place of the law of het-
erosexual coherence, we see sex and gender denaturalized by means of a
performance which avows their distinctness and dramatizes the cultural
mechanism of their fabricated unity. (138)

Hence, whereas Deleuze and Guattari find a virtue in schizo-society—in its
ability to avoid finally being coopted by capital—Butler et al. find virtue in,
a schizo-gender/sexuality. (Remember Butler agrees with Deleuze and
Guattari: "There are . . . as many sexes as individuals" [118].) In dis/respect
to the whole concept of Modernism (which works out of the negative and
which nostalgically longs to seize the phantasy of the real, essences, totality), the "drag" makes a sham of identity politics, of the way that we get
politically represented, while it simultaneously makes a virtue of Postmodern
resistances to and disruptions of capital's ready-made agent(s) and agency,
its recoded "consumers."

Butler sees that "there is a subversive laughter in the pastiche-effect
of parodic practices in which the original, the authentic, and the real are
themselves constituted as effects. The loss of gender norms would have the
effect of proliferating gender configurations, destabilizing substantive identity, and depriving the naturalizing narratives of compulsory heterosexual-
ity of their central protagonists: 'man' and 'woman' " (146). Outside of this
binary (machine) we will have taken a step toward *including* the "excluded
thirds," which will have been excesses. If the strategy of *ex*cluding the third
is a strategy of negative dialectic, the strategy of *in*cluding the third is a
strategy of denegating (libidinalizing) the negative. Butler concludes: "If
identities were no longer fixed as the premises of a political syllogism, and
politics no longer understood as a set of practices derived from the alleged
interests that belong to a set of ready-made subjects, a new configuration
of politics would surely emerge from the ruins of the old" (149).

Chapter 7

❧

Gorgias, "Some More," and Helens

. . . and so, what would this new (configuration of) politics—if, at all, correctly called "politics"—be like? Pagan politics! In dis/order to meditate on other possible answers and what promise they would have for reconfiguring Helen(s), it is necessary to return, ever again, to Nietzsche's views of affirmation and negation. (I am going to rely heavily now on Gilles Deleuze's reading of Nietzsche.) If Nietzsche reconfigures, remeasures, revalues, the ethico-political, it is along the lines of negating, or denegating, the negative. (Nietzsche calls it "self-overcoming." Bataille calls it "sovereignty.") Nietzsche sees the negative as a product of slave morality. Here he points a finger at Pauline Christianity; points a finger at Hegel's master/slave relationship, which is abstracted into dialectical thinking. Nietzsche writes:

> The slave revolt in morality begins when *ressentiment* itself becomes creative and gives birth to values: the *ressentiment* of natures that are denied the true reaction, that of deeds, and compensate themselves with an imaginary revenge. While every noble morality develops from a triumphant affirmation of itself, slave morality from the outset says No to what is "outside," what is "different," what is "not itself"; and *this* No is its creative deed. (1969, 36–37; Nietzsche's emphasis)

In simple terms, slave morality is defined by No; noble reality, by Yes. This "No" *is* a dialectical "No"/*Know*: Slave morality "says No to what is 'outside' "; it says "No" to what is outside its *genus*. In saying "No," slave (dialectical) morality expresses the will to Truth. At all costs. No matter what the *debt*.[1]

This slave morality, therefore, creates *a politics of revenge*. However, the will to such a politics is greatly mystified, for it is a politics that constructs an alibi (a forgetfulness) that allows for punishing, hurting Others. Therefore, politics, as practiced, is reactive. As Nietzsche explains, we today have "justice" so that we might exclude and punish (see 1969, 63; cf. 1968a, 211–14; Spivak 1989a, 217–18). (De Sade said we have Reason so that we can exclude and punish [cf. Klossowski, 1991; duBois 1991].) And, therefore, what does Nietzsche prescribe for this illness? This *burden*? He speaks of "self-overcoming" (1969, 160–61; 1968a, 225–28; cf. C. Scott, 1990), which can be achieved in a number of ways, but I would here insist on self-overcoming, or problematizing, by way of *one*, *two*, and *"some more,"* with the latter nonrational number (*"some more"*) referring to satyric dance, chance, and laughter. Which are themes, or *topoi*, of affirmation dis/engaged in by Nietzsche. (Again, self-overcoming = sovereignty.) This "some more" I will link up with new ways of thinking about subjectivity, with my ways of reconfiguring (refolding) Helen(s). In dis/order to discuss the ways of *"some more,"* I am going to spend some time on Deleuze's reading of Nietzsche's concept of affirmation, which is a rather complicated notion and, therefore, desires a processual, serial, intense unfolding.

Next, I am going to return to a discussion of subjectivity (agency) so that I might get on to two ways—similar to my ways of *"some more"*—of denegating subjectivity. I am going to discuss Charles Scott's linkage of Nietzsche's "self-overcoming" with the linguistic "middle voice." It is this linkage that will lead to ways of reconfiguring Helen(s) as an affirmative, radical multiplicity; and that will take her out of both the active (master, sadistic) voice and the passive (slave, masochistic) voice and that, consequently, will place her in the middle voice-cum-nonac*count*able-v(o)ices. In the muddle. The sounddance. (Into sovereignty.) In parallel fashion, I am going to discuss my (*some more's*) relinking of *Menelaius-Paris-Helen* (the political triangle) so as thereby to reach beyond to a relinkage of Deleuze's (Nietzsche's) *Theseus-Dionysus-Ariadne* (the self-overcoming, sovereign triangle). I would place the political burden into dispersion. The final linkage will be a negation of Theseus (who *is* the negative) and an affirmation of Dionysus (who *is* affirmation). The final linkage, however, will be realized with Ariadne, having already left Theseus, calling for (a third) Dionysus. Hence, a double affirmation: *Dionysus/Ariadne*. (As in chapter 1, we will end [rebegin] with a prayer to, lament for, Dionysus.)

IV. To Measure, To Value

Measure is alien to us; let us own it; our thrill is the thrill
of the infinite, the unmeasured.

—F. Nietzsche

As promised, let us forever again look closely at the problem of negation and affirmation, but first by way of "measuring." Then we will look even more closely at Deleuze's reading of Nietzsche's (double) affirmation. When

we look, however, we will glance, glance, glance "some more." The gaze—
the will to make a home for ac/counting—must be avoided. In *The Gay
Science*, Nietzsche writes: "The whole pose of 'man *against* the world,' of
man as a 'world-negating' principle, of man as *the measure of the value of
things* [my emphasis], as judge of the world who in the end places existence
itself upon his scales [of justice] and finds it wanting—the monstrous in-
sipidity of this pose has finally come home to us and we are sick of it. We
laugh as soon as we encounter the juxtaposition of man *and* world" (1974,
286).

Protagoras allegedly gave us the so-called "man-measure doctrine"
(Sprague 1990, 18). (Measure here means valuing. Giving an ac*count* of.)
Nietzsche's unfinished project was—and still *is*—a revaluing of value.
Protagoras, like his fellow lovers of wisdom, valued all things but valued
them negatively. (I must admit again, however, that Protagoras and others set the stage for the possibility of contradictory [twofold] arguments,
or of *dissoi logoi*, and therefore for deconstructive readings. This possibility is at best only *negative* deconstructive readings [reversal] and not
affirmative deconstructive readings [displacement], which I will continue
to make much of in relation to non-humanistic/non-reactive Helens.) In
many ways, Protagoras was one of the original nihilists, not only in relation to judging the world but also in relation to the question of the
gods: "Concerning the gods [he allegedly said] I cannot know either that
they exist or that they do not exist" (Sprague 1990, 20). Protagoras is
more of an agnostic in this statement than an epistemological/ontological
atheist.

There is little doubt, however, that Plato was a primary nihilist, when
he negated the phenomenal world (appearance), when he negated life itself,
in favor of what he called reality, or the real. Plato himself practiced a negative
deconstruction but absolutized it: Non-life (death) is life; life is non-life
(death). (Was Plato's, a strategic essentialism?) Therefore, in the original act
of valuing life, Plato devalues it. Nietzsche writes in the *Twilight of the Idols*:
"The characteristics which have been assigned to the 'real being' of things
are the characteristics of non-being, of *nothingness*—the 'real world' has
been constructed out of the contradiction to the actual world: an apparent
world indeed, in so far as it is no more than a *moral-optical* illusion" (1968b,
39; Nietzsche's emphasis). Christianity—as in St. Paul's appropriation of
Christ—simply follows suit; "Christianity is called the religion of *pity*. . . .
[O]ne has made of it *the* virtue, the ground and origin of all virtue. . . . [P]ity
is *practical* nihilism. . . . [P]ity persuades to *nothingness!*" (*The Anti-Christ*
1968b, 118; Nietzsche's emphasis). Why else does Nietzsche call "Platonism
. . . Christianity for 'the masses' "! (1966, 3). (Let us recall, ever recall Marx
and Engels's camera obscura.)

For Nietzsche—because "man" has killed the source of value, actually, because "man"/Plato killed affirmative value at the very moment he posited negative value)—"man" has consequently become *reactive* (having killed God) and *passive* (without now the possibility of any hope). Nietzsche sees *the engine of history* fed by nihilism—in fact, three kinds of nihilism: *negative nihilism* (killing God/foundationalism), *reactive nihilism* (feelings of *ressentiment*, apparent necessity for justice), and *passive nihilism* (willing *no more*) (see Deleuze 1983a, 151–52). This engine of history (these traditional and revisionary historiographies) must be denegated. Hence, the necessity for revaluing. However, this revaluing cannot be done by simply returning to "foundationalism," for to do so would be to return to the negative, to nihilism itself. (Along with the foundationalists, I also include the so-called "anti-foundationalist" who wish to work with local *nomoi*. Social-epistemic theorist are crypto-foundationalists. Remember, as Deleuze and Guattari say, what is wanted is not social[-epistemic] production but desiring-production [1983, 30]. Remember that the *physis*^{neg}-*nomos*^{neg} controversy is one that I would turn into a trilemma, i.e., add a third term to, unnamely, *physis*$^{nonpositive\ affirmation}$. Hence, desiring-production.)

Thus far, we have been discussing the problem of negation and affirmation in gross terms. I want to turn now to these *topoi* in yet more particular ways. The question remains, How is this urge for revaluing Helen—after all, I have been as I will have been *glancing* at Helen—to be reconfigured? (This urge is the most difficult and risky of tasks. Yet we cannot remain passive.) We now, therefore, must get to Deleuze's "Nietzsche," and begin to think through the question of rerealizing Helen and (perhaps) in the following ways. Let us recapitulate while simultaneously moving forward. I will rely on the future anterior.

First, *instead of value founded on negation, value must have been revalued in terms of affirmation*, without any remembrance of negation (1983a, 175).[2] (This in part is what is meant by affirmative forgetting, which is a forgetting that would make ressentiment, revenge, reactive thinking and action—history writing as such—no longer possible.) What will have been revalued is *life* itself, all (the "*some more*") of life: Its comedy, but mostly its tragedy, or its excesses; therefore, all of existence. (This revaluing would be an acceptance, in negative terms, of good and evil, but more so now, in affirmative terms, will have been an acceptance of what is *beyond* good and evil. This "beyond" (that is within, a refolding!) is what I see to be a third subject position. It is the "unmeasured," the "some more." This revaluing with its concomitant attitude is what Nietzsche means by accepting the ancient Greeks' "joyful pessimism" or by implementing his "gay science." Nietzsche's gay science—Walter Kaufmann says in his introduction to *The*

Gay Science—"is anti-German, anti-professional, anti-academic." Kaufmann writes that gay science "is also meant to suggest 'light feet,' 'dancing,' 'laughter'—and ridicule of 'the spirit of gravity' " [1974, 7; cf. Nietzsche 1968a, 303-07].) Affirmation would subvert any attempt to write history that would be traditional/reactionary (a.k.a. active nihilism); or to appropriate a Helen in a revisionary/reactionary manner.

Second, *the will to power*—the forces that we bring to bear on life—will have become affirmative (1983a, 176). (This view of the will to power must necessarily follow from the discussion of the first point.) What this means is that the forces—or attitudes of interpretation—must not have been determined by way of negation, which is traditionally and revisionally the case. Moreover, what this specifically means is that the forces must not have been determined or systematized by way of identifying the logical permutations and combinations. (It is in respect to this view of affirmation that Nietzsche should *not* be read in Burkean terms, in terms of a grammar, rhetoric, or symbolic. Burke is completely committed to the negative, though he attempts to ameliorate it by multiplying it. Burke, too, has his alibis, though he is awfully Nietzschean.)

If negation does not rule, then, *chance* and *amor fati* rule, if this can be called "ruling." This is sovereignty without traditional ruling (mastering). Heaviness (too much determined meaning) will have become lightness. In *The Gay Science*, Nietzsche writes: *"Amor fati*: let that be my love henceforth! I do not want to wage war against what is ugly. I do not want to accuse; I do not even want to accuse those who accuse. *Looking away* shall be my only negation. And all in all and on the whole: some day I wish to be a Yes-sayer" (1974, 223; Nietzsche's emphasis).

But we are getting ahead of ourselves here, for this view of yes-saying is more complicated because the first and second points do not rule out negation altogether: There is a form of *negation now that becomes a kind of affirmation*, without which, there could be no nonpositive affirmation. It would be incredibly wrong to think that Nietzsche does not—nor that I should not—dis/engage in a form of negation. As Foucault explains, there is a "transgression" that is not negative (1977, 35).

Therefore, a third point: *The "negative" being referred to now is the negation (or denegation) of negation itself.* Such a move (the double negative) is considered prepatory for a destructive, creative (hence, deconstructive) act. I emphasize "prepatory," preliminary, here (see Nietzsche 1974, 283), for we must continue on—as we will here to the concluding *excurses* that would be new beginnings—to an affirmative deconstruction. Deleuze writes: "The negative becomes a power of affirming: it is subordinated to affirmation and passes into the service of an excess of life. Negation is no longer the form under which life conserves all that is reactive in itself, but is, on the contrary, the act by which it sacrifices all its reactive forms" (1983a, 176; cf. 178–79, 180). Therefore, to capitulate: The will to power is affirmative. All that there is, is affirmation. However, to get to this creative point (or this excess), it is necessary to turn negation against negation, rationality against rationality, which is the initial creative urge.

As I intimated, this view of yea-saying is complicated, for there is yet a further possible misunderstanding, namely, that this negation (or denegation) of negation will be taken to be Hegelian. It is not; it has nothing to do with Platonic or especially now Hegelian notions of dialectics. Deleuze writes: "Anti-Hegelianism runs through Nietzsche's work as its cutting edge" (1983a, 8). As the will to power expresses itself in various forces (attitudes), this will and its forces desire "to affirm [their] difference. In its essential relation with the 'other' a will makes its difference an object of affirmation. . . . Nietzsche's 'yes' is opposed to the dialectical 'no'; affirmation to dialectical negation; difference to dialectical contradiction; joy, enjoyment, to dialectical labour; lightness, dance, to dialectical responsibilities" (9; cf. Watson 1985). What Deleuze—and Georges Bataille before him—see is Nietzsche's reaching for the *Übermensch* who is beyond the master/slave, dialectical relationship; is Nietzsche's reaching for a "sovereign" (or sublime) personage. What Nietzsche is attempting is a negation of Hegel's notion of "determinate" negation and an affirmation of "absolute" negation; is a negation of a "restrictive" economy (scarcity) and an affirmation of a "general" economy (excess).[3]

But things are still more complicated: There is yet the important theme of "burden." In *Thus Spoke Zarathustra*, Nietzsche has a number of animals such as the camel and ass (1968a, 137–39; 305–07). The camel and the ass— traditionally the beasts of burden—are both seen as creatures subject to negation, to the spirit of gravity. This willingness to accept burdens, Deleuze explains, is at first seen as a sign of strength and virtue, as "humility, acceptance of pain and sickness, patience towards the chastiser, taste for truth even if given acorns to eat and love of the real even if this real is a desert" (1983a, 180–81). While it appears that the camel and the ass (that says "Yea-Yuh" to everything) affirm life, they affirm only Nihilism and reactive forces. But how so? There are several possibilities, but I will concentrate on two.

The *first* deals with the theme of (political) *burden* in terms of the narrative of emancipation (liberation) from history/time, which from Zarathustra's (Nietzsche's) point of view is *the narrative of victimage*. This burden can be passive or active: Passive in the Christian sense of aggressively turning the other cheek, or doing *no-thing* but making an act of will to bear the burden, suffering; or active in a militant sense of aggressively attempting to seek *justice by way of redeeming the past*. The passive would write no history, but live the history of (the) suffering; the active would write with the sole purpose of creating guilt, then ressentiment, but consequently new victimage. Both the active and passive perpetuate aggression. In one of the most important sections of *Thus Spoke*, "Redemption," Zarathustra says:

> . . . every prisoner [of time] becomes a fool; and the imprisoned will re-deems himself [herself] foolishly. That time does not run backwards, that is his wrath; "that which was" is the name of the stone he cannot move. And so he moves stones out of wrath and displeasure, and he wreaks revenge on whatever does not feel wrath and displeasure as he does. Thus the will, the liberator, took to hurting; and on all who can suffer he wreaks revenge for his inability to go backwards. This indeed this alone, is what *revenge* is; the will's ill will against time and its "it was." (1968a, 251-52; Nietzsche's emphasis)

The camel and ass, then, have the need to redeem history by way of bring-ing justice—by way of punishing—the transgressors. (The camel and the ass would go to Troy to wage war.) However, Deleuze says, "this reality which unites the camel and its burden to the point of confusing them in a single mirage is only the desert, the reality of the desert, *nihilism*" itself (1983a, 182; emphasis mine). The only possibility for the camel, when he and she recall the past, is the past-as-real, as actuality. *History becomes a burden.* Here then, the ass understands "affirmation . . . as acquiescence in or adhesion to a consequence, the consequence of eternally negative premises, an answering yes, answering the spirit of gravity and all its solicitations. The ass does not know how to say no [to the past, or dis/engage in affirmative forgetfulness]; but first and foremost he [and she] does not know how to say no to nihilism itself" (182). In a word, the camel and especially the ass do not know how "to self-overcome." And it is this inability to say No to ni-hilism that drives the engine of thinking/action and of history. The engine that drives (revisionary) historiography itself. (Remember Spivak who in my earlier discussion of "Feminist Sophistic?" said that deconstruction forced us to say Yes to everything. Deconstruction does not, for it allows us finally to say No to nihilism. However, if someone's project gets its energy from nihilism/the negative, then, of course, such a critic's project is in jeopardy.)

If the first deals with the theme of political burden, the *second* deals with the theme of *possibility*, or the theme of *will to power* and its forces (attitudes) that would interpret the world. Deleuze explains that the camel and especially the ass engage in perverted forms of the will to power by assuming that there is *one* attitude to interpret the world, the attitude of the *real* as either predetermined by a common sense view of reality or as predetermined by the onto-theological (orthodox Platonic-Hegelian-Marxian) tradition. Deleuze writes: "These [political] burdens seem to [the camel and ass] to have the weight of the *real*. . . . This is why Nietzsche presents [them] as impervious to all forms of seduction [as persuasion or deception, *apate*] and temptation: they are only sensitive to what they have on their backs, to what they call real" (181; Deleuze's emphasis). They cannot through persuasion or falsehood (will to power) see the world as different, the opposite of common sense; see the world as light, the opposite of heaviness. In dis/order to see the world as light, they would have to remember that heaviness as real was initially an interpretation, but they cannot. Instead, the camel (traditional historians) would hold on to the so-called Aristotelian truth of the actual world, just as the ass (revisionary historians) would hold on to the so-called Marxist truth of the now demystified, material world.

Deleuze explains: "men [sic] of the present still live under an old idea: that everything heavy [serious and complete with meaning] is real and positive, that everything that carries it is real and affirmative" (182). As a case in point, and I quote at length, Terry Eagleton discloses:

> There has been, so far as I know, no Marxist theory of comedy to date; tragedy has been a considerably more successful contender for the attention of materialist criticism. And there are good enough reasons why Marxism has suspected the comic. . . . For Marxism, history moves under the very sign of irony: there is something darkly comic about the fact that the bourgeoisie are their own grave-diggers, just as there is an incongruous humour about the fact that the wretched of the earth should come to power. The only reason to be a Marxist is to get to the point where you can stop being one. It is in that glib, feeble piece of wit that much of the Marxist project is surely summarized. Marxism has the humour of dialectics because it reckons itself into the historical equations it writes; like the great heritage of Irish wit from Swift and Sterne to Joyce, Beckett and Flann O'Brien, it has the comedy of all "texts" that write about themselves in the act of writing history.
>
> Yet it is not of course true that all tragic contents are changeable, just as carnival is wrong to believe that anything can be converted into humour. There is nothing comic about gang rape, or Auschwitz. . . . Those who believe in the sacred and profane belong to a benighted past need only to consider whether they would be prepared to pronounce certain words about Auschwitz even as a joke. The mode in which sacred and profane *can* co-exist is the mode of satire: Swift's *Modest Proposal* utters the unspeakable in the context of therapeutic ridicule. But tragic situations are often unchangeable in at least one important respect—unchangeable for those who are their victims. . . . [W]e have a revolutionary chance *to redeem the past* [my emphasis] by imbuing it through political action with retroactive

meaning and value. But though this is a crucial *caveat* for those who would dogmatically absolutize tragedy, make the existence of Auschwitz rather than its destruction the definitive word, or arrogantly claim that the "modern world" is too shabbily unaristocratic to be tragic at all, it remains always individual tragedies, tragedies that persist like a forgotten bruise on the flesh of history, which no transcendence short of a Messiah could retroactively transform. (1981, 159–62; Eagleton's emphasis)

(The question of humor, I will take up intermittently, for it is the Nietzschean question of "joyful pessimism" and of *The Gay Science*. Here, in Eagleton's statement, is it not clear, that he favors *irony*, not *humor*? The latter, the most misunderstood!)[4]

Attempts to redeem the past are rife with cynicism and more crimes yet to be redeemed. Redemption is the machine that drives the cycle of re/vengeful history. If only the camel and the ass would cease saying Yes to No, if only the camel and the ass would say No to nihilism (denegate the negative), he and she (cum potentially "it") could, then, pass over into *the beyond of affirmation*. Again, by "beyond" I do not mean a Hegelian sublation, but a passing out of the binary or dialectic machine into a third subject perpetual repositioning of desiring-production, or as I will suggest, via Deleuze, a passing outside/inside the binary by way of a refolding. I mean a Nietzschean "self-overcoming." A sublime sovereign perpetual repositioning. And how is this to be realized? By understanding the will to power and its forces, by understanding Nietzsche's notion of an infinite play of differences and their affirmation, by understanding possibilities as nonpositive affirmation. (To which we will forever return.)

In sum then, for Nietzsche there is no Being behind things, as Deleuze and Guattari and, then, Butler respectively point out in relation to gender and sex. No fixed truth. No reality. No One. No heaviness or spirit of gravity, other than what we insist on by way of negation, nihilism. Instead, there is "life" and "living." As Deleuze writes: "the living world is will to power, *will to falsehood*, which is actualised in many different powers [forces]. To actualise the will to falsehood [instead of the will to truth, i.e., death] under any power whatever, to actualise the will to power under any quality whatever, is always to evaluate [to lie, to interpret, to measure!]" (1983a, 184; Deleuze's emphasis). Hence, the will to (*one*) truth = death, nihilism. The will to ("some more") power as falsehood = life. Nietzsche is everywhere very clear about this view of evaluation which must be revalued. Concerning art and an aesthetics of excess, he writes: "Art and nothing but art! It is the great means of making life possible, the great seduction to life, the great stimulant of life. . . . The will to appearance, to illusion, to deception, to becoming and change (to objectified deception) here counts as more profound, primeval, 'metaphysical,' than the will to truth, to reality, to mere appearance:—the last is itself merely a form of the will to illusion" (1968c, 452, 453).

"Redemption" (452) is, therefore, to be achieved not by way of traditional or revisionary politics but by ways of art/aesthetics: "Truth is Ugly. We possess *art* lest we *perish of the truth*" (1968c, 435; Nietzsche's emphasis). This is all another way of saying that we *unburden ourselves* (or overcome ourselves) by way of denegation or affirmation. By way of dis/engaging in deceptions (*apate*), by way of telling lies (re[e]valuating) in an extra-moral sense. By way, paradoxically, of denegating the so-called beautiful to accept the ugly, which is not ugly. (Recall Lispector, the roach, and becoming-animal.) I will close this section with Deleuze's assessment and reminder:

> To affirm is still to evaluate, but to evaluate from the perspective of a will which enjoys its own difference [that which is outside, the so-called ugly] in life instead of suffering the pains of the opposition to this life that it [as well as dialectic] has itself inspired. *To affirm is not to take responsibility for, to take on the burden of what is, but to release, to set free what lives.* To affirm is to unburden: not to load life with the weight of higher values [identity, species, genus], but *to create* new values which are those of life, which make life light and active. There is creation, properly speaking, only insofar as we make use of excess in order to invent new forms of life rather than separating life from what it can do. (1983a, 185; Deleuze's emphasis)

V. Nonpositive Affirmative (sublime, sovereign) Subjectivity

It is traditional both in the metaphysics of presence and in the metaphysics of absence, at bottom, to conceive of *being* by way of negation. Nietzsche, Deleuze writes, conceives of "Affirmation itself [as] being." He continues: "[B]eing is solely affirmation in all its power" (1983a, 186). Which returns us to the question of *What is subjectivity?*, or what is Helen as agent, or as possible agencies, in respect to this view of being-as-affirmation and affirmation-as-being? The way that this question, like so many questions comparable to it, is phrased, however, is dangerous, for it would lead us back to negation. (Remember questions of the *What is?* kind, as I discussed them in Chapter 1.) Perhaps it would be best, then, to rephrase it as *How is subjectivity, or How is Helen as agent?* The shift from *What* to *How* is still problematic, but at least it suggests awareness of the problem and suggests a movement from negative Being to affirmative, Dionysian becoming.

In dis/order to consider this question of *How?*—for I have been considering it thus far throughout and will continue to meditate on it since it is central to my entire discussion—I want now to turn, as promised, to a more specific discussion of subjectivity. (The previous discussion in Chapter 6 of Butler's view of gender as nonessentialist/negative but as "culturally performative"/affirmative should be recalled as we move through this discussion of affirmative Helen[s]. Moreover, Nietzsche's discussion of subjectivity [1966, 25–27, or no. 19], as a *pathos* of embodiment, an interpretive moment, an affect of command, then agency, should be kept in mind.)[5] Nietzsche's discussion is developed later by Foucault in terms of technologies of subjectivity or what Deleuze calls, using topology, four foldings (1988, 94–123; cf. 1993), which are a way of illustrating how forces (wills) are bent, given a slight twist, when confronting each other, or when one attends to the other. The result of the bending or refolding is something new, something that has been, in dis/respect to its previous shape, denegated. These foldings, however, are subject to the law. Desire, forces, wills to power are un/naturally, Deleuze (and Foucault) says, "too subjugated by Law" (1988, 105). It is the LAW, then, that would determine *What I can do*, *What I do know*, *What I am* (114–15). The LAW, of course, is ancient. (Recall Cixous's "He-Bible.") And yet, there is something that is more ancient.

To rebegin, I want to turn to and review Plato's and Aristotle's views of subjectivity (agency, *ethos*, *ethnos*). The LAW.

Plato, in Book 3 of the *Republic*, describes what a subject, fit for inclusion in his polity, should be. As Michael Serres has explained, this would be a republic maximally purged of noise (1982, 65–70). Moreover, we can say that it is a republic where men (and their Being) are men. Plato, therefore, writes: "We will not . . . allow our charges, whom we expect to prove good men, being men, to play the parts of women and imitate a woman . . . still less a woman that is sick, in love, or in labor" (1961, 640; or 395d–e). (Here is both maleness and femaleness as political categories that are not to be transgressed!) But the issue is not just to avoid imitating women but also "slaves" and "madmen" and "neighing horses and lowing bulls" (640–41; or 395e–396a–b). (Here is human and biological propriety as political categories!) And when it comes to a style (diction) for representing these subjects (or narratives), Plato identifies two: The first with few variations; the second, with manifold variations. He selects the former for his polity "because there is no twofold or manifold man ["some more"] among us, since every man does one thing" (642; or 397e). And especially since manifold men (beasts, barbars, Favorinus, the mad text of Marx, *pagani*) would automatically, along with the uncanny, be purged from the idea of a Republic. (And Kafka? and Cixous? and H. Miller? and Acker? and this my ["our"] book?)

In respect to subjectivity (*ethos*, ethics, habit) Aristotle in the *Nicomachean Ethics* is more intuitive (and tautological) than Plato; in other words, *ethos* is less understood as theoretical knowledge (or knowing) and more understood as action (or doing) (see 1941, bk. 2). Aristotle writes: "[W]e must become just [temperate, virtuous] by doing just acts; for if men do just and temperate acts, they are already just and temperate" (955–56; or 1105a 17–21).

However, still not tolerable enough (I want "some more"), Aristotle speaks against "excess" and "defect" in *ethos*, virtue, and in favor of the so-called golden "mean" (see bk. 2, chs. 6–7; cf. bk. 5, ch. 4). He writes, in relation to *doing* and *acting*, "a master of any art avoids excess and defect, but seeks the intermediate and chooses this—the intermediate not in the object but relatively to us" (958; or 1106b, 6–8). Excess or defect (ugliness) in the art(ist)—and the implication here for me would be life affirmed by way of art—is, then, to be "avoided" (repressed). Aristotle, agreeing with Pythagoreans, avers that it is possible to "fail in many ways (for evil belongs to the class [genus] of the unlimited . . . and good to that of the limited), while to succeed is possible only in one way" (958; or 1106b, 29–32).

Following this statement, Aristotle then engages in a wonderful example of species-genus analytics, further defining (limiting) what "mean" is in disrespect to the two vices of "excess" and "defect" (see 959; or 1106b, 36–1107a, 1–8). He then goes on to warn us of "the pleasant or pleasure"; he says: "We ought . . . to feel towards pleasure as the elders of the people felt towards Helen, and in all circumstances repeat their saying" (963; or 1109b, 9–10. See *Iliad*, 3, 156–60).

Finally and categorically, Aristotle warns us of "vice, incontinence, brutishness" (1145a, 16–17); about brutishness, he says: "I mean . . . the case of the female who . . . rips open pregnant women and devours the infants" (1044; or 1148b, 20–21). Aristotle is warning us of the Maenaids and of Bacchanalian excesses; but could as well be warning us of such contemporary brutish excesses as practiced by Lacan's (hysterical, uncanny) "ladies" such as the sisters, the maids, Christine and Léa Papin (see Clément 1983, Ch. 2, esp. 67–78). Or Aristotle could be warning us (futilely) against Bataille's excess, warning us against Bataille's Gilles de Rais (see Land 1992, 66–74).

Opposed to this view of subjectivity (*ethos*), in dis/respect to what is deemed good and evil, is Nietzsche's view as initially announced in *The Birth of Tragedy* and then further developed in later works such *Beyond Good and Evil* and *The Gay Science*. In *The Birth*, subjectivity is hailed by way of music and dancing. (Light- and cleft-footed dancing!) Subjectivity is neither constructed according to the principle of individuality or the principle of spectator (audience). Subjectivity is an orgiastic oneness (as in sovereign, nonpositive affirmative sublime, or "some more"). It is "an *affectivity*, a *pathos* of experience" (see Warren, 1988, 130). It is what is meant by the will to power. Nietzsche writes:

In the Dionysian dithyramb man [subject] is incited to the greatest exaltation of all his symbolic faculties; something never before experienced struggles for utterance . . . oneness as the soul of the race and of nature itself. . . . The essence of nature [Being of *physis*[nonpositive affirmation]] is now to be expressed symbolically. . . ; and the entire symbolism of the body is called into play, not the mere symbolism of the lips, face, and speech but the whole pantomime of dancing, forcing every member into rhythmic movement. (1967, 40)

The Apollonian consciousness—which Nietzsche calls "a permanent military encampment" and "a political structure so cruel and relentless" (47)—suppressed, repressed, politically oppressed this music that incited this dancing. Today (in Nietzsche's and in our day), therefore, a man or woman can only be "quite bewildered before this fantastic *excess of life* [recall Bataille], asking by virtue of what *magic potion* these high-spirited men [and women] could have found life so [pessimistically, sublimely] enjoyable that, wherever they turned, their eyes beheld the smile of *Helen*, the ideal picture of their own existence, 'floating in sweet sensuality' " (41; emphasis mine). The *smile* of Helen.

(Dear readers: Can you hear, understand, or are there still ears for this suppressed, repressed, politically-oppressed libidinal music, this music that so incited orgiastic dancing and "piercing shrieks" [1967, 46], in dis/order that Dionysian "Excess [once again will have] revealed itself as truth" [46]?—which is what we [the various nonpositive affirmative *WE*s] are about in this book!)

The Smile of Helen—Let Us Repeatedly "Glance" at it: However, as I have stated, the political trend has been and still is to turn Helen into an agent who would be humanist, who would be a subject/agent who acts (who would be *active*) and thereby would be potentially capable of authorizing her own destiny and, therefore, who, no longer, would be passive, subject to either men or the so-called irrational *logos/kairos*. This attempt to reconstruct Helen, however, would ironically and only refigure Helen as a subject of and to *negation*, which would mean a Helen, in Nietzschean terms, who would have an instinct for knowledge, an instinct cut off from the affirmative, or from excess, from an instinct for life and art. This Helen would be an *active nihilist*. An Enlightenment Helen, who would be, in Nietzschean terms, like Euripides and Socrates, "theoretical man" (1967, 94–95; cf. 76–81). This attempt, unfortunately, would return Helen to a mode of portrayal that is founded on either the principles of *individuality* or the *social*, which would be by way of a politics of identity and by way of consensus (*homologia*). Both principles rely on the dicta that to be good or beautiful everything must be "intelligible" (84) and "conscious" (86).

Therefore, what is to be done? Denegate the negative! as I have been suggesting. Let it flow, as I have been inciting! Let things refold.

For the most part, I have been suggesting in passing just a few tactics to realize denegation; now, I want to explore, again by way of suggestion, a couple more (some more) Nietzschean tactics. Both are tactics to reach for not the One (the principle of individuality) or the Many (the principle of heterogeneity homogenized, irony) but a radical many, a paratactic aggregate. As Nietzsche says: "My hypothesis: The subject as [radical] multiplicity" (1968c, 270, or no. 490; cf. Thiele, 1990, ch. 3). The subject is a *pathos* of existence. The subject is imcompossible.

The first is a tactic based on reclaiming the *middle voice*, the grammatical voice whose disappearance has left us with only the active and passive (nihilistic) voices, or the master/slave voices. The middle voice is the voice of perpetual Nietzschean "self-overcoming," the voice that will allow us to denegate our active/passive reactionary positions, our slave mentality, for a nonpositive affirmative third position.[6] (Helen would think and speak in this voice, which becomes sovereign, sublime voices.) The second is based on another Nietzschean tactic of recoupling Paris/Helen and Theseus/Ariadne by denegating the "masculine," reactionary Paris and Theseus and replacing them with Dionysus, who is, like Favorinus, the very embodiment of nonpositive affirmation and who is sexually ambiguous (see Kofman, 1991). Who is also a satyr, a becoming-animal. Hence, the result of the denegation would be the coupling of Dionysus/Helen and Dionysus/Ariadne.

The Subject now is the "Middle Voice" and Kairos: Recently much has been written about the loss of this voice. My readings of Eric Charles White's (1987) and of Charles Scott's (1990) separate but somewhat overlapping discussions of the middle voice have suggested to me that this voice might very well be the *locus* for a "subject" that would be denegated.[7] It would be a place that would avoid—denegate—either active and passive subject positions. Before exploring the possibilities of this *locus*, however, it will be necessary for me to discuss, what the middle voice is grammatically and rhetorically.

White's initial source, I take it, is Roland Barthes's essay "To Write: An Intransitive Verb?" (1972, 134–45, 145–56). (I began my discussion with Barthes's distinction among *topos, eutopos*, an *atopos* [the third position]. Barthes was continually searching for such third subject positions.) In his discussion of *diathesis* (voice), Barthes writes: "Diathesis designates the way in which the subject of the verb is affected by the action. . . ; this is obvious for the passive. . . . And yet linguists tells us that, at least in Indo-European, the diathetical opposition is actually not between the active and the passive, but between the active and the middle" (142). This linguistic phenomenon— the middle voice—that Barthes refers to is lost to us today. White explains: "The middle voice . . . disappeared as an identifiable linguistic form during antiquity when, as it were, a 'hardening' of grammatical categories led to its replacement by the fixed opposition of the active/passive dichotomy" (53; see Vernant in Barthes 1972, 152; Benveniste 1971, 148–49). Barthes focuses on the verb "to write," which, he says, "was traditionally an active verb, . . . But in our [French] literature the verb is changing status, if not form, and the verb *to write* is becoming a middle verb" (143). (Here, we have another example of the return of the repressed, the negated.) He argues: "[W]e should no longer say today *'j'ai écrit'* but, rather, *'je suis écrit'* [I am written], just as we say *'je suis né, il est mort, elle est éclose.* There is no passive idea in these expressions, in spite of the verb *to be,* for it is impossible to transform *'je suis écrit'* . . . into *'on m'a écrit'* ['I have been written' or 'somebody wrote me'] " (143). In pointing out that "in French certain verbs have an active meaning in their simple form . . . but take the passive auxiliary [*to be*]," Barthes characterizes these middle-voiced verbs as "bifurcat[ed]" (19).

Barthes is no mere student of language; his reason for writing about the middle voice (the hole, opening, in the grammar) is ethical-political *change.* When asked by Jean-Pierre Vernant if the middle voice is reappearing, Barthes indirectly replies: "[O]ne of the tasks of militant literature is to try often by extremely violent and difficult methods, to compensate for the falling away of linguistic categories." He continues: "One [the subversive writer] tries to rethink the lost category and to take it as a metaphorical model . . . to reclaim it by raising it to the level of discourse" (152). The lost, excluded, trace of a category, which is now a paracategory. A careful reading of everything that Barthes wrote, but especially his autobiography, will disclose that he constantly shifts between the Lacanian, Imaginary "I" (his image-repertoire, his *ethos*[neg.]) and the Symbolic "He" (both his *physis*[neg.] and *nomos*[neg.]) in perpetual search so as to reclaim the lost paracategory of the *middle voice* as a third locus (*physis*[nonpositive affirmation]) (see 1977, 119–20; see Vitanza 1994d).

Charles Scott further develops this view of a *bifurcated,* or linguistically ambiguous, voice, which Barthes finds in the middle voice, and in doing so, improves the conditions for the possibility of nonpositive affirmation as the *locus* for a new subjectivity. First, he associates the middle voice with Nietzsche's view of "self-overcoming," which "cannot be [accounted] for well in the active and passive voices." Therefore, he argues, "[t]he dominance of the active and passive voices makes inevitable the priority of the spectator-subject for philosophical thought, whereas the middle voice yields a *different way of thinking* that is marked by undergoing a *movement* rather than by either active assertion or passive reception" (1990, 18–19; emphasis mine). Though linguistically repressed, Scott argues, "[w]hat remains of the middle voice [in English] can be noted as a [movement or] *state of desiring*, a state of preference that issues in active choosing. The 'I will,' in the sense of I wish, comes from *a dispositional state rather than active deliberation and judgment*" (20; emphasis mine). This needs to be clarified: For this "active choosing" is not the everday *reactive* of the active-passive binary (machine), predicated on the negative, but the *active* of nonpositive affirmation, or desiring machines (series, intensities, assemblages), which would not be predicated, under the sign of negation.

The second point that Scott makes is that the middle voice is not just bifurcated (or disjunctive) but radically multiple. "When a word has several, even countervailing, meanings," he writes, "the middle voice can give expression to the word's multiple values without indicating a common, harmonizing meaning" (21). And again: "when a word has in its power several emphases and counterplays of meanings, such that none of its meanings can adequately express the other meanings, the word is then able to bring to expression a variety of registers, tones, experiences, and significatory chains as its play finds full voice" (21). When "events" are portrayed in the middle *locus*, Scott says, they "voice themselves in excess of the actions and meanings that constitute [or that would predicate] them" (21).

Scott, like Barthes, sees a subversive, militant possibility in the middle voice. He argues that this "different way of thinking" and "state of desiring" and these "counterplays of meanings" and "excess"—all fostered by the middle voice—are what make Nietzsche's *Genealogy of Morals* possible. Specifically, what Nietzsche discloses by way of *self-overcoming*, or *self-reflexive thinking* that perpetually problematizes, is that morality and justice are alibis for the repressed need to punish, to wreck havoc on Others. Scott writes:

> The history of the formation of morality, the fears and resentment, the profound oppression and suffering that are built into the attitudes and hierarchies of morality: these powers have the effect of *turning on themselves* when those inherent, *countervailing powers* are released to take their own directions in Nietzsche's genealogy. The *turning* of repressive powers on themselves . . . is a middle-voiced movement of self-overcoming. . . . [Nietzsche] places in question moral thinking . . . by maintaining in his language the countervalence of values [that which has been repressed] within morality. (25)

Like Barthes and Scott, White views the middle voice and its Nietzschean possibilities as means of resisting and disrupting traditional language-rhetoric, which has been made overly rational by the influence of, first Platonic, and, then, Aristotelian philosophies, and in our time by scientific protocols. Working from Jean Laplanche (1976), White develops the notion of *Kaironomia*. (The word is a linking of *kairos* and *nomos*.) This notion speaks for the perpetual reinvention, revaluing, of the self. White writes: "The middle voice suggests not a fixed and abiding selfhood but a sequence of discontinuous partial selves, or the self as a historical process." And: "[T]he middle voice would promote an activity of endless desiring metamorphosis" (1987, 52). And again: "The 'middle voice' [is] the *will-to-invent*" (63).

White's discussion of the middle voice is similar to Nietzsche's view of subjectivity that is in a perpetual state of self-overcoming, or self-reflection. Nietzsche speaks of the virtue of dis/engaging in "the most unscrupulous *polytropoi*" (1974, 282). Similarly, Nietzsche speaks of "Dionysian man [who] is continually transforming himself" (1968b, 73). In both contexts, Nietzsche is suggesting that through nonpositive affirmative "deception"—which is the middle voice and is the means of self-overcoming—we can free ourselves of the influence of negative deception that goes by the names of metaphysics, philosophical rhetoric, and traditional science, which, I might add, determine us to be—as Barthes, Scott, and White all argue—active/passive voices. Hence, whereas the will to truth is equated with the will to death, the will to invent (the middle voice, self-overcoming, deception) is equated here with the will to life.

By way of summary, I want to gather these various insights about the middle voice and comment more specifically on how Helen can be reportrayed-reconfigured along the lines of this voice, neither active or passive, but a middle that would be Dionysian.

What is most striking about White's and Scott's discussion is their linking of the middle voice with two extremely important concepts: White with *kairos*; Scott with self-overcoming. I would link all three (it's necessary to link but not how to link): Therefore, middle voice = *kairos* = self-overcoming. And the middle voice = *différance*, giving as *dépense*, as an economy without reserve (see Derrida 1982, 9, 18–21). And, lest we forget, the sun. The preference of such linkages will become evident as I proceed, especially in relation to "some more" Helens.

Let's rethink in terms of the problem at hand and how it would be (self-reflexively) problematized. The problem is that of binary-dialectical thinking, or of certain signifying practices or linguistic norms or protocols that determine a body and mind to be either male or female, either active or passive. (I have repeatedly labeled these signifying practices, etc. binary machines, after Deleuze and Guattari.) These practices, norms, or protocols accomplish this purpose by repressing, politically oppressing, the middle voice, which would, upon return, intervene by exploding such political categories as male/female, master/slave. (As Deleuze and Guattari say: "[T]here is no fixed subject unless there is repression" [1983, 26].) The middle voice intervenes by a preferential or dispositional discourse as opposed to an active, rational deliberative discourse, whose sole purpose is to solicit passivity. (It says: I prefer not to not!) Moreover, the middle voice intervenes by way of radical multiplicities, by way of the locus of excess (desiring machines), which would destroy the binary-dialectic of male/female, active/passive, master/slave, thesis/antithesis and thereby enable the return of Dionysian thinking. Desiring-production. (It says: I am all the names of history!)

This intervention of the middle voice, therefore, would be a self-overcoming, would be, in another word, the intervention of *kairos*. From Nietzschean points of view, which are expressed in the middle voice, this intervention has a profound countereffect on metaphysics, specifically in relation to either Platonic or Aristotelian notions of subjectivity in and for the *polis* and its history. This intervention forces not only metaphysics (*physis*[neg.]) but also the entire onto-theological tradition (nihilism) to question itself perpetually, to dis/engage by way of perpetual self-overcoming. This intervention into the onto-theological tradition with its canonized signifying practices questions subjectivity and content. It perpetually denegates this nihilistic tradition. Allow me to speak to these linkages and interpretations of ethical-political interventions more directly; here now, I will rely more heavily on Nietzsche's notion of *will to power* and finally on Nietzsche's influence on Untersteiner's interpretation of Gorgias and Helen.

First, at the level of metaphysics (*physis*[neg.]): I would now link up Nietzsche's important theme of the *will to power* to the previous linkages of middle voice, self-overcoming, and *kairos*. As Scott explains the linguistic phenomenon of the middle voice, there is a *movement* back and forth in Nietzsche's writing between *will to power* (dispersion) and the *eternal return of the same* (reintegration). (The way that I have parenthetically explained these complicated, highly problematic themes does not at all do justice to them; I oversimplify for the sake of a quick explanation. In one way, however, White analogically suggests a similar connection and interpretation with his blending of *kairos* and *nomos* in his neologism of "kaironomia." Analogically, White writes: ". . . *kairos* always defers in the end to *nomos*; the unforeseen opportunity of the present occasion is assimilated by the already known" [62]. The analogy, or ratio, then, is that *kairos* is to *nomos* as will to power/*dispersion* is to eternal return of the same/

reintegration.) As I was saying, the movement back and forth, the reflexive action, now in the words of Scott,

> breaks the privilege of the active-passive voices and, instead, privileges the movement by which the overcoming of metaphysics overcomes itself. When will to power is read primarily in the active voice, for example, it appears to be a quasi-subject that does something in and to specific situations of choice and affirmation. In the middle voice, however, will to power occurs as a self-overcoming movement of a specific, complex organization of countervailing values. (1990, 26)

Still speaking to these linkages and interpretations of ethical-political interventions more directly, I want now to focus more on the theme of the *will to power* (*physis*[nonpositive affirmation]); I want to suggest how the will to power would be both the middle voice and *kairos*, that is, the dispersive power. In a proto-Lacanian, but contrary way (after all, the tactic is "self-overcoming"), Nietzsche takes us as infants to and, once again, through "the mirror stage"; he denegates what Lacan has called the Symbolic (the cultural codes, laws, *nomoi*[neg.], such as Parmenidean, Platonic, Aristotelian contraries of male/female, active/passive). Holding us up to the mirror, Nietzsche (neither mother nor father) says:

> And do you know what "the world" is to me? Shall I show it to you in my mirror? This world: a monster of energy without beginning, without end . . . a sea of forces flowing and rushing together, eternally changing, eternally flooding back . . . blessing itself as that which must recur eternally, as a becoming that knows no satiety, no disgust, no weariness: this is my *Dionysian world* [emphasis mine] of eternally self-creating, the eternally self-destroying . . . my *"beyond good and evil,"* without goal, unless the joy of the circle is itself a goal. (1968c, 549)

What better description of *kairos*! My view of *kairos* is not Platonic or Aristotelian; is not a traditional view (see Kinneavy 1986). I am not referring here to *kairos* as the theological notion of a "moment of crisis" or a "time filled with significance" (Kermode 1967, 46–49) but more so as *many competing, contradictory voices.* (The middle voice = dispersion.) It is what I have been processually speaking of from my earlier discussion of the non-Kantian sublime to an aesthetics of excess. *Kairos* here is the nonpositive affirmative sublime. Which makes for Favorinus, the mad text of Marx, and Others—The sovereign subjects.

Kairos is often linked with *to prepon* (the fitting), which, as George Kennedy points out, "was to become one of the 'virtues' of style" (1963, 67). What would be fitting would be well defined by way of the Attic style. What

I am attempting to do, if not yet obvious, is to turn this *virtue* of style into wild (savage) *virtuosity*, just as a Gorgias—a further reintensified Gorgias—through the so-called Asiatic-cum-schizo style, will have attempted. Here comes the virtwo/cum/three-nosiocity.

> There is much that is strange, but nothing
> that surpasses man in strangeness [*to deinotaton*]
>
> —Antigone of Sophocles

> Here all things come caressingly to your speech and flatter you, for they want to ride on your back. . . . All being wants to become word here, all that is in the process of becoming wants to learn to speak from you.
>
> —Nietzsche

> With the very least residue of superstition within oneself, one could hardly know how to rid oneself of the idea that one is mere incarnation, merely a mouthpiece, merely a medium for powerful forces.
>
> —Nietzsche

Having linked up the middle voice with *kairos* and with the will to power and the sublime, I want now to turn to Untersteiner's view of *kairos*, or Gorgian *kai(e)ro(tic)s*. I made much of this view in chapter 6 when accounting for various subjectivities, mainly, for Helen(s).

For Nietzsche, knowledge is tragic. And yet, the gay science: "Even laughter may yet have a future. I mean, when the proposition 'the species is everything, one is always none' has become part of humanity, and this ultimate liberation and irresponsibility has become accessible to all at all times. Perhaps laughter will then have formed an alliance with wisdom, perhaps only 'gay science' will then be left" (1974, 74) of what is humanistically possible.

Some preparatory pastiches/assemblages of Nietzsche, Bataille, Gorgias, Untersteiner:

• We cannot know the Truth. (If it exits, we can only know it by Noing-it. [Bataille 1988b, 35.] Out of the impossible comes the possible; out of the possible comes the impossible.)
• What is even more tragic, however, is that we, nonetheless, pursue such Truth, which Nietzsche calls the *will to death* (negation, Nihilism). (If

we can No it, we cannot *communicate* it except semiotically across our wounds, lacerations, loss [27, 30–31, 34, 65–66, 68, 152], hence again, across our mutual, yet separate loss.)

(Most disturbingly, we are humorless, without laughter. Yes, to tragedy; No, to humor.)

• However, what we communicate is only part of Noing, for in Noing, we hide from ourselves that we are rotten with excess, which we cannot not spend. ("Future holiness will long for evil" [41]. Finally, catastrophe.)

As a case in point, Untersteiner—informed by this Nietzschean view of Gorgias and his hysterical "Helen"—reportrays Helen's struggling with a disjunctive proposition, or a dialectical (one), or a *dissoi logoi* (two). Helen is not unlike other tragic-hysterical characters, such as Antigone and Hamlet, "H. G." and Genet, who confront questions that *logos* cannot—or perversely, perhaps didactically, refuses—to answer. (No-ing sometimes gets us stuck, predisposing us to greater No-ing/violence. No-ing predisposes us to negate the excess that we are confronted with.) While Helen is hysterically struggling to resolve her dilemma—to go or not to go with Paris—a force (or power) intervenes in her deliberations: "will, decision," violently bursts forth. This *will* (to power, or excess) is, Untersteiner claims, "realised in a [*kairos*] endowed with the property of breaking up the cycle of the antitheses and creating *something new, irrational*" (1954, 161; emphasis mine. Cf. White 1987, 20). Hence, from One to Two to "some more." A nova occurs. The "caesura" of unreason (Foucault 1988, ix). Laughter.

Untersteiner points out that though "it must be . . . thought that a decision is carried out, . . . this famous woman could not have come to a rational decision" (1954, 161). Excess "decided" not to allow for a will-negating decision. Bataille would say that the possible cum impossible, or impossible cum possible, intervenes (1988b, 101). While Untersteiner suffers from nostalgia, as evidenced in his statement "It must be . . . thought," Bataille understands this *nostalgia*, and yet, is overwhelmed with "unbearable laughter" (1988b, 48). Nostalgia = homesickness. (Let us continue these pastiches/assemblages, so as in form, at least, to reach for the indeterminate.)

The precedence for such a strange, *uncanny* situation is Greek dramatic tragedy. It is this very force of *kairos*, or this will (to power), that remakes Helen and history. Helen, like Antigone, finds herself in the *uncanny* (strangest of strange) situation; however, unlike Antigone—and this is an important difference—she does not *decide*, as far as common sense notions of decisions go. In this sense, then, both Antigone and Helen can be seen as subject to, variously, *kairos*, the middle voice, the uncanny.[8] Which in turn can lead them to the irrational, or nonrational, to chance occurrence. If not Lord—from a theological point of view—of the compossible,[9] then, they can be seen as middle subjects of com/possible worlds. To decide or not to decide, however, makes for little difference between them, for each finds herself in the *uncanny* (strangest of strange) place. And yet, if, as Untersteiner argues, *it must be thought* that Helen has carried out a decision and simultaneously that she could not have come to a rational decision, it can equally be posited that it must be thought that Antigone finds herself in a similar situation. (Since neither is God and, therefore, the Lord of the compossible, both are subject to the impossible cum possible.[10] And once again, we might find ourselves laughing, or wailing with concealed laughter.)

As Heidegger points out, for human being to think that it decides, chooses, is only to "conceal" from itself "the uncanniness of language, of the passions, the powers by which man [*anthropos*] is ordained . . . as a historical being. . . ." (1959, 156). (Or to conceal from ourselves our sovereignty. Our compossibility. And to hide from ourselves that we are rotten with excess. Which we cannot not spend. And yet, future holiness will long for evil. And catastrophe. The *logos*, like Paris, has its way with Helen.[11] The Greeks with the Trojans. [Notice how we collectively begin to *anthropomorphize* this event into a narrative of exploitation, for which we must hold people *account-able*. Hence, the negative desire for revenge. In the face of the incompossible. Look at post-war Heidegger in his silence. And let us not forget that Gorgias, in speaking from the Helen-*topos*, is defending Helen against the charge of being responsible for men's deaths. And contemporary feminists argue—or should argue, given this anthropomorphizing—that the men are at fault for the rape, for the war, for blaming, once ever again, a woman; and for trafficking in women (for the gift had been stolen and, therefore, *potlatch*-as-war must be waged!, redemption, revenge waged). These are more than reasonable and life-furthering arguments. And yet, if we forget that we are anthropomorphizing in the face of the *logos*-as-irrational, or -nonrational, because excessive—because sun, exuberance, that cannot be reckoned—then, we hide from ourselves the other problem! And therefore cannot negotiate with these structures of violence. We conceal, un/namely, that we, human beings, are not masters of this situation. *Anthropos* is not in charge here or elsewhere. (And yet, as Untersteiner avers, it must be thought that we are in control.) And yet, Sovereignty? We are not at home, for, as Bataille says, we are will-negating, life-negating: "[Apollonian] Man is the animal that negates nature" (1993, 61). That is, negates excess. Moreover, because repulsed by [our] nature, we dis/engage from "sexuality" by engaging in "eroticism" (27).[12] That is, we negate our *animal sexuality* and take on human eroticism, which is a *limited eroticism*, which cannot not be expressed in *unlimited eroticisms*. Hence, we have a new three, or trilemma, here.]

Still parenthetical: Let us recall Helen, trying to decide between either tick or tock, tick or tock, but nonlogically finds herself in tock . . . tick, tock . . . tick. She is out of time. She is in the untimely. She is in *to apeiron* [the indeterminate]! Heidegger writes: "The essential [*physis*] is *not numbered*; the essential is the right time, i.e. the right moment, and the right perseverance" [1959, 206; emphasis mine]. That is, *kairos*. Heidegger, however, forgets this statement: He sets aside *to apeiron* [the indeterminate] for unity [determinate]. At other times, however, in silence, he listens to the *logos* for *kairos*, for the revelation.[13]

Interestingly enough—how is it that these things that I string together work out so fortuitously and analogically, yet discontinually?—Bataille says:

> Archic man endlessly posed the question of sovereignty; for him it was the primary question, *the one that counted as sovereign in his eyes*. It was not posed in his mind in a rational form. . . . For, in a way, he knew that sovereignty cannot be the anticipated result of a calculated effort. What is sovereign can only come from the arbitrary, from chance. There ought not exist any *means* by which man might *become* sovereign: it is better for him to *be* sovereign, . . . [He surpasses] the poverty of utility[.] Nothing sovereign must ever submit to the useful [1993, 226; Bataille's emphasis].

Bataille continues—again along the lines of Helen's experience and Heidegger's statement—

> We should calmly ask ourselves . . . if the world we have conceived in accordance with reason is itself a viable and complete world. It is a world of sequential duration; it is not a world of the moment. In it, the world is expressly nullified; the moment is nothing more than a kind of zero with which we no longer see that it is possible *to count*. It is the point, and the core, where the movement of knowledge, which always has elements distinguishable in duration as it object, runs aground and breaks apart.
>
> We have to realize finally that irrespective of any particular form . . . the problem of the sovereign moment (this moment whose meaning in no way depends on its consequences) is posed for us, not as a secondary form, but as a need to fill the void of the world of useful works. [227; Bataille's emphasis]

And what provisional conclusion [rebeginning?] would I draw from these discussions about time [the untimely, *kairos*, *to apeiron*, the sovereign moment, even haeccity[14]] and counting and, yes, utility? Un/namely, that Helen's experience with the *logos*, as Untersteiner redescribes it, is that of sovereignty. In fact, I would say that Helen's experience is the same as H. G.'s experience, in Clarice Lispector's *The Passion According to H. G.* [1988], un/namely, sovereignty. Helen, just like H. G. [and Cixous], in the words of

Bataille, is "the sovereign . . . [who] *is*, as if death were not. Indeed, [s/he] is the one who doesn't die, for [s/he] dies only to be reborn. [S/he] is not a [wo/man] in the individual sense of the word, but rather a god; [s/he] is essentially the embodiment of the one [s/he] is but is not" [1993, 222]. H. G. undergoes a metamorphosis from determinateness to indeterminateness. [Recall my having discussed this transformation in the excursus "Feminist Sophistic?"] Helen here dies out of rationality/utility—undergoes this denegation, this change to indeterminateness—so as to be reborn again in sovereignty. S/he is "an image of solar radiation" [223]. That is, excess energy. S/he is the return of the excluded middle [voice]. Or as logic [negated *logos*] would have it, *the muddle*. The s[o]undance. The expenditure of energy, noise, somatic rhythms—that cannot not be expended—in non-productive, wasteful ways. [Recall the perverse necessity here to denegate the three principles of man's logic: Identification, contradiction, excluded middle.] Whereas Helen's experience with the *logos* leads to war [extreme waste], her experience, nonetheless, shows the way to the other side of war, catastrophe. It shows that s/he is sovereign—in a nontheological sense—the Lord of the compossible. The indeterminate. And the means of avoiding the catastrophe. To which we will return, but first let us rev-up our regurgitation-machine so as to expel and recreate the conditions for our desiring machine. To Nietzsche. [End parenthesis.])

> But science spurred by its powerful illusion, speeds irresistibly toward its limits where its optimism, concealed in the essence of logic, suffers shipwreck. . . . When [men] see to their horror how logic coils up at these boundaries and finally bites its own tail—suddenly the new form of insight breaks through, *tragic insight* which, merely to be endured, needs art as a protection and remedy.
>
> —F. Nietzsche

The Uncanny (again): I want now to return, more forthrightly, to Nietzsche who speaks to the problem of the *uncanny*, but in terms of the clash between *Dionysian* and the everyday and the product of this clash, which is *nausea* (that which precedes vomiting). What I will attempt is a blending of Heidegger with Nietzsche, while favoring, as always, Nietzsche's nonpositive affirmation. The incompossible.

In *The Birth of Tragedy*, Nietzsche explains that the Helene "felt himself [sic] nullified [denegated] in the presence of the satyric chorus; and this is the most immediate effect of the Dionysian tragedy," un/namely, "unity leading back to the very heart of nature [as *physis* nonpositive affirmation]" (1967, 59). A *pathos* of experience.[15] In the midst of the chorus, the Helene loses the principle of individuation and of even the (political) social. Instead, this "chorus of satyrs" is "a chorus of natural beings who live ineradicably . . . behind all civilization and remain eternally the same, despite the changes of generations and of the history of nations" (59; cf. 56). If *a*political, the chorus is also *a*historical! Nietzsche says: "[T]he existence of the world is justified only as an aesthetic phenomenon" (22). (This characterization of the *a*political and *a*historical is an important one, which we will have to return to.[16] For now, however, I provisionally read both as being under negation—history is *history* neg.; politics, *politics* neg.—and, therefore, Nietzsche, in dis/order to avoid the negative [as in active political nihilism] and its narrative of emancipation-[redemption]-cum-revenge, speaks in terms of the satyric chorus, which is, as I would characterize it, *hystery* nonpositive affirmation, or perhaps the *hysterical sublime.*) Are you lost, Dear Reader? If so, I am saying, simply, that this chorus will appear to be apolitical and ahistorical, but is not! In the midst of this chorus, human being "comforts himself [sic]"; Nietzsche says: "Art [the satyric, tragic chorus] saves him, and through art—life" (59). This comfort is necessary; for both history and politics—active nihilism—lead only to *nausea*.

However, in speaking of the birth of tragedy, Nietzsche also speaks of its death, which is brought about because of the negative, because of an optimism in rationality (see 1967, 21). And yes, a political optimism predicated on rationalism (enlightenment)! Therefore, once the Helene steps out of the chorus into "everyday reality" (or history and politics as rational), and this reality, Nietzsche explains, "re-enters consciousness," then, what "is experienced [is] *nausea*: an ascetic, will-negating mood" (59–60; emphasis mine. Cf. 23).[17] There is no longer any comfort! Nietzsche writes: "Dionysian man [*Mensche*] resembles Hamlet: both have once looked truly into the essence of things, they have *gained knowledge*, and nausea inhibits action; for their action could not change anything in the eternal nature of things; they feel it to be ridiculous or humiliating that they should be asked to set right a world that is out of joint. Knowledge [*logos* neg., rationality] kills action" (60; Nietzsche's emphasis).

(Later in *The Genealogy of Morals*, this nausea, or "ascetic, will-negating mood" becomes morality—the ascetic mindset of the *thou shalt nots*, which set in motion guilt, ressentiment, a reactionary state [active nihilism], and victimage. This, as discussed, is the negating engine of history. It is this ascetic, Christian mindset, Nietzsche says, that predisposes us to have the void for our purpose than be void of purpose. For Heidegger, all this is owing to ontological guilt.)

It can be said that not only Hamlet, but also Antigone and Helen are all, as being outside of the chorus, confronted with the same question, What to do? (the question of praxis), and that all fall personally (socially?) powerless in the face of the other power, variously called here *kairos* (Untersteiner and Heidegger), the *uncanny* (Heidegger), and *nausea* (Nietzsche). To be sure, there are subtle differences among these three thinkers' concepts; but what they share in common is a claim that, when facing a question of *praxis*, human being is "decided" more than decides. Human being is the strangest of the strange. For Nietzsche, the only error is the history of the error of nihilism. For Nietzsche, who further develops what he had only initiated in *The Birth of Tragedy*, man or woman must avoid personal-lyrical and social-public (negative, Nihilistic) power, which is more often than not the will to one truth at the exclusion of the Others, and embrace the will to power, the infinite play of affirmations (of difference, chance, the irrational). If for Heidegger the ground (*Ab-grund*) of history is the abyss (impossible-cum-possible, death), for Nietzsche the ground of history, as Stephen Watson argues, is not "a negative ground [or abyss] for a positive emergence" (1985, 233; also see C. E. Scott 1990, 97). If not the *topos* of *impossible-cum-possible*, then, history is *possibilisms*, or the *compossible*: It is "a chasm of infinite alterity" and "the return of the Other, of becoming, of difference" (Watson 1985, 233).[18]

> But which *ought* we to choose? And how *ought* we to choose?
> It is yet another of Nietzsche's merits that he joins to his
> critique of Enlightenment moralities a sense of their failure
> to address adequately, let alone to answer the question: what
> sort of person am I to become?
>
> —A. MacIntyre

Choice/Becoming?: In sum, then, it is Nietzschean *kairos*, the middle voice, the will to power, possibilisms that are—is—the force that chooses for Helen and establishes the conditions for the compossible. Rationality balked, Helen experienced nausea, then, *kairos* acts. (If Helen had acted, it would most likely have been a reaction, which would have been based on, as discussed, the reactionary engine of history. Everyone else around Helen acts out reactionary fantasies that have terrible material results.) Helen, therefore, is more so a function of *kairos*, the middle voice, the will to power. *Kairos* is a force that makes Helen *subject to* it, but by breaking up the cycle of active-passive *physis*[neg.]/*nomos*[neg.] and by reestablishing the nonrational *physis*[nonpositive affirmation]. (Hence, a denegated, sovereign subject.) It is a force that makes Helen *subject to* it, but not by virtue of a passive voice, but by ill-virtue—against *to prepon*, what is fitting—of the middle voice. (Hence, a denegated subject!) It is a force that prefers—just as the middle voice does—to place subjectivity into infinite dispersion, into a "Dionysian world," into the middle voice, as Eric White characterizes it, of "endless desiring metamorphosis" (1987, 52). I have so long ago spoken of this metamorphosis in terms of a sovereign, sublime subject (as Favorinus and Hermaphroditus and "the desire named Marx," as the human species in Kafka becoming-animal, as the man and woman species in Cixous and Lispector attending to-becoming-other, as all undergoing metamorphoses). Dear Reader, is this all disconcerting? And, you may ask, How is this better than—this revaluing—what we have? And yet, What is it that we have, the illusion of choice? Is our choice today between either Heidegger or Nietzsche? Or Is our choice, as Alasdair MacIntyre asks, "*either* [to] follow through the aspirations and the collapse of the different versions of the Enlightenment project until there remains only the Nietzschean diagnosis and the Nietzschean problematic *or* must [we hold] that the Enlightenment project was not only mistaken, but should never have been commenced in the first place[?] [Is there] no third alternative[?]" (1984, 118; MacIntyre's emphasis; cf. Stout 1988, 191–219; Sloterdijk 1987). MacIntyre's third? Aristotle! No, we can't go home again: Our next door neighbor, after all, is de Sade (Klossowski 1991); or as Wolin puts it, quoting Habermas's critique of Heidegger: " 'man is "the neighbor of Being"—not the neighbor of man' " (1990, 149). Can we return to the values of the Enlightenment, as Habermas says we must, and rebuild the neighborhood of consensus? *Homologia*? What are we, the various "WEs," looking for?

More specifically now, What are WE looking for when it comes to WRITING HISTORIES OF RHETORICS, to rewriting Hellen(ism)? Do not look. About writing, Hélène Cixous says:

> Let yourself go! Let go of everything! Lose everything! Take to the air. . . . Go, fly, swim, bound, descend, cross, love the unknown, love the uncertain, love what has not yet been seen, love no one, whom you are, whom you will be, leave yourself, shrug off the old lies, *dare what you don't dare*, it is there that you will take pleasure, never make your here anywhere but *there*, and rejoice, rejoice in the terror, follow it where you're afraid to go, go ahead, take the plunge, you're on the right trail! Listen: you owe nothing to the past, you owe nothing to the law. *Gain* your freedom: get rid of everything, vomit up everything. (1991, 40; Cixous's emphasis; cf. 1993, 118)

And then? What might WE expect? Cixous says: "After that, you don't know. It's life that decides. Its terrible power of invention, which surpasses us. Our life anticipates us. Always ahead of you by a height, a desire, the good abyss, the one that suggests to you: 'Leap and pass into infinity.' Write! Write? . . . Live! Risk" (1991, 41).

Do not look. But jump. Leap. Refold. Stretch. Casuistically stretch. When writing the histories, hysteries, schizeries of Helen. Take the risk. Is there any other choice? Or, again, even a choice? (Is not the beetle, the cockroach, the *barata*,[19] older than the modern notion of choice?) If we look, and not glance, if we theorize, we will *see* (theorize) nothing. If thy eye/"I" offends you—Writers of The History of Helen—pluck it out. Give it to Helen. She will know what to do with it! Oh, Oedipus. We—Riders of the History—must get beyond Oedipus. Is there anyone here who can intuit how to refold, casuistically stretch Oedipus? Cixous writes: "I didn't seek: *I was the search*. In the beginning, there can be only dying, the abyss, the first laugh" (41; emphasis mine). Does anyone hear Oedipus-the search (he-who-searches-for-the-criminal-but-unwittingly-searches-for-himself/he who is *the search*, he-who-must-self-overcome) LAUGHING? What is the counter-option to tragedy? Nietzsche answers, the gay science (1974, 73–75). What is wanted is to write as if. The eyes, these "I"s. That must pass away so as to attend to the other. . . .

> I shall give birth to a centaur someday.
>
> —Fredrich Nietzsche

> I employ these words . . . with a glance toward the business of childbearing—but also with a glance toward those who, in a company from which I do not exclude myself, turn their eyes away in the face of the as yet unnameable which is proclaiming itself and which can do so, as is necessary whenever a birth is in the offing, only under the species of the non-species, in the formless, mute, infant, and terrifying form of monstrosity.
>
> —Derrida

Theseus/Ariadne and Dionysus/Ariadne: Having ruminated on the middle voice (self-overcoming, *kairos*, will to power) in relation to Helen(s), I want to continue—I am insatiable, I forever want "some more"—to discover way(s) to reconfigure Helen in nonpositive affirmative (Nietzschean) terms, or discover way(s) to place Helen not just in perpetual metamorphoses but now also in ever sexually ambiguous reconfigurations. Refoldings. (Therefore, neither female nor male, but sexual multiplicity, a third subject position. Therefore, from a stateless of animal "sexuality" to a state of limited "eroticism" to a *pagus*, *dépays*, of limitless "eroticisms" [see Bataille 1993, 81–83, 173–84].) I want to rebegin by briefly discussing the *Theseus/ Ariadne* coupling with the *Dionysus/Ariadne* recoupling. What Nietzsche attempts in his poem "Ariadne's Lament" (*Dionysian Dithyrambs*, qtd. in Krell 1986, 16–19) is a sub/version of Theseus and all that he represents, by way of his inclusion of Dionysus.

Allow me to explain further, for this is crucial to historiography: Theseus is the male hero who could kill the minotaur, the halfbeast/halfman, with the help of Ariadne and her continuous thread. What Nietzsche does, sub/versively, is to displace Theseus (the male-hero) with Dionysus (a god). But for what purpose? No doubt, there are numerous possibilities here, but the one that is of temporary interest to my narrative is that Dionysus is sub/versively necessary because, unlike Theseus, he *is sexually ambiguous* (see Kofman 1991, 196–99). While Theseus follows the thread, Dionysus has no need or desire for the thread and all that it represents. When Theseus is replaced with Dionysus, there is no necessity to kill the Minotaur. (Cf., Land 1992, ch. 10.) Nietzsche in his poem has Ariadne reject Theseus and call, as a lover in heat, for the god Dionysus, who itself is a radical multiplicity of creatures. (The reactionary male has been sub/verted.) Allow me to explain further by focusing on the imagery.

The thread serves as a metaphor for "rationality," as discursive reasoning would allow Theseus, the hero, to become master of his mind and, therefore, to be successful. It is this rationality, however, that is reactive. Deleuze explains: "Theseus is a representation of the higher man: he is the [negatively] sublime and heroic man, the one who *takes up* [moral, political] *burdens* and defeats monsters. But what he lacks is precisely the virtue of the bull, that is to say the sense of the earth when he is harnessed and also the capacity to unharshness, *to throw off burdens*" (1983, 187; emphasis mine). About Ariadne, Deleuze says: "As terrible mothers, terrible sisters and wives, femininity represents the spirit of revenge and the *ressentiment* which animates man himself" (187). The couple—the traditional linkage—of Theseus/Ariadne is reactionary. Both think and react by way of active nihilism.

The way that I read the exclusion of Theseus and the call for Dionysus, therefore, is that the exclusion is the negation, or denegation, of Theseus (male-hero). Correspondingly, the way that I am reading the call (a/vocation) for Dionysus (a god who is sexually ambiguous) is that this call is an affirmation of excess and life. Deleuze writes: ". . . in relation to Dionysus, Ariadne . . . is like a second affirmation" (187). Dionysus *is* nonpositive affirmation and, therefore, when calling to him, Ariadne announces a second affirmation. Hence, in my scheming, Ariadne signals the move from negation (*physis*[neg.] or *nomos*[neg.]) to a double affirmation (*physis*[nonpositive affirmation]).[20]

But there is much left unsaid here, especially in relation to the sexual ambiguity of Dionysus. By now the most obvious point should be that Dionysus represents a denegated (sovereign, sublime) subject, or a being who is perpetually becoming. Any lament of, or prayer to, Dionysus, or to affirmation, would signal, as a double affirmation, a reportrayal of a subject— in this case, Ariadne herself, who must become sexually ambiguous so as to avoid (negate) being reactionary. (Lest the ancillary point be lost here, what is being lost, or denegated, is subjectvity-negativity itself, or all Humanist, Enlightenment values, which are reactionary values. This point will have a profound effect on Helen who herself should be reportrayed so as to become, like the sub/versive Ariadne, nonreactionary.)

In further discussing the consequences of *Ariadne-Helen* becoming sexually ambiguous, becoming no longer a traditional or revised subject, no longer subject to active nihilism, I want now to turn to discussions by Jacques Derrida's *Spurs: Nietzsche's Style* (1979) and, as a followup, David Farrell Krell's *Postponements* (1986). The subject is woman, or the feminine. Which is a highly problematic subject (as I indicated in relation to Spivak in the excursis "Feminist Sophistics?"). Before starting, it needs to be acknowledged that Nietzsche is often critiqued for his (apparent) misogynist statements. He is, as he is aware himself, especially difficult to read and understand, given his aphoristic style (assemblages), and consequently is open to all kinds of interpretations. The *logos*, as Nietzsche well acknowledges, is uncanny. (And so are readers' interests.) As a case in point, he has commonly been read to be not only a misogynist but also a proto-Nazi. The charge that he hates women is the one that sticks more than the latter charge. As far as I am concerned, as well as growing scholarship devoted to these charges, Nietzsche is neither (see Graybeal 1990; P. Patton 1993; Burgard 1994).[21] If anything, Nietzsche is still posthumous writer, still waiting for readers who are capable of going with the flow and intensities of his aphoristic style.

That Nietzsche is not against "women," I would explain, is best understood in the light of his post-ontology and post-epistemology. As already suggested, Nietzsche did not work with the notion of *Being*[neg.] behind subjectivity; he was not a (negative) essentialist. When responding to "women," he is responding to the masculine-determined roles, or masks, that women played, or wore. He is responding to their roles semiotically performed across passive nihilism and active nihilism, both of which are reactionary states. In this sense and only in this sense is Nietzsche "against" woman. (Remember, again, that gender roles and masks for Nietzsche are, in the words of Butler, "cultural performances." Any revolt against the law [either *physis*[neg.] or *nomos*[neg.]], any revolt that is reactionary, is subject to that law, or is a subject that would be reactionary.) It is these roles and masks, therefore, that

Nietzsche attacks. At a social level, he also attacks feminism which he saw as male-determined, or thoroughly reactionary. Nietzsche (through Zarathustra-Christ-Dionysus) calls for and awaits the sovereign, sublime subject.[22]

If his attitude toward woman/feminism is understood in this light, then, we might possibly begin to understand a different perspective on why Nietzsche attempts to reach the *Ubermensch*, which should not be translated as "overman," for the German word is nongender specific. The *Ubermensch* is outside of the political categories, or the binary, of male/female; it is *a third subject position* (or not countable and therefore best described as sovereign, sublime, "some more"). The *Male/female* binary is the error apparently initiated by Parmenides (in his dividing practice, binary machine).

This error must be further explained now in terms of "the gay science" and of woman and the feminine. Plato says that there is One truth; Nietzsche says there is only the truth that there is *no* One Truth. Derrida says: "A joyful wisdom shows [that] there never has been *the* style, *the* simulacrum, *the* woman. There never has been *the* sexual difference" (1979, 139; Derrida's emphasis). Derrida is referring directly to Nietzsche's view of "feminine," which I wish to continue to emphasize now and especially, yet implicitly, in reference to *Ariadne-Helen*.

Nietzsche's Third "Woman": Let us rebegin with the opening lines of *Beyond Good and Evil*: "Supposing truth is a woman—what then?" (1966, 2). This opening statement is an attack on "dogmatism" (2, 3), but specifically on "Platonism" (and Christianity), which "[stood] truth on her head and [denied] *perspective*, the basic condition of all life" (3; Nietzsche's emphasis). The denial of all life is again a reference to Nihilism. But what does Nietzsche mean here by "woman"? Does Nietzsche mean biological, essential woman of the binary? *The* woman? Or *the* sexual difference? Or does he mean something else? Nietzsche is not an essentialist, specifically not a naive or "strategic" essentialist; Nietzsche does not think in Platonic terms of Being behind the mask[23] or role (see Nietzsche 1969, 45; cf. 1966, 23–29; 1968b, 48–50; 1968c, 267–71). He is not willing to take, for the sake of doing politics, the "risk of [negative] essence," say, as a Spivak and others are (see Spivak 1989b). This would only be a perpetuation of the history of an "error" (Nietzsche 1968b), and the conditions for the continuation of the history of a "burden." Derrida writes:

> That which will not be pinned down by truth is, in truth—*feminine*. This should not, however, be hastily mistaken for a woman's feminini*ty*, for female sexuali*ty*, or for any other of those essentializing fetishes which might

still tantalize the dogmatic philosopher, the impotent artist or the inexpe-
rienced seducer who has not yet escaped his foolish hopes of capture. (1979,
55; Derrida's emphasis)

The *risk* Nietzsche does take is that of *affirmative essence*, or "nonpositive
affirmation," which I have been signifying, throughout thus far, in terms of
Physis^nonpositive affirmation. (This is the risk that informs this book on historiographies of rhetorics. It's a risk that attempts to respond to the history of an
error in history writing, both traditional and revisionary.)

Working from the nonpositive affirmative, Nietzsche is searching for
ways of developing what some call a "third woman" (see Berg 1982;
Derrida 1979). Moving now from *Beyond Good and Evil* to *Twilight of
the Idols*, we can see more clearly this affirmative "woman." (Implicitly,
we might see how both Ariadne and the Helen can be avatars of this
woman.) Nietzsche continues to establish the conditions for the possibility of this third woman in *Twilight*, but specifically in that famous
section entitled "How the 'Real World' at last Became a Myth: History
of an Error." In the first part, after writing " 'I, Plato, *am* the truth',"
Nietzsche writes in the second part: "*it* [the real world, the truth] *becomes a woman*, it becomes Christian" (1968b, 40; Nietzsche's emphasis). About this amendment from the first to the second parts, however,
Derrida writes: "it is the idea that becomes woman. The *becoming-female*
is 'process of the idea' . . . and the idea a form of truth's self-presenta-
tion. Thus the truth has not always been woman nor is the woman always truth. They both have a history. . . . [T]heir history is history itself,
a history which philosophy alone . . . is unable to decode" (1979, 87;
emphasis mine. Cf. Deleuze and Guattari 1987, 232–309). What happens
then is that "Plato can no more say 'I am the truth' " (87). However, this
becoming-woman must be seen as being linked with "Christianity." What
"woman" might possibly offer, therefore, is once again negated, or as
Derrida says "castrated" (89). The passions return to being idealized or
spiritualized (91, 93). They become passive (acetic) nihilism.

Derrida now has Nietzsche move beyond this Christianized woman, who
is a second woman, and think in terms of a third women. In the section
entitled "Positions," Derrida distinguishes between what he sees are two
women in the first two sections of "How the 'Real World' at last Became a
Myth": The first two women, implicitly present, are the Platonic woman as
supplement and the Christian woman as supplement (97); or the first is
"castrated woman" and the second, "castrating woman" (101). Or passive-
nihilistic woman; active-nihilistic woman. (Remember the active-passive
voices.) About the inevitability of a third woman (based in part on Nietzsche's
styles), Derrida writes: "In the instance of the third proposition[,] beyond

the double negation of the first two, woman is recognized and affirmed as
an affirmative power, a dissimulatress, an artist, a *dionysiac*. And no longer
is it man who affirms her. She affirms herself, in and of herself, in man"
(97; my emphasis). But this man that she affirms herself in is not Platonic
(negative) man but Dionysian (nonpositive affirmative) "man." She (Helen)
will have become by way of a sovereign, sublime subjectivity; by way of leaving
behind active/passive voices, sadistic/masochistic voices by way of reaching
for a middle voice.

What Nietzsche is attempting is to write a philosophy of a third
woman and a third man, a philosophy that would be *beyond* these simply, but insidious, political categories. Here then, the heretofore "excluded
thirds" (Serres 1982, 65–70) become included in, at best, a post-philoso-
phy. The reportrayal that Nietzsche performs on the history of an error
(Platonic nihilism) is one that cannot not effect the representation of
subjectivity. This reportrayal/refolding can be seen as threatening the
stability of such notions as What is male? and What is female? However,
it threatens even more, namely, that which goes generally by the name
of feminism, or rather that which has come to be know as reactive feminism, that which engages in negative deconstruction. Alone. What is
wanted, instead, in Nietzschean terms, is a movement beyond such feminisms to a view of gender radically dis/informed by affirmative
deconstruction. If Helen is returned to agency, "she" will most likely be
a reactionary, who attempts to redeem the past.

Helen(ism) of the past "is what *revenge* is: the will's ill will against time
and its 'it was' " (*Thus Spoke*, 1968a, 252). Helen, like Ariadne, should not
join forces with, not link up with, Theseus, but with Dionysus. The third
woman as Ariadne (in Nietzsche's view) and as Helen (in my view) is
Dionysian. (Remember Dionysus is neither male or female, but sexually
ambiguous. Remember Dionysus is to return by way of Demeter, who is not
a female of the *polis* [negation] but of the *pagus* [nonpositive affirmation].)
Nietzsche continues to work toward the return of Dionysus, to move beyond,
to revalue value. In the fourth book of *Thus Spoke* ("The Magician" [1968a,
364–67]), Nietzsche begins the petition for Dionysus, spoken by the Magician. Later, in his rewriting of this petition, In the "Ariadne's Lament,"
Nietzsche shifts from male to female, this time with Ariadne calling for the
god Dionysus. Leaving Theseus (reactionary hero) behind, she wails like a
demon lover for Dionysus:

> Who will warm me, who loves me still? . . .
> Spread-eagled, shuddering . . .
> Racked, oh, by unknown fevers, . . .
>   shot by you, O thought!

> Unnameable! Veiled! Horrific! . . .
>   Thus I lie,
> turn, twist, tortured. . . .

Dionysus interrupts:

> Be clever, Ariadne! . . .
> You have little ears; you have my ears:
> stick a clever [creative] word in them!—
> Must one not first hate oneself [i.e., denegate, self-overcome,
>   undergo death]
>   in order to love [affirm] oneself? . . .
> *I am your labyrinth* [your abyss of an infinite play of affirmation]. . . .

A Postscript: Kofman and Irigaray: That the foregoing discussion of the "feminine" as three kinds (castrated, castrating, and affirmative) will not be satisfying to many readers is understandable. The literature on Nietzsche, Derrida, and *Spurs*—not including, of course, my appropriation of this literature—testifies to such dissatisfaction. I do not expect that this appropriation of mine will necessarily be received well either. For those feminists in historiography of rhetoric that demand an agent that can change history, my notion of third subject (sublime, sovereign) positions will be of no help and will be read very unsympathetically. Being aware of this difference of attitudes—as I indicated at length in the excursus "Sophistic Feminism?"— however, can be of value, I hope, if this difference is seen as not just male against female, or male against male, or female against female. There are feminists who engage in similar tactics as mine. I will not repeat the list that I have developed intermittently throughout my discussion.

However, we might think of a paradigm for difference between feminists themselves, say, in the contrary discussions of Sarah Kofman (1985, 1991) and Luce Irigaray (1991).[24] Kofman, in her article "Baubô: Theological Perversion and Fetishism," employs a *dissoi logoi*, or negative deconstructive, reading of Nietzsche, considering him as potentially a misogynist and as not one. Her conclusion is the latter. Irigaray, in her book *Marine Lover of Friedrich Nietzsche*, interrogates Nietzsche's works, attempting to demonstrate that he is misogynist. Her claim, among others, is that he desires to be creative *as* a woman, which he cannot be. As Bataille points out that Gide said that Nietzsche was "jealous of God" (1993, 374–79), Irigaray poetically states that Nietzsche envies her and other women (1991, 24). Womb envy! After reading Irigaray's inquisition of Nietzsche, I get the impression that, as analyst, she is doing an unintended parody of Freud interpreting Dora. She writes: "I want to interpret your midnight dreams, and unmask that phenomenon: your night.

And make you admit that I dwell in it as your most fearsome adversity" (25; emphasis mine). If Nietzsche were alive, he, too, like Dora, would give Irigaray a two-week notice, never to return.

And yet—comedy of comedies—we must eternally return.

*Excursus. Preludes to Future (anterior) Histories of Rhetorics
(From The Obsessive to the Hysterical and Third Schizo turns)*

The contemporary German poet Heinrich Müller asserts, "It
is good to be a woman, and no victor."

—C. Jan Swearingen

I would rather be a cyborg than a goddess.

—Donna Haraway

Beyond the Right and the Left ears: I am now and will have perpetually
been far Left of what is humanly (humanistically) possible. I will have hopped
out of the binary (machine) and *hoped* for. . . .

The Eternal Return of Difference: I need to get some things clear
before getting more unclearly clear and, un/namely, in dis/respect to my
notions of *hysteriography* and *schizography*. For some time I have been
espousing the desire to replace a modernist, disciplinary protocol of reading but especially writing with a hysteriography (1987a, 1987b, 1991b).
I have called this my "Hysterical Turn," as opposed to a mere linguistic
or ideological turn (1991a). As suggested intermittently here, I am now
less inclined to employ hysteriography by itself and more inclined to dis/
engage in excesses of schizography. My sense is, as Clément has suggested
(Cixous and Clément 1986), that hysteria or hysteriography can establish, at its best, a standoff. It is a terrific tactic of resistance and disruption, but the results appear to me a mere standoff. Especially, when used
without another tactic. And Baudrillard in *Seduction* ever reminds me
that since after the orgy all is in implosion, hysteria is no longer possible (see 1990). (Yet, contrary to Baudrillard, I would take up with
schizos. For the resistance.)

Dora-the-hysteric was effective against the Freudian research protocol;
the psychoanalytic protocol, however, was just as effective in neutralizing

307

Dora. It is true that Ida Bauer gave Freud a two-week notice (the amount of time given to a maid-servant); but as we well know, Freud, in playing the naming game, gave Bauer the pseudonym "Dora," which was the name of her sister's maid (see Moi 1985). This, then, is at best an hysterical standoff! (Freud himself believed he was becoming-hysterical.)

I will employ, therefore, the tactic of schizography more so than hysteriography. As Deleuze and Guattari tell us, "Freud doesn't like schizophrenics. He doesn't like their resistance to being oedipalized" (1983, 23; cf. 91). Schizos are de-oedipalized Oedipus. (Schizos neither ask riddles nor answer them; they *are* riddles. The old riddle was What goes by four, two, and three? [Riddles are questions about counting.] The new riddle, however, is While men and women have two ears, a schizo has how many ears?) It is to that strangest of strange, or that uncanniness, unhomeliness, that I will have nomadically gone and gone. Un/namely, the labyrinth of the ears. And you, *mes lecteurs?*, how many ears do you count?

> This victor over God and nothingness—he must come some day.—
>
> —Nietzsche

Up to this point, I have neglected Dona Haraway's sovereign subject as cyborg (1990, 1991; cf. 1992). (I would rather be a schizo and a cyborg than nothingness, than either a man or a god or a woman or a goddess!) For me, a *schizo* has much in common with a *cyborg*, for they both embody confusions of boundaries: They are both without fixed gender; both are outside salvation (reactionary) history; both are outside Oedipal (repressive-oppressive) narratives; both are half machine and human being (schizo = "desiring-machine"); both are half so-called lower animal and so-called human animal; both are half "reality" and half simulation (cf. Haraway 1990, 191–97).[1]

Let's look closer, and with Haraway's and Deleuze and Guattari's own words: For Haraway,

> Writing is preeminently the technology of cyborgs, etched surfaces of the late twentieth century. Cyborg politics is the struggle for language and the struggle against perfect communication, against the one code that translates all meaning perfectly, the central dogma of phallogocentricism. That is why cyborg politics insist on noise and advocate pollution, rejoicing in the illegitimate fusions of animal and machine. These are the couplings which make Man and Woman so problematic, subverting the structure of desire, the force imagined to generate language and gender and so subverting the structure and modes of reproduction of Western identity, of nature and culture, of mirror and eye, slave and master, body and mind. (1990, 218)

For Deleuze and Guattari, writing is

> inscribed on the very surface of the Real: a strangely polyvocal kind of
> writing, never a biunivocalized, linearized one; a transcursive system of
> writing, never a discursive one; a writing that constitutes the entire
> domain of the "real inorganization" of the passive syntheses, where we
> would search in vain for something that might be labeled the Signifier—
> writing that ceaselessly composes and decomposes the chains into signs
> that have nothing that impels them to become signifying. The one vo-
> cation of the sign is to produce desire, engineering it in every direction.
> (1983, 39)

With this initially said as an explanation for the importance of the un/
said, I-cum-a-radical-we would now turn to our excursus. But first, the death
of masculinity, mascuLeni(n)sts.

> Dear Victor,
>
> The other day I was trying to match the various rhetorics I
> have read with real structural objects. Spurred by a re-reading
> of McKeon's notion of rhetoric as a productive architectonic
> art, it occurred to me that while other rhetorics can be likened
> to the Great Pyramid (Kennedy), the Eiffel Tower (Murphy),
> the Sears Tower in Chicago (Leff), or the Tower of Pisa (Scott),
> yours derives its strength from the model afforded by the
> Tower of Babel.
>
> —John Poulakos, a letter, January 12, 1989

> I am not a man of ideas. I am a man of style. . . . This involves
> taking sentences . . . and unhinging them.
>
> —Louis-Ferdinand Céline

> In the beginning, there can be only dying, the abyss, the first
> laugh.
>
> —H. Cixous

The masculine subject—predicated on Capital's restricted economy,
on Hegel's determinate negation, on giving with expected returns—must
die (be denegated, self-overcome, undergo self-immolation, become nonhuman). This he must become desubjected according to a general economy
and an abstract negation.[2] That's all there is to it! HE must die. He is dying.

He will have been dead. The female subject, namely, that predicated on the male subject is dead, but if not dead, must also die (see Cixous 1993, 1–54). What must die is the determinate negative, that which brings us into being by way of suppression, repression, political oppression. To kill is to denegate. The subject of *One* must die, so as to become the subject that is not a subject, to become the subject of radical multiplicities (the sublime, sovereign subject). Out of *One* or *Two* must come *some more.* How shall we kill (sacrifice) such a One? By placing him in and through a desiring machine. He will have been multipl(i)ed beyond recognition. (Kafka like.) Paradoxically, s/he will have been, like Nietzsche, all the names of history.

I would (idiomatically speaking) denegate the proper (negating) name and, then, unravel and place, in dispersion, narrative.

Having said as much about the death of man (and woman), I desire now to return to Nietzsche, who has shown the way in his near to last letter to Jacob Burckhardt, January 6, 1889. Nietzsche—the crucified one, Dionysus—writes: "What is disagreeable and offends my modesty is that . . . I am every name in history" (1968a, 485–87).

Having said as much about multiplicities, as Cixous says as much, I, too, desire the return of the repressed. All the improper names, not to make them proper, not to reterritorialize them, but to return them to the conditions of the possibilities of series, intensities, and assemblages.[3]

What follows are some epistolary-post/scriptural, "continuing" thoughts, of my own, on *The* History of Rhetoric. These thoughts are a *"théorie-fictional"* dis/continuation of Nietzsche's letter, and include the How of giving and receiving in a general, libidinalized economy.

> During his seminars Lacan sometimes mused about how high his analysands could count.
>
> —Schneiderman

> In many languages of the world counting has never been developed. In some languages of New Guinea . . . people . . . count: *one thing, two things, many things,* and then must stop; one man translated his counting system into Pidgin English for me as *one fellow, two fellow, plenty fellow.*
>
> —Pike

> . . . all human . . . Desire . . . is . . . the desire for "recognition."
>
> —Kojève

. . . the worst thing is "being ignored."

—Octalog [Vitanza]

. . . I was wrong; for the worst thing is being recognized. It
is necessary to write as if recognized but not recognized. Such
would be the writing of denegation.

—Vitanza, a conversation, with Joshua Kretchmar and
Diane Mowery, April 27, 1994

. . . language is an operational superstructure on an erotic
base.

—N. O. Brown

I. "Some More" Difficult Beginnings

Making myselphs ac*count*able to my collig(gation)s: My last (rebeginnin'?)
excursus is about many things—too many scattered things—that have been,
heretofore, ignored (negated). But which no longer can be ignored. Altogether (but never together), my excursion is about *counting* and about what
has been and still is *ignored* in writing what is cavalierly referred to as *The
History of Rhetoric*. But my excursion, which is—as I've said, an excursion
about many-cum-scattered things—is not an excursion, therefore, that easily
follows (*poria*); in fact, for the most part, throughout the first half, there
will have been, for sure, one difficulty after another in following (*aporia*),
what it is that is being said here, if not mostly elsewhere. And why? Because
it's an excursion subject to *tmesis* (Barthes 1975, 10–11), that is, subject to
cutting up, to pastiche effects, to interruptions, to polygraphy. While my
excursion dis/engages in cutting up, it is nonetheless searching, forever
searching, for a locus cum loci of a third person who will *not* negotiate how
the pastiche effects might be revised for easy passage, but how they might
be recut up and repasted in yet still other (*aporetic*) ways. This task of
reading/writing, therefore, will not have been easy. For me or for other
readers/writers. And again, Why? For the simple reason that this excursion
is in search of "the excluded third man" (Serres 1982a, 67) and "third woman"
(Berg 1982), who have been excluded not only from *The* History of Rhetoric
but also from writing histories/hysteries of rhetorics. Therefore, what this
(my) excursion is searching for is what has been systematically excluded but
when finally included (if it so happens that the excluded third does "show

up") will not make my or any other reader/writer's task any easier. In fact, the appearance of the excluded third will make everyone's task more diffi- cult. What my excursion is searching for, then, is not *the*, or even *a*, reader cum author who could make sense of a history/hystery that would be finally liberatory, but "some more" readers cum authors, if authors at all, who would be perpetually revolutionary, perhaps anarchistic. (Yes, I use that dreaded word "anarchistic," if only to mislead, misdirect! Yes, once again we're waiting for the early Trotsky!) I'm, then, less a writer and more a *cacographist*. I would turn readers into an *epigraphists*. My excursion will be concerned, perhaps then, with the question, How many readers/authors (i.e., interrupt- ers) does it take to re/write, reinscribe, to cut up, the anathema that goes by the so-called proper name of *The* History of Rhetoric? And I do plan (scheme) to cut (it) up!

About Counting: A possible answer to this question of How many?, if an answer is needed, is to be un/founded in my view of counting, which is simply: *one, two,* and *"some more."* And no more. I'm using it as a concep- tual restarting place. In dis/order to restart *some-more talk* (of mine and my readers) about writing histories/hysteries of rhetorics. I've used it pre- viously in " 'Some More' Notes, Towards a 'Third' Sophistic," (1991a), which I have rewritten here in chapter 6, in dis/order to ac*count* for what has been displaced—and therefore ignored and held un/accountable—in writing *The* History of Rhetoric.[4] And what has been displaced (held in the clutches of negation)? Un/namely, a phenomenon of nonrationality (Gorgian, Nietzschean, Heideggerian, Lyotardian *kairos*) that creates the conditions of (what I call) *a Third Sophistic hystery*, which is radically oppositional and appositional to philosophical-rhetori*k*al history/hystery.

In dis/order to achieve this end (or beginning), relationships between *logos* and *kairos* have to be re/accounted for and then replayed: *Which can and must be done by way of what I have called hystery-writing.* Which, if it can be called "writing" (see note 10), has a profound effect on *logos*. (Or vice versa.) What an "excluded third man" and "woman" would say, then, is that hystery-writing can revive (tease out) that which was repressed in and lost to a Platonized or Aristotelianized *logos*. And again, Why was it lost to *logos*? In order to write *The* History. For some of the pre-Socratics (who were hysterics) *logos* was, on occasion, the ambivalence/confusion of both *physis* and *doxa*. With Plato and Aristotle, however, *logos* is reconceived, with *physis* as privileged and *doxa* as supplement. (What I'm talking about here is repression, suppression, political oppression.) A state of productive confu- sion, therefore, was lost, and remains lost. And the conditions of the pos- sibilities of hystery-writing (-speaking, -thinking) were displaced, or held (in their nonrational possibilities) unac*count*able. (See Heidegger 1959, 98–114;1984, 59–78. Also, Kofman 1987.)

The kind (or un/kind) of *logos* that I'm alluding to—it must be grasped—is highly problematic. In this view, then, both the so-called pre-Socratics *logos* and the Platonic or Aristotelian *logos* are both highly problematic. In the former, there is the acceptance of the confusion of language, and nothing is to be done to redeem it (hence, a tragic view of knowledge), whereas in the latter, especially the Platonic latter, there is the rejection of the confusion of language, except as practiced by, say, the Sophists, the *demos*, and barbarians, and everything is to be done to redeem it (hence, an optimistic view of knowledge). I'm thinking perhaps of the distinction that Nietzsche makes between the "cheerful pessimism" (the gay science) of the Greeks in the tragic age of philosophy and the "optimism" (of "theoretical man," Euripides/Socrates) in the post-tragic age of the Greeks (see Nietzsche 1967a). In my view, here and elsewhere, in my tragic but cheerful view, I must insist and incite that *logos* (discourse, language) is helpless as "guide" (*hegemon*) for rational, so-called Enlightenment history.[5] (And I might add that this "guide" is helpless in holding back hystery-writing. What has been, heretofore, repressed, eternally returns.) Such a "guide" is not always rational, or trustworthy. Human beings' possession of language is a dangerous possession (cf. White 1978, 265). Some of the pre-Socratics, especially Heraclitus, were well aware of the unreliability of the narrator of *logos* who would interpellate them and us. As a case in point: An agent or ethical subject—such as Gorgias's "Helen"—listens to the *logos* and, in listening, deliberates over whether to act or not to act, but is confronted with a logical dilemma and, therefore, does not act in order "to act or not to act." (Another case is Nikos Kazantzakis's Christ in *The Last Temptation* [1960], who is called *and* not called by God/*logos*.) As Mario Untersteiner says, however, "in every action . . . it must nevertheless be thought that a decision is carried out, even if not always consciously, because the power of one of the two alternatives may have been such as . . . to cancel out the other, as in the case of Helen, who deserves acquittal once it is shown by *a revival of the ambivalence of logos* [as both *physis* and *doxa*] that in any case this famous woman could not have come to a rational decision." What happens, then, Untersteiner explains, is that "epistemology . . . becomes will, decision, which was [for Helen] realised in a *kairos* endowed with the property of breaking up the cycle of the antitheses and creating something new, irrational" (1954, 161; cf. 177). [Laughter.]

In relation to counting and accountability: Helen has become overwhelmed by *kairos*, which extends the dilemma/binary, in which she finds herself, into a trilemma of *one*, then on to a *two*, and then finally moves past the dilemma into a destabilizing-nonrational *third* of "some more." The trilemma develops, as we might ac*count* for it in still other terms, from "one"- homogeneity through "two"-heterogeneity systematized finally to "some more"-radical heterogeneities, multiplicities. What *kairos* is, as I would characterize it now, is affirmative desire; it is un/founded on a metaphysics of excess, not lack. (See Deleuze and Guattari 1983.) *Kairos*, here then, denegates the negative informing, that is, suppressing, repressing, politically oppressing, *logos*. What *kairos/logos* would have us do, again then, in writing histories/hysteries of rhetorics, is to be dissatisfied with playing the *fort/da* game (the negative deconstructive game), and to search for third ways, which *kairos/logos* are always telling us (it is simply a matter of our learning how to listen, to record, and then to dis/cord).

Let me emphasize, it is the revival of the ambivalence/confusion of (or even deception [*apate*] inherent in) *logos* that is crucial here. As Heidegger says: "For the Greeks appearing belonged to being, or more precisely . . . the essence of being lay *partly* in appearing" (1959, 103). With this view of *logos* in mind, then, we can venture to revive, with the help of Untersteiner (and Kazantzakis [and Heidegger]) again, a hystery-writing and a concomitant subject (or *ethos*) as radically heterogeneous—with these most ethical subjects being engaged in a *dissoi logoi* (see Untersteiner 1954 , ch. 7) that would irrepressibly dis/engage in *dissoi* para*logoi* (see Vitanza 1987a and 1990; cf. Jarratt 1991.) and irrepressibly become poly*ethoi* (scattered schizo- subject positions).

At this point/less, it is necessary to turn toward a further set of *atopoi* (from *topos, e/utopos,* to *atopos*) that might prepare the future authors (epigraphists) of this excursus to interrupt *The* History of Rhetoric. The *atopoi* that "I" (the present so-called author) have in mind are "de/negation," "pastiche," and "hysteria/schizophrenia."

De/Negation: Another way of saying ("some more" of) all this about *searching for* a new conceptual restarting place, or a new way of *recount*ing history in dis/order to revive hystery, is to echo Hegel's but primarily Alexandre Kojève's view of history—namely, "human history is the history of desired Desires" (1969, 6). (I'm doing this kind of recalling, however, so that I can get beyond Hegel and Kojève to my "some more.") Therefore, Kojève says: "desire . . . is . . . a function of the desire for 'recognition' " (7). We want to be valued. But how is this desire for desire (desire for recog- nition, or to become Master) to be satisfied? Both Hegel and Kojève answer: By risking our life in order to negate anOther, that is, to create a Slave. (Master/Slave. Another dilemma, waiting to become a trilemma.) Hence, recognition (value) is based on *denial* (negation, oppression) *of anOther,* which must be *denegated*, as Kojève's Slave, in fact, *denegates* (*affirms*) its Being-for-itself (21–22). But is there not yet an/other way, waiting to express itself as a trilemma? From Master/Slave, Teacher/Disciple, Analyst/Analysand to a third kind of subject position: One, two, cum-a-radical-many subject positions? Sovereign positions? (I cum we think so, and will return to such thinking.)

However, in reflecting on this view of what drives history, Kojève writes: "Human Desire [therefore] tends to satisfy itself by *a negating . . . action*" (1969, 6). Now we're getting closer to my point, but without really ever reaching it. Therefore, my point/less. This *tendency to negate is the defining tendency of modernism* (see Lyotard 1984b, 77–82). What is lost to modernism (what is lost is reality, realism!), however, is regained (spoken and heard) by ill-virtue of negation. (Here, *No* means *Yes*.) Freud wrote of negation/disavowal as central to his hermeneutic (*SE* 1962, 19: 234–39). Marx wrote of disavowal/commodity fetishism as well (1977, 163–77). Kenneth Burke tells us that we ("inventors of the negative") cannot say what a thing is, but we can say what it is not (1966, 9). And thereby, paradoxically, say what it "is." This is a modernist questioning and inventing by way of negation. (Just think of Gorgias's "Nothing [of essence] Exists" [Sprague 1990]. Theodor Adorno's *Negative Dialectics* [1987]. Or Existentialism's existence precedes essence. Or John Dewey's "infinitation of the negative" (1938, 192). Or Jacques Derrida's metaphysics of absence with its posthermeneutic of "negative deconstruction." Or Paul de Man's "negative knowledge" [1983a]. The list goes on. The negative goes on. The beat of tick . . . tock, tick . . . tock goes on and on.) I would desire, however, even beyond Kojève's rereading of Hegel's Slave (1969, 21–22), or these other modernist-negative ways of reading/writing, a particular postmodern repositioning that would be *a double negative*—that is, a negating of the negative (a denegation) in dis/order to get to some nonsynthetic "some more." (You see, I desire *some-more hystery!*, to which I will have eternally returned.)

Pastiche: In this light of a double negation—or this darkness—my excursus is variously about the productiveness of postmodern/Dionysian thought for talking about *The* history, or more so, *hysteries of rhetorics*. My essay dis-counts Fredric Jameson's view of postmodernism and history,[6] and counts on Jean-François Lyotard's and Judith Butler's views among Others'. Specifically, then, along with a practice of double negation, my rebeginning reclaims and practices *pastiche* as a means of getting to what, heretofore, has been ignored. It is not parody that I engage in; for as long as there is a Marxist left (or a Kapitalist right), contrary to what Jameson tells us, there's both a need and opportunity to dis/engage in *pastiche* as a form of drifting.

Therefore: While my socialist "colligs" say, "Let's Party," I say: "Let's just-pastiche!" I reclaim/revive pastiche over parody on the same basis as Butler does: "Whereas parody, Jameson argues, sustains some sympathy with the original of which it is a copy, pastiche disputes the possibility of an 'original' or, in the case of gender, reveals the 'original' as a failed effort to 'copy' a phantasmatic ideal that cannot be copied without failure" (1990a, 157). Traditional *history-writing* works with, or suffers from the nostalgia of, an original that can be recovered; *hystery-writing*, however, paratestifies to the impossibility of an original of the real (which is the intractable, the impossible) and how it must be a-voided (denegated). *History-writing* presumes the ideal or actual whereas *hystery-writing* can assume impossibility, therefore, perpetual possibility. Hence, lack (a negative that is *de*negated) becomes excess. But this lack model must be demystified and (again) demystified. (To this point and its attendant problems, I will ever return.) It is assumed, Dear Reader, that the hystery-writer, or hysteric, simply needs the Master (or analyst) to help recall what was lost. The hysteric subject position, therefore, needs to be further demystified, perpetually demystified. Hence, the schizo.

Hysteria and Schizophrenia: My rebeginnin'—which is about *writing* (if it can be called "writing") *hysteries of rhetorics*—is also about hysteria (hysteriography) and schizophrenia (schizography)—but not the clinical kind—and about their perverse/*pharmakonic* value in creating the (future) conditions for the possibilities of history-cum-hystery: For the possibilities of exploding/fragmenting *logos* that would speak such hysteries, for exploding/fragmenting the *ethos* that would record such discord (and that would be its "subjects" matter, and for exploding/fragmenting *pathos* that would further dis/engage in such hysteries and schizographies. (Hysteria and schizophrenia, when combined, are ways of *de*negation.) The nova. Express. Hence, the three *atopoi*, so as to drift. And so . . .

Let's Drift (in atemporality): My essay (transitionally) is about just-linking (Lyotard 1988a) this point about hysteria/schizophrenia (timelessness) with the next point about temporality. (Cut and paste, recut and repaste. Where is Brion Gysin when we need him?) Postmodernism, like poststructuralism, generally eschews "temporality/historicism." However, after the grand narrative of *The* History has been—as nonrational desire wishes—*de*negated, fragmented, shattered, scattered, then, multiple provisional temporalities will have created the conditions of possibilities. The dividing/fading of grand temporality is, thereby, the de-struction of symbol, which, as Paul de Man says, "postulates the possibility of an identity or identification" and conversely the deconstruction of allegory, which "designates primarily a distance in relation to its own origin, and, renouncing the nostalgia and the desire [as rational and original] to coincide, it establishes its language in the void of this temporal difference" (1983a, 207).[7]

> Writing has nothing to do with signifying. It has to do with surveying, mapping, even realms that are yet to come.
>
> —Deleuze and Guattari

Let's Drift (in the future anterior): But this is only an initial step toward *rethinking time* in relation to history/hystery, *chronos/kairos*. My excursion, however, is less about de Man's view of allegory/irony in disrespect to symbolic temporality and is much more about what Jacques Lacan calls the "future anterior" (the tense that heals). After the fall, we must be healed, *but healed pharmakonically*. Lacan writes: "I identify myself in language, but only by losing myself in it like an object. What is realized in my history is not the past definite of what was, since it is no more, or even the present perfect of what has been in what I am, but the future anterior of what I shall have been for what I am in the process of becoming" (1977, 86; also see 1988, 158–59; cf. de Man 1983, 222; Kellner 1991). (I [personally, but socially] am *on the way to* becoming a [future-anterior] nomad. I would be "some more" of a nomad than any of the Sophists ever were. I would be a third Sophist.) What Lacan (and I) are saying is difficult to understand, especially in relation to a "libidinalized Marxism" or "libidinalized hystery," *if* a connection is not made between the future anterior and the eternal return of the repressed (or suppressed or politically oppressed). What has been negated (repressed) today, therefore, will have returned tomorrow. It is this way, I especially contend, with *The* History of Rhetorik.

Moreover, my excursion is similarly about what Lyotard calls "working without rules in order to formulate the rules of what will have been done," which is the paradox of the future (*post*) anterior (*modo*) (1984b, 81). My project is proleptic as well as paratactic and nomadic.

My attempt, therefore—in just-linking timelessness with new, but Third Sophistic, temporalities—is to bring together both aesthetics and politics, to create the conditions of the possibilities of eventually being able to bring together both post-Marx and post-Freud with Nietzsche, that is, the future after Nietzsche, and then being enabled (finally) to talk about *libidinalized Marxism*. My attempt, thereby, will have been to approach living within what Lyotard calls the *pagus* (the savage place, "a border zone where genres of discourse enter into [perpetual] conflict over the mode of linking [coupling]"

[1988a , 151]). Let us not forget: *Dépays*, T.A.Z.s, the folds, *les Domaines inférieurs*. We must not forget: "It is necessary to link," as Lyotard says, "but not how to link" (66; cf. 29, 80). (History, rationally founded, links according to rules; hystery, nonrationally un/founded, links to reach for "some more.") And so, let us reach for "some more."

When thinking *as a postmodernist*—resisting-critiquing modernism and its negative-lack model—I believe, like Deleuze and Guattari (1983, 25–29, 295, 311), that the unconscious has no "No" there. (Hence, again, one postmodernist activity is to denegate this negative that modernists, such as a Freud, have planted there in their perpetual acts of colonization.) But what did Freud do? He simply negated consciousness; hence, the *un*conscious. But what Freud did was more complicated, for in fact he *did* say that there is only affirmation in the unconscious: Dora's NOs meant YES (see *SE* 1962, 7: 57)! Freud, however, proceeded nonetheless to territorialize the *un*conscious. He specifically said, when he sailed to that country (where Id was there shall Ego be), that he found Oedipus there. Found Castration there. Found Lack there. The Oedipus story is a story of prohibition/of the negative. Of repression. Therefore, in the negative (the *un*conscious), Freud tells us, we have the negative (prohibition, lack). Which leads to negation in infinite regress. (At best, Freud *is* a hysteric! as he himself labels himself. [See *SE* 1962, 1: 262.] He is a hysteric, however, who dislikes schizophrenics because he cannot recode and thereby control them.)

But again, when thinking *as a postmodernist*, there is agreement that the conscious state is only, after all is said and undone, an epiphenomenon. But it is also a construct of hegemony, but no more a construct of hegemony than the unconscious itself can be and, indeed, is. As postmodernists, we must, therefore, not plant or find in the unconscious only another negative. Another hegemonic prohibition, or a law. (And to this statement, I have to include that we must not plant or find in the unconscious a universal lack of freedom and, then, politicize it as being realized only in the Master Narrative of class-struggle. [See Jameson 1981.]) We will find, instead, pure affirmative desire.

Let us sail from that country of our naive (conscious) thoughts; it's no place for sub/versives. (As Deleuze and Guattari say: "The schizophrenic voyage is the only kind there is" [1983, 224].) As postmodernists, let us understand, therefore, that we sail/negate *doubly*: By dismissing the conscious, we *denegate* the *un*conscious and let it flow freely, let it flow as it so desires, into our everyday—heretofore, called "conscious"—life. Such a flow of desire lets history become hystery. Let us float and drift on the free flow of desire, as you, my readers, must freely drift through this (my-cum-our) Rebeginnin'.

My approach, therefore, throughout (*a*) will not be a traditional disciplinary approach, nor will it be an attempt that is informed by a grand narrative metadisciplinary approach. Instead, my approach will be a borrowing of Louis Althusser's "wild/savage practice" (*"une pratique sauvage"*), which in turn is a borrowing from and commentary on Lenin's "wild answer," or response, to the "dividing practice" between Hegelian Idealism *and* Marxist materialism, between ideology *and* science. Althusser further characterizes: "A wild practice [is to be taken] in the sense in which Freud spoke of a wild analysis [see *SE* 1962, 11: 221–27], one which does not provide the theoretical credentials for its operations and which raises screams from the philosophy of 'interpretation' of the world, which might be called the philosophy of *denegation* [this term is translated as "denegation," but it is here simply "negation"[9]]. A wild practice, if you will, but what did not begin by being wild?" (1971, 66; cf. H. White 1978, ch. 7; Worsham 1993).

We advocate nothing, then, but a return to inclusiveness.

—K. Burke

My Wild/Savage Practice, or Response: . . . is in counterresponse to *The* History of Rhetorik, which is depicted (by way of a "dividing practice") as a grand narrative *and* as in conflict with *The* History of Philosophy. (Often the two are blatantly combined—via a Masterful deflection—to form The History of *Philosophical* Rhetorik.) Or my wild/savage practice, or response, is to Plato's "dividing practice" (*diaeresis*) between the party of one *and* the party of many (*Theaetetus* 160d, 180d). This "dividing practice," like all others in our field, only serves to deflect sophistries, magic in language, and all "savage/wild" uses of language (see Lyotard 1988a; Cixous and Clément 1986). This "dividing practice" deflects "counter-memory" (see Foucault 1977). This "dividing practice" negates "some more."

Therefore: Playing with Althusser's language—at first substituting my words for his words and then finally using his exact words—I would wildly/ savagely say: There are hysteries *in* rhetorik rather than The history *of* rhetorik: Hysteries of the displacement ["negation"] of the bodily, therefore indefinite, repetition of a null trace [a residue, excluded other] whose effects are, nonetheless, *real* (cf. 1971, 63). Hysteries of rhetorics speak through the savage *silences* of Dora, through the savage *miraculating body* of Schreber and savage *dreams* of the Wolfman, through the savage *acts* of Lacan's Christine and Léa Papin—all of which are excluded, through "negation" (repression/suppression) from *The* History of Rhetorik (oppression).[10] If included, they function solely as illustrations of deviant, *a*rhetorical behavior, only as examples of the *pathos of ugliness*, which must be forever excluded from the *polis*. For we would desire the beautiful. Not the sublime, or ugly, but The Beautiful. As Catherine Clément says: "Somewhere every culture has an imaginary zone for what it excludes, and it is that zone we must try to remember *today*. This is history that is not over" (Cixous and Clément 1986, 6; Clément's emphasis). And again as Clément says: "The same goes for women as for madmen: in a *manifest* position of exclusion, they keep the system together, *latently*, by virtue of their very exclusion" (1981, 134; Clément's emphasis; cf. N. O. Brown 1966, 160–61). Hence, the power of negation. We know who we are—We men and women of the *polis*—because we are *not* "one of them"! But, I would insist/incite, we are!

My central point/less (!)—further developed, in relation to this wild, savage practice of mine—is that though systematically deflected/silenced, *these hysteries* ("counter-memories") of Dora, the Wolfman, and the Papin sisters, nonetheless, can profitably be read in *The* History of Rhetorik. (As Deleuze and Guattari say: "A schizophrenic out for a walk is a better model than a neurotic lying on the analyst's couch" [1983, 2; cf. N. O. Brown 1966, 159–60]). As Lenin reads Hegel *as* a materialist, and Lacan and Feminists read Freud *as* a hysteric, we must come to read George Kennedy and James Murphy and Michael Leff not just as historicists but also *as* hystericists, as schizos, as deflectors of the most savage, misshapen forms of *letteraturizzazione* (see Kennedy 1988, 231). Yes, we must become, in an Althusserian-Leninist sense, "partisans" with them (Althusser 1971, 64), so as to "denegate" them, too. Our potential libidinalized comrades in reading hysteries of rhetorics.

Moreover (*b*), my approach will have been a "drifting" approach, from Michel Montaigne (the essayist), and from Lyotard, a drifter (see 1984a), but not from René Descartes. I am a drifter: The attempt (the essay) is foreign to finishing, completion, reaching a goal. I am a nomad. I'm, in Other's words, as I've said and said, a "cutup" (see Foucault 1977, 154; Copjec 1989).

My approach will have been, as it always already has been, an "hysterical" approach, from Hélène Cixous, the hysterical body-politic that laughs (see 1981). It will be a "schizo" approach, from Deleuze and Guattari (the schizo that radically, forever switches codes [see 1983, 15]). But I fear, as Nietzsche, "I am not the mouth for these [my readers'] ears" (1968a, 128). For I'm, for them, an *impropria persona*.

But most of all my approach will have been *the future after Nietzsche*: Nietzsche—the greatest advocate of a pessimism of cheerfulness (*amor fati*) and the most suspicious of thinkers (the aphorism that embodies nomadic thought). Which means? I do not wish to be the Apollonian, "theoretical man" (the harbinger of [historicist] optimism), but the Dionysian, "artistic Socrates" (see 1967a, secs. 14–15). I do not wish to be "the good man speaking," nor "the representative of seriousness," nor the traditional-escetic priest, but the satyr-speaking (see 1969, preface, sec. 6; first essay, sec. 3–6; third essay, sec. 11). And where does the Dionysian go to speak, the satyr go to write?

From the Polis *to a* Pagus: The *pagus* (the savage place of "some more" linkage) is a frightening place; it is from a Lacanian perspective the pre-oedipal place of primary narcissism, or from a Deleuzian perspective, "affirmative desire"; it is (especially in the latter) most threatening to the survival of the *polis*. (Father Freud felt the necessity to "negate" it, while brother Norm Brown wishes to revise Freud as a denegator.) *We now must denegate the (de)negation!* Thereby, letting (affirmative) desire flow excessively! We must move from science/history to hystery/fantasy effects. Freud, the scientist-hysteric, struggled with this distinction when writing about Dora. (But what of Marx and the *polis/pagus*? I read *The Eighteenth Brumaire* [1984], and I said: Oh, grandpapa Marx, I must leave you if I am ever to remain [a] revolutionary. And then, I asked for early Trotsky. Which is to say, I asked for "some more." But then, I also recalled what they [Stalin and company] did to Trotsky! But I would risk "some more.")

To use a coined phrase from C. S. Peirce, the *pagus* (the savage place) or "some more" is one of the places of places, of *"esperable uberty"*—that is, the place of the "expected" or "hoped for," the place of "rich growth, fruitfulness, fertility; copiousness, abundance."[11] (The place of "some more" *and* the places of Baubô!!). "Uberty," then—the compossible, like Robert Darton's/my "Possibilisms"[12]—is the "haunting" place of total, but un*count*able freedoms. "Uberty" is (impossible?-)"Liberty." It is, in its/my most hyperbolic radical of presentations, the place of Babel/babble, babylonianisms, the wildest heteroglossias. The f/arting of Baubô! It's a "nightmare" place for, and to be avoided by, Jürgen Habermas and his europocentric thinking! It's a place that Hayden White would call the locus of "the absurdist moment" (1978, 269). It's the place of a *physis* that has not been placed under negation, as Plato and then Aristotle have placed not only *logos* (as I previously discussed) but also *physis* under negation. (That I would also be a follower of a Heraclitean *logos* and a de Sadian *physis* is how I would differ from my sophistic "colligs" who would be followers of local *nomoi*. [Cf. Jarratt 1991.])

In speaking of the absurdist moment, White says that those "critics" who would engage in such a "moment" (as, yes, I would here and elsewhere dis/engage in it) . . . those "critics" would investigate "the dark side of civilized existence—that which, as Nietzsche said, had to be given up or repressed or confined or simply ignored [placed under negation], if civilization was to have been founded in the first place" (1978, 269). This dark, wild, savage side, I would insist and incite, "has simply been avoided by [historians of rhetoric] who define their principal task as the defense of civilization against all of these [savage] things [i.e., people and ideas]" (269). I would return us, then, to this dark side (the *pagus*, where denegated pagans, and *pagani*, gambol and satyr-ize, where *physis* is gat-in-tooth and cleft-in-hoof); and I would return us in dis/order to remind us all of how we have deflected it, and at what costs to Others and to ourselves. Hence, I would search for and perversely celebrate—when writing about hysteries of rhetorics—what White calls "such antisocial phenomena as barbarism, criminality, insanity, childishness" (269). This return I would see as part of the task of a Third Sophistic hysteriography. This return is my acknowledgement of Bataille's notion of necessary expenditure (*dépense*). If not Plato's philosopher-king, then Dora. If not Aristotle's judge, then Schreber. (I make much of all this "return" of the repressed in the second half of this paper.)

Counting "some more" and reaching a de/stabilized third via the Dilemma: Ferdinand de Saussure has given us the *di*lemma of *la langue* and *le parole*, or of *system* (community in language) and *a speaker's expression* (controlled by system-community-*polis*). Noam Chomsky as well has given us "Competence" and "Performance." (And there has been a whole [consecrated] host of analogous binaries/dilemmas, built on these two.)

Lacan (the *pagan* of all *pagani*), on the other hand, has identified the wild (screaming) place of the *third*, which turns the *di*lemma into a *tri*lemma. (I know, I know, Lacan generally speaks by ill-virtue of the negative, so what?) That wild, screaming place is *lalangue* (the place of Babel/babble, the place of the *pagus*, the place where the most "radical [of] multiplicities" dis/engage in, heretofore unknown, linkages). Few venture there. (See 1985, 80–82). But can and does *lalangue*—which I would insist on associating, in this instance, with the *pagus*, and which I associate with *Letteraturizzazione*—really threaten to *destabilize* the *polis*? I think not. I think that the systematizers of language, such as a Habermas, want us to think that Lacanian *lalangue*, or the *pagus*, is a threat, so that they can be "benevolent," but nonetheless a threat to us all in their dream (i.e., nightmare) of "benevolent," philanthropic ORDER.

After Lacan, there is Délire: Besides the Lacanian concept of *lalangue*, there is the Lecerclean concept of *délire*, which is *yet another* third place of "some more" (but a place that *negotiates for us* [we are passive, but protected!, in its midst]). It's a place situated between *lack* and the laughing face of "schizophrenic" *excess*. It perpetually attempts linkages here. *Délire*, as Jean-Jacques Lecercle says,

... is the frontier between two languages, the embodiment of the contradiction between them. Abstract language is systematic; it transcends the
individual speaker, separated from any physical or material origin, it is an
instrument of control, mastered by a regulating subject. Material language,
on the other hand, is unsystematic, a series of noises, private to individual
speakers, not meant to promote communication, and therefore self-
contradictory, "impossible" like all "private languages." (1985, 44)

This latter, I would interpolate here, is Nietzsche's *bodily rhythmic* view of
language (cf. Cixous and Clément 1986, 93; Lyotard 1984b, 22; Barthes 1975,
66–67). Lecercle continues:

[Material language] is an integral part of the speaker's body, an outward
expression of its drives. It imposes itself on the individual, controlling the
"subject": it is not the transparent medium which the instrumentalist describes, nor the means of consensus which the conventionalist conceives,
it is, to misquote a philosophical phrase a (material) process without a
subject.... This is a real contradiction. Neither of the two languages exists on its own, as an independent entity: material language is repressed
and returns to the surface as a disruptive force, and the "dictionary" is an
abstraction which denies the material expression of instincts. *Délire* is the
name for this contradiction.... Between the dictionary and the scream, or
in both at the same time, délire pervades the text, dissolves the subject,
threatens to engulf the reader in its disaster, yet saves him [and her]—and
the text—at the last moment, by preserving an appearance of order, a
semblance of linguistic organization. Even screams can become dictionary
items; and every word, even an entry in a dictionary, can be a scream. (1985,
44–45)

I'm (now) reminded of Cixous's Screams! Cixous's Laughter! And her
call: "Let's get out of here" (1981, 255). Her screams, her laughter, her calls
do get appropriated (in the Kapitalists' or Socialists' dic[k]tionary), don't
they? Which invites her, I assume, and others of us, in our individual, private
(Imaginary) ways, to return (to retrope) affirmatively even (at times) against
délire-as-the-Negotiator! And so . . .

As Burke Says, "Well, where are we now?": Let's get out of here and
end, so that we might begin again, on an/other affirmative note, by recalling Lacan's concept of the future anterior. Which is somewhat like délire-
as-the-Negotiator, but which is constantly *projecting nomadically* in its
search. It's a concept/tense that is postmodern. Clément, in her book on
Lacan, puts it well:

Lacan . . . fooling around with tenses found in grammar [a] resource, the
form whose function it is to span *the gap* between past and future *and link*
the two firmly together: the so-called future anterior, the future that comes
before like the *poetic life* imagined by Baudelaire. Only one tense is truly
dialectical: a logical shuttle between past and future. No one pays attention to it. But it is true that the locution 'I will have been,' oddly twisted
as it is, contains seeds of the future that one finds retroactively
[proleptically]. It is a memory curious about its own future. A memory with
a gift for science fiction, which refuses simply to repeat the old saw, "once
upon a time," over and over again. Everything is different if we say, "It will
have come to pass. . . ." The fairy, whether *good or bad*, wins in advance:
the story is already sketched out, *but it changes as it is being told*. As if
nothing had happened, *the future anterior alters history*: it is the miracu-
lous tense. *The tense of healing*. (1983, 123; my emphasis)

The tense of a (Third, eternally returning, nonrepressed) Sophistic.

II. Desire and the Social

Let's Begin again: What remains, then, in dis/order to get where we will have
desired to venture? What remains is what always remains: The social, with
its affirmative desires. (Most of what the reader will now "read" is fairly easy
to follow, and so if you, dearest of readers, are still with me, you will be
rewarded with "some [easier] more.")

I believe, like Deleuze and Guattari, that *"there is only desire and the
social, and nothing else"* (1983, 29; their emphasis). And "In the unconscious
there are only populations, groups, and machines" (283; for the influence
of Nietzsche, see Thiele 1990, ch. 3).

This view of desire, however, is not colonized by rationality, nor by the
negative. It's desire, as Kristeva, points out, that is deeply influenced by
rereadings of Hegel, Nietzsche, Freud, and Marx. It's desire that is resistant
to linguistic formulation/subjugation and, therefore, is desire that is disruptive of "a logical, normative basis for the speaking subject." It's a view of desire,
situated in a *newer ethic* (post-Aristotelian and -Kantian) that "crops up
wherever a code (mores, social contract) must be shattered in order to give
way to the free play of . . . jouissance" (Kristeva 1980, 23; cf. Rajchman 1991).

And why am I interested in this view of desire with its newer ethics of
resistance and disruption? I am focusing on *desire*-in-language (variously
Foucaultian "counter-memory" and Lacanian *lalangue* and sophistic
Letteraturizzazione and Bataille's excess) so as to ask sacred/profane questions
(and to ask them perpetually) about the *subjugated social* (the social, with its
desire, made rational, ac*count*able: rationality = the negative; *non*rationality

= denegation of the negative). Specifically, however, I am asking (de/ in*terrori*gating) questions about rewriting *The* History of Rhetorik, not in relation to Enlightenment heroes, but in relation to the Other's s/heroes, if they can still be considered s/heroes!, like Freud's Dora or Wolfman, or Deleuze and Guattari's Judge Schreber and Antonin Artaud, or still Others.[13] (We will eternally return to these uncelebrated [as in PM celibate] embodiments of radical heterogeneities; *for* there's no *epideictic* discourse [*no paignion/* for them. We will return in dis/order to recognize the desire of the Other. [Cf. Deleuze and Guattari 1983, 176; Cixous and Clément 1986, 84.]) For it is these Others, these "monsters," these outcasts/outlaws, these creatures of the uncountry (Cixous), the excluded thirds (Serres), with their hysteries, their schizzies (Deleuze and Guattari), that are the mis/representatives antidotes. It is them who are have crawled out of the abyss of *to apeiron* (the [almost] indeterminate). It is them that we must no longer exclude, but must join, link up, couple with. And Irresponsibly. Given Nietzsche's "Homer's Contest," given that I would again refold-reconfigure it, I would not just negate the Gen(i)us, but would exclude us all from the *polis* to the *pagus*. Or I would topologically turn the *polis* inside out. (This, then, is how I would avoid a reactionary relationship with the past [with time's "It was"]. It is not enough of making everything *present* but a matter of twisting the future around the past.)

In the Meantime: Here's something to ruminate on when struggling to let be written, *hysteries of rhetorics*: Lacan muses: "The Life experience of the paranoiac [by which he means, the schizo] and the world view it engenders may be thought of as *a novel form of syntax, which enlists its own peculiar means of comprehension for the purpose of affirming* the community *of mankind.*" Lacan is speaking of "*schizographie*," schizo-speaking/ writing, which has been, heretofore, *e*xcluded from the community. He continues:

> Understanding this syntax can, I think, provide an invaluable introduction to the symbolic values of art and, more particularly, to the problems of style—an introduction, in other words, to art's [and I would insist on adding, rhetorik's] peculiar virtues of conviction and human communica- tion as well as to the paradoxes attendant upon its creation. Those prob- lems will always remain beyond the grasp of any form of anthropology [Humanism or accountability] that has not yet freed itself from the naive realism of the object. (*Premier Écrits sur le paranoïa*, cited in Clément 1983, 57–58; my emphasis)

To be sure, some people will say, here, that I'm conflating poetics *and* rhetoric. They need that *alibi*. And ah, there's the rub. But what am I to do?

other than to insist that poetics *and* rhetoric were artificially separated, for example, by Plato and Aristotle. (And they were separated for reasons of *the game of knowledge, the game of power!*) Political discourse is poetics and vice versa. And it's the *vice* of our political "lives" that has been displaced, and *it's that "vice"* that I'm after! To separate them is to invite *an alibi* (an ex-cuse that provides the conditions) *of not understanding* (as I'm attempting to mis/understand via misprision, or a denegation of the de/negation) *how The History of Rhetorik is The History of Oppression.* (Like Heidegger, it is the end of philosophical rhetorik and the primacy of poetic speech that I am after. [See Grassi 1983, sec. 1; cf. N. O. Brown 1966, 160–61.])

The History of Desire/Power: But what is it specifically that *I mean* [Laughter] when I say that "The History of Rhetorik is The History of Oppression"? I mean—will have meant, let's give "some more" years—two things so as to get on to a sophistic third. (And it will take me a while to get to the second-cum-third, so don't hold your breath! as "we" *rescramble* around.) I mean that the history has been a representation of how rhetors have attempted to define, to obtain, and to keep *power.* And at the expense of Others. Desire/Power is defined across a scarcity (*negative, lack*) model. (In part, this has to do with separating poetic discourse from political rhetoric, to which I will eternally return—to this which has been eternally repressed.) What do I mean by scarcity model? There is this terribly dangerous notion in *The* History of Rhetorik that with the so-called origins of rhetorik, there was simultaneously the origins of *the promise of democracy*—which, in turn, meant the promise of changing the *scarcity/lack model* into a common one of equity, or equal distribution of rhetorical power and determination over one's life within the *polis.* (Except for the slaves and women and barbarians, of course!)[14]

Vincent Farenga, among others (see Althusser 1971, 67), *will have done* much to expel/dispel this dangerous notion. For Farenga, *Rhetoric arose out of the overthrow of tyranny only to return (us all, ironically) back to tyranny.* (That's the way it is when working with the lack/negative model: What is *de*territorialized only ends up being *re*territorialized. Hence, Deleuze and Guattari's and my Trotsky/ite perpetual *de*territorializations.) Farenga's statement about *The* History of Rhetorik is, to be sure, heretical; for the great majority of rhetoricians (both *classical* and *modern*), who tell the story of origins (or reorigins) would, instead, wish us to believe that rhetorik has contributed to and is the primary means of our "emancipation" (i.e., is [potentially] the means of an equal distribution of power through *equal access* to rhetorical deliberation) and that, for example, one *patron saint* of the history of rhetoric is "Korax"—though for these rhetoricians "Isocrates," or "Aristotle," or "Cicero," today, is the most revered.

The "story" (Grand Narrative of Emancipation) goes like this: Sicily was ruled by "Gelon and Hieron," two terrible tyrants, who eventually lost their control over the Syracusans. The two tyrants had forbad the Syracusans to communicate orally, but allowed them to communicate through *sign language*, that is, with their appendages via some sort of *proto-dance-pantomine*, via some sort of *somatic tropings*. (They are forced to be *aphonic!* [Cf. Freud *SE* 1962, 7: 39–41; Cixous and Clément 1986, 19–27].) The Syracusans, in hopes of overthrowing the tyrants, prayed to Zeus, who answered their prayers. But fearing a return to tyranny, the people wanted to have absolute control over all things, upon which they fell into a state of *disorder*. However, a person by the name of "Korax," who had been in "Hieron's" service—yes, Korax was/is a bureaukrat—*used speech to soothe the people back to a state of order* (!). As he spoke, *his speaking taught the people how to control (discipline) themselves*; as he spoke, he referred to the first part of his speech as "introduction," and subsequent parts as "narration," "argument," "digression," and "epilogue." By these means, he contrived to persuade (to teach, or as Althusser would say, "to hail/interpellate" [see "Ideology" in 1971], or as Deleuze and Guattari would say "reterritorialize") the people just as he used to persuade one other man—namely, the tyrant! (Farenga 1979, 1035–36).

What are we to think of such a story, such a history *of* rhetorik that has displaced *in* it a hystery? Are we to ask, at last, critically-cynically, who is this Korax? Would not our charge be that *he is* the culprit, or the goat whom *we-the-people* are *to sacrifice in dis/order to prepare (that is, to cleanse) ourselves for the "cure" or for the final solution/emancipation*? Is he not the tyrant behind the tyrant (the source of the dis-ease)? Is he not the bureaukrat? In a sense the answer is "Yes." It is an answer based, *however*, on *re*codification, or *re*territorialization. And, therefore, I think that such an affirmative answer (which proves actually to be another crypto-[displaced]-*negative* answer [simply recall Lenin/Althusser's concept of "de/negation"]) greatly silences an important point—namely, that "Korax" (or anyone else whom anyone wishes to put forth as "the father" or "the mother" of rhetorik, or as "the liberator" of woman or humankind) is only the narrative function of the will-to-(negative)-authority/power. Still more specifically, I would now say that ("philosophical," i.e., *classical* or *modern*) *rhetorik*, which espouses *a pragmatics of power* and its *control*, is similarly a function of the will-to-extract/abstract *techné* (*the game of knowledge*) from *physis* (see Jardine 1985, 72–73).

From a *postmodern* rhetorical vantage point, however, "Korax" must/ought to, or *will have been*, resisted/disrupted by way of radical (heretical) "little [i.e., radically heterological] narratives" played out by and through the game of (poetics, avant-garde) art. The *strategies* of that game are—in the words of Lyotard, comparable to Lacan's words—a para/activity "without rules in order to formulate the rules of *what will have been done*" (1984b, 81). But then, once the rules are known or account*able*, the future anterior must be reengaged again, and again, and again, perpetually. (And again, this reengagement is de*codification* and/or de*territorialization*, or *perpetual revolution*.) As Lyotard would say, such a game is *the game of the Just* (see Lyotard and Thebaud 1985). What is important to understand here is that Lyotard is *not-just* advocating the use of *local* (stable) *nomoi*. And why? I repeat: Because by placing "little narratives" in the future anterior (by placing them within the pragmatics of the game of avant-garde art) Lyotard is and I am advocating *non-homogenizable radical heterogeneities/multiplicities*. Or advocating, evoking, provoking, a perpetual drifting toward a Third (forever already destabilizing) Sophistic. Therefore, instead of controlling the flow of language/discourse/*logos*/speech/writing/thinking, we will have let it flow, as Heraclitus sees it always flowing.

Where are we now in Dis/respect to Writing The History of RhetoriK?: I hope that our ruminating *will have been taking* us to the idea of *the dispersion of power* in various ac*counts* and in my *ironic* (yet humorous) ac*counts* of writing histories-cum-hysteries of rhetorics. If classical and modern rhetors have attempted to define, to obtain, and to keep power, the new Third Sophistic rhetors (hysterians) *will have found* ways of *re*thinking power altogether, will have found ways of *not-just dispersing* it among all people equally (I hope that the Korax *misrepresentative antidote* disabuses us of this notion, or specifically why this dangerous notion of "equity" has been only a dangerous *displacement* [again, Althusser's "de/negation"] of where power really rests—namely, in the person ["Korax"] who does the "hailing"/"interpellating"). But more so, the new Third Sophistic rhetors *will have found* ways of *placing power in perpetual diaspora*. Power! And what is it *if not* at root *the love of fascism*. Have not Nietzsche and Foucault made this abundantly clear to us all?: As Nietzsche metaleptically says through Foucault, we must resist "not only historical fascism, the fascism of Hitler and Mussolini—which was able to mobilize and use the desire of the masses so effectively—but also the fascism in us all, in our heads and in our everyday behavior, the fascism that causes us to love power, to desire the very thing that dominates and exploits us" (Preface xiii, to Deleuze and Guattari 1983; cf. K. Burke 1968, 118).

Beyond "Local Nomoi" as Little Narratives to Third Schizo Narratives: *BUT* let's complicate this matter even further—with what I'm further attempting—and let's start talking (in Babel/babble) even more on several levels simultaneously. I'm talking about *scrambled-talking*. (Remember: It's necessary to link, but not how to link!) As I've said, I'm *not-just* talking about "linking" local (stable) *nomoi* with conventional poetic play/fantasy; I'm talking—more so, if not perversely—about an aesthetics (poetics) of excesses (see Weiss 1989) that is to be linked to politics. (KB writes: "a system of aesthetics subsumes a system of politics" [1968, 113].) Or I'm talking about . . . well, let's perversely imagine . . . "my writing"[15] epideictic (*paignions*) hysteries for such postmodern, Third Sophistic rhetors as Dora or the Wolfman, or Judge Schreber or Antonin Artaud, or Christine and Léa Papin; or better yet, writing hysteries as they will have written them. Which is what I will (not) have been doing!

Such *paignions* would be, at minimum, a step (and, to be sure, a stumble, a stutter in-"our"-languages) toward the hysteries of (nonpositive affirmative) desires—the hysteries that have been denied legitimacy, locked up, systematically oppressed. *Letteraturizzaziones!* Counter-Memories! These in/famous rhetors (Dora and the Wolfman, etc.) are the *lumpen/proletariat*, *la boheme* (see Marx 1976, 797; 1984[16]; cf. Vitanza 1993a), the *excluded thirds* (see Serres 1982a), that have, heretofore, been rounded up and sent to *the gulags* (they have been silenced [made *a*phonic like the tyrants' subjects], turned into *differends*, victims only furthermore victimized). What is it that I *will have been attempting*? Let us recall that the two tyrants—Gelon and Hieron—had forbad the Syracusans to communicate orally, but allowed them to communicate through sign language, that is, with their appendages via some sort of hysterical or proto-dance-pantomine, via some sort of somatic/ se*mantic* tropings. (But let's don't dance the tarantella!) What is it that *I will have been doing?* I will have been calling on (awkwardly put) what's (far) left over both from and in (heretofore) *the writing of The History of Rhetork*—un/namely, that which still *lies* (buried) *unrestfully silent*. (And buried deep in the "counter-memory" of languages of the body. And all across the surfaces.) I'm speaking of the somatic/mantic-bodily tropings. The hysteries (the body hysterics) that will have been written, but not written, are, as I eternally return to them, epideictic (*paignions*) hysteries of/for such postmodern, Third Sophistic, sub/versive rhetors as Dora or the Wolfman, or Judge Schreber or Antonin Artaud, or Christine and Léa Papin. In the Other's words, the question more generally, therefore, that I (will) have been asking and entertaining answers to (it's important, crucial to guard this question, to keep it always forever open) is WHAT WILL HAVE BEEN ANTI-OEDIPAL (De-Negated) HYSTERIES OF RHETORICS? WHAT WILL HAVE THEY LOOKED, SOUNDED, READ LIKE?

But let's further complicate all this discussion with another de/stabilizing allegory, and henceforth make it even more scrambled. When a historian, or "maker of history," like Ronald Reagan (a neo-Hieron) dumps these in/famous (the Dora*s* and Wolfmen, the "crazies") onto the streets-as-gulag, they still get ignored by us, right *under* our very eyes! We—my "colligs" and I—are Oedipus and in more ways than One! (Thebes is in the midst of *a famine*. We are in the midst of *the negative*. We are in the midst of, and have let *our*selves be defined by, the *LACK*.) I'm talking about the dispossessed, the disinherited, the *barbars* of the *pagus* in the streets of the *polis*! (All projected eighteen to twenty million of them—or us—by the turn of the century. All who have been denied a voice.) I'm also talking about the Anti-Oedipal*s*. I'm talking about those Others who resist the negative by engaging in the affirmative. Desire, no longer as lack, but as nonpositive affirmation. These are the subalterns whose stories can't be told, but in a nonhumanistic way "will have, nonetheless, been told."[17]

But not with, by, or through political discourse. (There is no longer a Korax who can hail/interpellate them.) If not through political discourse, then through pararhetorics. Such a discourse, political discourse, even in the midst of ideology critique—only displaces the *lumpen/proletariat*. Kristeva (1986) says that the story can be told with, by, or through psychoanalytic discourse. But what kind of discourse is this that she's alluding to? Certainly not Rogerian or Buberian discourses, which only invidiously/insidiously maintain the social bond/age, via reterritorialization. (And certainly not [again] Koraxian discourse.) Let me explain further, and in doing so, let's reexamine the notion of *the cure*, the notion of *philanthropy* (or the gift). (Which *gives* only with the contractual understanding of getting *a return*.) This all will require going back in dis/order to go forward.

Chapter One (about cure): Lacan tells us that when *psychoanalysis* came into being (because of female and male hysterics), it was unfortunately "discovered" by a medical doctor, a Dr. Freud, whose predisposition or "trained incapacity," was *to cure* (once and forever) the disorder. (See Heath 1978; cf. Schneiderman, who has Lacan against the cure, 1983, 47, 50, 57.) Freud's hermeneutic predisposition, however, prevented him from being suspicious enough, about his philanthropic motives. First, he for the most part withdrew his initial view that both males and females suffered from hysteric symptoms; he backed down because his "colligs" kept (paranoically) insisting that it was impossible for a male to suffer from hysteria (after all, a male has no womb, which can become nomadic!, so let's call it "shell shock" [see Showalter 1987, who speaks of eighty thousand male hysterics in the first war.]). Second, Freud insisted on (perhaps his trained incapacity again) employing only myopic/monological hermeneutical principles, such as the *oedipal complex* and *penis envy* (all based on lack). These first two only perpetuate the master/slave relationship between males/females. And third, Freud, as Deleuze and Guattari tell us, "doesn't [didn't] like schizophrenics. He doesn't like [them because of] their resistance to being oedipalized, and tends to treat them more or less as animals" (1983, 23). Freud, again, does not like schizos because of their resistance to the negative. As exiles, as *barbars*, outcasts from the *polis*, schizos like Artaud resist, disrupt, expel, vomit up "Papa, Mama" and "Korax"[18]—that is, the *Symbolic*—which is, in Deleuze and Guattari's view, a vomiting-as-resistance to being Oedipalized. I insist, as Deleuze and Guattari do, that this "vomiting" can be seen as not an illness, but a paracure! A *pharmakon*. (Therefore, I vomit up *The* History of Rhetoric. Vomit. Vomit. Vomit.)

Marx's cure—by which I mean a cure based on orthodox Marxists' readings of Marx's texts—is that the *lumpen/proletariat* ("pauperism," the lowest common denominator, which for me also includes the Jean Genets and Antonin Artauds of the world and includes the aesthetic of language, *Letteraturizzaziones*) will simply disappear, will wither away, with the dawning of (e)utopic socialism. In other words, philanthropy, or the cure, is built into dialectical/historical materialism. For these orthodox Marxists, the concept of the *lumpen/proletariat* is a vulgar-restricted economic category that defines *desire* exclusively in terms of lack, or the (modernist) negative. My "casuistic stretching" of this *negative concept of economics* is an attempt—on the extreme Left hand of the *a*phonic body—to establish the conditions of the possibilities of seeing what the *lumpen/proletariat* might/ could mean for us . . . *if* the *lumpen/proletariat* were *libidinalized*, or viewed in a radically heterodox economic category that defines *desire*, not in terms of "the negative," but in terms of a (postmodernist, denegated) "affirmative." (I'm *not* speaking here of a libidinal economy based on kapitalism, as unfortunately Lyotard [1993], much to his own chagrin, previously has.) If the *lumpen/proletariat* is seen as also including the Jean Genets and Antonin Artauds of the world, we will have begun to understand them not as something that is to be cured, but *as* a cure (a *pharmakon*) themselves. The *lumpen/proletariat*, as I have re/presented them here, will never disappear any more than the irrational/nonrational Doras will wither away. The *lumpen dejecta* is/are the excluded middle. Muddle. The desire in *logos* and human being (the strange creature). I have spoken of—as Cixous has spoken of—attending to the Other. The ugly. Repeatedly. In other terms, Denis Hollier puts it well in terms of Bataille's notion of "heterology." He writes: "Heterology is not a technique for provoking scandal" (1988, xix). I have not been attempting to be scandalous by saying that we must go with the excluded, *la bohème*, go to *les domaines inférieurs*, go to *dépays*. Go with the Wolfman, or Schreber, or the Papin sisters. In fact, we do not go there or with them, it/they come to us repeatedly as the return of the repressed. Even in their absence, they are (a) present. Again, Hollier says:

> Heterology is not a product of the aestheticization of the repugnant. Disgust here is not a modality of aesthetic experience but a fundamental existential dimension. Reactions of repulsion do not have to be induced: They are what is given to start with. But rather than discharging them outside (rather than getting rid of them), one should think them. *Heterology would be the theory of that which theory expels.* In its battle with the angel of repugnance, in the depths of darkness thought persistently faces the things that repel it. What unites men? The things that repel them. *Society stands upon the things it cannot stand.* (xix)

Hence, the modernists' necessity to cart off these people to the Gulags (both the pickpockets and the dissidents, both the paragrammaticism and contradictions, the human and linguistic roaches—all schizos), so that the rabid, vulgar, orthodox, "romantic socialists" (historians of rhetorik) can declare socialism a success. (At bottom, there's no difference between a logical positivist, in relation to language, and an [orthodox or, at times, heterodox] Marxist!) Again, if I am to remain (a) revolutionary, I must reject but reclaim Marxism. (Hence, a Libidinalized Marxism.)[19]

But—to be sure, let's turn the whirl even more around here—it's *not-just* "romanticized socialism" that's at fault. As I said earlier it's, *more so*, "romanticized kapitalism." When kapitalism is not teaching us to be political quietists, it's teaching us to be altogether blind to the *lumpen/proletariat* as "we" step over and over—and even occasionally "trip" over—them in the *pagus* in the midst of our *polis*. What is not understood by (orthodox) Marxists but is understood by Fifth Avenuists (and that's what makes the latter especially dangerous, because they are able "to capitalize" off of *and* "*re*territorialize" the *lumpen/proletariat* in more ways than One) is that *some* (a small, perverse percentage of) human beings engage in such "pauperism" and "dissidence" (schizoidness) and paragrammaticisms for reasons *other than* vulgar economics. (It is this few-cum-excess that I speak of! Not all.) The kapitalists are much closer to an understanding of the libido than the Marxists. That is why the kapitalists are so damn frightening. But then again, the Marxists' blindness to the libido is equally, if not more so, frightening.

What can *we learn* from the *lumpen/proletariat*? The *Letteraturizzaziones*? Specifically: What can we learn from how people respond to them? What can we learn from them concerning the cure and philanthropy? (How, in other words, can they be a para-cure?)

This first specific question—what can we learn from how people re-spond?—is of immense importance. Let us recapitulate: Recall my earlier reference to Kristeva's saying that there is a "Platonistic acknowledgment on the eve of Stalinism and fascism: A (any) society may be stabilized only if it excludes poetic language." She adds: "The question is unavoidable: if we are not on the side of those whom society *wastes* in order to reproduce itself, where are we?" And yes, let us remember what KB says: We must make "peace" with our "faeces" (1969a, 23). (If it is not obvious by now, when I talk about the *lumpen/proletariat* and *Letteraturizzaziones*, I'm talking about both language *and* people.) And Clément who says: "Somewhere every culture has an imaginary zone for what it excludes, and it is that zone we must try to remember *today*. This is history that is not over" (Cixous and Clément 1986, 6). (The imaginary zone can be a gulag or a ghetto or a septic tank.) And again she says: "The same goes for women as for madmen: in a mani-fest position of exclusion, they keep the system together, *latently*, by virtue of their very exclusion" (1981, 134).

I recall now, having read Burke's book review of Hitler's *Mein Kampf*, in which Burke points out how Hitler refers to the Habsburg Empire as a state of nationalities and the parliament, where the representatives met, as Babel/Babylon. (It is necessary that you, dear reader, *drift* with me here.) Burke writes: "The many conflicting voices of the spokesmen of the many political blocs arose from the fact that various separationist movements of a nationalistic sort had arisen within a Catholic imperial structure formed prior to the nationalistic emphasis and slowly breaking apart under its development." Burke continues and now more to my point: "So, you had this Babel of voices; and, by the method of associative mergers, using ideas as imagery, it became tied up, in the Hitler rhetoric, with 'Babylon,' Vienna as the city of poverty, prostitution, immorality, coalitions, half-measures, incest, democracy (i.e., majority rule leading to 'lack of personal respon-sibility'), death, internationalism, seduction, and anything else of thumbs down sort" (1957, 172). It is obvious where Hitler's vision is going, which is to keep the system together, blatantly, by virtue of exclusion. And as we well know by now, though KB was predicting then what was to come, Hitler did exclude, by silencing all the mixed voices as manifested in both lan-guage (*logos*) and people. Burke writes: "The wrangle of the parliamen-tary is to be stilled by the giving of *one voice* to the whole people, this to be the 'inner voice' of Hitler, made uniform throughout the German boundaries, as leader and people were completely identified with each other" (177; my emphasis).

And so do I need to spell out here what we have learned (but not learned) from how Hitler and his dupes responded to Babel/babble and Babylon? How, for example, the advocates of *The* genre of history (as this genre itself positions subjects and objects) excludes hystery? *The* history is not democratic; only the inclusion of the hystery of Babel/babble can be radically democratic! It is time to reconsider the whole concept of historical genre so that we might move beyond genre altogether.

The next specific question—What can we learn from the *lumpenproletariat* and *Letteraturizzaziones* concerning the cure and philanthropy?—is taken up again by Burke. In his *Counter-Statement* (1968), he makes a distinction between the "practical" and "aesthetic." (Here, I return to conflating the political and poetic.) For Burke, the *practical* favors "efficiency, prosperity, material acquisitions, increased consumption, 'new needs,' expansion, higher standards of living, progressive instead of regressive evolution, in short, ubiquitous optimism." By contrast, the *aesthetic* (the Bohemian) favors "inefficiency, indolence, dissipation, vacillation, mockery, distrust, 'hypochondria,' non-conformity, bad sportsmanship, in short, negativism" (110–11). He continues: "The 'Bohemian,' the 'aesthetic' . . . relegates enterprise to such inquiries and imaginings as serve to 'corrode' the practical—it is concerned with such intellectual vagabondage, such aspects of 'irresponsibility,' as constitute a grave interference with the cultural code behind our contemporary economic ambitiousness" (121). Yes, my dear comrades in *The* history of rhetorik, *I would, indeed, be irresponsible!* (Cf. Enos 1991.)

This all gets worse for better. KB writes (perversely): "A society is sound only if it can prosper on its vices" (1968, 114). "The aesthetic," or "the anti-practical," he continues, "would be driven back to democracy (a system of government based upon the fear that central authority becomes bad authority—democracy, organized distrust, 'protest made easy,' a babble of discordant voices, a colossal getting in one's own way—democracy, now endangered by the apostles of hope who would attack it for its 'inefficiency,' whereas inefficiency is the one thing it has in its favor" (114). But (Oh) let us continue: "The Fascists, the hopeful, the propounders of business culture, believe that the future lies in perfecting the means of control. The democrat, the negativist, the man who thinks of powers as something to be 'fought,' has no hope in perfection—as the 'opposition,' his nearest approach to a doctrine is the doctrine of interference" (115).

In Sum, KB writes: "The aesthetic would seek to discourage the most stimulating values of the practical, would seek—by wit, by fancy, by anathema, by versatility—to throw into confusion the code which underlies commercial enterprise, industrial competition, the 'heroism' of economic warfare; would seek to endanger the basic props of industry" (115).

KB, here a postmodernist before his time, espouses resistance to and disruption of the political status quo, and any forthcoming macropolitical activities, left or right.

Let us drop anchor now and listen to what we might hear from critics: I can hear some self-righteous leftist saying, "Victor, see, you are a neo-conservative. You hide behind all this talk about aesthetics, organized distrust, inefficiency, and do nothing at all for the street people, whom you mislabel as the *lumpen/proletariat.*" Such a response, I *can* mis/understand, given what is subjectively invested in being a leftist. Which is? Their way—which is their trained incapacity—is *the* way (see Jameson 1981).

My point, as previously announced is that we cannot socially engineer either language or people, because there will always be paraelements that will escape being engineered, paraelements that we more likely than not (given that we are, as KB says, "rotten with perfection") have to exclude (in the name of "thugs") in some gods-forsaken way. (We will have to take political prisoners; every *system* must have them.) Therefore, I have suggested that we (the so-called fortunate) not try to help-by-excluding on *our own terms* (because we always expect "a return" on our investment) but that we, instead, listen to and learn from what both (street) language and (street) people, what *Letteraturizzaziones* and the *lumpen/proletariat,* say they want/desire. (To this point, I will return.) Marx, on the other hand, said that we must listen to, learn from, the *proletariat.* There, then, lies our differences!

The *proletariat,* to be sure, are not in *The* History of Rhetoric, except by displacement; hence, they demand their rational inclusion. They point out the logical inconsistency, the inherent contradiction. (The birth of rhetoric and the birth of democracy should not be at odds!) But what of the *lumpenproletariat?* The "Some More"? They, the nonrational, push for even greater, more radical democracies. (Herein is where I differ most emphatically from Susan Jarratt's call for what I see as her liberal democracy, not a radical one at all [see Jarratt 1991].) How much—dear reader, you might ask—can *The* History of Rhetoric bear? My answer: As much as it takes to distend and finally explode *The* (speculative) genre of history. It is not inclusion into *The* history that I desire but radical, countless numbers ("some more").

Let Us Listen to what Lyotard Says: Marx "thinks he hears the demand of the proletariat, which is . . . *an ideal of reason,* namely an emancipated working humanity. The proletariat demands communism, the free linking of phrases, the destruction of genres. . . . This finality is signaled . . . by the enthusiasm which workers' struggles can arouse" (1988a, 171–72; my emphasis). Lyotard continues: "Marx understands the feeling of enthusiasm as a request emanating from an (ideal, emancipated) self. The referent of the Idea of communism is transcribed as a subject (addressor) who proscribes communism. The common being wants itself. This can be formulated [however] only within the speculative genre" (172). And, ah, there is the problem. "To let the proletariat 'speak' is to endow it with a historical-political reality. Marx built the International Association of Working Men. He interprets the sign that is the enthusiasm aroused by the Commune as if it signaled the political project of the *real* class and as if it outlined the organization of a *real* party" (172; my emphasis). The proletariat demands the end of genres, but its enthusiasm, if it is to become channeled into a political reality, must be *real*ized through "the speculative genre," or *the economic genre*. What has happened is what KB calls the "bureaucratization of the imaginative" (1984b, 225–29). What has happened is what Lyotard calls "central monopoly"—"the party assumes a monopoly over the procedures for establishing historical-political reality" (172). Which, in turn, gives us party-line history and politics. I would have what KB has called "a national 'Art Party' " (1968, xiii). I would be "the representative of 'the aesthetic' . . . who blurted out things in a somewhat violent fashion," while I would have my leftist/kapitalist "colligs" be the representative of " 'the practical' . . . who looked upon [their] adversary as a scandal" and while I would have you, my reader, be "one other figure . . . who suffered the wrangling of the two, . . feeling that both" of us had our "particular kinds of justification" (xiii).

What I hear, echoing back to Burke, is that we have much to learn—aesthetically and politically—in respect to writing histories-cum-hysteries of rhetorics. We have to learn what Walter Benjamin learned in the streets of Paris from the *flaneur*, the conspirator, the Boheme, the ragcollector, but also learn what he did not. We must learn that there is more than one economic system at work here. (There are, in fact, some more!) There are more ways than one to call for, or to go on, a strike! There are more ways than one to express desire. (Lacanian *lalangue*, which is embodied in our *polis*, is a perpetual strike, a perpetual expression of desire-as-cure.) Let us, therefore, learn how *to count* the irrational/nonrational number of ways so that we might a*void* the speculative genre of history. Let us set aside, for a while, the negative approach (of a genre of genres) and take up the affirmative approaches of non-ac*count*ability as "the free linking of phrases, the destruction of genres." Which means what? It means, in dis/order to understand, "we" must libidinalize (over-rationalized) Marxist texts! We must *de*territorialize them! After all is said and undone, *I am a libidinalized Marxist*, but by virtue (i.e., a radical ethical *areté*) of both Marx and Freud being "subsumed" within a Nietzschean irrational/nonrational few-cum-"some more." I am a Deleuzian/ Guattarian, radically heterodox Marxist, which is a negation of the nega- tive (orthodox) Marxists, so as to reach new perpetual states of affirma- tion. Which means what, in addition? It means we have more (a great deal "some more") to learn from "minoritarians" (embodied, *a*phonically, in the *lumpen/proletariat* of *lalangue* and in the *pagus*) than we have to give them. We must, then, with the help of the *lumpen/proletariat*, rethink benev(i)olence.

    Chapter Two (another Possible Cure): Deleuze and Guattari, in their *Anti-Oedipus* (1983), argue against *the orthodox cure*.[20] They write: "What are the most favorable conditions for the cure, it is asked? A *flow* that lets itself be plugged by Oedipus [or any Grand Narrative, Freudian or orthodox Marxist]; *partial objects* that let themselves be subsumed under the category of a complete object, even if absent—the phallus of castra- tion [the negative]; . . . For what is the meaning of 'so *that* was what *this* meant'? The crushing of the 'so' onto Oedipus and castration. The sigh of relief: you see, the colonel, the instructor, the teacher, the boss, all of this meant that: Oedipus and castration, 'all history in a new version' " (67). You see, my "colligs," in this scheme, to be sick *is* to LACK Oedi- pus, or an Oedipal (Social) metanarrative! (91). (Jameson, in the *Politi- cal Unconscious* [1981], says: for society to be sick is to LACK a Grand [Socialist/Marxist] Narrative of Emancipation!) As Deleuze and Guattari say: "Psychoanalysis is like the Russian Revolution; we don't know when it started going bad" [1983, 55].) They also say: "Oedipus [and who/what else? the proletariat?] is a means of *integration* into the group" (103; my emphasis). And then they also say: "Oedipus is something like euthana- sia within ethnocide" (169).
    Start making some simple substitutions here, folks, and you will begin more clearly to understand what I'm allegorically, ironically alluding to. Need "some more" help? The narrator of *The Unbearable Lightness of Being* tells us—in between discussing Oedipus and an allegory that Tomas wrote based on the myth—that: "Anyone who thinks that the Communist regimes of Central Europe are exclusively the work of criminals is overlooking a basic truth: the criminal regimes were made not by criminals but by enthusiasts [socialist romantics] convinced they had discovered the only road to paradise. [The elimination of all dissidence/dissonance. In the body- hysteric politic! The removal of the *pagus* from the *polis*.] They defended that road so valiantly that they were forced to execute many people. Later

it became clear that there was no paradise [great, good place], that the enthusiasts were therefore murderers" (Kundera 1987, 176). As Kundera's character Tomas says, they were like Oedipus and therefore should/ought to put their eyes out and leave Thebes. See all, read all, of this *théorie-fiction* so as in dis/order to see, again. Which will have put "us" in a position to have been able to ask forever again: WHAT WILL HAVE BEEN ANTI-OEDIPALized (de-negated) HYSTERIES OF RHETORICS? WHAT WILL HAVE THEY LOOKED, SOUNDED, READ LIKE? Or to ask affirmatively, WHAT, then, WILL HAVE LIBIDINALIZED-HYSTERIES OF RHETORICS LOOKED, SOUNDED, READ LIKE?

Chapter Three; or "Some More, Some More": What Deleuze and Guattari say about a *cure* is that *schizos are combatants against the orthodox cure* (remember Freud did not like schizophrenics). How do they resist? Deleuze and Guattari say:

> The schizos [have their] own system of co-ordinates for situating [themselves] at [their] disposal, because first of all, [they have at their] disposal [their] very own recording code, which does not coincide with the social [i.e., linguistic] code, or coincides with it only in order *to parody* [I would say "pastiche"] it. The *code of delirium or of desire* proves to have an extraordinary *fluidity*. It might be said that . . . schizophrenic[s] pass . . . from one code to the other, that [they] deliberately *scramble . . . all the codes*, by quickly shifting from one to another, according to the questions asked [them], never giving the same explanation from one day to the next, never invoking the same genealogy. . . . When [they are] more or less forced into it and [are] not in a touchy mood, [they] may even accept the banal Oedipal code, so long as [they] can stuff it full of all the disjunctions that this code was designed to eliminate. (1983, 15)

I see this statement as a postmodern *manifesto* for writing (future anterior) hysteries of rhetorics. What must be stuffed full of *disjunctions*—as "I will have been attempting"—is that code, or set of codes, that go by the banal proper name of *The* Tradition of *The* History of Rhetoric (see Bizzell and Herzberg 1990). The *schizophrenic hysteriographer* will have deliberately sought out the very limit of *The* Tradition: S/he will have been its inherent tendency brought to fulfillment, its surplus product, its *lumpen/proletariat* (the somatic tropings of the Doras and Wolfmen), and its paradoxical "exterminating angel." S/he will have scrambled all the codes and will have had been the transmitter of the decoded flows of nonpositive-affirmative *desire*. S/he will have been the eternal return of the repressed "counter-memory."

III. "De Beginnibus"!

. . . once more and innumerable times more. . . .

—Nietzsche

I began this long hysterical/allegorical-personal statement with the affirmative statement, "I believe, like Deleuze and Guattari, that *there is only desire and the social, and nothing else.*' " Why is it, again then, that I choose to trek with schizos? What do they, after all is said and undone, have to do with the social? What I'm against, as I have stated, is a *subjugated group*, and what I'm advocating at this moment, like Deleuze and Guattari, is a libidinalized *subject-group*.

A *subjugated group* is, in its structure (and everything else), *paranoiac*. It's structured in two ways: Either by *homogeneity* or by *heterogeneity homogenized* or by *both*. It's a group that gets its order from some other group or from "Korax" Inc. Socialist political formations tend to be *homogenized*; capitalist political formations, *heterogeneity rehomogenized* according to the needs of supply and demand (the negative, the lack). Paranoiac political structure is also called *molar*. Deleuze and Guattari write:

> It might be said that of the two directions in *physics*—the *molar* direction that goes toward the large numbers and the mass phenomena, and the *molecular* direction that on the contrary penetrates into singularities, their interactions and connections at a distance or between different orders— the *paranoiac* has chosen the first; [s]he practices *macro*physics. And it could be said that by contrast *the schizo* goes in the other direction, that of *micro*physics, of *molecules* [*micro*politics] insofar as they no longer obey the statistical laws [of a master group or narrative]: waves and corpuscles, flows and partial objects that are no longer dependent upon the large numbers; infinitesimal lines of escape, instead of the perspectives of the large aggregates. (1983, 279–80)

Then Deleuze and Guattari say: "It *would be a mistake* to contrast these two dimensions in terms of the *collective* and the *individual*" (280).

So where are we? The *molar* (paranoiac) is the *subjugated group*. The *molecular* (schizo) is the *subject group*, which is *radical multiplicities* or *heterogeneities*. Which disrupts all attempts by the *molar* socialists and capitalist rhetors to make desire conform to their flows, or "Korax's" schema, or disposition, for discoursing. Schizos (as desiring-machines, with heterogeneous parts) in a Marxist economy take the

modes of production, distribution, exchange, and consumption and produce an undifferentiated body (politic?) without organs. Schizos radically-
heterogeneously disrupt desiring (logical-binary) machines (1983, 5),
which are designed, as "Korax" would have them, to control the flow
(disposition) of desire. Schizos produce at a *molecular* level. What schizos
understand, contrary to "Korax," is that any attempt to return to the past
was/is only a return to domination; and any effort to appropriate state
control (ISA) is an effort to perpetuate despotism (to be, as Nietzsche says,
resentful and then reactionary); and any "political program" for *revision*
is a potential blueprint for *molar, paranoiac* investment of social desire
as lack. What is desired, then, is a *sub/version*, through a schizophrenic
process of affirmation (denegation), by rapidly switching codes, so as to
shatter the synecdochic (container and thing contained) system. Where
are we now? Or, Where *will we have been? "De Beginnibus"*![21]

Theirs/"Ours" should, therefore, be attempts at forming "transverse
relations among deterritorialized flows" so as to be able to include, in
"our" writing hysteries of rhetorics, those who, heretofore, have been
excluded (silenced, made into *differends*) such as Dora and the Wolfman
and Genet and Artaud who have *no papas, no mamas*, who have not been
oedipalized. I got no papa, no mama, no "Korax," no Plato, no Aristotle,
no Isocrates, no Cicero, no Quintilian, no. . . . Herein, No becomes Yes
and Yes, No. Becomes Nes/Yo!

"Some More" Radical Switching of Codes: A Loss of the Personal: We
have counted again from 1, 2, and "some more," and it's the schizo-social
that I am in flight with. That I am NoMadic with. I would lose/confuse the
personal in dis/order to be anOther "perfect hysteric." *Q*: What is hysteria?
A: It's a confusion concerning gender (and genre). It's not androgyny, which
is a synthesis. It's, instead, a productive confusion of such political categories as "male" and "female." It's gender as "cultural performance" (see J.
Butler 1990a,1990b). Therefore, like Nietzsche, in his last, *pastiched* letter
to Jacob Burckhardt (the individualist, Renaissance historian!), I to you all
say: "what is disagreeable and offends my modesty is that . . . *I* am every name
in history" (Nietzsche 1968, 686; also, see Deleuze and Guattari 1983, 21–
22; Vitanza 1994b).

AnOther Beginning: *"Measure* is alien to us [Be gone Prot*agora*s!]; let
us own it [our alienation]; our thrill is the thrill of the infinite, the unmeasured. Like a rider on a steed [let's now affirmatively forget Plato's *Phaedrus*]
that flies forward, we drop the reins before the infinite, we [post]modern
[wo/]men, like semi-barbarians—and reach *our* bliss only where we are
most—*in danger*" (which is *Beyond Good and Evil*, 1966, 153).

AnOther Beginning: "In the beginning, there can be only dying, the abyss, the first laugh. After that, you don't know. It's life that decides. Its terrible power of invention, which surpasses us. Our life anticipates us. Always ahead of you by a height, a desire, the good abyss, the one that suggests to you: 'Leap and pass into infinity.' Write! what? Take to the wind, take to writing, form one body with the letters. Live! Risk: those who risk nothing gain nothing, risk and you no longer risk anything. In the beginning, there is an end. Don't be afraid: it's your death that is dying. Then: all the beginnings" (Cixous 1991, 41)

And in the Beginning: "Even laughter may yet have a future. I mean, when the proposition 'the species is everything, one is always none' has become part of humanity, and this ultimate liberation and irresponsibility has become accessible to all at all times. Perhaps laughter will then have formed an alliance with wisdom, perhaps only 'gay science' will then be *left*" (1974, 74; my emphasis).

Or, AnOther Comic Beginning:

Dexter: Oh yes, yes, yes!
Sebastian: Funnier than that?
Dexter: Oh, absolutely. Yes.
Dexter: Now on the St. Louis team we have Who's on first,
What's on second, I Don't [NO] is on third . . .

On Third? Now, Dear Reader, ready or not, here we go to the whirl of the third millennium.

Notes

Introduction

1. Or *"différance,"* "writing," "power."

2. Cf. Deleuze and Guattari 1983, 26–27.

3. Our arguments are not only with the living but, perhaps more so, with the dead. (Hysterics suffer mainly from reminiscences. [Freud 1962, *SE* 2: 7].) Which poses a problem: How does someone argue with an other who was so much alive but who is now (the) dead? Paul Feyerabend, I think, puts it best:

> This essay is the first part of a book on rationalism that was to be written by Imre Lakatos and myself. I was to attack the rationalist position, Imre was to restate and to defend it, making mincemeat of me in the process. Taken together, the two parts were supposed to give an account of our long debate concerning these matters that had started in 1964, had continued, in letters, lectures, telephone calls, papers, almost to the last day of Imre's life and had become a natural part of my daily routine. The origin explains the style of the essay: it is a long and rather personal *letter* to Imre and every wicked phrase it contains was written in anticipation of an even more wicked reply from the recipient. It is also clear that as it stands the book is sadly incomplete. It lacks the most important part: the reply of the person to whom it is addressed. I still publish it as a testimony to the strong, and exhilarating influence Imre Lakatos has had on all of us. (1978, 7; Feyerabend's emphasis)

Similarly, I think of JB (Jim Berlin). Most of what I have written and published prior to this book, but including especially this book as well (and the sequel), are open letters to him and his thinking. This unorthodox introduction is, yes, a letter to Jim. Which can now never be delivered. Except to a third (audience).

There are yet other precedents for what I am VVariously doing here. See Schneiderman, *Jacques Lacan: The Death of an Intellectual Hero* (1983); and Clément, *The Lives and Legends of Jacques Lacan* (1983). Both writers remember (reminisce) by way of hysterical discourse. To be sure, the problem of remembering is the problem of forgetting, a *topos* that I intermittently deal with through out.

343

4. Literally translated means "What do you want?" It is a question that is asked by the unconscious. For a full discussion of this term and its Lacanian possibilities, see Zizek 1989, ch. 3.

Let us, however, not forget the question's Freudian possibilities! The question is hilarious, for it is, after all, historically a gendered question: Namely, What is it that women want? Does JB think that Vitanza is an hysteric? Or a "critical cross dresser" (Showalter 1987) or any variety thereof? How are we—the various WEs to take such a question that is a reversal? Further complications: Is the answer ("I want *desire*. . .") given by Vitanza to the question *a gendered desire*? Male desire? A Male fantasy of a female desire? Or is it, as Vitanza eventually says, via Deleuze and Guattari's social ontology, a desire unfixed, ungendered, denegated, a desire beyond/ prior to conventionally coded, inscribed, gendered desire? Is it possible that there is such a desire beyond feminine desire? Biology and cultural-social atrocities (against women) will in most cases determine the answers. I continue this questioning later here in relation to yet another question, which is How to give (gifts)?

5. The discussion took place at Takis Poulakos's and Barbara Biesecker's.

6. I am referring to "Critical Sub/Versions" (1987a).

7. Here and throughout this book, I capitalize *The* History of Rhetoric so as to signify the grand narrative, or what goes for the narrative. In opposition, I will later refer to histories, or even hysteries and schizzies, of rhetorics. Whereas the grand narrative is a unified One, the latter are minor histories. The first, I abhor; the latter (it is necessary to say?), I favor.

8. There is, I think, a remarkable parallel in views and practices of writing between Acker and Hélène Cixous, which I mention in the excursus entitled "Feminist Sophistic?"

9. A *rye* is a wandering male gypsy. As I progress, of course, "rye" becomes a rye comment in terms of gender.

10. The allusion to the corporate we is to Kenneth Burke (see 1969a).

11. Cf. Mark Taylor, *Nots* (1993).

12. This very important phrase is from Cixous, whom I take up in the excursus "Feminist Sophistic?" See Cixous and Clément 1986, 89.

13. Haraway speaks of One, two, and other: "The self is the One who is not dominated, who knows that by the service of the other; the other is the one who holds the future, who knows that by experience of domination, which gives the lie to the autonomy of the self. To be One is to be autonomous, to be powerful, to be God; but to be One is to be an illusion and so to be involved in a dialectic of apocalypse with the other. Yet to be other is to be multiple, without clear boundaries, frayed, insubstantial. One is too few, but two are too many" (1990, 219). Haraway's allusions are to Hegel's theme of lordship and bondage (in *The Phenomonology* [1977, 111–19]) and perhaps to Alexandre Kojève's reading of this theme (see Kojève 1986, ch. 1). Somewhat differently, Antonin Artaud speculates on counting (1965, 113–23). I

discuss *the thematics of counting* throughout, but especially in the excurses on aesthetics and in chapter 6.

William Desmond says, "Hegel counts to three, but in dialectically counting to three, he is finally counting to one; the third turns out to be the first; for the second, in dialectically turning into the third, also turns out to be the first; three turns out to be one, two turns out to be one, hence Hegel does not finally count beyond one at all" (1992, 11).

Luce Irigaray, about woman, says, "*She is neither one nor two*" (1985b, 27; Irigaray's emphasis). Nick Land speaks of zero and one (see 1992, 122). Etc., Etc., Etc. And see Vernant 1990. And the discussions on counting go on and on, as will become obvious throughout my discussion. (see Gamow 1988.)

14. Cf. Sutton 1994.

15. As I interpret *nomos* (a genus word), it *is*—if it is—always under the sign of negation. Hence, it cannot be denegated as *physis* or *logos* can. But of course it can be dispersed.

16. The allusion is to Heidegger's *What is Called Thinking?* (1968).

17. Cixous writes: "Beware, my friend, of the signifier that would take you back to the authority of a signified! Beware of diagnoses that would reduce your generative powers. 'Common' nouns are also proper nouns that disparage your singularity by classifying it into species. Break out of the circles. . . . Take a look around, then cut through!" (1981, 263).

18. Some of my readers often cite my " 'Notes' Towards . . ." (1987b) as such a grammar. This early article has been rewritten and updated as "Rudiments . . ." (see 1993b). It might be helpful to read the updated version as another way into the discussion of this present book. In the original version of this book, "Rudiments" was chapter 1.

19. I am alluding to Schiappa's "Sophistic Rhetoric: Oasis or Mirage?" (1991).

20. Of course, I have to say "should *break* loose" because it is up (or down) to the readers to determine how they are *to receive* what I have done here. The *break*-ing of the vessels, to be sure, can be read in terms of a potlatch creating the conditions for anger. Finally, it depends on the interests invested by each reader, that is, what they will (to) do with what I have done here. Readers who are faithful to the father (or mother) can, and *do*, reOedipalize a deOedipalization.

21. Something (species) *is* by being similar to other things (genus) that are similar because they *are not like* these other things (other species + genus); yet those things (species in a genus) that are similar (identifiably the same in a genus) *are so* by virtue of being different from each other.

22. Burke has written much on the negative. I borrow his line from the scholastics (1969a, 25), and in chapter 1, I call on his genealogy of the negative. Against Burke, I have written a lengthy more unfavorable view of the negative, but favorable view of denegating the negative in "On Negation—and yet Affirmation—in Dis/

respect to Critical Theory" (*The Society for Critical Exchange*. The PACT Project. October 1991).

23. See Rabinow (1984, 7–12); any work by Foucault (e.g., *Madness and Civilization*, 1965); and see Nye (1990, chs. 1–4).

24. Freud writes: "We are . . . obliged to recognize that the little girl is a little man" (*SE* 1962, 22: 118).

25. Burke has suggested ways of "refin[ing war] to the point where it would be much more peaceful than the conditions we would now call peace" (305). That's a hilarious statement, in more ways than one.

26. I am thinking of Paul Shorey, who is quoted by Kennedy at the beginning of his *The Art of Persuasion in Greece* (1963; cf. 1988, 232). Shorey wrote: "We are freed from rhetoric only by study of its history."

27. I know that this is rather an impolitic thing to say. But I am thinking of Nietzsche's notion of nausea, vomiting, and Derrida's (1981b), Kristeva's (1982), and Fourier's (vomiting as invention [Barthes 1976, 88]), etc. See Worsham 1994; Vitanza 1994c.

28. This argument is curious because it is Platonic: There is history (the "events" of the real or whatever), then historians (who write about the "events"), and thirdly the historiographers (who write about the historians who write about the "events"). Since I am three times removed from "reality," proper sort-of Platonists would not allow me in their Republic of historians. Through out my work and in this book, I have sought—have had to seek—third positions and audiences.

29. See Vitanza, "Interview with . . ." (1993a).

30. This is a Deleuzian and Guattarian switch. See *Anti-Oedipus* (1983).

31. See my article "Threes" (1994); also, see Zurbrugg 1993, 114–18.

32. I do understand, however, what and how it means, according to Deleuze and Guattari, to "become-woman" (see 1987).

33. I have discussed this point at length in "An Open Letter . . . " (1990).

34. By performative, I on occasion mean performative as a speech act. Only women can authoritatively say what they say by virtue of being women. Or more often than not, by performative, I have in mind Butler's discussion (see 1990) and her attack on identity politics or even Spivak's idea of "fabricat[ing] strategic 'misreadings' " (see 1983, 186). I am well aware that Butler has somewhat refined her position in *Bodies that Matter*, 1993. For an interesting discussion of feminism and performance, see Martin Jay (1994).

35. I am thinking primarily of Derrida (1981c, 1985a) and Gayatri Spivak (1989), who would say yes, twice, to Heideggerian texts.

36. Obviously, K. Burke would make much of these ambiguities, and yet he would systematize (grammatize) them (see 1969a, xviii, 55–58).

37. Freud says: "Negation is a way of taking cognizance of what is repressed; indeed it is already a lifting of the repression, though not, of course, an acceptance of what is repressed. We can see how in this the *intellectual function* is separated from the *affective process.* . . . To negate something in a judgement is, at bottom, to say: 'This is something which I should prefer to repress.' A negative judgement is the intellectual substitute for repression. . . ." (*SE* 1962, 19: 235–36; emphasis mine).

Let's look at an example: In the case history of Dora, Freud says that despite her refusal Dora wanted to accept Herr K's (amorous) advances:

> My expectations were by no means disappointed when this explanation of mine [that Dora desired K] was met by Dora with a most emphatic negative. The "No" uttered by a patient after a repressed thought has been presented to his [sic] conscious perception for the first time does no more than register the existence of a repression and its severity; it acts, as it were, as a gauge of the repression's strength. If this "No," instead of being regarded as the expression of an impartial judgement (of which, indeed, the patient is incapable), is ignored, and if work is continued, the first evidence soon begins to appear that in such a case "No" signifies the desired "Yes." (*SE* 1962, 7: 57)

38. The parapolitics of locations (*loci*) are discussed throughout and, therefore, these names will begin to take on more concrete meaning in the forthcoming chapters and excurses. However, for an interesting discussion on the politics of location, see K. M. Kirby 1993.

39. A *fold* is a term from topology. I am using this term as Deleuze uses it in discussing Foucault's technologies of subjectivity. I will return to this language, once again, in chapter 7 to discuss Nietzsche's notions of subjectivity, which Foucault and Deleuze appropriate. See Deleuze 1988. I wish to thank Lynda Hass for calling this chapter in Deleuze's book to my attention.

40. I say "Victor Vitanzan hope" not so as to indulge in self-aggrandizement, but out of a sense of "responsibility" to my most improper name. Allow me to explain: A couple of years ago, when I thought of distancing (exiling, dispersing) myselphs and giving birth (bestially, satyrically) to myselphs, that is, to a countersignature, I began by reexamining my own name, "Victor Vitanza." I spread wide my surname into "vita" and "anza." In Italian, "anza" signifies "against." (The "z," however, signifies Sicilian, not Italian, lineage.) I discovered, therefore, that, when reversed, my surname signifies "against life." (The "z," the most decadent letter of the alphabet, invites me to reverse my name.) This discovery—un/namely, that my name signifies literally "against life"—was, indeed, disconcerting. I recalled immediately, however, that my given name, "Victor," when linked with my surname, becomes literally "conqueror against life," or "conqueror of death."

All of this is to say that I discovered that I have a deconstructive name. I have the means of perversity, of resistance. And disruption.

But this name—this naming, hailing—business (of mine) in its uncanny ways continues. Quite recently, I was looking at *Finnegans Wake* (1976) and I discovered my name had been chosen, dreamed, and written years before my birth; had always already been, prior to my time. Yes, yes, yes, I found in the *Wake* my name, represented as "Victa Nyanza" (558.28). In this joycing, or in this dream of H. C. Earwicker (here comes everybody!), I discovered "myselphs" as Vico and Joyce and Earwicker would conceive (of) "me." However, as I found other references in the *Wake* based on this (my) name, "Victa Nyanza," I discovered that it, along with another companion name ("Albatrus Nyanzer"), referred to the two lakes (Victoria and Albert) that are the source of the Nile, the source of life itself. I also discovered the pun on "Nyanza" as being "No answer" (89.27).

You see, my name is a Third Sophistic name.

41. *To turn the lever* is a Derridian (and later a Gayatri Spivakian) term, which designates, among other possibilities, a reading (writing, thinking) strategy that is a negative deconstruction allowing us to promote our own interests while reading someone we wish to disagree with. Actually, it is what language does right before us—in its own self-referential deconstructions—sometime when we are reading (observing) it. (See Derrida 1981c, 39–96; 1982, 88–108, 117–36.) For example, at the end of "The Ends of Man," Derrida begins to use the word "eve" (from Nietzsche's German into French, and from French into English); after using it a few times, it becomes rather obvious that the word is taking on double meanings. The "Man" of the title is confronting a major shift and an end (*c'est fini*) in *evening time* and in *Eve* (the feminine?) (1982, 136). I will take up this reading strategy of turning the lever in the excursus "Feminist Sophistic?"

42. See C. Miller 1993.

43. The *last* sex is the *third* sex (centaur, hermaphrodite, cyborg, etc.).

44. Fausto-Sterling, a geneticist, says that there are five sexes (males, female, hermaphrodites, merms, and ferms). She says: "I would argue further that sex is a vast, infinitely malleable continuum that defies the constraints of even five categories" (1993, 21).

45. Kristeva, however, is predisposed to see the abject as the sign of negation; after all, she is Freudian and Lacanian. I do not see abjection as negation but in terms of a Nietzschean joyful affirmation.

46. A caveat: I have a number of variations on this game in the book. And yes, I step outside, and invite others to step outside of the circle of this game altogether, only for the opportunity (the untimely ones!) of returning refreshed to play the game anew. I am attempting to revalue this History that represents nihilism.

Parapolitics is a generic term here for not only "pagan politics" but also Foucault's "biopolitics" (1980b) and Haraway's "cyborg politics" (1990; 1991).

47. See Bataille 1988b, 47, 118–19.

Chapter 1. The Sophists

1. I use the word "readdress" so as to avoid Kerferd's concept of "reception" (1981). The word "readdress" has several puns in it that I prefer and implies an intersubjective possibility that the word "reception" does not.

2. I discuss this notion of the sublime at length beginning in the two excurses that follow chapter 1.

3. The problem with the concept of "fact" has been dealt with by numerous thinkers in modern times from Nietzsche through Thomas Kuhn and up to Baudrillard. I have not referred to Baudrillard here to the degree that I might have. Most important is his concept of simulacrum (seduction, hyperreality, and production versus seduction).

4. See, e.g., Burke 1973, 67–68; 1966, 44–62; 1969a, 84–85, 354–55, 415–16; Valesio 1980, 19–41.

5. As I have indicted previously (1987a), I have similar problems with Grice's or Habermas's pragmatics and its axioms.

6. The terms "ironist" and "metaphysician" are used extensively by Rorty in *Contingency, Irony, and Solidarity* (1989, 73–95). Simply put, the difference is between the attitudes of pragmaticists and beyond, on the one hand, and traditional philosophers, on the other. An ironist does not believe or trust any final vocabulary, whereas a metaphysician needs one. Eventually, with the help of Deleuze, I will make a distinction between "irony" and "humor."

7. Feyerabend similarly states: "Where arguments do seem to have an effect this is more often due to their *physical repetition* than to their *semantic content*" (1978, 24–25; Feyerabend's emphasis; cf. 256–57).

8. Rorty writes: "tossing a metaphor into a conversation is like suddenly breaking off the conversation long enough to make a face, or pulling a photograph out of your pocket and displaying it, . . . Tossing a metaphor into a text is like using italics, or illustrations, or odd punctuation or formats. All of these are ways of producing effects on your interlocutor or your reader, but not ways of conveying a message. To one of these is it appropriate to respond with 'What exactly are you trying to say?'. . ." (1989, 18, 19).

9. The article won the best article of the year award in *Rhetoric Review*.

10. If Schiappa pretends to be an earlier student of Rorty's, situating himself in respect to Rorty's two truncated philosophical historiographies, I will perversely here extend myself into becoming a later student of Rorty's, resituating myselves in respect to Rorty's sophistic notions of "self-creation and affiliation" (see 1989, 96–121).

11. I have used this nomenclature, a Third Sophistic, in several articles. See 1987a, 1987b, 1991a, 1991b, 1993, 1994a, 1994b, 1994c, 1994d. When I say "Third"

Sophistic, I mean it in a very specific sense, which I will develop through out this book in reference to my notion of "threes."

Many of my contemporaries write about the Sophists, and in doing so refer to a neo-Sophistic. E.g., Neel (1988), J. Poulakos (1983b, 1984, 1990, 1993), Schiappa (1990b, 1990c, 1991), Crowley (1979) or Feminist Sophistic (Jarratt 1991). That there is a renewed interest in the Sophists can be dated, at least, back to Funck-Brentano (1879). In his book, Funck-Brentano identifies John Stuart Mill and Herbert Spencer as Sophists. See Jarratt's dissertation (1985), in which Jarratt makes a similar parallel, but does not refer to Funck-Brentano. In our century, there are de Romilly (1975), in her last lecture, on twentieth-century French thought; Nelson (1983), in his discussion of political theory. Also see. E. C. White (1987). There are others.

12. What is suggested as a possibility here, though not pursued by Lyotard in the book, is an aesthetic of excess, which would be an aesthetic of affirmation, one that would work out of Nietzschean ways of thinking. It would be an aesthetic of excess, for it would allow for a way out of binaries by virtue of a third subject or object position. It would be an aesthetic of affirmation, for binaries such as male/female require negation, repression, and therefore a movement to a third position, to excess, would simply require a denegation of negation, i.e., affirmation. (I discuss this aesthetic fully in the two excurses following this chapter.)

13. The important word here is "necessary." (Not necessary how to link.) This lack of necessity, of course, is an antifoundational position, which means a working without fixed criteria. Someone might need to argue that it is necessary to link *responsibly*. I take responsibility to be a code word demanding that linkage must be done prescriptively/dogmatically. Someone might need to argue that it is *strategically necessary* to link. If so, it can become very difficult to tell the difference between necessary and strategically necessary (dogmatism). My position is that in both of these cases, in both phrases in dispute (say, not necessary how to link vs. strategically necessary how to link), no resolution of their differences should be attempted, for only a *differend* would result; that is, the rules and regimens of one phrase would determine the conditions of the other. And yet, there is a greater argument, for the very fact that there can be a strategic necessity is owing to the proposition "not necessary how to link." Because there are no necessary ways to link, then, strategic necessity or strategic essentialism can express itself.

14. I am well aware that Wittgenstein changes in his latter period, from the *Blue Book* on. This change is best discussed by Staten (1986), who compares Wittgenstein to Derrida. As I have stated, my method is to casuistically stretch.

15. It is necessary to emphasize here that Lyotard's *The Differend* (1988a) is a sublime predicated on the negative, while I eventually (in the excurses following this chapter) search for ways of denegating this Kantian/Lyotardian sublime. (Lyotard offers clues in his earlier book *Libidinal Economy* [1993].)

16. So much of what I will have said throughout this book will most likely get read as postmodern, which has become a kind of devil term in particular circles. That

I dis/engage, on occasion, in tactics that can be interpreted as postmodern, or that I identify, on occasion, with writers who are classified as postmodern, I will not deny. Unfortunately, since the word is a devil term, it is rejected without much thought by the would-be critic. Most authors of books whom I have read that are supposed to be critiquing postmodernism generally fail to announce that the term is highly and purposively problematic; the term is an acknowledgement that some terms refused to be limited. It would be better to think of postmodern(s) in plural terms. Of the critiques that I have read, John McGowan's (1991) is the best of the worst; like so many other critics, however, he inists on reading postmodernism in terms of Jürgen Habermas's argument based on performative contradictions. In the case of Lyotard and many other so-called postmodernists the so-called argument of contradictions simply should not hold, because the particular rule that Habermas followers would judge by is not applicable to so-called postmodern prose. Lyotard is not to be read semiotically across speech acts, but across just gaming, theatrics. McGowan, like others, creates a differend when reading/critiquing postmodernists. He reads/judges a phrase of one genre by the rules and regimens of another, thereby excluding. In other words he himself engages in a performative contradiction, which is a rule that he cannot violate!

17. This third concept, like all such concepts that I garner here, I associate with Plato's third order of representation, which of course he needs to purge from the Republic; and, need I say it here, we associate with the Sophists, whom, as seen, Schiappa needs to disassociate from The History of Rhetoric. And finally (beginningly?) I associate with my notion of a Third Sophistic.

18. Deleuze and Guattari, in their book *Kafka*, answer the question of What happened? during and after the Russian Revolution? in terms of reterritorialization. Moreover, they speak of a distinction between paranoid transcendental law and immanent schizo law. The paranoid reterritorializes and steals the revolution. Like Lyotard, Deleuze and Guattari are concerned with the question of justice. (See 1986, ch. 6.)

19. To be sure, Marx (with Engels) is not always a Humanist. In *The German Ideology* (Marx and Engels 1978), e.g., self-consciousness amounts to nothing, for history as dialectical materialism will have its way with us no matter what human beings desire. But I have emphasized the Humanism of Marx here—the kind that can be found in, e.g., Marx's *Eighteenth Brumaire* (1984)—because many people in our field (criticism, rhetoric) who claim to be "Marxists" still speak of choosing correctly, which means choosing exclusively by way of a "materialist" rationality. For me, such an exclusive view of Humanism leads paradoxically only to a further impoverishment of human beings and the environment.

20. Schiappa has written an article entitled "Arguing About Definitions" (1993). Schiappa's primary example is "death"! It is one thing to be able to make distinctions and to appear to understand distinctions and quite another to act on them. There is a difference between what Schiappa apparently knows in this later article and what he had forgotten when thinking earlier about the Sophists.

21. Again I want to point out that Deleuze and Guattari speak of these problems at great length in Kafka (1986). I will eventually refer to their specific views and anecdotes.

22. What Schiappa is suggesting, of course, when he says history should not be read backwards is that—e.g., in the case of the Sophists—we should not read them in our contemporary terms but in the Sophists's *own* terms. Hans-Georg Gadamer says, however, that we cannot but read history backwards. Gadamer would call Schiappa's view "romantic hermeneutics," while Nietzsche would call it a will to knowledge (death). One result of such a hermeneutic is the split between a truth effect and falsity effect, or between *logos* and *mythos*, history and fiction, or even authentic myth and poetic myth. (Schiappa necessarily, then, given his prejudice, says, " 'sophistic rhetoric' is largely a fiction" [1991, 14], which he uncovers because he employs a method of discovering truth (I allude to the ironic title of Gadamer's book!) Gadamer says that historical hermeneutics must always begin by way of a historian's prejudice, or perspective. A universal hermeneutic (the will to truth) does not and cannot exist, though many insist on it, such as E. D. Hirsch (meaning vs. significance) and Jürgen Habermas (pragmatics and consensus). Classical philology is saturated with prejudices. Looking through a Greek lexicon is looking through a set of well-established (e.g., roman-*eyez*-ed) prejudices. See Gadamer 1975, 153ff, 173ff, 213ff; Weinsheimer 1985, 133–212. Even Rorty agrees; see 1979, 357–64. It even gets worse, for Schiappa is confused when it comes to a reading of Nietzsche and Foucault. He writes: " 'Facts' figure crucially in the "power/knowledge' dynamic problematized by Michael Foucault. Eliminate *all* vestiges of the will-to-truth, and naught but the will-to-power remains. If power is all that writes history, then there is no basis [ground?] for reclaiming marginalized histories, no basis for critiquing establishment narratives, and no basis for curing cultural amnesia about past genocide [!], misogyny, and racism" (1991, 13). The problem here (again) is that Schiappa does not understand what *will to truth* and *will to power* mean. (He has got their meanings turned around, as he has so many other things.) It is the will to truth (fact as truth) that impoverishes the will to power; the former is only one of the perspectives (interpretations) that can be brought forth by the latter. Schiappa does not see his own position as only one facet of the will to power, while others' positions are other facets of the will to power. For Nietzsche and Foucault, power in general is not a negative term; on the contrary, it is an *enabling* term; it is negative only when power becomes impoverished in the name of the will to truth. Power is an infinite play of affirmations. That there is no basis, or ground, as Schiappa says, is accurate; for such a basis again is the will to truth, or the impoverishment of the will to power. Everything is contingent. Quite ironically, it is Schiappa who would *disenable* history-writing and historiography.

In response to his queries, I would, therefore, answer that we historians can *reclaim marginalized histories* by pointing out that the will to truth has cut off an expression of the will to power; we *critique establishment narratives*, such as Schiappa's, by pointing out that the will to truth, again, has cut off other so-called little narratives, such as those about the neo-sophists, or those of mine about a Third Sophistic; and we *cure cultural amnesia* by remembering what has been systematically forgotten by, yes again, recalling the various lost perspectives of the will to power, lost, e.g., by Schiappa's genus-cide (see Nietzsche 1968c; Lyotard 1990; Watson 1985).

23. There is a significant body of literature on the (apparent) death of rhetoric. See, e.g., Sutton 1986 (which has a selected list of other references to this theme), and 1994.

24. This is a reference to the philologist who attacked Nietzsche and his *Birth of Tragedy*. On the question of philology, see Nietzsche's "We Classicists" [Philologists] (1990).

25. I discuss Heidegger and this problem at length in chapters 4–5.

26. Later, in chapter 6, I will set them aside and move on to Nietzsche for thinking, reading, writing protocols, and for a new paraethic.

27. Spivak writes: "According to Derrida, if one looks at propriation in the general sense in Nietzsche, one sees a question that is 'more powerful than the question, "what is?" ', more powerful than 'the veil of truth or the meaning of being,' because before one can even say that *there is being*, there must be a decision that being can be proper to itself to the extent of being part of that proposition. . . . Outside of all philosophical game-playing, the irreducible predicament pointed at here is that the ontological question cannot be asked in terms of a cleansed epistemology, for propriation organizes the totality of 'language's process and symbolic exchange in general' " (1989a, 211; see Derrida 1979, 111, 113).

28. I take up the question of the concept-metaphor of "woman" later in the excursus "Feminist Sophistic?"

29. I have purposefully, strategically, called directly on Spivak and not Derrida here; moreover, I have mixed in Deleuze and Guattari as well. I am well aware that there are differences among this lot, which I take up in the excursus "Feminist Sophistic?"

30. There is a necessity for clarification here: This second—i.e., affirmative deconstruction—is not a second, but a third of "some more"; for the first—negative deconstruction—is both one and two, both privileged and supplement. With this problem cleared up, there is yet another possible misunderstanding that I am identifying with Spivak. I am not. Spivak favors negotiating with structures of violence, with negative deconstruction, because not to do so, she assumes, would place her outside of history and, therefore, the struggle. I, however, am not willing—at least, to the extent Spivak is willing—to negotiate with the negative; and I, consequently, do not have any fear of stepping outside of history into affirmation, when I am dis/engaging in schizography. Voiding the negative does not necessarily void history; voiding negative subjectivity does not necessarily void *Homo historia*. As Deleuze and Guattari say: "No one has ever been as deeply involved in history as the schizo, or dealt with it in this way. He [*sic*] consumes all of universal history in one fell swoop. We began by defining him [*sic*] as *Homo natura*, and lo and behold, he [*sic*] has turned out to be *Homo historia*" [1983, 21]. As I proceed, I will intermittently make this

Deleuzian point in favor of affirmative deconstruction, especially in the final chapter, with its excurses.)

31. It is extremely important to understand that in my attempt to denegate the narrative that I refer to Hermaphroditus initially here, though, to be sure, I will continue use of the metaphor intermittently. I agree with Helene Cixous when she writes that "Ovid's Hermaphrodite [is potentially] less bisexual than asexual, [is] not made up of two genders but of two halves. Hence, a fantasy of unity. Two within one, and not even two wholes" (in Clément and Cixous 1986, 84). It should also be understood that Hermaphroditus represents here, as many have argued, a castrated male. It is not beyond me to begin to rewrite The History of Rhetoric by way of a castration of phallocentrism. As I will say in passing later in the excurses "Feminist Sophistic?", I would help the new history to be born by castrating castration. Perhaps these are difficult tactics and strategies to follow, even at the conscious level. My tactics and strategies, or tactics without strategies, of redefining sexuality in terms of denegated desire will continue in the forthcoming excurses and chapters. Having said all this, I also want to make it unclearly clear that I move from hermaphrodite to becoming-animal. In all cases, however, the *locus* remains pretty much the same, metamorphoses.

32. I address this issue more fully in the excursus "Feminist Sophistic?"

33. I have been discussing Favorinus in the following way for some time now, at a conference (Speech Communication Conference, Chicago, 1992) and in print (see 1994d).

34. I have modeled this entire statement on Shklovsky's statement (see 1965, 30–31).

Excursus, The Negative, Aesthetics, and the Sublime (Terror)

1. I have previously written a rather lengthy, yet unpublished, article on this problem, "On Negation—and yet Affirmation—in Dis/respect to Critical Theory.")

2. Hayden White, in an excellent essay, has written: "the disciplining of historical thinking that had to be undertaken if history considered as a kind of knowledge was to be established as arbitrator of the realism of contending political programs, each attended by its own philosophy of history, had first of all to consist of *a rigorous de-rhetoricization*" (1987, 65; emphasis mine). The next thing historians had to do was to involve themselves in "the progressive demotion of the sublime in favor of the beautiful" (68). My approach, to be sure, is to do the absolute opposite; hence, my returning sophistic rhetoric and aesthetics as sublime to historiography. Also see Kellner 1991.

3. I am referring to Lyotard's *Libidinal Economy* (in French, 1974; in English, 1993). Supposedly he recants in his *Peregrinations* (1988b). Iain Hamilton Grant's introduction to the translation of *Libidinal Economy* raises questions about Lyotard's

attempt to recant. The issue of Lyotard's stand on his book cannot be reduced to any simple moral judgment. I later, in the second excursus, deal with Lyotard's general, libidinal economy.

4. The juncture of aesthetics and politics is being 'negotiated' in Speech-Communication. Actually, the two camps speak at cross purposes. Ever since our Speech colleagues walked out of the Modern Language Association, leaving departments of English, they have found aesthetics rather difficult. I have spoken of this at length (see 1993b). Most recently, as this book goes to press, the battle even within Speech Communication itself continues. See Whitson and Poulakos 1993; Hikins 1995; Whitson and Poulakos 1995.

5. In my discussion of aesthetics and politics in this excursus and the next, I do not call on Kenneth Burke and his *Counter-Statement* (1968); instead, I wait until the very final excursus. Perhaps by then my tactic-strategy will be more clear as to why I *will have waited*. Burke subsumes politics under aesthetics (113). He also attacks the idea of art for art's sake, while speaking of art for life's (all of life's) sake.

6. Bill Readings writes:

> The importance of Lyotard's work is not that it gives post-structuralism a decidable political dimension that it had otherwise lacked. Rather, Lyotard's refusal to think the political as a determining or determinate metalanguage, as the sphere in which the true meaning of false metalanguages (such as "aesthetic value") is revealed as "political effects," pushes him towards a deconstruction of the representational space of the political. . . . [T]his induces a shift from the political to the ethical, in the sense that the instances of dispute conventionally determined as political are seen to be more justly considered as sites for indeterminate judgment. Let it be clear that this is not an "aestheticization of the political" in the sense of the Fascist project. In Fascism, as Benjamin has demonstrated, the political remains as site of determinate judgment, by analogy with the determinant judgments of the beautiful which may be made about art. The political is conceived in terms of criteria which are claimed to be drawn from art (the ugly should be eliminated). For Lyotard, the aesthetic and the political are both sites for *indeterminate* (ethical) judgment *without criteria*. To find the grounds of the political in the aesthetic is not simply the determining ground of the political.

> Just as the aesthetic cannot provide the legitimating grounds of the political, so the political cannot legitimate the aesthetic. Rather, the analogy between the aesthetic and the political is that their grounds of legitimacy always *remain to be decided*. (1991, 86–87; Readings's emphasis)

I would reinclude the ugly and ALL.

7. Cf. Eagleton 1991; Chytry 1989; J. M. Bernstein 1992. These works have excellent bibliographies. I have especially benefited from Weiskel (1976) and Hertz (1985).

8. See Lyotard 1988a, no. 22; and "Aristotle" Notice, 3.4; cf. Freud *SE* 19: 234–39; Burke 1966, 9–13, 419–79; Lacan 1981, 167. For an interesting discussion of the theme of the impossible (the limit, the No) in various disciplines, see Davis and Park's *No Way: The Nature of the Impossible* (1987); also, see Bataille (1991).

9. See Spinoza 1985; Nietzsche 1967, 46; N. O. Brown 1959, 1966, 1991; Bataille 1985, 1988a; Deleuze 1983a , 1983b, 1988; Deleuze and Guattari 1983, 25, 42, 294–96; Irigaray 1985, 23–33; Butler 1990, 26–29, 118.

10. Forgive me, dear reader, for my various attempts at de/forming neologisms.

11. My view of affirmative action is similar to Rodriguez (1982), who argues that such action was established by lower-middle- and middle-class minorities, who wanted a piece of the Capitalist pie, while providing nothing for those minorities lower on the social-economic scale. In other words, affirmative action was no where radical enough to include all the rest who were still excluded from the pie.

12. Cixous also finds becoming-animal valuable. She appropriates Kafka and Clarice Lispector, specifically Lispector's character's eating of (consuming, identifying with) a cockroach. See Cixous 1991 75–77, 134; 1993, 86–87, 112; also, see her discussion on the laws of eating and the joy of the *imund* (to be unclean with joy), 1993, 111–20. For Lispector, see *The Passion According to G. H.* (1988). Lispector is the most important sovereign writer that I have read while preparing myself for this book. I return to the theme of the *imund* (the unclean, the abject, the other) and to Lispector in the next excursus and "Feminist Sophistic?"

13. Cixous, an ardent reader of Kafka, has a similar position on escape, which I will discuss in the excursus "Feminist Sophistic?" and a similar interest in becoming-animal (see 1993, 111–56).

14. Rosa Braidotti, in her *Patterns of Dissonance* (1991), would argue against Land's position (and most French thinkers'), specifically, against void-nothing-death as a primary starting and ending *topos*. Braidotti's position, however, takes a very black/white approach to this problem, one that Land himself does not take. Land, who is discussing Bataille, is no simple negative thinker. Obviously, I, too, am taking a position diametrically opposed to the negative, but, like Land—whom I differ with only in rhetorical strategy—I am aware that the problem of the negative is no easy one to dismiss. Hence, my "strategic" bravado when I am confronted with particular problems. Land and Bataille and I believe in the continuous flow of energy just as, say, Cixous does. I mention the latter because although she denounces, as we do, death as a male concept (see 1981, 255), she also, along with Lispector, speaks of death in terms of metamorphosis, most specifically as the death of individuation (a denegating of the negative) into the continuous (Cixous 1993, 1–54; Lispector 1988). And she also favors the new (general) economy (1981, 264). My point here is that there is even metamorphoses when speaking of and with such terms as *death* and *negative*. I discuss Cixous and Lispector at greater length intermittently throughout and especially in the excursus "Feminist Sophistic?"

15. And yet (ever again), I agree with Land: "Of course, the distinction between the organic and the inorganic is without final usefulness, because organic matter is only a name for that fragment of inorganic material that has been woven into metastable regional compositions. If a negative prefix is to be used, it would be more accurate to place it on the side of life, since the difference is unilateral, with inorganic matter proving itself to be non-exclusive, or indifferent to its organization, whereas life necessarily operates on the basis of selection and filtering functions" (1992, 50).

16. To be sure, there are many valuable discussions on the beautiful and sublime besides Kant and Lyotard's. since my concern, however, is with Lyotard's reading of Kant, I stick with these two for the most part. The reader may want, of course, to look at Edmund Burke's *A Philosophical Enquiry into the Origin of Our Ideas of the Sublime and Beautiful* (1958).

17. I take this phrase from Weiskel (1976, 44) and rely on his discussion as a guide through Kant.

18. I discussed this distinction between litigation and *differend* in chapter 1.

19. Besides *The Differend*, one should study Lyotard's *Lessons on the Analytic of the Sublime* (1994). This book, which I have read and studied, appeared after completion of my present study. Like *The Differend*, it is in the form of study notes. In a few cases here, I have made parenthetical citations to it, so that the reader might see supplementary discussions on the distinction between the beautiful and sublime, mathematical and dynamic sublime.

20. Behind Kant lurks Sade (see Klossowski 1991; Lacan 1989. Cf. Deleuze, 1991, esp. ch. 7; Barthes 1976, secs. Sade I and Sade II).

21. Cf. 1994, 64–76, 89–146. See Kant 127; or Bk II, "General Remarks." My sense here is that a negative presentation would not really be an escape from the cognitive at all if the cognitive is seen as the very seat of the negative. Instead of following the three basic laws of logic (identity, contradiction, and excluded middle), the cognitive would call on the power of logic to dis/engage in and byway of what Dewey calls "the infinitation of the negative" (1938, 192). I discussed this matter in the introduction and intermittently in this chapter.

22. Cf. Lyotard's "Nicomachean Erotics" (1993, 155–64).

23. Later, when I discuss Bataille's response to Hegel and especially Bataille's rethinking of *physis/nomos*, or nature/culture, I will return to Kant's conception of culture-*nomos* as benefactor, which Bataille interrogates fully.

Aristotle's view of *phronesis*, which is often appealed to my moderns (see MacIntyre1984; cf. Stout 1988), is founded on view of virtue which is not at all our view of virtue. I would submit that Aristotle's view will simply not work for us, especially in the light of how we have come to view contemporary problems of the speaking subject. I discuss Aristotle's view of ethics, in chapter 7.

24. There is always the possibility of some misunderstanding here. I have been discussing issues in terms of negative/affirmative, which sounds and reads like a binary (machine) itself. Occasionally I have introduced a third term, *nonpositive affirmation*. My own-going purpose has been to examine negation/affirmation, but not as a binary—which it is usually represented as—but as a trinary, specifically as mater-slave-sovereignty. Negation (*topos, e/utopos*) is always the result of dialectic and the law of noncontradiction. Nonpositive affirmation, as discussed here, is the result of "transgression," but not as a mere transgression against the law. (Such a transgression would always, therefore, be determined by, subject-ed to, the law.) As Foucault, in his homage to Bataille says, "transgression . . . is not related to the limit as black to white, the prohibited to the lawful, the outside to the inside"; and again, "[t]rangression does not seek to oppose one thing to another. Transgression is neither violence in a divided world (in an ethical world) nor a victory over limits (in a dialectical or revolutionary world); . . . Transgression contains nothing negative, but . . . affirms the limitlessness into which it leaps as it opens this zone to existence for the first time. But correspondingly, this affirmation contains nothing positive: no content can bind it, since, by definition [sic], no limit can possibly restrict it [i.e., define it]" (1977, 35–36).

25. There is a loose analogy between these two consciousnesses, recognitions—one dominant, the other subordinate—and Socratic/Platonic dialectics (see *Parmenides* 132e); and, I would go so far as to say, an even looser analogy, but nonetheless an important one, with Lyotard's distinction between a litigation (master/slave) and a differend (which is potentially either a master/slave or a sovereign).

26. I will save for later a discussion of Hélène Cixous, who speaks in three terms of negative, positive, joyous. The third term is the locus of the unclean, the waste by product of the thou shalt nots (see 1993a, esp. 107–56).

Excursus (cont'd.). The Negative, Aesthetics, and the Sublime (Terror)

1. I take up the issue of death in the excursus "Feminist Sophistic?" and the last excursus.

2. I will return to the theme of *to apeiron* when discussing Isocrates, Heidegger, and the *logos*. The theme is taken up by Nietzsche in *The Birth of Tragedy* in terms of the principle of individuation (1967). Also see Nietzsche's discussion of Anaximander in *Philosophy in the Tragic Age of the Greeks* (1987).

3. See Derrida 1978, 31–63; Spivak 1987, 197–221; 1988, 271–313.

4. What I am suggesting, perhaps in a caddy sort of way, is that Spivak has much invested in not thinking that the subalterns can speak for themselves. First of all "to speak for oneself" implies a humanist speaking-subject. And choice. My sense, that which I am steadily getting to, is that the libidinal body is always speaking for itself. It is that libidinal body that I would listen to.

5. I am deliberately going to *Death and Sensuality* and not *The Accursed Share* (esp. vols. 2–3) because, I think, that Bataille's discussion in *DS* is by far more intricate and revealing. Later I will pick up on *AS*. However, passages from *DS* are included in the second volume of *AS*. I will cross reference where desirable.

6. Bataille suggests with this sexist analogy and custom, which is obviously not limited to primitive cultures, that champagne/woman is semiotically coded to be consumed socially/exogamically and not individually/inogamically (1962, 204–05).

7. As we proceed, this statement will receive the further development that it deserves.

8. *Homeorrhesis* means to flow in one direction while resisting such a flow. See Serres 1982, 74–75.

9. The best example that I have found of the difference between man (woman) *and* animals is in Clarice Lispector's *The Passion According to G. H.* (1988). The entire work is an account—"according to"—the narrator, G. H., about her feelings of attraction and repulsion toward a cockroach that she finds in her home. The description of its repugnance is given in terms that directly suggest the sublime, the giving up of one's identity, and becoming-animal. G. H. expels her acceptance of the *beautiful* (that which is sanctioned, but which becomes in her *eyes* ugly) and desires the *ugly*. She eats/consumes the repulsive animal of ancient times, the cockroach (see 12, 75, 149–50). She, like Gregor Samsa, gives up human identifty and becomes-animal. (See the excursus "Feminist Sophistic?")

10. I want to stress that perhaps no where else, outside of Bataille himself, can one find this theme expressed as repulsively as it is than in Nick Land's book, *A Thirst for Annihilation* (1992).

11. This statement will be difficult for the reader to accept, especially the reader who has consciously lived through the 1980's (with its valuing greed and its further wasting of the environment). This statement will be difficult to follow, for Capital has turned everything upside down, creating the illusion—hence, making it difficult to move beyond its limits—that there is shortage, and that it drives the economy. In the eighties so much wealth (excess) was concentrated in so few hands. The general Marxist approach to that problem was to spread that wealth equally. I see both the Capitalist and the so-called Socialist view of economy as unacceptable: The first because it is incredibly immoral, based on scarcity; the latter, because it does not take the role of excess into consideration. What I would favor, then, is a libidinalized Marxism that would be way beyond the limits of Capital. (See my final excursus.)

12. The phrase, "light, desire, and politics," is from Land 1992, 28.

13. See Deleuze and Guattari (1983, 25–27).

14. The explanation is a great deal more complicated: Hollier says, Bataille " 'prefers' the sphinx. He refuses to have man be the answer. Instead he transforms man into a sphinx, into the riddle of his own contamination by animality" (85). Prefers

Zero. Because Oedipus answered, the sphinx took on a different character, a riddle. If Oedipus had forgotten—affirmatively forgotten—the question, What is X?, the sphinx would have remained a non-threatening enigma. The question concerned counting, accounting. Four, Two, Three. But No/Know, Oedipus wanted *to theorize* (to see) the riddle, to desire an answer. To deny his animality. Oedipus preferred One. Linnaeus, in his system of classification, his genus-cide, put man first: *Homo sapiens* (86). Man has science, has scientific *seeing* (theory). What is seen, is seen by way of homogeneity. The rule and regimen of the day is "homogenization, identification, reproduction" (86). One.

However, "Theory does not know or even encounter its other. The other escapes it" (87). Theory creates the conditions for the abject. Zero.

In his attempt to deny his animality, therefore, MAN fell into animality (incest). And from here on—despite the lesson of the tragedy that has, with Freud, become universalized—MAN (men, not females) see themselves as the center of Thebes, and the solver of all problems, *and yet* MAN, with his answer, is the polluter of the city. Pollution now is. The sun now is black. (Bataille counts from One to Zero.)

In the face of *homology* (a restricted economy: theoretical discourse, science, philosophy, orderliness and cleanliness), Bataille—and his colleagues at "the school of sociology" (Hollier 1988)—call for a practical *heterology* (a general economy of the abject: "undesirables, bodies, the unconscious, base matter, extravagant and excremental waste, and associated excitations, energies and disturbances" [Botting and Wilson 1993, 197]). It is this undercurrent of energy that must be exposed so as to expend it gloriously and not catastrophically.

And, therefore, Bataille in his fiction and essays and diagrams cuts off the head of MAN. (The headless man, *Acephalus.*) He has man—the philosopher, the scientist, the priest—rip out his eyes, or has them ripped out. He has a female demand that the eye of a priest be cut out so that she can insert it into her vagina, reunborn (see Bataille 1987, 83–84; cf. Irigaray 1985a, 147–51; Foucault 1980, 146–65).

The eye must now acknowledge *the blind spot*! (cf. Bataille 1988c, 110–11; 1987, 38–40,48, 61–62.)

Bataille finds the profane in the sacred, the heterogeneous in the homogeneous. As Bataille says, man is a fundamental contradiction. A paradox of substance. Our neighbor, Sade: Reason/rationality harbors madness; madness, reason (see Klossowski 1991). For example, the place of the beheading of the sun-king (bloody revolution) is the place of concord (spending/killing time, vacation, CaCa-pit-alist.) (see Hollier 1989, xxii–xxiii).

15. Marxism, in its traditional form, does not take this additional problem into consideration, for it believes in simply recodifying, reterritorializing the problem.

16. And yet, it is not just *animal*, but all *matter*. (See Land 1992, ch. 2.)

17. This latter point is difficult to understand and to accept. Both Capital and various Marxisms, socialisms, blind us from seeing what Bataille says we must come to see (cf. Habermas 1987b, 231–32). Logic must be wasted as well. I will return to this point, however, in a fuller discussion of the sacred.

18. One of Bataille's prime examples is Gilles de Rais (see *La Tragédie de Gilles de Rais* 1965; Land 1992, 66–72).

19. Cf. Marx's discussion of commodification. (See 1977, 125–77, or *Capital 1*, ch. 1).

20. I will later opt for a different way of designating *physis* denegated. To simplify matters, I am saying that *physis*[neg.] is artificial, that it is really *nomos*[neg.] that has forgotten that it was, prior to negation, *physis* without any reserve. In other words, *physis*[neg.] is only a form of *nomos*, which is always under negation. (There is no binary! as I will suggest later in chapters 6–7 that absence is presence and presence is absence.) My thinking is in parallel form here possibly with Derrida's (by way of Lévi-Strauss's thinking of the scandal of no difference between *physis/nomos*); Derrida suggests that "epistemic discourse" comes from "mythomorphic discourse" and the "engineer" comes from the "*bricoleur*" (see 1972).

21. Deleuze and Guattari in *Anti-Oedipus* have made much of this letter (see 1983, 21, 86, 278; cf. Vitanza 1994b), in relation to the psychiatric case histories of Judge Schreber and Antonin Artaud.

22. I am suggesting that both *physis* and *nomos* under negation are unacceptable. It might be thought, but somewhat misleadingly, that I am after a *physis* dispredicated on ignoble, wild savages.

23. I would at this point simply allude to the attempts to desexualize, "detropealize" language (*logos*) in The History of Rhetoric. See most notably Vickers (1990, 435–79).

24. As I have suggested, there can be an individual only if we return to Capital. The individual is an effect of Capital. Like Deleuze and Guattari, I would say there are only desire and the social (see 1983, 29).

25. Here again is an allusion to Heidegger.

26. The term simply means, in Freudian thought, that in the unconscious any and every idea , no matter how contradictory, can be together. Hence, Freud's notion that there is no No in the unconscious.

The term is from Leibnitz. If God had all possible worlds to choose from, he had to choose the best of all possible. God by definition is under negation, at least, in "man's" reasoning about God. However, when God (foundationalism) is dead, we might expect to be able to live in "compossible" (not systematized) worlds. See Lyotard, 1993, x–xi; Deleuze 1993, ch. 5)

27. I appropriate these terms from Nick Land.

28. Neil Hertz—in a brilliant article on the uncanny, on obsessive compulsion, and on the death wish—writes: "Whatever it is that is repeated—an obsessive ritual, perhaps, or a bit of acting-out in relation to one's analyst—will, then, feel most compellingly uncanny when it is seen as merely coloring, that is, when it comes to seem most gratuitously rhetorical" (1985, 102). This strategy of resistance by way

of delay (*Nachträglichkeit* [deferred action]) is seen as the principle of *thanatos* itself. Not only, in Lyotard's terms, is Marx engaging in it—after all, Marx, too, is subject to this dysfunctional display of the death wish—but also Lyotard himself, who writes about his book, "This book [*Libidinal Economy*] has been written in scandalous fashion. What is scandalous about it is that it is all rhetoric" (1985, 4). And my book?

29. I am thinking here of Lacan's demand/desire logic. Zizek explains: "The hysterical demand is 'I'm demanding this of you, but what I'm really demanding of you is to refute my demand because this is not it' " (1989, 111–12).

30. I discussed the *pagus* in relation to Kant and Lyotard. See Lyotard 1988a, 151.

31. Contrary to what G. Spivak says, Deleuze and Guattari do, in fact, have a theory of "interests/investment." See Spivak 1988, 273–75; and Deleuze and Guattari 1983,105, 116.

32. Let us not forget, however, that escape or "flight is [easily] challenged [by Capital] when it is . . . a movement of false liberty; . . . flight is affirmed when it is a stationary flight, a flight of intensity. [Escape or flight] is an "act of becoming" (Deleuze and Guattari 1986, 13; cf. 35, 71).

33. As a case in point, from Lyotard's historical viewpoint, when the *dispostifs* (or negative investments) take on "compromise-formations," they end not in social justice but in bureaucracies or centralisms. Later in *The Differend*, he makes this quiet clear: "To let the proletariat 'speak' is to endow it with a historical-political reality. Marx built the International Association of Working Men. He interprets the sign that is the enthusiasm aroused by the Commune as if it signaled the political project of the real class and as if it outlined the organization of a real party. [Then] the party assumes a monopoly over the procedures for establishing historical-political reality" (1988a, 172–73).

Chapter 2. Helen(ism)?

1. Again, to be sure, Plato and Aristotle are different, but I insist they are overly similar in their *use* of *diaeresis*. I do not see "Aristotle" or his modification of Platonic metaphysics as an acceptable compromise. (I place Aristotle in quotes because I wish to signify how he is generally read/interpreted by philosophers and by members of my field. I am against the Plato-Aristotle-Kant line (lineage) of thinking, which is always thinking by way of the negative.) The best discussion that I have found on species-genus analytics in Aristotle's *Poetics* is James Hutton's (1982) introduction.

2. In the *Panegyricus*, Isocrates invests an inordinate amount of time in discussing the myth of Demeter (as well as her daughter Korê [aka Persephone]) so as to purchase favor for Athens. (If Theseus was the founder of Athens, Demeter, the goddess of corn, is the sustainer of Athenian life.) Isocrates relates the myth of Demeter:

When Demeter came to our land, in her wandering after the rape of Korê, and, . . . gave these two gifts, the greatest in the world—the fruits of the earth, which have enabled us to rise above the life of the beasts, and the holy rite . . . —our city was not only so beloved of the gods but also so devoted to mankind that . . . she did not begrudge them to the rest of the world, but shared with all men what she had received. (1980, Vol 1: 135; or ll. 28–29)

Isocrates then continues by attempting to establish the grounds, or proof, for his genealogy, which traces and legitimizes Athens by having Demeter as its source of life. (As Page DuBois points out, Demeter is the goddess of production and reproduction. DuBois, though she does not explicitly reach my conclusion, nonetheless, can be extrapolated as saying that the land must be plowed, by way of mutual consent or by way of sexual violation, i.e., raped, in order to re/produce food. [See 1988, 49, 52–55, 59–61.]) Here then, in Isocrates's narrative-argument, we begin with Demeter, after the "rape" of her daughter. Demeter gives "two gifts" to human beings who will be the Athenians. In this narrative, which originates with rape—for Demeter would not be wandering unless her daughter had been raped—in this narrative, we have rape and gifts, both of which are ways of taking and taming women, both of which are means of exchange and communication. (I have in mind Mauss's [1967], Levi-Strauss's [1969], Bataille's [1962, 197–220], Rubin's [1975], and Irigaray's [1985b, 170–91] studies in the "trafficking in women.") The rape of Korê and the violation of the land, and then the gifts from Demeter in the form of corn, signify a sublimated, political economy—which I would say, then, makes up part of the narrative (exchange) logic of the founding and the legitimization of Athens. This political economy, however, continues, as Isocrates's narrative-argument takes on imperialist tones; for as Isocrates states, Athens "did not begrudge [the two gifts] to the rest of the world": "For most of the Hellenic cities, in memory of our ancient services, send us each year the first-fruits of the harvest, and those who neglect to do so have often been admonished by the Pythian priestess to pay us our due portion of their crops" (Isocrates, 1980, 137; or l. 31). Hence, we now move from rape and gifts to sharecropping.

But the development of this rape narrative still continues, which I take up in the monograph that I am presently writing, entitled *The History of Rhetoric, Canonicity, and Rape Narratives*.

3. In using the words gathering and laying and their German renderings, I am referring to Heidegger's lecture on Heraclitus's Fragment B50, on *Logos*. See Heidegger 1984, 59–78.

4. See Schiappa's "Gorgias's Helen Revisited" (1995a), which appeared as this book went to press.

5. For the concept of casuistic stretching, see Burke 1984, 229–32, 307.

6. I avoid the topic, for, though it is important to my discussion, it would require a lengthy discussion that would get me away from what, at this moment, is more important to me. I can say, however, that I generally disagree on what has been recently written on orality/literacy, say, the work of Ong (1982) or Swearingen (1991).

7. Isocrates's view of centralized education is far from Plato's; and, therefore, it can appear to many of us as an improvement. Earlier I argued similarly that Aristotle (good copy) looks better than Plato (bad copy). Often we are moved by what is the lesser of two evils.

8. I am well aware as I make these interpolations that most likely someone will bring a charge against me of being anachronistic. It is this very criticism, however, that has served as an alibi for our not thinking and saying what I eventually will say and at great length. If Poulakos is talking about consequences, so am I. Profound consequences! As I proceed with this discussion over the next two chapters, I will deal with this criticism.

9. Cf. Lyotard 1984b, 37. The allusion to E. M. Butler's book, *The Tyranny* (1958), can be misleading. I am suggesting here less a linear view, or a history of an idea (of education) as it progresses from Athens to Freiburg and more so a dominant will or force that has won out over other forces, or wills. In other words, I am thinking in Nietzschean terms.

10. Here, I refer to the classic three: Expressionism, cognitive psychologism, or social-epistemicism. See Berlin 1988.

11. As I have suggested already, my tactic is the same tactic as Kafka's. See Deleuze and Guattari's reading of K's tactic in the face (photo) of Oedipus/ Oedipalization (negation). They explain the strategy in terms of exaggeration, an exaggerated Oedipus. For a comic effect. Hence, I am using two tactics here: Burke's casuistic stretching and Kafka's exaggeration. And yet a third, metalepsis. My sense is that a thinker, such as myself, cannot rely on a single tactic, but several cum a radical multiplicity. Not a tactic, then, but tactics of intensities.

12. Isocrates's view, it should be understood, is not by any means unique; even today his view of *logos* is propounded by others and just as innocently. For example, Paulo Freire, in *The Pedagogy of the Oppressed*, writes of "the ontological vocation" (1987, 61), in other words, writes of the *logos* calling the oppressed to change the world and move toward freedom (see 12–13, 68). Isocrates had written similarly of the calling of the *logos*, which makes human beings human (i.e., Hellenic) and liberates them.

13. What I say here makes it sound as if Heraclitus, like Paul deMan, posits "negative knowledge," that is, *logos*[neg.]. I do not think that this is the case, but of course such a conclusion is contingent on whose interpretation one identifies with. Mine is Nietzsche's. (For deMan, see 1983, 75; for Heraclitus-Nietzsche, see Kofman 1987.)

14. My allusions here are, first, to K. Burke (1969a, 38–41) and to Nietzsche (1967).

15. I take this translation from Eugen Fink's "The oasis of happiness" (1968, 29). Besides this article, there is an excellent and extensive discussion of Fink's other thoughts on play in Krell (1972).

16. One of the few who have wrestled with this angel (devil [the laughter of the two]) is Milan Kundera throughout his fiction (especially, *The Book of Laughter and Forgetting* and *The Unbearable Lightness of Being*). Exclusion and/or all inclusion are both thematically balanced in Kundera. I agree with Rorty that it may only be possible to deal with this problem in the genre of the novel. (See my comment on this genre in my introduction.)

17. For an excellent discussion of various responses to and interpretations of Heraclitus, from Plato-Aristotle through Nietzsche-Heidegger, see Kofman 1987.

Chapter 3. Isocrates, the Paideia, and Imperialism

1. The projected title of that book is presently *Negation, Subjectivity, and Composition Studies*.

2. Concerning the opening quotes to this chapter, they also do and do not fit this discussion. But they—especially the latter—remind us that Nietzsche and Freud were teachers. Though I quote both Freud and Nietzsche, I have not forgotten Marx, whom I will reintroduce in the final excursus. There I will bring a Nietzschean Dionysus and a Freudian "libidinalization" to bear on Marx.

3. In general, master tropes are highly problematic, though perhaps inevitable; they tend to privilege one way of reading history at the expense of other ways. Burke selects irony as his master trope so as to insist on Nietzschean, multiple perspectives. (See Burke's 1969a, 503–17.)

4. I am indebted to Edward Schiappa for calling my attention to Mathieu's work.

5. Nietzsche has repeatedly warned his readers of the problems of German nationalism. (See, e.g., 1969, 319; 1974, 338–40; 1968b, 60–66.)

6. "counter-tradition"? To be sure, not counter in the sense of chronologically following, but in terms of privilege/supplement.

7. Nietzsche would have called it, the eternal return; Freud, the eternal return of the repressed; Marx, the eternal return of the oppressed.

8. This mentioning of Grammar Z is in reference to Donald Stewart having claimed that I write with Grammar B. (For Stewart's charge, see 1990, 174; for my response see, 1994a; 1994d.)

9. Yes, I would gossip! See Spivak 1987, 213.

10. Though I rely on Finley and Momigliano in my discussion of Jaeger, there are obviously others who level similar charges and put forth evidence of Jaeger's being an elitist and having flirted with fascism, etc. See for example the collection of articles entitled *Werner Jaeger Reconsidered: Proceedings of the Second Oldfather Conference.* . . . (Calder 1992), especially the articles by Chambers, Kahn, and White. The

latter points out that prior to leaving Hitler's Germany, Jaeger had direct connections and, it can be said, sympathized with the Nazis. This volume has numerous references to the discussions from 1930 to the present. In its introduction, Calder writes: "C. H. Kahn remarked at the end of the [Oldfather] conference 'I came admiring him [Jaeger]; I departed pitying him.' This was the feeling of most of us. Similar reactions were evoked at the Eduard Norden conference held in Bad Homburg in June 1991. The gulf between the ideals professed by Jaeger as the prophet of the Third Humanism and the petty compromises and betrayals that his *Sitz im Leben* elicited from him caused difficulties for some" (vii).

11. Jaeger, however, says: "It [*paideia*] was not a sum of several abstract ideas; it was Greek history itself, *in all its concrete reality.*" But then he alludes to the facts becoming abstract/conceptual: "the facts of Greek history would long ago have sunk into oblivion if the Greeks had not moulded them into a permanent form—the expression of their highest will, of their resistance to change and destiny" (xvi). And yet later he says: "Both [Greek and Roman] lives were based on the same principle, *an abstract timeless conception* of the mind as a realm of eternal truth and beauty. . ." (1965, xxv; my emphasis).

At this point in my discussion, I am reporting Finley's reading of Momigliano's reading of Jaeger. It is a convention in scholarly works to work with the primary source instead of hearsay. As far as I am concerned all history is hearsay. My reason for reading, at times, Finley's reports of Momigliano's attitudes concerning Jaeger is so that I might accentuate layers of historiographical views. While at times I read Finley's Momigliano, at other times I go directly to Momigliano.

12. Hence, again I examine layers of reports, in this case, my review of Finley's review of Momigliano's reviews.

13. Momigliano suggests that Italian historians, as well as other historians, must begin to employ and learn from other historiographical approaches, specifically sociological and anthropological; to learn, as Lévi-Strauss's learned, of the danger of using the ur-myth and of being ethnocentric (see Lévi-Strauss 1974. Cf. Derrida 1972).

14. See note 9.

15. The German word *Geschlecht* (variously translated as sex, race, species, genus, gender, stock, family, generation or genealogy, community) will play some importance in my discussion of Isocrates and (later) Heidegger. Derrida (1987) makes much of the word.

16. I have generally neglected the role of Hegel and Spirit (*Geist*) in this discussion. Cassirer (1966) has an excellent discussion of Hegel and his contribution to Prussian-German political destiny. E.g., Cassirer (273–74) quotes the following passage from *Philosophy of Right* (§ 340): "The world-spirit, in its onward march, hands over to each people the task of working out its own peculiar vocation. Thus in universal history each nation in turn is for that epoch (and it can make such an epoch only once) dominant. Against this absolute right to be the bearer of the present

stage of the development of the world-spirit, the spirits of the other nations are absolutely without right, and they, as well as those whose epochs are passed, count no longer in universal history." This, indeed, is a frighting statement, coming from such a philosopher. It is easy to see how Hegel could and did serve both the right and the left.

17. *Geschlecht*, as a dividing practice, has obvious political implications. The word *Geschlecht* is unstable, for when used in various contexts, it is hard to detect the difference that the word might have, as Derrida points out, in reference to "national and nationalism, that is, between the national and a biologicist and racist ideology" (1983, 165). Derrida quotes a letter written in 1945 by Heidegger, explaining that for him *Geschlecht* meant national, not nationalism (165). We will return to Heidegger view of blood and spirituality later when we examine his "Rector's Address."

18. The etymology of the word "banal" should be of special interest to us. It is of Germanic origin, signifying *summons to military service*.

19. Isocrates makes a similar claim in his work *Aeropagiticus* and offers solutions, to which we will eventually return; and of course Allan Bloom (*The Closing of the American Mind*, 1987) continues in this same tradition with his own solutions, to which there are no reasons at all for us to return.

20. For Isocrates the cause of decline was also a revolt against tradition, or elitism, in that there was far too much freedom in the new pure democracy, with elections by lot.

21. Another reason for Leavis's selecting Dante is that his is "a cultural order extremely different from that which has grown out of it" and "it would provide for the contemplation of the modern scene a measuring reference, . . a standing place, outside" (1943, 62).

22. Earlier and later, I mention Blake and others, who individually are social. Leavis's Blake is not my nor Georges Bataille's Blake who is under denegation.

23. I hesitate to call Finley a Marxist historian; for though many see him as a Marxist, there are many others, including Marxists, who consider him to be only a Liberal.

24. I will make a few gross distinctions: Aristotle is a philosopher—though, to be sure, unlike Plato. Aristotle in the works included in his organon, which of course does not include his *Rhetoric*, is closer, however, to Plato than he is to Isocrates. (But then, we must keep in mind that there is the scholarly view that Aristotle finally not only distanced himself from Platonic thought, but lost interest in metaphysics altogether.) Aristotle in his *Rhetoric* is closer to the Plato who wrote the *Phaedrus* and closer to Isocrates. Isocrates, however, most probably would find little value, if any, in the works of either the organon or metaphysical speculation.

For Isocrates, "Philosophy," in his special and exclusive sense, is "the power of conjecture," never certainty (*Antidosis* 1982, 271). Conjecture is realized through oratory/rhetoric—i.e., the "art" or "faculty" (*techné*) or the "power" (*dynamis*) of speaking well—which Aristotle also calls "power" and thoroughly gives an account of or systematizes (Bk. 1, Ch. 2). (The words *dynamis* and *techné* are interchangeable, but *techné* does *not* mean skill or technique in any modern, technological sense, but "knowledge" as the ability, faculty, or "power" again, to accomplish the embodiment of being in a work. Therefore, rhetoric/oratory is the power of bringing into being, into embodiment, the available means of persuasion.)

Isocrates, unlike Aristotle, does not give a systematic account of rhetoric. For Isocrates, speaking well can be accounted for—pure and simple—by, first, natural ability, second, practical experience, and last, formal training. Isocrates tells us: "Formal training makes . . . men more skillful and more resourceful in discovering the possibilities of a subject. . . . But it cannot fully fashion men who are without natural aptitude into good debaters or writers. . ." (*Against the Sophists* 1982, 15; cf. *Antidosis* 186–92).

In respect to Plato, Isocrates's redefinition of oratory/rhetoric as "philosophy" creates possibilities of political dissolution, which are possibilities that Plato continually warned of and perhaps eventually himself was disillusioned by. (I am thinking of Plato's intervention into Sicilian politics and his subsequent commentaries in the *Seventh* and *Eighth Letters*, which indicate his own disillusionment [see Finley 74–87, 1977; Voegelin 1966, 14–23]). But it is important to emphasize that, for Isocrates, Plato's view of philosophy, with its aspirations to *epistemic* knowledge, most assuredly *does* lead to dissolution. Such an aspiration would make man into God, which would more often than not give man the opposite, a demagogue or evil genus. It is true, for Isocrates, that men are above the beasts, because men have *logos*, which speaks through them, but it is equally true, for Isocrates, that men are not divine.

25. Finley does not directly refer to this work, but he does write out of it when he assigns the concept of "citizen élite" to Isocrates, which is a concept that progressively gets more concrete and narrow in Isocrates' work as he moves from *Panegyricus* through *Areopagiticus* and then finally to the oration *To Philip* and the letters to Philip.

26. Cf. Richard Rodriquez's autobiography, *Hunger of Memory* (1982). Every page illustrates the differences between education/pedagogy, learned/taught, *scholé/* school, inside elite/outside Other.

Chapter 4. Isocrates, the *Logos*, and Heidegger

1. Richard Wolin (1990, 87) writes: "According to Jaspers, Heidegger viewed National Socialism as standing in an essential relation to Being. And thus, he believed it should be his responsibility to 'lead the leader' . . . in the manner of a contemporary philosopher-king."

2. For Nietzsche's discussion on decadence, see *The Twilight of the Idols* (1968b, 29–34). I have chosen the word "decadence" because of its *paradoxical* meaning, its

reversal (or negative deconstruction) in Nietzsche's interpretation of Socrates. Nietzsche writes:

> I have intimated the way in which Socrates exercised fascination: he seemed to be a physician, a saviour. Is it necessary to go on to point out the error which lay in his faith in "rationality as any cost"?—It is self-deception on the part of philosophers and moralists to imagine that by making war on *décadence* they therewith elude *décadence* themselves. This is beyond their powers: what they select as an expedient, as a deliverance, is itself only another expression of *décadence*—they *alter* its expression, they do not abolish the thing itself (33–34; Nietzsche's emphasis).

3. E.g., the U.S. giving to India or Africa without expecting some political favor in return. For if we give and expect something in return, we create the conditions for potlatch and, hence, resentment and revenge and the terrible cycle of violence.

4. The allusion is to the tight rope walker in *Thus Spake*: "Man is a rope, tied between beast and overman—a rope over an abyss. A dangerous cross, a dangerous on-the-way, a dangerous looking-back, and dangerous shuddering and stopping" (Nietzsche 1968a, 126).

5. The combination of the two words (wild and savage, or a savage practice) has many sources. See Louis Althusser's "wild/savage practice" (*"une pratique sauvage"*), which in turn is a borrowing from and commentary on Lenin's "wild answer," or response, to the "dividing practice" between Hegelian Idealism *and* Marxist materialism, between ideology *and* science. Althusser further characterizes: "A wild practice [is to be taken] in the sense in which Freud spoke of a wild analysis [see *SE* 1955, 11: 221–27], one which does not provide the theoretical credentials for its operations and which raises screams from the philosophy of 'interpretation' of the world, which might be called the philosophy of *denegation* [this term is translated as "denegation," but it is here simply "negation"]. A wild practice, if you will, but what did not begin by being wild?" (1971, 66).

6. Zizek (1984, 174) writes: "It is not only Stalinism which is a linguistic phenomenon, but language itself which is a Stalinist phenomenon."

7. I have in mind here two kinds of philologies/linguistics/pragmatics. See, e.g., Deleuze and Guattari 1987, 75–110; Lecercle 1985, ch. 2.

8. Wolin (1990) makes a case for thinking analogically. He writes: "If one were to pursue the parallels Heidegger is seeking to draw concerning Fifth century Athens and the Germany of his day, Athens would become Berlin, Heraclitus Heidegger himself, and Pericles . . . Hitler!" (188, n. 53).

9. I do not wish to suggest, however, that Derrida is the only one who has dealt with the problem of misappropriation of texts. Wolin (1990, 186, n. 37) focuses briefly on this problem—in relation to Heidegger, Nietzsche, and Marx—by referring to Max Weber's *The Protestant Ethic and the Spirit of Capitalism* (1958), in which the sociologist discusses his concept of "unintended consequences" (181). Somewhat

similar to, but different from, Weber's thought is Kenneth Burke's "casuistic stretching" (1984, 229–232) and Edward Said's "traveling theory" (1983, 226–47).

10. I do not believe in this Santayanian doctrine that we must remember/know the past so that we will possibly not repeat our (its) mistakes. The assumptions behind this doctrine are immense and based on a view of subjectivity that I do not agree with. See Vitanza 1993, 205–06.

11. Similarly, though not speaking of ears, Herman Melville in *Moby-Dick* says that human beings are to model themselves after the whale, whose two eyes are never one in vision. I cannot help but recall that in the novel there are two Whales attached to the right and left of the *Pequod*: One whale, we are told, is called Locke; the other, Kant. If one is cut, the ship will capsize, lose equilibrium. Hence, in Melville's view it is necessary to keep both.

12. For an explanation of Nyanza, see the introduction, note 40.

13. I discussed Nietzsche, Freud, and Marx in chapter one under Ricoeur's rubric of the "hermeneuts of suspicion" (see 1978). I will discuss them again later in final (beginning?) excurses, though in different terms.

14. The only other contemporary historian who has attempted *a metaleptic reading* of the history of rhetoric—as I read this historian, for he does not consciously acknowledge such a reading—is William Covino, in his *Art of Wondering* (1988). What Covino has to say in chapter one about Plato, Aristotle, and Cicero makes little sense, given the canonical way of reading The History, *unless* the reader realizes that it is Montaigne and DeQuincey—their views of language and writing as set forth in chapters two and three—that make possible Covino's "strange" readings of Plato, Aristotle, and Cicero possible. (I applaud Covino, or perhaps this *my reading* of Covino's history.)

15. See respectively Vitanza 1987b, 1990, 1994b; cf. Jameson 1981, 9. And Vitanza 1987a, 51–61; 1993).

16. For *kairos*, see Kinneavy 1986. For Heidegger's view of *kairos*, see Gillespie 1984; B. Miller 1987. I see Nietzsche's will to power in terms of *kairos* and will elaborate on this connection in chapters 6–7.

17. But let us not confuse this map for the territory! I cannot help but be contra-*logos* here, for though I give, let's say, a map, I would write via Deleuze and Guattari's notion of *haecceity* (1987, 261–65, 296–97).

18. I am thinking of the allegory of the cave (*Republic*, bk. 7), in which those in the cave are away from the awfulness of the sun. (See Land 1992, 27.) I am also thinking of the Enlightenment, with its false promise of light.

19. That is, the Others. See Lyotard 1990.

20. This Platonic view of *logos*/reason and its complementary view of the State culminates, as discussed already by Finley, in a rigid view of education, separating

the people into three exclusionary, static categories [1975, 197]. Moreover, as Ijsseling points out, this latter view of *logos* as *episteme* culminates in the Judeo-Christian view of the divine word, or in Hegel's phenomenology of spirit and science of logic—both of which are visions of the end of history.

One misunderstanding that Ijsseling passes on, however, is that Heidegger blamed or held Plato, or even others, responsible for the shift to *logos* as Pure Reason. According to Heidegger it is not any human being who caused (or causes) such a shift, but Being itself rather mysteriously removes itself from human experience and moves into unconcealment; in other words, Being withdraws as a question and presents itself as answers, the kinds of dogmatic answers offered by Parmenides, some of the Sophists, and Plato (see Gillespie 1984, 143).

21. I am well aware that there are contrary readings of Plato's intent. I am responding to the traditional readings. There is no "Plato," only Platonism(s).

22. Ijsseling gives his own account of Cl. Ramnoux's *Pre-Socratics Studies*, in which she discusses three grand narratives, or *logoi*—distinctly, the *logos* of man, of the gods, and of the world (1976, 21–22). Plato resisted these *logoi*/stories, which he saw as "myth," or false words, though as any reader knows Plato, nonetheless, employed poetry, stories, myths in the dialogues as a means of explanation.

23. There are several poetic passages from Heidegger that further describe and lament this *separation*. (Which, as a separation, is an attempt to answer, *in a permanent decision*, the question of Being and of Man.) Heidegger writes: "Because being and appearance belong together and, belonging together, are always side by side, the one changing unceasingly into the other; because in this change they present the possibility of error and confusion, the main effort of thought at the beginning of philosophy, i.e., in the first disclosure of the being of the essent, was necessarily *to rescue being from its plight of being submerged in appearance to differentiate being from appearance*. This in turn made it necessary *to secure the priority of truth as unconcealment over concealment*, of discovery over occultation and distortion. But as it became necessary to differentiate being from the other and to consolidate it as *physis*, being was differentiated from nonbeing, while nonbeing was differentiated from appearance. The two differentiations do not coincide" (1959, 109–10; my emphasis).

24. Another typical comparison, in relation to the concept of *control*, is the binary (machine) of *physis/techné*, with *physis* being the secrets of nature, or the feminine, and *techné* as these secrets, or knowledge, having been methodized/controlled, or made into the masculine. (See Jardine 1985, 72–73; Heidegger 1959, 16.) Whereas Jardine and Heidegger overlap in their view of *physis/techné*, they do in one dramatic way differ on whether to interpret *techné* in the modern sense as "technique." Jardine favors such an interpretation.

25. Yes, Heidegger places some of the Sophists with Plato and Aristotle. Heidegger has Antiphon in mind. (See Heidegger 1959, 106; Gillespie 1984, 141, 142, 167.)

26. A caveat: This is Heidegger's view of *kairos*, or moment of vision, and not Nietzsche's view, which had no place for revelation as such. (See Gillespie 1984, 149–64.)

27. Here, I begin to slant my exposition of and narrative on Heidegger to suggest that his error in politics—the association with the Nationalist Socialist party—springs from basic tendencies in his thinking. These tendencies culminate, in my presentation, in "The Rector's Address." (I am attempting to establish a parallel between Isocrates's nationalistic-imperialistic thinking and Heidegger's.)

28. I am well aware that Heidegger would see this distinction as problematic. See 1959, 126.

29. See Heidegger and Fink, *Heraclitus Seminar* 3–14; Heidegger 1984, 59–78. Concerning the word *polemos*, see Heidegger's "The Rectorate 1933/34" 1985b, 488–89, to which I will return.

30. To be sure, Kenneth Burke has attempted to speak of this problem and its potential virtuosity. See his *Grammar of Motives* (1969a).

31. My allusion here is to MacIntyre's *After Virtue* (1984). The reader, of course, should consider Stout's *Ethics After Babel* (1988). Of special interest is Bernstein's discussion of Heidegger and his (apparent) lack of concern for ethics (1992, 79–141).

32. I casuistically stretch my point here. I am well aware, as I will mention later, that the pre-ontological, though nothing for Heidegger, is not the negative.

33. Isocrates speaks similarly of the origin of the *polis* (specifically Athens); he speaks similarly in mythic terms, without deliberation but in *polemos* (a rape and wars [see *Panegyricus* 1980, 28ff]). Isocrates goes back to the legend of the *wanderings of Demeter* who "came [he says] to our land, in her wandering after the rape of Korê, and, being moved to kindness towards our ancestors by services which may not be told save to her initiates, gave these two gifts . . . the fruits of the earth [and] and the holy rite. . . . [O]ur city was not only so beloved of the gods but also so devoted to mankind that . . . she did not begrudge them to the rest of the world, but shared with all men what she had received." The myth/story continues with Athens as the original city (33), forming alliances with other Hellenes so as to lead them in the fight against the barbarians and so as to claim territory and to colonize (34–37), but most importantly "to lay down laws and establish a polity" (40) The parallel between Heidegger's nomads and Demeter as wanderer is close enough for us to see, initially here anyway, both stories/myths of origins as attempts to establish a philosophy of history-telling/writing that will establish one's own country as not only superior to others but also as having a benevolent mission to civilize the barbarians or the rest of the world, bring culture to them all. (This connection between Isocrates-Heidegger will become more clear, especially as we come to Heidegger's "Rector's Address." What might help us now to make the connection is both Jaeger's and Heidegger's claim, which is not unusual for a German scholar to make, that there is an intimate bond between Greece and Germany, between their languages and mission. It is a claim

of "intellectual nationalism," if I may borrow a phrase from Jaeger himself (79), which sadly does become, in addition, "racial nationalism" for Heidegger, which is a significant departure from Isocrates. [See above, Finley's and Momigliano's critique of Jaeger; and Heidegger in 1959, 37–39; 57.]

Jaeger, however, has a relevant critique of this Isocratean attempt at Origins, a critique that will allow us to begin to understand further *the Isocrates-Heidegger connection*. Jaeger writes:

> [T]his journeying back into a legendary past allowed Isocrates to trace the origins of all culture to the soil of Attica, where . . . it was later to reach the highest stage of its development and spiritual power in the form of paideia. Every national and cultural myth is created in the same way—by narrowing the field of vision and extolling one particular nation's achievements to the pinnacle of the absolute. It can quite well be combined with full knowledge of foreign nations and foreign cultures—it would be a mistake to think that Isocrates knew nothing of Egypt, Phoenicia, or Babylon. It is his faith in the unique mission of Athenian culture that is triumphant in his philosophy of history, and above all in his interpretation of the legendary past. Isocrates' nationalistic ideology (in which Athens is the founder of all civilization), along with all the other ideas implicit in his paideia, was later taken over by humanism [and Heidegger, a non-humanist] as part of its general view of history. (1986b, 77)

34. Derrida takes a different slant on Heidegger (1993) in respect to struggle (*polemos*).

35. As I have repeatedly stated, the style of this discussion of Isocrates and Heidegger is metaleptic and, no doubt, difficult to follow. It can be no other way and still get at what desires to be said and heard here. Have I yet said that I have had to reinvent the style of historiography as hysteriography because it had no style? One mis/manifestation of this my reinvented style is what I have called here, therefore, the "tactic of the uncanny," which I have intermittently employed throughout and will more so continue to employ well through the final (beginning?) excursis. It cannot but be other/wise. (See Hertz 1985, 97–121).

36. I take this description from Gillespie 1984, 173–74.

37. In this way, his view is comparable to Nietzsche's *amor fati*. See e.g., *The Gay Science* 1974, 223, No. 276; *Ecce Homo* 1969, 258, Sec. 2, No. 10. Also, see Heidegger's lecture "Moira" in 1984.

Chapter 5. Heidegger, *Wesen*, and "The Rector's Address"

1. For the most part Heidegger remained in silence. However, of special interest to the reader is Heidegger's interview with *Der Spiegel* (1990).

2. See work, e.g., already done by Sheehan (1988, 1993); Farias (1989); Ferry and Renaut (1990); Zimmerman (1990); Wolin (1990); Derrida (1989); Lacoue-Labarthe (1989); Neske and Kettering (1990); Gadamar et. al (*Critical Inquiry* 15.2 [Winter 1989]), Lyotard (1990).

3. When I make this statement, I have Foucault's preface to *Anti-Oedipus* (1983) in mind.

4. In my reading of the address, I am indebted to Charles Scott (1990) especially and to Wolin (1990).

5. I am referring here to Isocrates's hymn to *logos* in *Nicocles* (1980, 79, line 6). The word *eggenomenou* is translated as "implanted," but could be translated as "to be born with."

6. I am relying here, in part, on Norlin's discussion of Isocrates. Norlin's treatment of Isocrates is less hyperbolic than mine. See Norlin's introduction to Isocrates 1980, xxxii–xlvi. In the light of my discussion, it is important also to keep in mind Isocrates's *Nicocles or the Cyprians*, in which he argues "one man rule is more efficient" (1980, 89). As is well known, Isocrates steadily grew against full democracy, and moved to favor a limited one.

7. Further explaining this passage, Wolin argues that it is double-edged: While "it eliminates a liberal democratic interpretation of the university's independence," it also "claims authority for the university by appeal to *its* essence, not to a state authority" (1990, 150; Wolin's emphasis). This argument supports Heidegger's later explanation that he was attempting to outmaneuver the National Socialist Party in an attempt to win over autonomy for the university and its faculty and students (see 1985, 483–84)

8. I am referring to the first German edition of the first volume of the *Paideia* trilogy, which I discussed earlier in this chapter.

9. This view of aesthetics, or what de Man calls "aesthetic ideology," can be extremely dangerous, leading to totalities, or totalitarianism. See de Man 1984, 263–90; Norris 1988.

10. Derrida (1993) has written of Heidegger's musings on ears.

11. The reference here to Skinner is more fully discussed in chapter 1. (There I take the reference from Rorty 1984.) To be sure, there is always a surplus of possible meanings in what we say. However, it must be understood and granted that if a thinker has such a surplus (with all kinds of hidden, latent agendas) so does the refuter or audience. Ideology always already precedes thinking and counterthinking.

12. My allusion here is to *repetition* as discussed in *Being and Time* (1962, 436–39) and in "The Rector's Address": Specifically in the latter as "But doesn't this beginning [i.e., Greek science, knowledge, which was not realized] by now lie two and a half millennia behind us? . . . But this does not mean that the beginning has been overcome, let alone brought to nought. . . . The beginning has invaded our

future. There it awaits us, a distant command bidding us catch up with its great-ness" (1985b, 473). Here, Heidegger is working with the future anterior. Which must be redone (or undone, as in dispersion) so that it no longer suffers from nostalgia, homesickness, for *Heim* (home), or unity, which, indeed, Heidegger suffers from. I attempt such an *undoing* in chapter eight.

13. In *Being and Time*, Heidegger writes: *"Keeping silent* is another essential possibility of discourse, and it has the same existential foundation. In talking with one another, the person who keeps silent can 'make one understand' . . . and he can do so more authentically than the person who is never short of words. . . . Keeping silent authentically is possible only in genuine discoursing. To be able to keep silent, Dasein must have something to say—that is, it must have at its disposal an authen-tic and rich disclosedness of itself" (1962, 208; Heidegger's emphasis).

14. I am not going to continue with Heidegger's defense of his address, but the reader is encouraged to read both the address and the defense in their entirety. And to also see Farias, chs. 8–14.

15. I am alluding to Heidegger's view of *Dasein* (Being-there) and its *negative* possibilities of revealing the truth. (See Heidegger 1962, 183; 1977, 196.)

Not only Heidegger but also Paulo Freire (1970, 12, 61) speak favorably of the "ontological vocation" that will finally free human beings.

16. And Derrida and Spivak, as they perform affirmative deconstructions.

17. Heidegger in his "Letter on Humanism" modifies these earlier statements concerning Greece, Germany, and nationalism (see 1977, 218–19).

Excursus. A Feminist Sophistic?

1. Here, I leave Poulakos and discuss Schiappa in passing and Jarratt more competely because of my discussions of and references to Poulakos in the previous four chapters. To my knowledge, Jarratt has not in print distinguished her position from Schiappa's.

2. My first reading may be typical of a larger group of readers; for a number of people, both male and female, reported to me that they similarly read Jarratt as an essentialist, by which they meant a naive essentialist. What at first proved to be the big stumbling block among readers, however, was, more so, the analogy between the Sophists and feminists (see Poulakos and Whitson). Not until readers get over their hangups with analogies will this analogy be read with some sympathy; what has to be seen, I think, is that Jarratt is very careful to use analogy *as a heuristic* that will allow her—and consequently, her readers—to explore "the possibility" of the relationship between the two culturally excluded groups (see *Rereading*, 63).

3. Unfortunately, the term "liberal" has negative connotations. My sense is that all of us—even those of us who would be against what goes for liberalism—are

liberals. Similarly, though various of us are against modernism or postmodernism, we nonetheless are both simultaneously.

4. Jarratt's identifying herself with this group of theorists/pedagogues is especially curious. Why would she select a group of men instead of the numerous examples of feminists developing new pedagogies? And why would she align herself so forthrightly with a continuation of late Frankfurt school thinking!

5. There is a growing body of literature by men and women concerning Nietzsche as establishing the conditions for feminist theory. See, e.g., Graybeal; Patton; Burgard.

6. The text in question is from *Spurs*, in which Derrida writes about Nietzsche's understanding of woman: "There is no such thing as the truth of woman, but it is because of that abyssal divergence of the truth, because that untruth is <<truth>>. Woman is but one name for the untruth of truth" [51].

I find this particular interpretation of "Woman" as unacceptable, perhaps not for the same reasons as Jarratt, but because it is one more example of the master *topos, out of the impossible* [the negative] *comes the possible*. This *topos is* the problem! This is, indeed, a *topos* to be found in Nietzsche, but it is one that he goes on to revalue in non-negative terms, and which his readers such as Deleuze and Guattari have denegated. My sense, here, is that Nietzsche is the messenger bringing bad news of the event of Nihilism; Nietzsche, however, goes on to attempt to revalue the sad condition that we human, all too human species find ourselves in.

Nietzsche opens the preface to *Beyond Good and Evil* with "Supposing truth is a woman—what then? Are there not grounds for the suspicion that all philosophers, insofar as they were dogmatists, have been very inexpert about women?"

Cixous speaks of another passage in Nietzsche that she objects to. In "The Laugh," she writes: "Woman is obviously not that woman Nietzsche dreamed of who gives only in order to. Who could ever think of the gift as a gift-that-takes?" (259). My response is that Nietzsche is not dreaming of any dream woman, but of woman as reactionary, just as man is reactionary. He finds in certain women, women who would be men, instead of dis/engaging in becoming-woman, just as men have to dis/engage in becoming-minoritarian, all of us have to dis/engage in. . . .

7. Jarratt does not mention Judith Butler and Dona Haraway, who are major exceptions.

8. Qtd. from Morot-Sir's translation of "Les fins de l'homme"; see in Spivak 1983, n13, 193; cf. Bass's translation, Derrida 1982.

9. Spivak writes: "Women armed with deconstruction must beware of becoming Athenas, uncontaminated by the womb, sprung in armor from Father's forehead, ruling against Clytemnestra by privileging marriage, the Law that appropriates the woman's body over the claims of that body as Law" (1983, 174).

10. This statement was made in 1988, published in 1990. See Spivak 1990, 133, 137.

11. I am forced to make such a 'provisionary' statement, of course, because of the conditions of strategic feminism and strategic masculinism. Such a position is analogous with the arguments about sovereign nations. It is, indeed, the thinking of the political. And yet our sense of ethics/morality, etc., call on us to intervene in the name of humanity when something goes wrong within a so-called soverign entity. This is the condition of the negative: congreation purchased by way of segreatation, which then reestablishes the conditions for intervention.

12. It is important to understand, however, that I take this advice only provisionally at this point in my discussion, for later I will trek more so with Cixous's advice, which is quite different.

13. To this point, I will eventually return and offer an explanation for why Spivak does not think there is a possibility outside of the narrative of violence.

14. It is not clear as to whether narrative means all narrative, or the narrative of the history of philosophy (thinking). See Cummings (1991) who suggests that tightly woven narratives are violent towards woman; also see Mulvey (1985).

15. Braidotti (1991) has written against "the becoming-woman of philosophy," specifically, against Derrida's *Spurs* and similar writings of others. Her discussion pales in comparison to Spivak's.

16. Spivak is very open about having learned from both Paul de Man and from Derrida; and she, when calling on them, does not reverse or lower them to the supplementary position of less than herself (see 1990, 107–08).

17. The best source for an exposition of such strategies is, I think, still Derrida's own description of them—which he calls, as I have said, a *"relever"* or a "double gesture"—in the interview in *Positions* (1981c, esp. 37–96; also, see Krupnick 1983, 10–15). The particular interview of the book's title, "Positions," was conducted, in part, by Jean-Louis Houdebine, a Marxist, who keeps urging Derrida in various followup questions to say that *différance* is really another word for contradiction. As Krupnick points out, "although Derrida insists on the subversiveness of his method, he spends most of the interview distinguishing his 'positions' from the 'position' (dialectical materialism) of the single-minded interviewer" (13). Herein lies the différance between a wedding between deconstruction and Marxism and an orthodox Marxism.

18. Derrida himself often substitutes the words "spur" or *"différance"* for whatever term is privileged such as "man." See Derrida's playful title and discussion of "The Ends of Man" in *Margins* (1982).

19. E.g., having already destroyed the name of "man" in the article "The Ends of Man," Derrida turns in a punning (double gesture) on the word "eve" to both the eve-ning of man, his decline, and to the eve (Eve replacing Adam) of "the day that is coming." Derrida asks, "Is there an economy of the eve? Perhaps we are between these two eves, which are also two ends of man. But who, we?" (1982, 136). As I read this passage, Derrida not only problematizes man but also woman (eve) when he asks

the question of the economy of eve. But then, it is not necessary for Derrida to problematize both, for they are already made problematic by Nietzsche, as Derrida acknowledges and explores later in *Spurs*. (The first was originally published in 1972; the latter in 1978.)

20. Nietzsche's reasoning is rather simple: Men think that they have the Truth but it is not in Woman; then, when they discover that they do not have the Truth, that it is the History of an Error, truth becomes a woman, un/namely, that which is Untruth; and yet, "woman" is only one name for Untruth. Man is untruth, woman is untruth, *différance* is untruth, power is untruth, etc. There is no proper name for Truth. It does not exi(s)t!

21. Which is again curious, for to be substantial is to be under negation (see K. Burke 1969a). Truth, even strategic truth or politics, is always under the sign of untruth, only masquerading as Truth, strategic or otherwise. Strategic masquerading? What's the difference?

22. Towards the end of her discussion, Spivak is very careful to insist that it is better in the long run *to lose* altogether the concept metaphor "woman," for it will discover itself inevitably "open to traditional masculism" (1989a, 217). One way that feminists can be open to traditional masculism is to aspire to justice in the name of "woman" when not being aware that such justice can be only an alibi to punish. Spivak's explanation of this point is rather lengthy. She writes:

> . . . we have to bring our understanding of the relationship between the name 'woman' and deconstruction into crisis. If we do not take the time to understand this in our zeal to be "political," then I fear we act out the kind of play that Nietzsche figured out in *The Genealogy of Morals*: in the interest of giving an alibi to his desire to punish, which is written into his way of being, in other words in the interest of a survival game, man produces an alibi which is called justice. And in the interest of that alibi, man has to define and articulate, over and over again, the name of man. It seems to me that if *we* forget that *we* cannot have a deconstructive feminism which decides to transform the usefulness of the name "woman," itself based on a certain kind of historical anxiety for the graphematic structure, into a narrative, and thus take up arms against what we sometimes call essentialism, *then* we might be acting out this particular scenario, adequately contradicting and thus legitimizing it—by devising newer names of woman—in the interest of giving the desire to punish the alibi of justice. (217–18)

23. A reader of Spivak's may complain that this is all too philosophical; Spivak is well aware, at least, twice in her discussion of being too "ethereal." And yet, states that even the other in her own way understand what she means and would not complain (1989a, 215, 218). Spivak's understanding of preconditions as inevitable reminds me of K. Burke's acceptance of these conditions as well. See 1969a, 21–58.

24. I am well aware of the articles against Derrida and McDonald's "Choreographies" (of more than two sexes). They are gathered in defense of only two sexes

by N.K. Miller (78–90). But I am also well aware of Butler's and Haraway's work. And of Cixous's work, which I will get to here.

25. The source, among others, is Derrida's "The Ends of Man" (1982, 135) and 1985a.

26. See Feyerabend (1978); Rorty (1989).

27. I am alluding to Derrida's "A Number of Yes."

28. Jarratt's linking of Nietzsche and Darwin is innovative to say the least. As far as Nietzsche is concerned, he does not want to be interpreted as a Darwinist, or evolutionist. See 1968c, 361–66, or nos. 684–687. Also, see Kaufmann 1974. And yet, I admit to the possibilities of casuistic stretching!

29. I.e., published after Jarratt's book.

30. This is a highly questionable point made by Jarratt, for Cixous is quite explicitly against culture-*nomos* (see 1993a, 128–31). Cixous does not favor either a negated nature nor a necessarily negated *nomos*, but a denegated nature. Whereas Jarratt continues to work in binaries, Cixous does not. Cixous does not find liberation of the species by way of culture but by way of an Ovidian free-flowing nature. I will return to this point later.

31. There are women who are under the sign of the phallus or who are phallus-mothers (see Cixous 1981, 262–63); and there are women who are not in the feminine at all (see 1993a, 113).

32. Cixous writes: "I make a point of using the *qualifiers* of sexual difference here [i.e., masculine and feminine] to avoid the confusion man/masculine, woman/feminine: for there are some men who do not repress their femininity, some women who, more or less strongly, inscribe their masculinity" (Cixous and Clément 1986, 81; Cixous's emphasis).

Conley also argues: "The term 'woman' is not a natural term. It is a 'trap-word.' Men and women have been caught in a historical configuration in a theatre of representation. A word is never neutral just as the body is never natural but is always socially ciphered. Therefore, strictly speaking, there can be no essentialism. But the question is slippery. The attributes 'masculine' and 'feminine' do not refer to men and women. Nouns solidify. They become objects to be studied. Although still used for historical reasons, 'masculine' and 'feminine' will hopefully, she argues, be replaced soon by others, by colour adjectives" (1992, 40). Also, see Shiach 1991, 17–20. Also see Cixous 1991, 148–50.

33. Concerning the question of whether or not men are excluded automatically and women are included automatically: In *Three Steps*, Cixous speaks of birds as being associated with "woman"; birds represent the waste, abomination, the forbidden. She writes: "Those who belongs to the birds and their kind (these may include some men), to writings and their kind: they are all to be found—and a fair company it is—outside; in a place that is called by Those Bible [the book of thou shalt nots], those who are the Bible, abominable. Elsewhere, outside, birds, women, and writing gather. *Not all*

women however; quite a number of this kind linger inside, as we realize daily, and identify with 'those-He-Bible' and their kind. Outside we shall find *all* those precious people who have not worried about respecting the law that separates what is and is not abominable according to Those Bible" (1993a, 113).

34. As Cixous says: "Difference would be a bunch of new differences" (Cixous and Clément 1986, 83).

35. A Nietzschean concept, becoming-woman, is discussed at length by Deleuze and Guattari *A Thousand Plateaus* (1987, 232–309), whose writings Cixous is familiar with.

36. Like Bataille and influenced by Bataille's discussion of the gift and exchange and the necessity for a general economy with expenditure and waste, Cixous writes: "Every woman has known the torture of beginning to speak aloud, heart beating as if to break, occasionally falling into loss of language, ground and language slipping out from under her. . . . The logic of communication requires an economy both of signs—of signifiers—and of subjectivity. The orator is asked to unwind a thin thread, dry and taut. We like uneasiness, questioning. There is waste in what we say. We need that waste. To write is always to make allowances for superabundance and uselessness while slashing the exchange value that keeps the spoken word on its track. That is why writing is good, letting the tongue try itself out—as one attempts a caress, taking the time a phrase or a thought needs to make oneself loved, to make oneself reverberate" (Cixous and Clement 1986, 92–93). See Conley 1992, 32–33; 38–39; Shiach 1991, 21–22, 81–82.

37. Actually, this should read "I owe my life to Lynn Worsham, who introduced me to Cixous many years ago."

38. To write the *imund* would be to return all that which is unfit back into The History. I will practice Spivak's suggested rage and Cixous's writing the *imund*, but mostly the latter. This will become clear as we continue.

39. See 1993a, 113.

40. The parallels between Deleuze and Cixous are numerous. Their common indebtedness to Nietzsche perhaps binds them. In *"Coming to Writing"*, she writes: "Aren't you the very demon of multiplicity? All the people I caught myself being instead of me, my un-nameables, my monsters, my hybrids, I exhorted them in silence" (1991, 29).

On the question of thousands, there can always be raised the problem of the ineffectualness of a splintered subject. See, e.g., Jardine 1985, ch. 10; also, Grosz 1993b, who claims to be very critical of Deleuze and Guattari's *Anti-Oedipus* (1983) and its sequel. I say *claims*, because I suspect strongly, given what and how Grosz says it, that she is still enamored with Deleuze and Guattari's project. The first part of her article is an attack on them, the second part is an exposition of their basic ideas in *A Thousand Plateaus* (1987), the final part is a provisional acceptance. Curiously enough, Grosz says some rather unqualified positive things about Deleuze and Guattari in her article "Nietzsche and the stomach for knowledge" (1993a, 69n1).

Along the same lines, Braidotti opens her *Patterns of Dissonance* (1991), saying a few positive things about Deleuze in regards to his refusal to accept a negative ontology (the void), but quickly then she disagrees with him because of his concept of "becoming woman" and becoming minoritarian. Whereas at first she accepts a denegated nature (*physis*), she later "strategically" (?) falls back into negating women. Her arguments against Deleuze are typical and perhaps establish a "strategic" (?) *differend*.

41. Cixous herself refers to her notion of libidinalized economy/education. See 1991, 148–49; 1993a, 120–21. Also, see Irigaray 1985a.

42. In relation to this discussion of *dépays* (uncountry), recall Lyotard's *pagus* (*country* that is an uncountry of experimental linkage [see 1988a, 151]). As Cixous continues her discussion, she begins to sound more and more like Deleuze and Guattari and they, like her. They all mirror each other. She begins to talk about becoming-dog, about the author's sex, about the text's sex.

43. Her characters? Dora, Pierre Goldman, the Mandelas, the victims at Hiroshima, the victims of Central and South America, of Vietnam and Cambodia, etc. Pierre Goldman, alleged murderer, in France in the mid-1970s, is championed by Cixous. See her *Un k. incompréhensible: Pierre Goldman* (1975). Also see Conley 1992, 46–48.

44. One way of summing up this difference is to say that while Cixous is for establishing a general-libidinal-economy, Spivak is more so, as long as she hands on to her political position as limited, a restricted economy.

45. It is rather clear, after my reading *The Post-Colonial Critic* (1990), that the last thing in the world that Spivak wants are disciples. But she, too, cannot help but inadvertently produce them.

46. But there is another danger in terms of this dividing practice, and that is the apparent impossibility of "legitimately" constructing one. Here is how I see the problem: Given Nietzsche/Derrida's and Spivak/Cixous's post-philosophical, post-humanist views, there appears to be no way to say, here is *woman-as-real*, so as to distinguish "her" from woman-as-concept-metaphor (along with "*différance*," "writing," "power," etc.). For even those of us who understand and theoretically inhabit this post-philosophical, post-humanist space, it is difficult. To complicate matters, there is very much the need, nonetheless, to think such a strategic space in terms of the *real*. As Spivak says nostalgically-ambivalently-ambiguously, "Incanting to ourselves all the perils of transforming a 'name' to a referent—making a catechism, in other words, of catechresis—let us none the less name (as) 'woman' that disenfranchised woman whom we strictly, historically, geo-politically *cannot imagine*, as literal referent" (1989a, 220). This "woman," however, is the "gendered subaltern" (220, 218), not a "high feminist," not white females who are concerned for the most part with tenure in the university or equity of numbers at conferences, but the subaltern, post-colonial woman, whom we-academic-wo/men cannot imagine except as a new orientalism (see 1990, 117–19). Spivak continues: "Let us *divide* the name of woman so that we see ourselves as naming, not merely named" (1989a, 220; emphasis mine).

47. This distinction between social- and desiring-production is one made by Deleuze and Guattari in *Anti-Oedipus* (see, e.g., 1983, 28–30 and chs. 3–4).

48. Virginia Woolf? or the Wolf-Man (Sergei Constantinovitch Pankeiev)? or ?

Chapter 6. Gorgias, Accounting, and Helen

1. There is an intriguing book on counting that I discovered after the writing of this book; see Gamow 1988. My starting point for counting to three as "plenty" was un/found in Pike 1982.

2. I discussed Helen(ism) in chapter 2, and discussed it even more specifically and at greater length in the chapters on Isocrates.

3. I am presently working on a monograph (polygraph) on this subject, tentatively entitled *The History of Rhetoric, Canonicity, and Rape Narratives*.

4. Cf. Darton's notion of "possibilism" (1989), which he defines as being "against the givenness of things" (10).

5. E.g., see Untersteiner (1954), Gomperz (1955), Zeller (1955), Levi (1966), Grote (1869), Bowersock (1969), Guthrie (1971), Classen (1976), Kerferd (1981), Rankin (1983).

6. I am not overlooking a basic similarity between the two groups. Both were (for the most part) engaged in "rational theories of human nature" (Cassirer 1966, 56) and in providing *techné*. They were both proto-scientists. I would have to exclude, however, Gorgias from this group. (Given my agreement with Untersteiner's interpretation of this Sophist, as "a tragedian" [1954, 143]. For me, though, Gorgias is, more so, a tragic-comedian, as "impossible-possi*babl*[e]ist.")

7. My understanding of the *physis/nomos* distinction is from Guthrie (1980, ch. 4) and Kerferd (1981, ch. 11). I say that the Sophists "generally" associated themselves with *nomos* because there are Sophists such as Antiphon and Gorgias who, contrary to other Sophists, do work with the notion of *physis*. As I proceed, I will discuss the implications of these even greater differences.

8. There are alternative views to Gorgias's view of *physis/non-physis*, and the are Callicles's and Antiphon's views of *physis*—respectively, "as the right of the stronger" and "as enlightened self-interest" (see Guthrie 1971, 101ff). These positions should not be confused with Gorgias's, nor should they, as far as I am concerned, be confused with Nietzsche's as E. R. Dodds (1986) has. The attacks made on Nietzsche are similar to the attacks made on the Sophists. Both are seen as being for a dangerous *relativism* and being for the *individual* in the worst sense of these words. Dodds's particular parallels between Nietzsche and Callicles are striking but Nietzsche's notion of the superman (the man beyond *ressentiment*) and of the transvaluation of values should not be confused with Callicles's right of the stronger. At

a gross level of comparison the two thinkers appear to be similar; upon closer examination, however, they are not. I am in in general agreement with Deleuze's more favorable view of Nietzsche, for (by implication) it draws closer ties with Gorgias's view of epistemology as tragedy/comedy (joyful pessimism).

9. Whatever I say about the Sophists—since they cannot really be grouped together, except as a molecular agglomerate, or paratactic aggregate—and how they might "count" is going to be either heretical (at lest, I hope so) or open to contention . . . hope so); therefore, allow me to say, and perhaps with less hereticalness, that the Sophists—because many of them were interested not in universal perceptions, which can be linked with *physis*, but individual perceptions, *nomoi*—were open to counting to *Two*, such as one person experiencing the wind as cold, another as hot. The experiencing was done semiotically across linguistic contraries (see Kerferd 1991, ch. 9).

10. Poulakos cites in the *Rhetoric*, 1396a 4; 1354a 4–6; 1356a 4; and 1404a 5–6.

11. Poulakos has very recently somewhat refined his earlier position (1984). In his most recent article entitled "Terms for Sophistical Rhetoric" (1993), which is a chapter in his book manuscript on the Sophists, his use of *kairos* suggests the beginning of a fundamental change, but it is not at all clear in his discussion how his view of *kairos* (which he borrows from E. White) is Heideggerian or otherwise. Poulakos gives no indication of the problem of the negative at all. White, as I will point out in the next chapter, calls on *kairos* as a means of discussing the middle voice, which I explore. The middle voice, however, is only one means, among other possible analogues, to reach radical multiplicities. To return to Poulakos: His article, as the title suggests, is formalist in design as much of Kenneth Burke's is. It is an attempt to systematize/grammatize frames of acceptance/rejection and most assuredly to validate novelty. My interests, more hyperbolically expressed here, are way beyond formalisms, of giving an account of.

12. I am well aware that in the excursus "Feminist Sophistic?" I praise Spivak for looking around corners, for constantly undergoing metamorphosis. Am I contradicting myself? Different contexts, different redescriptions. And yet, I stand against Spivak's strategic essentialism.

13. See Warren 1988, 126–32. For a discussion of Nietzsche and the body, see Grosz (1993).

14. See the introduction (note 40) for an earlier explanation for these puns from my name.

15. The translation of Parmenides's poem that I am using is Kathleen Freeman's (1983). I have consulted other translation as well (Kirk and Raven 1957; Nye 1990).

16. The translation of Plato's *Sophist* that I am using is F. M. Cornford's in Hamilton and Cairns' collection (1961).

17. See Derrida on Heidegger and negative theology (1992a, 1992b).

18. The "there is no difference" is a deliberate pun.

19. This dancing with tears in one's eyes is reminiscent of Kenneth Burke's entitled response to Wayne Booth (see Booth 1979, ch. 3). I have referred to this connection earlier (see 1989). Burke, like Heidegger, is deeply indebted to Nietzsche but attempts to distance his thinking from Nietzsche. Recently, a graduate student in my Burke seminar informed me that the line is from a 1920s or 30s song entitled "Josephine."

20. I am aware of the literature by feminists that has been generated by this interview between McDonald and Derrida, specifically on the innumerable. In part, it is summarized and documented by N. K. Miller (see 1991, 78–90).

21. The innumerable for Derrida is *Four* (see 1981a, 305–12).

22. Baudrillard (1993) appears to be critiquing Deleuze and Guattari's discussion of molecular sexuality as "the hell of the same" (see 113–23). There is the possibility that such a critique might stick for some readers; however, for me, it does not. Whereas Baudrillard wants to get rid of the idea of the unconscious altogether, Deleuze and Guattari want to perpetually deterritorialize it. These two views, however, can be seen as the same.

23. Still, the best discussion of original and copy (simulation) is to be found in Baudrillard (1983, 1–78). It is not a matter of choosing original over copy, as Baudrillard points out, for all is now copy.

Chapter 7. Gorgias, "Some More," and Helens

1. I have spoken in chapter one of species-genus analytics and Adorno's assessment of this exclusionary procedure in *Negative Dialectics* (1987).

2. By "affirmative," I mean, as previously stated, a nonpositive affirmation.

3. I discussed this notion of sovereignty, determinate and absolute negations, and restrictive and general economies at length in the excurses following chapter 1.

4. I have discussed irony and humor in the excurses. Often ironists will attack— by way of active nihilism—their enemies by claiming that they do not care for the suffering of the others. The nihilistic activity, with its alibi, is not a concern for the other at all, but only a concern for punishing, hurting others.

5. Mark Warren (1986, 126–29) has an excellent discussion of agency in Nietzsche.

6. K. Burke comes close on occasion to speaking about a middle voice. In his searching out for a third term, himself, he speaks of Yes, No, and Perhaps (Maybe).

This triad is important even in his early work, e.g., *Counter-Statement* (1968) and *Attitudes Toward History* (1984). From this triad, Burke in the latter book especially begins to speak in terms of frames of acceptance and rejection, in term of the notion of being a "meliorist" (see 1984, 19). I will pick up later in the final excursis, Burke's notion of the Bohemian voice, ranting and raving, in opposition to the conservative voice, and then the audience that is to see value in both. Yes, No, Maybe. Burke is a Sophist par excellence.

7. Also see Vincent Pecora's "Ethics, Politics, and the Middle Voice" (1991), which concentrates on Derrida's discussion of "Différance" with the middle voice, general economy, and the gift (1982, 9).

8. Yet another way of explaining the phenomenon that Helen is confronted with is in terms of Paul Virilio's notion of speed *and* "picnolepsy" (see 1991). The former means the speed of immediate acceptance, e.g., of the compelling force toward a logical conclusion, without ever ruminating over it; the latter literally translated means *frequent sleep*. As Virilio explains, a newborn is more often than not in a state of picnolepsy (little sleeps, deaths). As the child grows into consciousness, however, it is a growing into reason while picnolepsy is progressively all but eliminated (1991, 31, 101). Reason/rationality, the immediate acceptance of reason and its impact on time, is always already there. Another logic, or paralogic, is not easily available to us. In other words, the timely dominates the untimely, at least, when it comes to understanding our subjectivity in the world. We live in a Dromology, an empire of immediacy.

Similarly, Deleuze and Guattari refer to the untimely by the name of "haeccity (for example, chromaticism, aggregates, and complex notes, but already the resources and possibilities of polyphony . . .)" (1987, 297). The untimely is "unhistorical," "becoming," "the innocence of becoming (. . . forgetting as opposed to remembering, . . . the rhizome as opposed to arboresence)" (296). Haeccity is out of time (like picnolepsy); it "breaks its ties to memory," that is, history (296). Or again, an empire of immediacy.

What Helen—as Gorgias depicts her and Untersteiner interprets Gorgias's depiction, I would argue—experiences is a "picnoleptic interruption" or an event known as the Untimely (either Nietzsche's or Deleuze's haeccity) in the face of pure (speed) logic/*logos* (Virilio and Lotringer 1983, 34), or of rape.

Helen is best here understood, then, as an hysteric or schizo (caught up in the untimely, in a sleep from reason, so that something new, irrational might happen). Virilio explains: A "schizophrenic model of subjectivity corresponds to the great esthetic of the collage. The ego is not continuous, it's made up of a series of deaths [picnoleptics] and partial identities [in between becomings] which don't come back together, or which only manage to come back together by paying the price of anxiety and repression [as in the proper name of The History of Rhetoric]" (1991, 38).

What better way for Gorgias to depict her as someone cum many who needs multiple defenses. Virilio indirectly explains that someone like Gorgias's Helen [he does not refer to Helen] "confirms the Sophist idea of *apate*, the suddenness of this possible entry into another logic 'which dissolves the concepts of truth and illusion, of reality and appearance and which is given by the *kairos* that one might call 'opportunity'" (1991, 35).

By falling (to sleep, so to speak) Helen falls out of time, history. She leaves Being and enters Becoming, loses identification and enters the middle voice, perpetually becoming-something else.

9. Compossible plays off of possible/impossible. It is here a third term. I referred to it earlier in the second excursis on aesthetics. See note 26.

10. I redescribe God here not as usually described. God, given human beings' limited understanding, can only be incompossible, for if otherwise, HE would contradict himself. God, however, the *logos*—it wants to be thought—is compossible, or contradictory. I have in mind Kazantzakis's *The Last Temptation of Christ* (1960), in which the *logos* speaks compossibly to Christ. As for Helen, so for Christ.

11. What I am saying here about force/violence could be said in terms of *"Bia."* For an excellent article on the relationships among *Bia, Peitho,* and *Eros,* see J. T. Kirby 1990.

12. Bataille explains: "I am referring to the associations and judgments that tend to qualify sexually objects, beings, places and moments that by themselves have nothing sexual about them, nor anything contrary to sexuality: the meaning attached to nudity, for example, and the prohibition of incest. In this sense, chastity itself is one of the aspects of eroticism, that is, of properly *human* sexuality" (1993, 27).

13. I have discussed these issues about Heidegger in chs. 4–5.

14. I discuss haeccity in note 8. I am sure that there will be someone who will be greatly annoyed with my conflating all these terms!

15. Unity here is not the unity of fascism, for this unity comes about by excluding nothing, whereas the unity of fascism/totalitarianism is forced by way of exclusion. The latter, then, is a congregation by way of exclusion.

16. I should caution my reader, however, that the chorus (the dionysian) is not apolitical/ahistorical. For now, see Strong 1988; Sloterdijk 1989; and Cresap 1993; also, see Love 1986; Warren 1988.

17. Though not the same, but perhaps similar enough, Grassi's discussion of character and chorus and rhetoric and philosophy, should be considered. See 1976, cf. 1980.

18. I am led to temper what I say here, because of Sloterdijk's discussion (see 1989, ch. 2), but will not be moderate.

19. Cixous writes: "In Brazilian the word for cockroach is *barata*, and it is feminine" (1993, 112).

20. The parallel that I have in mind—mostly out of mind—here is the metamorphosis, or movement, that takes place from Theseus to Dionysus and from H. G. to cockroach. The latter, as I have discussed it, is in Lispector's novel (1988).

21. In this collection edited by Patton, there is a rather remarkable article by Keith Ansell-Pearson that treats reading Nietzsche doubly: When Nietzsche is a sexist, misogynist, Ansell-Pearson is being a literal reader; when a critic of Nietzsche suggests that there is saving grace in these statements if read in a certain way, given Nietzsche's style and clues, Ansell-Pearson is a tolerant reporter. It is a curious piece, especially in its personal, ad hominem attack on Derrida as being totally insensitive, blind, and stupid in relation to women. The response is quite reactionary and damages an article that has some information in it that might be useful to those not familiar with some of the literature on the subject of feminist who are Nietzscheans.

22. There will be for many of my readers a sense that this is just not enough of an explanation. My purpose is not to defend Nietzsche at all, but to summarize ways of pulling the lever to read him otherwise, so as to attend to the other in his texts. Why some readers would have as their purpose to attack him is not difficult to understand. Every philosophy or movement has to have a goat.

23. I suggested in the Introduction, concerning masks, Deleuze would find the concept generally unacceptable. Nietzsche, however, uses the word, or its English equivalent.

24. For a discussion of Kofman and Irigaray, see Berg's "The Third Woman" (1982).

Excursus. Preludes to Future (Anterior) Histories of Rhetorics

1. Among the writers that I have called upon, there are two, along with Haraway, who have speculated on what will have become of the human species when it becomes nonhuman (I prefer non- to in- for, I hope, obvious reasons). See Deleuze's appendix, "On the Death of Man and Superman" in 1988; and Lyotard's "Introduction: About the Human" and "Can Thought Go on Without a Body?" in 1991a.

2. If by now forgotten, these concepts are discussed at length toward the end of the first excursus. See the sections *Bataille's Deconstruction of Hegel, a Return to the Two Negatives* and *Bataille's Sovereignty*. K. Burke has an excellent discussion of killing, self-immolation, in *The Rhetoric of Motives* (see 1969b, 3–48).

3. I will not define these terms but perform them. For a discussion, see Deleuze and Guattari 1986, chs. 8–9; and 1987.

4. Actually, I have used this approach previously (1987b; 1991b), and have used it in the improper name of "the excluded third" (1990; 1993; 1994a). Lacan, according to Schneiderman (1983), learned to *re*count to *three* (as in "Imaginary, Symbolic, and the Real") and then to *four* (as in "four fundamental concepts"). Cf. Ragland-Sullivan (1984). John Poulakos (1984) similarly counts to *three* ("Ideal, Actual, Possible"). Other people count, as well.

5. I have deliberately (further) confused matters here by using the word *hegemon* more appropriately associated with Isocrates rather than Plato. I have worked out the implications of this word in relation to Plato, Isocrates, and Heidegger in a chapter on Isocrates in a book that I am writing on historiography.

6. For Jameson, see "Postmodernism and Consumer Society" (1983), or for a longer version (1984), or for the still longer discussion (1991).

7. I have discussed proper names and narrative at length and by way of Kristeva's mother phallus and my counter-reasons and have performed against proper names and narrative. See 1994a, 405–06.

8. This position, I have ruminated on at great length (see 1991b). It is, to be sure, a modernist position that reaches for postmodernist radical multiplicities. I nomadically stated: The Impossible-cum-Possibilisms! This is home—i.e., such States of Possibilisms—as much as there can be a home for "the unhappy [nomadic] consciousness" (Hegel).

9. *A Caveat*: For Althusser, "denegation," which is translated from *negation* to *denegation* (see "Glossary," Althusser 1987, 312), is a displacement, a deflection, which is "an unconscious denial masked [through ideology] by a conscious acceptance, or vice versa. There is a potential confusion here, however, with what I have already and will again refer to later as "*de*negating the negative," which I borrow recklessly from N. O. Brown (1959). Therefore, *denegating* will mean (hereafter) *the denegating of the denegation, or negation*, so as to let be heard what (heretofore) has been systematically/ideologically negated, silenced, represented as *lack*; to let flow, in other words, non-rational *desires*, and to let them linguistically flow in *excess*.

10. For this cast of characters, see Freud on Dora (*SE* 1962, 7: 3–122); Schreber (1988); Wolf Man (1971); Clément on the Papin sisters (1983). They are all variously discussed by Deleuze and Guattari (1983).

11. See Sebeok, "One, Two, Three, Spells UBERTY" (1988, 1). The article is important because of its concentration on stabilizing "threes," which is a concept that I began this article with, but in a contrary fashion. Searching for de/stabilizing thirds in dis/order to breakup the binaries is my paraproject (see Vitanza 1994d).

12. Darton discusses the *Possibilism* as "against the givenness of things" (1989, 10). See Vitanza (1991b). On occasion, I have used the term *compossible*.

13. The question of the Other is most difficult and rife with problems. My reading of Baudrillard's *The Transparency of Evil* (1993, 140–42) has recently reminded me of this problem. There is the notion of the Other that is internalized (as in the unconscious) and there is the notion that everything is Other. The first is predicated on psychology; the second, on a fatal universe (gods, magic). Which do I work with? Intermittently, both.

14. By way of explaining the concept of "desire," one must understand, *first*, why it is that we more often than not desire being duped by preferring slavery over

freedom. *What is it, at these times, that we Desire?* Deleuze and Guattari see that what we Desire is Our Oppression/Domination. For them, however, Desire should be pure affirmation; they resist Freud, who sees/saw Desire in terms of Lack/the Negative. Freud had defined Desire semiotically across the Oedipus story, i.e., across a prohibition. And therefore attempted to control the flow of Desire. I will discuss this later. But for now here is a passage from *Anti-Oedipus*, in which the authors (and Reich) are wise to the problem of negative Desire: "Even the most repressive and the most deadly forms of social reproduction are produced by desire within the organization that is the consequence of such production under various conditions that we must analyze. That is why the fundamental problem of political philosophy is still precisely the one that Spinoza sees so clearly, and that Wilhelm Reich redis-covered: *'Why do men fight for their servitude as stubbornly as though it were their salvation?'* How can people possibly reach the point of shouting: 'More taxes! Less bread!'? As Reich remarks, the astonishing thing is not that some people steal or that others occasionally go out on strike, but rather that all those who are starving do not steal as a regular practice, and all those who are exploited are not continually out on strike: *after centuries of exploitation, why do people still tolerate being humiliated and enslaved*, to such a point, indeed, that *they actually want humili-ation and slavery not only for others but for themselves?* Reich is at his profoundest as a thinker when he refuses to accept ignorance or illusion on the part of the masses as an explanation of fascism, and demands an explanation . . . formulated in terms of desire: no, the masses were not innocent dupes; at a certain point, under a cer-tain set of conditions, they wanted fascism, and it is this perversion of the desire of the masses that needs to be accounted for" (1983, 29; emphasis mine). It is, *then*, necessary to understand the differences between the concepts of "Desire-as-lack" (the negative/scarcity model based on acquisition) *and* "Desire-as-pure-affirmation" (the impossible made possible, based on free-flowing production). Deleuze and Guattari (1983, 22–35) are the best in explaining this difference, as they take on that long tradition of dialectics (which creates the negative) from Plato through Adorno to Lacan (cf. J. Butler 1987).

Elsewhere (1991b), I have extended Deleuze and Guattari's argument, specifically against Lacan, by extending my own rereading (or *de*territorialization) of Lacan, in which I extend Lacan's view of the impossible-as-lack to a view of the impossible-cum-possible-as-excess. (As Lacan writes: "The unconscious is that chapter of my history that is marked by a blank or occupied by a falsehood: it is the censored chapter" [1977, 50]. Or otherwise put: It is the *negated*, modernist chapter. For additional statements by Lacan, on "the impossible," see 1978, ix, 51; and 1977, 331, specifically the refer-ences listed under "Epistemology.") In 1991b, I paradoxically accept/do not accept lack. Which is how I perpetually, hysterically-situate myselphs here, if the reader catches my drift. Sometimes a postmodernist, other times a modernist, but always a postmodern modernist—I have functioned very much as a *bricoleur* throughout as well as a "drifter." In a paper written a year after this present article, I develop a contemporary genealogy of the negative and discuss two ways toward affirmation; see 1991a. (The paper was presented to the PACT project [The project for affirmation in critical theory, associ-ated with the Society for Critical Exchange].)

15. This kind of "writing" is under erasure. No One can write it; *They*, who are ever catachrestic (without reference), write themselves, or are written by their bodies. But I would, on the left hand, send my reader to Lyotard (1988a), in which he talks about how someone of us must bear witness to *differends* (in part, the loci of exclusion) and discover idioms for them, and we must do so "without criteria." (See 1988a , 10, no. 13.)

16. Marx speaks of the *lumpenproletariat* most specifically in The Eighteenth Brumaire of Louis Bonaparte: Marx writes of such outlaws (outsiders) as

> vagabonds, discharged soldiers, discharged jailbirds, escaped galley slaves, swindlers, mountebanks, *lazzaroni*, pickpockets, tricksters, gamblers, *maquereaus* [procurers, pimps], brothel keepers, porters, *literati*, organ-grinders, ragpickers, knife grinders, tinkers, beggars—in short, the whole indefinite, disintegrated mass, thrown hither and thither, which the French term *la boheme*. (75)

I insert a slash between the two main words—hence, lumpen/proletariat—to distinguish my use of the term from Marx's.

17. At this point, we reach one of the *pharmakons* of this my book. "The street people." What have we to learn from them? (Spivak, whom I will refer to later, would have major reservations, about their being able to speak for themselves; we, for sure, cannot speak for them! Anymore than we can speak/write for the Other. Hence, the statement in note 15. Let me now complicate the argument: I agree that the "subalterns," as Spivak develops the argument (1987; 1988), cannot speak for themselves, nor we for them. I agree with Spivak's reverse on this point, however, that the displaced can and do speak (1989a, 218). The concept of the *lumpen/proletariat* that I am using, however, in associating it with schizos and body hysterics, can and do speak uncontrollably for themselves, though we cannot speak for them. Here lies my difference with Spivak. And then, there are the street "people" of the *logos*. Here lies my negation of the negative.

Deleuze and Guattari have much to say on this subject (which I have called with a special sense the *lumpen/proletariat*) and again in respect to desire-as-lack. They write: "Desire . . . becomes this abject fear of lacking something. But it should be noted that this is not a phrase uttered by the poor or the dispossessed. On the contrary, such people know that they are close to grass, almost akin to it, and that desire 'needs' very few things—*not those leftovers that chance to come their way, but the very things that are continually taken from them*—and that what is missing is not things a subject feels the lack of some where deep down inside himself [sic], but rather the objectivity of man, the objective being of man [sic], for whom to desire is to produce, to produce within the realm of the real" (1983, 27; their emphasis). Remember this is the real not as impossible, but as possible, as a paramodel of desire-as-affirmative-production.

Let me finally note that Spivak's concern with speaking for the Other is really Derrida's prior concern (see "Cogito and the History of Madness" in 1978, 31–63) with Foucault's position in *Madness and Civilization* (1988). For a discussion of the

Foucault-Derrida debate, see Boyne (1990). My other most explicit concern with this 'problem' and my favoring Foucault's attempt is put forth in 1994b.

18. Kristeva puts it graphically: "I imagine a child who has swallowed up his parents too soon, who frightens himself on that account, 'all by himself,' and, to save himself, rejects and throws up everything that is given to him—all gifts, all objects. He has ... a sense of the abject" (1982, 5–6).

19. For some time, now, I have been developing this stretched idea of the *lumpen/proletariat* as the trace of history (as excluded third, the waste, the nonpositive affirmative) and doing so intuitively (see 1987b, 1990, 1991a, 1994a, 1994b, 1994c). It was not until I had written most of this book that I discovered Jeffrey Mehlman's *Revolution and Repetition* (1977). Mehlman argues the same position that I incite by saying that Marx in *The Eighteenth Brumaire* is not as optimistic as some people, especially my colleagues, such as Berlin (you, Jimmie!) read him to be.

First, the movement is not just from tragedy to comedy but to a third term, *farce* (or Bonapartism). I have been reading the *Brumaire* this way for some time (see most recently 1994d). My book is farce in that at times it blends a tragedy/comedy into something farcical, or it calls for a repetition (as if it has to be called for!) of what Nietzsche called joyful pessimism. Farce, Mehlman writes, is "a genre which excites a different kind of laughter than (*petit bourgeois*) comedy, and which, in its absurdity, elicits tears unknown to (proletarian) tragedy, free of every promise of redemption" (13–14).

Second, "The lumpen-proletariat," not the proletariat, is "a *third* element which in its heterogeneity, asymmetry, and unexpectedness, breaks the unity of two specular terms and rots away their *closure*" (19; Mehlman's emphasis). It is "a crude peasant joke" (16). It, the return of the repressed third, is the result of repetition, or an *Unheimlich*, the uncanny (20). Mehlman continues: "But what is repressed is by no means a synthesis of the two positions [tragedy and comedy] or a compromise between their contents. For the 'content' *represented* in and by each ideology exists only in order to repress or mask a 'desire'—for the parliamentary republic—which is entirely incompatible with that content. Thus, for Marx as analyst ... reading entails endavoring to affirm a tertiary instance breaking with the registers of specularity and representation. It is the degree zero of polysemy, the fundamentally *heterogenizing* movement of dissemination" (22). Mehlman pretty much says, as I do, that we must go with, as if there is a choice, this third element: *Lumpen* dejecta.

And third, Mehlman associates this moment of repetition (the uncanny in terms of the return of the repressed third element, the *lumpen* dejecta) with Bataille's notion of expenditure (*dépense*, waste), of a general economy. And yet, he points out that when Bataille was a member of the School of Sociology, he spoke against Bonapartism (see 24–30). Mehlman mentions (22) that the Bataille's text is to be published in Hollier's *The College of Sociology, 1937–39*, which is now in print. The only text, in the collection, that Mehlman could be referring to is a fragment that says really very little (see Hollier 1988, 351–52).

20. E.g., 17, 65–67, 91, 167–68, 332. Limitations of space do not allow me to give an adequate exposition of Deleuze and Guattari. It might be helpful, therefore,

to read Bogue's (1989), Holland's (1987), and Massumi's (1992) discussions of Deleuze and Guattari and how the para-philosopher and para-psychoanalyst resist Marxist [socialist] and Freudian [say, capitalist] master narratives and hermeneutics. On Deleuze, see Hardt (1993). I am well aware of the work of René Girard (1977) and especially his critique of *Anti-Oedipus* ("Delirum"1988, 84–120); I am not particularly moved by what he says other than to think that he himself exemplifies sacrificial rivalry when it comes to Deleuze and Guattari. A critique of Girard that I agree with is put forth by LaCapra (see 1983, 296, n. 11).

21. "De Beginnibus" is the title of a commencement address that K. Burke delivered at Bennington College in 1962 (see Burke 1984a).

Works Cited

Acker, Kathy. 1982. *Great Expectations*. N.Y.: Grove Press.

———. 1990. *In Memoriam to Identity*. N.Y.: Pantheon Books.

Adorno, Theodor W. 1987. *Negative Dialectics*. Translated by E. B. Ashton. N.Y.: Continuum.

Althusser, Louis. 1971. *Lenin and Philosophy and Other Essays*. N.Y.: Monthly Review Press.

Anchor, Robert. 1967. *The Enlightenment Tradition*. Berkeley: University of California Press.

Aristotle. 1941. *The Basic Works of Aristotle*, ed. Richard McKeon. N.Y.: Random.

Arrowsmith, William. 1990. Introduction to Friedrich Nietzsche, "We Classicists." In *Unmodern Observations*, 307–20. New Haven: Yale University Press.

Artaud, Antonin. 1965. *Anthology*, ed. Jack Hirschman. San Francisco: City Lights Books.

Auerbach, Erich. 1969. "Philology and *Weltliteratur*." Translated by Marie and Edward Said. *The Centennial Review* 13.1: 1–17.

Barthes, Roland. 1972. "To Write: An Intransitive Verb?" *The Structuralist Controversy: The Languages of Criticism and the Sciences of Man*. Baltimore: The Johns Hopkins University Press.

———. 1975. *The Pleasure of the Text*. Translated by Richard Miller. N.Y.: Hill and Wang.

———. 1976. *Sade Fourier Loyola*. Translated by Richard Miller. NY: Hill and Wang.

———. 1977. *Roland Barthes by Roland Barthes*. Translated by Richard Howard. N.Y.: Hill and Wang.

———. 1978. *A Lover's Discourse: Fragments*. Translated by Richard Howard. N.Y.: Hill and Wang.

393

————. 1983. "Inaugural Lecture, College de France." In *A Barthes Reader*, ed. Susan Sontag, 457–78. N.Y.: Hill and Wang.

————. 1987. *Michelet*. Translated by Richard Howard. London: Basil Blackwell.

————. 1988. "The Old Rhetoric: an aide-mémoire." In *The Semiotic Challenge*, 11–94. Translated by Richard Howard. N.Y.: Hill and Wang.

Bataille, Georges. 1962. *Death and Sensuality: A Study of Eroticism and the Taboo*. Translated by Mary Dalwood. N.Y.: Walker.

————. 1965. *La Tragédie de Gilles de Rais*. Montreuil: J.-J. Pauvert.

————. 1985. *Visions of Excess: Selected Writings, 1927–1939*. Translated by Allan Stoekl. Minneapolis: University of Minnesota Press.

————. 1987. *The Story of the Eye, by Lord Auch*. Translated by Joachim Neugroschel. San Francisco: City Lights Books.

————. 1988a. *The Accursed Share*. Translated by Robert Hurley. Vol. I. N.Y.: Zone Books.

————. 1988b. *Guilty*. Translated by Bruce Boone. Venice, Calif.: The Lapis Press.

————. 1988c. *Inner Experience*. Translated by Leslie Anne Boldt. Albany: State University of New York Press.

————. 1991. *The Impossible: A Story of Rats followed by Dianus and by The Oresteia*. Translated by Robert Hurley. San Francisco: City Lights Books.

————. 1993. *The Accursed Share*. Translated by Robert Hurley. Vols. 2 and 3. N.Y.: Zone Books.

Baudrillard. Jean. 1983. *Simulations*. Translated by Paul Foss, Paul Patton, and Philip Beitchman. N.Y.: Semiotext(e).

————. 1988. *Selected Writings*, ed. Mark Poster. Stanford, Calif.: Stanford University Press.

————. 1990. *Seduction*. Translated by Brian Singer. N.Y.: St. Martin's Press.

————. 1993. *Transparency of Evil*. Translated by James Benedict. N.Y.: Verso.

Benjamin, Walter. 1969. *Illuminations*. N.Y.: Harcourt, Brace and World.

Bennington, Geoffrey. 1988. *Lyotard: Writing the Event*. N.Y.: Columbia University Press.

Benveniste, Emil. 1971. *Problems in General Linguistics*. Translated by M.E. Meek. Coral Gables, Fla.: University of Miami Press.

Berg, Elizabeth L. 1982. "The Third Woman." *Diacritics* 12: 11–20.

Berlin, James A. 1988. "Rhetoric and Ideology in the Writing Class." *College English* 50.5: 477–94.

Bernheimer, Charles. 1985. "Introduction." In *In Dora's Case: Freud-Hysteria-Feminism*, ed. Charles Bernheimer and Claire Kahane, 1–18. N.Y.: Columbia University Press.

Bernal, Martin. 1987. *Black Athena: The Afroasiatic Roots of Classical Civilization*. Vol. I. New Brunswick, N.J.: Rutgers University Press.

———. 1991. *Black Athena: The Afroasiatic Roots of Classical Civilization*. Vol. 2. New Brunswick, N.J.: Rutgers University Press.

Bernasconi, Robert. 1993. "Justice and the Twilight Zone of Morality." In *Reading Heidegger*, ed. John Sallis, 80–94. Bloomington: Indiana University Press.

Bernstein, J. M. 1992. *The Fate of Art: Aesthetic Alienation from Kant to Derrida and Adorno*. University Park: The Pennsylvania State University Press.

Bernstein, Richard J. 1992. *The New Constellation: The Ethical-Political Horizons of Modernity/Postmodernity*. Cambridge, Mass.: The MIT Press.

Bey, Hakim. 1991. *T.A.Z.: The Temporary Autonomous Zone, Ontological Anarchy, Poetic Terrorism*. Brooklyn: Autonomedia.

Biesecker, Susan. 1991. "Feminist Criticism of Classical Rhetorical Texts: A Case Study of Gorgias' *Helen*." In *Realms of Rhetoric: Phonic, Graphic, Electronic*, ed. Victor J. Vitanza and Michelle Ballif, 67–84. Arlington, Tex.: Rhetoric Society of America.

Bogue, Ronald. 1989. *Deleuze and Guattari*. N.Y.: Routledge.

Booth, Wayne C. 1979. *Critical Understanding: The Powers and Limits of Pluralism*. Chicago: University of Chicago Press.

Botting, Fred, and Scott Wilson. 1993. "Literature as Heterological Practice: Georges Bataille, Writing and Inner Experience." *Textual Practice* 7.2: 195–207.

Bowersock, G. W. 1969. *Greek Sophists in the Roman Empire*. Oxford: Clarendon Press.

Boyne, Roy. 1990. *Foucault and Derrida: The Other Side of Reason*. London: Unwin Hyman.

Braidotti, Rosi. 1991. *Patterns of Dissonance: A Study of Women in Contemporary Philosophy*. Translated by Elizabeth Guild. N.Y.: Routledge.

Brown, Norman O. 1959. *Life Against Death*. Middletown, Conn.: Wesleyan University Press.

———. 1966. *Love's Body*. Berkeley: University of California Press.

———. 1974. *Closing Time*. N.Y.: Vintage.

———. 1991. *Apocalypse and/or Metamorphosis*. Berkeley: University of California Press.

Burgard, Peter J., ed. 1994. *Nietzsche and the Feminine*. Charlottesville: University Press of Virginia.

Burke, Edmund. 1958. *A Philosophical Enquiry into the Origin of Our Ideas of the Sublime and Beautiful*, ed. James T. Boulton. London: Routledge and Kegan Paul.

Burke, Kenneth. 1966. *Language as Symbolic Action*. Berkeley: University of California Press.

———. 1968. *Counter-Statement*. Berkeley: University of California Press.

———. 1969a. *A Grammar of Motives*. Berkeley: University of California Press.

———. 1969b. *A Rhetoric of Motives*. Berkeley: University of California Press.

———. 1970. *The Rhetoric of Religion: Studies in Logology*. Berkeley: University of California Press.

———. 1984a "De Beginnibus." In *Reclaiming the Imagination*, ed. Ann E Berthoff, 29–37. Upper Monteclair, N.J.: Boynton/Cook.

———. 1984b. *Attitudes Towards History*. Third Edition. Berkeley: University of California Press.

Butler, E. M. 1958. *The Tyranny of Greece Over Germany*. Boston: Beacon Press.

Butler, Judith P. 1987. *Subjects of Desire*. N.Y.: Columbia University Press.

———. 1990a. *Gender Trouble: Feminism and the Subversion of Identity*. N.Y.: Routledge.

———. 1990b. "Gender Trouble, Feminist Theory, and Psychoanalytic Discourse." In *Feminism/Postmodernism*, ed. Linda J. Nicholson, 324–40. N.Y.: Routledge.

———. 1993. *Bodies That Matter*. N.Y.: Routledge.

Butler, Judith, and Joan W. Scott, ed. 1991. *Feminists Theorize the Political*. N.Y.: Routledge.

Calder, William M., III, ed. 1992. *Werner Jaeger Reconsidered: Illinois Classical Studies, Supplement 3*. Atlanta: Scholars Press.

Camus, Albert. 1955. *The Myth of Sisyphus*. Translated by Justin O'Brien. N.Y.: Knopf.

Carroll, David. 1987. *Paraesthetics: Foucault, Lyotard, Derrida*. N.Y.: Methuen.

Cassirer, Ernst. 1966. *The Myth of the State*. New Haven: Yale University Press.

Chytry, Josef. 1989. *The Aesthetic State: A Quest in Modern German Thought*. Berkeley: University of California Press.

Cixous, Hélène. 1981. "The Laugh of the Medusa." In *New French Feminisms*, ed. Elaine Marks and Isabelle de Courtrivron, 245–64. N.Y.: Schocken Books.

————. 1989. "From the Scene of the Unconscious to the Scene of History." In *The Future of Literary Theory*, ed. Ralph Cohen, 1–18. N.Y.: Routledge.

————. 1991. *"Coming to Writing" and Other Essays*, ed. Deborah Jenson. Translated by Sarah Cornell, Deborah Jenson, Ann Liddle, Susan Sellers. Cambridge, Mass.: Harvard University Press.

————. 1993a. *Three Steps on the Ladder of Writing*. Translated by Sarah Cornell and Susan Sellers. N.Y.: Columbia University Press.

————. 1993b. "We Who Are Free, Are We Free?" *Critical Inquiry* 19: 201–19.

Cixous, Hélène, and Catherine Clément. 1986. *The Newly Born Woman*. Translated by Betsy Wing. Minneapolis: University of Minnesota Press.

Classen, Carl Joachim, ed. 1976. *Sophistik*. Darmstadt: Wissenschaftliche Buchgesellschaft.

Clément, Catherine. 1981. "Encslaved Enclave." *New French Feminism: An Anthology*. Ed. Elaine Marks and Isabelle de Courtivron. N.Y.: Schocken: 130–36.

Clément, Catherine. 1983. *The Lives and Legends of Jacques Lacan*. Translated by Arthur Goldhammer. N.Y.: Columbia University Press.

Conley, Verena Andermatt. 1992. *Hélène Cixous*. Toronto: University of Toronto Press.

Connors, Robert J. 1991. "Writing the History of Our Discipline." In *An Introduction to Composition Studies*, ed. Erika Lindemann and Gary Tate, 49–71. N.Y.: Oxford University Press.

Consigny, Scott. 1991. "Sophistic Freedom: Gorgias and the Subversion of Logos." *PRE/TEXT* 12. 3–4. 225–35.

Cope, Edward M. 1970. *The Rhetoric of Aristotle with a Commentary*, ed. and rev. J. E. Sandys. 3 vols. Hidesheim: Olms.

Covino, William A. 1988. *The Art of Wondering : A Revisionist Return to the History of Rhetoric*. Portsmouth: Boynton/Cook-Heinemann.

Cresap, Steven. 1993. "Nietzsche as Social Engineer: *The Birth of Tragedy*'s Critique of Action." *Rethinking Marxism* 6.3: 102–16.

Crowley, Sharon. 1979. "Of Gorgias and Grammatology." *College Composition and Communication* 30.3: 279–83.

Cummings, Katherine. 1991. "Principled Pleasures: Obsessional Pedagogies or (Ac)counting from Irving Babbitt to Allan Bloom." In *Texts for Change: Theory/Pedagogy/Politics*, ed. Donald Morton and Mas'ud Zavarzadeh, 90–111. Urbana: University of Illinois Press.

Curtius, Ernst Robert. 1953. *European Literature and the Latin Middle Ages*. Translated by Willard R. Trask. N.Y.: Harper and Row.

Darton, Robert. 1989. "What Was Revolutionary About the French Revolution?" *The New York Review of Books*. 35.21–22: 3–4, 6, 10.

Davis, Philip J., David Park, ed. 1987. *No Way: The Nature of the Impossible*. N.Y.: W. H. Freeman.

Deleuze, Gilles. 1977. "Nomad Thought." In *The New Nietzsche*, ed. David B. Allison, 142–49. N.Y.: Dell.

————. 1983a. *Nietzsche and Philosophy*. Translated by Hugh Tomlinson. N.Y.: Columbia University Press.

————. 1983b. "Plato and the Simulacrum." *October* 27: 45–56.

————. 1988. *Foucault*. Translated by Seán Hand. Minneapolis: University of Minnesota Press.

————. 1991. "Coldness and Cruelty." In *Masochism*, 9–138. N.Y.: Zone Books.

————. 1993. *The Fold: Leibniz and the Baroque*. Translated by Tom Conley. Minneapolis: University of Minnesota Press.

Deleuze, Gilles, and Felix Guattari. 1983. *Anti-Oedipus: Capitalism and Schizophrenia*. Minneapolis: University of Minnesota Press.

————. 1986. *Kafka: Toward a Minor Literature*. Translated by Dana Polan. Minneapolis: University of Minnesota Press.

————. 1987. *A Thousand Plateaus: Capitalism and Schizophrenia*. Minneapolis: University of Minnesota Press.

Deleuze, Gilles, and Claire Parnet. 1987. *Dialogues*. Translated by Hugh Tomlinson and Barbara Habberjam. N.Y.: Columbia University Press.

De Man, Paul. 1983a. *Blindness and Insight*. Minneapolis: University of Minnesota Press.

————. 1983b. "Hegel on the Sublime." In *Displacement: Derrida and After*, ed. Mark Krupnick,139–53. Bloomington: Indiana University Press.

————. 1984. *The Rhetoric of Romanticism*. N.Y.: Columbia University Press.

Derrida, Jacques. 1970. "Structure, Sign, and Play in the Discourse of the Human Sciences." In *The Languages of Criticism and the Sciences of Man: The Structuralist Controversy*, ed. Richard Macksey and Eugenio Donato, 247–64. Baltimore: The Johns Hopkins University Press.

————. 1978. *Writing and Difference*. Translated by Alan Bass. Chicago: University of Chicago Press.

————. 1979. *Spurs: Nietzsche's Styles*. Translated by Barbara Harlow. Chicago: University of Chicago Press.

———. 1980. "The Law of Genre." In *On Narrative*, ed. W. J. T. Mitchell, 51–78. Chicago: University of Chicago Press.

———. 1981a. *Disseminations*. Translated by Barbara Johnson. Chicago: University of Chicago Press.

———. 1981b. "Economimesis." *Diacritics* 11: 3–25.

———. 1981c. *Positions*. Translated by Alan Bass. Chicago: University of Chicago Press.

———. 1982. *Margins of Philosophy*. Translated by Alan Bass. Chicago: University of Chicago Press.

———. 1983. "*Geschlecht*: sexual difference, ontological difference." *Research in Phenomenology* 13: 65–83.

———. 1985a. *The Ear of the Other: Otobiography, Transference, Translation*. Translated by Peggy Kamuf. Lincoln: University of Nebraska Press.

———. 1985b. "Racism's Last Word." *Critical Inquiry* 12.1: 290–99.

———. 1987. "*Geschlecht* II: Heidegger's Hand." In *Deconstruction and Philosophy: The Texts of Jacques Derrida*, ed. John Sallis, 161–96. Chicago: University of Chicago Press.

———. 1988. "A Number of Yes." *Qui Parle* 2.2: 120–33.

———. 1989. *Of Spirit: Heidegger and the Question*. Translated by Geoffrey Bennington and Rachel Bowlby. Chicago: University of Chicago Press.

———. 1990. "Interpreting Signatures." In *Looking After Nietzsche*, edited by Laurence A Rickels, 1–17. Albany: State University of New York Press.

———. 1992a. "How to Avoid Speaking: Denials." In *Derrida and Negative Theology*, ed. Harold Coward and Toby Foshay, 73–142. Albany: State University of New York Press.

———. 1992b. "Of an Apocalyptic Tone Newly Adopted in Philosophy." In *Derrida and Negative Theology*, ed. Harold Coward and Toby Foshay, 25–71. Albany: State University of New York Press.

———. 1993. "Heidegger's Ear: Philopolemology (*Geschlecht* IV)." In *Reading Heidegger: Commemorations*, ed. John Sallis, 163–218. Bloomington: Indiana University Press.

Derrida, Jacques, and Christie V. McDonald. 1982. "Choreographies." *Diacritics* 12: 66–76.

Desmond, William. 1992. *Beyond Hegel and Dialectic: Speculation, Cult, and Comedy*. Albany: State University of New York Press.

Dewey, John. 1938. *Logic: The Theory of Inquiry.* NY: Holt.

Diselet, Gregory. 1989. "Nietzsche Contra Burke: The Melodrama in Dramatism." *Quarterly Journal of Speech.* 75: 65–83.

Dodds, E. R. 1986. "Socrates, Callicles, and Nietzsche." In Plato, *Gorgias. A Revised Text with Introduction and Commentary*, 385–91. Oxford: Clarendon Press.

DuBois, Page. 1988. *Sowing the Body: Psychoanalysis and Ancient Representations of Women.* Chicago: University of Chicago Press.

Durrell, Lawrence. 1969. *Justine.* N.Y.: E. P. Dutton.

Eagleton, Terry. 1981. *Walter Benjamin or Towards a Revolutionary Criticism.* London: Verso and NLB.

———. 1991. *The Ideology of the Aesthetic.* Cambridge, Mass.: Blackwell.

Ebert, Theresa L. 1991. "The 'Difference' of Postmodern Feminism." *College English* 53.8: 886–904.

Eco, Umberto. 1984. *Semiotics and the Philosophy of Language.* Bloomington: Indiana University Press.

Farenga, Vincent. 1979. "Periphrasis on the Origin of Rhetoric." *MLN* 94: 1033–55.

Farias, Victor. 1989. *Heidegger and Nazism*, ed. Joseph Margolis and Tom Rockmore. Translated by Gabriel R. Ricci. Philadelphia: Temple University Press.

Fausto-Sterling, Anne. 1993. "The Five Sexes: Why Male and Female Are Not Enough." *The Sciences* (March/April): 20–25.

Ferry, Luc, and Alain Renaut. 1990. *Heidegger and Modernity.* Translated by Franklin Philip. Chicago: University of Chicago Press.

Feyerabend, Paul. 1978. *Against Method.* London: Verso.

Fichte, Johann Gottlieb. 1968. *Addresses to the German Nation*, ed. George Armstrong Kelly. N.Y.: Harper and Row.

Fink, Eugen. 1968. "The oasis of happiness: Toward an ontology of play." *Yale French Studies* 41: 19–30.

Finley, M. I. 1975. *The Use and Abuse of History.* N.Y.: Penguin.

———. 1977. *Aspects of Antiquity.* 2nd ed. N.Y.: Penguin.

———. 1987. *Ancient History.* N.Y.: Penguin.

Foucault, Michel. 1977. *Language, Counter-Memory, Practice.* Translated by D. F. Bouchard and Sherry Simon. Ithaca, N.Y.: Cornell University Press.

———. 1980a. *Herculine Barbin.* N.Y.: Pantheon.

————. 1980b. *Power/Knowledge*, ed. Colin Gordon. Translated by Colin Gordin, Leo Marshall, John Mepham, and Kate Sopher. N.Y.: Pantheon.

————.1988. *Madness and Civilization*. Translated by Richard Howard. N.Y.: Vintage.

Freire, Paulo. 1987. *Pedagogy of the Oppressed*. N.Y.: Continuum.

Freud, Sigmund. 1961. *Civilization and Its Discontents*. Translated by James Strachey. N.Y.: Norton.

————. 1962. *The Standard Edition of The Completed Psychological Works of Sigmund Freud*. Translated by James Strachey. London: Hogarth Press.

Fuss, Diana. 1989. *Essentially Speaking: Feminism, Nature and Difference*. N.Y.: Routledge.

Gadamer, Hans-Georg. 1975. *Truth and Method*. N.Y.: Crossroads.

Gamow, George. 1988. *One, Two, Three ... Infinity*. N.Y.: Dover.

Gasché, Rodolphe. 1989. "In-Difference to Philosophy: de Man on Kant, Hegel, and Nietzsche." In *Reading de Man Reading*, ed. Lindsay Waters and Wlad Godzich, 259–96. Minneapolis: University of Minnesota Press.

Gillespie, Michael Allen. 1984. *Hegel, Heidegger, and the Ground of History*. Chicago: University of Chicago Press.

Girard, René. 1977. *Violence and the Sacred*. Translated by Patrick Gregory. Baltimore: The Johns Hopkins University Press.

————. 1988. "Delirum As System." In *"To Double Business Bound": Essays on Literature, Mimesis, and Anthropology*, 84–120. Baltimore: The Johns Hopkins University Press.

Gomperz, Theodor. 1955. *Greek Thinkers: A History of Ancient Philosophy*. Vol. I. London: John Murray.

Graff, Gerald. 1987. *Professing LIterature: An Institutional History*. Chicago: University of Chicago Press.

Grassi, Ernesto. 1976. "Rhetoric and Philosophy." *Philosophy and Rhetoric* 9: 200–16.

————. 1980. *Rhetoric as Philosophy: The Humanist Tradition*. University Park: The Pennsylvania State University Press.

Graybeal, Jean. 1990. *Language and "The Feminine" in Nietzsche and Heidegger*. Bloomington: Indiana University Press.

Grosz, Elizabeth. 1993a. "Nietzsche and the stomach for knowledge." In *Nietzsche: Feminism and Political Theory*, ed. Paul Patton, 49–70. N.Y.: Routledge.

————. 1993b. "A Thousand Tiny Sexes: Feminism and Rhizomatics." *Topoi* 12: 167–79.

Grote, George. 1869. *A History of Greece*. Vol. 8. London: John Murray.

Guthrie, W. K. C. 1971. *The Sophists*. N.Y.: Cambridge University Press.

Habermas, Jürgen. 1979. *Communication and the Evolution of Society*. Translated by Thomas McCarthy. Boston: Beacon.

———. 1987. *The Philosophical Discourse of Modernity: Twelve Lectures*. Translated by Frederick Lawrence. Cambridge, Mass.: MIT Press.

Haraway, Donna. 1990. "A Manifesto for Cyborgs: Science, Technology, and Socialist Feminism in the 1980s." In *Feminism/Postmodernism*, ed. Linda J. Nicholson, 190–233. N.Y.: Routledge.

———. 1991. *Simians, Cyborgs, and Women*. N.Y.: Routledge.

———. 1992. "The Promises of Monsters: A Regenerative Politics for Inapproprite/ d." In *Cultural Studies*, ed. Lawrence Grossberg, Cary Nelson, and Paula A. Treichler, 295–337. N.Y.: Routledge.

Hardt, Michael. 1993. *Gilles Deleuze: An Apprenticeship in Philosophy*. Minneapolis: University of Minnesota Press.

Havelock, Eric A. 1982. *The Literate Revolution in Greece and Its Cultural Consequences*. Princeton, N.J.: Princeton University Press.

Heath, Stephen. 1978. "Difference." *Screen* 19: 50–112.

[Hegel, G. W. F.] 1974. *Hegel's Lectures on the History of Philosophy*. Translated by E. S. Haldane and Frances H. Simson. 3 vols. N.Y.: The Humanities Press.

———. 1977. *The Phenomenology of Spirit*. Translated by A. V. Miller. Oxford: The University Press.

Heidegger, Martin. 1959. *Introduction to Metaphysics*. New Haven: Yale University Press.

———. 1962. *Being and Time*. Translated by John Macquarrie and Edward Robinson. N.Y.: Harper and Row.

———. 1968. *What is Called Thinking?* Translated by J. Glenn Gray. N.Y.: Harper and Row.

———. 1977. *Basic Writings*, ed. David Farrell Krell. San Francisco: Harper and Row.

———. 1982. *On the Way to Language*. Translated by Peter D. Hertz. San Francisco: Harper and Row.

———. 1984. *Early Greek Thinking*. San Francisco: Harper and Row.

———. 1985a. "The Self-Assertion of the German University: Address, Delivered on the Solemn Assumption of the Rectorate of the University of Freiburg." Translated by Karsten Harries. *Review of Metaphysics* 38: 467–80.

————. 1985b. "The Rectorate 1933/34: Facts and Thoughts." Translated by Karsten Harries. *Review of Metaphysics* 38: 481–502.

————. 1990. "*Spiegel* Interview with Martin Heidegger." In *Martin Heidegger and National Socialism*, ed. Günther Neske and Emil Kettering, 41–66. N.Y.: Paragon House.

————. 1991. *Nietzsche*. 4 vols. Translated by David Farrell Krell. San Francisco: Harper.

Heidegger, Martin, and Eugen Fink. 1979. *Heraclitus Seminar, 1966/67*. Translated by Charles H. Seibert. University, Ala.: University of Alabama Press.

Hertz, Neil. 1978. "The Notion of Blockage in the Literature of the Sublime." In *Psychoanalysis and the Question of the Text*, ed. Geoffrey H. Hartman, 62–85. Baltimore: The Johns Hopkins University Press.

————. 1985. *The End of the Line: Essays on Psychoanalysis and the Sublime*. N.Y.: Columbia University Press.

Hikins, James W. 1995. "Nietzsche, Eristic, and the Rhetoric of the Possible: A Commentary on the Whitson and Poulakos 'Aesthetic View' of Rhetoric." *Quarterly Journal of Speech* 81 (1995): 353–77.

Holland, Eugene W. 1987. " 'Introduction to the Non-Fascist Life': Deleuze and Guattari's 'Revolutionary' Semiotics." *L'Esprit Createur* 27.2: 19–29.

Hollier, Denis, ed. 1988. *The College of Sociology (1937–39)*. Translated by Betsy Wing. Minneapolis: University of Minnesota Press.

————. 1989. *Against Architecture: The Writings of Georges Bataille*. Translated by Betsy Wing. Cambridge, Mass.: The MIT Press.

Hutton, James. 1982. "Introduction and Notes." In *Aristotle's* Poetics. Translated by James Hutton. N.Y.: Norton.

Ijsseling, Samuel. 1976. *Rhetoric and Philosophy in Conflict*. The Hague: Martinus Nijhoff.

————. 1992. "Heidegger and Politics." In *Ethics and Danger: Essays on Heidegger and Continental Thought*, ed. Arleen B. Dallery and Charles E .Scott with P. Holley Roberts, 3–10. Albany: State University of New York Press.

Irigaray, Luce. 1985a. *Speculum of the Other Woman*. Translated by Gillian C. Gill. Ithaca, N.Y.: Cornell University Press.

————. 1985b. *This Sex Which Is Not One*. Translated by Catherine Porter with Carolyn Burke. Ithaca, N.Y.: Cornell University Press.

————. 1991. *Marine Lover of Friedrich Nietzsche*. Translated by Gillian C. Gill. N.Y.: Columbia University Press.

Isocrates. 1980. *Isocrates*. Translated by George Norlin. Cambridge, Mass.: Harvard University Press.

———. 1982. *Isocrates*. Translated by George Norlin. Cambridge, Mass.: Harvard University Press.

———. 1986. *Isocrates*. Translated by George Norlin. Cambridge, Mass.: Harvard University Press.

Jaeger, Werner. 1965. *Paideia: The Ideals of Greek Culture*. Translated by Gilbert Highet. 2nd ed. Vol. 1. Oxford: Oxford University Press.

———. 1986a. *Paideia: The Ideals of Greek Culture*. Translated by Gilbert Highet. 2nd ed. Vol. 2. Oxford: Oxford University Press.

———. 1986b. *Paideia: The Ideals of Greek Culture*. Translated by Gilbert Highet. 2nd ed. Vol. 3. Oxford: Oxford University Press.

Jameson, Frederic. 1981. *The Political Unconscious*. Ithaca, N.Y.: Cornell University Press.

———. 1983. "Postmodernism and Consumer Society." In *Anti-Aesthetic: Essays on Postmodern Culture*, ed. Hal Foster, 111–25. Port Townsend, Wash.: Bay Press.

———. 1984. "Postmodernism; or, The Cultural Logic of Late Capitalism." *New Left Review* 146: 53–92.

———. 1991. *Postmodernism; or, The Cultural Logic of Late Capitalism*. Durham: Duke University Press.

Jardine, Alice A. 1985. *Gynesis: Configurations of Woman and Modernity*. Ithaca, N.Y.: Cornell University Press.

Jardine, Alice, and Paul Smith. 1987. *Men in Feminism*. N.Y.: Methuen.

Jarratt, Susan Carole Funderburgh. 1985. "A Victorian Sophistic: The Rhetoric of Knowledge in Darwin, Newman, and Pater." Diss. University of Texas, at Austin.

Jarratt, Susan C. 1990. "The First Sophists and Feminism: Discourses of the 'Other.' " *Hypatia* 5.1: 27–41.

———. 1991. *Rereading the Sophists: Classical Rhetoric Refigured*. Carbondale, Ill.: Southern Illinois University Press.

Jay, Martin. 1992. " 'The Aesthetic Ideology' as Ideology; or, What Does It Mean to Aestheticize Politics?" *Cultural Critique* 21: 41–61.

Jay, Nancy. 1981. "Gender and Dichotomy." *Feminist Studies* 7.1: 38–56.

Jed, Stephanie H. 1989. *Chaste Thinking*. Bloomington: Indiana University Press.

Joyce, James. 1976. *Finnegans Wake*. N.Y.: Penguin.

Kant, Immanuel. 1949. *Critique of Practical Reason and Other Writings in Moral Philosophy*. Translated by Lewis White Beck. Chicago: University of Chicago Press.

———. 1991. *The Critique of Judgement*. Translated by James Creed Meredith. Oxford: Claredon Press.

Kaufmann, Walter. 1967. "Translator's Introduction." In Friedrich Nietzsche, *The Birth of Tragedy and The Case of Wagner*, 3–13. N.Y.: Vintage.

———. 1974. *Nietzsche: Philosopher, Psychologist, Antichrist*. 4th ed. Princeton, N.J.: Princeton University Press.

Kazantzakis, Nikos. 1960. *The Last Temptation of Christ*. N.Y.: Simon and Schuster.

Kellner, Hans. 1980. "A Bedrock of Order: Hayden White's Linguistic Humanism." Beiheft 19. *History and Theory* 19.4: 1–29.

———. 1991. "Beautifying the Nightmare: The Aesthetics of Postmodern History." *Strategies* 4/5: 289–313.

———. 1994. "After the Fall: Reflections on Histories of Rhetoric." In *Writing Histories of Rhetoric*, ed. Victor J. Vitanza, 20–37. Carbondale, Ill.: Southern Illinois University Press.

Kennedy, Geroge A. 1963. *The Art of Persuasion in Greece*. Princeton, N.J.: Princeton University Press.

———. 1988. "Some Reflections on Neomodernism [a response to Vitanza]." *Rhetoric Review* 6.2: 230–33.

Kerferd, G. B. 1981. *The Sophistic Movement*. Cambridge: Cambridge University Press.

Kermode, Frank. 1967. *The Sense of an Ending*. N.Y.: Oxford University Press.

Kinneavy, James L. 1986. "*Kairos*: A Neglected Concept in Classical Rhetoric." In *Rhetoric and Praxis*, ed. Jean Dietz Moss, 79–106. Washington, D.C.: The Catholic University of America Press.

Kirby, John T. 1990. "The 'Great Triangle' in Early Greek Rhetoric and Poetics." *Rhetorica* 8.3: 213–29.

Kirby, Kathleen M. 1993. "Thinking Through the Boundary: The Politics of Location, Subjects, and Space." *Boundary 2* 20:2: 173–89.

Kirk, G. S., and J. E. Raven. 1957. *The Presocrtics Philosophers: A Critical History with a Selection of Texts*. Cambridge: The University Press.

Klossowski, Pierre. 1991. *Sade, My Neighbor*. Translated by Alphonso Lingis. Evanston, Ill.: Northwestern University Press.

Kofman, Sarah. 1985. *The Enigma of Woman: Woman in Freud's Writings*. Translated by Catherine Porter. Ithaca, N.Y.: Cornell University Press.

———. 1987. "Nietzsche and the Obscurity of Heraclitus." *Diacritics* 17.3 39–55.

———. 1991. "Baubô: Theological Perversion and Fetishism." In *Nietzsche's New Seas: Explorations in Philosophy, Aesthetics, and Politics*, ed. Michael

Allen Gillespie and Tracy B. Strong, 175–202. Chicago: University of Chicago Press.

Kojève, Alexandre. 1986. *Introduction to the Reading of Hegel*. Translated by James H. Nichols, Jr. Ithaca, N.Y.: Cornell University Press.

Kott, Jan. 1973. *The Eating of the Gods: An Interpretation of Greek Tragedy*. Translated by Boleslaw Taborski and Edward J. Czerwinski. N.Y.: Random House.

Krell, David Farrell. 1972. "Towards an Ontology of Play: Eugen Fink's Notion of *Spiel*." *Research in Phenomenology* 2: 63–93.

———. 1986. *Intimations of Mortality: Time, Truth, and Finitude in Heidegger's Thinking of Being*. University Park: The Pennsylvania State University Press.

Kristeva, Julia. 1980. *Desire in Language: A Semiotic Approach to Literature and Art*. Translated by Thomas Gora et al. N.Y.: Columbia University Press.

———. 1982. *Powers of Horror: An Essay on Abjection*. N.Y.: Columbia University Press.

———. 1989. *Black Sun: Depression and Melancholia*. Translated by Leon S. Roudiez. N.Y.: Columbia University Press.

Kroker, Arthur, and Marilouise Kroker, ed. 1993. *The Last Sex: Feminism and Outlaw Bodies*. New York: St. Martin's Press.

Krupnick, Mark. 1983. "Introduction." In *Displacement: Derrida and After*, ed. Mark Krupnick, 1–20. Bloomington: Indiana University Press.

Kundera, Milan. 1986. *Life is Elsewhere*. N.Y.: Penguin.

———. 1987. *The Unbearable Lightness of Being*. N.Y.: Harper and Row.

Lacan, Jacques. 1981. *The Four Fundamental Concepts of Psycho-analysis*, ed. Jacques-Alain Miller. Translated by Alan Sheridan. N.Y.: W. W. Norton.

———. 1989. "Kant with Sade." *October* 51 (Winter): 55–75.

LaCapra, Dominick. 1983. *Rethinking Intellectual History: Texts, Contexts, Language*. Ithaca, N.Y.: Cornell University Press.

———. 1989. *Soundings in Critical Theory*. Ithaca, N.Y.: Cornell University Press.

Laclau, Ernesto, and Chantal Mouffe. 1985. *Hegemony and Socialist Strategy. Towards a Radical Democratic Politics*. N.Y.: Verso.

Lacoue-Labarthe, Philippe. 1989. *Typography: Mimesis, Philosophy, Politics*. Cambridge, Mass.: Harvard University Press.

Land, Nick. 1992. *The Thirst for Annihilation: Georges Bataille and Virulent Nihilism*. N.Y.: Routledge.

Lanham, Richard. 1976. *The Motives of Eloquence*. New Haven: Yale University Press.

———. 1988. "The 'Q' Question." *SAQ* 87.4: 653–700.

Leavis, F. R. 1943. *Education and the University: A Sketch for an English School.* London: Chatto and Windus.

———. 1972. *Nor Shall My Sword: Discourses on Pluralism, Compassion and Social Hope*. N.Y.: Barnes and Noble.

Lecercle, Jean-Jacques. 1985. *Philosophy Through the Looking-Glass*. La Salle, Ill.: Open Court.

Lechte, John. 1993, "An Introduction to Bataille: The Impossible as (a practice of) Writing." *Textual Practice* 7.2: 173–94.

Leff, Michael C. 1988. "Serious Comedy: The Strange Case History of Dr. Vitanza." *Rhetoric Review* 6.2: 237–45.

Levi, Adolfo. 1966. *Storia della Sofistica*. Naples: Morano Editore.

Lévi-Strauss, Claude. 1969. *Elementary Structures of Kinship*. Translated by James Harle Bell, John Richard von Sturmes, and Rodney Needham. Boston: Beacon Press.

———. 1974. *Tristes Tropiques*. N.Y.: Atheneum.

Lispector, Clarice. 1988. *The Passion According to G. H.* Translated by Ronald W. Sousa. Minnesota: University of Minnesota Press.

Loraux, Nicole. 1986. *The Inventions of Athens: The Funeral Oration in the Classical City*. Translated by Alan Sheridan. Cambridge, Mass.: Harvard University Press.

Love, Nancy S. 1986. *Marx, Nietzsche, and Modernity*. N.Y.: Columbia University Press.

Lyotard, Jean-François. 1984a. *Driftworks*. N.Y.: Semiotext(e).

———. 1984b. *The Postmodern Condition: A Report on Knowledge*. Translated by Geoff Bennington and Brian Massumi. Minneapolis: University of Minnesota Press.

———. 1988a. *The Differend*. Translated by Georges Van Den Abbeele. Minneapolis: University of Minnesota Press.

———. 1988b. *Peregrinations: Law, Form, Event*. N.Y.: Columbia University Press.

———. 1990. *Heidegger and "the jews."* Translated by Andreas Michel and Mark Roberts. Minneapolis: University of Minnesota Press.

———. 1991a. *The Inhuman: Reflections on Time*. Translated by Geoffrey Bennington and Rachel Bowlby. Stanford: Stanford University Press.

———. 1991b. "*Sensus communis*: The Subject in *statu nascendi*." In *Who Comes After the Subject?*, ed. Eduardo Cadava, Peter Connor, and Jean-Luc Nancy, 217–35. N.Y.: Routledge.

———. 1993. *Libidinal Economy*. Translated by Iain Hamilton Grant. Bloomington: Indiana University Press.

———. 1994. *Lessons on the Analytic of the Sublime*. Translated by Elizabeth Rottenberg. Stanford, Calif.: Stanford University Press.

Lyotard, Jean-François, and Jean-Loup Thébaud. 1985. *Just Gaming*. Translated by Wlad Godzich. Minneapolis: University of Minnesota Press.

MacIntyre, Alasdair. 1984. *After Virtue*. 2nd ed. Notre Dame, Ind.: University of Notre Dame Press.

Marcus, Steven. 1985. "Freud and Dora: Story, History, Case History." In *In Dora's Case: Freud-Hysteria-Feminism*, ed. Charles Bernheimer and Claire Kahane, 56–91. N.Y.: Columbia University Press.

Marcuse, Herbert. 1962. *Eros and Civilization*. N.Y.: Vintage.

Marrou, H. I. 1964. *A History of Education in Antiquity*. Translated by George Lamb. N.Y.: Mentor.

Marx, Karl. 1977. *Capital*. Vol. 1. New York: Vintage.

———. 1984. *The Eighteenth Brumaire of Louis Bonaparte*. N.Y.: International Publishers.

Marx, Karl, and Friedrich Engels. 1978. *Marx-Engels Reader*, ed. Robert C. Tucker. 2nd ed. New York: W. W. Norton.

Mason, Jeff. 1989. *Philosophical Rhetoric*. London: Routledge.

Massumi, Brian. 1992. *A User's Guide to Capitalism and Schizophrenia: Deviations from Deleuze and Guattari*. Cambridge, Mass.: MIT Press.

Mathieu, Georges. 1925. *Les Idées Politiques d'Isocrate*. Paris: Les Belles Lettres.

Mauss, Marcel. 1967. *The Gift: Forms and Functions of Exchange in Archaic Societies*. Translated by I. Cunnison. N.Y.: Norton.

McGowan, John. 1991. *Postmodernism and Its Critics*. Ithaca, N.Y.: Cornell University Press.

Mehlman, Jeffrey. 1977. *Revolution and Repetition: Marx, Hugo, Balzac*. Berkeley: University of California Press.

Miller, Bernard A. 1987. "Heidegger and the Gorgian *Kairos*." In *Visions of Rhetoric: History, Theory and Criticism*, ed. Charles Kneupper, 169–84. Arlington, Tex.: Rhetoric Society of America.

Miller, Christopher L. 1993. "The Postidentitarian Predicament in the Footnotes of *A Thousand Plateaus*: Nomadology, Anthropology, and Authority." *Diacritics* 23.3: 6–35.

Miller, Henry. 1981. *Tropic of Cancer*. N.Y.: Grove Wiedenfeld.

Miller, Nancy K. 1991. *Getting Personal*. N.Y.: Routledge.

Moi, Toril. 1985. "Representation of Patriarchy: Sexuality and Epistemology in Freud's Dora." In *In Dora's Case: Freud-Hysteria-Feminism*, ed. Charles Bernheimer and Claire Kahane, 181–99. N.Y.: Columbia University Press.

Momigliano, Arnaldo. 1955. *Contributo alla storia degli studi classici e del mondo antico*. Rome: Edizioni di Storia e letteratura.

———. 1966. *Terzo contributo alla storia degli studi classici e del mondo antico*. Rome: Edizioni di Storia e letteratura.

———. 1969. *Quarto contributo alla storia degli studi classici e del mondo antico*. Rome: Edizioni di Storia e letteratura.

———. 1982. *Essays in Ancient and Modern Historiography*. Middletown, Conn.: Wesleyan University Press.

Montaigne, Michel. 1965. *The Complete Essays of Montaigne*. Translated by Donald M. Frame. Stanford, Calif.: Stanford University Press.

Mulvey, Laura. 1985. "Visual Pleasure and Narrative Cinema." *Screen* 16.3: 6–18.

Naegel, Thomas. 1979. *Mortal Questions*. Cambridge: Cambridge University Press.

Neel, Jasper. 1988. *Plato, Derrida, and Writing*. Carbondale, Ill.: Southern Illinois University Press.

———. 1995. *Aristotle's Voice: Rhetoric, Theory, and Writing in America*. Carbondale, Ill.: Southern Illinois University Press.

Nelson, J. S. 1983. "Political Theory as Political Rhetoric." In *What Should Political Theory Be Now?*, ed. J. S. Nelson, 176–93. Albany: State University of New York Press. 176–93.

Neske, Gunther, and Emil Kettering, ed. 1990. *Martin Heidegger and National Socialism: Questions and Answers*. N.Y.: Paragon House.

Nietzsche, Friedrich. 1966. *Beyond Good and Evil*. Translated by Walter Kaufmann. N.Y.: Vintage.

———. 1967. *The Birth of Tragedy and The Case of Wagner*. Translated by Walter Kaufmann. N.Y.: Vintage.

———. 1968a. *The Portable Nietzsche*. Translated by Walter Kaufmann. N.Y.: Vintage.

———. 1968b. *Twilight of the Idols and The Anti-Christ*. Translated by R. J. Hollingdale. N.Y. Penguin.

———. 1968c. *The Will To Power*. Translated by Walter Kaufmann and R. J. Hollingdale. N.Y.: Vintage.

———. 1969. *On the Genealogy of Morals and Ecce Homo*. N.Y.: Vintage.

———. 1974. *The Gay Science*. N.Y.: Vintage.

———. 1987. *Philosophy in the Tragic Age of the Greeks*. Translated by Marianee Cowan. Washington, D.C.: Regency Gateway.

———. 1988. "On the uses and disadvantages of history for life." *Untimely Meditations*, 57–124. Translated by R. J. Hollingdale. Cambridge: Cambridge University Press.

———. 1989. "Truth and Lying in the Extra-Moral Sense." In *Friedrich Nietzsche on Rhetoric and Language*, 246–57. Edited and translated by Sander L. Gilman, Carole Blair, David J. Parent. N.Y.: Oxford University Press.

———. 1990. "We Classicists." In *Unmodern Observations*, 321–87. Translated by William Arrowsmith. New Haven: Yale University Press.

Nolan, Mary. 1988. "The *Historikerstreit* and Social History." *New German Critique* 44: 51–80.

Norris, Christopher. 1988. *Paul de Man: Deconstruction and the Critique of Aesthetics Ideology*. N.Y.: Routledge.

Nye, Andrea. 1990. *Words of Power*. N.Y.: Routledge.

Octalog. 1988. "The Politics of Historiography." *Rhetoric Review* 7.1: 5–49. [Position statements by and discussion among James Murphy, James A. Berlin, Robert Connors, Sharon Crowley, Richard Leo Enos, Victor J. Vitanza, Susan Jarratt, C. Jan Swearingen, Nan Johnson]

Ovid. 1967. *Metamorphoses*. Translated by Rolfe Humphries. Bloomington: Indiana University Press.

Patton, Paul, ed. 1993. *Nietzsche, Feminism, and Political Theory*. N.Y.: Routledge.

Pecora, Vincent P. 1991. "Ethics, Politics, and the Middle Voice." *Yale French Studies* 79: 203–30.

Pefanis, Julian. 1991. *Heterology and the Postmodern*. Durham, N.C.: Duke University Press.

Perelman, Chaim, and L. Olbrechts-Tyteca. 1961. *The New Rhetoric: A Treatise on Argumentation*. Notre Dame, Ind.: University of Notre Dame Press.

Philostratus and Eunapius. 1968. *Lives of the Sophists*. Cambridge, Mass.: Harvard University Press.

Pierssens, Michel. 1980. *The Power of Babel: A Study of Logophilia*. Translated by Carl R. Lovitt. London: Routledge and Kegan Paul.

Pike, Kenneth L. 1982. *Linguistic Concepts*. Lincoln: University of Nebraska Press.

Plato. 1961. *The Collected Dialogues*, ed. Edith Hamilton and Huntington Cairns. Princeton, N.J.: Princeton University Press.

Poulakos, John. 1983a. "Gorgias' *Enconium on Helen* and the Defense of Rhetoric." *Rhetorica* 1: 1–19.

————. 1983b. "Toward a Sophistic Definition of Rhetoric." *Philosophy and Rhetoric* 16.1: 35–48.

————. 1984. "Rhetoric, The Sophists, and the Possible." *Communication Monographs* 51: 215–26.

————. 1986. "Gorgias' and Isocrates' Use of the Encomium." *Southern Speech Communication Journal* 51: 300–07.

————. 1989. "Early Changes in Rhetorical Practice and Understanding: From the Sophists to Isocrates." *Texte* 8–9: 307–24.

————. 1990. "Interpreting Sophistical Rhetoric: A Response to Schiappa." *Rhetoric and Philosophy*. 23.3: 218–28.

————. 1993. "Terms for Sophistical Rhetoric." In *Rethinking the History of Rhetoric: Multidisciplinary Essays on the Rhetorical Tradition*, ed. Takis Poulakos, 53–74. Boulder, Colo.: Westview Press.

Poulakos, John, and Steve Whitson. 1990. "The Search for an Alliance Between the Greek Sophists and Postmodern Feminists: A Response to Jarratt and Grogan." Unpublished paper presented at the 11th Annual Temple University Conference on Discourse Analysis.

Rabinow, Paul. 1984. "Introduction." In *The Foucault Reader*, ed. Paul Rabinow, 3–29. N.Y.: Pantheon Books.

Ragland-Sullivan, Ellie. 1984. "Counting from 0 to 6: Lacan and the Imaginary Order." Working Paper No. 7, 1–26. Center for Twentieth Century Studies. University of Wisconsin, Milwaukee.

Rajchman, John. 1991. *Truth and Eros*. N.Y.: Routledge.

Rankin, H. D. 1983. *Sophists, Socratics, and Cynics*. Totowa, N.J.: Barnes and Noble.

Rapaport, Herman. 1989. *Heidegger and Derrida: Reflections on Time and Language*. N.Y.: Columbia University Press.

Readings, Bill. 1991. *Introducing Lyotard: Art and Politics*. N.Y.: Routledge.

Richmond, Michele H. 1982. *Reading Georges Bataille: Beyond the Gift*. Baltimore: The Johns Hopkins University Press.

Ricoeur, Paul. 1978. *Freud and Philosophy*. Translated by Denis Savage. New Haven: Yale University Press.

————. 1983. *Time and Narrative*. Vol. 1. Translated by Kathleen McLaughlin and David Pellauer. Chicago: University of Chicago Press.

Rodriguez, Richard. 1982. *Hunger of Memory: The Education of Richard Rodriguez*. N.Y.: Bantam.

Romilly, Jacqueline de. 1975. *Magic and Rhetoric in Ancient Greece*. Cambridge, Mass.: Harvard University Press.

Rorty, Richard. 1979. *Philosophy and the Mirror of Nature*. Princeton, N.J.: Princeton University Press.

———. 1984. "The Historiography of Philosophy: Four Genres." In *Philosophy in History: Essays on the Historiography of Philosophy*, edited by Richard Rorty, et al., 49–75. Cambridge: Cambridge University Press.

———. 1989. *Contingency, Irony, Solidarity*. Cambridge: Cambridge University Press.

Rosen, Stanley. 1983. *Plato's Sophist: The Drama of Original and Image*. New Haven: Yale University Press.

Rosenmeyer, Thomas G. 1955. "Gorgias, Aeschylus, and *Apaté*." *American Journal of Philology*. 76: 225–60.

Rubin, Gayle. 1975. "The Traffic in Women: Notes on the 'Political Economy' of Sex." In *Toward an Anthropology of Women*, ed. Rayna R. Reiter, 157–210. N.Y.: Monthly Review Press.

Schiappa, Edward. 1990a. "Did Plato Coin *Rhetorike?*" *American Journal of Philology* 111: 457–70.

———. 1990b. "History and Neo-Sophistic Criticism: A Reply to Poulakos." *Philosophy and Rhetoric* 23.4: 307–15.

———. 1990c. "Neo-Sophistic Rhetorical Criticism or the Historical Reconstruction of Sophistic Doctrines?" *Philosophy and Rhetoric* 23.3: 192–217.

———. 1991. "Sophistic Rhetoric: Oasis or Mirage?" *Rhetoric Review* 10.1: 5–19.

———. 1993. "Arguing About Definitions." *Argumentation* 7: 403–17.

———. 1995a. "Gorgias's *Helen* Revisted." *Quarterly Journal of Speech* 81: 310–24.

———. 1995b. "Isocrates' *Philosophia* and Contemporary Pragmatism." In *Rhetoric, Sophistry, Pragmaticism*, ed. Steven Mailloux, 36–60. Cambridge: Cambridge University Press.

Schiller, Friedrich. 1967. *On the Aesthetic Education of Man, in a Series of Letters*. Translated by Elizabeth M. Wilkinson and L. A. Willoughby. Oxford: Clarendon Press.

———. 1968. *Dialogue on Poetry and Literary Aphorisms*. Translated by Ernst Behler and Roman Struc. University Park: The Pennsylvania State University Press.

Schneiderman, Stuart. 1983. *Jacques Lacan: The Death of an Intellectual Hero*. Cambridge, Mass.: Harvard University Press.

Schreber, Daniel Paul. 1988. *Memoirs of My Nervous Illness*. Cambridge, Mass.: Harvard University Press.

Scott, Charles E. 1990. *The Question of Ethics: Nietzsche, Foucault, Heidegger*. Bloomington: Indiana University Press.

Scott, Robert. 1988. "Non-Discipline as a Remedy for Rhetoric? A Reply to Victor Vitanza." *Rhetoric Review* 6.2: 233–37.

Sebeok, Thomas A. 1988. "One, Two, Three Spells UBERTY." In *The Sign of Three*, edited by Umberto Eco and Thomas A. Sebeok, 1–10. Bloomington: Indiana University Press.

Serres, Michel. 1982. *Hermes: Literature, Science, Philosophy*. Baltimore: The Johns Hopkins University Press.

Sheehan, Thomas. 1988. "Heidegger and the Nazis." *New York Review of Books* 35 (June 16): 38–47.

―――. 1993. "A Normal Nazi." *New York Review of Books* 40 (June 14): 30–35.

Shiach, Morag. 1991. *Hélène Cixous: A Politics of Reading*. London: Routledge.

Shklovsky, Victor. 1965. "Sterne's *Tristram Shandy*: Stylistic Commentary." In *Russian Formalist Criticism: Four Essays*, translated by Lee T. Lemon and Marion J. Reis, 25–57. Lincoln: University of Nebraska Press.

Showalter, Elaine. 1987. "Critical Cross-Dressing: Male Feminists and the Woman of the Year." In *Male Feminism*, ed. Alice Jardine and Paul Smith, 116–32. New York: Methuen.

Skinner, Quentin. 1969. "Meaning and Understanding in the History of Ideas." *History and Theory* 8: 3–53.

―――, ed. 1985. *The Return of Grand Theory in the Human Sciences*. Cambridge: Cambridge University Press.

Sloterdijk, Peter. 1987. *Critique of Cynical Reason*. Minneapolis: University of Minnesota Press.

―――. 1989. *Thinker on Stage: Nietzsche's Materialism*. Translated by Jamie Owen Daniel. Minneapolis: University of Minnesota Press.

Soper, Kate. 1986. *Humanism and AntiHumanism*. La Salle, Ill.: Open Court.

Spivak, Gayatri Chakrovorty. 1983. "Displacement and the Discourse of Woman." In *Displacement: Derrida and After*, ed. Mark Krupnick, 169–96. Bloomington: Indiana University Press.

―――. 1987. "Subalterns Studies: Deconstructing Historiography." In *In Other Worlds: Essays in Cultural Politics*, 197–221. N.Y.: Methuen.

―――. 1988. "Can the Subalterns Speak?" In *Marxism and the Interpretation of Culture*, ed. Cary Nelson and Lawrence Grossberg, 271–313. Urbana: University of Illinois Press.

————. 1989a. "Feminism and deconstruction, again: negotiating with unacknowledged masculinism." In *Between Feminism and Psychoanalysis*, ed. Teresa Brennan, 206–23. N.Y.: Routledge,

————. 1989b. "In a Word. *Interview.*" *Differences: A Journal of Feminist Cultural Studies* 1 (Summer): 124–56.

————. 1989c. "The New Historicism: Political Commitment and the Postmodern Critic." In *The New Historicism*, ed. H. Aram Veeser, 277–92. N.Y.: Routledge.

————. 1990. *The Post-Colonial Critic: Interviews, Strategies, Dialogues*. N.Y.: Routledge.

Sprague, Rosamond Kent, ed. 1990. *The Older Sophists*. Columbia: University of South Carolina Press.

Staten, Henry. 1986. *Wittgenstein and Derrida*. Lincoln: University of Nebraska Press.

Stewart, Donald C. 1990. "The Nineteenth Century." In *The Present State of Scholarship in Historical and Contemporary Rhetoric*, ed. Winifred Bryan Horner, 151–85. rev. ed. Columbia: University of Missouri Press.

Stout, Jeffrey. 1988. *Ethics After Babel*. Boston: Beacon Press.

Strong, Tracy B. 1988. "Nietzsche's Political Aesthetics." In *Nietzsche's New Seas: Explorations in Philosophy, Aesthetics, and Politics*, ed. Michael Allen Gillespie and Tracy B. Strong, 153–74. Chicago: University of Chicago Press.

Sutton, Jane. 1986. "The Death of Rhetoric and its Rebirth in Philosophy." *Rhetorica* 4.3: 203–26.

————. 1994. "Structuring the Narrative for the Canon of Rhetoric: The Principles of Traditional HIstoriography (an Essay) with Dead's Differend (a Collage)." In *Writing Histories of Rhetoric*, ed. Victor J. Vitanza, 156–179. Carbondale, Ill.: Southern Illinois University Press.

Suzuki, Mihoko. 1989. *The Metamorphoses of Helen: Authority, Difference and the Epic*. Ithaca, N.Y.: Cornell University Press.

Swearingen, C. Jan. 1991. *Rhetoric and Irony: Western Literacy and Western Lies*. N.Y.: Oxford University Press.

Taylor, Mark C. *Nots*. Chicago: University of Chicago Press, 1993.

Thiele, Leslie Paul. 1990. *Friedrich Nietzsche and the Politics of the Soul*. Princeton, N.J.: Princeton University Press.

Trimbur, John. 1989, "Consensus and Difference in Collaborative Learning." *College English* 51: 602–16.

Ulmer, Gregory L. 1994. *Heuretics: The Logic of Invention*. Baltimore: The Johns Hopkins University Press.

Untersteiner, Mario. 1954. *The Sophists*. Translated by Kathleen Freeman. N.Y.: Philosophical Library.

Valesio, Paolo. 1980. *Novantiqua: Rhetorics as a Contemporary Theory*. Bloomington: Indiana University Press.

Vernant, Jean-Pierre. 1982. *The Origins of Greek Thought*. Ithaca, N.Y.: Cornell University Press.

———. 1990. "One . . . Two . . . Three: *Eros*." In *Before Sexuality: The Construction of Erotic Experience in the Ancient Greek World*, ed. David M. Halperin, John J. Winkler, and Froma I. Zeitlin, 465–78. Princeton, N.J.: Princeton University Press.

Vickers, Brian. 1988. *In Defense of Rhetoric*. Oxford: Claredon.

Virilio, Paul. 1991. *The Aesthetics of Disappearance*. Translated by Philip Beitchman. N.Y.: Semiotext(e).

Virilio, Paul, and Sylvjere Lotringer. 1983. *Pure War*. Translated by Mark Polizzotti. N.Y.: Semiotext(e).

Vitanza, Victor J. 1987a. "Critical Sub/Versions of the History of Philosophical Rhetoric." *Rhetoric Review* 6.1: 41–66.

———. 1987b. " 'Notes' Towards Historiographies of Rhetorics; or the Rhetorics of the Histories of Rhetorics: Traditional, Revisionary, and Sub/Versive." *PRE/TEXT* 8.1–2: 63–125.

———. 1988. "Cackling With Tears in My Eyes; or, Some Responses to 'The Gang of Three': Scott-Leff-Kennedy." *Rhetoric Review* 7.1: 214–18. (This is a much abbreviated version of a longer, unpublished response.)

———. 1989. "What's 'at stake' in the Gorgian Fragment on Seriousness/Laughter." *PRE/TEXT* 10.1–2: 107–14.

———. 1990. "An Open Letter to My 'Colligs': On 'Counter'-Ethics, Para/Rhetorics, and the Hysterical Turn." *PRE/TEXT* 11.3–4: 237–87.

———. 1991a. " 'Some More' Notes, Towards a Third Sophistic." *Argumentation* 5: 117–39.

———. 1991b. "Three Countertheses: A Critical In(ter)vention into Composition Theories and Pedagogies." In *Contending With Words*, ed. Patricia Harkin and John Schilb, 139–72. N.Y.: MLA.

———. 1993a. "Interview with Victor J. Vitanza." *Composition Studies* 21.1: 49–65.

———. 1993b. "Some Rudiments of Histories of Rhetorics and Rhetorics of Histories." In *Rethinking the History of Rhetoric*, ed. Takis Poulakos, 193–240. Polemics Series. Denver, Colo.: Westview Press.

———. 1994a. "An After/word: Preparing to Meet the Faces that We Will Have Met." In *Writing Histories of Rhetoric*, ed. Victor J. Vitanza, 217–57. Carbondale, Ill.: Southern Illinois University Press.

———. 1994b. "Concerning a Post-Classical Ethos, as Para/Rhetorical Ethics, the 'Selphs,' and The Excluded Third." In *Ethos: New Essays in Rhetorical and Critical Theory*, ed. James S. Baumlin and Tita French Baumlin, 389–42. Dallas, Tex.: Southern Methodist University Press.

———. 1994c. "Taking A-Count of a (Future-Anterior) History of Rhetoric as 'Libidinalized Marxism' (A PM Pastiche)." In *Writing Histories of Rhetoric*, ed. Victor J. Vitanza, 180–216. Carbondale, Ill.: Southern Illinois University Press.

———. 1994d. "Threes." In *Composition in Context*, ed. W. Ross Winterowd and Vincent Gillespie, 196–218. Carbondale, Ill.: Southern Illinois University Press.

———. 1995. "Feminist Sophistic?" *JAC: A Journal of Composition Theory* 15.2: 321–49.

———. 1996. "Two Propositions: On the Hermeneutics of Suspicion and on Writing the History of Rhetoric." In *Discourse Studies in Honor of James Kinneavy*, ed. Rosalind Gabin. Potomac, Md.: Studia Humanitatis.

Voegelin, Eric. 1966. *Plato*. Baton Rouge: Louisiana State University Press, 1966.

Warren, Mark. 1988. *Nietzsche and Political Thought*. Cambridge, Mass.: The MIT Press.

Watson, Stephen H. 1985. "Abysses." In *Hermeneutics and Deconstruction*, ed. Hugh J. Silverman and Don Ihde, 229–46. Albany: SUNY P.

Webber, Sam. 1985. "Afterword: Literature—Just Making It." *Just Gaming*, Jean-François Lyotard and Jean-Loup Thébaud. Translated by Wlad Godzich. Minneapolis: University of Minnesota Press: 101–20.

Weinsheimer, Joel C. 1985. *Gadamer's Hermeneutics: A Reading of* Truth and Method. New Haven: Yale University Press.

Weiskel, Thomas. 1976. *The Romantic Sublime*. Baltimore: The Johns Hopkins University Press.

Weiss, Allen S. 1989. *The Aesthetics of Excess*. Albany: State University of New York Press.

White, Eric Charles. 1987. *Kaironomia: On the Will-To-Invent*. Ithaca, N.Y.: Cornell University Press.

White, Hayden. 1973. *Metahistory: The Historical Imagination in Nineteenth-Century Europe*. Baltimore: The Johns Hopkins University Press.

———. 1978. *Tropics of Discourse*. Baltimore: The Johns Hopkins University Press.

————. 1981. "The Value of Narrativity in the Representation of Reality." In *On Narrative*, ed. W. J. T. Mitchell, 1–24. Chicago: University of Chicago Press.

————. 1984. "The Question of Narrative in Contemporary Historical Theory." *History and Theory* 23.1: 2–33.

————. 1987. "The Politics of Historical Interpretation: Discipline and De-Sublimation." In *The Content of Form*, 58–82. Baltimore: The Johns Hopkins University Press.

Whitson, Steve, and John Poulakos. 1993. "Nietzsche and the Aesthetics of Rhetoric." *Quarterly Journal of Speech* 79: 131–45.

————. 1995. "Rhetoric Denuded and Redressed: Figs and Figures." *Quarterly Journal of Speech* 81: 378–85.

Wittgenstein, Ludwig. 1968. *Philosophical Investigations*. N.Y.: Macmillan.

————. 1977. *Tractatus Logico-Philosophicus*. Translated by D. F. Pears and B. F. McGuinness. London: Routledge and Kegan Paul.

Wolin, Richard. 1990. *The Politics of Being*. N.Y.: Columbia University Press.

Worsham, Lynn. 1993. "Reading Wild, Seriously: Confessions of an Epistemophiliac." *Rhetoric Society Quarterly*. 22.1: 39–62.

————. 1994. "Eating History, Digesting Rhetoric, Purging Memory, and Writing the Future: A Remunation on Roland Barthes' *Gastronomie*." In *Writing Histories of Rhetoric*, ed. Victor J. Vitanza. Carbondale, Ill.: Southern Illinois University Press.

Zeller, Edward. 1955. *Outlines of the History of Greek Philosophy*. 13th ed. Revised by Wilhelm Nestle. Translated by J. R. Palmer. N.Y.: The Humanities Press.

Zimmerman, Michael E. 1990. *Heidegger's Confrontation with Modernity: Technology, Politics, Art*. Bloomington: Indiana University Press.

Zizek, Slavoj. 1989. *The Sublime Object of Ideology*. N.Y.: Verso.

————. 1993. *Tarrying with the Negative*. Durham: Duke University Press.

Zurbrugg, Nicholas. 1993. *The Parameters of Postmodernism*. Carbondale, Ill.: Southern Illinois University Press.

Index